A LIFE OF PICASSO

Volume I: 1881-1906

JOHN RICHARDSON
with the collaboration of Marilyn McCully

PIMLICO

PIMLICO

20 Vauxhall Bridge Road, London SW1V 2SA

London Melbourne Sydney Auckland Johannesburg
and agencies throughout the world

First published by Jonathan Cape 1991
Pimlico edition 1992

Printed and bound in Great Britain by
Butler & Tanner Ltd, Frome and London

ISBN 0-7126-5337-6

Frontispiece: Picasso. *Self-Portrait.* Barcelona, 1899.
Charcoal on paper, 47x53.2cm. Private Collection.

Opposite: Picasso. Decorated frame. Barcelona, *c.*1902.
Oil on wood, 122.8x82cm. Museu Picasso, Barcelona.

PIMLICO

57

A LIFE OF PICASSO

John Richardson was born in 1924. He studied art at the Slade School. In 1949 he moved to Southern France, where he and Douglas Cooper, the collector, bought and transformed the Château de Castille near Avignon into a private museum of cubist painting. For the next ten years he lived in France, where he became a friend of Picasso, Braque, Léger and Cocteau, and embarked on an analytical study of Picasso's work, now part of this biography.

In the early 1960s Richardson went to live in New York, where he was appointed head of Christie's. He organised various exhibitions, including a major Picasso retrospective in 1962. He is the author of books on Manet and Braque and is a contributor to *The New York Review of Books* and *Vanity Fair*.

P. Ruiz Picasso

In Memory of
Douglas Cooper
February 20, 1911—April 1, 1984

Acknowledgments

SO LONG AS PABLO PICASSO AND his wife, Jacqueline, were alive, they gave me every encouragement in this project. My deepest thanks to both of them. Thanks, also, to the artist's children: Claude and Paloma and her husband, Rafael López Sánchez; to his daughter-in-law, Christine Picasso; to his nephew, Javier Vilató; to his family in Málaga, Manuel Blasco and Ricardo Huelin; and to Jacqueline's daughter, Catherine Hutin-Blay, for all their help.

I am enormously indebted to Dominique Bozo, the first curator-in-charge of the Musée Picasso, who was unfailingly supportive; to his successors, Pierre Georgel and Gérard Régnier; to Marie-Laure Besnard-Bernadac for scholarly assistance of inestimable value; also to Brigitte Léal, Laurence Berthon-Marceillac, Christine Piot, Michèle Richet and Hélène Seckel, for solving any number of problems. The librarian, François Chapon, and staff of the Bibliothèque Littéraire Jacques Doucet have likewise been of great service. In supplying photographs, untiring efforts to satisfy the needs of the book were made by Maria Teresa Ocaña, the director, and Margarita Ferrer at the Museu Picasso, Barcelona, Montserrat Blanch at the Arxiu Mas and Caroline de Lambertye at the Réunion des Musées Nationaux, Paris.

Gratitude also to my friends at the Museum of Modern Art for their co-operation. The backing of William Rubin, director emeritus of the museum and most assiduous of Picasso scholars, has been especially heartening. In addition, Kirk Varnedoe, director, and Kynaston McShine in the department of painting and Clive Philpot, the librarian, have been unfailingly helpful. At the Metropolitan Museum of Art, William Luers, the president, and Philippe de Montebello, director, have given me every assistance. Special thanks to William S. Lieberman for all his advice; also to Sabine Rewald, Gary Tinterow, John Brearley and the staff of the restoration department.

My publishers, both American and English, have given me a remarkably free hand, for which many thanks: especially to Harry Evans of Random House for his unflagging support and to my editor, Jason Epstein, who had the courage to commission this biography. I would also like to express my gratitude to the eagle-eyed Jean McNutt, who started the final editing of these pages, and to Virginia Avery, who took over from her. At Jonathan Cape I would like to thank Tom Maschler, David Godwin, Jenny Cottom and Margaret Clark for seeing the book through the English press.

Congratulations to my agent, Robert Tabian of I.C.M., for saving the day when it looked as if the book might appear unillustrated.

The more scrutiny a project of this nature receives from critical minds, the better. In this respect I have been exceedingly fortunate: among the friends who have gone over my manuscript I am proud to be able to thank Robert Hughes, Donald Munson, Angelica Rudenstine, Robert Silvers, Susan Sontag and Richard Wollheim. Fortunate, too, in being able to count on the editorial skills and moral support of Sharon Delano.

Besides the above I would be remiss if I failed to acknowledge all the stimulus and kindness I received from the late Daniel-Henry Kahnweiler and his associates, the late Louise Leiris and Maurice Jardot; from my old and valued friend John Golding, whose eye for the finer points of Picasso's work is so sharp and perceptive; from Lydia Gasman, whose exploration of the artist's imagination and psyche has been a constant inspiration to me; from Robert Rosenblum and the late Gert Schiff, whose forays into hitherto unexplored areas have greatly facilitated my own task; from Ron Johnson, who has generously put his unpublished study of Picasso and the poets at my disposal; from Billy Klüver and Julie Martin who have been tireless in elucidating iconographical problems. Special thanks also to the late Pancho Murature for tracking down the memoirs of Picasso's fellow student, Francisco Bernareggi; to Lewis Kachur for drawing my attention to the unpublished Picasso/Apollinaire interview; to Peter Perrone for research in New York libraries; to Renata Propper for her analysis of Picasso's handwriting; to Angel Padín, for generously making his research concerning Picasso's art school days in Corunna available; to Teresa Sauret for her enormous efforts on my behalf in Málaga; to Gerrit Valk for giving me access to his unpublished study concerning Picasso and Tom Schilperoort's stay in Holland; and to the Casanovas family in Olot for allowing me to consult the correspondence between Enric Casanovas and Picasso.

From all over Europe and America hundreds more people have helped to make this book possible. To them and to anyone whose name I may have inadvertently overlooked, my warmest thanks: William Acquavella; Pierre Marcel Adéma; Santiago Alcolea; Hon. Charles Allsopp; Thomas Ammann; Fernando Arenas Quintela; Lily Auchincloss; Jorge de Barandiaran; Janine Barbey; Mr and Mrs Sid Bass; David Batterham; William Beadleston; Comte Henri de Beaumont; Heinz Berggruen; Rosamond Bernier; Ernst Beyeler; Bill Blass; Suzanne and Max Bollag; Gilbert de Botton; Jacqueline Boucher; Jonathan Brown; Tina Brown; Timothy Burgard; Christopher Burge; Françoise Cachin; Nane Cailler; Eugenio Chicano; Lucien Clergue; Desmond Corcoran; Judith Cousins; Gérald and Ines Cramer; Pierre Daix; Marjorie Delpech; James DeVries; Douglas Druick; Grace, Countess of Dudley; David Douglas Duncan; Lee V. Eastman; Mr and Mrs Ahmet Ertegun; Sarah Faunce; Maxime de la Falaise; Theodore H. Feder; Jack Flam; Jane Fluegel; Sandra Fisher; Edward Fry; the late Victor Ganz; Sally Ganz; Pierrette Gargallo; Joan Gaspar; Paul Gayot; Christian Geelhaar; Oscar Ghez; Françoise Gilot; Colette Giraudon; Danièle Giraudy; the late Jurgen Glaesemer; Peter Glenville; Jacqueline Gojard; Didier Gompel; James Neil Goodman; Assumpta Gou Vernet; Lydia Hagner; Dr Kosei Hara; Anne d'Harnoncourt; Michael Harvey; Mildred Hathaway; Joseph H. Hazen; Drue Heinz; Niall Hobhouse; David

Hockney; Didier Imbert; Wil Janssen; James Joll; Count Rupert de Keller; R. B. Kitaj; Jean Kisling; Rolf Kreib; Ulrich Krempel; Monsieur and Madame Gilbert Krill; Dorothy Kosinski; Monsieur and Madame Jan Krugier; François Lachenal; Carolyn Lanchner; Monsieur and Madame Claude Laurens; Quentin Laurens; Jane Lee; the late Michel Leiris; Jean Leymarie; Alexander Liberman; Nancy C. Little; Cindy Mack; Joan Antoni Maragall; Françoise Marquet; Jaime Martínez García; Alain C. Mazo; Stephen Mazoh; Boaz Mazor; William McCarty-Cooper; Mr and Mrs Paul Mellon; Cristina Mendoza; Leonardo Mondadori; Isabelle Monod-Fontaine; Lane Montgomery; Beatrice di Monti; Nelida Mori; Charlotte Mosley; David Nash; Enrique Negri; Stavros Niarchos; Javier Ordóñez Vergara; the late William S. Paley; Josep Palau i Fabre; Vinyet Panyella i Balcells; Francesc Parcerisas; Alexandra Parigoris; María Angeles Pazos Bernal; Penelope Pepper; Anthony Penrose; the late Roland and Lee Penrose; Klaus Perls; the late Boris Piotrovsky; the late Anatoli Podoksik; Lilian Poses; Lionel Prejger; Nancy Boyle Press; Stuart Preston; Mr and Mrs Joseph Pulitzer, Jr; Edward Quinn; Theodore Reff; Mr and Mrs Oscar de la Renta; David Rockefeller; Angela Rosengart; Baronne Cécile de Rothschild; James Roundell; Nicole Rousset-Altounian; John Russell; Charles Ryscamp; Florene Schoenborn; María Carmen Serantes López; Nicholas Serota; Romana Severini; Roger Shattuck; Anthony Sheil; Josep Sindreu Fernández; Alan Solomon; Mariuccia Sprenger; Werner Spies; Christine Stauffer; Francis Steegmuller; Leo Steinberg; Jean Stralem; Jeremy Strick; Charles Stuckey; Simon Studer; Rosa Maria Subirana; Jaume Sunyer; the late Denys Sutton; David Sweetman; David Sylvester; Maria Victoria Talavera; Patty Tang; Eugene V. Thaw; Samir Traboulsi; Shelley Wanger; Roseanna Warren; John W. Warrington; the Earl of Warwick; Margit Weinberg Staber; Betsey Whitney; Beverly Whitney Kean; the late Ian Woodner; Nicole Worms de Romilly; Kristen Zaremba; Peter Zegers.

Lastly my greatest debt of all: to Marilyn McCully whose unwavering faith and encouragement has kept this project from foundering on more than one occasion. As well as contributing her vast knowledge of Picasso's early years, of *fin-de-siècle* Barcelona and Catalan cultural history, she has done most of the research for this volume and come up with a mass of new material (notably on Picasso's years in Corunna and his 1905 trip to Holland). She has also contributed many of her own ideas and taken over such routine tasks as checking sources and marshalling notes, thereby leaving me free to focus my energies on the writing. Because we seem instinctively to arrive at similar conclusions, we have had the happiest and most fruitful of collaborations. I thank Marilyn with all my heart.

Marilyn's husband, Michael Raeburn, has played a no less crucial role in the actual making of the book. He has assembled hundreds of illustrations, single-handedly designed the layout, set the type and taken care of the technical details. His forbearance in the face of successive setbacks has been an inspiration. No author could have been better served.

Contents

A LIFE OF

PICASSO

VOLUME I: 1881–1906

Pour John
son ami aussi

Introduction

Opposite top: Picasso, Mateu de Soto and Carles Casagemas on the roof of 3 Carrer de la Mercè, Barcelona, where Picasso and his family lived. Photo, *c.*1900, inscribed to the author.

Opposite bottom: Douglas Cooper, Picasso and John Richardson at the Château de Vauvenargues, 1959. Photo: Jacqueline Picasso.

THIS BIOGRAPHY HAS ITS ORIGINS in a project conceived some thirty years ago. After seeing at first hand how closely Picasso's personal life and art impinged on each other, I decided to try charting his development through his portraits. Since the successive images Picasso devised for his women always permeated his style, I proposed to concentrate on portraits of wives and mistresses. The artist approved of this approach. Anything that might cast light on the mystery of his creative process—a mystery he was always trying and failing to fathom—intrigued him. And so long as he was not badgered with too many searching questions, he was most forthcoming. Apropos the flanges of fur-like hair in a certain portrait, he confessed that this was a 'pun' on the floppy ears of his Afghan dog—a reflection on the animal nature of the woman in question. He would go over a sequence of paintings and show how changes from angst to radiance, angularity to voluptuousness, would announce the onset of a new passion. It must be painful, Picasso would say with more pride than guilt, for a woman to watch herself transformed into a monster, or fade from his work, while a new favourite materializes in all her glory. He showed me how two—sometimes three or even four—women might be present in a single image; how many of the still lifes were in a manner of speaking portraits (a stocky jug would actually look like the artist; a bowl of peaches would conjure up the girl). The same with certain bullfight scenes. Virtually all of Picasso's output, I began to realize, had this anthropomorphic element. Better abandon the portrait project and write a biography that would be broader in scope: one that would set the artist's life and work in relation to each other and in the broader context of cultural history.

'My work is like a diary,' Picasso used to tell biographers, as if this facilitated their task. 'It's even dated like a diary.' Picasso was right; however, we have to tread carefully. Much of what the 'diary' chronicles is self-explanatory, but other parts are arcane or in code. And then we should remember that diaries are none the less interesting for fantasizing, embroidering and reordering the truth. This is very much the case with Picasso. He was such a mass of contradictions that, according to his son, he used to repeat again and again, 'Truth is a lie; truth is a lie . . .' No wonder so much of what has been said about Picasso turns out to be equally true in reverse. Since quicksilver would be easier to nail down than his precepts, methodologies have proved unequal to the task. I have therefore tried wherever possible to respect this ambivalence, to present the artist's life, inside and outside the studio, in the light of it. Even the one apparent constant in Picasso's character—his Spanish *duende* (soul): so intense, so black, so shot through with flashes of apocalyptic lightning—turns out to have its antithesis: a Mediterranean effulgence. Paradox, it turns out, is a specifically Andalusian phenomenon.

* * *

Picasso. *The Masks*. Vallauris, January 25, 1954. Wash on paper, 24×32cm. Whereabouts unknown.

My friendship with Picasso dated from the end of 1953. I had recently moved to Provence, where I shared a house with one of the artist's old friends, the English collector Douglas Cooper. The two of us would drive over to Vallauris, where Picasso lived in an ugly little villa, called La Galloise, hidden away behind a garage. The apartment above the garage belonged to a mad old dancing mistress who loathed the painter and used to come out on her balcony and yell that this was where she, not Picasso, lived. To his delight she put up signs to this effect—signs that scared off anyone who wanted to find La Galloise. Only those in the know could track him down.

By the autumn of 1953 Picasso's life was in turmoil. The departure of Françoise Gilot, his mistress of the last ten years, with their two children, Claude and Paloma, had left him desolate. To exorcise his anguish, the artist set about doing a series of drawings (December 1953–January 1954)—'the pictorial journal of a detestable season in hell,' Michel Leiris called it—that analyse with eerie detachment and irony the problems besetting an old painter with a young mistress. At the same time he cast around for a new companion. Waiting in the wings was Jacqueline Roque, a twenty-seven-year-old woman who had left her husband, a colonial official in the Upper Volta (now Burkina Fasso), and was working as a salesgirl for Picasso's potters, the Ramiés. She was the target of such snubs on the part of other contenders that Cooper and I felt sorry for her and bought her a present (a Dior wrap adapted from a bullfighter's cape). When Jacqueline moved in with the artist a few months later, we were handsomely rewarded. Picasso brought back the Dior box; inside was a marvellous drawing of a naked girl that I had admired when it was tacked to the studio wall. Sycophants were already deluging the new favourite with presents, but nothing could make up for past slights. 'People used to pretend I wasn't there; now they arrive bearing gifts,' she said. 'It makes me very nervous.' Jacqueline never forgot the wrap and would make a point of wearing it, ten, twenty, thirty years later, whenever we met.

Picasso. *Seated Nude* (Geneviève Laporte). Vallauris, December 4, 1953. Pencil on paper, 24×20cm. Stolen from the author and Douglas Cooper.

Our friendship with Picasso was based on more than an exchange of presents. Cooper had established himself as the preeminent authority on cubism, and the Château de Castille, which he and I shared until the early 1960s, housed what was probably the finest cubist collection in France. Picasso enjoyed visiting the house and reviewing his own work in the context of Braques, Légers and Grises of the same period. There was a further inducement. Castille was conveniently close to Nîmes and Arles, where Picasso regularly attended bullfights in the Roman arenas. After the corridas he would bring his entourage to dine. Once or twice he tried to buy Castille. 'Think of the paintings I would give you!' We finally (1958) persuaded him to buy the Château de Vauvenargues instead.

Dora Maar (Picasso's companion from 1936 to 1945) had pointed out to me that when the woman in the artist's life changed, virtually everything else changed. And, sure enough, over the next six months I was able to observe how the arrival of a new mistress triggered a new style. Soon there was also a new house, a new poet, a new group of friends (who provided the admiration, understanding and love that were as vital as his daily bread), a new dog, new servants and, not least, new kinds of food. By virtue of their function certain associates were exempt from this process: among them, Jaime Sabartès, Picasso's black shadow of a secretary, Daniel-Henry Kahnweiler, his principal dealer, and Christian and Yvonne Zervos, who were responsible for compiling the thirty-three-volume catalogue of his work. Sometimes old favourites would be reinstated after being banished by an earlier *maîtresse-en-titre*. But by and large, the tone, mood and atmosphere of Picasso's life and work would be utterly different each time there was a new regime.

Poets exerted an especially formative influence. Max Jacob is the one we associate with Picasso's earliest years in Paris, Guillaume Apollinaire with the Rose period and cubism. Jean Cocteau was the catalyst for the neo-classical period (1918–25)—'*l'époque des duchesses*', Jacob called it —presided over by the artist's first wife, Olga Kokhlova; André Breton and the surrealists for the 'metamorphic' period, when the teenage Marie-Thérèse acted as muse; Paul Eluard both for the Dora Maar (1936–45) and Françoise Gilot (1945–53) periods; and Cocteau again (early 1950s until his death in 1963) for the first half of *l'époque Jacqueline;* and, at the very end of his life, the one and only Spaniard, Rafael Alberti.

Picasso. *Self-Portrait with Angel de Soto and Sebastià Junyer Vidal.* Barcelona, 1902. Pen on paper, 14×9cm. Museu Picasso, Barcelona.

As for Picasso's group of friends, this was modelled on the Spanish *tertulia*—a circle of mostly professional cronies, who would meet day after day in a particular café and pass the time, gossiping, arguing, exchanging jokes and more often than not boring each other to distraction with their all too familiar views. The artist's father had been the centre of one such *tertulia* in Málaga. The son followed suit. By the time he was seventeen, Picasso was the young star of a Barcelona *tertulia*. And within a few months of moving to Paris he managed to establish a comparable group in Montmartre. The *bande à Picasso*, as it became known, included some of the most gifted young writers of their time—Jacob, Salmon and Apollinaire among them—and in one form or another it survived until the artist's death.

Cocteau had previously courted Françoise Gilot, and she had succumbed, but not as wholeheartedly as Jacqueline now did, to the magical patter of the old conjuror. Jacqueline also succumbed to the attentions of Francine Weisweiler, the generous patron who seldom left Cocteau's side and who would transport him and his entourage (his adopted son, Edouard Dermit, his adopted son's sister and the occasional disciple) to bullfights in two black Bentleys. From the height of his ancient Hispano Suiza, Picasso would look down on '*la famille Cocteau*' with sardonic amusement, not entirely shared by Jacqueline.

Thirty years had passed since Cocteau had provided Picasso with any literary stimulus (the crystalline pessimism of his beloved friend Michel Leiris was much more in line with his darkening view of life); however, he was the ideal court jester, the ideal foil for the painter's barbs. I will never forget the gestures and mimicry with which this raconteur of genius

described a visit to Rome culminating in a ceremony at St Peter's, where the cardinals, recently docked of their trains by Pope John, looked askance at one of their number who had sewn all the cut-off bits onto his own robes. The jester was careful not to upstage or mock the master. On the contrary, Cocteau always made a point of deferring to him. 'As an academician,' he would announce as we went into dinner, 'I take precedence over everyone except a prince of the Church and of course Picasso.'

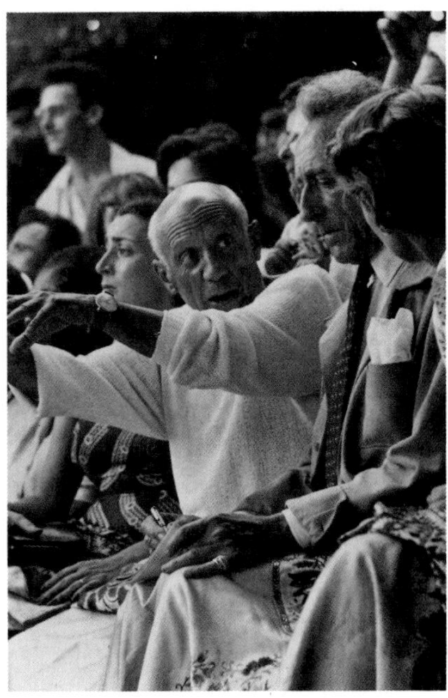

Jacqueline, Picasso and Jean Cocteau at a bullfight at Vallauris, 1955. Photo: Brian Brake. Auckland City Art Gallery.

In the paltry spaces of La Galloise, Cocteau had felt out of his element, but in Picasso's lavish new villa back of Cannes—a Beaux Arts monstrosity called La Californie—he found it easier to preen. There the poet and the artist would fantasize about the previous tenant, the former queen of Albania, who turned out to have been a sister-in-law of one of Douglas Cooper's sisters-in-law. Madame Weisweiler would help Jacqueline receive or dismiss the admirers who had wangled an entrée to the studio. Jacqueline took fierce pride in her new role of *maîtresse de maison*, and rapidly made herself so indispensable that Picasso would never let her out of his sight, not even to have a badly needed operation. In revenge, Jacqueline became maniacally possessive and took to addressing him as 'Monseigneur' and treating him, not entirely in jest, as a monarch. The artist, who had once inscribed a self-portrait, '*Yo el rey*', went along with this charade. The spoof ceremoniousness helped melt the ice engendered by dazzled strangers. Also the illusion of a crown boosted Picasso's morale at a time when many of his former constituents were rallying to the banners of neo-dadaism and minimalism.

A sense of drama was an essential part of Picasso's birthright. It enabled him to switch from style to style and role to role, like an actor, without ever losing his identity; it also enabled this surprisingly shy man to confront the world while hiding from it. Hence the masks, exotic hats and headdresses—disguises that came to be perceived as Picassian trademarks. The photographers who thronged La Californie cannot be blamed for taking advantage of the photo opportunities that the artist unwittingly provided. Unfortunately, the coffee-table books and magazine features that resulted from Picasso's clowning promoted a false perception. The artist came across as an ancient Grock, who had had his day, instead of a great artist in the throes of an exultant regeneration. The moment the visitors and photographers left, Picasso would turn back into his usual sardonic self —good-humoured or bad-humoured, depending on the state of his work. Back in the studio, he was as driven and indefatigably inventive and prolific as ever.

By 1961, the year of Picasso's eightieth birthday and his marriage to Jacqueline, La Californie had become impossible to defend against invasive hordes of photographers and tourists and the encroachment of high-rise buildings. Picasso left the treasure-filled villa in the hands of a caretaker and instead of moving to Vauvenargues—too far from the Mediterranean for comfort—he took refuge in Notre-Dame-de-Vie, a handsome property outside Mougins, where stricter security could be enforced. Henceforth his studio became a microcosm of the universe—what Gert Schiff has called Picasso's Theatrum Mundi. In the last decade of his life Picasso's thoughts turned more and more to Spain. Despite the presence of French friends and associates, the atmosphere of the last *tertulia* became decidedly Spanish. Spanish became something of a secret language

Opposite: Picasso in his studio at La Californie around 1960. Photo: Edward Quinn.

that Picasso would speak so convolutedly and fast that Jacqueline, not to speak of French friends, would be kept perversely and pointlessly (mystification for its own sake) in the dark.

Picasso had always enjoyed having Spanish or Spanish-speaking friends around. Manuel Pallarès, a Catalan who had been a friend since he was fourteen, would come and spend two weeks in a nearby hotel. In true *tertulia* style the two old cronies would gossip for hours in Catalan about the minutiae of life in turn-of-the-century Barcelona or the high sierra. Jacqueline found all this very tedious. She far preferred the company of the artist's Catalan publisher, Gustau Gili, or his fellow Andalusian, the celebrated bullfighter, Luis Miguel Dominguín. Although Picasso loved to discuss bullfighting with Dominguín, he was taken not so much with his professional prowess—'his real arena is the Place Vendôme,' he told Cocteau:[1] 'One thinks he's not like the others, but he's exactly the same' —as with his personal allure. Picasso had a short man's envy of people who were tall; and Dominguín was the inspiration for the slender, elegant torero in most of the later bullfight scenes. In his lively text *Toros y Toreros*, Dominguín likens his relationship with Picasso to the great Pedro Romero's with Goya. He sees Picasso as a bull and quotes the popular Andalusian poet Rafael Alberti's paean to him: 'You the only matador / in Picassian pink and gold / with Pablo Ruiz Picasso as the bull / And me as picador.'[2]

Picasso. *Matador*. Vauvenargues, April 3, 1959. Ink on sketchbook page. Published in *Toros y Toreros* by Picasso and Luis Miguel Dominguín.

Alberti, who had lived in exile for many years, was a welcome addition to the last *tertulia*. As a young man, he had been the first person to whom Picasso declaimed his first poetry (in the 1930s); and he would be the last of the artist's laureates. During the three winters he spent at Antibes (1968–72), Alberti wrote a number of poems about the artist,[3] including a prologue to Picasso's 'play', *The Burial of Count Orgaz*. His macho adulation is typically Andalusian in its excess: 'For you every day begins like a powerful erection, an ardent / lance pointing / at the rising sun.'[4] Even 'Lullaby for Picasso' honours the artist as a bull: '*Niño, niño, torito, Jacqueline / este niño / es un toro que piensa que es un niño*' ('Child, child, little bull, Jacqueline / this child / is a bull who thinks he is a child'); but it ends on an irreverent note: '*Toro jodido este, Jacqueline*' ('He is a fucked-up bull, Jacqueline').[5] Alberti is the only one of Picasso's literary mentors to have had the prescience to recognize the painter as a major Spanish poet—something that is taken for granted in Spain now that his extensive writings have been published.

Manuel Garvayo. Caricature of Picasso and Alberti. Pen on paper, 25×16cm. 1972. Private collection.

Another Hispanic attachment was the engaging Argentine film-maker, photographer and adventurer Roberto Otero, who appeared at Notre-Dame-de-Vie in the mid-1960s to make a documentary film. After filling twenty-eight notebooks with records of the artist's conversation and taking some two thousand photographs, he abandoned the project and used the material for a day-to-day chronicle of the artist's life between 1966 and 1972. Otero reveals Picasso at his most genial, delighting in friends who could take him back in spirit to Spain. With Otero and Alberti, Picasso felt once again part of an authentic Spanish *tertulia*. Together they created an imaginary village (see pages 106–7) called Navas de Malvivir, and would spend hours concocting scurrilous gossip about the inhabitants: the same sort of scurrilous fantasies that provide the subjects—or should one say plots?—of the last great series of prints.

Picasso. Etching from *Suite 347*. Mougins, May 16, 1968. 9×12.5 cm. Museu Picasso, Barcelona.

Picasso. *Village near Toledo*. 1901. Pastel on paper, 36×22 cm. Private collection.

Picasso. *Lovers with a Cat*. Barcelona, 1902–03. Pencil, watercolour and coloured crayons on paper, 18×26.5cm. Museu Picasso, Barcelona.

More often than not these prints—one of the glories of the late period—are set somewhere in Spain. As death drew near, Picasso returned to the locations that we will visit in the course of these pages: the gypsy shacks above Málaga, the lighthouse at Corunna, the high sierra of Horta de Ebro and Gósol. But it is above all Barcelona that Picasso evokes: the brothels of the Barri Xino, the cabarets of the Paralelo, the street fairs of the Ramblas and, of course, the bullring. He also resurrects many of the people who will appear in the course of this volume: his gentlemanly father, don José, his first girlfriend, the equestrienne Rosita del Oro, the procuress Carlota Valdivia, and assorted painters, writers and hangers-on.

Picasso's late paintings are less anecdotal, less illustrative than the prints, but like the prints, they, too, hark back to Spain: not so much the Spain of the artist's youth as the Spain of Velázquez, El Greco, Góngora and Cervantes. In their blackness of spirit as well as hue, these late works have much in common with the black paintings that the aged Goya did in retirement at his quinta outside Madrid. Like Goya, Picasso suffered from deafness (though not so seriously); he was likewise preoccupied with mortality. However, being Andalusian, he was apt to be at the mercy of this obsession, just as he was at the mercy of that other Andalusian obsession, the *mirada fuerte* (literally, 'strong gazing'). 'In Andalusia the eye is akin to a sexual organ . . . looking too intently at a woman is akin to ocular rape.'[6] So is painting a woman, especially when Picasso wields the brush. The *mirada fuerte* is the key—the Andalusian key—that helps unlock the mysteries of Picasso's late work, and of his work as a whole. It helps us understand his recurrent references to voyeurism; the way he uses art and sex—painting and making love—as metaphors for each other; and his fascination with genitalia—all those ocular penises, those vaginal eyes. 'Why not put sexual organs in the place of eyes and eyes between the legs?' he once asked.

David Gilmore's recent study of the ambivalence of Andalusian machismo and related phenomena makes no reference to Picasso; nevertheless it enables us to understand the artist's disconcerting oscillations between tenderness and cruelty, as well as other paradoxical manifestations. Sex in phallocentric Andalusia, Gilmore claims, is still a 'masculine monopoly. Man the furrowing plough, woman the fertile soil. . . . [The Andalusian man's] phallic aggression fused with sexual love and with a curious sexual hate born of centuries of defeat unites him to the world, as it protects him from the world.'[7] Gilmore's analysis of the *mirada fuerte* is particularly relevant to Picasso:

> If you mention something valuable to an Andalusian, he wants to see it, wants to eye it. To express that something is good or true, he points to his eye, tapping the side of his head [a characteristically Picassian gesture]: he needs to see it and in seeing to experience it, feel it. . . . When the Andalusian fixes a thing with a stare, he grasps it. His eyes are fingers holding and probing. . . . The *mirada fuerte* has elements of curiosity, hostility . . . and envy. But the sexual element is present also. . . .The light of the eyes is highly erotic. . . . In a culture where the sexes are segregated to the point of mutual invisibility, the eye becomes the erogenous zone par excellence.[8]

Picasso. *Head*. Mougins, July 3, 1972. Coloured crayons on paper, 66×50.5cm. Galerie Rosengart, Lucerne.

And Gilmore cites an Andalusian voyeurs' club whose members would check on the marriage banns, then peep in at night on the newlyweds.[9] Although Picasso's psychological make-up was infinitely more complex, he is a supreme embodiment of these theories—the *mirada fuerte* especially—above all in old age, when his imagination reverted to his Andalusian roots. 'The eyes of that Andalusian are killing me':[10] these lines by Góngora, Picasso's favourite Spanish poet, could be written on the gravestones of all the women in the artist's life. 'You should wear a black dress,' he once told Françoise Gilot, 'with a kerchief over your head so that no one will see your face. In that way you'll belong even less to the others. They won't even have you with their eyes.'[11]

For Picasso this demonic Andalusian birthright would be a lifelong source of anguish, also a lifelong source of power.

Picasso. *Bullfighters* (detail). Málaga, 1900. Pen on paper, 15.9×21.8cm. Museu Picasso, Barcelona.

1

Málaga

José Ruiz Blasco. *The Pigeon Loft*. Oil on canvas, 102×147 cm. Málaga, 1878. Ayuntamiento, Málaga.

Opposite: The port of Málaga with the cathedral behind, *c*.1880. Archivo Temboury, Málaga.

On the occasion of Picasso's eightieth birthday in 1961, a delegation of worthies from Málaga journeyed to Cannes to pay their respects. With some difficulty they wheedled an invitation to luncheon, during which they handed Picasso one of his painter father's sketches of a pigeon. Would he finish it? 'Choked with emotion,' according to the Spaniards, he nodded his approval. They never saw the pigeon again. Instead, they received a postcard with a drawing of a pigeon signed 'the son of José Ruiz Blasco' (Picasso's father's name).[1]

Ten years later, when Picasso reached the age of ninety, the city fathers of Málaga once again decided to honour their most illustrious son. In October 1971, a deputation made its way to Notre-Dame-de-Vie to present the aged genius with a gift they believed would move him greatly: his father's *chef-d'œuvre*. The municipality had acquired this work, *The Pigeon Loft*, for 1,500 pesetas in 1878, the year it was painted. This time the Malagueños were not even allowed through the artist's electrically controlled gate, nor was their gift. Picasso was probably in a cantankerous mood; he usually was on his birthdays—the last few milestones on the road to death. And he would have hated being manoeuvred into handing over one of his own works—a precious early one most likely—for this daub. In any case, he already owned more than enough parental pigeons. So the Malagueño envoys were kept cooling their heels in a hotel in Mougins, sending plaintive cables to the mayor of their city asking how to deal with this unanticipated snub.[2] The artist did not relent.

This churlishness was dictated by Picasso's lifelong resentment of his birthplace—resentment of the backwardness, listlessness and air of defeat that characterized the beautiful southern province where he spent the first ten years (1881–91) of his life. Later he had come to think of himself as a Catalan and his city as Barcelona, even though he did not move there until after his thirteenth birthday. And since Picasso's memories often involved an element of wish fulfilment, a Catalan he became. The progressive Catalans were apt to look down on people from the south. This is why the artist, who treasured the company of his fellow Spaniards, indeed of almost anyone who spoke Spanish, and treated them with unfailing courtesy, hospitality and generosity (his rebuffal of the city fathers notwithstanding), accorded a warmer welcome to Catalans than Malagueños. In the 1950s he even went so far as to counsel his secretary, Jaime Sabartès, to donate the bulk of the Sabartès collection, including an archive and a lifetime of major gifts from Picasso—to Barcelona, and not, as he had originally intended, to Málaga.[3]

Picasso's repudiation of Málaga and everything associated with it, except the *cante jondo* of the gypsies (the only music he really liked), is at first sight puzzling, for his childhood there had apparently been happy, sheltered, free and easy, full of love. From the moment he was born he had been indulged by his weak, kindly father and his strong, warm-hearted, typically Andalusian mother. And although the family was obliged to live on his father's miserable salary as an art teacher, they were never in actual want, thanks to a network of prosperous relatives. However, the stigma of being a poor relation permanently bruised Picasso's pride. He resented charity, above all the niggardly charity of his rich uncle Salvador, the benefactor who stood for the bourgeois hypocrisy and stuffiness that Picasso associated with Málaga.

Triumphal arch built for the 1888 Universal Exhibition in Barcelona, which marked that city's rise to international fame. Photo, *c.*1900: Mas.

Family resentment aside, there were other reasons to prefer Barcelona to Málaga. In the 1890s Barcelona was a city of opportunity. Despite an undercurrent of social strife, its avant garde looked ahead to the twentieth century with an optimism that was positively Utopian. As well as being a centre of advanced ideas in art and architecture, not to speak of politics both separatist and anarchist, the city was far more prosperous, international and stimulating than any other in Spain. (It had much the same relationship to the rest of the country as New York has to the United States.) In stagnant Málaga, by contrast, local artists or writers or, for that matter, businessmen had to decide between a life of idleness and frustration or flight. The fact that Picasso's pigeon-fancying father was the complacent victim of this situation made the son all the more eager to disavow his dismal heritage.

Picasso could not have come into the world at a less propitious time for Málaga. Earlier in the century the city had been one of the richest in Spain, thanks to its agriculture, ironworks and strong trading links with Britain and America. But in 1878 phylloxera, the American grape disease that had crossed the Atlantic in 1865 and destroyed French vineyards, finally reached the south of Spain and wiped out not only Málaga's extensive wine business but also the area's lucrative raisin crop.[4] The vines that supported Picasso's maternal family never recovered. Cotton—the other principal crop—also suffered, and the closure of textile factories put many more people out of work. Meanwhile, the local iron industry had gone into a decline—done in by the foundries of the north, which had devised cheaper methods of smelting. And the market for sugar, another staple of the region, was undercut by cheap imports from the Caribbean and the even cheaper substitution of beets for sugarcane. Wages in Andalusia had always been lower than anywhere else in Spain, but all of a sudden there was very little work. A series of strikes (1868, 1869 and 1890) and a succession of epidemics (cholera claimed 1,705 victims in 1885) made for disaster. This beautiful Mediterranean harbour was dying. Eventually tourism would bring the area back to prosperity: at first as an elegant winter resort for elderly Madrileños; later (after 1950) as the centre of one of the most overrun and overexploited holiday areas on the Mediterranean. But by then Picasso had long abandoned not only Andalusia but Spain itself.

Bernardo Ferrándiz and Antonio Muñoz Degrain. *Allegory of the History, Industry and Commerce of Málaga;* ceiling design for the new Teatro Cervantes. Oil on canvas, 190×170 cm. 1870. Museo de Málaga.

* * *

Above: Textile mills and the ironworks of La Constancia on the outskirts of Málaga in the mid-nineteenth century. Archivo Díaz de Escovar, Málaga.

Right: Warehouse in the fishing port at the western end of Málaga harbour, July 1886. Manuel Blasco collection.

On his father's side, Picasso was descended from a knight of legendary courage—Juan de León, the owner of an estate near Valladolid, who was killed in the battle of Granada in 1481. Thanks to an archaic custom that preserved the father's name for an eldest son by permitting a younger son to adopt a maternal or other family name, Picasso's ancestors by the end of the seventeenth century bore the far less distinguished name of Ruiz. Ruizes they remained. In the eighteenth century, Picasso's great-grandfather, José Ruiz y de Fuentes, married the aristocratic María Josefa de Almoguera, whose family had provided the church with an archbishop of Lima and captain-general of Peru in the seventeenth century and a saintly hermit in the nineteenth. At this point the Ruizes dropped from the ranks of the landed gentry. Although they were both descended from Córdoban landowners, don José and doña María Josefa left their native region, for no reason that has been discovered, and settled first in Morón de la Frontera, then in Málaga. The family did not prosper in the south, possibly because times were troubled. Napoleon had invaded Spain, and a regiment commanded by General Sebastiani occupied Málaga. To make matters worse, don José's eldest son, Diego (Picasso's grandfather), then aged eleven, threw a sharp stone at a French officer in one of Sebastiani's parades. The family maintained that Diego was out to avenge the insult to Spanish honour that the French occupation represented. The French treated the child's prank as an act of rebellion; the culprit was so badly mauled by a trooper that he was left for dead. But Diego recovered, and forever after lived off the kudos of this exploit.

Don Diego courted and ultimately (1830) married María de la Paz Blasco y Echevarría, who was partly Aragonese (Blasco) and partly Basque (Echevarría). They produced eleven children, of whom José, the artist's father, was the ninth. Although of noble descent on both sides (Blasco was an ancient name associated with privilege in Aragon), don Diego joined the ranks of the bourgeoisie by becoming a glove-maker, working hard to keep his large family fed, clothed and educated. Nevertheless he ended up an embittered man, as he had always wanted to be a musician or a painter rather than a tradesman. The only pictures of don Diego portray an old curmudgeon who looks highly strung and quick to anger. But he was also 'intelligent . . . humorous, spirited, musical (he played double bass in the local orchestra) and artistic to the extent that he liked to draw.'[5] In October 1876, at the age of seventy-seven, don Diego went to Halama, near Granada, to take a cure. His son Salvador, who accompanied him, reported that, 'he may have lost the use of his legs, but not that of his tongue. He talks more than a parakeet.'[6] A few days later Picasso's grandfather was dead of a stroke.

Don Diego was survived by four sons and four daughters (one girl died of cholera in 1860, one as an infant, one aged nineteen). Picasso's father, José Ruiz Blasco, was not the youngest, but he was certainly the most spoiled. He was thirty-eight when his father died, and still lived at home, fussed over by indulgent sisters. While his three brothers bettered themselves, José eked out a meagre living as an art teacher and painter of the pigeons that he devoted much of his time to breeding. His other passion was for the bulls, *los toros*—a passion he passed on to his son. Except for a family tradition that José's early manhood had been blighted by the death of a great love, there is no record that this assiduous frequenter of

Picasso's grandfather, Don Diego Ruiz y Almoguera. Oil on canvas. Ricardo Huelin collection.

Picasso's uncle, Diego Ruiz Blasco, Ricardo Huelin collection.

Picasso's uncle, Canon Pablo Ruiz Blasco. Musée Picasso, Paris.

local brothels had any romantic attachments. Bachelordom seems to have been a pretext for avoiding the responsibilities of marriage—a fate he managed to put off until well into middle age. José's elegance, charm and wit, his fair hair and complexion (which earned him the nickname of 'the Englishman'), are traits that Picasso would always remember with pride. He also envied his height. All his life the artist regretted that he looked less like his 'aristocratic' father than his homely mother. His father's 'English' distinction would, for Picasso, be forever enshrined in a set of eighteenth-century Chippendale-ish chairs that José bought at the sale of an English wine-merchant's house in Málaga. These seem to have constituted his paternal inheritance, and they would always be an important feature of his household.

Picasso's father, don José (known to friends and family as Pepe), had a twofold problem: the inclination to be an artist but not the gifts, and the temperament of a gentleman of leisure but not the means. The good things cancelled out; not, however, the bad things. If the family failed to oppose José's choice of a career, which was hardly in accord with their bourgeois standards and for which he was ill-equipped, it was because he was a charmer who usually got his way. Besides, most of the Ruiz family were sympathetically disposed towards the arts. Picasso's grandfather, don Diego, was not only a musician but a draughtsman, who enrolled two of his sons, José and Pablo, for a free course in drawing at the Instituto de Enseñanza.[7] Pablo subsequently forsook the study of art for the priesthood, but he continued to collect devotional paintings and sculpture. Their older brother and don Diego's namesake painted still lifes, images of saints and copies of Rubens and Velázquez; one of the sisters, Matilde, is said to have been 'artistic', and Salvador prided himself on being 'a lover of all the arts',[8] and of having married the daughter of a noted sculptor.

Picasso's uncle, Dr Salvador Ruiz Blasco. Manuel Blasco collection.

José's brothers all distinguished themselves in the classic professions of the bourgeoisie: Diego, the eldest, may not have reached the highest rungs of the diplomatic corps—accompanying the Spanish ambassador to Russia (in what capacity we do not know) was his finest hour—but Salvador became a most respected doctor in Málaga, and Pablo, by virtue of being a doctor of theology and canon to the cathedral, could look forward to a bishopric. José, however, had no financial sense, no inclination to follow his father into trade, and no aptitude for 'the professions'. A modest talent for drawing had been nurtured by enrolment (in 1851, when he was twelve or thirteen) at Málaga's newly founded Escuela de Bellas Artes. *Faute de mieux*, José drifted into art.

The school began as 'a second grade academy for minor studies' and was principally designed for adult pupils—factory workers, stonemasons, carpenters and the like—who studied technical subjects. It was so successful that in 1868—after José had left as a pupil but before he returned as a teacher—it was upgraded.[9] The Provincial Council of Málaga put it under the direction of a reputable painter from Valencia, Bernardo Ferrándiz. He was succeeded in 1879 by his better-known friend (likewise from Valencia), Antonio Muñoz Degrain, who would become José's 'oracle' and revered friend. Muñoz Degrain and Ferrándiz formed the nucleus of what came to be known as the 'School of Málaga', which flourished in the 1870s.[10] Ferrándiz, who assumed the role of leader, promoted the painterly techniques he had learned from his famous

Picasso's father, José Ruiz Blasco. Ricardo Huelin collection.

Antonio Muñoz Degrain. *Portrait of a Lady*. 1885. Oil on canvas, 65×52cm. Museo de Málaga.

contemporary the Catalan Marià Fortuny: accurate recording of detail combined with *preciosismo* (the virtuoso rendering of shimmering surfaces —silk and satin, gold and silver—so as to give a sparkle to subjects that might otherwise tend to be drab). Both at the school and in his studio on a hill above the city Ferrándiz surrounded himself with disciples, among them Picasso's father. In all this he was seconded by Muñoz Degrain, whose enthusiasm for landscape painting inspired local artists to work— not very successfully—out of doors.

The other influential artist in José's life was the Andalusian Joaquín Martínez de la Vega, who had escaped his home town, Almería, to study in Madrid, where he was considered the most promising pupil at the Academy. His appointment as teacher of young ladies at the Liceo (an arts club catering to local society) brought a badly needed touch of sophistication to Málaga; so did the fashionable portraits he did, with their overtones of Carolus Duran. Although at odds with Muñoz Degrain and the stuffier teachers, Martínez de la Vega became a great friend of don José, who would always revere him as the first serious artist to recognize the budding genius of his son Pablo. The stagnation of Malagueño life eventually did him in; he took to drink and drugs and died in 1905.

Beyond being a disciple of Muñoz Degrain, and a hanger-on at Ferrándiz's studio, Picasso's father never became a luminary of the School of Málaga. True, he won prizes at the Liceo's annual exhibitions in 1862 and 1871, but he did not take his art seriously, either as a vocation or as a lucrative career. Nor for many years was there any pressure on him to do so. José's life revolved around cultural activities at the Liceo (located in the old convent of San Francisco) and the handsome new (1870) Teatro Cervantes. Like his double-bass-playing father, he frequented the Philharmonic Society and the Conservatory of Music. Thanks to his looks and charm, José also became a popular figure in cultivated liberal circles, with a reputation for being 'somewhat vague'. Years later Picasso recalled his father returning from the house of a local marquesa in some embarrassment; he had not noticed that in the course of luncheon he had managed to button a napkin into his fly.

Diego Ruiz Blasco. *Portrait of a Lady*. Oil on canvas. Private collection.

Surviving members of the Ruiz Blasco family remember being told that the easygoing—one suspects feckless—José dawdled much of the day away in cafés, where he was celebrated less for his prowess as a pigeon painter than his conversation, which exemplified 'the Malagueño vein of light-hearted and rather fantastic irony, with a certain boyish thread of braggadocio running through it.'[11] However, Sabartès, Picasso's secretary and principal myth-maker, surely exaggerates when he acclaims don José's 'audacity, his picaresque adventures, his unspeakable series of high jinks triggered by a fertile imagination and carried out with the help of his friends, Aldana, Castillo and Juan Carreño . . . whose *bons mots* could bring down the government like a house of cards.'[12] Picassian hyperbole! Failure would give an increasingly sardonic edge to José's fabled irony—a trait that he passed on in good measure to his son. If he continued to entertain his cronies, it was with barbs rather than *boutades*. Don José's last words are a measure of his querulous disdain. To the insensitive concierge, who came too close to his deathbed, he said, 'What have things come to? Are there no more frontiers?'[13]

Right: Bernardo Ferrándiz. Sketch for the drop-curtain of the Teatro Cervantes. Oil on canvas, *c.*61×125cm. Private collection.

Below: José Denis Belgrano. *Scene in the Liceo.* Málaga, *c.*1900. Oil on canvas, 39×24cm. Private collection.

The studio of Martínez de la Vega, *c.*1900. Teresa Sauret collection.

Of Málaga's numerous cafés, José's favourite was the famous Café de Chinitas[14]—a place of very mixed pleasures; originally a café-concert, it was later known for cockfighting in the afternoons, debates in the evenings, followed by dancing and pornographic 'entertainments': women, naked under cloaks, performing with bananas. Like most Spaniards of his class, José belonged to a *tertulia*: in his case a distinguished one consisting of politicians, lawyers, doctors, writers and a few artists, who are said to have relished his sharp wit. *Tertulias* were not limited to cafés: José frequented similar gatherings in Ferrándiz's studio, the Liceo and the local pharmacy. After the *tertulia*, young men of the bourgeoisie would go whoring. Most of the *casas malas* were situated near the churches—unlike the more plebeian sailors' brothels that were located near the harbour. The whorehouse most frequented by don José was 'Lola la Chata', where the girls would sit around knitting, sewing or reading 'in a conventional sitting-room almost as if they were daughters of the bourgeoisie.'[15] A century later, José's penchant for these establishments inspired his son to depict the frock-coated father in the guise of Degas, imperturbably inspecting and on occasion drawing the whores in a brothel, which is a cross between 'Lola la Chata' and Maupassant's Maison Tellier.

Preparatory Education: a dancer's admirer backstage. Cartoon from the Málaga satirical magazine, *El País de la Olla,* January 29, 1883. Library of the Ayuntamiento, Málaga.

It was not until 1875, when he was thirty-seven, that José took a regular job—as assistant teacher to his friend Serafín Martínez del Rincón, at the Escuela. And just as well, for on don Diego's death the following year the family's house was sold. All the same, José still refused to set up on his own. He simply moved in with his brother Pablo—by a now a canon —who also welcomed two of the spinster sisters, Josefa and Matilde, into his house on the Calle Granada. It was only a temporary measure, for the canon insisted that José find a wife. Not one of don Diego's eleven children had as yet produced a son and heir—a shameful state of affairs in Andalusian eyes. For lack of initiative on José's part, the family decided to come up with a girl called Amelia Picasso (sister of the future general Juan Picasso González), who was thought to have attracted José. But he was still in no hurry to marry, and the more the brothers insisted that he court the Picasso girl, the more he procrastinated. Finally, in 1878, José proposed—not to the family's candidate (he prided himself on his freedom of spirit), but to her cousin, María Picasso López: a very short, very lively girl seventeen years younger than himself, and a rung or two below the Ruizes in the social hierarchy.

All of a sudden disaster struck both families. First phylloxera put an end to the modest income the Picasso family derived from agricultural rents. María's sisters were reduced to making gold braid for the caps of railway workers. As for the Ruiz family, the saintly and supportive Canon Pablo died in 1879 at the early age of forty-six, and José's parasitic life ended. From now on he would have to fend for himself. Meanwhile, mourning would prolong his engagement for a further year.

Fortunately José had another, equally protective, brother, Salvador, who was six years younger.[16] Salvador was the most ambitious and hardworking of the Ruiz brothers: already a very successful doctor whose wife had borne him two daughters, Concepción (Concha) and María de la Paz. This bourgeois paragon took the two spinster sisters he had inherited from Canon Pablo, Matilde and Josefa (Picasso's aunt Pepa), to live with him in his large house on the Plaza de la Aduana, down by the harbour. And in his piety he did his best to look after his unworldly brother José.

The early death of his wife had left the pious Salvador more pious than ever. He devoted himself increasingly to good works: supplying free medical attention to two orders of nuns, and protecting them—once at the risk of his life—from outbreaks of religious persecution. The doctor's special concern was a French community of Augustine nuns who had been brought to Málaga by a pious grande dame, doña Amalia Heredia y Livermore, Marquesa de Casa Loring.[17] So grateful was this powerful lady for Dr Salvador's services to 'her' French nuns, as well as for the great care he took of her sickly son, Tomás Heredia, that she would eventually (1896) marry him off to her plain, forty-year-old niece, Adelaida Martínez Loring. This grand match would be a source of snobbish pride to the rest of the Ruizes—not however to Picasso, who would be made to feel more than ever like a poor relation. He never had a good word for his sanctimonious uncle.

José Ruiz Blasco. *The Fish Vendor:* copy after Leoncio Talavera's prize-winning painting of 1877. Oil on canvas. Private collection.

In 1879, however, Salvador was not yet in a position to give his brother much financial help. Fortunately José won a modest promotion (July 13, 1879) at the Escuela: he was made general assistant teacher of drawing (at 1,500 pesetas a year, though without tenure). Then, thanks to his friendly rapport with the influential Muñoz Degrain and also to his brother's connections with the municipality, he acquired yet another source of income to support his bride-to-be.[18] Early in December 1879, José was appointed curator of the new municipal museum, which Muñoz Degrain had founded in the former Augustine monastery. The salary was small, 125 pesetas a month; still, it effectively doubled his income.[19]

José's responsibility lay less in administration (the new museum was virtually never open to the public) than conservation, specifically in the restoration of the grubby old canvases that formed the nucleus of the collection. José knew no more about conservation techniques than anyone else in Spain at the time, but at least he was an experienced copyist and trainer of copyists. A secondary attraction of this job was the studio that José could use for his own work. Not that his daubs found many buyers. Apart from the city, the only recorded purchasers of his work were a certain Ildefonso Ruiz (who owned one canvas) and Enrique Padrón Arteaga, a brother-in-law's brother and estate manager for the Larioses, the foremost local landowners; Padrón owned four of the canvases José had exhibited at the Exposición de Bellas Artes de Málaga in 1877.[20]

José Ruiz Blasco. *Still Life.* Oil on canvas. Private collection.

José's work attracted so few buyers not because he confined himself to the life of the pigeon (his only known portrait—of his brother Diego—was destroyed during the Civil War), but because he was such an execrable painter. Even by the bourgeois standards of the period, his taste was beyond kitsch: he depicted his pets anthropomorphically in terms of domestic bliss or homely allegory; and his style was unoriginal to the point of banality. A hundred years later we can see, through the prism of his son's work, that this tastelessness has a certain negative force—a view later echoed by Picasso, who was always ready, like Goya, to see beauty in ugliness. But to his contemporaries with their penchant for chocolate-box prettiness, chocolate-box ugliness was unacceptable.

* * *

Picasso's grandmother Inés López Robles, with her daughters Aurelia (left) and María Picasso López. Musée Picasso, Paris.

Picasso's maternal grandfather, Francisco Picasso Guardeño. Musée Picasso, Paris.

After the mandatory period of mourning for Canon Pablo was over, José married María. The wedding took place on the Feast of the Immaculate Conception, December 8, 1880, in the parish church of Santiago, where his brother Pablo had served as priest before his appointment to the cathedral. The bride was twenty-five years old, and although the husband was forty-two, from expedience, vanity or vagueness, he claimed on his marriage certificate to be thirty-six.[21] The choice of sponsors for the 'veiling'—in southern Spain friends or relatives veil the couple in the course of the nuptial mass—was not without significance: one of José's maternal cousins, Juan Nepomuceno Blasco Barroso, and his wife, María de los Remedios Alarcón Herrera. According to their son, Manuel, the Blasco Barrosos had been picked because they were younger, more socially acceptable and better off than José. (For the same reasons this couple was asked, a year later, to act as godparents to José's son, Pablo.)

María Picasso López was more typically Mediterranean than her English-looking husband. She was very short and a bit plump, but pretty, with delicate features, dark eyes and blue-black hair. She was vivacious, good-humoured and incorrigibly optimistic—qualities that would carry her and her family relatively unscathed through much poverty and hardship, and would make for a remarkably cheerful and fully occupied old age. For all her charms, María was not a good catch—nor, for that matter, was her husband. In the chauvinistic eyes of the Malagueños, María was a 'foreigner' in that her grandfather had been an Italian immigrant.[22] And, although they had arrived from Genoa at the beginning of the century, the Picassos had never bothered to take out Spanish citizenship. This lapse may explain the puzzling fact that the family continued to register with the British consulate. Why the British consulate? There is no record of the Picassos having any British blood. Was there a business link? Probably, for María's father (Picasso's grandfather), Francisco Picasso Guardeño, had been educated in England—something that was unusual for a middle-class Spanish (or for that matter, Italian) boy of the period. Francisco is a mystery in other respects. Next to nothing is known about this bizarre gentleman with the staring eyes and outsize walrus moustache beyond the fact that he married a plump young woman from the province of Málaga, Inés López Robles, rumoured to be a Marrana (of Jewish descent);[23] that he fathered four girls (Aurelia, María, Eladia and Eliodora) and abandoned his family, though not definitively, for a career in Cuba.

In 1883, after some years as a customs official in Havana—a job for which his languages would have qualified him—don Francisco announced that he was returning home, presumably to retire. Luggage, which was shipped on ahead, arrived as expected, but not don Francisco. Fifteen years would pass before the Picassos learned of his fate: before leaving Havana, he had gone to the port of Matanzas to take leave of an old friend. Yellow fever had broken out; don Francisco caught it and died in a local hotel. The body had been buried in haste, and the death had gone unrecorded.

Rents from the family vineyards and whatever her husband managed to send from Cuba enabled María's mother to support her young family during the long years of grass widowhood, at least until 1878, when phylloxera wiped out her main source of income. And so, far from providing José with a badly needed dowry, his bride brought him, materially speaking, nothing but liabilities: an impoverished mother-in-law and two young sisters-in-law, who never married and were thus a drain on the family's straitened finances. The other sister-in-law, Aurelia, fared better: she married Baldomero Ghiara, a jeweller (also of Italian descent), who would, along with José's brother Salvador, briefly finance Picasso's studies in Madrid. Fortunately, hardship had prepared María for the poverty that lay ahead. She was a constant source of energy and knew just how to scrimp and improvise to keep her family fed and clothed and resilient.

Despite their reduced circumstances, the Picassos—like the Ruizes—could boast of at least one distinguished connection: María's first cousin, General Juan Picasso González, who won fame in the African campaign of 1893. Later (1921), General Picasso was chosen to head an inquiry into the military disaster at Annual. But his report—a volume of seven hundred pages known as the 'Picasso File'—compromised so many important friends of Alfonso XIII that it was suppressed. After the king's abdication there was again talk of making the 'Picasso File' public, but it would have implicated too many people in the new regime, and was once and for all hushed up.[24] Picasso took ironical pride in the career of this gallant cousin—who resembled him in being 'small, energetic, witty and intensely bright'[25]—and in the fascists' suppression of the famous file, just as he would always take ironical pride in the fact that both sides of his impoverished family reached into the higher echelons of the Spanish establishment and that he was descended from an illustrious line of knights and clerics.

The witnesses at the wedding of José Ruiz Blasco and María Picasso López: María Alarcón Herrera and her husband, Juan Nepomuceno Blasco Barroso. Manuel Blasco collection.

2

Pablo Ruiz Picasso, Son and Heir

The church of Santiago, where Picasso was baptised. It stands a short distance from the Plaza de la Merced in the Calle de Granada, the street where don José had lived (at no.8) with his family before his marriage. Archivo Díaz de Escovar, Málaga.

Opposite: Plaza de la Merced, Málaga. The apartment where Picasso was born is behind the trees at centre, on the corner by the church of La Merced. Archivo Temboury, Málaga.

HIS MOTHER, DOÑA MARÍA, Picasso claimed, was no more than conventionally pious; however, she had a special devotion to the Virgin de la Merced, and belonged to the Hermandad de la Victoria, a lay sisterhood. Realizing that everyone's hopes were pinned upon her, she prayed hard to have a son—the first male heir for either side of the family. Her prayers were answered on October 25, 1881, when Pablo was born. If she had given birth to the Messiah, the family could hardly have been more joyful. In later years Picasso gave precise but conflicting information as to the hour of his birth: 'half past nine P.M.', he wrote on the flyleaf of Geiser's copy of his catalogue of Picasso's engraved work;[1] 'midnight' is what he told others. According to his birth certificate, the artist was born at 11:15 P.M. It was a difficult birth, and the baby showed so little sign of life that the midwife concluded he was stillborn, and left him lying on a table while she attended the mother. He would have died, Picasso said, if his uncle Salvador had not been present. 'Doctors . . . used to smoke big cigars and my uncle was no exception. When he saw me lying there he blew smoke into my face. . . . I immediately reacted with a grimace and a bellow of fury.'[2] 'This story so often told in childhood,' Penrose has written, 'of how death was so forcefully present at birth lurked in Picasso's imagination throughout his life.'[3]

There has also been confusion as to exactly where Picasso was born. The birth certificate gives the address as an apartment on the third floor of 36 Plaza de la Merced (alternatively known as Plaza de Riego).[4] All that Picasso remembered is that he was born in a house that 'belonged to don Antonio Campo, or Campos, [and] that the apartment into which [the family] moved later, overlooking the square, was in the same building.'[5] Although the census confirms Picasso's recollection, it has been questioned.[6]

Despite his harrowing start, the baby flourished. Since the mother was slow to regain her strength, the christening did not take place within forty-eight hours, as was the local custom, but was put off until November 10, 1881. The parish church of Santiago, where the parents had been married eleven months earlier, was the scene of the baptism, and the same priest, Father José Fernández Quintero—a friend of the late Canon Pablo—officiated. Besides being named Pablo after his uncle, the baby was given an impressive string of names in the Malagueño manner: Diego (after his paternal grandfather and eldest uncle), José (after his father), Francisco de Paula (after his maternal grandfather), Juan Nepomuceno and María de los Remedios (after his cousins, Juan Nepomuceno Blasco Barroso and María de los Remedios Alarcón Herrera, who were also his godparents), Crispín Crispiniano (after the two shoemaker saints whose feastday falls on October 25), and Santísima Trinidad (added by Andalusians as an ultimate reverential flourish).

Picasso's aunt Eloísa and her husband, Antonio Suárez Pizarro. Ricardo Huelin collection.

Doña María's mother and the two braid-making sisters, Eladia and Eliodora, were probably a later addition to the Ruiz Blasco household. Their names appear on the census of 1885 as residents of 32 Plaza de Riego, so they presumably did not move in until the family left no. 36 for the larger apartment. These women, whom Picasso remembered as a permanent feature of his childhood, deserve recognition for having beguiled their nephew's inquisitive eye with the minutiae of their ornate craft. The artist's ironical use of embroidery-like arabesques and foliate patterns, which are a recurrent feature of 'rococo' cubist still lifes and decorative passages in prints and drawings as late as the sixties, can be traced back to the encrustations of gold braid with which the aunts adorned the caps of provincial station-masters.

A paternal aunt, Eloísa, also played an important role in Pablo's upbringing, as did her husband, Antonio Suárez Pizarro. This couple had gone to live with Uncle Salvador after the death of his first wife. Eloísa acted as housekeeper, the emasculated Antonio as a kind of nanny to the children. Uncle Antonio, who was fat and greedy and liked to make candy, used to include Pablo on his morning walks with Uncle Salvador's two daughters down by the harbour. Pablo liked Antonio, but don José had typically Andalusian reservations: this in-law was the reverse of macho; he was a parasite; he was also a Jew. Although a man of moderate opinions, don José was in sympathy with the anti-Semitic ideas then prevalent in Spain—at least according to his son,[7] who was a lifelong foe of anti-Semitism.

Below: Entry from the census of 1884/5 listing the residents of 32 Plaza de Riego: don José Ruiz Blasco and his sons, Pablo, aged 3, and José, aged 1; doña María Picasso López, doña Inés López Robles and her other two daughters, Eladia, aged 21, and Eliodora, aged 19, and the servant Mariana. Ayuntamiento, Málaga.

TÉRMINO MUNICIPAL DE MÁLAGA

Núm. de la casa.	NOMBRES Y APELLIDOS DE LOS VARONES	Edad — Años.	Estado.	Profesion.	Sabe leer	Sabe escribir	PUEBLO de su naturaleza.

Biographers have inevitably made much of Pablo's predominantly female upbringing, but this was (still is, in working-class families) an Andalusian custom. Gilmore has described how pre-adolescent boys 'spend most of their time in [the] female sphere, a place which their fathers and older brothers scrupulously avoid as feminine. The older men spend virtually all their free time in the totally segregated male world of the bars and taverns. Young sons are therefore effectively separated from adult male kinsmen and are surrounded from birth by often dominant mothers, older sisters and grandmothers. These women monopolize all aspects of child-rearing and socialization.'[8] This was especially true of Pablo, who had no young male relatives—brothers or cousins—with whom to play.

In fact Picasso may not have been as brotherless as we have been led to believe. The artist never mentioned the existence of a sibling, nor has anyone else. However, the 1885 census records that the Ruiz household included a second male child, named José, aged one, who was listed as having been baptized in the church of Santiago. Research in local archives has failed to confirm whether this child existed and died in infancy or was merely a clerical error.[9]

Picasso's typically Andalusian upbringing at the hands of a doting mother and grandmother abetted by two doting maternal aunts, a succession of doting maids (first Mariana Montañés, then the masculine-looking

Scene in the 'Chupa y Tira' quarter below the castle, painted in 1881 by Rafael Blanco, a student at the Escuela de Bellas Artes. Watercolour on paper, 25×16.1 cm. Museu Picasso, Barcelona.

NICIPAL CALLE

NOMBRES Y APELLIDOS DE LAS HEMBRAS | Edad Años | ESTADO | PUEBLO de su naturaleza | PARROQUIA en que se bautizó

and moustachioed Carmen Mendoza), and, on occasion, by don José's no less doting spinster sisters, is in keeping with his subsequent alternations of misogyny and tenderness towards women: his insatiable need for their love and attention on the one hand, his affectionate though sometimes heartless manipulation of them on the other. Machismo, we would do well to remember, is a concept specifically associated with Andalusia; it is not surprising to find women bringing it out in the adult Picasso. It was the only possible attitude for an artist, he once said, when challenged. As an artist and an Andalusian, he felt entitled to have women cater to his deepest psychic needs as well as his childish caprices. To demonstrate this point, the great man would time and again turn back into a fractious child and oblige his wife or mistress to indulge his infantile rituals and tantrums—as for instance when setting out on a journey—just as the infant Picasso obliged the women of the Plaza de la Merced to submit to his will. His eyes, which gaze implacably out at us from his earliest photograph, were already endowed with *la mirada fuerte*.

According to doña María, Pablito, as she usually called her son, could draw before he could speak, and the first sound that he made was '*piz, piz* . . .'—baby language for *lapiz*, i.e., pencil.[10] When given a pencil, the infant would apparently draw spirals that represented a snail-shaped fritter called a *torruela*. None of the earliest drawings have survived, so these accounts have to be taken on faith. Picasso himself remembered that while other children played under the trees of the Plaza de la Merced, he would make drawings in the dust—a habit he recalled years later, when he would divert and at the same time dismay his companions (especially art dealers) by tracing elaborate compositions on a sandy beach and watch with sardonic glee as the sea washed away his handiwork.

As he grew up Pablo would forsake the more prosperous quarters of the city, where 'the Victorias of the Madrid aristocracy rolled up and down . . . and sleek, jingling horses and gleaming spokes flickered by under the lattice of the plane trees',[11] for the Moorish castle of the Gibralfaro and, below, the picturesque Alcazaba with its Arab labyrinth of hanging gardens and crumbling walls and flocks of peacocks. In the shadow of the Alcazaba were the shacks of 'Chupa y Tira', where beggars and gypsies 'sat de-lousing one another in the sun among whiffs of orange flower and drying excrement [and] children up to the age of twelve ran naked.'[12] The neighbourhood was called 'Chupa y Tira' (Suck and Throw) because 'the people were so poor', Picasso told Sabartès, 'that all they could eat was a chowder made with clams. And all their backyards were filled with clamshells which they had thrown out of their windows after having sucked out . . . their very souls.'[13] Picasso's love for *cante jondo* originated in the 'Chupa y Tira.' But that was not all the gypsies taught him. Unbeknownst to his family, he learned not only how to smoke but how to smoke with a cigarette up his nostril; he also learned how to dance rudimentary flamenco. 'There was no end to the tricks I learned from the gypsies,' he would say mysteriously.

A few days before doña María gave birth to another child, Málaga was struck by a severe earthquake. The tremors began at eleven o'clock on Christmas night, 1884, and lasted for several days. Some six hundred people were killed and many more seriously injured. There was vast devastation, not least to the cathedral and the hospital. When the first

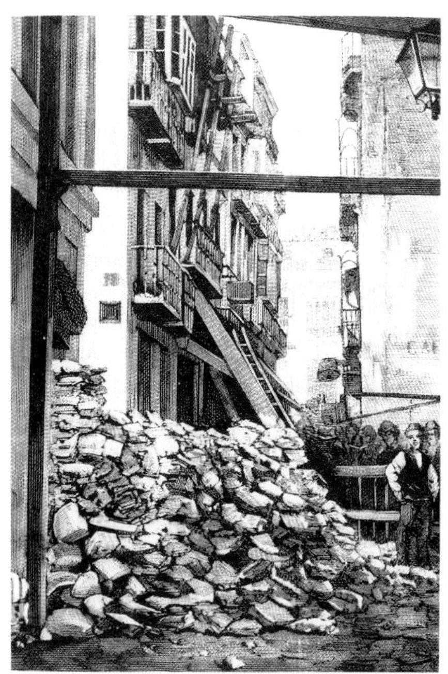

Ruined house in the Calle de Granada after the earthquake in Málaga in December 1884. From *La Ilustración Española*.

tremors struck, don José was talking to friends in a neighbourhood pharmacy. As the chemist's jars and bottles crashed down, he rushed back home to his third-floor apartment and told his pregnant wife to throw on some clothes and follow him to a safer place.

Although Pablo was only three, he claimed to recall exactly what had happened: he remembered his mother putting a scarf round her head—a peasant-like gesture that he had never seen before; he remembered his father flinging a cape over his shoulders, then snatching him up and wrapping him in its folds until only his head peeped out.[14] At first don José thought of heading for his brother Salvador's house, but this was some way off—buildings might collapse on top of them. On second thoughts he decided to make for somewhere closer and safer: the studio of Muñoz Degrain, who was away in Rome on a painting trip. Muñoz Degrain's studio was in a well-built house on the Calle de la Victoria, which don José knew to be built on a rocky outcrop. There the Ruiz Blasco family found shelter; and there, on December 28, doña María gave birth to a daughter. Despite the drama of the earthquake, mother and daughter suffered no harm.[15]

On January 10, after things had more or less returned to normal, the child was christened María de los Dolores Joaquina Josefa Juana Teodora de la Santísima Trinidad—Lola for short. Her godparents were Muñoz Degrain's wife, María de los Dolores Sánchez, and son Joaquín (because Muñoz Degrain himself was away in Rome). Later in life Picasso enjoyed giving a spirited account of these events, and he would finish his tale in characteristically mocking fashion with a description—which certainly originated from don José—of how, a few days after the earthquake, Alfonso XII paid a state visit to the devastated city; and how Muñoz Degrain and his companion, Moreno Carbonero, the well-known painter (whom Picasso remembered watching at work on an elaborate academic painting in the bullring), happened to return by train from Rome the same day as the king arrived from Madrid, and were convinced that the flags and bunting were in their honour, not the king's.

* * *

Most of what we know about Picasso's early childhood comes from Jaime Sabartès, for sixty-five years his fanatically loyal friend and from 1936 onwards his secretary. Most of what Sabartès says comes from Picasso. And as Picasso's cousin (Dr Salvador's grandson) Ricardo Huelin y Ruiz Blasco has pointed out, Sabartès was often led astray by the artist's Andalusian embellishment.[16] Picasso's memory, factual as well as visual, was prodigious; but in certain sensitive areas, childhood, for instance, we have to make allowances for hyperbole or fantasy—not that this makes his recollections any the less revealing. Most of the stories concern Picasso's impatience to be an adult. According to Sabartès, the artist was very proud of having learned to walk upright like an adult (by pushing a large tin of Olibet biscuits round the room) instead of toddling about like most infants. This was done to please his family as much as to satisfy himself.

There is a similar element of wish fulfilment in Picasso's frequently reiterated claim that, just as he never walked like a child, he never drew like a child: 'I have never done children's drawings. Never. Even when I was very small. I remember one of my first drawings. I was perhaps six, or even less [i.e., 1887]. In my father's house there was a statue of Hercules with his club in the corridor, and I drew Hercules. But it wasn't a child's drawing. It was a real drawing, representing Hercules with his club.'[17] Wishful thinking played him false. Picasso had forgotten that the drawing in question is dated November 1890—that is to say, three years later than he thought. The execution and conception are no more or less mature than one would expect of a gifted nine-year-old. In the circumstances it is suspicious that nothing has survived that might confirm Picasso's claim to have bypassed the instinctive phase of childhood perception. On the evidence of the Hercules drawing, however, it would seem that Picasso—unlike certain composers (Mozart, for instance)—conforms to the rule that no great painter has ever produced work of any serious interest before puberty. However, his legend obliged him to have been a genius from earliest days. He was not joking when he later said there was no such thing as a bad Picasso; some were more or less good than others. By virtue of being by him, everything—even his earliest scribbles—had to be in some degree the work of a prodigy if not a genius.

Picasso. *Hercules*. Málaga, November 1890. Pencil on paper, 49.6×32cm. Museu Picasso, Barcelona.

Virtuosity is conspicuously absent from what, so far as is known, are Picasso's first extant works: two little paintings and two or three drawings (1889–91).[18] Except for the Hercules, these are all that survive from his first ten years of life. Tempting as it is to see the germ of great art in Picasso's juvenilia, they are once again what one would expect from a reasonably gifted child. True, if we turn one of the drawings upside down, we find a row of competently executed pigeons, but since the style is so much slicker than the rest of these tentative sketches, they are either copies after, or wholly or partly the work of, don José. The other items are more interesting for their iconography than for their artistry. For instance, the principal figures are seen in profile, facing right as opposed to left, which would be the instinctive attitude for a right-handed draughtsman to choose. This left-handed approach may have been dictated by the stance of the model, if these sketches were indeed done from life. But from his earliest years he preferred to fight against what comes naturally and to do things the hard way. Only by making things as difficult as possible would he be able to set himself challenging problems and, what is more, solve them. The only other point of interest is the bullfight subject matter. The painting of a picador and the drawing of a torero tossed by a bull provide the first pictorial record of Picasso's lifelong *afición*—a legacy from his father, who had such a passion for corridas that he started taking his son to the bullring as soon as he could walk.

> I must have been ten years old when my father took me to see El Lagartijo fight. I remember his hair was white, snow white. In those days bullfighters didn't retire so young as they do now. Well, the bulls were different then too, huge—and they charged the horses as much as twenty times. And the horses dropped like flies, their guts everywhere. Horrible! Those days were different, and so was the bullfight. . . .
>
> I also knew Cara Ancha, even if I never saw him fight. I was very young and my father, a great *aficionado*, took me to his hotel room in Málaga, either before or after the bullfight. I can't remember. It's one of my most vivid childhood recollections: I was on his lap looking at him, overwhelmed.[19]

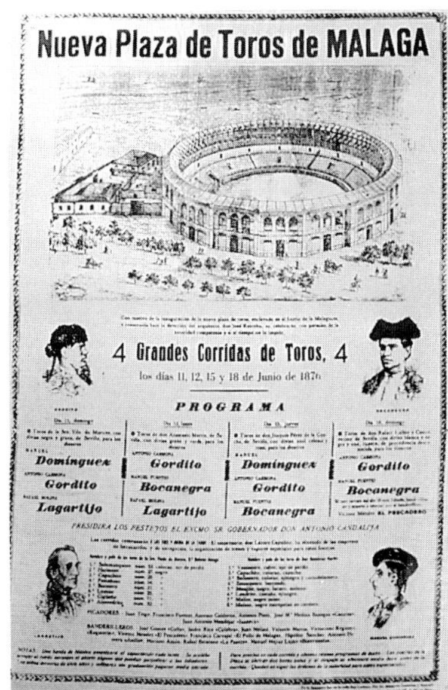

Poster for four corridas to inaugurate the new bullring in Málaga in June 1876. The toreros are Domínguez, Gordito, Lagartijo and Bocanegra. Ayuntamiento, Málaga.

Top: Picasso. *The Port of Málaga.* Málaga, *c.*1890. Oil on panel, 18×24cm. Private collection.

Above: Picasso. *Bullfight; Pigeons.* Málaga, *c.*1890. Pencil on paper, 13.5×20.2cm. Museu Picasso, Barcelona.

Right: Picasso. *Picador.* Málaga, *c.*1890. Oil on panel, 24×19cm. Heirs of the artist.

The little works that record Picasso's first enthusiasm for bullfighting look ahead to a vast oeuvre that covers every aspect of the art. This obsession would not end for another eighty years, and then with great éclat in one of his last masterpieces, *The Black Torero* (1970), inspired by a final visit to a corrida at Fréjus. These images look far ahead to periods of deep personal identification with both the bullfighter and the bull, not to speak of that vulnerable monster the minotaur. 'Pablo is a bullfighter at heart,' Luis Miguel Dominguín would say. 'The bulls are in his very soul,' Picasso's friend Hélène Parmelin has written. 'The bullfighters are his cousins. The bullring is his home.'[20] He equated the family with the corrida.

It is strange that so little work has survived from these early years, especially since family members recall that he used to

> draw for hours on end, provided people let him be and . . . his cousins, if present, didn't distract him from his favourite pastime. Otherwise he would get them to concentrate by asking them again and again, 'What do you want me to do?' [Cousin] María would ask him to do a donkey, her favourite animal, but starting with the spine. Then [María's sister] Concha would ask him to do another for her, but this time beginning with the ear, and so on without stopping until he was exhausted.[21]

Picasso. *Dog*. Málaga, *c*.1890. Paper cut-out, 6×9.2cm. Museu Picasso, Barcelona.

Thanks perhaps to his cousins' promptings, Picasso fell into the habit of starting work from some arbitrary point of departure, continuing in an apparently illogical way and always ending up 'mysteriously' (his word) with a pictorially coherent image. This procedure—first chronicled by Sabartès—was a perpetual source of puzzlement to the artist. 'I have no idea what imperatives my hand obeys,' he would say. And even when Georges Clouzot filmed Picasso at work (*Le Mystère Picasso*, 1955) on surfaces set up in such a way that he appeared to be drawing or painting on the camera lens itself, he still found his own creative processes '*un mystère totale*'. Did the ear of Concha's donkey hold the key? These seemingly haphazard processes, he could only conclude, were ordained by some instinctive system over which the intellect had little or no control.

Young Pablo's artistry was by no means confined to drawing. Sabartès describes how the seven-year-old boy used to borrow his aunt Eloísa's embroidery scissors and do *papiers découpés*, and how his 'skilful hands cut out animals, flowers, strange garlands and groups of figures. At first he did this to please himself. Later he took pleasure in submitting to Concha or María's wishes. 'Do us a portrait of Tola Calderon's Newfoundland dog.' Or he would be asked to do the cock that Aunt Matilde had sent from Alhuarinejo and which awaited the sacrificial hour tethered by a foot.'[22]

Picasso. Cut-out dolls made for the artist's daughter Maya. *c*.1937.

Picasso would profit from these juvenile games in later life, when he put his scissors to the most inventive use: in 1912 for the *papiers collés* and paper sculptures of cubism; and in the 1950s for the cut-out maquettes—heads of Jacqueline, pipe-playing fauns and bulls—that he would later magnify and execute in sheet metal. He would also use his scissors for fun: for whimsical paper dolls to divert his children; for paper chains made of torn-up paper napkins to amuse guests in restaurants; or for ties and crowns contrived of cut-out cartridge paper with which to dress up friends: 'a dress-making technique I acquired as a child.'

* * *

Five days after Pablo's sixth birthday, that is to say on October 30, 1887, doña María gave birth to a second girl. She was christened María de la Concepción Josefa Aurelia Salvadora Angela Simona de la Santísima Trinidad, but was known to the family as Concha or Conchita. The godfather was her paternal uncle Dr Salvador; the godmother her aunt Aurelia (married to Baldomero Ghiara). Pablo preferred his younger sister to Lola, the sister who was nearer to him in age. The six years between him and Concha precluded any rivalry; also she showed signs of developing into a beauty, the only one of the children to take after don José. Both Françoise Gilot and Jacqueline remarked on the obsessive tenderness Picasso evinced for the memory of Conchita, who died at the age of seven—this girl who had been so blonde, so slender, so vulnerable.[23] His feelings for the Andalusian-looking Lola were more conventionally fraternal. Still, Pablo was very much the little pasha with his sisters and aunts—a nursery harem.

Pablo, aged four. Author's collection.

Pablo was only weaned away from this household of over-indulgent women when he was packed off to school shortly after his fifth birthday. Because it was cheap and conveniently situated, the family chose a municipal school next door to the old Augustinian monastery where don José had his office and studio. Pablo loathed the place. He told Sabartès it was damp and gloomy; the discipline was harsh, the teaching imbecilic; and he had to be dragged there kicking and screaming by his father or the moustachioed maid.[24] He also said that once the lessons started he would dash to the window and try to catch the eye of one of his uncles who lived opposite, and have him come and rescue him.[25] The devoted Sabartès never questions the contradictions in these stories, never seems to realize that Picasso—even more than most adults in their memories of childhood—was out to dramatize himself as both victim and victor of one set of circumstances after another. To believe Picasso, he finally escaped from school by falling ill. The doctor (his uncle?) diagnosed inflamed kidneys and insisted the child be removed from the insalubrious municipal school. Pablo exulted—not, however, for long. Anxious that their recalcitrant son should have a proper education, his parents sent him, as soon as he was better, to the more up-to-date Colegio de San Rafael, headed by a family friend called don Pesies.

Pablo, aged seven, with Lola. Musée Picasso, Paris.

Picasso boasted to Sabartès that he manipulated not only his parents but the headmaster of his new school. Every morning there would be tearful tantrums, complaints that he was feeling ill and reasons of every sort (Gilot describes the same pattern of behaviour years later) as to why he shouldn't leave the house—couldn't he, for instance, stay at home and draw? Pablo extorted elaborate, outrageous pledges and bribes. He refused to set off for school without being given his father's favourite walking stick or a pigeon—something precious that would oblige don José to return on the dot of one o'clock to collect his son. 'Supposing he forgets,' Picasso remembered thinking. 'Had he left me his brushes I would have felt more confident.' Back home, he would be rewarded with a pencil, brush or some drawing paper. Or his mother would give him one of the cakes—a 'baba made of eau de vie flour aniseed sugar and olive oil' (to quote a poem he wrote in January 1936)—that he specially liked and that she would continue to send him over the years. During class he would take advantage—so he claimed—of the teacher's friendship for his family, or solicitude for his supposedly delicate health, to draw his father's pigeons instead of attending to his lessons. Or he would wander off to the kitchen and watch the headmaster's wife tend the fire or peel potatoes —anything rather than sit at his desk. In despair the family called in a private tutor, but 'the results were not remarkable'—at least, so we are told.[26]

Pablo was not of course the dunce he made himself out to be. Why, then, did he claim that he could not remember how or when he learned to read or write—not before the age of ten, if we are to believe Sabartès —and that he could never recall the correct order of the alphabet? The answer would seem to lie in Picasso's ambivalence: he chose to see himself as a prodigy of infantile backwardness on the one hand and a prodigy of adult perception on the other; as a child who took pride in having learned virtually nothing since he emerged from his mother's womb, and yet an artistic virtuoso who sprang fully developed from his father's head. As for forgetting the circumstances of his earliest lessons, someone as mimetic and intuitive, as visually and mentally alert as Picasso would have learned to read and write as effortlessly as he mastered any other mental endeavour.

Picasso's pretensions to ignorance turn out to have been unfounded: for instance, the long, virtually verbatim account Sabartès has given of the nine-year-old's comical attempt to pass the entrance exam for secondary school. 'What do you know?' asked the examiner, who was a friend of the family. 'Nothing,' Picasso claimed to have replied. 'In order to assist him, the teacher asked a few questions. . . . When the boy failed to answer he decided that perhaps he had gone over his head. It did not occur to him to ask him to read; he supposed . . . that of course he knew how to do that, like everybody else. To write . . . why ask that? Better not try.'[27] Unfortunately for the veracity of Picasso's memory, his exam papers have come to light, and they tell a very different story.[28] The examiner did indeed ask Pablo to take dictation, which he did quite passably. As for his account of the arithmetical test, this is all the more revealing for diverging from the truth. According to Picasso, the examiner gave him some simple addition to do, but on realizing that Pablo had no mathematical aptitude whatsoever, he left the answer to the problem lying on his blotter. Sabartès, that martyr to poetic licence, has inflated this incident into a touching tale, which has been much quoted, especially the whimsical ending: 'When I get home . . . Papa will surely let me paint. I'll copy the little pigeon . . . ' Sabartès goes on to describe Pablo's return:

> . . . holding tightly to his certificate . . . he thought only of his mother's joy. He was happy, too, because he understood at last the importance of concentration: had he not concentrated he would not have noticed the slip of paper on the teacher's desk, he would not have been able to memorize the total. . . . 'Now maybe Papa will lend me the brushes. . . . They'll see how I can concentrate. I won't miss a single detail. . . . The little eye of the pigeon is round like an 0. Underneath the 0 a 6. Underneath that a 3. The eyes are like 2's, and so are the wings. The little feet rest on the table, as if on a horizontal line. . . . Underneath it all the total.'[29]

In fact the mathematical test involved division rather than addition. Not that it matters, for once again the partly apocryphal story is interesting for the insights it provides into the artist's labyrinthine mind rather than for

Pablo's examination paper, 25 June 1891. On the left is a short passage of dictation, on the right the answers to some arithmetical questions. Diputación Provincial de Málaga.

José Ruiz Blasco. Musée Picasso, Paris.

the information it provides about his schooldays. Interesting, too, because it shows how, in memory at least, he transformed abstract symbols into figurative or pictorial terms, unlike a later generation of artists who would reverse this process.

The exam to which Sabartès devotes so much attention was necessitated by a sequence of blows that befell the Ruiz Blascos. Although he had organized exhibitions and served on juries, don José was never elected to the local academy; and he was passed over for the top job at the Escuela, which went to his great friend, the infinitely more qualified Muñoz Degrain. The blow to his pride and pocket was such that don José decided to leave Málaga. He had heard of a position at Corunna: he would be a professor of drawing. But he was turned down for this job, and was turned down again in 1887, when he made a second request. To make matters worse, his position as museum curator was jeopardized by municipal cutbacks. Sure enough, the following year (1888), after a review of the city's finances, don José's salary was stopped. In exchange for the use of a studio, he continued to do light curatorial chores as well as some restoration (many of the paintings damaged in the 1884 earthquake still required patching up). Testimonials were his only recompense, such as the following in the 1888 guidebook to Málaga: 'José Ruiz Blasco, curator of the Municipal Museum where he has his studio, is a true artist and a dedicated worker. His pigeons proclaim the presence of nature, since Ruiz Blasco reproduces what he sees, and he sees perfectly.'[30]

At the end of 1890 the collapse of the local economy closed the museum doors once and for all. Don José no longer had a studio in which to paint pigeons. And he could no longer rely on his brother. Dr Salvador may have been well-off by the standards of the day, but he had children of his own to support and was too tight-fisted to be counted on for lavish handouts. Since don José's income from teaching was barely enough to feed his family, let alone keep up appearances—all-important in bourgeois Málaga—the unfortunate artist, now fifty-two, had no choice but to press yet again for a transfer.

This time strings were pulled in earnest—thanks to his Loring connections, Dr Salvador had a lot of influence—and don José's transfer went through. He was appointed teacher of drawing at the da Guarda institute in Corunna on April 4, 1891, at a salary of 3,000 pesetas a year. Protocol obliged him to make a special trip to Corunna and present himself to the principal of the institute—a mere formality, but it enabled him to find somewhere for his family to live. Since he did not have to take up his duties until the academic year began in the autumn, he returned forthwith to Málaga to pack up his possessions and make his farewells. Pablo never forgot how heartrending this was. Don José dreaded the prospect of leaving his birthplace and all that it represented: his large but close-knit family and his *tertulia*; he also dreaded leaving the extreme south for the extreme north, the sun and blue sky for rain, fog and gales. For despite his English airs, don José was essentially Andalusian—Mediterranean born and bred. After the Costa del Sol, Corunna's Atlantic promontory was as inviting as Antarctica. To don José the move to Corunna amounted to defeat. 'My father', Picasso told an interviewer, 'suffered the same sweat that Napoleon must have suffered when he moved to Saint Helena. He sweated when he embarked; he sweated during the voyage. . . . Any adaptation was impossible for him.'[31] Corunna was to prove far, far worse than don José anticipated. '*Ni Málaga, ni taureaux, ni amis, ni rien*' is how Picasso summed up his father's reactions to this place of exile.[32]

Plaster casts in the Escuela de Bellas Artes, Málaga. Teresa Sauret collection.

3

Corunna

The 'Tower of Hercules' at Corunna. Photo: Blanco.

Opposite: Picasso. *Coast at Corunna*, Corunna, *c*.1894. Oil on panel, 10.3×15.4cm. Museu Picasso, Barcelona.

CORUNNA, THE PRINCIPAL PORT OF the ancient province of Galicia, is as far northwest as it is possible to go on the Iberian peninsula (close to Finisterre, Spain's Land's End), and has a reputation for foul weather, especially with southerners. But it is in fact a city of paradoxical beauty, battered by Atlantic gales yet warmed by the Gulf Stream, girt by bleak rocks yet abounding in lush vegetation. And, in common with Santiago de Compostela some miles inland, the city is paved with large flagstones that glisten after the frequent showers like faceted jet. Corunna's cultural background is as idiosyncratic as the climate: a sum of opposites. Originally settled by the Armorican Celts—hence bagpipes and other Celtic remnants—the strategic harbour was later colonized by successive invaders, each of whom left their mark: Phoenicians, Greeks, Romans, Suevians and, lastly, Moors, who were expelled by the Asturian kings. According to legend, the city was founded by Hercules; hence the famed local landmark—the great golden granite lighthouse originally erected by the Phoenicians, rebuilt during the reign of Trajan and restored many times thereafter—has been known since antiquity as the 'Tower of Hercules'. In the Dark Ages a belief grew up that this tower housed a miraculous mirror which reflected anything that happened anywhere in the world —a belief that stemmed apparently from a confusion between the Latin words for watchtower (*specula*) and mirror (*speculum*). Picasso retained fond memories of the 'Tower of Caramel' (the family's nickname for the Tower of Hercules): 'the place heightened my sensations . . . the tower was also a retreat for lovers . . . and I spent hours making drawings there even when it rained.'[1] Virtually none of these drawings have survived. This remote monument, this all-seeing, all-reflecting phallus that sheltered lovers, had a permanent place in the memory of this artist for whom the acts of looking, painting and making love would eventually become metaphors for one another.

* * *

The journey from Málaga to Corunna must have been very rough on a family that had rarely, if ever, left its hometown. Uncle Salvador had obtained special rates on a cargo boat for don José, his wife and three children (the grandmother and aunts stayed behind in Málaga). The boat—headed for England, via the Strait of Gibraltar, Cadiz, Vigo and Corunna

—weighed anchor sometime in October 1891. It was a bad season for storms, and sure enough, as they approached Vigo, an Atlantic gale of such force bore down on their small vessel that don José insisted on disembarking and continuing the journey by rail to Santiago de Compostela, and then by coach to Corunna. 'A new road to Calvary' is how Picasso described the voyage seventy years later. Exhausted and demoralized, the family arrived in Corunna at about the time of Pablo's tenth birthday.

The apartment don José had taken occupied the second floor of 14 (today 12) Calle de Payo Gómez. There were not quite enough rooms for five people but it was spacious, high-ceilinged and well appointed. The rent was low, and it boasted not one but two of those elaborate glassed-in balconies that are such an attractive feature of Corunna's houses. The back balcony gave don José access to his rooftop dovecotes; the front balcony provided the children with a lookout place, as Picasso remembered with delight. The address conformed to don José's notions of respectability, and it was only half a block from the da Guarda institute, a new building that was opening its doors for the first time not only to don José but to pupils of an art school, a music school and a secondary school. And, no less convenient, it was across the street from a newish villa in the French style belonging to don Ramón Pérez Costales—former Minister of Public Works, with responsibility for the fine arts, and a promi nent supporter of liberal causes—who was to play a leading role in the lives of don José's family.[2] This proximity was no coincidence: a doctor as well as a politician, Pérez Costales had once been a quarantine official and is thought to have lived in Málaga in the early 1880s when he was out of political favour. He almost certainly knew the eminent Dr Salvador, who would have asked him to help his indigent brother settle in Corunna.

Cantón Grande, one of the principal streets of Corunna, with typical glazed balconies overlooking the Alameda and the port. The Calle de Payo Gómez is a turning a little further to the left. Lithograph published by Ferrer at the turn of the century. Arenas collection, Corunna.

Don José and doña María could not have had a more genial, sympathetic or powerful protector than don Ramón. He assumed the role that Uncle Salvador had played in their chronically impoverished life. Besides wielding considerable influence—national as well as local—he was a charitable man who devoted part of his fortune to supporting a kindergarten. 'I remember his noble carriage and his cordiality,' Picasso recalled, '. . . that moustache which curled was so impressive. I remember him better than my playmates. With him I discussed things and exchanged views. And for a child, that was important. I sold him my work to earn a *duro* [five pesetas] so that I could amuse myself with my friends. . . . Every painter must remember his first collector with gratitude. Pérez Costales was my maecenas.'[3] Don Ramón's first acquisitions seem to have been old cigar-box lids that he paid Pablo to paint for him.[4] There are also a couple of family portraits, one of which evokes the charm and authority of this white-whiskered patron, while another depicts his illegitimate son, Modesto Castillo.[5] He wanted to be painted in a burnoose but didn't have one, Picasso told me, 'so I made him wear a terry-cloth robe.'[6] At the same time Pablo executed two fanciful little paintings of the lavishly upholstered rooms in the Pérez Costales apartment—very redolent of the *confort cossu* of the period. Surprisingly, he never painted don Ramón's attractive French wife, although she gave him his first taste of French culture and probably helped him with the French lessons he was taking.

* * *

Picasso. *Interior of the Pérez Costales House*. Corunna, 1895. Oil on canvas, 9.9×5.5cm. Museu Picasso, Barcelona.

Above: Picasso. *Modesto Castillo as a Moor*. Corunna, 1895. Oil on canvas, 43×25cm. Private collection.

Left: Picasso. *Portrait of Ramón Pérez Costales*. Corunna, 1895. Oil on canvas, 52×37cm. Heirs of the artist.

Picasso. *Don José with his Brushes and Palette.* Corunna, 1894–95. Pencil on sketchbook page, 19.5×13.5cm. Museu Picasso, Barcelona.

Picasso remembered his father's life in Corunna as a disaster from the start. 'My father never left the house,' he told Sabartès, 'except to go [and teach at] the Escuela. Upon returning home, he amused himself painting, but not so much as before. He spent the rest of the time watching the rain through the windowpanes.'[7] Picasso exaggerates. Don José made every effort to establish himself in Corunna's artistic circles: he was a founder member of the Academia Gallega; he courted local collectors; and he also did his best to participate in academic life. He even took on the additional responsibilities of school secretary in 1892—probably to earn extra income. Life in Corunna had not proved as economical as don José and doña María had hoped, and Picasso never forgot how his mother worried perpetually about finances, and how he learned to watch out for any cheap take-out meals that might be advertised, such as one that stuck in his memory: 'soup, stew and a main course for one peseta and served at home.'

Although don José sold some of his work to friends of Pérez Costales, he did not make much effort to endear himself to the local establishment. Lacking a *tertulia*, he ceased going to cafés and became more and more bitter and melancholic. This formerly passionate *aficionado* refused even to go to corridas—so inferior to Andalusian ones, he rightly said. Nevertheless his son turned into an assiduous follower of local bullfights.

Nor was don José encouraged by local reactions to his work. In the hope of making extra money, he showed some of his paintings in shop windows on the Calle Real—the main street, where pictures were often put up for sale. Nobody paid much attention. In March 1894 he exhibited with his assistant Navarro and a young artist, Gonzalo Brañas. But Barrero, the critic of *La Voz de Galicia*, reviewed his work, including the painting of an orange branch, less enthusiastically than the local artists' canvases. He had slightly better luck in June, when he exhibited yet again with Navarro and another Galician friend, Souto. But in October, when he showed with Sanz at a stationer's on the Calle Real, he was once more damned with faint praise. ('Two abandoned blooms' is how Barrero dismissed his attempt at a flower piece.) In the face of small-town chauvinism don José decided to exhibit no more. It was beneath a professor's dignity to be compared unfavourably with his assistant.

Meanwhile don José's professional pride was being put to another disagreeable test. A power struggle had broken out at the institute and don José found himself on the losing side—the side of the establishment. The administration was under attack from the more progressive teachers, headed by one González Jiménez, 'a known trouble-maker'. Throughout 1894 the fight rumbled on, as we know from minutes—kept by don José—that came to light only recently (1988), when the art school moved to new premises. González Jiménez eventually won the support of a majority of his colleagues, who seem to have declared some sort of strike. Formal complaints were made against the director, Emilio Fernández Deus, and the matter was aired in the local press. In the end González Jiménez forced Fernández Deus's resignation and was appointed acting director in his place. Don José was appalled at the upstart's brusqueness, and he castigates his 'scandalous behaviour' in the minutes that he kept. If this were not enough, don José's sight had begun to deteriorate. This, coupled with a loss of steadiness in his hand, was the more galling in

Picasso. *Bullfighting Scenes*. Corunna, 1892. Pencil and gouache on paper, 13×21 cm. Heirs of the artist.

view of his son's burgeoning skills. No wonder he lapsed into despair. The more the father came to loathe Corunna, the more the son came to love it—so much so that he eventually learned enough dialect to recite poems by Rosalia, the Galician laureate, and to sing songs in Galego.

In old age Picasso chided the Galicians for forgetting all about the formative years he had spent in their midst—at the outset such happy years.[8] Corunna provided him with his first taste of freedom. In Málaga the ladies of the parental household, helped by countless aunts, uncles, cousins and friends, had kept their precious Pablo under constant surveillance. In Corunna, life was very different. Despite his mother's watchfulness, Pablo was growing up rapidly and by the age of eleven, running wild:

> My friends and I spent our time chasing stray cats with shotguns. Once on Calle de Damas we caused a real massacre. The alarm which spread among the neighbours was phenomenal. This escapade was reported and afterwards I was supervised more closely. My mother . . . worried what I was up to in the street. But any vigilance on her part was limited because . . . in order to watch me [she] had to climb on top of the water closet. She stood on tiptoe and through a small crack could observe our games . . . There in the Plaza de Pontevedra, in front of the Instituto [where don José taught], we organized our own bullfights. I used to teach the other boys how to handle the bull and our jackets would serve as capes. It was great fun, and if one of those childhood friends is still alive he'll remember it.[9]

Picasso. *Scene Backstage at a Theatre*. Corunna, 1894. Pen on paper, 16×11.2 cm. Heirs of the artist.

Eighty years later, Picasso could still recall a few of the friends who played in the mock corridas. They were of the same bourgeois background as himself. Antonio Pardo Garcia, son of Gumersindo Pardo Reguera (a professor of physics and natural history at the institute), who became a pharmacist and died in 1928; Angel Sardina Muiños, a brilliant seminarian, who forsook the church for the law, and then the law for the church, and died, aged thirty-five, in 1919; and Jesús Salgado Rios, who eventually moved to Argentina and became an unsuccessful painter and restorer. These corridas were the first step in Picasso's identification with the matador (the word means 'killer') and the bull. But the corrida would not become a metaphor for Picasso's own dilemmas until he was well into middle age and identified with the bull as both aggressor and victim —a far cry from the squally alleyways of Corunna.

One of Picasso's most valuable gifts was an ability to dramatize and heighten whatever he was depicting. Drama was in his blood. It shows up early on in his handwriting. It is also reflected in his precocious taste for the theatre, a taste that went into temporary eclipse when he moved to France and had difficulty following the dialogue. One drawing suggests he was allowed backstage. At the Teatro Principal he saw the celebrated Andalusian actor Antonio Vico perform in Calderón's play about peasant honour, *El Alcalde de Alamea*, and in romantic melodramas by the popular dramatist José Echegaray. At the same time Pablo and Lola attended dances for children at the Círculo de Artesanos. More to his and his mother's taste was the ocean. 'Although I come from far away, I am a child and have a desire to eat and to swim in salt water,' he wrote of Corunna in his first (1935) long autobiographical poem.[10] Pablo loved to play in the surf on the wonderful local beaches. The Riazor beach was only a block away behind the da Guarda institute, and Orzán a little farther to the north. He played but did not swim. In spite of his lifelong obsession with the sea (so long as he was in it, or near it, rather than on it), neither then nor later did Pablo learn to swim. 'I swim very well up to my knees,' he would tell his second wife.[11] And at the age of eighty-five he amazed Otero by the dexterity with which he mimed being a champion swimmer while keeping his feet on the bottom.[12]

At Riazor or Orzán Pablo had his first exposure to female nudity. Playing near the bathing huts on the local beach as a very small child, he found himself standing next to a naked woman, his eyes level with her pubic hair. The voyeuristic excitement associated with this occasion is something that Picasso never forgot. Forever afterwards beach cabanas would be associated with the mystery of sex, especially in the late 1920s, when the little bathing huts at Dinard—the scene of his amours with the teenage Marie-Thérèse Walter—recur again and again in paintings (also poems) that are ostensibly playful and yet imbued with a mixture of sexuality and angst.[13]

Since his supposedly backward days at Málaga, Pablo had done well at school. During his first year at Corunna, he was too young to enrol at the School of Fine Arts, but the exam he had passed in Málaga entitled him to attend classes at the secondary school next door. Beyond the fact that his teachers were priests, one of whom, Benito Jerónimo Feijoo, taught him Latin, we know virtually nothing about his education. The only evidence consists of four textbooks that survive in the Museu Picasso: a book of Latin exercises, a Castilian grammar, a vast tome on literary analysis and a copy of *Literatura Preceptiva o Retórica y Poética*—plus a French primer, with seventy-six words translated in Pablo's hand. To judge by dates in them, these books must have been given to Pablo when he was ten or eleven years old: further evidence that he was not as backward or analphabetic as he pretended, even if the only word in the Latin grammar to be underlined, 'latrocinor' ('*I serve as a mercenary, I am a brigand or pirate*'), suggests an interest in adventure rather than Latin. More revealing are the drawings and doodles that cover margins and flyleaves: pigeons, doves, cats, an actor, the Eiffel Tower, inkblots transformed into figures and a drawing of a donkey mounting an ass to illustrate a schoolboy's bawdy quatrain. These thumbnail sketches are remarkably observant and spirited, but they do not testify to the passion for drawing that Picasso boasted about sixty years later:

> For being a bad student I was banished to the 'calaboose'—a bare cell with whitewashed walls and a bench to sit on. I liked it there, because I took along a sketch pad and drew incessantly. . . . I think I provoked situations so that professors would punish me. I was isolated and no one bothered me—drawing, drawing, drawing. I could have stayed there forever drawing without a stop. True, all my life I've been in the habit of drawing, but in that cell it was a special pleasure—difficult to explain. It's not that I wanted to excel, rather to work—that's what one must always do.[14]

Curiously enough, virtually nothing from the early days in Corunna survives among the mass of juvenilia in the Museu Picasso. The drawings may well have been destroyed to preserve the legend that the artist never drew like a child.

*   *   *

Picasso. *Man and Nude Woman in a Forest.* Corunna, 1895. Pen and watercolour on paper, 20×15.5cm. Galerie Jan Krugier, Geneva.

Opposite top: Postcard of 1890 with views of Corunna: (top left) theatre; (top right) iron jetty and port; (bottom left) lighthouse; (centre) da Guarda institute and school; (centre bottom) tomb of Sir John Moore in the botanic garden. Arenas collection, Corunna.

Picasso. *Bather with a Parasol.* Juan-les-Pins, 1930. Pencil on an opened out envelope, 23.5×28.3cm. Musée Picasso, Paris.

Opposite: Riazor Beach. Photo: Blanco.

Recuerdo de La Coruña.

CORUNA

Above: Picasso. *Profile Studies.* Corunna, 1892–93. Conté crayon on paper, 23.7×31cm. Heirs of the artist.

Left: Picasso. *Seated Male Nude.* Corunna, 1893. Conté crayon on paper, 51.8×36.5cm. Heirs of the artist.

Below left: Picasso. *Plaster Cast of a Leg.* Corunna, 1893–94. Charcoal on paper, 54×27cm. Heirs of the artist.

Below: Picasso. *Plaster Cast of an Arm.* Corunna, 1894. Charcoal and conté crayon on paper, 45×34cm. Museu Picasso, Barcelona.

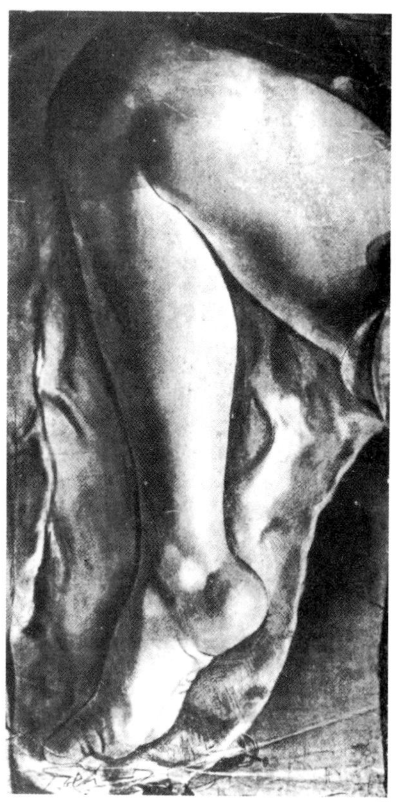

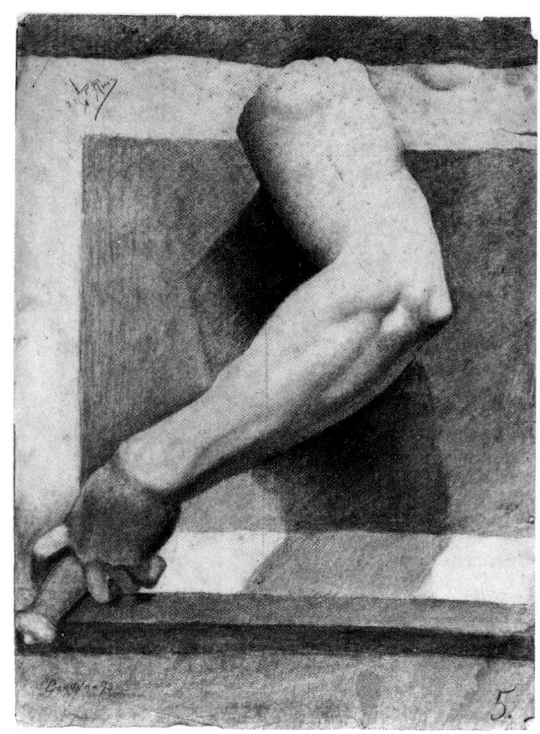

Pablo could not be enrolled in the art school until his second year at Corunna. Just prior to his eleventh birthday he was accepted as student number 88 in his father's class of ornamental drawing, but he was still obliged to attend secondary school. The deadly grind of copying plaster casts and drawing by rote—anathema to most students—never bored him. Pablo's earliest art-school drawings are nothing if not competent, but the temptation to foresee future triumphs in the tea leaves of juvenilia must be resisted. Palau, for instance, claims that there are presentiments of Cézanne and 'something of the future creator of cubism, albeit in embryonic form' in a drawing (1893) of a bearded man reduced to a simplistic diagram.[15] Far from looking forward to a new form of pictorial notation, mechanical shortcuts such as this look backwards—to the crude charts found in old-fashioned manuals that taught drawing by formula rather than observation. If Picasso was destined for greatness, it was despite rather than because of these rigid precepts. As for his father's teaching: don José was an exemplar by virtue of his ineptitude rather than his skill, Picasso once joked.

Picasso. Drawing and bawdy verse on the page of a schoolbook. Pencil on paper. Museu Picasso, Barcelona.

One of the most puzzling early drawings depicts a male nude seated on a crate with his head in his hands. The technique is so assured that it cannot be reconciled with the childish script of the signature, date (1893) and enrolment number. It may have been reworked at a later time; it may have been copied from an illustration that his father or one of his other professors had shown him. The most likely candidate is the painter and sculptor Isidoro Modesto Brocos, who had worked in Paris. He favoured Pablo enough to give him one of his Parisian sketchbooks,[16] and years later Picasso remarked that Brocos had been 'an exceptional teacher'. The pages of this sketchbook are so diverse in style and competence that some are almost certainly by his students. The sketchbook fails to substantiate the claim that Brocos opened Picasso's eyes to impressionism.[17] Insofar as this ever happened, it was not before 1899. However, a group of charming little watercolours by this artist in the museum at Corunna reveals the source of the boy's growing interest in the medium. The heavily shaded charcoal drawings of plaster casts that date from Pablo's second year (1893–4) likewise suggest that he had fallen under the aegis of a more competent teacher than his father.

Isidoro Modesto Brocos. *In Thought*. Watercolour on paper. Don Julio Estrada Gallardo collection, Corunna.

These drawings, with their dramatic, seemingly candlelit chiaroscuro, are the ones that Picasso took such pride in showing his friend Brassaï some fifty years later. For a twelve- or thirteen-year-old, their precision frightened him, he declared.[18] He also had them in mind when he visited an exhibition of children's drawings organized by the British Council in 1946 and boasted that 'as a child I would never have been able to participate in a show of this kind: at the age of twelve I drew like Raphael.'[19] Once again the compulsion to have been a genius from his earliest days was upon him. By making such an uncharacteristically portentous claim, Picasso does himself an injustice. What really distinguishes these disembodied arms, legs and feet from run-of-the-mill academic studies is not so much their accomplishment, which is far from Raphaelesque, as their intensity—the eerie sensuousness that shines through the art-school polish.

Compared with his academic exercises, the drawings that Pablo did for his own pleasure are not particularly skilful—naive in conception, faulty

Picasso. *Self-Portrait*. Corunna, 1894. Pencil on sketchbook page, 19.5×13.5cm. Museu Picasso, Barcelona.

Picasso. *Lola Embroidering*. Corunna, 1894. Pencil on sketchbook page, 19.5×13.5cm. Museu Picasso, Barcelona.

in scale, clumsy in execution—but they abound in boyish fantasy and high spirits. Nowhere is this boyishness more evident than in the handwritten 'newspapers' he produced at Corunna. He modelled them, he said, on *Blanco y Negro*, Spain's most popular weekly magazine of the period, and a theatrical journal, *Teatro Crítico*, to which his family subscribed, and to which he wanted to contribute. 'But how was I going to contribute something done by a child? So I decided to make myself editor, illustrator, writer and director of my own publications. It was a means of communicating with my family in Málaga. Actually they were letters but I gave them the form of journals with titles, notices, publicity.'[20]

The earliest of Pablo's 'journals', which are handwritten and limited to a single copy, is called *Asul* (sic) *y Blanco* No. 1 (blue, *azul*, and white, *blanco*, are the colours of Galicia) and is dated October 8, 1893; a second and third number, with the title correctly spelt, came out the following year on September 24 and October 28, 1894; and a fourth 'issue' came out at Christmas 1895. The two others are *La Coruña*, dated September 16, 1894, and *Torre de Hercules*, which has not survived. 'I remember a sentence that impressed me a lot that I used at the foot of my drawings: "the wind has started to blow again and will continue as long as Corunna exists." I did them with the following notice added: "Pigeons of guaranteed genealogy wanted to buy"'[21]—a reference to don José's passion for these birds, which he not only painted but bred in Corunna as well as Málaga. These journals are said to have been the father's method of improving the son's handwriting.[22] And, it is true, besides sharply observed caricatures, cartoons and comic *culs de lampe*, the pages feature lively chronicles of daily life laboriously written out in a dogged attempt at cursive script, very unlike the boy's habitual scrawl. However, a neat hand can only have been incidental to the principal purpose of these journals, which was to impress that potential fount of patronage, Uncle Salvador, with Pablo's diligence. Sure enough, the first number of *La Coruña* is dedicated to him. To the same end the 'news'—above all Pablo's spirited little rubric entitled 'Festivities in Corunna'—is humorously slanted to persuade the 'folks back home' that, contrary to the truth, all was well in Galicia.

Pablo's preoccupation with periodicals did not last much more than a year. After the Christmas 1895 issue of *Azul y Blanco*, he abandoned this childish pastime for the more adult pursuit of family portraits. Conchita was still too young to serve as a model, so he concentrated on his schoolgirl sister, Lola. Like Pablo, Lola had originally been destined to study at the da Guarda institute—music, not art—but in the absence of any real gift, she had never bothered to take the necessary entrance exam. This left her all the more time to pose for her brother. 'I drew her all day long,' Picasso remembered years later; 'my drawings were a perfect diary of her getting up, going to bed, helping my mother in the kitchen, doing errands in her school uniform, playing with friends.'[23] Once again Picasso may be exaggerating. There are very few early (i.e., Corunna) Lolas among the drawings in the Museu Picasso or in the two albums—Picasso's first known sketchbooks—that chart the boy's laborious emergence from the chrysalis of academic clichés.

The first of these two albums (early 1893–94) reveals suspiciously few traces of the academic technique that distinguishes most of Pablo's art-

Picasso. *Asul* (sic) *y Blanco,* no.1; double page of manuscript newspaper. Corunna, October 8, 1893. Pen on paper, 20.2×26.3 cm. Museu Picasso, Barcelona.

Picasso. *La Coruña;* double page of manuscript newspaper. September 16, 1894. Pen, sepia and pencil on paper, 21×26 cm. Musée Picasso, Paris.

school work. Did Pablo, who would have been twelve to thirteen at this time, fall back under the shadow of don José once he had returned home? Certainly the views of Corunna and its environs suffer from the niggling touch that is a badge of his father's style. And the flights of fancy are not much more competent: facile variations on magazine illustrations. The only glimmer of things to come is provided by the nicely observed portraits of Pablo's mother and father and the fact that pages are signed and dated and localities identified ('the fritter-seller's house on the Camino Nuevo')—first intimations of the artist's compulsion to pin down his work to a specific time and place.

Picasso. *Doña María*. Corunna, 1894. Conté crayon on sketchbook page, 19.5×13.5cm. Museu Picasso, Barcelona.

The drawings in the second of these albums (dated October 1894–early 1895) are much more mature. Even the signatures have a confidence and brio that is no longer childish. Family portraits in black chalk are passable likenesses and reveal an eye for character that had probably been brought out by Brocos. Such shortcomings as there are—a certain glibness and slickness, for instance—appear to be parental in origin. But these adolescent drawings bear out that, far from being the innately gifted prodigy of legend, Pablo had to work very, very hard. Hard work, however, came naturally, thanks to the energy and concentration that he had inherited from his mother. Still the road to competence, let alone mastery, was far more arduous than is usually thought. And Picasso would always see that it remained as arduous as he could possibly make it. 'I believe in nothing but work,' the artist said at the height of cubism. 'You cannot have an art without hard work: manual as well as cerebral dexterity.'[24]

More than any other great artist, Picasso harnessed his sexuality to his work. Indeed, he would ultimately come to equate the creative with the procreative act. To what extent his dawning sexual awareness affected his artistic awareness we cannot say. But the pressures of puberty must surely have heightened his perceptions and vision and intensified his emotional responses. Years later, he recalled a frequent adolescent dream: he was an eagle and could fly. In old age Picasso maintained that his sex life started when he was a child, that in sex as in work he missed out on adolescence, and went directly from childhood to manhood. Andalusian machismo again. We only have to turn to his work (which is either dated or easily datable) to find evidence of a more normal adolescent progression. Between the ages of twelve and thirteen caricature gives way to portraiture; playfulness to a self-conscious gravity that bespeaks the earnest schoolboy. There is a much greater physicality. There is also a gradual increase in the scale of the figures that Pablo does for his own pleasure. They are seen closer-up and cover far more of the page. Even plaster casts are drawn with a sensuousness suggestive of flesh.

Around this time Pablo must also have realized that, compared with other bourgeois families, his parents were poor and *déclassé*, and that his beloved father was a pathetically bad teacher and painter. This realization would have dealt Pablo's pride a grievous blow. His response was embodied in a determination to exorcise the stigma of parental failure by a triumphant display of his own gifts, something that can only have increased his guilt towards his father. Of all the routine chores of a student's training, the discipline of drawing came the most naturally to him and gave him the greatest sense of fulfilment. As Picasso told Jacqueline some seventy years later, 'much as I despise academic methods, "Ecole de Dessin" should be emblazoned on every artist's door. Not, however, "Ecole de peinture".' His teachers, Picasso recalled, 'made us write in a notebook: "one must learn to paint," and to repeat it several times. I did just the reverse. I wrote, "one must not learn to paint."'[25] Whether or not he actually did this, it confirms that Picasso—at any rate in retrospect—saw himself initially as a draughtsman. It also accounts for the scarcity of paintings until the last few months of his stay in Corunna, when, as we will see, he appropriated, in imagination at least, the parental brushes.

Pablo's *amour propre* must also have been tested by his short stature. Far from attaining the height that was his father's pride, he took after his mother, whose feet barely reached the floor when she sat down. Whether or not this accounted for the artist's mammoth will, self-consciousness about it is reflected in his work. Heads out of all proportion to bodies, and features out of all proportion to faces, are only some of the devices that Picasso will use to conjure up monumentality. He will enlarge one small detail—the bridge of a nose, a toe, an eyelid—at the expense of another. He will cram a figure so tightly into the picture space that it looks ready to burst out of the top of the frame. To demonstrate how a small image could have the impact of a colossus, Picasso told me that a shipper with nothing but a photograph to go on sent a large truck to pick up a gouache of a bather a few inches square. He was very proud of the trick he had unwittingly played on the shipper's perception; it was as if he had aggrandized himself in the process.

Picasso. *Don José*. Corunna, January 1, 1895. Pencil with white chalk on sketchbook page, 13.5×19.5cm. Museu Picasso, Barcelona.

*　　　*　　　*

In the last days of 1894, don José had further cause to take a grim view of life. Diphtheria broke out in Corunna. Pérez Costales was a specialist in the disease, but despite his surveillance, the beloved Conchita fell ill. The doctor had heard of a new anti-diphtheria serum that was being developed in Paris and wired for some to be sent immediately. Lest the seven-year-old patient realize how sick she was, Epiphany (the culmination of the Christmas season) was celebrated, presents exchanged, as if nothing were amiss. A macabre charade, not least for Pablo, who adored his younger sister. Until the serum arrived, there was little the family could do but pray, and pray they did, even if, except for doña María, their devotions had lapsed now that they were away from Uncle Salvador's supervision. 'My family practised their religion,' Picasso said in 1968, 'but not in any very strict sense; they went to mass from time to time, but they never obliged me to go.'[26] Conchita's illness seems momentarily to have ignited Pablo's faith, which was in the combustible state peculiar to hypersensitive boys around the age of fourteen. In a burst of adolescent piety he vowed to God that he would never paint or draw again if Conchita's life was spared.

Picasso. *Conchita*. Corunna, 1894. Pencil on sketchbook page, 19.5×13.5cm. Museu Picasso, Barcelona.

Jacqueline told me this 'dark secret' some years after Picasso's death. She had no idea, she said, whether the vow had been made to a priest, at the instigation of his parents or out of some inner urge. If it was pre-emptive, Pablo might well have given way to temptation and painted. All the more reason for guilt. Another myth? Unlikely; Picasso seems not to have told Sabartès, his principal legend-monger. He confided it only to wives or mistresses.[27] Jacqueline found the implications ominous, as well she might. The shadow thrown by the ineffectual vow stretched far enough ahead to darken her own life.

Despite Pérez Costales's efforts (for which he was later rewarded with one of don José's rare flower pieces), the child slipped beyond reach of her brother's bargain with God, and died at home at five in the afternoon on January 10, 1895. Twenty-four hours later, the serum arrived.[28] The fact that Picasso was still torn by guilt and remorse over Conchita's death fifty-odd years after the event suggests that he had little confidence in his ability to keep this vow.[29]

Picasso. *The Sick Woman*. Corunna, 1894. Oil on panel. Heirs of the artist.

Broken or kept, the vow illuminates some otherwise dark areas: it reveals why a sick or dying girl is the principal subject of his work between 1897 and 1899—specifically his two most ambitious early paintings, *Science and Charity* (1897) and *Last Moments* (1899). It also casts light on Picasso's identification with Gauguin's *Spirit of the Dead* in a drawing of himself watching over a recumbent nude (1902–03),[30] as well as all those other scenes of a man gazing at a sleeping girl with a voyeurism both tender and predatory (see illustrations, p.265 and p.316). It casts light, too, on the way Conchita, the spirit of innocence, will, years later, be reincarnated in the guise of Picasso's young mistress, Marie-Thérèse Walter: in one case as a beautiful blonde girl clutching one of don José's pigeons and leading a blind minotaur by the hand. Guilty feelings for the women in his life seem to have been bound up with guilty feelings for his dead sister. Conchita's death left Picasso with a permanent terror of illness, especially in women. 'It's always women's fault if they're ill,' he used to say, as if to ward off the guilt to which the vow had left him susceptible. It may also have prompted his eventual identification with a minotaur, the legendary monster to whom young girls had to be sacrificed. In the role of minotaur, Picasso would manoeuvre the woman he loved into sacrificing not just her body and her will but, in the case of Dora Maar, her peace of mind and, in that of Jacqueline, her sanity and life to his art.

Picasso. *Blind Minotaur Guided by a Little Girl in the Night*. 1934. Aquatint, 24.7×34.7cm. Musée Picasso, Paris.

Conchita's death was made even more painful for the family by the shabbiness of her funeral and burial. An obituary notice records that the body was interred in the beautiful San Amaro cemetery overlooking the sea.[31] The family could not afford a burial plot, let alone a headstone. Four years later Picasso refers to this shameful embarrassment in *The End of the Road* (see illustration, p.151), one of his very few overtly polemical scenes. It contrasts two funeral processions—one rich, one poor—wending their way to a cemetery. 'At the end of the road death waits for everybody,' Picasso explained the subject to me, 'even though the rich go in carriages and the poor on foot.'

The death of Conchita—the only one of his children to take after him—convinced don José that Corunna was to blame for his misfortunes. He had to get away: not just from daily reminders of his daughter's deathbed, but from townspeople with whom he had no rapport and colleagues who had a low opinion of him and insufficient faith in his son's promise. The contrast between Pablo's ever-growing gifts and his own ineptitude made don José's sense of loss and despair the harder to bear. Just when his fortunes had reached their nadir, there was a glint of hope. Román Navarro—the Galician artist who had been don José's assistant and fellow exhibitor—was anxious to leave La Llotja in Barcelona, where he had gone to teach drawing. He wanted to return to his home town, and take over as director of the da Guarda institute. Don José and Navarro applied to change places. On March 17, 1895, by royal decree, Román Navarro was appointed to head the institute in Corunna, and don José to the lesser, but for him better paid, post in Barcelona. Don José was given a month's leave (March 16–April 16) in order to visit Barcelona and make arrangements for the move.

Román Navarro. *Scene of the Peninsular War in Galicia.* 1899. Painting reproduced in *Hispania*, October 15, 1899.

* * *

When don José's self-esteem was at its lowest, an event took place that would have as profound an effect on Pablo as the loss of Conchita. One evening don José asked his son to help him finish the painting of a pigeon that had been giving him trouble. His eyesight was no longer sharp enough for the intricate bits, he said, so he chopped off the claws, nailed them to a board and set Pablo to paint them. When don José returned from his evening stroll, he found the claws had been painted with such skill that there and then he handed over his palette, brushes and paints to his prodigy of a son. He declared that he would never paint again. Biographers have taken this story of renunciation at its face value and come to some curious conclusions: Sabartès and Penrose both see don José's gesture as a form of religious penance. Sabartès compares don José to his late brother, Canon Pablo, who 'offered his mortifications up to God, while he [José] offered his up to the devil.'[32] Penrose sees his self-denial as 'not unlike similar gestures among his pious Andalusian ancestors.'[33]

These pious interpretations might carry more weight if don José had in fact renounced painting, but he went on wielding his feeble brush until well into the twentieth century, portraying the pigeon of the year for Barcelona's Colombofila Society, of which he was president.[34] Was this gesture of self-denial an empty one? Or are we confronted with yet another legend? Some small incident seems to have been magnified by Picasso, embroidered by Sabartès and taken much too seriously by one credulous biographer after another—ultimately by the artist himself. Whether or not it actually happened, don José's gesture loses much of its lustre when seen in the darkness of his failing vision. Any lingering doubts are dispelled by Manuel Pallarès, who met Pablo a few months later and remained a lifelong friend both to him and to his father (Pallarès and don José later taught together at La Llotja). Pallarès always maintained that the father never renounced painting in favour of the son. 'Made up out of whole cloth,' he said.[35] And when informed that Picasso himself had recounted the story, Pallarès 'accused Sabartès, whom he disliked—the antipathy was mutual—of being responsible for the Picasso legends.'[36]

This story is the more revealing for being founded on fantasy rather than fact. Pablo's love for his father evidently had a patricidal tinge to it. Like the vow that put Conchita's life on the scales with his art, it suggests why Picasso's art and life involved successive sacrifices: the sacrifice of woman after woman in commemoration of Conchita's; the sacrifice of man after man in commemoration of his father's. By dint of charisma and charm, Picasso had no difficulty in disarming and enslaving (and sometimes destroying) one not very gifted man after another: Pallarès, Sabartès,

Picasso. *Still Life with Pigeons* (detail). Sorgues, 1912. Oil on canvas, 46×65cm. Museo del Prado, Madrid (ex-Douglas Cooper collection).

Casagemas, his son Paulo and a host of minor figures would all end up his besotted and only very occasionally resentful victims. Picasso's tyranny was the more effective for being tacit. He never forced anyone to sacrifice a wife, mistress or career. They were the ones who insisted on doing so. That the myth of don José's renunciation of his brush should have been perpetuated by Sabartès is ironical. It was Sabartès who renounced his career as a journalist to become Picasso's secretary; it was Sabartès who thenceforth subordinated the loyalty he owed his beloved wife to the loyalty he owed his beloved master. And it was Sabartès who resigned himself to the humiliation and conspiratorial closeness that being a stand-in for don José entailed.

Picasso kept the story of his debt to his father very much alive. In the 1950s, when his dove of peace became a world-famous icon, he claimed to 'have repaid him in pigeons.' Appropriately, this claim was made in front of the cubist *Still Life with Pigeons* of 1912 that he so much admired in Douglas Cooper's collection—a painting in which the *trompe-l'œil* verisimilitude of the bird's amputated claws points up the cubist idiom of the rest of the composition. Yes, don José did have a hand in it, Picasso observed; these were souvenirs of the famous claws that launched his career at the expense of the father's—concrete figments of the artist's fantasy.

Whether or not fantasies about the sister's death and the father's renunciation were responsible, there was an immediate improvement in Pablo's skill and power. Hitherto of little more than average promise, his work came into its own, not just his drawing but his painting. The transformation can be appreciated in a dozen or so vivid portraits dating from immediately after Conchita's death, among them a clumsy, grimacing image that catches the ferocity of the father's grief. Apart from a painting of the family maid, the other portraits depict picturesque models: a barefoot peasant girl, a young tramp, a bearded 'pilgrim', an old fishwife—locals who were ready to pose for a pittance.

José Ruiz Blasco. *Pigeons*. Oil on canvas. Private collection.

These Corunna portraits are the first Picassos that can be taken seriously as works of art as opposed to juvenilia. They have been too often praised for their precocious virtuosity—a view that pleased Picasso more than it should have done. The fact that the artist was a boy of thirteen is irrelevant; it raises the issue of meretriciousness. The fervour and urgency of these works—of the awkward ones more than the glib ones—is what counts, not their revelation of the artist as a prodigy. One is reminded of certain very early Cézannes, where the sense of struggle— what Picasso called 'anxiety'—takes over as the subject of the painting. For all the intensity of these portraits, for all the fitful brilliance, the technique is still erratic. Far more practice would be required before Pablo's accomplishment could compensate for his father's lack of it. Picasso's statement to Kahnweiler many years later that these paintings, which are so much more accomplished than any of don José's, 'were done under the sole advice of his father' is baffling.[37] Was he giving his father the credit for Brocos's influence? Or was it simply that don José had come up with a new set of father figures? Certainly the collective shadow of Velázquez, Zurbarán, Ribera, Murillo, lies heavily on these portraits. The 'sole advice' of don José (and Brocos) was surely to concentrate on studying masterpieces of Spain's Golden Age (in reproduction), so that his son could paint himself into the great tradition of Spanish art.

Picasso. *Portrait of Don José*. Corunna, 1895. Oil on canvas, 29×20 cm. Heirs of the artist.

Picasso. *Girl with Bare Feet*. Corunna, 1895. Oil on canvas, 75×50 cm. Musée Picasso, Paris.

Not the least Spanish aspect of these early paintings is their limited perception of colour. Don José and his colleagues may have imparted rudimentary notions of form, tone and design to Pablo, but when it came to colour, they saddled him with a taste for the umbers, ochres and bituminous browns that are traditional to Spanish painting. Pablo was quick to perceive the disadvantages—just as later on he would perceive the advantages—of monochrome; and he compensated for the time-honoured drabness with bold applications of vermilion. A red dress or shawl or cloak brightens most of the portraits in this group. For all its effectiveness, this simple remedy indicates that an instinctive feeling for colour was still a long way off. But then, as Picasso would later tell Apollinaire, colours for him were 'only symbols'.[38]

Picasso. *Beggar in a Cap*. Corunna, 1895. Oil on canvas, 72×50cm. Musée Picasso, Paris.

The absence of foreign influence from the early work is also typically Spanish. Even to the painters of the Golden Age the Italian Renaissance had been somewhat suspect. Picasso inherited a full share of this chauvinistic prejudice against the classic Italian masters. 'People are always talking about the Renaissance,' he would tell his dealer, Kahnweiler, half a century later, 'but it's really pathetic. I've been seeing some Tintorettos recently. It's nothing but cinema, cheap cinema. It makes an impression . . . but how bad it is, how vulgar, without any real understanding.'[39] As for the Sistine Chapel, he thought it looked 'like a vast sketch by Daumier'.[40] Spanish art was his first love, and despite his subsequent annexation of Poussin, Ingres, Delacroix, Manet, Gauguin and Cézanne, to name but the greatest of his French exemplars, Picasso should always be seen primarily as a Spanish artist.

Picasso considered his Corunna portraits superior to the student work he did later in Barcelona.[41] Sometimes he even rated them more highly than works of the Blue or Rose periods. And it is true the Corunna portraits are refreshingly free of the self-pity and mannerism of the Blue period. No wonder the *Beggar in a Cap* and the bluff portrait of the artist's bluff patron, Pérez Costales, became talismans that stayed with him through seventy-five years of moving house. There would be a proud glint in his eyes as he showed them off: 'they still smell of Corunna,' he would say. Not the least of these portraits is the one of his dog, Clipper, the first of a succession of pets to figure in his work. Picasso painted Clipper with as much insight as he devoted to human models, catching the questing sharpness, the *qui vive* of the mongrel's eye. The dog wins out over St Antony of Padua, who can just be discerned under the paint to the right of Clipper's cocked ear. Such was Pablo's pride in his new paintings that he decided to follow his father's example and show some of them in shop windows on the Calle Real. Picasso later implied that one of these modest displays was a one-man show:

Picasso. *Clipper*. Corunna, 1895. Oil on canvas, 21.7×33cm. Museu Picasso, Barcelona.

> It frightened my parents that their child dared exhibit his work, but don Ramón [Pérez Costales], my protector, was the one who supported me. Some friends chose a place, an umbrella shop [belonging to the Hernández family] at Calle Real, no. 54. Actually it was more of a junk-shop where they sold everything from headscarves to suits of clothes. There was even a review in the papers . . . and my friends found the things of great quality. . . . In spite of the cheap prices, the sales . . . were not great. I would not have sold a thing had it not been, as always, for the generosity of Pérez Costales and my father's friends.[42]

Local newspapers tell a slightly different story. According to *La Voz de Galicia* (February 21, 1895), Pablo first exhibited two studies of heads in the window of a furniture shop belonging to Joaquín Latorre at 20 Calle Real. Ten days later (March 3, 1895) the same newspaper records that Pablo (wrongly named Ruiz Blasco, instead of Ruiz Picasso) exhibited a single painting, *Beggar in a Cap*, in the window of the junkshop at 54 Calle Real.

More revealing than the inflated stories about these so-called first exhibits is the local critic's perceptive and enthusiastic reaction to Pablo's work as opposed to his father's. These reviews, which have never been reprinted outside Corunna,[43] are worth quoting:

> [The two oil studies of heads] are not badly drawn and are forceful in colour, the tonal values are well handled, considering the age of the artist. The overall quality is excellent. But what is surprising is the will and confidence with which the heads have been painted; and we do not hesitate to predict that if he continues painting like this he is on the right track. . . . We do not doubt that he has a glorious and brilliant future ahead of him. [February 21, 1895]

> This is a fresh test of his pictorial gifts. The painting represents a beggar who is well known in La Coruña in the act of soliciting alms, and the execution denotes real courage as if the brushes had been handled by an artist of considerable experience instead of a neophyte. [March 3, 1895]

Shops on the Calle Real, Corunna, 1890. Photo: Blanco.

A few weeks after the last of these 'shows', don José received confirmation of his appointment in Barcelona. He immediately applied for Pablo to be examined ahead of his class; this would secure him automatic admission to the higher courses at the art school there. Don José's plan went awry, not surprisingly, given the tensions and the ill-feeling against him that had recently come to a head. His adversary, González Jiménez, had been appointed acting director on March 1. This probably explains why Pablo was permitted to sit for the figure-drawing examination (his father's course), which he passed with ease, but not for the painting exam. To his father's chagrin, Pablo did not obtain the coveted certificate. This could have been González Jiménez's revenge.

Meanwhile Pablo had been courting—apparently with considerable ardour and some success—a girl who was one of only two female pupils at the da Guarda secondary school. The girl's family, said to have been 'important', disapproved of her involvement with so young and undistinguished an admirer. Her name was suppressed by Luis Caparrós Muñoz, who first divulged the relationship;[44] however, on the strength of the initials and other cryptic annotations scrawled in one of Pablo's textbooks, she has been identified as Angeles Mendez Gil.[45] Angeles's parents put an end to the romance by sending her away, but Pablo continued to pine. Inscriptions in an early sketchbook reveal that Angeles remained on his mind long after Pablo had left Corunna. That this was more than an ephemeral crush is confirmed by a passionate scrawl, '*Gloria esperanza/Angeles/Mendez*', written four years later on a page of sketches,[46] one of which may well portray Angeles herself. (By no means the last time that Picasso would express his adoration for a particular girl by inscribing his work with her name.) Significantly, this precocious romance coincides with the first glimmer of greatness in Picasso's work.

Picasso. *Girl Surrounded by Cupids* (detail). Corunna, 1894–95. Pen on paper, 13×20.7cm. Museu Picasso, Barcelona.

4

The Move to Barcelona

'Barcelona that beautiful and intelligent [city] where I have left so many things hung round the altar of joy to which I now add some of the pigeon's throat colour of melancholy.' (Picasso)[1]

Picasso. *The Jester Calabacillas,* after Velázquez. Madrid, 1895. Pencil on sketchbook page, 12×8cm. Museu Picasso, Barcelona.

SOMETIME IN THE SPRING OF 1895—probably late April or early May—the Ruiz Blasco family packed up and left Corunna for good. Before moving to Barcelona, they took a prolonged summer holiday in Málaga. After the horrors of their previous boat trip, there was no question of going by sea. Instead they went by train and stopped for the better part of a day in Madrid so that don José could take Pablo on his first visit to the Prado. This was the first time that Picasso had been exposed to great art in the original, and for a fourteen-year-old boy who had been encouraged to have an almost divine belief in his own powers the experience must have been a challenging one. No wonder (as he remarked to Kahnweiler) his work was so much more confident before he left Corunna than it was after. It must have been daunting for someone so prodigiously competitive to see what he had to measure himself against if he was to realize his dreams of mastery. The Prado would always be as much a goad as a revelation to Picasso. Hence his ambivalent attitude to the institution when he returned to study at the Academy of San Fernando in 1897, and when he came back to edit *Arte Joven* in 1901. Hence also his euphoria when the Republican government appointed him director of the Prado in 1937. 'All those artists finally belonged to me,' he said.

Their time in Madrid was limited to a few hours between trains, so Pablo could make only two sketches after Velázquez.[2] He did not choose the master's more obvious or familiar works but copied the heads of a court dwarf and a jester. Interesting, because it was this group of portraits (notably the one of Sebastián de Moro, with his stumpy little legs jutting out at us) that inspired the last references to Velázquez in Picasso's work: two paintings begun on the same day (August 2, 1969). One of these depicts the dwarf as an adolescent—roughly the same age as the artist was on this first visit to the Prado; the other depicts an old, Picasso-like man holding a sword and a flower. A passion for Velázquez spanned virtually the entire gamut of the artist's career.

On arrival in Málaga, they installed themselves in Dr Salvador's house, 97 Calle Cortina del Muelle. For don José the homecoming was fraught with failure. It fell to Pablo, the child prodigy and still the only male offspring on either side of the family, to compensate for the disappointments and miseries of life in Corunna. Don José and doña María invited relatives and friends as well as teachers from the Escuela to see Pablo's recent paintings, but the most important person to impress was rich

Opposite: Picasso aged fifteen. Musée Picasso, Paris.

Uncle Salvador; and Uncle Salvador was impressed to the extent that he gave his nephew an allowance of five pesetas a day and a room in the office part of his house to use as a studio. He also provided him with a model: a picturesque old sailor named Salmerón, one of the objects of the doctor's charity. Salmerón would be the pretext for another of the artist's strange boasts about speed. 'What caused consternation to Uncle Salvador,' Picasso said sixty years later, 'was that the [portrait of Salmerón] was finished far too soon and he was obliged to search for other sitters.'[3] Once again the boast is difficult to reconcile with the facts: in this case the dates on some of the portrait sketches—'June' and 'August 14'. These confirm that the model was available to Pablo for most of his stay. Doesn't the fact that these sketches were executed over a period of two months suggest that Uncle Salvador's 'consternation' resulted from his nephew's dilatory use of the model provided for him? If haste was involved, it was surely because Pablo had to finish the old mariner's portrait in a rush before the family left for Barcelona at the beginning of September or face his uncle's displeasure. Compared with the models he had portrayed so dispassionately in Corunna to please himself, the Salmerón portrait suffers from being done to please his demanding uncle. It recalls the slick paintings of fisherfolk that are still churned out for tourists in southern Spain or Italy.

Dr Salvador Ruiz Blasco and his daughters. Ricardo Huelin collection.

In a further effort to keep his nephew busy, Uncle Salvador commissioned him to do a portrait of his slightly mad, half paralysed and excessively pious eldest sister, Josefa (Picasso's aunt Pepa). Neither the artist nor the subject, who was notorious for saying 'no' to everybody, was keen on this assignment. Reluctant to approach the old spinster himself, Uncle Salvador suggested that Pablo do so. He accordingly called on this frightening hag, who lived in a secluded wing of her brother's capacious house. Her room was filled with the effigies of saints, a *purísima* virgin dressed in gold, as well as a shrine to the memory of her favourite brother, the erudite, art-loving Canon Pablo, whose household she had once supervised. Mementos of the loved one included his 'collection': a seventeenth-century crèche in terracotta, bronze urns studded with precious stones, some antique ecclesiastical silver and empty bottles of *amict de nipi*, the cologne that the austere but elegant canon had always worn. As usual Aunt Pepa—who, incidentally, had never learned to read—was at her devotions; when she heard what her nephew suggested, she accompanied her usual 'no' with a blow. Pablo fled. Later, however, the old lady changed her mind and emerged unexpectedly from her apartment, dragging her paralysed leg behind her. She had dressed in her Sunday best: a winter cloak, a lace veil made by her sister and the canon's gold watch on a heavy gold chain. Pablo was playing with his cousins in the courtyard and not in the mood to paint the difficult old lady, but his diplomatic mother insisted that he do so for Uncle Salvador's sake. A piece of cardboard was produced from the Sanitation Department, which was housed in the doctor's office, and Pablo set to work. According to legend, the portrait was completed in less than an hour.[4] But speed has as little bearing on the quality of the painting as the artist's age.

Picasso's aunt Pepa. Ricardo Huelin collection.

The portrait around which Picasso and Sabartès have woven this circumstantial tale is not in fact on cardboard but canvas; and its bravura style bears far more resemblance to the artist's work of 1896 than 1895.

Picasso. *Portrait of Baldomero Ghiara*, Corunna, December 1894. Oil on card, 9×12 cm. Private collection. Inscribed to the sitter.

Left: Picasso. *Male Portrait,* (Uncle Salvador?). Málaga, 1895. Pencil on sketchbook page, 12×8cm. Museu Picasso, Barcelona.

Right: Picasso. *Portrait of Aunt Pepa.* Málaga, 1896. Oil on canvas, 57.5×50.5cm. Museu Picasso, Barcelona.

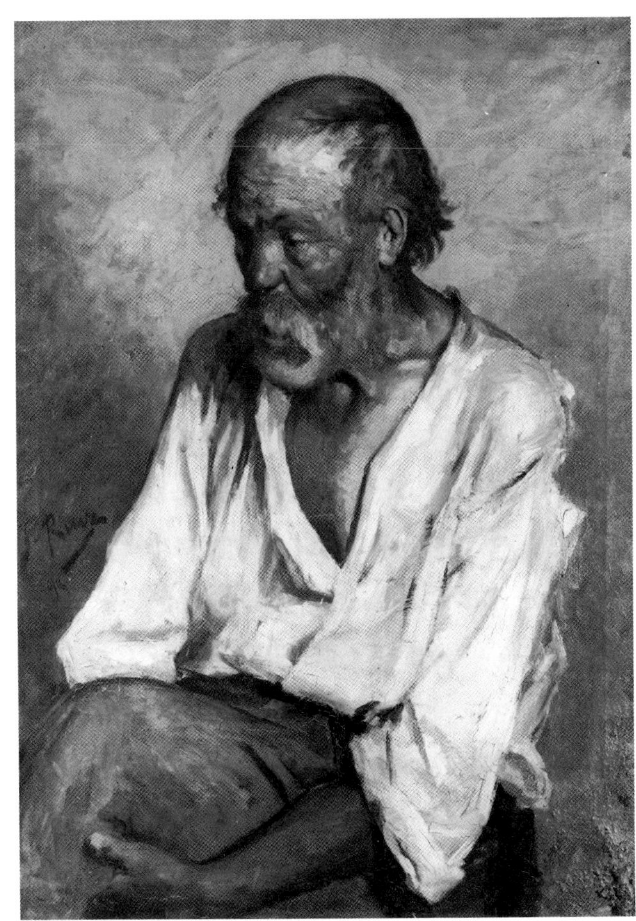

Left: Picasso. *Aunt Pepa.* Málaga, 1895. Pencil and conté crayon on sketchbook page, 12×8cm. Museu Picasso, Barcelona.

Right: Picasso. *Portrait of Salmerón.* Málaga, 1895. Oil on canvas, 82×62cm. Sala Collection, Abbey of Montserrat.

Left: Picasso. *Salmerón.* Málaga, June 1895. Pencil on sketchbook page, 12×8cm. Museu Picasso, Barcelona.

Picasso. *Still Life with Fruit*. Málaga, 1895. Oil on canvas, *c*.110×80cm. Whereabouts unknown.

In the circumstances we can only conclude that the portrait on cardboard has disappeared or, more likely, that Picasso and Sabartès were mistaken as to the date and type of 'support'. To judge by a somewhat hesitant drawing of Aunt Pepa in one of the Museu Picasso sketchbooks (signed and dated 1895), Pablo did not paint the done-in-less-than-an-hour portrait until the following year.

One work that Pablo evidently did execute this summer of 1895 with a view to pleasing don José is a hideous *Still Life with Fruit*. In 1968 Picasso recalled 'that painting as if I had done it yesterday. Do you see the grapes? While I was painting, I ate all the ones on the other side, the side that doesn't show in the painting. . . . The only grapes left were the ones you see. . . . It was a Herculean task to arrange this bunch of grapes so that I could paint them as if I hadn't eaten a good half of them.'[5] The kind of vulgarity—what the Spaniards call *cursi*—that is such a feature of this conglomeration of fruit, flowers, silver, china and basketwork, would always intrigue Picasso. He never lost his taste for bad taste, and knew exactly how to make it work for him. In June 1956, for instance, he allowed an ineffably *cursi* flower arrangement, which had been sent to him for his birthday eight months earlier, to wither and its silvered jardinière to fall apart so that he could use the tawdriness of the florist's set piece to his own advantage. 'I wanted to do a Manet,' he said, and came up with a *vanitas*.[6]

Having demonstrated to his father and uncle a mimetic gift for Salon still life, the fourteen-year-old Pablo turned his attention to another academic genre. Never one to waste expensive canvas, he scraped down a flower piece and substituted a fustian costume scene, *Columbus at the Monastery of La Rábida*, loosely based on a composition of the same subject by José Ponce Fuente recently installed in Málaga's town hall. *Columbus* demonstrates the boy's facility for the kind of history painting that don José and Dr Salvador found almost as ennobling as religious art. An important consideration this, for Pablo was more than ever dependent on his uncle's goodwill, more than ever mindful of the strings attached to it. Nothing less than the financing of his future career was at stake. He had to watch his step, for Uncle Salvador was turning melancholic—much like don José—and was more than ever insistent on social and religious obligations. So that Uncle Salvador could attend, Pablo's first communion had been put off until the family's return to Málaga. One aspect of this ceremony gave the boy certain pleasure: he was dressed, according to Spanish custom, in the role of boy-bishop. Less to his taste was Uncle Salvador's insistence that, if Pablo skipped communion, 'he wouldn't take me to the bullfight. I would have gone to Communion twenty times for the chance of going to the bullfight.'[7] Some clumsy but expressive little sketches that he dashed off at one of the corridas that summer testify to his growing *afición*.

Besides doing oil sketches of Málaga harbour, Pablo is thought to have worked at the Escuela where his father had formerly taught. Although the place was closed for the summer, something of the sort would explain an academic study, a male nude, and a painting and drawing of the same Andalusian-looking model, this time clothed. Years later, Picasso said this young man was probably 'a relative'.[8] He was in fact a friend of the family: a local photographer named José Román, according to an

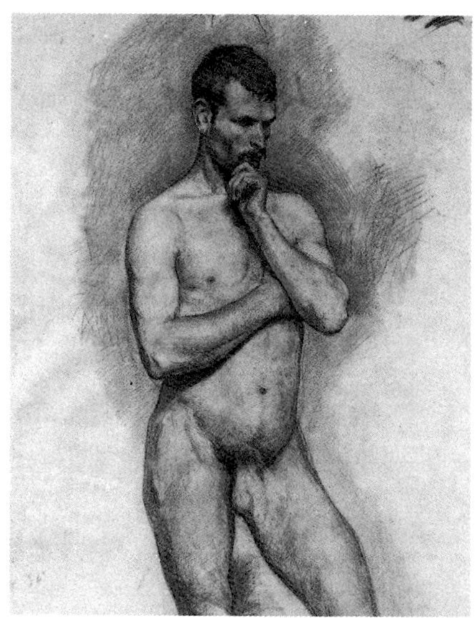

Picasso. *Nude Study of José Román* (detail). Málaga, 1895. Charcoal and conté crayon on paper, 43.5×47.4cm. Museu Picasso, Barcelona.

Picasso. *Self-Portrait with José Román*. Málaga, 1895. Oil on canvas, 60×46cm. Marina Picasso collection.

Picasso. *Ship's Captain*. 1895–96. Oil on panel, 15.6×10.1cm. Museu Picasso, Barcelona.

annotated photograph of him with a dressmaker called Manuela and the three Blasco girls.[9] Also present in this photograph and others taken at a picnic this summer is a youth believed by Blasco to be Pablo. However the youth in question looks remarkably unlike the self-portrait with hair *en brosse*—as a precaution against lice, boy's heads were kept shaved in the summer—alongside another head of José Román. After the accomplishment of the Corunna portraits, the works of this summer are a bit feeble. Doubtless Pablo felt he was on holiday and entitled to relax before the tests that faced him in Barcelona.

*   *   *

On Friday, September 13, 1895, the Ruiz Blasco family set forth once again to make a new life for themselves. Despite the ominous date and bad memories of their previous voyage, they went by sea. Once again Dr Salvador had arranged cheap rates. The small cargo boat, *Cabo Roca*, took eight days to reach Barcelona, stopping at Cartagena, Alicante, Valencia and Tarragona. Compared with the Atlantic, the Mediterranean was calm, and Pablo did run-of-the-mill oil sketches of their ports of call, also of the captain and his dog. On Saturday the 21st, the family arrived safely in Barcelona and installed themselves in an apartment near the art school, where the father was to teach and the son to study. There is some disagreement as to the family's first address in Barcelona.[10] In any case they stayed there only a month. Arrangements had been made to take over the apartment at 4 Carrer Llauder,[11] where don José's predecessor at La Llotja, don Román Navarro, had lived before moving back to Corunna.

By the time the Ruiz Blascos arrived in Barcelona, Catalonia had become the most industrialized and up-to-date region of Spain. Iron foundries and textile mills, which were failing in Andalusia, were thriving in Catalonia. Workers poured in from the south to share in the boom, only to find that urban poverty in the north was little better than rural poverty in Andalusia; and the dissident groups they formed were more often than not proscribed. The bourgeoisie, however, flourished. They were on the whole enlightened, liberal, dynamic and obsessively conscious of being Catalans. They still resented the loss of their autonomy that resulted when their vast territories (minus the province of Roussillon, which went to France) had been absorbed into the kingdom of Spain at the end of the fifteenth century. They resented even more the tyrannical regulations—censorship, suppression of their national language and songs—that were imposed by Madrid. *Catalanisme* was constantly boiling over into violence. This in turn provoked savage reprisals on the part of the authorities —reprisals that increased in savagery after the anarchists began to make their presence felt in the 1880s. It was above all in the ranks of the workers' organizations that anarchism took hold—a hold that the collapse of the economy in the wake of defeat in the Cuban War (1898) was to make stronger than ever. True, there were activists, even terrorists, among the bourgeois intelligentsia, but for the students, whose ranks Pablo was about to join, anarchism was apt to be a modish fad, and they were not taken very seriously by the workers or hard-core adherents.

Although Catalonia had produced little art of distinction since the Middle Ages and its capital had no museums to speak of, the Catalans

José Ponce. *Portrait of Don José.* Málaga, *c.*1895. Oil on canvas. Whereabouts unknown. Inscribed to the sitter.

Exterior of La Llotja, the old Barcelona stock exchange, where the art school was situated. Photo: Mas.

prided themselves on being more cultivated, more avant garde than other Spaniards. They prided themselves on their language and literature and their efforts at reviving it; also on their magnificent Romanesque and Gothic monuments, altarpieces and sculptures and their efforts at restoring them. Local piety had engendered a *Renaixença*: a Catalan 'rebirth' (nothing Italianate about it), which Picasso would come to support, though never as fanatically as some of his friends. This *Renaixença* involved everything from arts and crafts to puppetry, but it was principally in architecture that it came to epitomize Catalan aspirations. From the 1870s onwards, local architects and politicians (often one and the same), canny businessmen and starry-eyed local patriots set about extending Barcelona's medieval limits, developing new urban areas and erecting buildings in a 'national', that is to say Catalan, style.[12] They were determined to create a great new modern capital—a rival to Madrid—that would compensate for Catalonia's loss of status as a nation. And in 1888 they organized a spectacular Universal Exhibition as the apotheosis of this dream. Catalan architects and designers turned to traditional techniques as well as the glories of their Romanesque and Gothic past for inspiration; at the same time they culled the latest ideas from all over Europe—primarily Paris, for which they had far more affinity than Madrid, also Vienna and Munich, Brussels and Glasgow. The 'national' style of architecture and design that evolved has rightly been hailed as a major precursor of the modern movement, although many of the ideas behind it were the reverse of modern. Antoni Gaudí, to name but one of the leading lights, was adamantly anti-liberal: his ideal was a medieval guild with high-minded craftsmen working together for the greater glory of God. He despised and distrusted the progressive young artists of Barcelona, who would soon include Picasso. Nor did the young artists have much sympathy for him. For Picasso, Gaudí's famous church, the Sagrada Familia, was something of a joke—more to Salvador Dalí's taste, he once commented, than his. In the living room at La Californie there used to be an enormous *panettone* that mice had reduced to a ruin: 'Gaudí's model', he would say.

No sooner had they unpacked than father and son hastened to register at the School of Fine Arts, or La Llotja (literally 'exchange'), as it was familiarly known because it was housed on the second floor of the stock exchange. Don José felt even more of an outsider than he had in Corunna: La Llotja seethed with separatist fervour. At the new professor's first staff meeting (September 26) the principal topic was the trouble a non-Catalan teacher, Díaz de Capilla, was having with local students whose chauvinism was out of control.[13] Profiting from his disastrous experiences in Corunna, don José kept his thoughts to himself—even in the privacy of the family circle. 'All equal,' he announced cryptically of the colleagues with whom he hoped, for a change, to work in amity.

The day before this meeting, Pablo, who had failed to acquire the requisite diplomas in Corunna, was obliged to sit for an entry exam to La Llotja. The famous legend launched by his friend and biographer Roland Penrose and repeated by virtually every other authority—that this 'test, for which one month was prescribed, was completed by [Picasso] in exactly one day'[14]—does not stand up to investigation. Although the standard Llotja test involved three drawing categories, there was no question

Above: Drawing class at La Llotja in the early twentieth century. Photo: Mas.

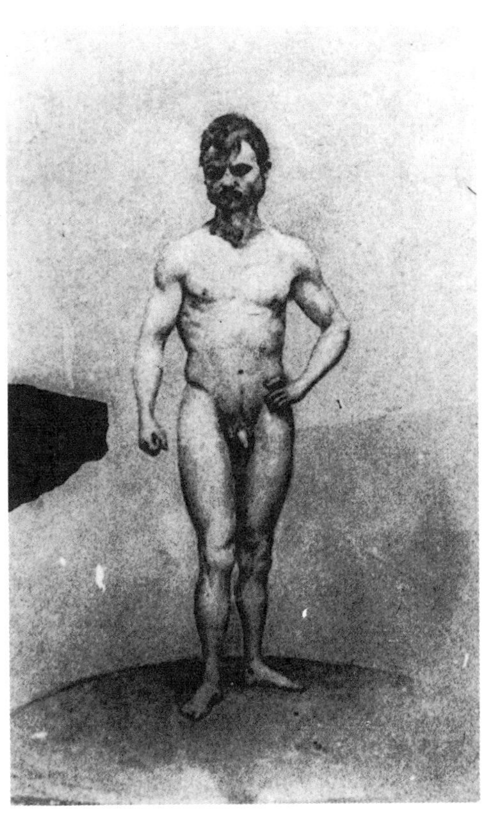

Right: Picasso. *Male Nude;* drawing for entrance exam to La Llotja. Barcelona, September 25, 1895. Conté crayon on paper, 50.2×32.5cm. Heirs of the artist.

Above: Picasso. *Study of Plaster Cast;* drawing for entrance exam to La Llotja. Barcelona, September 25, 1895. Charcoal, conté crayon and pen on paper, 47.4×61cm. Museu Picasso, Barcelona.

Right: Picasso. *Draped Male Model;* drawing for entrance exam to La Llotja. Barcelona, September 30, 1895. Conté crayon on paper, 47×31.2cm. Heirs of the artist.

of its taking a month, least of all in the case of Pablo, who was, apparently in view of his youth, let off with doing two studies of a model and a drawing of a plaster cast (a fragment of a male nude from the western pediment of the Parthenon). Any half-way gifted student could have completed these drawings in a day, but two days were allotted for the task. The drawing of the cast is dated September 25, as is the first life study, which portrays an ugly little runt of a model naked; the second one is dated September 30, and portrays the same man draped in a sheet masquerading as a toga. Penrose maintains that members of the jury 'were at once convinced that they were faced, for the first and perhaps the last time, with a prodigy,'[15] but there is no evidence of any such conviction; nor do these run-of-the-mill drawings proclaim the prodigy. The brilliance of the portraits done at Corunna in the spring is conspicuously lacking, which suggests the boy was ill at ease sitting for an exam. The peculiar proportions—the large head compared with the dwindling extremities—have the effect of minifying the scale of the model. (Interesting, given Picasso's aggrandizement of figures in years to come by magnifying specific features.) Penrose's loyalty does him credit: 'the technical ability . . . is enhanced by a brutal disregard for the idealized classical canons of human proportions. . . . Without effort [Picasso] had proved himself capable of mastering the academic standards required of a fully fledged art student, but [academicism] was no more than a step backwards for Pablo Picasso, who began life as a master.'[16] However, by perpetuating Picasso's retrospective view of himself as a prodigy who was endowed from earliest days with the mastery of a Raphael, Penrose belittles the young artist's unremitting efforts to perfect his technique. We need only compare these curiously tentative 'test' drawings with ones done the following year to see that Picasso's development depended at least as much on the infinite pains he took as on the infinite gifts with which he was born.

The drawings Pablo submitted to the examiners, as well as the time he had spent working from plaster casts in Corunna, entitled him to pass directly into the more advanced class at La Llotja: Antique, Life, Model and Painting. (The official records of the Academy for the year 1895–96 list Pablo Ruiz Picano [*sic*], as number 108 of 128 pupils.) Although the Catalans prided themselves on being familiar with the latest developments in European art, the teaching at La Llotja proved to be almost as stultifying as at Corunna—otherwise don José would not have been employed there—but this did not, at first at least, bother Pablo. Antiquated notions that stemmed from the debased classicism of the Spanish Nazarenes were pretty much what don José had accustomed his son to expect. Indeed, Pablo actually respected the director of the school—an indifferent portraitist called Antoni Caba—respected him for insisting that students draw and draw from the model, a discipline that Picasso advocated to his dying day. Picasso may have despised academicism; he did not despise academic teaching. And as long as he was not made to feel beholden to Uncle Salvador, he was ready to submit to it.

Picasso. *Male Nude*. Barcelona, 1896. Charcoal and conté crayon on paper, 60×47.4cm. Museu Picasso, Barcelona.

What Pablo enjoyed about La Llotja was the unlimited supply of live models, as opposed to the plaster casts which he had hitherto been condemned to copy. Besides portraying their bodies (always male; female models were not permitted), Pablo made a point of characterizing their faces—one of the reasons that his academic studies look much more real and human than most of their ilk. When the models had left for the day, he would go home and get his accommodating father or sister—seldom his mother: she was too busy—to pose for him. If family members could not be coerced into sitting, he would make do with a mirror; a recurrent phenomenon of the next decade is the succession of self-portraits that constitute an autobiography of sorts, albeit of a dramatizing, wishful-thinking kind.

Soon after enrolling, he applied to the principal of La Llotja for permission to make copies in the Museo del Establecimiento.[17] He was almost certainly put up to this by don José—an old hand at copying—who regarded this activity as an essential part of a student's training. He may have hoped to sell his son's copies, but since the only surviving example is a back view of a nude in a frothy figure study by Mas i Fondevila, it is more likely that the absence of female models at La Llotja left Pablo with no alternative but to use nudes by another artist.

The stimulus in an art school is generated as much by the pupils as the teachers. This was particularly true of La Llotja, where ethnic pride encouraged students to be more fractious and lively than their counterparts elsewhere in Spain. Except for Pablo, the class of 1895 at La Llotja was short on artistic talent but long on energy, enthusiasm and openness to ideas. And although they tended to be chauvinistic towards southerners, they welcomed Pablo. He was after all only thirteen years old when he enrolled: five or six years younger than most of them. Instead of feeling threatened by his gifts, fellow students soon succumbed to his mercurial charm and physical magnetism—the huge, all-devouring eyes, the small wiry frame, the cool Andalusian swagger—and accepted him as one of themselves, just as they would come to accept him as a paragon.

Pablo never had trouble attracting friends. The first day he attended Tiberi Avila's anatomy class, he found himself sitting next to a second-year student, Manuel Pallarès i Grau, a farmer's son from a remote village in the mountains of southern Catalonia. Although Pallarès was nineteen —almost six years older than Pablo—the two students became instant friends. Pablo's earliest portraits of him (winter, 1895–96) reveal Pallarès to have been an ordinary-looking, clean-cut, fair-skinned young man—more like a student of law than an art student. Pablo was drawn to him because he was solid and supportive, a big brother all too willing to take him under his wing; he was also extremely amenable: a born disciple. Pallarès introduced his new friend to other students, also to girls and night-life. And this odd couple were soon spending their days together. In the mornings, they would go to La Llotja or take walks in the Ciutadella park, where Pablo would paint views on cigarbox lids. In the evenings, they would wander up and down the Ramblas: the tree-lined chain of boulevards bustling with bird and flower markets, theatres, cafés and bars that is still the palpitating heart of the city. They would always end up at the Eden Concert, a raucous cabaret which was to become Pablo's favourite haunt. In return Pablo insisted that his family entertain Pallarès at home on Sundays. At first don José disliked the idea: he suspected Pallarès of leading his boy astray. But Pablo was already adept at manipulating his parents, and he made their hospitality a condition of spending Sundays at home. They soon came round to accepting this new friend and would

Picasso. *Nude,* copy after Mas i Fondevila. Barcelona, 1895. Oil on panel, 22.3×13.7 cm. Museu Picasso, Barcelona.

Picasso. *Portrait of Manuel Pallarès.* Barcelona, 1895. Oil on board, 35.3×25. Ex-Pallarès collection.

Picasso. *Doña María*. Barcelona, 1896. Pastel on paper, 49.8×39cm. Museu Picasso, Barcelona.

Top: Picasso. *Don José*. Barcelona, 1896. Watercolour on paper, 25.5×17.8cm. Museu Picasso, Barcelona.

Above: Picasso. *Self-Portrait*. Barcelona, 1896. Oil on canvas, 32.7×23.6cm. Museu Picasso, Barcelona.

invoke the steadying influence of Pallarès whenever they needed to curb their wilful son. Pablo already had a very strong personality, Pallarès said some seventy-five years later:

> He was way ahead of the other students, who were all five or six years older. Although he paid no apparent attention to what the professors were saying, he instantly grasped what he was taught. His phenomenal curiosity made up for his lack of artistic culture: he absorbed things in the blink of an eye and remembered them months later. He was unlike the others in every respect. Sometimes he got very excited; sometimes he would go for hours without a word. He was quick to anger, just as quick to calm down. He was well aware of his superiority, but never showed it. He often seemed melancholy, as if he had just thought of something sad. His face would cloud over, eyes become dark. At fifteen he neither looked nor acted like a boy his age. He was very mature.[18]

Manuel Pallarès. *Picasso*. Barcelona, *c*.1895–96. Conté crayon on paper, 63×47.5cm. Museu Picasso, Barcelona.

As usual with Picasso, the reverse is also true. He may have boasted that 'just as he never drew like a child, he never acted like one,' and that when he was fourteen he passed for twenty. However, he had a childish side—one that he kept hidden from everyone but his family and Pallarès. Pablo would take Pallarès up to the flat roof of his studio building and together they would watch the passers-by: 'a popular pastime that nobody goes in for,' Picasso recounted over half a century later.[19] 'One day we decided to play a joke: attach a coin to the end of a string and throw it down onto the pavement.' They roared with laughter when a workman bent down to pick up the coin, only to have it fly past his nose; and when a woman with a basket of fish on her head nearly lost her balance, as she brandished her fist at them. They were less amused when an outraged gentleman in top hat and tailcoat insisted that the concierge take him up to the studio, where the two boys were hiding behind the large canvas of *Science and Charity* (see illustration, p.81). However, the painting so impressed him that he beat a retreat, 'unable to believe that it was the work of a fourteen-year-old'. In fact, Pablo would have been fifteen at the time—a bit old for these pranks, one might have thought, as was the twenty-year-old Pallarès. In later years childishness would be a weapon that Picasso manipulated with diabolical deftness, as more than one of his mistresses would complain.

Pallarès is the only witness to have left a record of Pablo's early days at La Llotja.[20] Too bad he was an uninteresting man, and most of what he tells us is trivial or beside the point. We learn, for instance, that the two students took part in the carnival on February 16, 1896, dressed as Moors. Or was it women? Pallarès says that he might have confused their 1896 costumes with their 1897 ones. Whichever year it was, Pablo entered into the spirit of travesty so successfully that he made a male conquest—a most persistent one—who had to be dispatched with a right to the jaw.

Stuffy though he was, Pallarès was an ardent womanizer; indeed, he had recently been thrown out by his landlady, who was also his aunt and a tale-bearer to his family, for having a mistress. It was almost certainly Pallarès who introduced the fourteen-year-old Pablo to the local brothels, although he was well below the legal age for such activity. When questioned much later about his earliest sexual experience, Picasso claimed that his sex life had started very early on: '"Yes," he says smiling, with a sparkle in his eye, "I was still quite small"—and he indicated a diminutive

Interior of the Eden Concert, Barcelona, in the early years of the twentieth century. Among the artistes billed to appear is La Bella Chelito.

Picasso. *Female Nude* and other sketches. Barcelona, *c.*1896. Pen on paper, 14×10.2cm. Museu Picasso, Barcelona.

height with his hand. "Obviously I didn't wait for the age of reason. If I had I might not have begun at all!"'[21] He was not exaggerating. Given his precocity, Picasso's sexual initiation might have occurred in Corunna, but more likely in one of the whorehouses in the Barri Xino, Barcelona's labyrinthine red-light district, whose amenities rivaled Marseille's *vieux port*. Where the boy found the cash for prostitutes is a mystery. His pocket money would not have sufficed. Did older friends like Pallarès treat him to the occasional girl, or were his boyish charms such that the motherly whores did not charge him? All those loving older women must have brought back his childhood in Málaga. These early experiences in the brothels of Barcelona seem to have reinforced Picasso's Andalusian misogyny. The fact that he would often treat his mistresses as whores tends to bear this out. So does the work, not least *Les Demoiselles d'Avignon*, a group of whores whom he chose to identify as his women friends. Thirty years later, in image after image, the misogynistic pasha would endlessly reduce his teenage mistress, Marie-Thérèse Walter, to a thing of flesh and orifices in works of orgasmic explosiveness. Again at the end of his life, when the sexual act and creative act become metaphors for each other, the work gapes with vaginas, which the artist's loaded brush—his surrogate penis—would remorselessly probe. And where does the aged Picasso go back to in imagination but the Barri Xino, which he evokes again and again in prints and drawings that depict the artist's studio in terms of a brothel, or a circus, or a mixture of all three?

Besides frequenting brothels, the precocious Pablo found himself a mistress, Rosita del Oro. He seems to have met her through Joaquim Bas i Gich, one of two brothers—friends of Pallarès—who studied at La Llotja. Poor Rosita! Even the dependable Palau describes her as Picasso's 'favourite girl in one of the brothels'[22] when in fact she was a well-known circus performer—well enough known to merit her own poster. The conquest of this star equestrienne by a boy just turned fifteen says a lot for his personality and sexual magnetism. Nor was this a short-lived adolescent fling; it was a relationship that lasted on and off for a number of years (seemingly until Rosita met with a serious accident). Apart from one drawing and a caricatural sketch of 1900 (see illustration, p.151), no identifiable portraits of Rosita have survived, although the bareback riders of the Rose period were partly inspired by memories of her. At the very end of his life (1970), however, Rosita comes back to haunt Picasso, as do many other figures from his youth. In one of the most complex and beautiful of the late engravings, the artist, in the guise of an ancient child armed with a kite or a shield emblazoned with the mask of Rembrandt, is accompanied by a big-bosomed, wasp-waisted equestrienne of the 1890s. She towers over him through nine states of a mythological comic strip. Picasso's lifelong passion for the circus, his identification with acrobats and clowns, stems from this early romance.

For all his fascination with the circus and the Eden Concert, Pablo did not neglect La Llotja. He may have cut lectures on art theory or history, but he seldom missed an opportunity to draw and occasionally paint from life. And to judge by datable drawings, he made considerable technical strides during his first few months in Barcelona. Figure studies of early 1896 are far more confidently drawn and deftly characterized than the ones that won him entry into the school; and there is an attempt to

Picasso. Etching and scraping (detail). February–March 1970. 51×64cm. Galerie Louise Leiris, Paris.

evoke space. The quick sketches that he did at home, in cabarets or on walks round the city are also sharper and more disciplined now that he was learning how to channel the random energy of a first impression into a formally coherent image. Meanwhile, the fifteen-year-old Pablo would reward himself for days of grinding drudgery with nights of libidinous release. He came to love Barcelona and would continue to do so until his dying day. The life of the city—the Ramblas, the Paralelo, above all the Barri Xino—will be evoked in his late work more than any other place.

Poster advertising Rosita del Oro's equestrian act at the Tívoli Circus, July 30, 1897. Private collection.

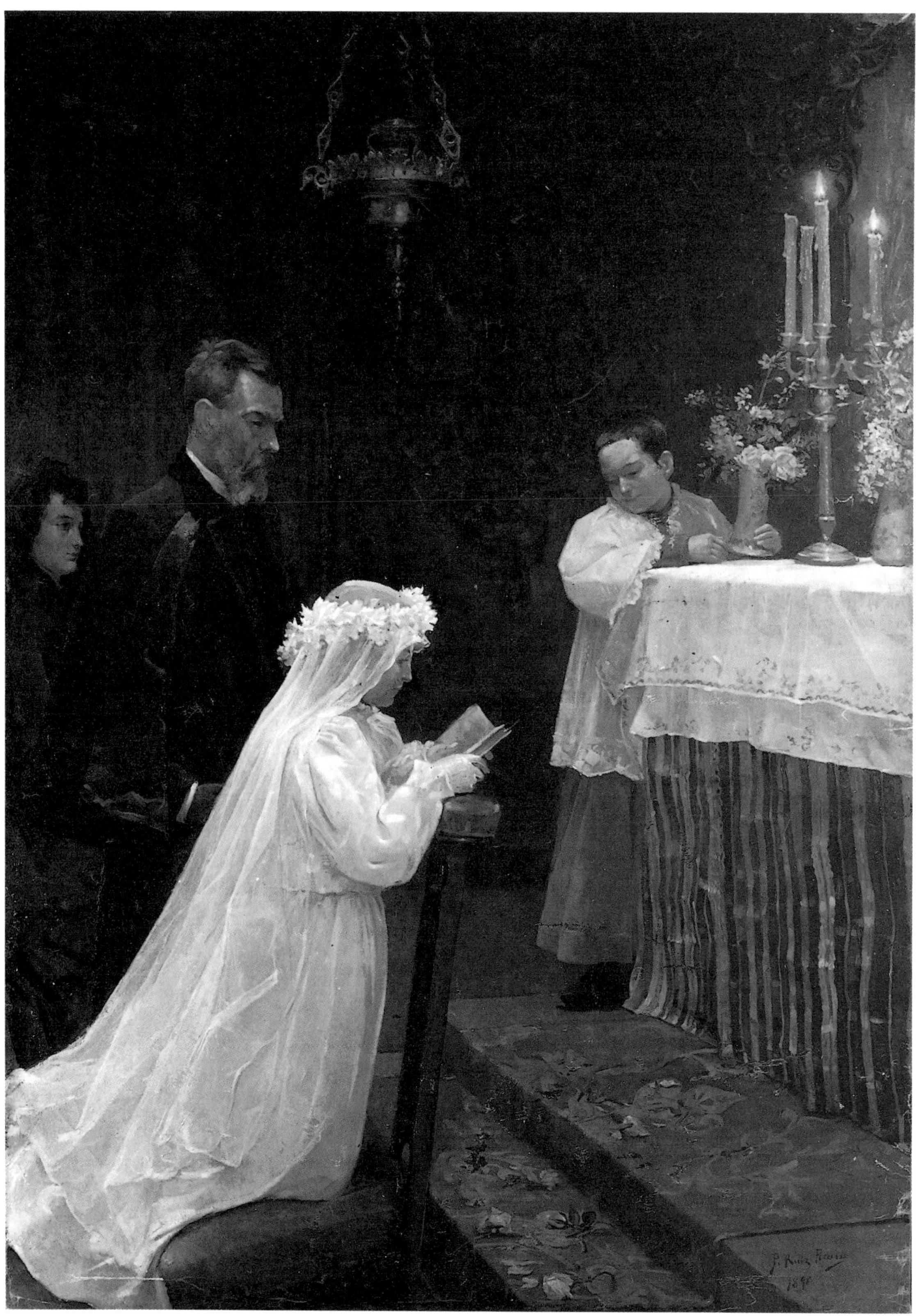

5

Sacred Subjects

'How can you make religious art one day and another kind the next?' (Picasso)[1]

José Garnelo Alda. *First Communion.* Valencia, 1893. Oil on canvas, 91×68cm. Private collection.

Although don José had little but the lesson of his failure to instil into his son, he insisted on supervising his development, encouraging him to train like a champion and envisage a lucrative career as an academic painter. His own chosen subject, the pigeon, had found little favour with the public, so he steered his son in a direction that was more serious, and potentially more profitable: religious art. Although anti-clericalism was on the rise and the Spanish church had been stripped of much of its power and wealth, there was more demand than ever for *bondieuseries*—devotional paintings and artefacts of all kinds. What an appropriate career for a canon's nephew; and how relieved pious Uncle Salvador would be if the wayward Pablo devoted his gifts to God. And so don José arranged for his son to work, after La Llotja closed, in a large studio belonging to his principal teacher. José Garnelo Alda was an Andalusian painter of sacred and moralizing subjects, whose younger brother Manuel was a fellow student and reasonably good friend of Pablo's. His vast atelier at 5 Plaça de la Universitat was as full of scenery and props as an old-time movie studio. When he went to work there, Pablo found the place decked out as the grotto at Lourdes, with models posing for the Virgin and Bernadette. Garnelo's studio also boasted a baroque altar in front of which this *pompier* artist could stage elaborate religious ceremonials and allegorical scenes. This altar, which had recently served as a backdrop for Garnelo's colossal *Flowers for the Blessed Virgin* (the centrepiece of his Sala Parés exhibition that year), seems to have served as a setting for Pablo's *First Communion*, his debut as a religious genre painter.

Executed early in 1896 in Garnelo's studio, *First Communion* was destined for the Exposición de Bellas Artes y Industrias Artísticas (the third of a series to be held in Barcelona's Palace of Fine Arts), which was due to open on April 23 (the feast of San Jordi, patron saint of Catalonia). Garnelo and don José had decreed that a contemporary but pious subject featuring a child would be within range of Pablo's adolescent sensibility and likely to win a prize, or at least sell. There are numerous preliminary drawings; the earlier ones portray an acolyte giving holy oil to an old woman accompanied by a girl dressed for her first communion. Pablo also executed a large painting of an altar boy holding a candle snuffer (see illustration, p.86).[2] But the theme of the definitive composition is his sister's first communion.[3] Lola is portrayed all in white—wreath, veil, dress, gloves—kneeling in front of an altar on a red-leather prie-dieu.

Opposite: Picasso. *First Communion.* Barcelona, 1896. Oil on canvas, 166×118cm. Museu Picasso, Barcelona.

Enrique Simonet. *Stumbling in the Choir of Málaga Cathedral.* 1888. Oil on canvas, 55×45cm. Ayuntamiento, Málaga. A characteristic example of the choirboy paintings so popular in Picasso's home town.

Picasso. *Christ Appearing to Blessed Marguerite Marie Alacoque.* Barcelona, *c.*1896. Oil on canvas, 24.4×18.5cm. Museu Picasso, Barcelona.

Presiding over the altar is not, as one might expect, a priest, but a boy of the same age as the painter: an acolyte robed in red and white. *First Communion* is saved from banality by Pablo's sharp observation of the figures—none of them, except for Lola, family members. We do not know who modelled for the mother (or godmother), but the father (or godfather) was impersonated by a family friend called Vilches. His son, Pedro, posed for the acolyte, the clumsy youth who looks as if he is about to upset the flowers and gives this sanctimonious scene a dash of verismo. Stilted as it is, *First Communion* remained a source of pride to the artist. He had hit on something 'real', he felt—something more real, if we can believe him, than is to be found in his Blue period paintings. More than twenty years later, he took an affectionate backward look at *First Communion* when he painted a couple of neo-classical variations on the subject.

The fact that two of the candles are lit and two have gone out is puzzling. This could be a realistic or anecdotal touch; I think it is more likely to be a symbolic one. Tempting as it is to see these candles as a reference to Pablo's guttering faith, we should put credence in the 1885 census that records the Ruiz Blascos as having a second, presumably short-lived, son, José. The candles could then stand for the two living and two dead children. Combined with the rose petals, emblems of mortality, that are scattered on the altar steps, this device would suggest that this *First Communion* is also a *vanitas*—a *memento mori* that could commemorate the dead Conchita as well as the living Lola. Be that as it may, this painting served another all-important purpose: Pablo was commissioned to do two altarpieces for a Barcelona convent.

Little or no attention has been paid to the quantity of sacred subjects in Picasso's work during his first year or so at La Llotja. The artist himself was reticent about them, as if these pious lapses of his youth might tarnish his atheistic image. But anyone who peruses the early sketchbooks and drawings in the Museu Picasso cannot fail to be struck by the variety of religious references, also by the knowledge of Catholic iconography that Garnelo instilled into his pupil. Among the saints portrayed are Peter, Sebastian, Antony of Padua, Ildefonso, Eulalia and Agnes. Sketchbooks likewise abound with martyrdoms, mostly of female saints, that have yet to be identified. These images of saintly suffering should not be dismissed as juvenilia, for they lingered on in the artist's memory, and re-emerged in the tear-filled eyes and scream-filled mouths of *Guernica*, not to speak of Picasso's harrowing portrayals of his own personal martyrs—Dora Maar, and his wives, Olga and Jacqueline.

More prevalent even than martyrdoms are scenes from the life of Christ: among them several Annunciations, the Education of Christ, the Supper at Emmaus, the Last Supper, the Taking of Christ, the Crucifixion, the Deposition, the Entombment, the Resurrection and Veronica's Veil. Since Pablo was studying under Garnelo, such subjects are to be expected. All the same, it sometimes seems that the boy is referring to himself in those scenes, that there may be a self-referential aspect to this sudden obsession with the life of Christ.[4]

One subject that crops up several times, notably in an oil sketch, can, I believe, be identified as *Christ Appearing to Blessed Marguerite Marie Alacoque*, the vision that engendered the enormously popular cult of

Picasso. *Annunciation*. Barcelona, *c*.1896. Oil on panel, 22.4×13.7cm. Museu Picasso, Barcelona.

Picasso. Sketch for an altarpiece. Barcelona, *c*.1896. Pen on paper, 10.8×11.9cm. Museu Picasso, Barcelona.

the Sacred Heart. So highly finished is the oil sketch, so numerous the preparatory drawings, that we can reasonably conclude they relate to one of the altarpieces. Hitherto, nobody has managed to cast any light on this project.[5] Thanks, however, to an unpublished statement by Picasso that has materialized among the Apollinaire papers in the Bibliothèque Doucet, it is no longer a mystery:

> The first pictures I ever sold [Picasso informed Apollinaire, *circa* 1910] were to a convent in Barcelona. I was fifteen years old when I did them, and it was a terrible blow to discover they had been burned during the troubles in Barcelona in 1909. The nuns had commissioned me to copy two altarpieces by Murillo; the idea bored me, so I copied them up to a point, then rearranged things according to my own ideas. Considering my age, I must admit feeling very satisfied.[6]

Marguerite Marie Alacoque's vision of the Sacred Heart of Jesus occurred in 1675, but it was not until she was beatified in 1864 that her cult, formerly opposed by the Jansenists, attracted a world-wide following. Coming as it did at a time of widespread defections from the church, the two-hundredth anniversary of the miraculous vision was exploited to the maximum by Church authorities, especially in Spain. The Sacred Heart became a rallying point for the traditionally devout, so much so that a million of the faithful petitioned Pius IX to dedicate the universe to it. This charismatic cult would have had great appeal to the Barcelona nuns, as would the prospect of having the vision of Christ appearing to the saintly nun commemorated by a child prodigy whose fee would have been less than that of an established artist. For Pablo the subject would have been ready-made, since he could work in Garnelo's studio, which was currently the setting for another miraculous vision.

To judge by the drawings, Picasso's Sacred Heart composition had very little in common with Murillo. Although, as he told Apollinaire, he transposed the master's work '*à ma manière*', the Christ figure was Murilloesque enough to satisfy the nuns. Moreover one of the preparatory drawings, the so-called *Revelation of the Miraculous Medal*, is a pastiche of Murillo's famous altarpiece in the Prado, *San Ildefonso Receiving the Chasuble from the Virgin*. This may well have been the original idea for the altarpiece that Pablo submitted to the nuns: he has simply substituted Christ for the Virgin and a French nun for the Spanish archbishop. The second painting presents more of a problem. It may have been an Annunciation, given a number of drawings of this subject. There is also a revealing little pen-and-ink sketch of a three-fold altarpiece. The centre panel appears to be a Resurrection—interesting in that Pablo had done a largish oil sketch after Murillo's *Resurrection* in the San Fernando Academy. Each of the side panels portrays two figures: the one on the left could easily be the Sacred Heart; the one on the right an Annunciation or a Visitation. Notes in a sketchbook for an art-school project suggest another possibility: 'Subject, sketch for an altar: Sta. Eulalia; Magdalen at the sepulchre on Easter Day.'[7]

Pablo was apt to make fun of sacred subjects: he used the figure of Christ in an 1896 watercolour on the Sacred Heart theme[8] as the model for a subsequent caricature of his friend Sabartès (see illustration, p.116). Sabartès is crowned with a wreath instead of a halo, holding out a flower instead of a medal, emblazoned with crosses instead of lilies and blasphemously inscribed '*Poeta Decadente*'. Picasso also had the Sacred Heart in mind twenty years later, when he made a series of pictorial puns of an anatomical nature on the form of a heart; these encoded his sexual passion for the teenage Marie-Thérèse Walter while concealing it from his wife; the emblem sanctified his love while desecrating whatever was left of his faith.

Picasso. *Revelation of the Miraculous Medal*. Barcelona, *c*.1896. Pen and watercolour on paper, 31×24cm. Museu Picasso, Barcelona.

Despite a thorough search, no photographs have been found of these altarpieces, which were burned in the Setmana Tràgica. The 'Tragic Week' of 1909 unleashed such a wave of anti-clerical violence that scores of religious institutions were destroyed. There is no knowing which one commissioned Pablo's altarpieces. A possible clue is the fact that the artist's parents had a friend from Málaga, Sister Josefa González, who worked in a Barcelona poorhouse known as the Asilo de la Granja. This nun could have been instrumental in obtaining the altarpiece commission, since a year later (1897) she took enough interest in Pablo's work to lend him one of her habits (for the figure of Charity in his *Science and Charity*). This habit is the same as the one worn by the nun in the Sacred Heart sketches. The convent may therefore have belonged to the Order of Saint Vincent.

Later in life Picasso would cannibalize only those painters—Velázquez, Ingres, Delacroix, Manet—who represented a supreme challenge to him. At the age of fourteen, as he himself admitted, Murillo already 'bored him'—and for good reason. The popular cult of Murillo's work, outside as well as inside Spain, depended primarily on its southern sweetness and softness: qualities that Picasso came to distrust, not least, I suspect, because he had to combat them in himself. Although both artists were Andalusian, they were the antithesis of each other. While Murillo spent his entire life happily ensconced in his home town (Seville), Picasso kept far away from his. Both artists took their mother's name in preference to their father's, but while Murillo celebrated women as Madonnas and won fame glorifying the Immaculate Conception, Picasso would celebrate whores as Madonnas and win fame portraying women as anything but 'immaculate'. Both artists owe too much of their popularity to picturesque scenes of poverty, but while Murillo oversentimentalizes the playfulness of his ragamuffins, Picasso would oversentimentalize the woefulness of his mendicants. And lastly, both artists emerged at periods of Spanish history that were culturally propitious yet socially ominous; but while Murillo's life coincided with the first phase of decline in Spanish fortunes, Picasso's coincided with the debacle. The two centuries separating their lives had seen all too little change, to judge by the following description of late seventeenth-century Seville, which could well have been written about late nineteenth-century Málaga, or even the more progressive Barcelona:

Murillo. *San Ildefonso Receiving the Chasuble from the Virgin*. *c*.1650–55. Oil on canvas, 309×261cm. Museo del Prado, Madrid.

> There was an affluent elite . . . there was also a vast poverty-stricken sub-world of underemployed—vagabonds, rogues, street-urchins, casual labourers, dock workers, hawkers, pedlars, water-sellers, all of them anxiously wondering where and how to get a square meal. According to Sancho Panza's grandmother, 'there are only two races in the world, the haves and the have-nots,' and the distinguishing criterion was food.[9]

Murillo's lack of *duende*—Spanish 'soul'—was not congenial to Picasso's already darkening spirit; and after the conventual commission there is only one later reference to the master of Seville: some drawings of 1906 that poke gentle fun at his *Prodigal Son Amidst the Swine*. Instead Picasso turned for inspiration to El Greco, whose Counter-Reformation spirituality and mingling of mannerism and mysticism was more to his taste than Murillo's rose-tinted cult of the Virgin, his optimistic *alma Sevillana*. El Greco's art with the religion left out but the *duende* left in is what he would seek to emulate. Picasso would always try to endow his subjects, no matter how ordinary or trivial, with the miraculous power that had hitherto been the prerogative of devotional painting. Later he would appropriate the sacred fire of tribal art, but first he had to appropriate the sacred fire of Christian art and throw out all, or almost all, the trappings and apparatus that went with it. El Greco would help Picasso exploit the ecstasy, anguish and morbid sense of sin of his black Spanish faith—a faith that no amount of atheistic protestations or blasphemy could ever entirely exorcise. As Picasso's great friend Michel Leiris wrote, 'One must never flatter oneself that one has altogether escaped the absurd power of Christian morality':[10] words that the artist knew well—words that sound just like him in old age, when defiant impiety went hand in hand with compulsive superstition. Apropos Picasso's religious views, his widow, Jacqueline, told me that, despite incessant avowals to the contrary, '*Pablo était plus catholique que le pape*.' To prove her point she showed me a sketchbook done in 1959. One series of drawings depicts Jacqueline in baroque splendour as a royal figure on a prancing horse out of Velázquez (one of them inscribed 'Jacqueline *reine*'), also as Dolores, Our Lady of Sorrows, with tears embellishing her cheeks and the seven swords of dolour transfixing her heart. A second series was probably inspired by the legend (cited in Lorca's essay on *duende*) that 'Saint Teresa had stopped an angry bull with three magnificent passes';[11] it depicts Christ descending from the cross to save the life of a gored torero, and using his loincloth as a cape to distract the bull.[12] 'Hardly the drawings of an atheist,' she said: true, except that, as usual with Picasso, irony makes for ambivalence.

Picasso. *Rest on the Flight into Egypt*. Barcelona, 1895. Oil on canvas, 50×36cm. Heirs of the artist.

Then again, as Jacqueline emphasized, the piety that Pablo railed against was a family trait. Not only Canon Pablo, his uncle, but his great-uncle Perico (Brother Pedro de Cristo) had conferred a measure of sanctity on the Ruiz family. Uncle Perico had not only pushed through clerical reforms, he had heroically nursed cholera victims and forsaken his career as a priest to live on alms as a hermit in the mountains of Córdoba. There he had died—revered as a holy man—in 1855, at the age of eighty-two. Still further back was another illustrious antecedent, the Venerable Juan de Almoguera y Ramírez, who had risen to the apex of spiritual and earthly power by becoming archbishop of Lima as well as viceroy and captain-general of Peru before he died in 1676. To Picasso, these pious forebears were a source of sardonic amusement, equally a source of sardonic pride.

Picasso's great-uncle, the hermit Pedro de Cristo Almoguera. In a frame painted by don José in 1879. Whereabouts unknown.

Don José did well to push his son into religious painting. The conventual commission justified his insistence that Pablo prove himself by exhibiting *First Communion* at the Exposición de Bellas Artes y Industrias Artísticas in 1896. The ridiculously high price of 1,500 pesetas that don José set on this work was the equivalent of half his annual salary, also three times as much as an established artist like Isidre Nonell was

Alexandre de Riquer. Poster for the 1896 *Exposición de Bellas Artes y Industrias Artísticas* in Barcelona. 99×150cm. Museu d'Art Modern, Barcelona.

Juli González. *Flowers*. *c*.1896. Iron, ht: 29.4cm. IVAM, Centre Julio González, Generalitat Valenciana.

Opposite: Group of prize-winning paintings included in the 1896 Exhibition. Rusiñol's won one of the first prizes (other winners included Mas i Fondevila, Simonet and Stuck), while the other three illustrated were awarded second prizes.

asking for a painting. The idea was presumably to obtain a maximum fee if and when ecclesiastical or municipal commissions materialized. With so much patronage in the offing, these hopes were anything but vain. The Exposición was generating excitement at all levels of Catalan culture. There was disappointment in official circles when the queen regent, María Cristina, was prevented from presiding over the opening (April 23, 1896) by the disastrous state of Spain's affairs (the collapse of the dwindling economy at home and the collapse of the dwindling empire beyond the seas); disappointment, too, in anti-royalist circles at being deprived of such a promising target for their discontent. In the face of national disaster the exhibition was all the more a showcase for promoting a new school of Catalan art—a school in which Picasso would assume a leading role, but not for another four years.

Apart from Picasso, the Exposición included two other artists who would make their names in the modern movement: Joaquín Torres García, an Uruguayan of Catalan descent, recently graduated from La Llotja, and Juli González, scion of a celebrated clan of metalworkers and goldsmiths, almost all of whom were represented in the Exposición. González exhibited a *Bouquet of Flowers* made of burnished wrought iron—a forerunner of the brutal iron blooms that González would help Picasso weld thirty years later. The most discussed exhibit was the garish *Rector's Orchard* by Joaquim Mir, leader of the 'saffron' group of open-air painters, who owed their nickname to their taste for yellow and orange sunset scenes. This orchard scene impressed Pablo to the extent that he tried half-heartedly to copy 'saffron' colours later that summer. Besides Mir, the Exposición included all the progressive Catalans— Ramon Casas, Ricard Canals, Isidre Nonell, Ramon Pichot, Santiago Rusiñol, Joaquim Sunyer, Sebastià Junyent—who were soon to form the Quatre Gats group: the group that Picasso's name would ultimately make famous. To these artists' more sophisticated eyes *First Communion* must have seemed the acme of kitsch, but Picasso would soon catch up and come to regard their work in an equally disdainful light. Apart from Nonell, the Quatre Gats painters are remembered outside Spain only by virtue of their association with Picasso.

First Communion failed to sell, failed to engender further commissions and failed to attract more than a brief, though polite, mention by Miquel i Badia in the *Diario de Barcelona* (May 25, 1896): 'the work of a novice in which one perceives sensibility in the principal figures. Parts [of the canvas] are painted with strength.' A more progressive critic, Raimon Casellas, attacked the exhibition (*La Vanguardia*, May 12, 1896) for including so many anecdotal genre scenes and history paintings, such as don José and Garnelo were urging Pablo to paint. Casellas advocated the arts-and-crafts theories of William Morris and the stylized work of Franz von Stuck (also included in the exhibition); and he singled out the decorative compositions of Santiago Rusiñol for eulogy. Such notions were anathema to don José, who insisted that his son follow up his not-very-promising Barcelona debut with an even larger, more edifying set piece. He still saw Pablo's career as an extension of his own. Pablo was too young and too dependent on his father to disabuse him.

*   *   *

Right: Santiago Rusiñol. *Allegory of Poetry*. 1895. Oil on canvas, 140×194 cm. Museu Cau Ferrat, Sitges.

Above: Joaquim Mir. *The Rector's Orchard*. 1896. Oil on canvas, 100×126 cm. Museu d'Art Modern, Barcelona.

Above right: Isidre Nonell. *Morning Sun*. 1896. Oil on canvas, 71×90 cm. Private collection.

Right: Ramon Casas. *Afternoon Dance*. 1896. Oil on canvas, 170×232 cm. Cercle del Liceu, Barcelona.

As a relief from the overcrowded life class and the stiflingly ecclesiastical atmosphere of Garnelo's studio, Pablo tried working in the open air. Accompanied either by Pallarès or his mother, who would sit crocheting on a nearby bench, he would set up an easel in the Ciutadella park and sketch its kiosks, ponds, palm trees and the miniature man-made mountains that were supposed to resemble Montserrat but looked like an abandoned stage set. He also painted vignettes of the harbour, quaint old corners of Barcelona (the cathedral cloister and Sant Pau del Camp) and fleeting impressions of sea and sky on cigar-box lids. Though painterly, these exercises confirm that nature would never replace mankind as the artist's primary concern. But then, Spaniards had never excelled at landscape painting; in over twenty years of existence impressionism had made virtually no headway south of the Pyrenees—unlike symbolism. The few Spanish artists who tried to paint the harsh light of the south were too inherently insensitive to colour to register its dazzle. The inaptly named Luminists from Sitges never cast off the influence of Marià Fortuny and the Italian Macchiaioli, and the School of Olot derived inspiration from Barbizon rather than Argenteuil.[13] Moreover, the short-lived saffron group (Mir, Nonell, Gual and Vallmitjana) were more interested in painting gaudy sunsets than in using complementary colours to register the shimmer of light. Travellers' reports and black-and-white illustrations in magazines were all that students at La Llotja knew of Renoir or Monet. Pablo's timid attempts at plein-airism evoke Whistler (whose work was widely reproduced) and, sometimes, Mir, rather than the iridescent colour harmonies of the impressionists. Nor in years to come would Picasso show the slightest interest in exploiting impressionist light effects in daring new ways; he left that to Matisse and the Fauves. True, Picasso would tell Apollinaire that 'I love light above all,' but this should not be construed as an impressionist avowal, for he went on to claim: 'Colours are only symbols and reality can exist only if there is light.' (*'La realité n'est que dans la lumière.'*)[14] Why else did Picasso use chiaroscuro rather than prismatic colour to generate light; why else find the high wattage of a naked electric bulb more to his taste than the sun; why else paint shadows black instead of an impressionist blue?

Picasso. *View of the 'Mountains' in Ciutadella Park*. Barcelona, 1895–96. Oil on panel, 10×15.6cm. Museu Picasso, Barcelona.

This inability to flood a painting with light is the more noticeable when Pablo sets out to do so, as in the two would-be luminous paintings of a quarry he executed during the family's summer holiday at Málaga in 1896. Far from being light-filled in the manner of Monet's paintings of the Creuse, which they superficially resemble, they are lightless. The blue of the sky above finds no answering Mir-like sparkle in the energetic stippling of the red earth below. As yet Pablo had no idea how to juggle with the spectrum. Blobs of colour remain blobs of colour; sunlight fails to materialize. But at least these loosely painted scenes of arid rock and scrub, empty of figures like most of Picasso's later landscapes, fly in the face of the deadly precepts taught by don José and his colleagues at La Llotja. For once there are no traces of academic blight. These *Quarries* are the boy's first conscious attempt to paint a modern picture.

Picasso. *Quarry*. Málaga, 1896. Oil on canvas, 60.7×82.5cm. Museu Picasso, Barcelona.

The family's Málaga holiday in the summer of 1896 did not last more than six weeks—mid-June to the end of July—as we know from paintings which the artist inscribed with the time and place of execution. Compared with previous summer visits, this one appears to have involved more work than play, more painting than drawing. Besides the quarry scenes, Pablo probably did the *Portrait of Aunt Pepa*, usually assigned to the previous summer, but more likely—on the grounds of confidence and brio—to date from 1896. He also dashed off a couple of small paintings of bulls that are important only insofar as one of them—a large black beast seen sideways on—is the archetypal Picassian bull, the one with which the artist comes to identify.

Picasso. *Bull and Head of a Bull.* Málaga, June 1896. Oil on panel, 13.7×22cm. Museu Picasso, Barcelona.

On the family's leisurely return trip along the Mediterranean coast to Barcelona at the end of July, the boat stopped, as it had the year before, at Cartagena and Valencia. Once again Pablo recorded the trip on cigar-box lids. His parents had curtailed their holiday by a month. They were in a hurry to get back and move house: from the sunny but damp apartment on the Carrer Llauder to a less sunny but larger one on the first floor of 3 Carrer de la Mercè, which was conveniently near La Llotja. The Carrer de la Mercè apartment would be a permanent home to Pablo as long as he lived in Barcelona; and for all his subsequent moves from studio to studio, that is where, often as not, he slept. At the same time don José gave in to his son's request for a studio of his own and rented a room for him and Pallarès on the top floor of 4 Carrer de la Plata. It was not very large but it had a skylight and it was half-way between the parents' apartment and La Llotja. This was a mixed blessing. Don José was forever dropping in, and although he was still very close to his father, Pablo had come to resent his managerial guidance almost as much as his abysmal precepts (don José had a lot in common with Leopold Mozart). Picasso loathed painting the set pieces his father imposed. And it was with some ambivalence that he regarded the large canvas propped against the wall that don José had specially stretched for him: the price to pay for the new studio. Once more he would be obliged to prove himself publicly with one of the outmoded genre scenes that his mentors regarded as the *summum* of art.

Pablo's first painting in his first studio, *The Bayonet Charge*, has the ring of his taste rather than his father's. The story that the canvas was so large it had to be lowered on ropes from the studio window seems to be without foundation: Picasso could not remember this happening.[15] Since *The Bayonet Charge* has vanished, we have no way of knowing, although x-rays may one day discover it lurking under a later work. A couple of sketchbook pages of confused battle scenes presumably relate to it.[16] Newspaper accounts and illustrations of the war in Cuba were the inspiration: also Marià Fortuny's mammoth *chef d'œuvre, The Battle of Tetuan* (1863),[17] the most celebrated Spanish painting of its period, which had a place of honour in the halls of the Diputació (the provincial government). Pablo may also have derived inspiration from another source: moving pictures. These were shown in Barcelona for the first time on December 4, 1896, when two local photographers, the Fernández brothers (nicknamed 'The Napoleon Brothers', after the Cinematográfico Napoleon, where the films were shown) organized a screening of several short features, including a much applauded *Cavalry Charge*. Since Picasso and Pallarès went as often as possible to the Cinematográfico Napoleon,[18] it is unlikely that this future movie buff would have missed out on such a sensational new experience. *The Cavalry Charge* would have catered to the boy's penchant for violence, just as a TV rerun of *The Bengal Lancers*

Picasso. *Battle Scene*. Barcelona, 1896. Pen on paper, 12.5×18cm. Museu Picasso, Barcelona.

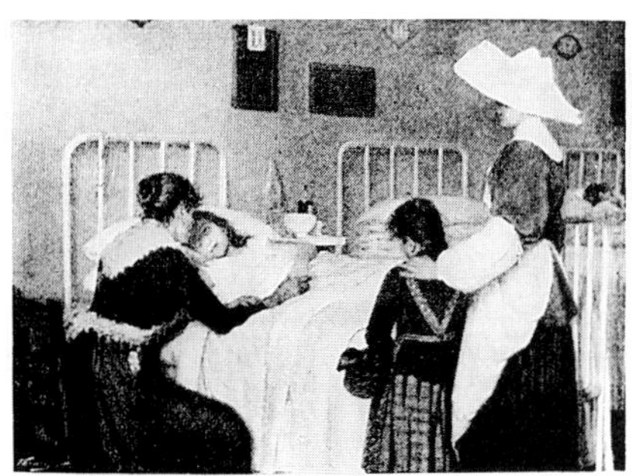

Enrique Paternina. *The Mother's Visit.* 1896. Oil on canvas. Private collection.

would delight the aged artist in 1962, when he was denouncing and at the same time revelling in violence, as witness his *Rape of the Sabines* paintings. Curious that trouble between Cuba and the United States should have inspired him once again.

The large newly stretched canvas was destined for yet another genre scene. *A Visit to the Sick Woman*, the subject was originally called. However, don José elevated it to *Science and Charity* to impress the jury of Madrid's Exposición de Bellas Artes, as well as Uncle Salvador who, in his brother's eyes, was the embodiment of these qualities. Like its predecessor, *Science and Charity* is a quasi-devotional work that revolves around the figure of a girl—this time a proxy rather than an actual family member—and three attendants. The death of Conchita suggested the theme, but there are at least three well-known Spanish paintings[19] of the period that could have inspired this maudlin sickroom set piece. *Science and Charity* is closest to a painting called *The Mother's Visit* by Enrique Paternina, a celebrated Castilian painter of the day. This depicts a nun watching a mother embrace her sick child in a hospital ward. But whereas Paternina plays on our feelings by conveying a sense of consolation, Pablo does the reverse and endows the waxwork scene that recapitulates (except for the invalid's age) the circumstances of Conchita's fatal illness with an almost Dickensian sense of foreboding. Oil sketches—eerily ex-voto-like—reveal that the doctor, with his grey hair and whiskers, originally resembled Dr Pérez Costales, who attended Conchita on her deathbed. All the more reason for seeing this composition in the light and shade of family tragedy. It then takes on a depth of meaning that transcends don José's pretentious allegorical concept. However, Pablo was becoming increasingly resentful of parental guidance. Why should his father insist on expressing his hollow aspirations, ventriloquially, through his son's gifts. When he reverts to the subject of a dying girl two years later, Pablo explores his guilt and grief in his own deep, dark way.

The setting for *Science and Charity* recalls Garnelo's amateur theatricals, but on the cheap. Pablo's tiny studio was divided more or less in two by the huge canvas (approximately 200×250cm), which the artist took most of March (1897) to complete. Crammed into the rest of the garret was a truckle bed on which lay a local beggar woman, who posed for the doomed invalid (although paid ten pesetas for her services, she stole the sheets off the bed). On one side of her a boy, masquerading as a nun in a starched coif and habit—loaned by a family friend, Sister Josefa González—holds the beggar woman's child and represents Charity. On the other side don José, impersonating a frock-coated doctor (his successful brother?), represents Science. The models make appropriate gestures—the 'doctor' takes the invalid's pulse; the 'nun' offers soup—but there is something ambivalent about the allegory. Whether or not this was his intention, Pablo kindles little faith in the efficacy of either science or charity. The girl looks apprehensive, as if she has no confidence in vows or vaccines and is doomed to suffer Conchita's fate. There is a further anomaly: the lighting. Why is this heavily shuttered room so brightly lit? The sun poured in through Pablo's skylight.

Despite the stilted concept, there are one or two prescient passages in *Science and Charity:* the brown paint on the bolted shutters that stains the whitewashed wall below with utterly real dribbles. Here the artist

Right: Picasso. Sketch for *Science and Charity*. Barcelona, March 1897. Oil on panel, 19.5×27.2 cm. Museu Picasso, Barcelona.

Below: Picasso. *Science and Charity*. Barcelona, 1897. Oil on canvas, 197×249.5 cm. Museu Picasso, Barcelona.

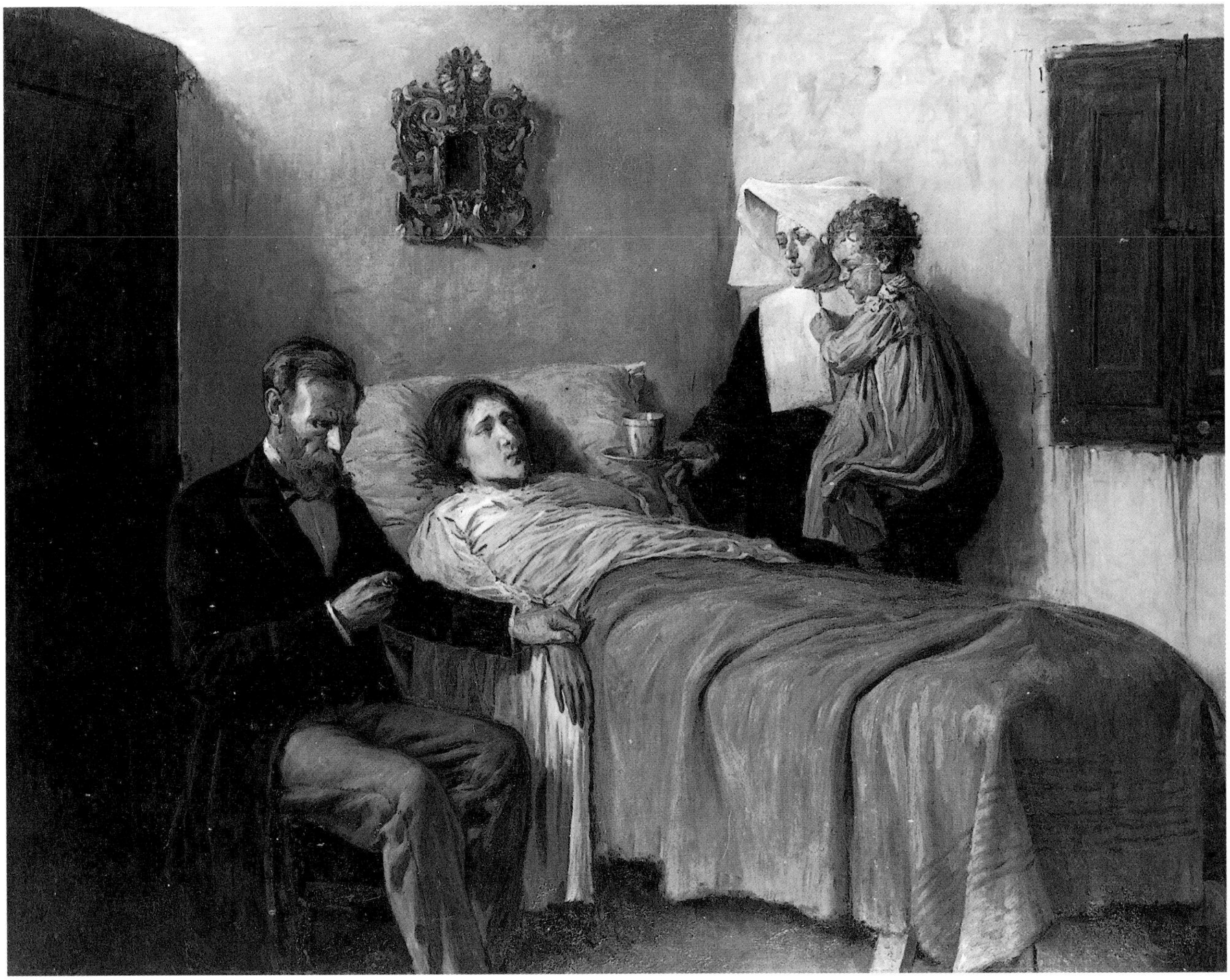

speaks with his own and not his father's voice. Only someone impervious to prettiness, someone destined to advocate reality (as opposed to realism) at all costs, could have come up with such a succinct and painterly evocation of shabbiness. The truth of these trickles carries far more conviction than the artful effects in Paternina's prototype. Another typical touch: instead of the crucifix he had hanging above the bed in the earliest sketches, Pablo has substituted a small mirror in a coarse baroque frame; and he has painted the volutes with a relish that leavens the ominousness of the scene. A mirror very like it (if not the same: Picasso always cherished things inherited from his father) crops up in several still lifes of 1943–44.

Picasso. *Don José*. Barcelona, 1896. Pen and watercolour on paper, 15×16.5cm. Museu Picasso, Barcelona.

While working on *Science and Charity*, Pablo honed his skills in portraits of his family and himself. Portraits of the father inevitably outnumber those of his mother: the much-put-upon doña María had ever less time to spare from household duties, whereas don José—never the most energetic of men—was always ready to serve as a model, and double as a mentor. Also, the mother had matured into a dumpy matron, whereas the father had aged into a figure of patriarchal distinction, gloomily handsome as an El Greco saint. Pablo's portrayals of don José are more than routine studies of a picturesque model. Filial tenderness, pride, pity and the mixture of guilt and gratification that a sensitive young pupil feels for the dear old teacher he overtakes are only some of the conflicting feelings they convey. Especially poignant is the contrast between the arrogant casualness of the son's virtuosity and the melancholy dignity of the old father whom he more than once portrays as faceless. At the end of Picasso's life, when so many early obsessions came back to roost, Picasso would make amends by depicting don José in a less doleful light: in a superb series of engravings devoted to brothel scenes, where he is flatteringly disguised as Degas.[20] Picasso was out to improve his father's circumstances for him, just as he would soon be doing for another beloved failure, his fellow student Angel de Soto. Equating his father with Degas is the ultimate example of this ameliorative process. But then, as the artist once said, all the men in his work are to some extent his father.[21] He might have gone on to say that most of these men, and even some of the women, are also to some extent Picasso himself—if we go by the eyes. Still there is no denying that long after the sheer force of genius had released the son from the father's grasp, the image of don José—so profoundly internalized in adolescence—repeatedly manifests itself in his art.

Picasso. *The Artist's Family*. Barcelona, *c.*1896. Oil on panel, 13.8×22.1cm. Museu Picasso, Barcelona.

* * *

Pablo portrayed his sister, Lola, almost as frequently as his father; after all she was the only girl model available to him on a regular basis. His likenesses of her are consistently affectionate and emphatically Andalusian. Compared with the dark allegories that memorialize the dead Conchita (*Science and Charity* is merely the beginning of a series of sickroom and deathbed scenes), the Lolas have more surface charm than psychic depth. Pablo occasionally sees his own features reflected in hers (for instance, in the Ensor-like portrait of her with a boyish tan and an aggressively animate stare that is contrasted with the inanimate stare of her doll). He also does his best to bring out in Lola the distinction of her Ruiz father, rather than the homeliness of her Picasso mother—a tentative beginning to the manipulative tricks he would play on the looks and identities of one woman after another. In the end Pablo seems primarily interested in exorcising the schoolgirl and visualizing his sister as a stylized Andalusian in a mantilla, shawl or bright red scarf, hair piled up in a chignon—pretty as a picture-postcard 'Manola'. Around 1899 the girl this image idealizes became the *novia* of Dr Juan Vilató, a young neurologist. We know this from a sketchbook page obsessively inscribed with his and her names.[22] When Lola embarked on the ritual of *noviazgo*—a long-drawn-out courtship that would in her case last some ten years—she had less time for her brother. After she finally married Dr Vilató (in Málaga on August 18, 1909), the brother and sister were seldom able to see each other.[23] But they remained on the best of terms. In due course, Lola had seven children, one of whom died in infancy. After don José died, doña María moved in and helped the Vilatós bring up their family. Although their life was conventionally bourgeois, it was far from stuffy, thanks to the Andalusian exuberance of the mother and grandmother; thanks also to the good sense of Dr Vilató, whose successful career culminated in his appointment as head of all the psychiatric services and institutions in Catalonia. The Civil War and World War II cut Pablo off from his devoted, outgoing sister, but they telephoned regularly, often daily, until Lola's death in 1958. Lola's younger sons, Javier and Fin, who fled to France in 1939, were especially close to their uncle.

Picasso. *Lola with a Doll*. Barcelona, 1896. Oil on panel, 35.5×22.5cm. Heirs of the artist.

Most revealing of the youthful works are the self-portraits. Picasso's claim that he had 'never been too concerned with my own face'[24] is not borne out by his work. As teenagers do, Pablo took narcissistic delight in scrutinizing his looks in a mirror, but, thanks to his sense of drama, he was able to develop this adolescent scrutiny into a metamorphic power and record himself in different roles as nonchalantly as if they were different hats. Something Picasso said in old age about his switches of style casts light on his switches of identity. He was not one 'of those painters', he observed, who lock themselves 'into the same vision, the same technique, the same formula for years and years. . . . I myself thrash around too much, move too much. You see me here and yet I'm already changed. I'm already elsewhere. I'm never fixed.'[25] And so if in the space of a single year (1896–97), Pablo's self-portraits take extraordinarily diverse forms—child genius with unkempt hair, eighteenth-century nobleman in powdered wig, dashing young dandy in stiff collar and stock—it is because he wanted to 'thrash around': to fantasize and dramatize himself, and manipulate his own identity and appearance.

This self-dramatizing, chameleon-like sense would remain with him all his life. On occasion it lent itself to misinterpretation, for instance in those much-published photographs of the old artist playing the clown. These photographs gave the false impression he had degenerated into a quick-change artist or an exhibitionistic buffoon. They played into the hands of pharisaic critics who saw Picasso's innocent delight in dressing up as a symptom of identity crisis. To friends this was, on the contrary, a strategy to camouflage the impatience, embarrassment and boredom that he experienced day after day (above all at La Californie in the 1950s) in the face of unknown, tongue-tied, camera-wielding admirers who could not speak his languages, Spanish, French and Catalan, but insisted on an

Picasso. *Self-Portrait in a Wig*. Barcelona, *c*.1897. Oil on canvas, 55.8×46cm. Museu Picasso, Barcelona.

audience with him. By switching masks—disguising himself as an Indian chief, clown or torero—Picasso defused the awe and shyness (his own as well as his admirers') that these occasions generated, and avoided having to play the great man. This was not at all how he behaved '*dans l'intimité*'.

* * *

Science and Charity was finished by the end of March 1897. It was time, don José had decided, for Pablo to graduate from La Llotja to the Royal Academy of San Fernando in Madrid. The new composition was expected to facilitate this project. Pablo's candidacy would be bolstered if, besides painting two altarpieces, he had already exhibited a major work; better still, if he had won a medal at Spain's most prestigious show, the Exposición General de Bellas Artes, which was to open in Madrid on May 25. Since his old friend Muñoz Degrain was on the jury, don José had reason for optimism. Everything went according to plan. The painting was accepted and, thanks probably to Muñoz, awarded a *mención honorífica*. Mention in the press was less gratifying: a Madrid critic, who signed himself '*El Sastre de Campillo*' (the tailor of Campillo), wrote a lampoon comparing the invalid's hand to a glove: 'Before so much grief I regretfully laugh like a bandit . . . isn't the doctor taking the pulse of a glove?' Pablo has indeed overdone the lifelessness of the elongated fingers, just as he often would during the Blue period. *Science and Charity* fared better at its next stop: the Exposición Provincial in Málaga. A jury composed largely of don José's friends and former colleagues awarded the painting a gold medal. And when Pablo returned to Málaga for the usual family holiday, it was on the strength of this honour that Martínez de la Vega (the popular local artist who taught the daughters of the bourgeoisie how to draw) baptized him a painter by pouring champagne over his head at a gathering in the Liceo.[26] This accolade, which parodied induction into a medieval guild, did as much for don José's *amour propre* as it did for his son's. Martínez de la Vega was the most sophisticated artist around; and his death eight years later did not go unobserved by Picasso.

Certificate for the Honourable Mention won by *Science and Charity* in Madrid, June 1897. Sala Gaspar, Barcelona.

Back in Málaga for the summer of 1897, the Ruizes found the family's circumstances much changed. Now that he had married into the local aristocracy (his new wife was Adelaida Martínez Loring),[27] Uncle Salvador had moved to a grander house: 49 Alameda, the best address in Málaga. As a suitable offering *Science and Charity* was presented to him as soon as the exhibition closed and accorded a place of honour in his new front hall,[28] next to a painting by Francisco Morales y González, the Granada artist whose sister-in-law had been Dr Salvador's first wife. Notwithstanding this handsome gift, don José and his family no longer had their accustomed place in the brother's house. This was now under new management. Aunt Eloísa and her emasculated husband, who used to preside over the household, had been sent packing; and the Ruiz Blascos were obliged to put up in an apartment on the Plaza Mitjana (near the artist's birthplace) that belonged to 'Mama Iñés', Pablo's maternal grandmother, the extravagant spinner of weird tales. Lola and her mother remembered how on hot afternoons Pablo used to watch enthralled as a woman in a neighbouring apartment wandered from room to room 'wearing nothing but a corset'.[29]

The Alameda, Málaga, where Dr Salvador lived, at the turn of the century. Archivo Temboury, Málaga.

Dr Salvador continued to patronize his brother's family as poor relations; but, thanks to don José's appointment to La Llotja, he was no longer perceived as a failure. Back in Málaga the former pigeon painter briefly became 'the Englishman' again—the urbane wit of the fashionable Liceo—and he regaled his old *tertulia* with endless tales of his son's prowess.

Heartened by the reception of *Science and Charity*, don José pressed forward with arrangements for Pablo's enrolment at Madrid's San Fernando Academy, the most prestigious art school in the country. The expense was more than don José could afford, so Uncle Salvador's blessing and financial help were essential. Picasso later accused his uncle of being excessively parsimonious, of envisaging his future career in terms of 'purchasing stock in an oil well or a mine at a time it was cheap because nobody wanted it'.[30] He had nothing but scorn for the doctor's proposal that don José and another uncle, don Baldomero Ghiara—the jeweller, whose wife was doña María's sister—should share the costs of Pablo's studies in Madrid. 'A mere vile pittance' is how Picasso later described these contributions, eked out with one peseta a month from 'nearly everyone else in the family, including the two spinster aunts'. Once backing was forthcoming, Pablo made his application to the Academy. On the entry form he listed himself, falsely, as 'a pupil of Muñoz Degrain'. The fiction would have had the master's approval. After leaving the Málaga art school, don José's crony had become one of the principal teachers at the Academy. Acceptance soon came through, subject to the usual tests. Muñoz Degrain saw that the fee for all this was waived.

Don Baldomero Ghiara. Foto: Grecia.

Forever after, Picasso would hold his uncle's charity against him: there was not enough of it and there were too many strings attached, Sabartès maintained. However, Uncle Salvador's grandson, Ricardo Huelin, has questioned the 'Catalan secretary's' account.[31] He accuses Sabartès of blindly believing the artist when he was merely out to provoke or amuse or bite the hand that had once fed him—one of 'the most generous hands' in Málaga, to believe Huelin. The grandson has a point; all the same he is obliged to admit that his grandfather disapproved of his headstrong nephew; disapproved specifically of the way he now signed his work: *P. Ruiz Picasso* or, worse, *P. R. Picasso*. This flew in the face of family pride and elevated the not very distinguished Picassos at the expense of the well-connected Ruizes. Doña María did her best to keep her son's rebellious nature hidden, but Dr Salvador's suspicions were not allayed, and animosity smouldered away. The 'poor relation' syndrome exacerbated Pablo's resentment even further, until the pompous, pious uncle came to stand for everything the nephew loathed about Málaga—provincial hypocrisy, snobbery, stinginess.

That summer Pablo went through the first of his 'fallow' phases—a phenomenon that would recur again and again after bouts of intense activity. The only painting he is recorded as doing at Málaga is a portrait of his first cousin Mariquita Padrón, the daughter of don José's sister, María de la Paz. 'A grotesque daub,' she said and later destroyed it.[32] For Pablo the summer of 1897 was a time to rest on his laurels and be fêted before leaving his family and moving to Madrid. It was also a time for dalliance. Pablo had always liked his pretty cousin Carmen Blasco Alarcón and had even given her one of his earliest paintings, *The Old Couple*

Picasso. *Don José Wrapped in a Blanket*. Barcelona, December 1895. Watercolour on paper, 10×14cm. Museo de Málaga. Inscribed to Muñoz Degrain.

Picasso. *Kitchen at Málaga*. Málaga, 1896. Oil on panel, 9.9×15.5cm. Museu Picasso, Barcelona.

Picasso. *Altar Boy*. Barcelona, 1896. Oil on canvas, 76×50cm. Sala Collection, Abbey of Montserrat.

Picasso's cousin Carmen Blasco. Manuel Blasco collection.

(1894). But now, to the delight of his Málaga relations, he began paying court to this nice conventional girl. As the family's only male heir, he was expected to waste no time perpetuating the Ruiz line, even though he was only fifteen. So he obediently took her to '*dar el paseo*'—walking arm-in-arm up and down the Camino de la Caleta like countless other courting couples—and she obediently fell for him. And why not? For all his lack of years and stature, Picasso exuded amazing vitality; he was also remarkably seductive: quick and funny and, if need be, romantic—the huge eyes mockingly bright or wistfully dark. However, the charms of Rosita del Oro and the thrills of the Barri Xino had left Pablo immune to the genteel appeal of a provincial cousin and the interminable rigmarole of Andalusian courtship. He played at being assiduously flirtatious but his hard young heart was 'not touched'. Both sides of the family were anxious to promote a match that would keep Pablo in Málaga to carry on their dynasty. Only down-to-earth doña María, who understood her son and his innate rebelliousness better than anyone else, realized that nothing would come of this idle bourgeois dream. And so at the end of the summer everybody's hopes but hers were dashed when Pablo left Málaga without making any commitment to Carmen beyond the symbolic gift (it has since disappeared) of a tambourine with a bunch of roses painted on its membrane. The spirited young prodigy, grappling with a precocious sense of destiny, was not about to saddle himself with a boring bride and stagnate in this southern backwater.

Pablo was eager enough to escape his father's tutelage and see what the academy and the capital might offer. It was a time of turmoil. The old order in Spain was finally unravelling. In August the prime minister, Cánovas del Castillo (who had formerly owned El Greco's *Apocalyptic Vision*—a painting that would exert such a formative influence on *Les Demoiselles d'Avignon*), was assassinated by an anarchist. Meanwhile a disastrous war with America was brewing. Back in Barcelona at the end of September, Pablo spent a couple of weeks packing up his studio, before departing in the second half of October for a new life in Madrid. He had just turned sixteen.

6

Madrid 1897–98

Picasso. *Portrait of Muñoz Degrain*. Madrid, 1897–98. Sanguine on sketchbook page, 20×12cm. Museu Picasso, Barcelona.

Opposite: Picasso. *Self-Portrait and Two Cats*. Madrid, 1897–98. Charcoal and brown crayon on sketchbook page, 13×22cm. Heirs of the artist.

The story of Picasso's acceptance by the Royal Academy of San Fernando has become as corroded with legend as the account of his acceptance by La Llotja. He 'passed the entrance exam . . . with the same astonishing rapidity as [*sic*] he had displayed in Barcelona,' as if candidates were timed and judged on speed.[1] He 'passed the examination with stupefying ease.'[2] Once again hero-worship carries Penrose away: 'a performance of brilliance equal to that of La Llotja. In a single day he executed drawings that satisfied the most obstinate of his examiners.'[3] Since the drawings in question have yet to materialize, we have no record of Pablo's performance beyond boasts made by Sabartès many years later. They may well have manifested the utmost brilliance, but one thing is certain: Muñoz Degrain and his fellow examiners would not have been 'obstinate'. As for Pablo's performance after entering the Academy, we have virtually no record of that either. He said he avoided the place 'after the first few days'—legend again.

The eight or nine months (October 1897–June 1898) he spent at the San Fernando Academy is one of the more puzzling periods of Picasso's early life. It is not just that facts are sparse and contradictory; for the one and only time in his life, he faltered—failed to live up to his own, not to speak of his family's, expectations. He, who had been so desperate to broaden his vision and fine-tune his technique, lost momentum. Without don José's encouragement and faith, Pablo's energy and concentration dwindled. Compared with the Corunna portraits done so short a time before, the Madrid paintings lack confidence and character. The mournful, autumnal scenes of the Retiro park owe too much to similar subjects by a man who would later become a good friend, Santiago Rusiñol; the portrait of a man in pince-nez (surely Muñoz Degrain) is facile; and the copy after Velázquez's Philip IV undistinguished. And the unevenness and stylistic diversity of the drawings likewise hint at adolescent bewilderment. For once there are virtually no academic studies (only one, at any rate, has survived), which is odd, for although Pablo may have avoided the life class at the Academy, he spent his evenings at the Círculo de Bellas Artes, a less formal institution, where he would not have had Muñoz Degrain breathing down his neck. A likely explanation is a sudden conscious urge to become a modern artist. Instead of concentrating on academic exercises, he would set about adapting his work to the latest fad, *modernisme*: the blend of art nouveau, symbolism and *Jugendstil* favoured

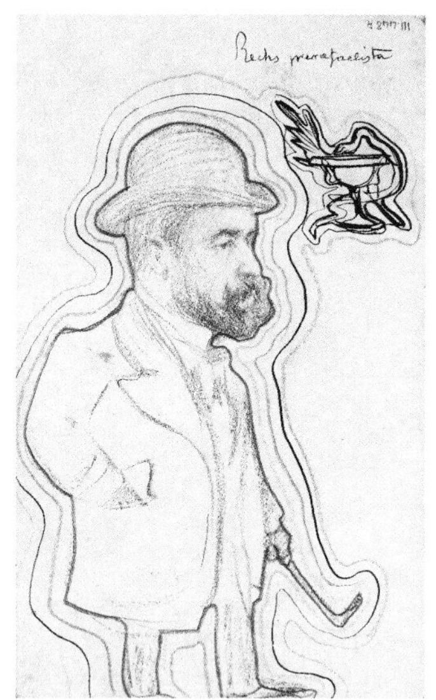

Picasso. *'Rechs Prerafaelista'*. Madrid, 1898. Coloured crayons on sketchbook page, 19.5×12 cm. Museu Picasso, Barcelona.

by the younger graphic artists in Madrid and Barcelona. He started stylizing his forms and enveloping them in heavy outlines, or a cocoon of curvilinear contours like those that indicate altitudes on a map: for instance the caricature of a bearded man (a doctor or chemist) in a trilby, inscribed '*Rechs Prerafaelista*', although it is about as Pre-Raphaelite as a cartoon by 'Spy'. He also did trite likenesses of girls (anonymous Carmens and Manolas); sketches of dogs and cats and horses in the manner of the popular French illustrator Steinlen; copies of Goya (one of the *Caprichos* and the portrait of his father's hero Pepe Illo, whose manual on bullfighting Picasso would illustrate in 1959); one or two brilliant bullfight scenes; notes of Velázquez compositions (*Las Meninas* and *Los Hilanderos*); and glimpses of street violence and café life. So disparate are these drawings, they could be by different hands.

The delusion that family members had purchased shares in him as a business venture determined Pablo to deny them any foreseeable profit. And while the growing distance between him and his father may have liberated Pablo, he seems to have felt lost and distraught—a sixteen-year-old making the difficult transformation from overprotected prodigy to underprotected adult performer. Furthermore, the San Fernando Academy did not live up to don José's encomiums. Its collection of masterpieces of Spain's Golden Age, its hoard of Goya drawings were magnificent, but the teaching was as pedestrian and rigid as La Llotja's, and the students lacked the liveliness and camaraderie. Moreover, Muñoz Degrain turned out to be depressingly hidebound, also a gossip who sent don José censorious reports about his son. At the same time the disastrous war against America shrouded Madrid in defeatism and despair, especially during the freezing winter of 1897–98. For Pablo, loneliness, poverty and, in due course, illness, made things even worse.

Disenchantment set in almost immediately. Respectable lodgings had been found for him in a run down apartment on the second floor of 5 Calle de San Pedro Martir, in one of the seedier quarters. Drawings in a Madrid sketchbook reveal the place to have been a typical *pension de famille*. Pablo had a bleak little room with a brass bedstead. He was obliged to eat with the household at a communal dining table set for six. The dinginess of his lodging was as irksome as the dinginess of the Academy. To his friends, however, Pablo overflowed with excitement slightly tinged with disappointment, to judge by a long letter (dated November 3, 1897) to his Barcelona friend Joaquim Bas. Besides revealing considerable impatience with the teaching, the letter is a manifesto of Picasso's early beliefs.

Picasso. *Flamenco Dancers*. Madrid, *c*.1898. Charcoal on paper, 29×21 cm. Private collection.

> Madrid, 3rd November '97.
> My friend,
> Today I am writing to you on rose-coloured paper, that might as well be gold.
> [The teachers here] . . . haven't a grain of common sense. They just go on and on, as I suspected they would, about the same old things: Velázquez for painting, Michelangelo for sculpture, etc., etc. The other night at his life class Moreno Carbonero told me that the figure I was doing was very good in proportion and drawing, but I ought to use straight lines. . . . He means you should construct a kind of box around the figure. It's incredible that anyone should say something so stupid . . . but he is the one who draws the best around here, because he studied in Paris. . . . But make no

Picasso. Drawings after Velázquez. Madrid, 1897–98. Conté crayon on paper, 15.7×21.8cm. Museu Picasso, Barcelona.

Picasso. *Portrait of Pepe Illo,* after Goya. Madrid, 1898. Brown crayon and sanguine on sketchbook page, 17.5×10.5cm. Museu Picasso, Barcelona.

Picasso. *Salón del Prado.* Madrid, 1897. Oil on panel, 10×15.5cm. Museu Picasso, Barcelona.

Picasso. *Bullfight,* after Goya. Madrid, 1898. Sanguine on sketchbook page, 17.5×10.5cm. Museu Picasso, Barcelona.

Picasso. *Dining-Room in the Pension.* Madrid, 1897–98. Sanguine on sketchbook page, 20×12cm. Museu Picasso, Barcelona.

Right: Picasso. *Street Fight.* Madrid, 1897. Conté crayon on paper, 20.1×26.2cm. Museu Picasso, Barcelona.

mistake, here in Spain we are not as stupid as we usually appear, we are just very poorly educated. That is why . . . if I had a son who wanted to be a painter, I wouldn't keep him here in Spain for a moment. And I certainly wouldn't send him to Paris (though that's where I would gladly be myself) but to Munik (if that is how you spell it), for that is a city where painting is studied seriously without regard for dogmatic notions of pointillism and so on . . . not that I think that sort of painting necessarily bad . . . just because one painter has made a success of a certain style, all the others don't have to follow suit. I don't believe in following one particular school, all it leads to is mannerism and affectation in those who tag along.

The [Prado] Museum is beautiful. Velázquez first class; some magnificent heads by El Greco; as for Murillo, to my mind not all his pictures carry conviction. There is a very fine *Mater Dolorosa* by Titian; Van Dik [*sic*] has some portraits and a really terrific *Taking of Christ*. Rubens has a painting (*The Fiery Serpent*) that is a prodigy; and then there are some very good little paintings of drunkards by Teniers; I can't remember anything more now. And everywhere in Madrid there are *majas* that not even the prettiest girls in Turkey could outshine.

I am going to do a drawing for you to submit to *Barcelona Cómica*, if they buy it, you'll have a good laugh. *Modernista* it will have to be, as that is what the magazine is all about. Neither Nonell nor the Young Mystic, nor Pichot, nor anybody else has ever done anything half so shocking as my drawing is going to be. You'll see.

And so good-bye. Sorry not to have taken leave of you in Barcelona.

Kisses to [Rosita del Oro]

An embrace from your friend P. Ruiz Picasso . . .

Goodbye [in Catalan]

After sealing the envelope, I realized I hadn't told you where I live. It is Calle de S. Pedro Mártir no. 5, second floor on the left. That is where one has a room—or humble abode, as a fancy lady would say.[4]

Picasso. *Couple in the Retiro Park*. Madrid, 1897–98. Oil on canvas, 53.4×44.5cm. Private collection.

Hesitant notes in sketchbooks reveal that Pablo could not write the simplest letter without a preliminary draft, so these fluent pages must have involved much effort. Bas was presumably expected to show the letter around La Llotja and reassure everyone that the arrogant Madrileños had not dampened their former comrade's bravado. How deceptively cocksure he seems, especially when he steps into a father's shoes and points out don José's error in having him study in Spain instead of Munich, the goal of so many *fin-de-siècle* painters.[5] No less revealing is Pablo's instinctive distrust of theory—of drawing taught diagrammatically (Carbonero's straight lines and boxes) and 'dogmatic notions of pointillism'—and, above all, his unorthodox preference for the freakish El Greco (whose rehabilitation had just begun) over the sacrosanct Murillo, whose work he had recently been copying. And his declared desire to do a 'shocking' drawing is the first manifestation of an impulse that will soon become an *idée fixe*.

Loathing the Academy and lacking a studio, Pablo trundled his easel round the streets. As long as the weather allowed, he worked in the Retiro park, doing melancholy studies of autumnal tints, shuttered kiosks, leaden ponds and occasional drawings of rich children in big bonnets and coats embellished with tiers of capes. As the icy Madrileño winter set in, Pablo loitered in cafés—the Café Numancia and the Café del Prado—and worked inside in the warmth. A note in a sketchbook confirms a trip some ten kilometres outside Madrid to what was said to be the geographical centre of Spain, where he drew a ruined hermitage and a

El Greco. *Burial of Count Orgaz*. 1586–88. Oil on canvas, 460×360cm. Church of Santo Tomé, Toledo.

shepherd and his dog. He also made expeditions to Aranjuez and the Escorial and visited Toledo with Moreno Carbonero and some pupils to copy El Greco's *Burial of Count Orgaz*. 'Instead of reproducing the original faces [Picasso] gave the figures the faces of his teachers, beginning with Moreno Carbonero's. This trick did not amuse that teacher at all. Picasso's sense of discipline was beginning to waver.'[6] No copy or parody of El Greco's masterpiece has survived. However, in the course of this visit and subsequent ones to Toledo, Pablo developed a preoccupation with this painting that lasted all his life. Its spiritual power would ultimately evoke the reverse of reverence. From gently mocking Count Orgaz's pallbearers as teachers or father figures, Picasso ended by transforming them into grotesquely named clowns—don Rat, don Blood-sausage, don Geriatric—in the demonic little farce, *El entierro del Conde de Orgaz*, he wrote some seventy years later. A spoof *tertulia* or family group, according to Picasso, that should be seen in the light of a '*corrida* or primitive postcard humanity'. Later still (1968), Picasso carries this process even further in a print that transforms the armoured corpse of Count Orgaz into a roast chicken. This is being served up by El Greco's son Jorge Manuel (who is portrayed pointing at the body in the original painting) as if to say, like Christ, 'This is my body.' The Virgin has undressed, descended from Heaven and taken a glass of wine. Meanwhile, Picasso has substituted a self-portrait of himself for the one that is known to be El Greco's.[7] If Picasso propels himself into the heart of one of Spain's noblest and most sacred images on the wings of a black joke, it could also have to do with the fact that the Orgaz family name, like his own, was Ruiz.

Picasso. Aquatint and etching. Mougins, June 30, 1968. 45×53.5 cm. Galerie Louise Leiris, Paris.

Left to himself in Madrid, Pablo spent ever more time in bed, ever less time at work. He cannot be blamed: having Muñoz Degrain as a professor was bad enough; having him *in loco parentis*, and being treated as the naughty child the professor had known in Málaga ten years earlier, was intolerable. Maybe this highly respected *pompier* sensed that his youngest, brightest pupil would soon overturn everything he held sacred. He certainly manifested uncanny bias. When Pablo showed him a view he had painted in the Retiro park, Muñoz Degrain dismissed it: looks like a poached egg, he said. Worse, he reported to don José that his son was idle: cutting classes. Worse still, this information was passed on—more likely by Muñoz Degrain than don José—to Uncle Salvador. Only this would explain the doctor's disastrous decree that he and the rest of the family would contribute nothing more to Pablo's keep. Don José's faith in his son never wavered; despite this dereliction, he continued, insofar as he could, to provide for him.

'In deciding to pay for his studies in Madrid,' Sabartès recorded,

> his family . . . had reckoned . . . he would win travelling scholarships, the Prix de Rome, grants . . . prizes in exhibitions, a professorship if he so desired, like his father and his father's friends, and following all this would be fame and money, commissions from the state and portraits handsomely paid for, like those of Moreno Carbonero and Muñoz Degrain, who would not deny him their support and sponsorship. In winning fame for himself he would win it for the family. . . . 'You can well imagine, they took advantage of [my independence] to stop my allowance and that was that. My father, who was [now] contributing the major part of it, went on sending me whatever he could—poor fellow!'[8]

Joaquín Sorolla. *Portrait of Muñoz Degrain*. 1898. Oil on canvas, 103×70 cm. Museo de Málaga.

Picasso. *An Artist Sketching in the Street*. Madrid, 1897–98. Coloured crayon on paper, 47×37cm. Marina Picasso collection.

Picasso. *Bernareggi Copying in the Prado*. Madrid, 1898. Brown crayon on sketchbook page, 19.5×12cm. Museu Picasso, Barcelona.

Back in Barcelona the family suffered as never before—a sacrifice that Picasso never forgot, although, he later said, the pittance he received was barely enough to keep him alive—'just enough to keep me from starving to death, no more'.

* * *

Sabartès would have us believe that the landlord rather than Pablo fell on evil times, and that the boy loyally moved with him and his family down the social scale: from the Calle San Pedro Mártir to the Calle Jesús y María, then to the Calle Lavapiés, and, finally, 'as their affairs went from bad to worse, from street to street in a rather small perimeter round the Plaza del Progreso'[9]—a rowdy working-class quarter near the famous El Rastro flea market. This unlikely tale of the landlord's precipitate collapse is probably another of Sabartès's legends. Researches into these successive addresses suggest that Pablo was obliged to leave his original lodgings because he, rather than the landlord, was in financial straits and his bohemian ways were not to the liking of respectable boarding-house keepers.[10] Constant changes of residence were not conducive to steady work, nor was Pablo's first taste of dire, as opposed to genteel, poverty and all that goes with it: cold, hunger, fear, illness, despair. This was the harder to bear since he no longer had the love and care of his doting parents. His loneliness is reflected in brooding self-portraits in which he suddenly looks older: he has started to grow a beard. Inner conflicts were exacerbated by social strife. As the sickly empire disintegrated, riots broke out ever more frequently. When Pablo and a fellow student tried to sketch the fights in the streets, they were set upon by the resentful mob and chased away.

As usual Pablo had no problem making friends—men friends, that is. He was in no position to court a respectable girl, and too poor for whores. His two inseparable companions were outsiders like himself: Francisco Bernareggi y González Calderón and Hortensi Güell i Güell. Bernareggi (nicknamed Pancho), whom Pablo had known at La Llotja, was a not-very-gifted painter from Argentina. In later years he would divide his time between South America and Mallorca, where he died in 1959. Pablo portrayed Pancho in the Prado, muffled up against the cold of the icy galleries, and perched on one of the special ladder-like constructions that enabled students to copy very large paintings. As Picasso told Rafael Alberti, the Spanish poet, he had never 'decided to go to' (i.e. study at) the Prado. 'How can you even imagine such a thing, Rafael! God, no! The truth is that I did go there a few times to visit my friend Bernareggi, an Argentine of about my own age who was copying Goyas and other famous paintings.'[11]

This is not how Bernareggi remembered things in reminiscences dictated to a friend in 1946. Whether or not Pablo bothered to attend the Academy after the first few days (when asked by Sabartès whether he attended classes, Picasso was derisive: 'I should say not! What for?'),[12] he certainly studied at the Prado:

> From Barcelona I went to Madrid with Picasso [Bernareggi relates]. I painted and studied in the Prado and lived a picturesque life in various districts of Madrid. What times of happiness, work and bohemianism! I studied the

great painters of every school. I copied Velázquez, Goya, the Venetian masters and El Greco. It was a period of rebellion against 'history painting' that [at this time] was triumphant. . . . Because Picasso and I copied El Greco in the Prado, people were scandalized and called us *Modernistes*. We sent our copies to our professor in Barcelona [Picasso's father]. All was well so long as we worked on Velázquez, Goya and the Venetians—but the day we decided to do a copy of El Greco and send it to him, his reaction was: 'You're taking the wrong road.' That was in 1897, when El Greco was considered a menace. . . . We spent our days (eight hours a day) studying and copying in the Prado and at night we went (for three hours) to draw from nude models at the Círculo de Bellas Artes. On holidays the Prado was closed to copyists and on those occasions we went out to the countryside to paint. This change of atmosphere and light—so different from what we found in the museum—gave us new inspiration, new artistic perspectives. The arguments we had with the copyists of Murillo! The disagreements we had with our fellow students in the life class were also unending because so many of them were dedicated to history painting of the most theatrical kind. We put our theories into practice on the street, in the café, at concerts, theatres, bullfights, everywhere we could, making notes of details and of more ambitious scenes. I remember one of our albums was lost and our pencils broken by groups of demonstrators while we were making sketches of the mob. Those were the days of Cuba's liberation. In addition we made trips to the Escorial, Aranjuez and Toledo. The hours we spent admiring and studying the *Burial of Count Orgaz*![13]

Picasso. *Life Class at the Círculo de Bellas Artes*. Madrid, 1898. Conté crayon on sketchbook page, 13.5×9cm. Museu Picasso, Barcelona.

Bernareggi's flat account of student life in Madrid is redeemed by the startling confession Picasso made to him at the time: '*En el arte hay que matar al padre*' ('In art one must kill one's father').[14] This Oedipal maxim lies at the heart of Picasso's creative process. No wonder he fantasized that don José had relinquished his brushes and palette to him. Now it turns out that the son was after more than the tools of the father's trade. Don José's very life had to be sacrificed if the son's work was to bear fruit. For the next year or so Pablo chose to be away from Barcelona, so he did not have to face up to the implications of his threat. Nor, when he returned home early in 1899, would he do much more than dissociate himself from his father's precepts. Only when the twisted sentimentality of the Blue period takes over Picasso's imagination does his work develop a patricidal edge. Seventy-five years later the artist would still on occasion fuel his art with Oedipal guilt.

Bernareggi and Picasso commemorated their friendship in a composite drawing: the two of them seated in a Madrid café, Pablo by Bernareggi and Bernareggi by Pablo. Each makes a point of portraying the other—flatteringly and improbably—as a prosperous boulevardier in stiff collar, Homburg, smart overcoat. Two other drawings depict Bernareggi more convincingly as a nondescript, muffled-up student. One of these includes the artint's hands and sketchbook in the foreground—a device Matisse frequently used in the 1930s.

Picasso. *Bernareggi*. Madrid, March 17, 1898. Pen and conté crayon on sketchbook page, 17.5×10cm. Museu Picasso, Barcelona.

Whereas Bernareggi was a cheerful, extrovert art student, Pablo's other close friend, Hortensi Güell i Güell (no relation of Gaudí's famous patron of the same name), was a neurotic, self-destructive aesthete—the first of many to latch on to the artist. Three years older than Pablo, Güell hailed from Reus in the south of Catalonia. After studying painting in his home town, he became an associate of the 'Luminist' Mir, and churned out

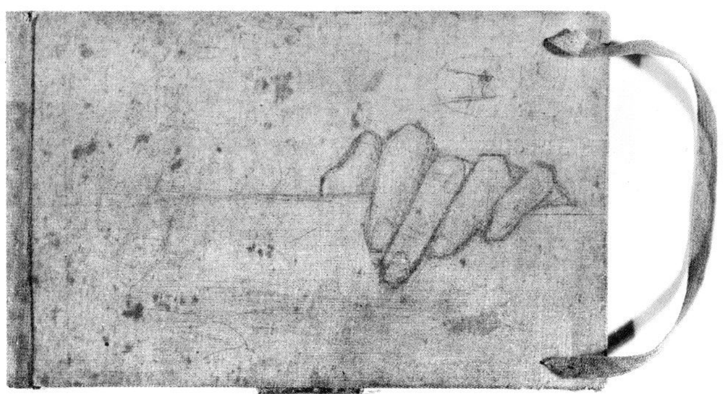

Cover of one of Picasso's Madrid sketchbooks. 1897–98. Pencil and conté crayon, 13.9×23.3cm. Museu Picasso, Barcelona.

Picasso. *Lola.* Madrid, May 1898. Conté crayon on paper. Private collection.

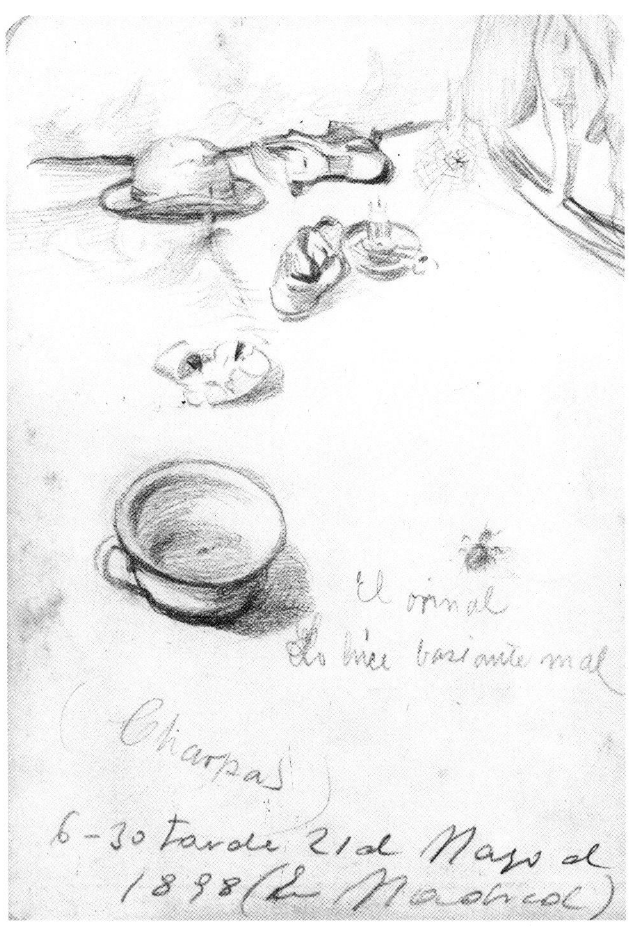

Picasso. *Drawing from the Artist's Sickbed.* Madrid, May 21, 1898. Pencil on sketchbook page, 18.5×13cm. Museu Picasso, Barcelona.

sunny scenes in a would-be impressionist idiom. The painting he gave Pablo (Museu Picasso) is of very minor interest; however, his writing had already been published in *La Renaixença*, the newspaper of the Catalan revival, which gave it a certain cachet. Güell regarded himself as an intellectual; he wrote art criticism, and probably kept Pablo, who was infinitely curious about literary as well as artistic matters, informed about symbolism, neo-impressionism, *Jugendstil* and other developments outside Spain. For all his gifts, this soulful young man (to judge by Pablo's soulful drawing of him) was too flawed with *fin-de-siècle* melancholia to apply himself to work, let alone life. And like other precociously world-weary artists and poets, he celebrated the end of the nineteenth century by committing suicide: throwing himself off the rocks at Salou (near Valencia) towards the end of 1899. Why did these doomed young men gravitate towards him? Picasso once asked—as if he had no say in his choice of victims. In his unfocused brilliance, his indulgence in decadence, and his sharp, dark looks, Güell was a blueprint for Carles Casagemas, Pablo's boon companion of the next two years, who would also kill himself. Then in 1908 it would be the turn of another psychotic admirer, the German Wiegels.

Joaquim Mir. *Portrait of Hortensi Güell*. Madrid, June 1895. Oil on canvas, 41×31 cm. Private collection.

Undernourished and debilitated, Pablo fell seriously ill sometime in the spring of 1898. Red blotches appeared all over his body and his temperature soared. The doctor diagnosed scarlet fever, a disease that was often fatal.[15] If there was nobody to nurse them, victims were packed off to an isolation hospital, but Pablo remained in his lodgings; someone must have looked after him. Partly because of the absence of records, partly because of Picasso's contradictory statements and the erroneous assumptions they engendered, the dates of his illness are in doubt. However, we have only to study the surviving drawings to establish what happened.

A drawing dated May 21 records that Pablo was well enough to sit up in bed and sketch the floor of his room, which was littered with a chamber pot and other domestic objects.[16] And so the fever, which usually lasted about forty days, probably manifested itself in mid-April. With Conchita's death from diphtheria in mind, don José and doña María would hardly have failed to send someone to look after their precious son. Pablo's life was in danger; he was living far from home in poverty and squalor and had no one to care for him. A portrait of Lola, dated May 1898, suggests that she came from Barcelona to nurse her brother and, when he was convalescing, sat for him.[17] This sequence of events is borne out by the artist, who asserted that he stayed on in Madrid to attend the *verbena* of St Antonio de la Florida on June 12.[18] There is no need to doubt him: Picasso preserved vivid memories of this lively bacchanalian festival, which was celebrated on the eve of the saint's day and held on terraces below the church with the great Goya frescoes he remembered so well. It would have been a spectacle after his own heart. He could then return to Barcelona, the city he had come to regard as his own, with at least one pleasant recollection of the callous capital that he never, now or later, warmed to, even when he returned in triumph twenty years later and was received in audience by the king.

L 8

7

Horta de Ebro

Picasso. *Head of Pallarès*. Horta, 1898. Conté crayon on paper, 21.8×15.6cm. Museu Picasso, Barcelona.

Opposite: Picasso. *The Artist Drawing*. Horta, 1898. Charcoal on paper, 33.1×23.4cm. Musée Picasso, Paris.

COMPARED WITH THE DEMORALIZED Madrileños, the Catalans were raring to fight. On his return from Madrid, Picasso found them digging trenches and installing batteries at Bonavista and Camp de la Bota to defend Barcelona against imminent invasion by American men-of-war. Half a century later this crisis continued to colour Picasso's view of the United States. Did Yankee companies still control Cuba, he sarcastically asked David Douglas Duncan, 'as they did in the days of Maquinli and the Maan [*sic*]?'[1] (He meant President McKinley and the *Maine*, the warship whose sinking precipitated the war between the United States and Spain.) Conscription was being rigidly enforced, but the war was so unpopular that hordes of young men went to ground. Pablo was still below military age, unlike his best friend, Manuel Pallarès, who decided to hide out at Horta in the Alta Terra—the remote uplands between Catalonia and Aragon—where his family had their ancestral farm.[2] When he suggested that Pablo come with him and recuperate, the Pallarèses were delighted: delighted to have the stalwart Manuel—the only one of their four sons to have deserted the land—back for the summer to help his siblings (Josep, Carme and Salvador) tend the olive trees and the *moli d'oli*, the mill, which still produces fine oil; delighted, too, to return the hospitality of Pablo's parents by having their son spend the next months helping out on the farm while recovering his strength.

Exposure to prosperous peasant life had an exhilarating effect on Pablo. His upbringing in three maritime cities had left him street-wise and more in tune with the sea than the land. The countryside was a mystery to him, and he was soon revelling in its unfamiliar pleasures. He

> walked in the woods, cleaned out the stables, tended the animals—and painted. To buy a pair of corduroys he walked many miles. He wore espadrilles like the peasants, learned to take care of the chickens and a horse, draw water from a well . . . tie a proper knot, balance the load on an ass, milk a cow, cook good rice, light a fire in an open fireplace, and so many other things that he often says: 'all that I know, I learned in Pallarès's village.'[3]

Among the 'other things' Pablo learned was to be almost as good a shot as his hosts. Years later he would amaze Jacqueline with the prizes he won at fairground shooting galleries; and when in 1958 he bought the Château de Vauvenargues, which was supposed to have good rough shooting, he would bring out an elaborate shotgun he had been given and talk of all the game he was going to bag—not that he ever did so.

It was not just rustic skills that Pablo acquired in Pallarès's village. Away from his overprotective parents, he finally grew up. The confidence that had ebbed away in Madrid poured back into his work. Even having to speak Catalan (obligatory in Horta) was an advantage. It helped Pablo get over being an Andalusian 'foreigner'; helped him put down Catalan roots. After the sadness and sickness of Madrid, the summer breeze and tranquillity of the Alta Terra healed the artist as it healed the man.

Above: Pallarès. *Mountain at Horta.* Oil on canvas. Whereabouts unknown.

Opposite: Picasso. *Mountain Landscape.* Horta, 1898–99. Oil on canvas, 28.2×39.5cm. Museu Picasso, Barcelona.

We do not know the exact date of the departure for Horta, but it was probably around the end of June 1898. This would have given Pablo time to organize his affairs and get together the things he needed for the trip. The two men took a train to Tortosa, where Pallarès's elder brother, Josep, met them with a mule that each rode in turn. They had to hurry: there were twenty-five miles to cover before nightfall. At first the going was easy—up the valley of the Ebro and then its tributary, the Canaleta —but the higher they climbed, the rougher the terrain became. Forever after, Picasso's trip to the Alta Terra—the mountain streams that had to be forded, the eagles circling overhead, the wild boar rooting in the forest, the almost audible silence of the uplands—would be enveloped in a golden haze. Illness had left Pablo unrecognizably skinny, as we know from dramatic *modernista* drawings of himself bearded and bare to the waist, and the journey to Horta exhausted him. Not so Pallarès, who had inherited a full measure of peasant robustness. But even he looked forward to a few days' relaxation at Can Tafetans, the rambling courtyarded house of his family, before setting off for the mountains. Can Tafetans was, indeed still is, one of the largest houses in this fortified hilltop village—situated just off the arcaded plaza on the corner of what is now known as Carrer Pintor Ruiz Picasso. Pablo felt instantly at home there and the Pallarèses accepted him into the family as a fifth son.

Above: Pallarès. *Main Square at Horta.* Oil on canvas. Ex-Pallarès collection.

Opposite: Picasso. *Houses in Horta.* Horta, 1898. Oil on canvas, 27×39cm. Heirs of the artist.

The childish spirit of adventure that had been a bond between the Andalusian wunderkind and the stolid farmer's son in Barcelona reasserted itself in Horta. Their escapades (as recounted by Pallarès) have the picaresque innocence of a boys' magazine story about city kids living out a fantasy of life in the wilds—with overtones of Jean-Jacques Rousseau. Up in the mountains the friendship deepened; it fulfilled needs on both sides. Pablo had become so reliant on don José's belief in him that he never outgrew the need for a devoted male friend whose loyalty, understanding and patience would constantly be put to demanding tests, someone who would be prepared to set Picasso ahead of everyone else. Pallarès was the first of these devoted dogsbodies. Besides being father figures, they had to be don José figures: ungifted, artistic, but basically bourgeois; and, of course, Spanish. On his side, the provincial Pallarès was only too happy to spend the rest of his days tending a shrine to the genius he had been one of the first to recognize. He turned a room in his large Barcelona house into a miniature Picasso museum and filled it with the portraits they had done of each other, as well as with books, photographs and memorabilia. The rest of the mansion was a shrine to the owner. To his credit, Pallarès never tried to force his work into a Picassian pattern. True to his provincial nineteenth-century vision, he remained an academic hack and after graduating returned to be a professor at La Llotja. That Pablo's father and this father figure should end up as colleagues is only fitting.

For years at a time the two friends would not see each other, but they kept in close touch, and in old age they resumed their rapport, much to the jealousy—a feeling Picasso enjoyed fanning—of the other Catalan crony, the secretary Sabartès. Every year Pallarès and his son, René, a dentist, would take the train from Barcelona and spend two weeks in a hotel at Cannes. There could be no question of their staying at Notre-Dame-de-Vie. One of Picasso's countless superstitions was that old men symbolized decay and death. He was terrified that if Pallarès slept under his roof, he might die and contaminate himself and his house.[4] Every morning Picasso would send a car for them, and the two octogenarians would chat away in Catalan for hours on end, while Jacqueline would fulminate at having to entertain the dentist. Pallarès had seemingly lost whatever spark he once had, but Picasso was remorseless in inflicting him on his friends. Whether they liked it or not, he obliged them to take account of this last remaining lifeline to his distant past, to *fin-de-siècle* Catalonia of treasured memory. Picasso commemorated sixty years of camaraderie by chalking over one of David Douglas Duncan's photographs of the two of them and transforming it into a geriatric bacchanale: two Silenuses in togas crowning each other's bald heads with vine leaves. The devotion of the two men in this farcical but touching souvenir is almost palpable. Pallarès's tough peasant upbringing stood him in good stead; he outlived Picasso, not dying until 1974, at the age of ninety-eight.

Picasso and Pallarès, *c.*1967. Photo by David Douglas Duncan drawn over by Picasso.

* * *

As soon as Pablo had recovered from the strain of the trek up to Horta, he and Pallarès left for the monastery of San Salvador and the mountain of Santa Barbara above it. They set up house in a cave and spent the next few days sketching before returning to Horta to prepare for a more ambitious expedition. Accompanied by Salvador, youngest of the Pallarès brothers, as well as a ten-year-old boy, a mule packed with provisions, camping impedimenta, artists' equipment and a dog, they set off for the Ports (passes) del Maestrat and the mountains called Roques d'en Benet that tower over them. Progress was slow. The rugged terrain is crisscrossed with gorges, often in spate, and can be negotiated only by means of logs clamped to the cliff face like pitons.[5] After eight miles of very rough going, they lit a fire and bivouacked for the night. The next morning Pablo and Manuel left the boy and dog in charge of their gear while they went in search of motifs to paint. Since he knew every escarpment from boyhood shooting expeditions, and since his convalescent friend assured him that he could keep up, Pallarès raced ahead. Suddenly there was a yell: Pablo had stumbled and was slithering helplessly down some rocks towards a seething torrent. Agile as a mountain lion, Pallarès managed to save his companion (no swimmer) from drowning; he also rescued the precious painting materials. This incident set a further seal on their friendship. Although passed over in silence by the jealous Sabartès, it became a legendary feat in the Picasso mythology. 'I'll never forget how you saved my life,' was a ritual statement that the artist would make whenever Pallarès reappeared.

Picasso. *Goatherd*. Horta, 1898. Black chalk on paper, 32×24cm. Musée Picasso, Paris.

Near the source of this particular torrent the two painters came upon a boulder that formed a natural shelter. They decided to return the following day and camp there for the rest of the summer. Back at their base, further trouble was in store for them: the boy had drunk most of their wine and passed out, leaving the dog to devour their dinner.[6] Fortunately Salvador reappeared the following day with the rest of their provisions. They then trekked to the boulder—'the cave', they called it—where they spent the next few weeks. With only the occasional poacher to see them, they went native, Picasso recalled.[7] They daubed their cave with paint, threw off their clothes and stayed naked. At night they slept on a huge bed of hay they had cut; they washed under a waterfall; they cooked the rice, bacalao, chick-peas and occasional game that Salvador delivered over a bonfire. There was a farmhouse nearby, the Mas del Quiquet, that Pablo painted in the yellows and pinks of the saffron group, but with far more sensibility. When Salvador came to spend a night with them, the farmers supplied them with bread and a large hare. Painting things, when not in use, were bundled up in the safety of a tree. The precious knife, with which Pablo sharpened pencils, trimmed wicks and skinned hares, was still in use at Notre-Dame-de-Vie sixty years later. It was a trophy of one of the most idyllic periods of his life. Indeed the large composition of the Ports del Maestrat that he now decided to paint was actually called *Idyll.* A letter was sent off to don José, and in due course a sizeable roll of canvas and a stretcher arrived at Horta, whereupon it was packed onto muleback and delivered to the cave.

Picasso. *Mas del Quiquet.* Horta, 1898. Oil on canvas, 27×40cm. Museu Picasso, Barcelona.

Idyll was Pablo's paean to the pastoral life of the Alta Terra. It represented a shepherd with a crook courting a shepherdess with a lamb, both in local costume. The background was one of the ravines that gouge these windswept heights: a refreshing contrast to the airless interior settings devised by don José. To judge by a brilliant oil sketch—all primrose sky and plum-coloured rocks—working in the open encouraged Pablo to experiment with colour and try out daring mannerist contrasts. And to judge by the drawings for *Idyll,* he had discovered how to harness art-school accomplishment to the demands of his imagination. Sketchiness no longer implied clumsiness, and a high finish no longer implied lifelessness. Pablo's painting had suddenly become fluent and eloquent. So had his Catalan.

Late summer storms put an abrupt end to life and work in the open air. Torrential rain deluged the cave; a day or two later a gale ripped apart the large version of Pablo's *Idyll,* Pallarès's no less ambitious *Woodcutter* and much else besides. The two of them made a bonfire of the stretchers and, next day, returned to the shelter of the village with the little they could salvage. Since hardly any of Pablo's Horta work has survived, it is not surprising that this period has been overlooked, despite the artist's insistence on its significance. Back in Horta they discovered that the war in Cuba had ended disastrously—the island had become a republic—and conscripts had been shipped home in a wretched state. Picasso was horrified that local conscripts were returning to their villages with nothing to wear but flimsy cotton trousers and straw hats.[8]

Picasso. Studies for *Idyll.* Horta, 1898. Conté crayon on paper, 24.7×16.3cm. Museu Picasso, Barcelona.

Pablo stayed on in Horta for another six months, until February 1899, earning his keep by shovelling manure, tending olive trees, drying figs. The only diversions were expeditions to Gandesa, a market town some

Picasso. *Josefa Sebastià Membrado.* Horta, November 1898. Black chalk on paper, 32×29.5cm. Musée Picasso, Paris.

Picasso. *Procession to the Hermitage of San Salvador, near Horta.* Horta, 1899. Oil and pastel on canvas, 60×71cm. Heirs of the artist.

twenty miles away, to buy clothes and, maybe, get together with a girl. Otherwise he had to rely on the one and only local café and the Pallarès brothers for distraction. Entertainment was limited to religious festivals and saints' days: the occasion for processions and pageants, for feasting and drinking. Pablo was never—then or later—much of a drinker, but it was hard to remain sober when the entire village was celebrating All Saints' Day or Epiphany or St Antony's Eve; and Pallarès remembered finding his friend passed out on the steps of the family house after a particularly drunken feast day. One of these fiestas is commemorated in a painting—peasant women processing through fields to the monastery of San Salvador. But its *modernista* stylizations suggest that it was probably executed back in Barcelona.

For the rest of his stay in Horta Pablo immersed himself in peasant life. Hence the usual repertoire of rural subjects: smithy, horse fair, wash house, mill, village street. We do not know what he did for girls, but a striking drawing of a smouldering local beauty, Josefa Sebastià Membrado (no doubt a relation of Joaquim Membrado, with whom Picasso would play cards at the café when he returned to Horta in 1909), indicates where his interest lay.

Picasso. Study for *Aragonese Customs*. Horta, 1898–99. Conté crayon on paper, 24.7×16.5cm. Museu Picasso, Barcelona.

Towards the end of his visit Pablo embarked on yet another large composition: an apotheosis of his months in the country—probably a sop to his father, who still envisaged his son's progress in terms of eye-catching set pieces submitted to official exhibitions, and who would have expected his son to bring back a major work from Horta. *Aragonese Customs*, as the painting was later called, depicted a man in local costume (breeches, sash, kerchief on head) chopping wood and a woman washing dishes in the background. We know the work only from scrappy sketches and a caricature by Xaudaró published in *Blanco y Negro* (May 13, 1899), when it won an honourable mention at the Exposición de Bellas Artes in Madrid. After a subsequent showing at Málaga, *Aragonese Customs* disappeared, probably under one of the large paintings done a few years later when there was no money for a large new canvas. The reference to Aragon as opposed to Catalonia is baffling, all the more so since Picasso later claimed that the title and subject were entirely Pallarès's idea.[9] Horta is so close to the frontier that the two friends frequently strayed into Aragon, and once found themselves the objects of inimical scrutiny. However, to judge by the caricature in *Blanco y Negro*, there is nothing specifically Aragonese, or for that matter Catalan, about the subject. If anything, Xaudaró's spoof (the woodcutter is metamorphosed into an executioner about to decapitate a crouching peasant woman) likens *Aragonese Customs* to a black Goya. The pile of skulls in the cartoon gave Pablo his first taste of the mockery that he, more than any other artist in history, would suffer at philistine hands.

716. *P. Ruiz Picasso.*

Con equidad y limpieza
y aseo y economía,
¡ay madre del alma mía
te cortaré la cabeza.

Joaquim Xaudaró. Caricature of *Aragonese Customs*, from *Blanco y Negro*, May 13, 1899.

*　　　*　　　*

One incident at Horta distressed Pablo. Pallarès took him to watch an autopsy on an old village woman and her granddaughter who had been struck by lightning. The dissection took place at night in the gravedigger's shed. The *sereno* (sheriff) proceeded to saw the girl's head in half so that the doctor could probe around—all the time puffing on a blood-spattered cigar—and confirm the cause of death. Pablo was nauseated and left before the men could get to work on the grandmother. Given this revulsion, it is difficult to accept the bizarre idea put forward by a biographer that 'the vertical dissection [may] have had some effect upon [Picasso's] own treatment of the human head in later days'.[10] Double profiles have a pictorial, not an autopsical, origin. Far from affecting Picasso's style, this grisly spectacle is more likely to have reactivated the trauma of Conchita's death and—who knows?—the trauma of his own bloody birth, in which cigar smoke had played an important part.

Picasso. *Self-Portrait*. Horta or Barcelona, 1899. Conté crayon on paper, 33.6×23.5 cm. Heirs of the artist.

In the aftermath of scarlet fever Pablo grew more than a fresh layer of skin. Self-portrait drawings done at Horta suggest that he had come to see himself as a new man—confident, forceful, moustachioed. Now that he felt reborn, artistically as well as physically, he began to think seriously about adopting a new name, or at least shortening his baptismal one. He continued to sign himself 'P. Ruiz Picasso' off and on for another year or so, but doodles in his sketchbooks show that ever since he had gone to Madrid and cut loose from his father he had played around with his mother's name, trying out different versions of it (Picas, Picaz, Picazzo, Picasso) sometimes with, more often without, the patronymic Ruiz.[11] On occasion he would also add the prefix '*Yo*' (I)—an indication of his concern with ego and identity. Sabartès's suggestion that Pablo changed his name as a 'gesture to his Catalan friends who found it more colourful to call him Picasso instead of Ruiz'[12] is hard to believe. He seems to have felt that exceptional gifts warranted an exceptional name. As he later fantasized, what attracted him to his mother's name 'was the double s, which is very rare in Spanish. . . . Can you imagine me being called Ruiz? Pablo Ruiz? Diego-José Ruiz? Or Juan-Nepomuceno Ruiz? . . . Have you ever noticed that there is a double s in Matisse, in Poussin, in Rousseau?'[13] The truth is surely that the loyal Sabartès was unwilling to admit that Ruiz was as common as any name in Spain and, by virtue of being don José's, one that connoted failure. To someone as superstitious as Picasso this would have been a bad omen. A change had to be made. Horrified, Uncle Salvador did everything to discourage Pablo from signing his work 'Picasso' instead of 'Ruiz', but since the rich uncle no longer supported Pablo, he no longer had any control over him. Pablo's renunciation of his patronymic dealt an unforgivable blow to don José's pride.

In January 1899, as soon as the paint was dry on *Aragonese Customs*, the seventeen-year-old Picasso made his way back to Barcelona. Although the Pallarèses urged him to return as soon as possible, he did not do so until the summer of 1909, at another crucial juncture in his development. Once more the peace and quiet of the uplands would work its magic. For Picasso this place would always stand for Spain, and though he never went back yet again, he frequently returned in spirit. Its beautiful situation probably inspired his great starlit backdrop of a Spanish village in the mountains for the ballet *Le Tricorne* in 1919. And the Spanish characters and settings that figure in many of the late prints and drawings and poems refer back to life at Can Tafetans.

Nearly seventy years later, Picasso and his friend Otero, the photographer, would improvise gossip about a fictitious Spanish village that they had named Navas de Malvivir.[14] Otero invented a character for himself, don Enrique Salgado; Picasso was don Hilario Cuernajo Nuñez de Vaca.

And the scandal that the sardonic 'don Hilario' recounted about his fellow 'villagers' had its roots in memories of Horta. Similar memories play a part in Picasso's poems, above all the later ones. Picasso told Otero, 'critics have said that I was affected by Surrealist poetry as well as by family problems. Absolute nonsense! Basically I've always written the same way . . . Poems about the postman or the priest.'[15] Although this disclaimer should not be taken too seriously, especially with regard to surrealism, there is no question that Picasso, like Lorca, derived inspiration for his verse from 'the glooms and glints' of life in a Spanish village. Take the following lines from *Dibujos y Escritos* (January 1959):

> then came the postman later the tax-collector applause and *olés* and the blind man
> from the parish and the blackbird the
> daughters of Ramón and those of Doña
> Paquita the eldest a spinster
> and the priest all strange iciness
> painted in saffron and greens loaded
> with noodles and dark cotton grapes
> and fat aloes and very
> perfect, well-ripened radishes and
> a frying-pan round with eggs and potato
> and cowbells and the question over the shoulder rich and poor carried along by the storm
> over the wheat burning wet
> his hailstone shirt dirty clothes.

This is surely Horta.

Picasso. Notebook page with text from *Dibujos y Escritos,* January 9, 1959. Musée Picasso, Paris.

Right: Picasso. *Pallarès Seated.* Horta, 1898. Conté crayon on paper, 24.7×16.3cm. Museu Picasso, Barcelona.

8

Barcelona 1899

Picasso. *Don José*. Barcelona, 1899. Paris crayon on paper, 30.5×24.7 cm. Museu Picasso, Barcelona.

Opposite: Picasso. *Lola by a Window*. Barcelona, 1899. Oil on canvas, 151×100 cm. Marina Picasso collection; Galerie Jan Krugier.

When Picasso returned to Barcelona in 1899, he was a far more forceful and independent character than he had been when he left for Madrid eighteen months before. He was no longer prepared to submit to the dictates of his father or the teachers at La Llotja. Dismayed to find his son slipping away from him, don José begged Pallarès, who had stayed behind at Horta, to persuade him to re-enrol at La Llotja. To no avail. Picasso, as he now signed himself, relented only to the extent of joining the Cercle Artístic, which was as unstructured as a Parisian '*académie libre*'. This meant he was free of his stultifying professors: he could teach himself to draw, and the work done over the next few months reveals an astonishingly rapid advance not just in acuity of observation and technique but in drama and style. Everything has more of an edge to it. The tendency to overdo emphatic outlines and mechanical hatching suggests that Picasso wanted to give academic exercises a dash of bravura. His diligence soon won round his father. 'I am pleased to hear that Pablo is working and above all that he is not missing his classes [presumably at the Cercle Artístic],' don José wrote his wife from Madrid (March 14, 1899), where he had gone to examine scholarship candidates for the Academy.[1] While in Madrid, don José had taken the opportunity of showing some of Pablo's drawings to Muñoz Degrain, whom he still considered the ultimate academic arbiter. To his relief, the professor 'liked [them] very much, but he told me that last year [Pablo] did nothing useful; however all that's over and done with.'

A story has been put about that the seventeen-year-old Picasso left home after a fight with his family and spent several weeks in a brothel: 'Since he cannot have paid the girls in cash, he repaid their kindness by decorating the walls of the room in which they sheltered him. The location of the murals [covered over long since, no doubt] . . . has eluded the researches of even Josep Palau.'[2] Toulouse-Lautrec's familiar shadow cannot be allowed to fall so picturesquely across Picasso's early life—least of all at this juncture—for there is no evidence that he left home, no evidence that he lived in a brothel. The fact that Picasso's mistress Rosita del Oro has been described as a whore instead of an equestrienne could well have given credence to this bordello rumour.[3] Whether or not he was on good terms with his father, Picasso seems always to have had the support of his mother, and as long as he lived in Barcelona the family apartment would be his base. Evenings spent in whorehouses or with a

Advertisement for *La Emperatriz* corsets, appearing in *La Exposición*, May 1888.

Casas in his studio with the critic Raimon Casellas (whose portrait hangs on the wall at left), the engineer Josep Codina (the artist's cousin) and a model, *c.*1900. Photo: Mas.

mistress were an accepted way of life and would not have involved a break with his parents.

It did not take long for Picasso to find somewhere more or less respectable to work and sleep when he did not feel the urge to go home: a tiny studio at the end of a long corridor in an apartment belonging to the painter Santiago Cardona—later well known in Argentina—who had been a fellow student at La Llotja. He chose well: Cardona and his sculptor brother, Josep, were most hospitable; and his apartment was the meeting place of a bohemian *tertulia*. Picasso's studio-room—at 1 or, more likely, 2 Carrer d'Escudillers Blancs—was in the same building as a small corset workshop run by the Cardonas' mother. 'El Perfill' was the name of the establishment, and it manufactured the 'Emperatriz' line of stays. Picasso is said to have amused himself 'punching eyelets in the corsets with a machine designed for the purpose. While doing this . . . he would observe the gestures of the operators and the motions of the machines. Then he would return to his room and sketch or paint . . . indefatigably.'[4] None of these paintings or drawings of corset-makers have survived. There is, however, a largish chiaroscuro painting of Josep Cardona—an elegant figure in a white shirt and floppy bow tie theatrically lit by an oil lamp—that is executed with all the aplomb of Ramon Casas or Joaquín Sorolla, the best-known society portraitists of the day. This flattering likeness—presumably done in lieu of rent—endows the corset-maker's provincial son with a decidedly cosmopolitan allure. Picasso had evidently wasted no time in mastering the bravura manner that was expected of a fashionable portrait painter. For sheer brio, the Cardona portrait cannot be faulted. If no commissions ensued, it can only have been because the necessary social contacts were lacking. And so Picasso turned his attention to another style. Emphatic art-nouveau contours, modish hatching and self-consciously artistic composition proclaim a determination to subscribe to the latest Catalan fad, *modernisme*.

Modernisme is a style as vague as its label. It can best be described as Catalan art nouveau with overtones of symbolism; it is also very eclectic and diverse, encompassing everything from puppets to posters, from *fin-de-siècle* decadence to folkloric gentility. *Modernisme* is in essence an intellectual, literary and artistic movement born out of the *Renaixença*: the recognition that Catalonia, with its own language and cultural history, was closer in its progressive attitudes to the rest of Europe than to the disintegrating empire within whose boundaries it had the misfortune to be situated.

The *modernista* movement owed its peculiar artistic identity to the promotional flair of three gifted young artists of the Catalan bourgeoisie: Santiago Rusiñol, who derived a sizeable fortune from his family's textile factory; Ramon Casas, whose father had made his money in Cuba; and Miquel Utrillo—more of a writer than a painter—whose family was involved in engineering and printing. Although they had known one another as students in Barcelona, their close association began in Paris, where in 1891 the three of them moved into an apartment above the Moulin de la Galette. In the spirit of the age, all three were united in their contempt for the materialistic values of the bourgeoisie from which they sprang. They envisaged a cultural *Renaixença* that would parallel the recent industrial one. And yet they saw that ethnic pride was not enough.

Picasso. *Woman Dressing Her Hair.* Barcelona, 1899. Pastel on paper, 50.2×30.5 cm. Private collection.

Picasso. *Portrait of Josep Cardona.* Barcelona, 1899. Oil on canvas, 100×63 cm. Private collection.

Above: Miquel Utrillo. Poster for the première of Morera's opera *La Fada* at the Fourth *Festa Modernista* at Sitges, February 1897.

Above left: Santiago Rusiñol. *Alfredo Sainati in 'L'Alegria que passa.'* 1899. Charcoal on paper, 62.5×41cm. Museu d'Art Modern, Barcelona.

Above right: Ramon Pichot. *Portrait of Santiago Rusiñol.* 1898. Conté crayon on paper, 51×32.6cm. Museu Cau Ferrat, Sitges.

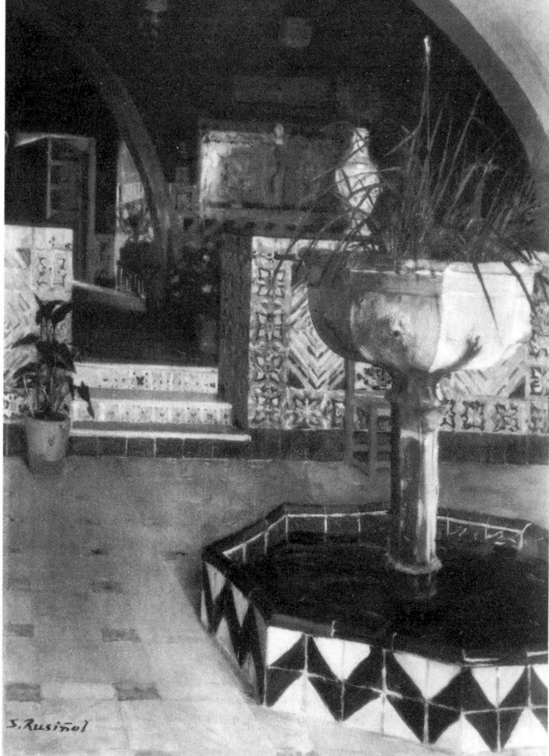

Right: Santiago Rusiñol. *Interior of the Cau Ferrat. c.*1895. Oil on canvas. Private collection.

Catalan primitives and Romanesque architecture were all very fine, but Rusiñol and his friends were sufficiently progressive to realize the need for French modernity as an antidote to Spanish *retraso* (backwardness). Unfortunately they did not understand what modern French art was about. They reacted to impressionism with wonder, to most of post-impressionism with alarm, and played for safety by opting for the timid classicism of Puvis de Chavannes and the drab realism of Raffaëlli (a minor figure who was not really an impressionist although included in the original impressionist exhibitions). Despite their good intentions and contributions to Catalan culture, Rusiñol and Casas ended up owing too much to too many different styles. Rusiñol veered erratically from realism to intimism to symbolism, while Casas tried and failed to reconcile social realism with a career as a social portraitist. For a year or two Picasso zig-zagged in their *modernista* wake.

Ramon Casas. *Miquel Utrillo*. From *Pèl & Ploma,* May 26, 1900. Museu d'Art Modern, Barcelona.

Besides being a painter, Rusiñol was a public-spirited impresario. His first project was to renovate a handsome Gothic villa he called Cau Ferrat ('The Iron Lair,' after the collection of antique wrought iron that it housed) in the still unspoiled seaside village of Sitges, twenty-five miles south of Barcelona. He then opened it as a museum and showplace for Catalan arts and crafts. Rusiñol chose Sitges because it was already the centre of a group of dedicated if insipid landscape painters who called themselves (they were not the first) 'Luminists.' They were delighted to be taken in hand by the enterprising Rusiñol, who helped them organize a group exhibition in 1892. Under Rusiñol's dynamic leadership, this project grew into a 'Festa Modernista' of music and drama as well as art; it was such a success with Catalan art lovers that it was repeated in 1893 and 1894. On the occasion of a performance (in Catalan) of Maeterlinck's *The Intruder* at the second Festa Modernista (César Franck was another attraction), Rusiñol made a rousing speech that gives an idea of what *modernisme* aspired (rather than what it was able) to achieve. The rhetoric anticipates the bombast of the manifestos—the menacing 'we' of Marinetti, Tzara and Breton—that would soon promote rebel art movements all over western Europe. After inveighing against rival ranters ('rhetorical sighs and rented tears; inflated speeches . . . shouted monologues'), Rusiñol concludes by saying 'what we have often dared not say' about *modernisme*:

> [We aim] to translate eternal verities into wild paradox; to extract life from the abnormal, the extraordinary, the outrageous; to express the horror of the rational mind as it contemplates the pit . . . to discern the unknown, to foretell fate. . . . As Casellas has said, 'the aesthetic form of this art is radiant and nebulous, prosaic and great, mystic and sensual, refined and barbaric, medieval and *modernista* at the same time'.[5]

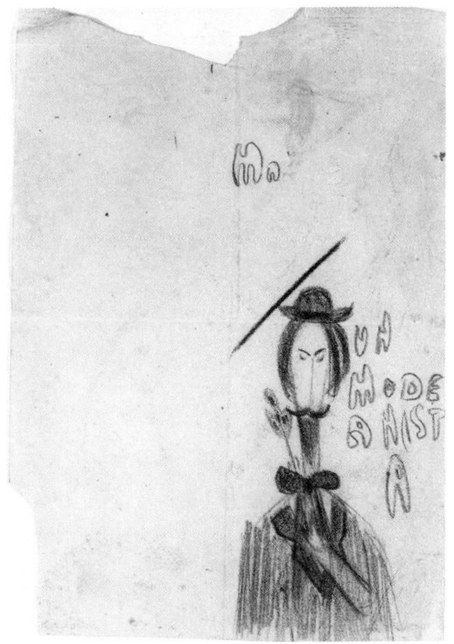

Picasso. *A Modernista*. Barcelona, 1899–1900. Conté crayon on paper, 22×15.9cm. Museu Picasso, Barcelona.

At the opening of the third Festa Modernista, Rusiñol came up with more in the same vein: 'We prefer to be symbolists and unstable, and even crazy and decadent, rather than fallen and meek. . . . Common sense oppresses us; there is too much cautiousness in our land.'[6]

Challenging words! Alas, neither Rusiñol nor Casas nor any of the other *modernista* painters had sufficient skill, originality or imagination to live up to them. To their pride and eventual envy, Picasso did. He never officially joined the movement, although from 1897 until his first trip to

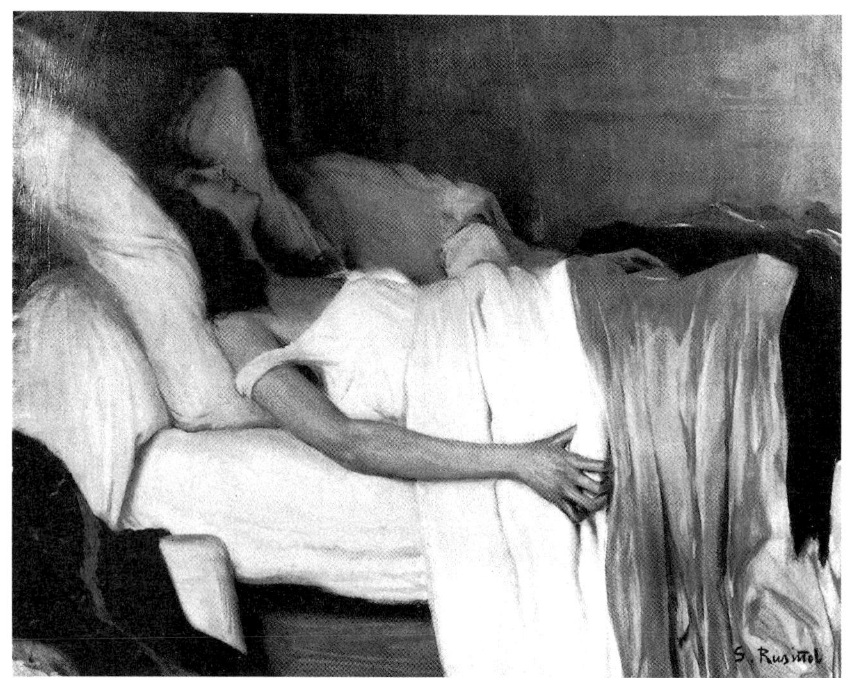

Left: Santiago Rusiñol. *The Morphine Addict.* Paris, 1894. Oil on canvas, 87.3×115cm. Museu Cau Ferrat, Sitges.

Below: Ramon Casas. *The Garrotting.* Barcelona, 1894. Oil on canvas, 127×166.2cm. Museo Español de Arte Contemporáneo, Madrid.

Paris in 1900 much of his work stemmed from it: Rusiñol, whose more interesting works depict death or morphine addiction (for which he himself had to be treated), confirmed Picasso in his morbid preoccupations. Casas, who was more accomplished and stylish, opened his eyes to the possibilities of graphic portraiture.[7] If Casas was the most renowned of the *modernista* painters, it was because he was so protean. He won over the more progressive elements in Barcelona with vast modern history paintings that are academic in style but liberal in sympathy; he delighted the bourgeoisie with portraits that could be as fashionable or informal as the sitter required; and he delighted the general public with the boldness of his posters and (later) the *joie de vivre* of his decorations for Els Quatre Gats and the Liceo. However, Casas confined himself to painting, unlike Rusiñol, who was a poet, dramatist, actor, journalist, impresario and public collector as well as a painter. In the course of 1899 these two men were to exert a formative influence on Picasso: Rusiñol on his imagination, Casas on his style. Indeed Rusiñol and Casas can be said to stand for the two tendencies that now developed in Picasso's style: the one so dark, the other so bright: the morbid Spanish genre painter preoccupied by gloom, disease and death on the one hand; the virtuoso portraitist out to capture the spirit of his bohemian circle, on the other. Picasso's ambivalence corresponds to *modernisme*'s.

Picasso. *Portrait of Angel de Soto.* Barcelona, 1899. Oil on canvas, 61.5×51 cm. Private collection.

Now that he had finally managed to establish a distance between himself and his father, and now that Pallarès, the boon companion who had taken don José's place, was away (for most of 1899) with his family at Horta, Picasso looked elsewhere for the male companions for whom he would always have a need. Picasso's Andalusian origins did not initially endear him to the clannish Catalans, but his charm, brilliance and vitality and the trouble he had taken to learn their language soon overcame their chauvinism. Within a few months of returning to Barcelona he had become the 'legendary hero' (Sabartès's words) of a small group of devotees who had not chosen him as much as he had chosen them—at least to believe Sabartès: 'Picasso . . . chooses [friends] as he chooses his colours when painting a picture, each one at its proper time and for a particular purpose.'[8]

* * *

Of all the new friends Picasso made in Barcelona, the Fernández de Soto brothers—Angel, an idler, and Mateu, a sculptor—were the most congenial. Strictly speaking, they were only half Catalan, for their father was a Castilian functionary who worked in Barcelona, but they had become fervent local patriots.[9] Picasso was so taken with Angel's stylishness and intransigence that they became inseparable. When they wished to make a fashionable impression they would share their one and only pair of gloves, each of them keeping the uncovered hand in a pocket while conspicuously gesturing with the gloved one.[10]

Picasso. *Portrait of Mateu de Soto.* Barcelona, 1900. Charcoal on paper, 50×33.5 cm. Private collection.

Although sometimes described as a painter, Angel did not take painting at all seriously. Picasso described him as 'an amusing wastrel', who worked unhappily for a spice merchant. Years later, I asked Picasso why he had depicted this penniless friend as a foppish man-about-town in white tie and tails. Angel was a dandy who sometimes eked out his small salary by hiring out as an extra at theatres, he explained, and the spectacle of him improbably attired in borrowed finery as an elegant boulevardier, dashing officer or habitué of Maxim's inspired these fanciful portrait drawings. Despite these disguises, Angel is always instantly recognizable, thanks to the lantern jaw and sardonic expression that Picasso catches so affectionately, even when he depicts him clutching a naked whore, who masturbates him with one hand while holding a champagne glass in the other (see illustration, p.291). Angel apparently shared Picasso's passion for the Barri Xino. '*On faisait la bringue ensemble*' ('we used to raise hell together'), he told me. In 1902 and again in 1903 they shared a studio, but Angel was so gregarious that the studio was always full of people, especially at night, when Picasso liked to work. The artist moved out, but they remained very close. Although only marginally better off than Picasso, Angel would always pay the rent or share whatever he had. In later years they rarely met, but they never lost touch. When Picasso was named director of the Prado in 1937, Angel was appointed a deputy of the arts. He was killed in the Civil War in 1938.

Picasso. *Portrait of Sabartès ('Poeta Decadente')*. Barcelona, 1900. Charcoal and watercolour on paper, 48×32cm. Museu Picasso, Barcelona.

The sculptor brother, Mateu, was the antithesis of Angel: reserved and serious with 'the sad fanatical expression of one of Zurbarán's monks'.[11] Picasso shared Mateu's studio for a short while in 1899; however, their close friendship dates from 1900, when both were in Paris.[12] 'Picasso liked Mateu more than the other [Catalans in Montmartre], perhaps out of pathos. He was small, slight, pale and shabby and spoke French like a Spanish cow.'[13] He always seemed to be starving and was reduced to doing the rounds of the Spanish colony every morning for contributions to his lunch. A major link between Mateu and Picasso was Jaime Sabartès, the man who would, some thirty-five years later, become the artist's secretary. Mateu had been so impressed by his first glimpse of Picasso, sketching away in the Eden Concert, that he had not been able to resist introducing himself and, later, Sabartès.

Sabartès was very proud of his ancient if not very distinguished ancestry, and full of Catalan disdain for anyone Andalusian—a word, he claimed, that was 'never pronounced at home without a grimace of repulsion. . . . Andalusian means a bullfighter, a gypsy, a "dago" who drinks and dances flamenco . . . tight trousers, short jackets, Córdoban hats and cock-and-bull stories. Ugh!'[14] Sabartès condescended to visit Picasso in his little room above the corset factory. He came away stunned. 'I still remember my leave-taking,' Sabartès wrote fifty years later. 'It was noon. My eyes were still dazzled by what I had seen. Picasso . . . intensified my confusion with his fixed stare. While making my exit, I made a kind of obeisance, stunned as I was by his magic power, the marvellous power of a magus, offering gifts so rich in surprise and hope.'[15] Given such a mystical revelation, it is odd that the only painting Sabartès remembered seeing in the studio was the far from stunning *Science and Charity*. The art seems to have had less to do with his initial reaction than the man.

Sabartès reports that although he and Mateu de Soto spoke almost constantly about Picasso, he saw little of him at first. 'I studied him from afar and after we discovered our affinities and differences we began to realize that we could understand one another and we were pleased to meet . . . in his studio . . . in the street . . . often in the house of the sacristan of the Iglesia del Pino, Señor Vidal, the father of a studio comrade.'[16] Sabartès

Picasso. *Sabartès Seated*. Barcelona, 1900. Charcoal and watercolour on paper, 48.4×32.5cm. Museu Picasso, Barcelona.

was pathologically submissive and eager to play Dr Watson to Picasso's Sherlock Holmes. He claimed to be the best friend with whom to converse because he did not impose his point of view: 'the sort of friend you can have fun with when you are broke.'[17] Despite the low value he set on himself, he set an even lower one on the other hangers-on who accompanied Picasso to bullfights, cafés, bars and brothels. The animosity was mutual. Even doña María, who liked most of her son's friends, could never abide Sabartès.

Sabartès lacked talent, charm and looks (he resembled a myopic sacristan, but with large, sensual lips); he hid his formidable qualities—diligence, honesty and loyalty—behind pride that was prickly to the point of paranoia. Before meeting Picasso, he had already failed as a sculptor (his *Head of a Child* was exhibited at the Sala Parés in 1901): 'When I discovered Egyptian sculpture,' he later said, 'I knew that was what I would have wanted to do, but I could never have hoped to do it that well. So I gave up the idea.'[18] In 1899 he was trying, and again failing, to make a name as a *decadente* poet, just as later he would fail as a novelist. However, like many of Picasso's Barcelona friends, Sabartès came from a prosperous family and did not have to worry about earning his living. As the artist recalled:

> The grandfather was completely illiterate but he had made a fortune . . . first as a scrap-metal dealer and then, later on, in some more respectable business. He could neither read nor write nor even count above the most rudimentary level, but no one could ever cheat him. If he was supposed to receive one hundred iron pots and only ninety-nine showed up, he knew it, even without being able to count that high. He took an interest in Sabartès from his very early childhood and decided to educate him, with the idea that when Sabartès knew how to read and write and especially count, he would take him into the business and from then on have no worries about being robbed by wily competitors. By the time Sabartès was nine years old he was handling all his grandfather's correspondence. Soon after, though, he had a very serious eye illness which resulted in his going nearly blind. That ended his usefulness to his grandfather.[19]

Picasso. *Sabartès and Esther Williams*. Cannes, May 23, 1957. Coloured crayons on printed colour pin-up, 35.6×26.5cm. Museu Picasso, Barcelona.

Sabartès's bourgeois bohemianism, melancholy aloofness, sardonic humour and fanatical supportiveness must have reminded Picasso of don José. His obsession was such that in years to come he would be more ashamed than proud of the success of his young cousin Joan Miró. The relationship with Picasso took priority over all others. There was another reason why this dismal man endeared himself to the artist. Sabartès was the perfect butt for his sadistic jokes and 'not least, scapegoat' when things went wrong.[20] Right from the start Picasso made fun of Sabartès's *decadente* pretensions, which were at such odds with his appearance, by depicting the myopic poetaster, in a portrait ironically inscribed '*Poeta Decadente*', as a greenery-yallery aesthete holding a lily. Later (1901) he painted a more touching, nevertheless mocking portrait (*The Poet Sabartès*) of his friend as a soulful poet—mocking because the untalented Sabartès could never aspire to fill this role (see illustration, p.216). Fifty years later, Picasso would still delight in ridiculing his old secretary by portraying him in dashing guises—flamboyant bullfighter, aristocratic courtier, horned satyr, sexual athlete (superimposed on movie pin-ups)—to which he was particularly ill-suited. If Pallarès had been around, Sabartès might never have insinuated himself into Picasso's affections, but by the time the former favourite returned to Barcelona in October 1899 it was too late. Henceforth Pallarès was obliged to share the role of good companion with Sabartès, and ultimately relinquish it to him. For the rest of their very long lives Sabartès and Pallarès loathed each other—an antipathy that Picasso fanned. He liked to divide and rule.

In 1904, Sabartès would emigrate to South America—first Buenos Aires, then Guatemala—and remain there for some thirty years. However, he stayed in constant contact with Picasso by mail,[21] and even made at least one trip (1927) to Paris to see him. By 1935, he had given up his job as a journalist in Guatemala City and returned with his wife to Europe. He visited Picasso in Paris and then, it seems, went to Madrid to pursue his career as a journalist and Berlitz teacher. At some point the longed-for summons came. On November 12, 1935, Sabartès arrived at the Gare d'Orsay, where Picasso awaited him. Henceforth he would move in with the artist and be his secretary. 'From that day on the course of my life followed his . . . we had decided it would be forever.'[22] Picasso told Sabartès that he wanted to escape his marital problems and 'other anxieties' and return in spirit to the simple camaraderie of their youth in Barcelona. He even had Sabartès write to him as 'Pablo Ruiz'—'like when we were young'. 'Forever' lasted for just over a year. By January 1937, Sabartès 'had the feeling that [he] was getting to be a hindrance.'[23] He left Picasso's employment. But on November 3, 1938, the artist persuaded him to return. This time it would be forever.

Picasso. *Decadentes.* Barcelona, 1899–1900. Pen on paper, 20.5×12.7cm. Museu Picasso, Barcelona.

* * *

If Sabartès saw himself as the 'good' companion, he had no compunction about seeing Carles Casagemas, Picasso's other new friend of the period, as a bad one. A dedicated *decadente* in life as well as art and literature, Casagemas came of a more sophisticated family than most of Picasso's other friends. His father is said to have been American consul in Barcelona and a figure of some official standing.[24] He and his rich wife (born a Coll from Sitges) had had three daughters and a son, who died young. Twenty years after the birth of their youngest daughter, they produced another son, Carles, who was inevitably spoiled—ultimately destroyed—by the women of the house. Problems started early on. Barely out of adolescence, Carles claimed to have fallen in love with the daughter of one of his sisters, but the girl—Nieves, she was called—married someone else. Although destined for the Navy, the boy was not in the end called up. Whether for physical or psychological reasons, or because the war with the United States would have put the son of an American representative in an invidious position, we do not know. Instead he studied art and stage design and quickly contrived a *modernista* style. Casagemas's hand was heavy; but he had a more original spirit than any of his Catalan contemporaries. A determination to be *outré* at all costs put too much strain on his technique: however, there is a fantasy and anguish to his work that can sometimes be disturbing. Casagemas was charming and bright but incurably self-destructive: one of those weak, demanding people who cannot survive without a friend to cling to. For the next eighteen months Picasso was fated to be this friend.

Picasso. *Casagemas as a Dandy.* Barcelona, 1900. Ink and watercolour on paper, 18.5×14.5cm. Whereabouts unknown.

Casagemas met the seventeen-year-old Picasso in the spring of 1899. Although only a year older, he was already desperately striving to be *decadente*, already addicted to alcohol and morphine,[25] and convinced his work, poetry as well as painting, was a sacred cause. Unlike Picasso, who was still apolitical, he felt no less fervently about social issues: *anarquismo* as well as *Catalanisme*. During a student riot at the university, Casagemas had joined the fray, wrested a truncheon from a policeman and belaboured him with it. Fearing that the frail Casagemas would get hurt, a friend picked up a chair and felled his opponent. Some of the students wanted to kill the policeman, but another friend saved the situation by shouting: 'Leave him alone! He's one of us!' His parents allowed Casagemas to use part of their large apartment on the Carrer Nou de la Rambla as a studio as well as a bohemian salon, where other *decadentes* and *anarquistas* from the university and art school would gather on Sunday afternoons to drink coffee laced with flaming brandy, recite poems, dabble in artistic experiments and sing '*Els Segadors*', the outlawed marching song of the Catalans.

Picasso. *Portrait of Casagemas.* Barcelona, 1899–1900. Oil on canvas, 55×45 cm. Museu Picasso, Barcelona.

For the next eighteen months Casagemas and Picasso were seldom apart. Early in 1900 they took a studio together in Barcelona (Riera Sant Joan). When they visited Paris later in the year, they continued to be roommates. This intimacy lasted until Casagemas went to pieces in January 1901—a month later he would commit suicide, and Picasso would hold himself partly responsible. What was he like, this man whose life and death obsessed Picasso's early years? According to Manolo, Casagemas flattered himself that he looked like Chopin, and did everything he could to accentuate this resemblance;[26] however, there is little trace of Chopin's noble features in the numerous, mostly caricatural portraits Picasso did of his friend. These show a raffish-looking student dandy, whose abruptly receding chin vanishes into an exaggeratedly high starched collar; and whose dark-ringed eyes are too close to his long nose for comfort. Surviving accounts suggest that Casagemas was a manic-depressive whose swings of mood were exacerbated by drink and drugs and sexual frustration. His work zigzagged between *fin-de-siècle* nocturnes and expressionistic caricatures, between eerie short shories and whimsical prose poems, such as this one about electricity, entitled 'Lightning':

Santiago Rusiñol. *Anarchists Indicted in the Montjuich Trials,* 1896. Pencil on paper, 20.5×27 cm. Museu Cau Ferrat, Sitges.

> Ray from heaven! Here in the city man has conquered you, wired you down so that you can summon the cook, drive cars, propel trams, and heat the food. Ray from heaven, you make me laugh.

Rather more revealing of Casagemas's ambivalence—not least towards Picasso (presumably the friend of 'repugnant appearance')—is an autobiographical 'poem', 'Dream', published in *Joventut* (July 1900). It also ends in hollow laughter:

> It was a large room—immense, white, vaulted—and its door was locked in a peculiar way. I found myself in the midst of a heavy cloud, feeling drowsy.
>
> A ghost I knew passed, fog-like, through the door. This was the friend with whom I had just dined; he materialized as a fluid through which I saw an infinity of dark variegated spots (like brushstrokes); these spread around and made him look repugnant. But he stared at me and we spoke, and according to what he said the spots moved nearer to, or farther from, his body.

> A little later, two other ghosts entered. I took a moment to recognize them. My brothers. Spots like the first ones covered them. I saw not only large black spots, but even some that amused me.
>
> . . . a new mist came through the door. It was my father—I also saw the same black spots. . . .
>
> From within the room, another ghost materialized. . . . It seemed strangely unfamiliar. I saw no spots and instinctively found him agreeable . . . [and] I felt a certain sympathy for him.
>
> 'Tell me who you are? You who seem so pure!'
>
> And in a deep, mocking voice he replied,
>
> 'I am you yourself.'
>
> And all the ghosts laughed heartily, repeating,
>
> 'Pure! Pure!'

Carles Casagemas. *A Couple*. *c*.1898. Black ink and coloured crayons on paper, 21.5×14.5cm. Private collection.

Dreadful stuff, but clinically interesting. Surviving drawings and paintings (two of which, *La Rue* and *La Place du Marché*, were listed in Picasso's estate) reveal Casagemas's painting to be less awful than his poetry. Despite or because of his shortcomings, Casagemas fascinated Picasso. However, Picasso did not share this defiantly free spirit's belief that excessive quantities of alcohol and drugs were the only key to artistic revelation, nor his simplistic view of life as either intensely heroic, ugly or absurd. His feeling for caricature—Casagemas had studied the French illustrators Steinlen and Caran d'Ache as well as the caricaturists of *Jugend* and *Simplicissimus*—would rub off on Picasso. So would some of the twisted anguish diagnosed by his friends. One of them, Manolo Jaumandreu, was appalled by the combination of tragedy and perversity in Casagemas's work: there was 'a kind of hateful masochism—in one canvas the eyes, in another the mouth, in another the breasts and hands, always the hands.'[27]

This self-destructiveness prepares us for Casagemas's suicide in February 1901, a month after Picasso eased him out of his life as too much of a liability. Impotence has always been cited as the cause of suicide: specifically Casagemas's inability to perform sexually with his 'fiancée', Germaine Gargallo. But this explanation does not stand up to investigation, nor does Picasso's unfounded claim that Casagemas's impotence was confirmed by a post-mortem.[28] No such thing took place, and even if it had, this condition would have been impossible to establish scientifically.[29] Did Picasso perhaps feel that proof of Casagemas's impotence would absolve him from having abandoned his desperate friend in his hour of need? Given the absence of medical evidence and the loose way in which the term 'impotence' was, indeed still is, used, we must be careful with our assumptions.

If Casagemas is unlikely to have been physiologically impotent, what was the nature of his sexual problem? Why did he accompany Picasso and his friends to brothels and never avail himself of a whore? Why should an impotent man kill himself over a woman who failed to arouse him? Oedipal conflicts or homosexuality might explain Casagemas's inability to perform with women; his reliance on drink and drugs; his choice of a married niece as a love object; his view of the opposite sex as threatening; above all his infatuation with Picasso and his attempt to find a substitute for this infatuation in Germaine. A dawning understanding of this situation would account for Picasso's ultimate flight from Casagemas,

Picasso. *Self-Portrait*. Barcelona, 1899–1900. Charcoal on paper, 22.5×16.5cm. Museu Picasso, Barcelona.

when the latter was headed for suicide. Hence the legend of the autopsy; hence all Picasso's posthumous portraits and commemorative paintings of Casagemas—paintings that combine the soulfulness of El Greco with a mockery that reeks of guilt.

Whatever the solution to the mystery, Picasso could not have found a more willing victim than Casagemas. Besides flattering the artist's eighteen-year-old ego, his devotion and hero worship would have fulfilled Picasso's urgent need for a subservient friend. There were also intellectual, not to speak of financial, considerations. Of all the young Catalans Picasso knew, Casagemas was probably the least provincial, the best informed about symbolist art and literature (Maeterlinck was a special passion, and Verlaine something of a role model). He was also better off than most of his peers and ever ready to help out Picasso, who was chronically penniless. Manolo recalled in his memoirs that when he arrived in Paris without a penny, a day or two before the suicide, the 'elegant' Casagemas had promised financial support.[30] No less important, unlike the stolid, unimaginative Pallarès or the sarcastic, censorious Sabartès, Casagemas was diverting and unpredictable. With Casagemas around, anything could happen.

On one occasion Casagemas took Picasso on a trip to Sitges, where his mother's family, the Colls, had a villa on the Sant Sebastià beach. After visiting the parental house and going to see Rusiñol's newly restored Cau Ferrat, they got very drunk and made the rounds of the brothels. Their visit to the Casagemases' family estate at Badalona (known as Cal General, because it had belonged to an Irish general who had fought Napoleon) was ominous. Casagemas insisted on going to the cemetery to paint, but none of the vistas suited him. They ended up in the family villa, where Casagemas persuaded Picasso to sit for his portrait. After some time, Picasso got up to see the result: Casagemas had done absolutely nothing.

Picasso. *A Couple*. Barcelona, 1899. Conté crayon and pencil on paper, 31.5×22cm. Museu Picasso, Barcelona. Annotated '– *Oscar Vilde – autor ingles este siglo*.'

Sometime before he blew his brains out Casagemas is said to have tried to stab himself;[31] indeed he seems to have conducted much of his short life in the shadow of death. In the wake of Conchita's demise and his own sickness, Picasso was also becoming preoccupied with the fashionable, *fin-de-siècle* subject of mortality—one that was setting off an epidemic of suicides. In 1899 the local journal *Luz* devoted an article to the suicide of the well-known Spanish writer Angel Ganivet in Sweden as a consequence of illness and marital troubles; and Picasso's friend from Madrid days Hortensi Güell had drowned himself—supposedly 'as a result of his intense identification with Ibsen, especially with . . . The Lady from the Sea.'[32] And although Aubrey Beardsley was not a suicide, his premature death from tuberculosis the year before at the age of twenty-six cast a pall over his many Catalan admirers, not least Picasso, to judge by the first issue of *Joventut* in February 1900. This journal, which derived much of its inspiration from *The Yellow Book*, included a lengthy tribute to Beardsley by its artistic director, Alexandre de Riquer. Picasso, incidentally, knew *The Yellow Book*. An inscription, '*Oscar Vilde* [sic] *autor ingles este siglo*' in the margin of a drawing of this period, suggests that he also read Oscar Wilde, probably his influential essay, 'The Soul of Man under Socialism', which had recently been translated into Spanish. Its defence of sin as 'an essential element of progress' would have appealed to Picasso.

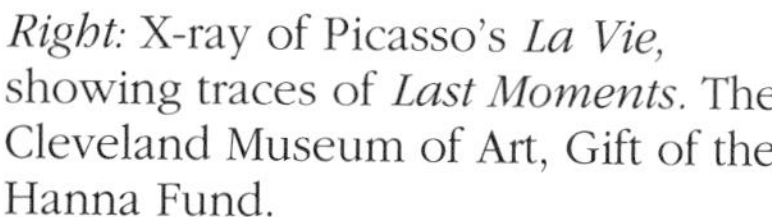

Right: X-ray of Picasso's *La Vie,* showing traces of *Last Moments.* The Cleveland Museum of Art, Gift of the Hanna Fund.

Below: Picasso. *Hospital Scene.* Barcelona, 1899–1900. Charcoal and conté crayon on paper, 32×48.5cm. Museu Picasso, Barcelona.

Picasso. *Kiss of Death*. Barcelona, 1899–1900. Conté crayon on paper, 15.9×24.3cm. Museu Picasso, Barcelona.

Death was much on Picasso's mind when, in the spring of 1899, he embarked on a phase that can best be described as tenebrism—the term that is usually applied to the dark, religious work of the Spanish masters Ribera and Valdes Leal. Picasso's tenebrism begins with another large sickroom composition: a successor to *Science and Charity*, which still took up much of the space in his garret studio. Once again he set out to exorcise the trauma of his sister's death. He did a group of drawings and watercolours and an oil sketch of a small, sick child in bed; by her side kneels a despairing young mother, hair down her back, praying to a crucifix on the wall. Compassion, even faith, is far more convincingly and economically evoked than in *Science and Charity*, and the idiom is manifestly more sophisticated and *modernista*. A possible source of influence is Munch, who had likewise harnessed his grief over the death of a much-loved younger sister to his art. Munch's work was well known in Barcelona through magazine illustrations, but then so was the work of countless other European artists who were drawn to the subject of death and the maiden, a subject that seemed appropriate to the demise of the old century.

Picasso. *Deathbed Scene with Violinist*. Barcelona, 1899–1900. Conté crayon on paper, 16.1×24.8cm. Museu Picasso, Barcelona.

Picasso never carried the sick child subject to a full-scale conclusion. Instead he executed variations on the theme of a dying person—sometimes a man, sometimes a woman, sometimes attended by a skeleton forcing an embrace on its victim, sometimes by a violinist—an echo of Arnold Böcklin's self-portrait (1872) with a grinning skeleton looking over the artist's shoulder and playing a fiddle. When he came to execute a definitive version of this macabre subject, Picasso transformed the attendant into a priest, for whom one of the Soto brothers posed (Picasso says Angel; Sabartès, Mateu).[33] Inevitably the victim ends up a girl—no specific girl, although Picasso may have recalled the recent death from tuberculosis of a young singer called La Caterina, who had been the mistress of one of his Barcelona friends.[34] Coming soon after the first performance (1898) in Barcelona of Puccini's sensational new *verismo* opera, *La Bohème*, the young singer's demise took on added poignancy and drama. But whether Picasso had La Caterina or Puccini's Mimi or his sister Conchita in mind, or whether he intended to allegorize youth cut off in its prime, we cannot judge. The composition, entitled *Last Moments*, has disappeared under the masterpiece of the Blue period, *La Vie*. We know it only through x-rays,[35] and a description in *La Vanguardia* (February 3, 1900): 'a young priest standing with a prayer book in his hand, looking at a woman on her deathbed. The light of the lamp radiates weakly and is reflected in patches on the white quilt covering the dying woman. The rest of the canvas is in shadow, which dissolves the figures into indecisive silhouettes.' The x-rays reveal that Picasso's technique has become far more confident, far less tightly academic than before. The composition is bolder; the forms are more emphatically defined in the *modernista* manner; and the melancholy mood and monochromatic colour look forward to the Blue period. Tempting as it is to see psychological links between *La Vie*, which commemorates the life and death of Casagemas, and the vanished *Last Moments* lurking beneath it,[36] the immolation of this painting could also be attributed to Picasso's dissatisfaction with the cliché-ridden conception of an earlier work, or, more likely, a poor artist's need to recycle old canvases.

Picasso. *Woman Praying at a Child's Bedside*. Barcelona, 1899–1900. Conté crayon on paper, 17×23cm. Heirs of the artist.

* * *

While working on *Last Moments* Picasso submitted his large Horta painting, *Aragonese Customs* (which has also vanished), to the Exposición General de Bellas Artes in Madrid. It was accepted and, like *Science and Charity*, received an honourable mention. Because a storm damaged the exhibition building, the show closed prematurely on June 10. At some point in the course of the next month Picasso left with Casagemas for a hitherto unrecorded trip to Málaga.[37] Given the outings to the Casagemases' Villa Coll and Cal General, what more natural than that Picasso should want to show Carles his home town?

There were other reasons for this journey. Thanks to the unexpected closure of the Madrid exhibition, Picasso was able to include *Aragonese Customs* with two other works, *Last Moments* (exhibited as *Last Rites*) and a *Portrait*, in the summer show at the Málaga Liceo. The portrait must have been either the large one of Cardona that had just been finished or another recent, even larger painting, Lola in front of a window, that is perhaps Picasso's most successful *modernista* work (see illustration, p.108). Since he would have been eager to demonstrate his phenomenal progress to the family as well as the local art world, he is unlikely to have submitted any but his latest work.[38] To his dismay, local critics paid very little attention to his three entries—another reason for coolness towards his birthplace. Picasso never exhibited there again.

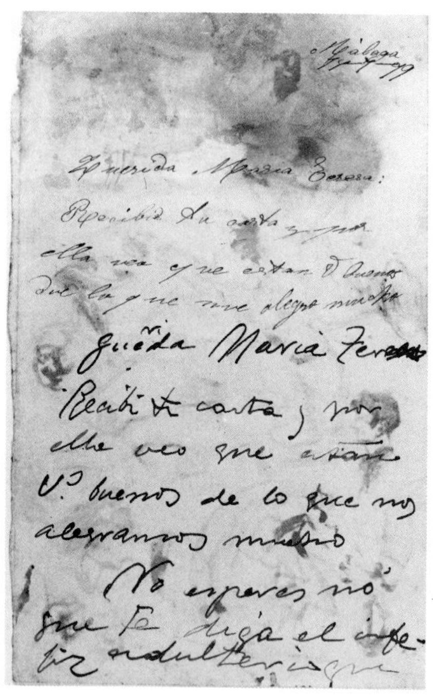
Málaga

Querida María Teresa:

Recibí tu carta y por ella veo que están Vds buenos de lo que nos alegramos mucho

No esperes no que te diga el infeliz adulterio que

Picasso. Drafts for a letter to Teresita Blasco, dated 'Málaga, July 14, 1899' and confessing his 'unhappy adultery'. Museu Picasso, Barcelona.

Picasso also needed to visit Málaga to tell his cousin Carmen Blasco that he had no intention of marrying her. For all his artistic courage, Picasso lacked moral courage—conspicuously so in this case. Rather than tackle his *novia*, he wrote to her sister, Teresita Blasco, and used a mistress (Rosita del Oro?) as a pretext for wriggling out of his obligations. 'Don't expect me to tell you anything about the unhappy adultery that . . . ' is how the draft of his letter reads.[39] Whether it was mailed we do not know. Picasso has been accused of trying to disillusion Carmen 'with his outlandish appearance and mortifying behaviour.'[40] On the contrary, he and Casagemas made a very favourable impression on this visit, according to another cousin, Concha Blasco Alarcón.[41] If Carmen refused to be seen with her former suitor—'Go away, I don't want to be seen with you,' she reportedly said—this was surely out of wounded pride and future marital strategy.

How long Picasso and Casagemas remained in Málaga we do not know. Time enough to do drawings of bullfights, a local fish vendor (*Senaller*), a rape scene (one inscribed 'Málaga, July'), and some whores, including a watercolour of a scrawny gypsy, 'La Chata'—possibly, 'Lola la Chata', the local madam. Hitherto these works have been assigned to Barcelona, but now that the 1899 trip has been established, they can be reassigned to Málaga.[42] This trip also accounts for the atypical theme of *The Andalusian Patio*, for which Picasso did studies in Málaga and an oil sketch back in Barcelona.

The Andalusian Patio, also entitled *Courtship* (it portrays a courting couple dressed in local costume seated at a table in an arbour), is unusual for the period in being cheerfully rather than morbidly sentimental. The greeting-card triteness might well be the reason that the studies never culminated in a large-scale composition. Picasso conjures up the Málaga of his childhood—even the pair of pigeons cooing in the foreground honours don José—at the same time as bidding the place farewell. It is the

Picasso. *Bullfighters*. Málaga, 1899. Pen on paper, 11.6×17.5 cm. Museu Picasso, Barcelona.

Right: Picasso. *Fish Vendor* and other sketches. Málaga, 1899. Pen on paper, 20.5×12.9 cm. Museu Picasso, Barcelona.

Above: Picasso. Preliminary version of *Courtship*. Barcelona, 1899. Oil on canvas, 36.8×49.7 cm. Museu Picasso, Barcelona.

Right: Picasso. *La Chata*. Málaga, 1899. Charcoal, watercolour and wash on paper, 31.6×7.6 cm. Museu Picasso, Barcelona.

Picasso. Sketch for *Poor Geniuses*. Barcelona, 1899–1900. Conté crayon on paper, 33.6×23.6cm. Museu Picasso, Barcelona.

Picasso. *Prostitute*. Barcelona, 1899–1900. Oil on canvas, 46×55cm. Heirs of the artist.

Picasso. Sheet of drawings with copies of signatures: 'Steinlen' and 'Forain'. Barcelona, *c.*1899. Conté crayon on paper, 22.8×31.8cm. Museu Picasso, Barcelona.

last overt reference to Andalusia in his work. *The Andalusian Patio* is conceived in the *modernista* manner—flat decorative shapes, heavy outlines, bright, pleasing colours—that he had flirted with earlier that year, in marked contrast to the 'tenebrist' manner of *Last Moments*, which he would revert to in the autumn.

* * *

On returning to Barcelona later in the summer, Picasso concentrated more intently than ever on becoming a *modernista*. Ideas poured forth in such spate that his brush could not keep pace with his pencil, and only one of the more ambitious projects materialized. After failing to come up with a large version of the colourful *Andalusian Patio*, Picasso failed to come up with a large version of a composition provisionally named *Poor Geniuses*. Once again there is a deathbed, but for a change the victim is male, likewise the dejected bohemians—Verlaine's 'poètes maudits' by the look of things. A likely concept, since Casagemas identified with it. Apart from some powerful and moving sketches, nothing came of *Poor Geniuses*, at least for the time being. (The theme will surface again in the self-pitying self-portraits of the Blue period.) Meanwhile Picasso had turned his attention to low life. Sketches in various media of whores in a tavern suggest that he envisaged a Barri Xino scene in the manner of Toulouse-Lautrec's Moulin Rouge paintings. Apart from a raw little study of a bedraggled whore obscenely gesturing at the stains on her dress, no paintings resulted from this project either. Picasso would not explore this vein in any depth until he went to Paris and saw Toulouse-Lautrec's work in the original a year later.

In addition to envisaging and very occasionally executing major paintings, Picasso persisted with commercial work—magazine illustrations, posters, brochures—in the hope of earning extra money. He saw himself becoming another Steinlen: the successful illustrator whose contributions to *Gil Blas* and *Le Rire* so impressed Picasso that he imitated Steinlen's signature over and over again in a sketchbook. And not only the left-wing Steinlen: on the same page he imitated the signature of that other famous illustrator, the die-hard reactionary Forain. These imitations have nothing to do with forgery. They are about shamanism: Picasso was out to assume the powers of other artists, to assimilate them into his own voracious psyche. He was also in search of an artistic identity. Trying out these signatures was a token of this need.

In the case of Ramon Casas, Barcelona's leading painter, Picasso not only imitated his signature, he ended up appropriating his style as a portraitist and totally transcending it. He was not so successful when he challenged Casas in the field of posters, where the latter excelled. When the magazine *Pèl & Ploma* offered a prize for the best poster announcing the 1900 carnival, Picasso came up with an arresting image. His final version has not survived, but enough drawings and a finished sketch in colour show that he was more concerned with mourning the dying century than in celebrating the one about to dawn. The colour sketch depicts a pierrot in white with a chalk-white, skull-like face, a champagne glass in his right hand, with a skinny soubrette in a black mask and long black gloves (like Yvette Guilbert in Toulouse-Lautrec's lithographs) on his

Picasso. Drawing for Carnival poster; self-portrait; copies of signatures: 'R. Casas' and 'J. Mir'. Barcelona, 1899–1900. Watercolour and conté crayon on paper, 48×43cm. Museu Picasso, Barcelona.

right arm; all this and the date, 1900, in *modernista* lettering against ominous darkness.

The young and sympathetic judges (they included Mir and Manolo) were impressed but not sufficiently charmed by Picasso's poster to give it first place. This went to a painter named Roig. The anonymous critic of *La Publicidad* (January 9, 1900) sided with them: 'Rather less cheerful is the one signed by P. Ruiz Picasso which has a group of masks in the centre, full of style and spontaneity. Too bad the poster looks dirty and lacks expression. Even more confused but similar in quality is the third signed by S. Cardona i Turró.' In the end no one, not even Roig, was found worthy of the prize, according to *La Veu de Catalunya* (February 8, 1900), which lists the runners-up as 'Don Carles Casagemas and Sr Ruiz Picasso'. (The different modes of address speak for themselves.) By this time, however, the outcome of the competition hardly mattered. Rusiñol, Casas and Utrillo, the leaders of the *modernista* movement, had promised him an exhibition in the main hall of their bohemian tavern, Els Quatre Gats. Recognition by them was recognition indeed. And how propitious that the début of Picasso's great career should coincide with the start of the new century.

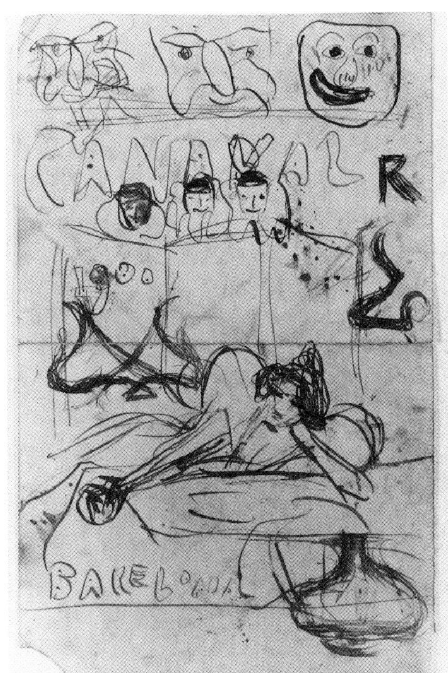

Above: Picasso. Study for Carnival poster. Barcelona, 1899. Pen on paper, 21×13.5cm. Museu Picasso, Barcelona.

Right: Picasso. Design for a Carnival Poster. Barcelona, 1899. Oil and black chalk on paper, 48.2×32cm. Musée Picasso, Paris.

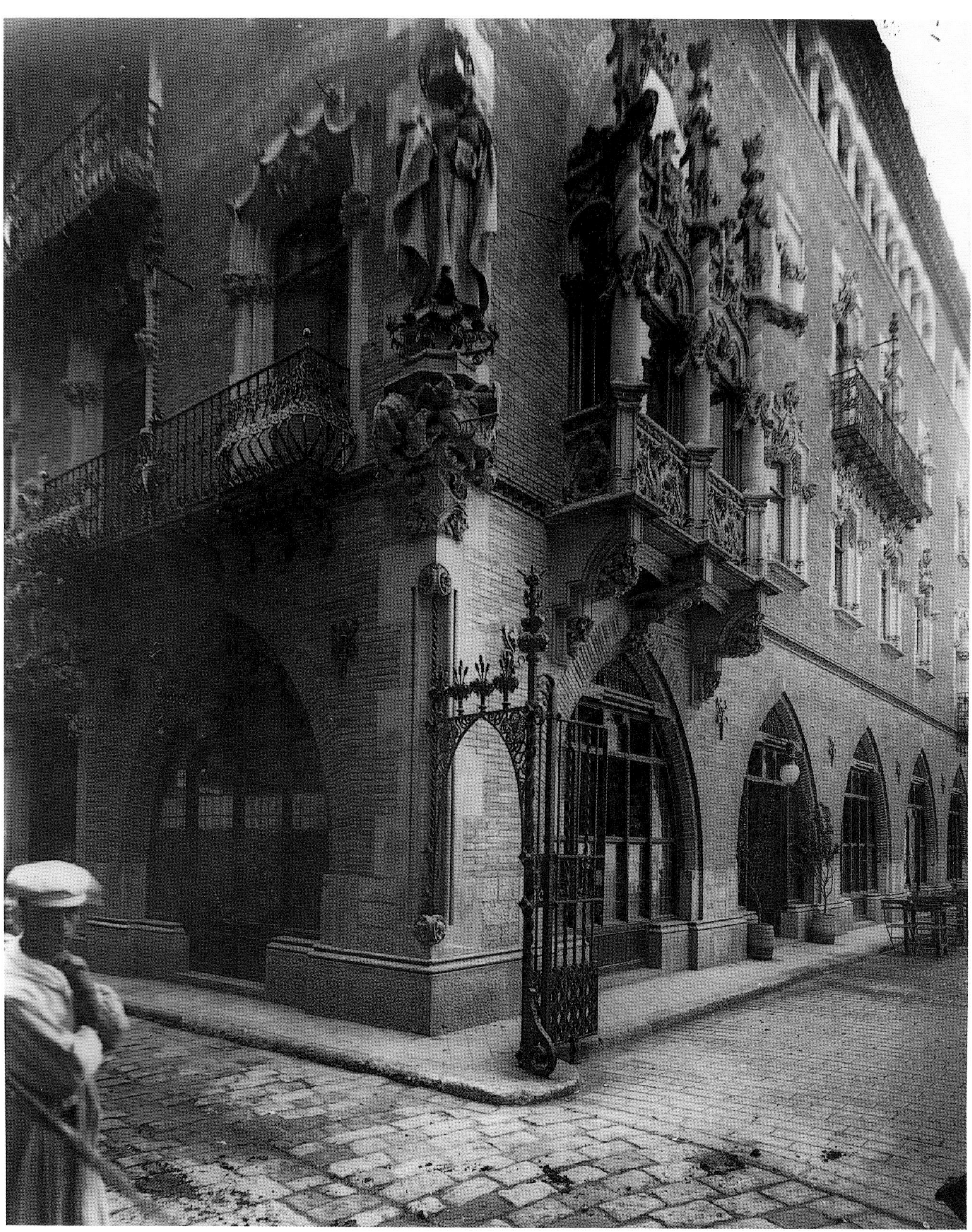

9

Els Quatre Gats

Beer mugs from Els Quatre Gats decorated with the emblem designed by Casas: the heads of Pere Romeu and of four cats. Private collection.

FOR ALMOST AS LONG AS PICASSO REMAINED IN Barcelona, the Quatre Gats tavern was the focal point of his life. This is where he learned about the latest developments in literature, philosophy, music and politics: about Verlaine, Nietzsche, Wilde, Wagner and Kropotkin, the principal heroes of the young, would-be intellectual habitués. If he learned less about the latest developments in painting, it was because the *modernisme* of Els Quatre Gats artists was a provincial offshoot of symbolism and art nouveau rather than an authentically modern movement. The work of Picasso's Quatre Gats period begins by reflecting the preoccupations and aspirations of his Catalan cronies; in the end he would repudiate almost everything they stood for. A few remained lifelong friends, but besides himself, only González, the sculptor, and Torres García made any contribution to the modern movement.

Els Quatre Gats, which opened on June 12, 1897 and closed in July 1903, advertised itself as a *'cerveseria-taverna hostal'* (beerhall-tavern-inn), but it was in fact modelled on the bohemian cabarets of Montmartre—establishments that attracted avant-garde writers and painters and made money out of their prosperous hangers-on. Its handsome *modernista* building, Casa Martí (which has recently been restored and reopened as a café), was the first important commission of a young architect, Puig i Cadafalch, a fervent regionalist who later became a pioneer historian of Catalan Romanesque. The Casa Martí was 'a mixture of archaeology and *modernisme* . . . of love for the old and a passion for the new'.[1] Besides a row of oversized Gothic arches giving onto the street, the principal façade featured a wealth of elaborate stone carving and wrought-iron work on the upper floors. Above the main entrance hung a mobile metal inn sign emblazoned with two cats. One was black on one side, white on the other; the other was grey on one side, yellow on the other—i.e., 'four cats'.[2] There was none of the sawdust-floored scruffiness of Parisian cabarets. Els Quatre Gats was a showplace—inspired by Rusiñol's Cau Ferrat—for local arts and crafts. Like the building, the furniture had been specially designed by Puig i Cadafalch; the decoration included fanciful arrangements of local tiles, some of them traditional, some designed by Casas. Walls were covered with an array of trophies and ceramics, as well as paintings and drawings—mostly portraits or caricatures of the clientele. Dominating the main wall of the *sala gran* was Casas's large poster-like painting of Pere Romeu, the proprietor, and himself (smoking a cigar

Opposite: The Casa Martí, where Els Quatre Gats occupied the ground floor, after 1900. Photo: Mas.

Eliseu Meifrèn. Shadow-puppet figure representing the writer Pompeu Gener. Cut-out black card and metal, ht: 20 cm. Carolina Meifrèn de Jiménez collection.

stuck into a pipe—his emblem) on a tandem bicycle. The inscription (in the upper right-hand corner, now painted over) read, 'When riding a bicycle, don't keep your back straight'—that is to say, if you want to forge ahead, put all your energy into it. Sometime after 1900 Casas replaced the bicyclists with more topical motorists: the same two men muffled in huge fur coats, racing into the new century in an automobile with a dog perched on the hood.

'Four cats' is a colloquial Catalan expression meaning 'only a few people'. It also stood for the four principal animators of the establishment: Pere Romeu, Santiago Rusiñol, Ramon Casas and Miquel Utrillo. These men had formed the nucleus of a bohemian Catalan group in Montmartre and had all (especially Utrillo) frequented Le Chat Noir: the small, sophisticated cabaret whose pioneering proprietor, Rodolphe de Salis—impresario, editor, puppeteer, eccentric—had recently died. Besides de Salis, their principal inspiration was the singer and songwriter Aristide Bruant, owner of another cabaret, Le Mirliton, and the subject of some of Toulouse-Lautrec's most striking posters. Romeu, who managed Els Quatre Gats, did his best to fill Bruant's boots, but the piratical panache, the cascade of whiskers and the big black Córdoban hat were all camouflage. Underneath, Romeu was gentle, melancholy, a bit vacant. If Els Quatre Gats had been run by someone with more flair, it would not have petered out so soon.

Romeu had been born around 1862 in Torredembarra, a small coastal town south of Barcelona. In the early 1880s, he had gone to Paris, where he made friends with his future collaborators. Romeu and Utrillo had apprenticed themselves to the shadow-puppet theatre, the most celebrated feature of Le Chat Noir. *Ombres chinoises* these were called, and they consisted of cut-out paper figures, often by well-known artists (Forain and Jacques-Emile Blanche, for instance), which were projected onto a screen lit by acetylene gas lamps, to the accompaniment of satirical, often scabrous dialogue. In 1893, Romeu and Utrillo joined Léon-Charles Mârot's shadow-theatre group, *Les Ombres Parisiennes*—a spin-off of Le Chat Noir—when it crossed the Atlantic and became one of the attractions at the Chicago World's Fair. Back in Catalonia in the mid-1890s, Romeu helped organize, or disorganize (he was a hopeless administrator), Rusiñol's *modernista* festivals at Sitges, before realizing his dream of founding a *rendezvous des artistes* in Barcelona. Els Quatre Gats was to be a rallying-place for supporters of the Catalan *Renaixença*, whether they were *modernistes*, *anarquistas* or *decadentes*, whether interested in symbolism, Kropotkin or Oscar Wilde. This diversity, which was one of the tenets of Els Quatre Gats, is summed up by Rusiñol in his manifesto-like 'invitation' to the tavern:

> An inn for the disillusioned . . . a corner full of warmth for those who long for home . . . a museum for those who look for illuminations for the soul . . . a tavern . . . for those who love the shadow of butterflies and the essence of a cluster of grapes; a gothic beer-hall for lovers of the North, and an Andalusian patio for lovers of the South . . . a place to cure the ills of our century, and a place for friendship and harmony. . . . [3]

Far from attracting the chosen few, Romeu and company were determined to cater to the widest possible clientele. And they succeeded to the extent

Ramon Casas and Miquel Utrillo. Poster advertising the shadow puppets at Els Quatre Gats, 1897. To the left of the screen are Casas and Rusiñol (both bearded), Utrillo and Zuloaga (one holding, the other smoking a pipe) and Eliseu Meifrèn; Pere Romeu stands on the right. Private collection.

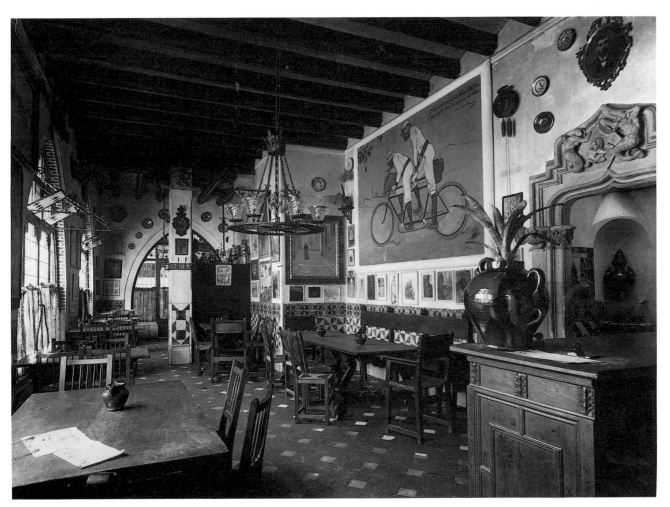

Sala Gran of Els Quatre Gats, *c.*1899. Photo: Mas.

Casas. *The Editors and Manager of Pèl & Ploma: Utrillo, Casas and Galceran.* 1900. Charcoal on paper, 52×39cm. Museu d'Art Modern, Barcelona.

Picasso. Poster design for *Dramas Criollos* at the Quatre Gats puppet theatre. Barcelona, 1900. Charcoal and pastel on paper, 57.8×38.1cm. Staatliche Museen zu Berlin. Inscribed to Pujulà i Vallès.

that 'the well-off of Barcelona filled the restaurant and their children filled the puppet theatre'.[4] To drum up attendance they were forever papering the walls of Barcelona with art nouveau posters. They put on regular exhibitions, starting with a group show (October 1897). Its catalogue idealistically invited 'citizens to come and see [the exhibits] and say what they think'. They also published their own magazine. The first journal, *Quatre Gats* (edited by Pere Romeu), lasted from February to May 1899, but in that short period fifteen issues came out. This was superseded by the more ambitious and sophisticated *Pèl & Ploma*, inspired by the Parisian magazine *La Plume.* Utrillo was literary editor and wrote nearly all the copy, and a very accomplished journalist he proved to be. Casas was art editor and responsible for most of the illustrations; he also allowed his studio to be used as an editorial office, which was managed by the watercolourist Celestí Galceran, with Utrillo also providing financial backing.

Although written in Catalan,[5] *Pèl & Ploma* was more than a vehicle for *Catalanisme.* It made a point of reprinting digests of articles and reviews from foreign periodicals such as *La Plume, L'Art Décoratif* and *The Studio* so as to cover cultural events all over Europe. There were perceptive articles on Toulouse-Lautrec (November 1901), Whistler (July 1903), Gauguin (August 1903) and other modern painters. There were also articles devoted to promising young artists from the tavern's own ranks, notably Picasso (June 1901). *Pèl & Ploma* ceased publication for six months in the second half of 1902 but started up again and outlived the tavern (its last issue appearing in December 1903, five months after the place closed). In the final number, Utrillo announced that *Pèl & Ploma* would be replaced by a new magazine called *Forma*, which would also include the occasional article on contemporary art. Instead *Forma* ended up concentrating on art history—a reflection of Utrillo's changing interests and the split-up of the four founding cats.

Els Quatre Gats also sponsored lectures, evenings of modern music, including concerts by Albéniz and Granados, and meetings of an active Wagner Society, poetry readings and theatrical productions, as well as *Sombres Artístiques* based on de Salis's *ombres chinoises.* Miquel Utrillo excelled at this. Like so many of the Quatre Gats group, he was good at many different things, not quite good enough at any one of them. *Sombres Artístiques* called for exactly the diversity of talents that in the end doomed Utrillo to a lack of fulfilment. Although innately gifted as an artist, he had first trained as an engineer, then joined the staff of a scientific journal (1879–80) while studying agronomy in Paris. Agronomy bored him, so he devoted himself to art criticism—he was Paris correspondent for the Barcelona newspaper *La Vanguardia.* The Montmartre cabarets were his other passion. Thanks to his engineering experience and knowledge of electricity and animation, Utrillo ultimately revolutionized the technique of shadow puppetry. For this he was hailed by Rusiñol as a genius, who 'knows how to bring together art and science as brothers, to obtain rare contrasts of colour with changing effects of light.'[6] A generation later, his diverse gifts would have qualified him for a successful career in films, the entertainment that superseded these shadow displays.

In his early days (1883) at Le Chat Noir, Utrillo had given a two-hour demonstration of the Ball del Ciri, a ritual candle dance performed by

Miquel Utrillo. *Portrait of Suzanne Valadon*. Paris, 1894. Conté crayon and sanguine on paper, 30.5×19.7cm. Museu Cau Ferrat, Sitges.

outgoing Catalan church wardens. In the audience was a beautiful young model, Suzanne Valadon, who had begun life in a circus but, after falling from a trapeze, earned her living as an artists' model (for Puvis de Chavannes and Renoir, among others). Utrillo and Valadon were introduced by her current lover, the cabaret's pianist—none other than Erik Satie (who would work on *Parade* with Picasso). A stormy romance developed. The handsome Catalan soon made his mistress pregnant, and on December 26, 1883, she gave birth to a son, who would win fame as Maurice Utrillo.[7] Since Valadon became the model and friend of Toulouse-Lautrec and, through him, of Degas (who taught her drawing and print-making), she turned out to be an asset to her former lover Utrillo, now that he was dividing his time between art criticism and Toulouse-Lautrec-like illustrations. Back in Barcelona in the mid-nineties, Utrillo was perceived as the quintessence of Parisian sophistication. Picasso would be flattered to have a friend who was a friend of Toulouse-Lautrec.

Although they became very friendly, Picasso never collaborated with Utrillo on the shadow puppets that were his specialty. But he participated in another more traditional form of puppetry that was no less popular at the tavern: Juli Pi's Punch-and-Judy shows (*Putxinellis* in Catalan), to the extent that he did a superb poster, embellished with gold dust, for one of Pi's performances, *Dramas Criollos*. In the course of attending these performances Picasso learned the tricks of Utrillo's trade. Years later he would exploit these silhouettes in countless different ways: in *papiers collés*, ballet décors and, most suitably, for the *memento mori* profile of his Catalan friend Pichot in *The Three Dancers* (1925). His experience of puppets also stood Picasso in good stead when he made a model theatre for his young son Paulo. The inclusion of this toy with its scaled-down décor in the middle of the great still life of 1925 in the Museum of Modern Art, New York, has puzzled many an uninitiated eye.

Besides introducing him to the Catalan avant garde, Els Quatre Gats provided Picasso with a *tertulia*. It was for Picasso what Málaga's Café de Chinitas had been for his father. Just as this aspect of don José's life had always been exclusively masculine, so it was with his son. For all the founders' liberal notions, this was still nineteenth-century Spain. Women and children were really welcome only at afternoon performances of the Punch-and-Judy shows, as we know from Rubén Darío, the well-known Nicaraguan writer who described a visit he made on January 1, 1899, to Els Quatre Gats:

> I arrived just as the performance was starting. The house was almost full and it was a pleasure to see various young ladies there, intellectuals I was told—but rather than being coiffed or dressed in the Botticelli or . . . Beardsley manner, they signified 'snob'.[8]

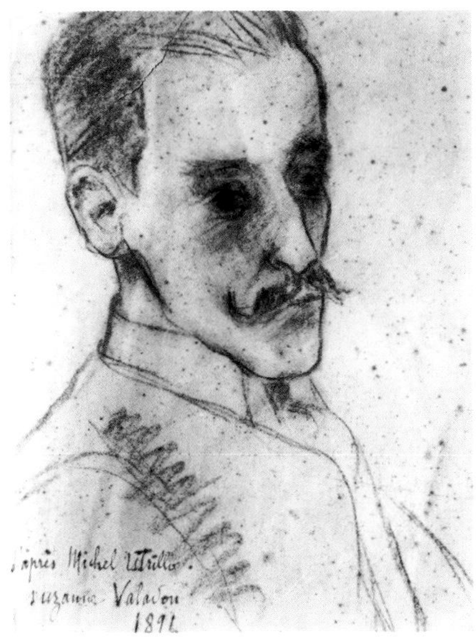

Suzanne Valadon. *Portrait of Miquel Utrillo*. Paris, 1891. Charcoal on paper. Private collection.

In the evenings, these 'snobbish' young ladies are unlikely to have been seen at Els Quatre Gats, even in the company of a husband or other family member; the ambiance of the place was that of a men's club. By the same token, the subjects of virtually all Picasso's early portraits are men; women turn out to be his sister or whores. Lluisa Vidal, the only woman painter in the Quatre Gats group, is conspicuously absent from the sitters. What has come to be called male chauvinism will be even more in evidence when Picasso devotes himself to painting women rather than men. The unpalatable truth is that machismo—a specifically Andalusian term—made for some of Picasso's most powerful work.

Some of the younger habitués—probably the Bas brothers or the Cardonas—had introduced the sixteen-year-old Picasso to Els Quatre Gats as early as 1897, the year of its opening. But it was only after he returned to Barcelona from Horta early in 1899 that he was welcomed into the inner circle. His proficiency in Catalan proved useful, but the young outsider was obliged to tread carefully and conceal the ferocity of his ego behind a mask that was shy and a touch soulful. The future art historian Joaquim Folch i Torres gives us an adolescent peep:

> The arches of the café were filled by great leaded panes of glass, across which hung curtains concealing whoever was seated . . . inside. By going very close . . . my brother Lluís, who was taller than I (I was still growing), could see the whole of the interior . . . I couldn't. However, by standing on tiptoe . . . on the window-sill . . . I too could glimpse the group at the corner table. 'The one with the sad eyes is Picasso,' my brother told me.[9]

Joaquim Mir. *Returning Veteran.* *c.*1899. Charcoal and watercolour on paper. Private collection.

Thanks to his tact and charm, Picasso was soon accepted and acclaimed rather than resented by those less gifted than himself. Romeu, Rusiñol and Utrillo were delighted to welcome this prodigy into their fold, and even Casas, who would have the most reason to dislike this potential rival, was friendly and encouraging and allowed Picasso to work in his studio. Casas had great generosity of spirit.

* * *

Of the younger painters in the Quatre Gats group the most gifted were Joaquim Mir, Isidre Nonell and Ricard Canals—intimate friends who were dedicated to painting everyday life, preferably out-of-doors. Although still in their twenties, they were a generation older than Picasso. The subject of countless drawings by Picasso, Mir had studied at La Llotja and Lluís Graner's academy. He had then joined the School of Olot,[10] but soon defected. With fellow art students Nonell and Canals, he had started up the Colla del Safrà (saffron group),[11] whose aim was to carry the naturalism of the School of Olot a stage further by substituting bright colours for the traditionally gloomy tones of Spanish painting. Understanding nothing of impressionist colouristic theory, they came up with landscapes that are garish rather than light-filled. Mir's socially conscious slices of local life have much more bite. In the winter of 1904–05 Mir suffered a serious nervous collapse—to the dismay of his Barcelona colleagues. Although they despaired of his sanity, he survived to become the best-known Spanish landscape painter of his day. To a non-Spanish eye, Mir's facile scenes seldom rise above the level of travel posters—a verdict Picasso would not have contradicted.

Picasso. *Joaquim Mir.* Barcelona, 1899–1900. Pen on paper, 31.5×21.6cm. Museu Picasso, Barcelona.
The dog carrying pots of cadmium yellow paint and the jealous sun are references to Mir's membership of the saffron group.

Some of Picasso's very early landscapes had been influenced by Mir, but by the time they met in 1899, their work had nothing in common, nor were they ever very close. Why then did he do so many portraits and caricatures of Mir? Picasso may have coveted Mir's popularity; he may have been flattered by a proposed exchange of paintings; or he may have been anxious to meet Mir's rich uncle, Avelino Trinxet, who was an important patron of the arts and famously generous to his nephew.[12] But the truth is surely that Picasso found Mir an irresistibly picturesque subject. With his boot-button eyes, shock of black hair and pipe permanently protruding from below an upturned nose, he looks like a bearded L'il Abner—one of the most instantly recognizable members of Els Quatre Gats. Picasso developed an extraordinary knack for internalizing a face or persona—usually a wife's or a mistress's—and then making endless variations on it. So it was with Angel de Soto and Casagemas; so it was with Mir. Time and again his endearing image pops up, sometimes accompanied by a hound. And then he disappears from the Picassian scene: he did not follow the rest of the group to Paris; later Picasso's solar power would have threatened Mir's small star with extinction.

Nonell and Canals, the two other up-and-coming members of the saffron group, spent most of 1898–99 and the first six months or so of the new century in Paris,[13] so Picasso would hardly have seen them. However, they were more innovative, more socially concerned than most other local artists, above all more successful—and in Paris rather than Barcelona. Both artists, Picasso realized, had something he could use, especially Nonell, who was more original, more steeped in *duende*.

Canals. *Isidre Nonell*. Paris, 1897–98. Charcoal on paper. Published in *Luz*, December 1898.

Unlike most of the Quatre Gats group, who tended to come from solid middle-class stock, Nonell was born into the lower echelons of the Catalan bourgeoisie—the son of a pasta merchant from a poor neighbourhood. After a stint with the Colla del Safrà, he went his own anarchistic way. Leaving the other *modernistes* to practise art for art's sake, Nonell turned his back on middle-class respectability and took up with gypsies, vagabonds, beggars and the down-and-out veterans of the Cuban war. These outcasts became his favourite subjects. Originally inspired by Daumier and Goya (especially the *Disasters of War* and the 'black' paintings), he leavened his gloomy Spanish vision with some of Forain's and Steinlen's journalistic spark. Nonell's cartoons of society's victims resemble Käthe Kollwitz's (seven years older than Nonell): for all that the artist's humanitarianism does him credit, his images tend to be a bit contrived.

In 1896 Nonell startled Barcelona with his *Cretins de Bohí*: drawings of goitrous idiots indigenous to Caldes de Bohí, a primitive thermal establishment in the backwoods of Catalonia. These drawings were published in *La Vanguardia* and exhibited in that journal's offices; and they excited young artists by demonstrating that magazine work could be artistically and politically progressive as well as prestigious and lucrative. Nonell followed up the *Cretins* with an even angrier set of drawings—anti-state as well as anti-war—entitled *España después de la guerra*, that were included in his exhibition at Els Quatre Gats in December 1898. Since Picasso was away from Barcelona for all but a week or two of this year, he would have missed this exhibition. After his return to Barcelona, however, he would have met this large genial bohemian through his admirer and imitator Casagemas, whom Nonell would visit whenever he returned from Paris. The two artists soon developed a warm regard for each other and each other's work, and Picasso later exempted Nonell from his aspersions on *modernista* painting. At Casagemas's they used to amuse themselves on Sunday afternoons making *dibujos fritos*—drawings that were fried in oil in order to give them the patina of age. Nonell was expert at this old faker's trick and passed it on to Picasso, hence the Nonellish look of the latter's only surviving *dibujos fritos* (see illustrations,

Nonell. *Cretins of Bohí*. 1896. Conté crayon, colour and powder on paper, 46×31 cm. Private collection.

Above: Nonell. *Repatriated Soldier.* 1899. 'Fried' drawing, 29.2×25.7cm. Museu d'Art Modern, Barcelona.

Top right: Picasso. *El Divan.* Barcelona, 1899–1900. Charcoal, pastel and coloured crayon on paper ('fried' drawing), 26.2×29.7cm. Museu Picasso, Barcelona.

Right: Canals. *Street Scene. c.*1901. Etching and aquatint, 37.5×26.5cm. Private collection.

pp.136, 163). The foggy chiaroscuro of *Poor Geniuses* and *Last Moments* seems to have rubbed off Nonell's drawings of the 1890s.

For all the sensation that Nonell's drawings of goitrous cretins and the human debris of war made in Barcelona, his paintings enjoyed even more success in Paris. A Spanish flavour in art as well as music and literature was perennially popular in Paris. Nonell's shows in the late 1890s had done so well that he had taken a studio in Montmartre. And over the next few years he divided his time between Paris and Barcelona. Whichever studio was not in use would be made available to friends. Picasso, who aspired to follow in the footsteps of Nonell and Canals, would benefit from this arrangement on his first visit to Paris. It was not until the year before his early death from typhoid (1911) that Nonell had the success he deserved in Spain. The impact of his exhibition at the Faianç Català shop in 1910 was all the greater for being belated. His studies of gypsies in the gloaming, as well as the later, lighter-toned figure paintings—crouching *gitanas* enveloped in shawls—established Nonell as perhaps the finest painter of his generation working in Spain.

Nonell. Invitation to the exhibition of drawings at Els Quatre Gats, December 1898.

Nonell's great friend Ricard Canals was a less exciting, less innovative artist, but he was a subtle colourist with an instinctive understanding of French *belle peinture*, of Renoir, Degas and Manet. He was also a man of exceptional charm—someone Picasso would come to like enormously. Canals played a liberating role in Picasso's development: he encouraged him to emerge from his tenebrist phase and experiment with colour. Most important, he introduced him to print-making—a field that Picasso would transform more radically than any other artist. Canals was an effective teacher. Picasso's very first print—a picador with an owl at his feet—reveals how quick he was to assimilate the etching technique.[14] His inexperience is reflected in a minor slip. By putting the pike in the picador's right hand, he assumed that it would come out that way round in the print. Of course it didn't. To account for the picador using the wrong hand, he ingeniously named the plate *El Zurdo* (the left-hander). Quite apart from this gaffe, Picasso was disappointed in the result and did not feel any urge to use the technique again.[15] It would be another four years before Canals overcame this prejudice against the etching process—'with the help of a simple pin'. The result would be that famous icon *The Frugal Repast* (see illustration, p.301).

Picasso. *El Zurdo*. Barcelona, 1899. Etching, 11.8×8cm. Alain C. Mazo collection.

After leaving La Llotja, Canals had headed for Paris, where he had a modest success with his scenes of low life, cabarets and cafés. His forte was upbeat gaiety, as opposed to that of his fellow exhibitor Nonell, whose forte was downbeat gloom. In Paris Canals had met a beautiful Roman girl, Benedetta Coletti (or Bianco)—thought to have modelled for Renoir and Degas—whom he eventually married, and he now spent as much time in Paris as in Spain. When Picasso settled in Paris in 1904 Canals would become his inseparable companion. A further link between them was the long-standing friendship between Benedetta and Picasso's mistress, Fernande Olivier, likewise a former model. Benedetta was an excellent cook, famous for her variations on macaroni, which is about all the two ménages could afford.[16] Although a gifted painter, Canals ended up churning out Andalusian kitsch for Durand-Ruel's less discriminating clients; later still, he went in for run-of-the-mill portraits. If Canals's flame guttered, it is not altogether surprising. With Picasso's star ever growing

Ricard Opisso. *Ricard and Benedetta Canals*. 1899 or later. Charcoal and crayon on paper. Private collection.

Picasso. *Ramon Reventós* (detail). Barcelona, 1899–1900. Pen and watercolour on paper, 16.4×17.8cm. Museu Picasso, Barcelona.

Picasso. Drypoint for *El Centaure Picador*. Golfe-Juan, February 17, 1948. 33×25.7cm. Sala Gaspar, Barcelona.

in brilliance, the lesser lights of *modernisme* can hardly be blamed for fading out. Some of them would bear him an undying grudge. Not, however, Canals. Canals's son Octavi still owns the drawing of himself as a baby that commemorates the fact that Picasso was his godfather. A second son, Ricard, recalls Picasso's return to his parents' house in Montmartre after a drunken night on the town, firing a volley of shots into the ceiling.[17]

* * *

The numerous members of the Quatre Gats group tend to blur. We should, however, try to distinguish among them, because each in his different way was an indispensable source of the admiration, support and stimulus that fuelled the early stages of Picasso's rocket-like ascent. In this respect two families stand out from the rest: the Reventóses and the Pichots. Picasso met the Reventós brothers through Angel de Soto. Ramon (Moni) was an aspiring writer reduced, like Angel, to earning his living at the spice shop; his brother, Jacint (Cinto or El Cintet), was a medical student. The Reventós house on Carrer Claris was 'where everything began', Picasso later said. The father, Isidre, was not only a prominent architect but a theatre critic and a force in cultural affairs (he had sat on the jury of the 1896 exhibition that had accepted Picasso's *First Communion*). He and his wife maintained an informal salon for artists and intellectuals of all ages and opinions, among them Rusiñol, Utrillo, Nonell, Gargallo (the sculptor) and Eugeni d'Ors (the up-and-coming literary pundit). Picasso felt that Ramon Reventós's writing was, if anything, too sensitive, precious and sentimental, for instance his esoteric play, supposedly called 'Flowers with twisted necks that a bit of water will revive'. Its humour was so far above the heads of the suburban audience summoned to a try-out that Moni did not dare take a curtain call. 'The author cannot be with you because he has already left,' Ramon announced and fled. Picasso held the work of his old friend in enough esteem to copy out two of his stories (*El Centaure Picador* and *El Capdevespre d'un Faune*) some fifty years later: 'I decided to make his work known in Paris,' he told Ramon's nephew, 'because he never achieved the recognition he deserved [Ramon died prematurely in 1923]; it was during the [Second World] war. I used to spend days in the Bibliothèque Nationale—I went on foot with all the dangers that that involved—just to copy these two stories, and I copied them by hand. One day I will show you my handwriting.'[18] If Picasso went to all this trouble at the height of the Occupation, there had to be a reason. Ramon's two stories enabled him to escape in imagination to the liberated days of his Catalan youth. But they would also play a major part in Picasso's return to classicism in 1946. Ramon's fauns and centaurs inspired the dramatis personae of the *Antipolis* series.

Ramon's brother, Cinto, was if anything closer to Picasso—'We were never separated very much during this time,' he told Cinto's son.[19] And indeed this was the friend to whom Picasso and Casagemas sent their reports from Paris in the autumn of 1900, and to whom Picasso confided his woes in 1905. The fact that Cinto was a medical student would prove useful to the artist in 1902, when he was again working on sickbed scenes and in search of morbid local colour. They drifted apart, but came

Picasso. *Portrait of Jacint Reventós.* Barcelona, 1900. Charcoal and oil wash on paper, 42×34cm. Fundación Reventós, Barcelona. Inscribed to the sitter.

together over fifty years later. In February 1956 Picasso gave Cinto the portrait he had done in 1900, inscribed in Catalan, '*per al meu Cintet*' ('for my Cintet').[20]

The Pichots were also deeply involved in Picasso's life. Like the Reventóses, they were all exceptionally gifted, free-spirited and hospitable. A sprawling apartment on the Carrer de Montcada—the handsome street of mostly sixteenth-century *hôtels particuliers*, two of which now house the Museu Picasso—is where they had their headquarters and ran a salon. But they used to spend their summers in their grandfather's villa at Cadaqués, or at another family house at Conrexia. Of the young Pichots, Ramon, a painter, was the brother who would be most intimately involved with Picasso. But it was his brother-in-law Eduard Marquina who introduced him to the family.[21] Marquina, who had married Mercedes Pichot, was already making a reputation in Catalan as a poet and *modernista* playwright, but he would later become a well-known writer in Castilian.[22]

Ten years older than Picasso and taller even than don José, whom he resembled, Ramon Pichot was another proxy father to the artist. Pichot even allowed him to move in with him for some weeks in 1899. A less than gifted painter, he had helped set up festivals at Sitges and, in 1898, had illustrated Rusiñol's *Fulls de la Vida* ('Pages of Life') with eerie black chalk drawings.[23] That Pichot was above all a man of the sea emerges in the numerous drawings and caricatures Picasso made of this genial, outgoing character. The nautical air was not a pose. Pichot had a boat, the *Nabucodonosor*, and rather than paint, he spent his summers sailing up and down the Catalan coast—at least until 1899, when he settled down and had Miquel Utrillo design a primitive house—two wings that formed an *L*, known as Sos Pitxot—at Punt del Sortell. There he would dabble in landscapes and seascapes, when he wasn't entertaining cronies from Els Quatre Gats. Like Picasso, Pichot would go to Paris in 1900. And after marrying Germaine Gargallo, the girl involved in Casagemas's suicide, he settled in a Montmartre house, called La Maison Rose. There he stayed until 1918. Pichot kept in closer touch with his famous compatriot than any of the other Catalans, except, much later, Sabartès.

Pichot. Illustration for the 'Friends of the Ceiling' chapter in Rusiñol's *Fulls de la Vida.* Conté crayon on paper, 27×29.6cm. Museu Cau Ferrat, Sitges.

Pichot crops up at important junctures in Picasso's life: he was around when Picasso visited the Exposition Universelle on his first trip to Paris in 1900; he attended the Rousseau banquet in 1908, where 'he danced a wonderful religious Spanish dance ending in making of himself a crucified Christ upon the floor';[24] he joined Picasso and Braque at Cadaqués in 1910, a crucial time for cubism; he was at Céret in May, 1912, when Picasso switched mistresses. And he was finally memorialized in Picasso's masterpiece *The Three Dancers*. Although Pichot returned to live in Spain after World War I, he continued to visit Paris to buy books. The painter had turned into a bibliophile, and worked for an American collector combing Parisian auctions and libraries for rare volumes. On one of these trips, May 1, 1925, Pichot suddenly died. The shock unleashed Picasso's darkest fears. To fight back at his arch-enemy, death, he included his former father figure as a black silhouette in the great balletic composition that he had recently begun in Monte Carlo. Although this work came to be called *The Three Dancers*, Picasso hated the title. He said the painting was a response to the misery he had suffered on hearing of his old friend's death.[25]

Right: Picasso. *At Els Quatre Gats.* Barcelona, 1899–1900. Pen on paper, 21×13.5cm. Museu Picasso, Barcelona. In the group on the left are the Soto brothers and Casagemas; on the right are two waiters.

Below: Picasso. *At Els Quatre Gats.* Barcelona, 1900. Oil on canvas, 41×28cm. Private collection.

Above: Picasso. Menu for Els Quatre Gats. Barcelona, 1899–1900. 21.8×16.4cm. Museu Picasso, Barcelona.

Above: Picasso. *Ramon Pichot.* Barcelona, 1900. Pen and watercolour on paper, 9.8×8.9cm. The Metropolitan Museum of Art, New York, Gift of Raymonde Paul, in memory of her brother, C. Michael Paul, 1982.

Right: Picasso. *Pere Romeu.* Barcelona, 1900. Pen and watercolour on paper, 7×8.6cm. The Metropolitan Museum of Art, New York, Gift of Raymonde Paul, in memory of her brother, C. Michael Paul, 1982.

Such were the members of Els Quatre Gats. So delighted were Romeu and his partners with their new recruit that they entrusted him with the design of menu cards and flyers for the tavern. Pere Romeu wanted to promote the restaurant and its regional specialities—*tripa a la Catalana* and *bacalao a la Viscaina.* The heavy outlines and stylized simplifications of Picasso's designs were evidently inspired by English greenery-yallery: Kate Greenaway, Walter Crane and the more up-to-date Beggarstaff Brothers (known in Barcelona thanks to *The Studio*). The menu card portrays Els Quatre Gats patrons in Biedermeierish costume: top hats and redingotes for the men; poke bonnets and crinolines for the women. If this nostalgic 1830-ish look might seem an aberration on Picasso's part, he was not alone: it would soon manifest itself in the early work of Kandinsky and Feininger, as well as of designers such as Bakst. In any case, Picasso's images transcend their modishness. However, if Els Quatre Gats is remembered today, it is not for menu cards but because Picasso portrayed so many of its habitués.

Mayo. | Junio. | Julio. | Agosto | Sbre. | Obre | CUOTA DE | RECAUDACION MENSUAL. | ANTICIPO | TOTALES | OBSERVACIONES.

Cts. | Pesetas. | Cts. | Pesetas. | Cts.

CD34.14

10

Yo el Rey

Casas's exhibition at the Sala Parés, October 1899. Published in *Pèl & Ploma,* November 11, 1899.

Opposite: Picasso. *Manola with a Fan.* Barcelona, 1900. Charcoal on page of a ledger, 31.5×22cm. Musée Picasso, Paris.

CASAS'S TRIUMPHANT SHOW AT THE Sala Parés (October 1899), Barcelona's most fashionable gallery, was a challenge. Anything Casas did Picasso knew he could do better—had he not had the run of his studio? And so, just as earlier in the year he had shown himself master of the bravura technique in his painting of Cardona, he now set about showing that he could outdo the facile charcoal portraits that had become Casas's principal claim to fame. Of the more than 150 works in the Sala Parés show, 132 were portraits of local leading lights—'a Barcelona iconography' as a critic described them.[1] Local society longed to be drawn by Casas, and it was—by the hundred. Casas combined a free use of charcoal with a variety of media (watercolour, pastel and coloured powders). Most of his earlier portraits were done from life; most of the later black-and-white ones, all too evidently, from photographs.

Picasso's principal supporters—Casagemas, Pallarès, Sabartès, the Sotos—were convinced that their young champion could do better than Casas. They relished the idea of setting him up in opposition to 'the idol of Barcelona' and teasing the public, not to speak of the idol himself. Their young champion accepted the challenge as if by right and devoted the next three months to portraying not just the Quatre Gats group but other friends, and friends of friends—anyone who might buy a drawing of himself, or commission something more important. Pallarès claimed that his was the first of the portraits: done in the autumn of 1899 just after he returned from Horta to continue at La Llotja.[2] It certainly has the same ineffably bourgeois air—the hand in the overcoat pocket, the rakish fedora—as the drawings Picasso had done of his father earlier in the year. The urban backgrounds that are a feature of the first portraits disappear as Picasso hits his stride (some days he must have done at least two or three). Right from the start he surpasses Casas in suppleness, sharpness of observation and the pleasure he takes in his own virtuosity. He also has fun deriding Casas's stylish manner by applying it to unstylish sitters, in one case going so far as to mock Casas's precious use of colour by adding a rich brown wash from his coffee cup to Vidal Ventosa's portrait (see illustration, p.245).

The subjects of some of these portraits also figure in vivid little vignettes that hover on the brink of caricature. But rather than poke physiognomical fun at people, Picasso comes up with neatly rounded character studies—terse as epigrams. Except for family members (himself included), nobody

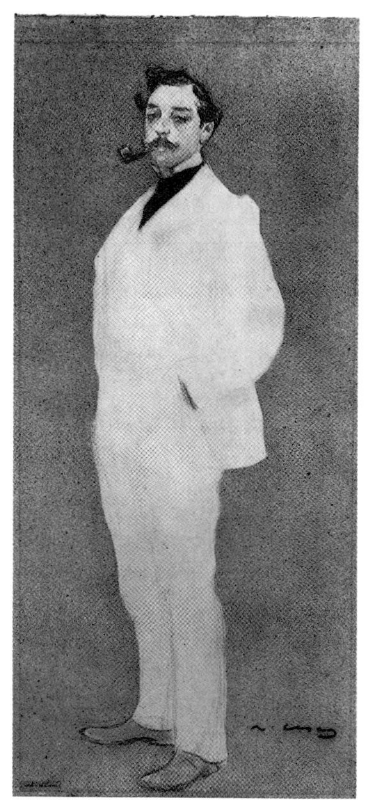

Above: Casas. *Self-Portrait.* Published in *Pèl & Ploma*, November 11, 1899.

Opposite: Casas. Portraits. 1899. Museu d'Art Modern, Barcelona.

Top (left to right):
Ramon Pichot. Charcoal, pastel and watercolour on paper, 64×30 cm.

Pompeu Gener. Charcoal and white wash on paper, 64.5×34 cm.

Joan Baptista Parés. Charcoal and pastel on paper, 62×28.5 cm.

Bottom (left to right):
Maurici Vilomara. Charcoal and powdered ground on paper, 58×24 cm.

Antoni Mas i Fondevila. Charcoal and watercolour on paper, 58×24 cm.

Antoni Utrillo. Charcoal and pastel with powdered ground on paper, 62×30 cm.

was safe from Picasso's probing eye. Cabaret performers, *boulevardiers*, workers, whores, priests, painters, street orators, musicians, ballet dancers, toreros, poets, enemies as well as friends: the whole spectrum of local life is depicted with wit and irony and economy. Sometimes he makes random grabs at people on the prowl, but he never doodles. Even the most playful of these five-finger exercises are miracles of trenchant observation. Picasso always arrives at an image that encapsulates character and reveals a subject in a candid new light. One sees why Utrillo dubbed him 'le petit Goya'. This gallery of bohemians, hovering on the verge of a humdrum future, is a unique accomplishment. The friends to whom Picasso introduces us—macho lady-killer, good doctor, doomed poet, nice dullard, smug hack, oily sponger, café anarchist—are types we are accustomed to meeting in turn-of-the-century fiction (Baroja, Joyce, Svevo, to name the most obvious writers), but never en masse in art. By comparison the people in Casas's 'Barcelona iconography' look like waxworks. Their eyes are lifeless, whereas Picasso always registers the sitter's gaze; and he diagnoses ambition or anguish, slyness or faint-heartedness, with insight and wit that has yet to acquire a lethal edge.

Sabartès disdainfully dismisses these subjects, who included all his closest friends, as 'a group of nonentities, badly dressed for the most part, and all looked upon askance . . . because not one did anything worthwhile . . . at best either apprentice journalists or merely people who like to associate with artists.'[3] This comes oddly from a future journalist who made a career out of his association with an artist. As for the shabbiness of his sitters, Picasso must have improved their appearances out of all recognition. For the mystery is not how badly but how well dressed these bohemians and *decadentes* look, with their starched collars, cravats, three-piece suits, bowlers and Homburgs. The most nonchalantly elegant is, of course, Picasso himself, for all the world like a romantic lead in a musical comedy. The self-portrait (which recalls the stylizations of the Beggarstaff Brothers) is again inscribed '*Yo*' ('I'), as if to settle any doubts as to the identity of this glamorous figure. This is not the first time Picasso gives himself pictorial airs, nor the last. As he was to murmur over sixty years later, when shown a particularly highfalutin photograph of himself, '*Comedia!*'.

Picasso was eighteen years and three months old when he showed these portraits: his first serious exhibition. It opened, auspiciously enough, on the first day of the first carnival of the new century. Compared with the Sala Parés, the Els Quatre Gats installation was amateurish. Picasso's portraits were pinned—unmounted, unglazed, unframed— onto the walls of the *sala gran*. Friends rallied round and nailed them up as best they could, cramming them together, when space ran out. One row was not enough, so they put in another above. The net effect was rough-and-ready, but the installation had cost nothing.[4] According to an unsigned review (*Diario de Barcelona*, February 7, 1900), three paintings were also included in the show, one of them *Last Moments*. The horrified critic (probably the forgotten hack Sebastià Trullol i Plana) accused Picasso of having 'an obsession with the most extreme form of *modernisme* . . . a lamentable derangement of the artistic sense and a mistaken concept of art,' but granted him talent and 'intuition and knowledge of the expressive power of colour'. Some of the portraits, he said, 'stand out by virtue

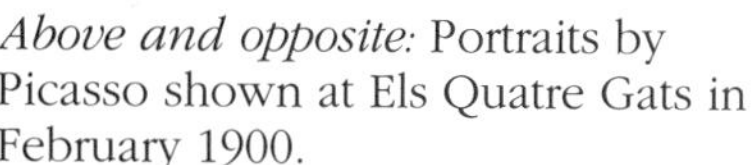

Above and opposite: Portraits by Picasso shown at Els Quatre Gats in February 1900.

Top (left to right):

Josep Cardona. Conté crayon and oil wash on paper, 51.8×36.5cm. Heirs of the artist.

Unidentified Man. Conté crayon and oil wash on paper, 48.5×32cm. Heirs of the artist.

Manuel Pallarès. Charcoal and oil wash on paper. Whereabouts unknown.

Bottom (left to right):

Daniel Masgoumeri. Charcoal and watercolour, 48.5×31.2cm. Marina Picasso collection; Galerie Jan Krugier.

Evelí Torent. Charcoal on paper, 48.8×32.3cm. Detroit Institute of Arts.

Unidentified Man. Conté crayon and oil wash on paper, 47×37cm. Marina Picasso collection; Galerie Jan Krugier.

Opposite top (left to right):

Angel de Soto. Charcoal and coloured ground on paper, 43×24cm. Whereabouts unknown.

Joan Fonte. Charcoal and oil wash on paper, 46.8×27.5cm. Fogg Art Museum, Harvard University, Bequest of Meta and Paul J. Sachs.

Ramon Reventós. Charcoal, conté crayon and watercolour on paper, 66.5×30.1cm. Museu Picasso, Barcelona.

Opposite center (left to right):

Josep Rocarol. Charcoal and oil wash on paper, 47×31cm. Fogg Art Museum, Harvard University, Gift of Arthur Sachs.

Unidentified Man. Charcoal and watercolour on paper, 47×30cm. Private collection.

Opposite bottom (left to right):

Unidentified Man. Barcelona, 1900. Charcoal and watercolour on paper, 47.2×31.3cm. Private collection, New York.

Unidentified Man. Crayon and oil wash on paper, 47.5×28.3cm. Heirs of the artist.

Mateu de Soto. Mixed media on paper. 51.4×23.5cm. Ian Woodner Family Collection, New York.

Picasso. *Self-Portrait 'Yo'.* Barcelona, 1900. Pen and watercolour on paper, 9.5×8.6cm. The Metropolitan Museum of Art, New York, Gift of Raymonde Paul, in memory of her brother, C. Michael Paul, 1982.

of the assurance of the drawing, but this . . . gallery of melancholy, taciturn and bored characters leaves the spectator with a feeling of . . . compassion for their unsympathetic portrayal.'

Another anonymous review in the more progressive *La Vanguardia* (February 3, 1900) was a bit more appreciative, but ultimately damning: 'True, Picazzo [*sic*] is a young man, almost a boy [who] displays extraordinary ease in his handling of pencil and brush . . . master, too, of . . . gracefulness of execution, a useful trait, but one that may become a handicap if it takes priority over . . . long and steady practice.' The critic accuses the artist of being uneven, inexperienced, careless and, above all, derivative—presumably of Casas: he advises him to take a different direction if he wants to 'avoid picking up the master's crumbs'. The sole value of this review is that the penultimate paragraph provides the only contemporary account of the vanished *Last Moments*.

Had *La Vanguardia*'s review been written by their regular critic, Alfred Opisso, it might have been even worse. Opisso's son, Ricard, and Picasso were two of the youngest Quatre Gats painters, and they disliked each other, more than ever now that Picasso had been accorded an honour denied to Opisso. The father's strategy was to refrain from reviewing Picasso's show, while exalting the work of his friends (e.g., Casagemas's vastly inferior exhibition a month later);[5] also to see that whoever wrote in his place would attack his son's rival. Hence the choice of Manuel Rodríguez Codolà, a peevish, admonitory man who was an assistant lecturer in aesthetics at La Llotja. Too bad that no journal published the review by an anonymous admirer that exists in draft in the Museu Picasso. The writer, who was evidently a good friend (Ramon Reventós?), commends Picasso's psychological understanding of his sitters, and his 'inspired fever reminiscent of the best works of El Greco and Goya, the only indisputable divinities for Picasso'.[6]

Disparaging reviews kept people away. Sabartès says 'the most assiduous visitors were ourselves, since nearly all of us had the time to drop in . . . if only for a cup of coffee and a friendly chat.'[7] However, in the two weeks the show lasted quite a few drawings sold—and no wonder: they cost from one to five pesetas. Very few of the buyers can be identified.[8] What became of the exhibits that failed to sell is unclear. There were originally as many as a hundred and fifty portraits, but fewer than a third have survived. A batch of unsold drawings is said to have passed to Pere Romeu, who distributed them to the sitters; after his death his widow sold the remainder.[9] Others found their way back to the family and were included in the gift to the Museu Picasso in 1970; many more stayed in the artist's possession and were eventually inherited by his heirs.

Casas seems to have reacted to Picasso's challenge with amused tolerance. He cannot have been altogether pleased; however, since his exhibition had been such a triumph, and Picasso's, by comparison, a failure, this paternal figure did not feel resentful: but then, he was not a vainglorious man. Nor did Casas apparently mind a further blow to his pride. On February 24, shortly after Picasso's show ended, newspapers announced the choice of Spanish paintings to be shown in the Exposition Universelle—the mammoth world's fair with which the city of Paris was going to celebrate the arrival of the twentieth century, and which was due to open in May. Picasso's *Last Moments* was included, but Casas's far larger and more ambitious canvas *La Carga* (The Charge), which portrays a typical confrontation between the Guardia Civil and a mob of workers, was turned down, doubtless for political reasons.[10]

Far from bearing Picasso a grudge, Casas did everything he could to support him. In 1901 he and Utrillo would arrange an exhibition of Picasso's pastels alongside Casas's drawings at the Sala Parés. In honour of the occasion Casas did a drawing of his co-exhibitor (see illustration, p.191), that was a measure of his status in the Barcelona art world. Casas, it would seem, had come to regard Picasso as someone who would assume his mantle, and at the same time rejuvenate the *modernistes*. This would leave the older artist free to devote himself to fashionable (on occasion royal) portraiture; devote himself, also, to the service of Charles Deering, a Maecenas from Chicago who became his patron. Unfortunately, as patrons often do, Deering killed his protégé with kindness. He took him to America, where he made a fortune flattering rich mid-westerners and Washingtonians, not least the President, with his facile brush. But as another Catalan, Salvador Dalí, would discover thirty years later, nothing tarnishes talent faster than commercial success in the United States, and Casas soon came to be regarded as a hack. Meanwhile Deering had recruited another leading *modernista*, Utrillo, to form a collection of Spanish masters, including the magnificent El Grecos now in the Art Institute of Chicago. To house his treasures he had Utrillo restore the old hospital at Sitges, which he renamed Mar-i-cel. Later (1916), Deering fell out with Utrillo and moved his collection, including Casas, to an even more handsome setting, the Castle of Tamarit in Tarragona. Casas flourished—the rooms of his country estate at San Benito de Bagès were crammed with works of art, the garages with his other passion, expensive motor cars—but by the time he died, in 1932, even Catalans had forgotten that this prosperous old gentleman had once been the hero of the *modernista* movement.

Casas. *La Carga* (detail). 1899. Oil on canvas, 298×470.5cm. Museu d'Art Modern, Olot.

*　　　*　　　*

The Quatre Gats portraits mark a turning point in Picasso's approach to work. Hitherto he had gone along with paternal strategy and envisaged his career in terms of successive set pieces that would make successive splashes at major exhibitions. While 'the big picture' would remain an obsession, he now embarked on a lifetime habit of working serially. He would seize on some subject or theme, devise an appropriately expressive idiom and abandon himself to its development. Just how this creative process functioned is a mystery that would puzzle him all his life. Sometimes, he said, he would exhaust the concept in the space of a sketchbook; sometimes he would return again and again to the attack over a period of months or years, until he had extracted every last drop of meaning, every last pictorial twist, from it. As Gertrude Stein wrote, 'Picasso was always possessed by the necessity of emptying himself, of emptying himself completely, of always emptying himself . . . and the moment he has completed emptying himself he must recommence emptying himself, he fills himself up again so quickly.'[11] So it was with the Quatre Gats portraits; so it would be with the bullfighting scenes that followed, and again and again in the future; only very occasionally would there be a brief backward look, a retracing of steps.

Just as he had emptied himself of his father and his precepts a year earlier, Picasso now emptied himself of Els Quatre Gats—Casas and *modernisme* included. He had grown fond of his Catalan cronies, but as he later confessed, virtually all of them except Nonell were losers. And so, after about a year, most of these provincial bohemians disappear from his work. Picasso would continue to do portraits of himself, his mistresses and his closest friends; he also accepted a few commissions in exchange for clothes or other commodities. But as he set about forging a new syntax, portraiture as such played less and less of a role in his work. Almost two decades were to pass before Picasso reverted to doing naturalistic likenesses of friends. Next time his sitters—chosen from the ranks of Diaghilev's Ballets Russes and Cocteau's *le tout Paris*—would be infinitely more prestigious. For all the differences in the sitters' milieu, these two series share certain qualities: detachment, sharp focus, quirkish insights, technical bravura; and, last but not least, they constitute an iconography of the artist's friends—his *tertulia*—at a specific time. There is one enormous difference: in Barcelona, Picasso matched himself against the living leader of a minor modern movement, Casas; twenty years later in Paris, he pitted himself against a far more formidable predecessor: the neo-classical master Ingres.

* * *

For Picasso the new century, which he more than any other artist would come to personify, started propitiously. Besides having his first serious exhibition, he finally had a proper studio of his own. About time, too, since for almost a year he had been a cuckoo, disrupting one hospitable nest after another. How long he remained in Cardona's little room we do not know; but in the course of 1899 he moved three times. At one point he went to stay with Ramon Pichot, and in no time had brought in so much stuff, made himself so much at home and established such a formidable presence in the studio that the place became his. The Pichot house was large enough to permit these liberties; other people were not always so forbearing.[12] Later in the year Picasso had settled into Mateu de Soto's studio on the Carrer Nou, where he shared everything but the rent. In the absence of congenial shelter, he could always work in the cramped room in his parents' apartment. Now, thanks to his better-off companion Casagemas, he moved into an *obrador* (loft) that they had found on the top floor of a dilapidated building at 17 Riera Sant Joan, a winding alley in the old part of the town that has now been pulled down and redeveloped.[13] Despite its poverty, this quarter—still known as the 'Reforma' —had a raffish charm. Picasso did not avail himself of the Academia Baixas (an *académie libre*, a few doors away), but he enjoyed the neighbouring Santa Caterina market. He remembered how, as the stars faded, the porters would light bonfires in the surrounding streets to keep themselves warm. The annual toy and book fair that took place in June on the Riera Sant Joan was another event he did not forget.[14] A more depressing feature of the neighbourhood was the army of beggars who lived off market refuse. Some of them were crippled veterans of the colonial wars;

Picasso. *Riera Sant Joan*. Barcelona, 1900. Charcoal and conté crayon on paper, 34.8×26.1cm. Museu Picasso, Barcelona.

Picasso. *The End of the Road.* Barcelona, 1900. Watercolour and conté crayon on paper, 47.8×30.8cm. The Solomon R. Guggenheim Museum, New York.

Picasso. *Presenting Rosita to Casagemas.* Barcelona, 1900. Pen and wash on paper, 14×10cm. Private collection.

many more were victims of disastrous conditions on the home front. These spectres of suffering will crop up repeatedly in the Blue period, but they make only a fleeting appearance in 1900: in the watercolour entitled *The End of the Road*, the allegory inspired by Conchita's wretched funeral.

Casagemas paid most, if not all, the rent of the studio. But as there was money only for the barest essentials of furniture, Picasso resorted to *trompe-l'œil.* Visitors panting from the climb would find the walls on the final flight of stairs 'frescoed' with a running frieze of caricatural figures. Inside the loft Picasso had used his brush to conjure up an *embarras de richesse.* Console tables groaned with fruit and flowers and piles of gold coins, bookcases with shelves of richly bound volumes. The walls were lined with a suite of grand furniture, an elaborate bed and even a safe for valuables. There was also a page to run errands and a voluptuous maid with mammoth breasts to look after the *maîtres de maison.* Casagemas collaborated on the large allegorical 'masterpieces' and facetious inscriptions that covered the walls of the studio. This décor was yet another example of Picasso's playful urge to improve his (and Casagemas's) circumstances pictorially. There will be many more examples of this compulsion to impose his stamp on new quarters—sometimes quite temporary ones—by covering the walls with fantastic embellishments: a studio in Montmartre (1900); a studio in Barcelona (1904); a dining room at Sorgues (1913); a bedroom at Biarritz (1918); a garage at Antibes (1921); a bathroom at Vauvenargues (1959). And then there were the decorations he contrived for friends and mistresses: not least the menacing flies he painted on the walls of Dora Maar's apartment during World War II.

In March (March 26–April 10) it was Casagemas's turn to show at Els Quatre Gats. His work received a fulsome notice from Opisso: 'Nothing is more pleasing than discovering new talents, and that is why it gives me great pleasure to speak of Señor Casagemas' (*La Vanguardia*, April 18, 1900). In the eyes of most of the group, Picasso was far more gifted and original than Casagemas; infinitely more so than Opisso's son, Ricard, who is remembered, if at all, as a run-of-the mill illustrator of slum life. His crude portraits of some of the better-known habitués of Els Quatre Gats (including Picasso) are not even of iconographical interest, since most were done from memory years later than the dates they bear.

Once their exhibitions were over, Picasso and Casagemas could concentrate on the trip to Paris that was the culmination of every Catalan student's dream. Parents had to be won over; money set aside; a studio borrowed. Meanwhile, Picasso relaxed. He continued to see his equestrienne girlfriend, Rosita del Oro, as we know from a drawing of him introducing her to Casagemas. Besides looking in on Els Quatre Gats, he and Casagemas explored the infinite variety of entertainment—from Zarzuela to sex shows—to be found in the theatres and cabarets on the Paralelo and in the Barri Xino brothels. This interlude coincided with the opening of the bullfighting season; hence a series of tauromachian subjects, mostly pastels, dating from the spring and summer of 1900. Never before had Picasso done his *afición* such credit. These scorched bullfight scenes are a tremendous advance not only in bravura but in colour. This is now as shrill and sharp as the trumpets heralding the rush of the bull into the ring. Picasso has finally discovered how to paint light. The tenebrism of *Last Moments* has given way to a garishness that is Andalusian rather than

Right: Picasso. *Bullfight*. Barcelona, 1900. Pastel and gouache on paper, 16.2×30.5cm. Museu Cau Ferrat, Sitges.

Below: Picasso. *Entry into the Arena*. Barcelona, 1900. Pastel on cardboard, 51×69cm. Private collection. In the background is the Barceloneta bullring.

Catalan: a garishness of gypsy shawls, cheap religious trinkets and toreros' suits of light. But *art populaire* is not the only source of these cacophonous mauves, lime greens, sugar pinks and saffron yellows; they recall the high key of El Greco's mannerist palette. The polarity that now develops in Picasso's colour is essentially Greco-like, essentially Spanish: monochrome and halftones on the one hand, and acid brilliance on the other. Henceforth he will zigzag—not just from dark sickrooms to sunlit bullfights but from the Blue period to the Rose period, from cubist monochrome to the local colour of labels and posters, from the grisaille of *Guernica* to the Day-Glo maquillage of certain Dora Maars.

This ambivalent feeling for colour is reflected in the way Picasso seems to conceive a subject as a draughtsman or a sculptor does, in monochrome, and then impose a colour scheme, like a composer orchestrating a piano score. The numerous colour charts and diagrams in the sketchbooks confirm that Picasso's sense of colour was not instinctive; it was calculated. As well as invoking the assistance of El Greco, he would over the next few years derive inspiration from the palettes of artists as different as Puvis de Chavannes, van Gogh, Gauguin and, above all, Cézanne—never the impressionists. At the same time, he would continue to take refuge in monochrome—blues early in life, later neutral colours.

* * *

The painter who had opened Picasso's eyes to the painting of light such as we find in the bullfight scenes was Ricard Canals. Canals had just returned from Paris, where his ability to enliven picturesque Spanish subjects with a shimmer of French light had won him a modicum of success. Picasso set about cultivating Canals: he was the living proof that a Spaniard could have more success with colourful paintings of Iberian life in Paris than at home. *Hispagnolisme* it was called, this mania for things Spanish that Canals was exploiting. It had found favour in France since the 1830s. Over the next fifty years, *Hispagnolisme* was kept in fashion by figures as disparate as Merimée, Bizet, the Empress Eugénie and La Belle Otéro. By the end of the nineteenth century, Spanish subjects in painting, literature, music and theatre—from the heights of sophistication to the abyss of kitsch—were more than ever à la mode. Galleries that catered to bourgeois taste abounded in snarling Carmens and primping Manolas, and even the Durand-Ruels would occasionally forgo an exhibit of afternoons on the Seine for nights in the gardens of Spain. Why else did this gallery send Canals back to Spain in 1900, and again in 1902, if not to bring back picturesque genre scenes drenched in local colour? In the hope of emulating Canals's success, Picasso set about painting eye-catching Spanish subjects. He was not going to arrive in the city where he hoped to find fame without saleable samples of his work. This would turn out to have been a sensible move. Sales of his bullfight pastels would pave the way for his first show in Paris.

Canals. *Fauna Flamenca.* Drawing reproduced in *Hispania,* February 1899.

These bullfight scenes also enhanced Picasso's reputation in Barcelona. During July he hung four of them in the main room at Els Quatre Gats, and he made at least one sale, to the Basque painter Ignacio Zuloaga, who would soon be a close friend, and later a bitter enemy. The little pastel that Zuloaga bought (along with a number of other Picasso

Picasso. *Frederic Pujulà i Vallès.* Barcelona, 1900. Pen and watercolour on paper, 12.4×9.2cm. The Metropolitan Museum of Art, New York, Gift of Raymonde Paul, in memory of her brother, C. Michael Paul, 1982.

Casagemas. *Leaving the Theatre.* c.1900. Pastel on paper, 23.5×19cm. Private collection.

drawings that he acquired over the next two years, and eventually sold to Rusiñol, in whose museum they still hang) is a dazzling scene of a torero and his cartel scrutinizing a baffled bull—a scene that looks ahead to Picasso's studies of Luis Miguel Dominguín of the 1950s. The exhibition of these pastels resulted in Picasso's first perceptive review in *Las Noticias* (July 23, 1900). The writer was the young critic Frederic Pujulà i Vallès, whose portrait Picasso had included in his show earlier that year:

> Let us welcome this youth, who has begun with such talent and courage but is so little appreciated by the establishment—old 'mannerists', who are respected for their grey hairs and nothing else. . . . Nobody of that ilk is going to pay any attention to Ruiz Picasso. . . . The last thing these degenerate old sages would do is praise a boy who is achieving more than they are.
>
> He exhibits four canvases [*sic*] . . . of the bullring. The effect of the blinding light beating down on the rows of seats is unbelievable: so are the silhouettes of the bullfighters and the clusters of spectators in the stands. . . . Most poetic is the one that shows the last bull being dragged off. It is the hour when the light is already fading and the few spectators, on a poorly attended day, are wandering off in groups . . . their spirits drained by this Spanish spectacle.[15]
>
> If anyone doubts our opinion, he should go see for himself; if he disagrees let him say so and we will be happy to defend our view. We need to redress the balance in favor of the young, if the young think and act like men.

A week or two after Picasso's show, Casagemas had a similar exhibit that included two interiors of sordid café-concerts, two street scenes and a caricature.[16]

In order to finance his Paris trip Picasso tried doing illustrations for magazines. Such sales as he made brought in very little. Certain magazines did not even bother to return the drawings he submitted. On going through files some years later, the new owner of *L'Esquella* discovered a self-portrait and two drawings by Picasso in an envelope marked 'Do not publish. Too poor.'[17] Picasso's first commissioned drawing was an illustration to a poem entitled 'The Call of the Virgins', by the almost forgotten symbolist poet Joan Oliva Bridgman. This came out in the July 12, 1900, issue of a new *modernista* magazine *Joventut* (Youth). Bridgman insisted that Picasso work from a photograph of a strapping Nordic model which he had already used as an illustration for another of his poems. As a result, the artist's image of a woman dreaming onanistically of her phantom lover is decidedly stilted, just like the poem—a tepid invocation to free love. Nonetheless the editor and author liked it enough to commission another illustration—a figure rowing a boat in a stormy sea—to another bad poem, 'To Be or Not to Be', which appeared in *Joventut*. Picasso also contributed illustrations to the Castilian edition of *Pèl & Ploma*; and to *Catalunya Artística*. The only inspired example of his early hackwork is an ink-wash illustration to a morbid short story by a writer named Surinyac Senties, entitled '*La Boja*' (*The Madwoman*). This demonic woman looks back at Nonell's cretins; it also looks ahead to the outcasts of the Blue period. Unlike the other illustrations, this one hints at the greatness to come.

Picasso also had another go at posters—a field in which *modernista* artists triumphed. Despite his persistence, none were ever printed. Sketches, some quite elaborate, exist for a variety of projects: to promote periodicals

Right: Picasso. *The Call of the Virgins.* Drawing reproduced in *Joventut,* July 12, 1900.

Far right: Picasso. *La Boja* (The Madwoman). Barcelona, 1900. Charcoal, ink and gouache on paper, 13.5×9.5cm. Private collection. Drawn for reproduction in *Catalunya Artística,* September 6, 1900.

Below: Picasso. Study for *Art.* Barcelona, 1900. Conté crayon on paper, 33.9×23.5cm. Museu Picasso, Barcelona.

Below right: Picasso. Study for *Caja de Previsión y Socorros* poster. Barcelona, 1900. Conté crayon on paper, 48×31.3cm. Museu Picasso, Barcelona.

Picasso. *Toreros, a Manola and Two Dogs.* Barcelona, 1900. Charcoal on page of a ledger, 31.5×22cm. Museé Picasso, Paris. Inscribed 'Goya' (twice).

Picasso. *Couple on a Sofa.* Barcelona, 1900. Charcoal and blue crayon on page of a ledger, 31.5×22cm. Museé Picasso, Paris. Inscribed '*Yo el Rey.*'

of record, like *Joventut* or *El Liberal*; to promote other periodicals *(Gente Nueva* and *Art*) that never seem to have appeared; to advertise a savings bank (Caja de Previsión y Socorros); also to launch various exhibitions, including a two-man show, 'Picasso y Pallarès', that never materialized. Picasso may even have decorated the façade of a grocer's shop on the Carrer Nou, but there is no firm record of this.[18]

Commissions bored him. Picasso's mastery can best be gauged from work done out of some inner compulsion. One of the most revelatory series of images has been locked away in a large ledger listing local property-owners; its pages are covered with black chalk sketches that blot out the columns of figures and names. Picasso evidently treasured this sketchbook: he kept it a secret from everybody, including Zervos. It came to light only after Jacqueline's death, and is now in the Musée Picasso. Some seventy masterly drawings bring turn-of-the-century Barcelona to life. Manolas in mantillas ply their fans; girls undress as a Peeping Tom looks on; men piss in the gutter; street musicians in chef-like hats entertain passers-by; couples kiss; people in traditional costume attend a bullfight (these pages are signed 'Goya'); a funeral carriage and a figure with a scythe evoke death; and there are numerous portraits—Casas, Pere Romeu, the painter Vallhonrat and a girl who is certainly Rosita del Oro. A note on one of these pages lists 'One portrait: 10 pesetas; three drawings: ten pesetas. Received 0,00 pesetas; struggle for 20 pesetas.' Scrawled with flamboyant pride across one of the pages are the words '*Yo el Rey*' ('I, the king').

Although the artist did not take his customary holiday in the summer of 1900, he could always escape the bustle of Barcelona by spending a few days at one of the Casagemas properties—at Sitges or Badalona—one of the Pichot family's houses by the sea, or at the Reventóses' country estate. But all his energy went into scheming to get himself to Paris in the autumn. Years later Picasso could still recall the endless discussions he had with his parents. There was no problem with doña María: she had total faith in her son's gifts and aspirations; she knew that he knew what was best for him. Don José was another matter: he still expected his son to follow in his footsteps, train to be a teacher and then make a name for himself in Spain. Instead of rushing off to Paris (don José said), Pablo should go back to La Llotja and finish his schooling. 'With a little effort he could become an instructor like himself. Then he could teach in Barcelona or, if he preferred, Madrid. Don José had enough contacts to take care of his future. Later he could paint as he pleased.'[19] This sort of talk made the son all the more determined to leave.

There were other arguments: the family could ill afford the expense; they were scared, too, that their son would be so entranced by Paris that he would never return. However, Picasso knew how to manipulate his parents: by turning back into an attentive son, he got his mother to win over his father, who eventually agreed to pay his return fare. It was not as if he were going to Paris on his own: the trustworthy Pallarès, who came to Barcelona for a few days in early autumn to buy paints and brushes, had agreed to accompany him. As for Casagemas, Picasso had turned his friend's increasingly precarious state of mind to his own advantage. What Carles really needed was a change, he told the parents. In the hope that this would alleviate their son's nervous state, the indulgent couple provided the necessary funds. As things transpired, they might as well have signed his death warrant. In his euphoria at going to Paris, Picasso drew a self-portrait (now lost; formerly Collection Junyer Vidal) that he inscribed, not once but three times, '*Yo el Rey*', as if to establish in the world's eyes as well as his own that he, Picasso, was the king, the messiah of the new century.

When everything was finally settled, Picasso and Casagemas went to a local tailor and ordered identical suits of black corduroy: they consisted of very loose jackets with collars that buttoned to the neck, so as to hide the absence of a waistcoat and, if the worst came to the worst, the lack of a shirt. The trousers were narrow but had vents at the bottom that fastened with two buttons.[20] Picasso sent word to Horta for Pallarès to hurry up and join them, but he was still busy decorating the walls in the village church. He promised to come to Paris as soon as he had finished. Years later, Picasso told Sabartès how don José and doña María came to the Estación de Francia to buy their son a ticket and see him off. 'When they went home, all they had left was the loose change in [my father's] pocket. They had to wait until the end of the month before they could get straight. My mother told me long after.'[21]

Picasso. *Casagemas on the Beach.* 1900. Watercolour on paper, 20.5×18cm. Baltimore Museum of Art. Cone Collection.

Right: Picasso. Drawing for a poster for a projected exhibition with Pallarès. Barcelona, 1900. Pen on paper, 13.3×21cm. Museu Picasso, Barcelona.

algunas nits anem pels
cafés concerts ó teatres idem
es bastant bonic pró
casi sempre resulta bestia.
Devegades fan com qui
balla espanyol y
ahi una s'ens
va engegar ant
un pet ó 'Ollé! Ollé
Carambá! Cagambá!'
qu'ens va deixar
frets y ens va fer
duptar de nostre
procedencia..
També está mol en
boga el genero militar.
"En todas partes
cuecen habas".
Digas á en
Romeu qu'es
un ximple
per que no vé á plan-
tar la botiga aqui;
que aqui els quartos
d'honrat guanyen, que sobri
matí y anessini
que ho faria tot, per axó
que aqui faria diners

11

First Trip to Paris

Picasso. *Carles Casagemas*. Barcelona, 1900. Pen and watercolour on paper, 21×15cm. Private collection.

Opposite: Picasso. *Café-Concert Singer*. Paris, 1900. Charcoal and coloured crayon on paper, 21×13cm. Page of letter to Ramon Reventós from Casagemas and Picasso, October 25, 1900. Fundación Reventós, Barcelona.

PARIS HAD NOT BEEN HIS ORIGINAL GOAL, Picasso told Penrose when he visited England fifty years later, but 'merely a halt on a journey which would take him north, to London'.[1] His father's taste in English furniture and clothes and his own penchant for Burne-Jones and the Pre-Raphaelites had imbued him with great admiration for England, which dated back, he said, to his childhood in Corunna. There he had learned all about the local hero, Sir John Moore (commemorated by a colossal tomb above the city), who had saved the city from Napoleon's hitherto victorious armies and then died of his wounds with the name of his mistress, the Orientalist Lady Hester Stanhope, on his lips. Picasso told Penrose that the Moore legend prompted an interest in this intrepid woman. He determined to investigate the country that fostered such a heroine, and only failed to do so because Paris detained him.

This story should not be taken seriously. Picasso may have fantasized about going to London to see the Pre-Raphaelites, but not on account of Hester Stanhope. When questioned years later by Cooper about his cult of this lady, he had only the vaguest idea who she was. This rigmarole suggests Andalusian hyperbole at its most convoluted: Picasso's way of paying England and his English host an ironical compliment in the face of the barrage of philistine hate with which the nation's establishment, headed by the president of the Royal Academy, had welcomed his first postwar London exhibition.[2] Paris was always Picasso's one and only destination. He was determined to see *Last Moments* in the Spanish pavilion and all the other special exhibits, national and international, before the Exposition Universelle closed; determined to experience modern French art and *la vie de bohème* at first hand and join, if only briefly, the much-envied band of Catalan expatriates in Montmartre. His lack of French mattered little because he moved almost exclusively in Spanish, or rather Catalan, circles; and in any case Casagemas spoke adequate French. In London, where neither he nor Casagemas had friends, they would have been utterly lost.

Picasso's date of arrival in Paris is not certain; it was probably just before his nineteenth birthday, on October 25.[3] When he and Casagemas stepped off the train at the newly opened Gare d'Orsay, they made for Montparnasse, where a friend, the stage designer Oleguer Junyent,[4] had a studio at 8 rue Campagne Première. An inexpensive studio was available in the same building, Junyent told them, so they went ahead and

Picasso. *Self-Portrait*. Paris, 1900. Pen on paper, 32×22cm. Museu Picasso, Barcelona. To the left of the head (upside-down) is a drawing of Alexandre Riera and to the right of Pompeu Gener ('Peio').

Picasso. *Alexandre Riera*. Barcelona, 1900. Pen on paper. Private collection.

rented it. Having paid a deposit and refreshed themselves, they set off across Paris to see Nonell, who had a spacious studio at 49 rue Gabrielle, high up on the Butte de Montmartre. They were idiots to settle in Montparnasse, Nonell said; it was far less congenial than Montmartre, which, as well as being the headquarters of the Catalan colony, was the centre of bohemian nightlife. Why didn't they take over his studio, when he returned to Barcelona in a few days? This was a much more attractive idea. And so back they traipsed across Paris for their luggage. They even persuaded the landlord to refund part of their deposit. En route, Picasso was spotted by Marcel Duchamp's brother, Jacques Villon, who had met him earlier that day—presumably at Nonell's.[5] The spectacle of this unknown young Spaniard trundling a cartload of baggage at dusk up the rue Lepic could mean only one thing: he was making a moonlight flit. Villon's mocking laughter made this misapprehension all too obvious. Picasso's Spanish pride was wounded; years later he still held this laugh against Villon. Picasso and Casagemas would have been on their way to the Hôtel du Nouvel Hippodrome on rue Caulaincourt, their quarters while waiting for Nonell to leave. The hotel was probably a *maison de passe*. The picturesque rue Caulaincourt was lined with brothels on one side and the rickety shacks Rusiñol had painted on the other.

As soon as they moved into Nonell's vast, barely furnished studio, Picasso and Casagemas settled down seriously to work as well as play. The letter that Casagemas wrote Ramon Reventós and Picasso signed and embellished with drawings gives their first impressions of Paris. Since Nonell took it to Barcelona in person, this letter must have been written the very day they took up residence in his studio.

> We have already started work and have a model. Tomorrow we are going to light the stove and work furiously for we're already thinking about the painting we're going to send to the next Salon. Also . . . to exhibitions in Barcelona and Madrid. . . . So long as there is daylight . . . we stay in the studio painting and drawing. . . . Peio[6] is here and . . . sent us a *pneumatique* giving us a midnight rendezvous at Ponset's tavern.
>
> . . . He treated us to beer and sandwiches and when we were about to leave Utrillo and Riera turned up and it lasted until the early hours. The following day we all got together at Petit-Pousset, which is not the same as Ponset's place, and got drunk. Utrillo wrote nursery rhymes, Peio sang bawdy songs in Latin, Picasso made sketches of people, and I wrote verses of 11, 12, 14 and more syllables. We mailed it all to Marquina. . . . Tomorrow there's going to be a meeting of Catalans and non-Catalans, illustrious and not so illustrious. We'll eat at the brasserie. There's a Catalan fellow here with fig-leaves called Cortada, loaded with millions and a miserly bastard. He often eats with us and considers himself an intellectual, but he's an arsehole.[7] The local intellectuals have more little deals going here than in Barcelona. They are pompous bachelors and not even Christ would have anything to do with them. None of them can compete with the serious way we gossip about people. Have you met Nonell yet? He's a nice man, and he and Pichot are the only two decent men around. Today we met Iturrino who also seems like a good fellow. I think Rusiñol is dying and maybe when you get this letter he'll be dead. We'll be very sorry. What about Perico?[8] Is he very bored? Tell him to come to Paris, and Manolo too, because there's room for everybody and money for anyone who works. Our studio is turning out well. Some nights we go to café-concerts or the theatre. . . . They think they're doing Spanish dances and yesterday one of

Cabaret des Quat'z'Arts on the Boulevard de Clichy, Montmartre. Photo, *c*.1905: Bibliothèque Nationale, Paris.

Place du Tertre, Montmartre. Photo, *c*.1904: Bibliothèque Nationale, Paris.

Picasso. *Group of Catalans in Montmartre* (left to right: Pichot, Mañach, Casagemas, Brossa, Picasso, Gener). Paris, 1900. Oil on paper, 23×17 cm. Barnes Foundation, Merion Station, Pa. Inscribed to 'Odet'.

them came up farting away, *ollé ollé caramba/cagamba*, which left us cold and in doubt about our origins. . . . Tell Romeu that he's crazy not to come here and open up—he must . . . rob, kill, assassinate, do anything to come because here he'd make money. The boulevard de Clichy is full of crazy places like Le Néant, Le Ciel, L'Enfer, La Fin du Monde, Les 4 z'Arts, Le Cabaret des Arts, Le Cabaret de Bruant and a lot more that have no charm but make lots of money. A Quatre Gats here would be a goldmine. . . . Pere would be appreciated and not at the mercy of the milling throng as he is in Barcelona.

There's nothing as good [as Els Quatre Gats] nor anything like it. Here everything is fanfare . . . tinsel . . . and papier-mâché stuffed with sawdust. But at least it has the advantage of deplorable taste—*cursi, vaja, bunyol, carquinyol*. The Moulin de la Galette has lost all its character and *l'idem* Rouge costs 3 francs to enter and some days 5. . . . The cheapest places and cheapest theatres cost one franc.

Had it not been for Nonell's trip we wouldn't have written you such a long letter because a letter like this is just extra baggage.

If you see Opisso tell him to come for the sake of his soul—tell him to send Gaudí and the Sagrada Família to hell. Soon the Exhibition will close and we still haven't seen more than the painting section.

Yesterday we saw a horror show at the Théâtre Montmartre. There were lots of deaths, shootings, conflagrations, beheadings, thefts, rapes of maidens, and other dire deeds, and then there was an announcement in huge letters of a scene superior to all the rest—a poor man, the Marqués de Siete Iglesias, a Spaniard who died being crushed by a roof that was coming down, down. . . . If it amuses you to know where we sit, lie down, write, paint, and what we look at, here is a little inventory . . .

One table, one sink, two green chairs, one green armchair, two chairs that aren't green, one bed with extensions, one corner cupboard that isn't corner-shaped, two wooden trestles that support a trunk, one oil lamp, one mat, a persian rug, twelve blankets, one eiderdown, two pillows and a lot of pillow cases, four more pillows without cases, some cooking utensils, glasses, wineglasses, bottles, brushes, a screen, flowerpots, W.C., books and a pile of other things. We even have a mysterious utensil for private use by ladies only.

In addition we have a kilo of coffee and a can of peas. Goodbye, and next time I'll be more lengthy.[9]

Casagemas did not report that a trio of easygoing girls came with the rue Gabrielle studio; 'models', they called themselves. They had been friendly with Nonell and his former roommate, Canals, as well as other members of the Catalan clan. Two of them were sisters: Germaine Florentin (née Gargallo) and Antoinette Fornerod.[10] Although no relation of Picasso's sculptor friend Pau Gargallo, Germaine was Spanish, or partly Spanish, to believe Gertrude Stein, who had it from Fernande Olivier.[11] This would explain her popularity with Catalan painters, few of whom spoke much French. As for her sister, Antoinette, we cannot be sure of her nationality, because (again to quote Stein): '[Germaine] had many sisters. She and all of them had been born and bred in Montmartre and they were all of different fathers and married to different nationalities, even to Turks and Armenians.'[12] The third girl, Odette (real name: Louise Lenoir), was the only one who spoke no Spanish; nevertheless she very soon became the mistress of Picasso, who spoke no French. Even if Odette (according to another letter of Casagemas's) 'had the good habit of getting drunk every night' and was 'raucous' to boot,[13] she was sexually attractive and sufficiently tolerant of the artist's promiscuity to be his principal girlfriend for the rest of his trip. Germaine, likewise, moved in, or stayed on, at the behest of Casagemas. He had developed an instant passion for her, and in his frantic all-or-nothing way had decided that although she already had a husband, she should become his wife.

Ten days or so after the move to Nonell's studio, Pallarès reached Paris, wearing—as agreed among the trio when they originally planned the voyage—a black corduroy suit of the same cut and from the same tailor as the others. The letter announcing Pallarès's time of arrival did not reach Paris until after he did, so there was nobody to meet him at the Gare d'Orsay, and he had to spend the first night on the studio couch. Next day the enterprising Germaine went out and bought another bed—cheap, but wide enough for two. Although he was supposedly faithful to his Spanish *novia* (ten years would pass before he married her), Pallarès—egged on by Germaine—embarked on an affair with her sister, Antoinette. Probably egged on, too, by Picasso; Pallarès really fancied Odette.

Picasso. *Picasso and Pallarès Arriving in Paris*. Paris, 1900. Pen on paper, 8.8×11.1 cm. Museu Picasso, Barcelona.

For most of the next two months or so the three couples lived on top of one another, in an admittedly large studio. Picasso's contribution to another joint letter to Reventós describes how the business-like Pallarès ('Pajaresco') nailed up a schedule for working and eating and even '*per grapejar*' (for fucking). Otherwise this 'dirty arcadia', as Casagemas called it, would not have functioned, and no painting would have been done. Now that each of the trio had a mistress, they decided to say 'good-bye to bachelor life: as of today we are going to bed at 10 and we're not going out anymore to the [brothels of the] calle de Londres.'[14] The girls, it seems, were faithful to Picasso and Pallarès in what Gertrude Stein later called 'the fashion of Montmartre'—that is to say both parties had a basic understanding with each other, while feeling free to amuse themselves on the side. This was fine with Picasso, who preferred his relationships to be casual and carnal; not, however, with Casagemas, whose feelings for the 'lady of his thoughts', as he called Germaine, were neither the one nor the other. The more this ill-adjusted couple were together, the more desperate and frustrated they both became. This was the first time in his life that the 'impotent' Casagemas had regularly shared a bed with a woman (let alone a sexually demanding one). To be doing so in the same room as his hero—especially one who hoped to transform him into a priapic heterosexual like himself—would have courted failure.

Despite her complaints of his shortcomings as a lover, Germaine was fond of Casagemas—fond enough to offer him the loan of thirty francs, which he had too much hidalgo pride to accept—but then, the promiscuous Germaine had a gentle, compassionate side. She hung around the circus, where she found the roustabouts she preferred as lovers. Gertrude Stein reports that she was 'the heroine of many a strange story. She had once taken a young man to the hospital, he had been injured in a fracas at a music hall and all his crowd had deserted him, Germaine quite naturally stood by and saw him through.'[15] Unable to provide the sex Germaine craved, Casagemas started to go to pieces and took more than ever to drink. His companions were too busy working or enjoying themselves to spare time for his problems. Casagemas may have been footing

Germaine Gargallo, *c.*1900.

many of the bills—he said they were spending between fifteen and twenty pesetas a day, which was more than enough for survival[16]—but Picasso had decided that on this, his first trip to Paris, his one and only obligation was to himself. Nor would he ever change in this respect.

Financially speaking, things were working out better for Picasso than he had expected. Nonell had put him in touch with Pere Mañach, a thirty-year-old Catalan who had quarrelled with his father—a safe-and-lock manufacturer in Barcelona—and set up in Paris as a dealer in modern Spanish art. Shortly after his arrival, Picasso had visited Mañach, who was much impressed by his bullfight scenes, and even more impressed when he managed to sell the three pastels he had taken on consignment within a matter of days for a hundred francs. The buyer was Berthe Weill. This dynamic dealer with an infallible eye for '*la jeune peinture*' turned the pastels over almost immediately to Adolphe Brisson, publisher of the *Annales Politiques et Littéraires*, for a hundred and fifty francs. A few days later, Mañach made an appointment for Weill to visit Picasso at the rue Gabrielle studio. But when she appeared, he failed to answer the door, so she returned a little later with Mañach. To her surprise Picasso turned out to have been hiding in bed with one of his friends.[17] Undeterred by this childishness, she proceeded to go through his work and make several more purchases.

Picasso. *El Arrastre* (Removal of the bull). Barcelona, 1900. Charcoal and pastel on paper, 15×22 cm. Private collection.

Of the motley bunch dealing in modern art when Picasso first arrived in Paris, Berthe Weill was virtually the only one who never took advantage of his chronic penury. Her funds were very limited, so she was unable to pay him or her other artists as much as she would have liked. But she prided herself on her fairness. When she made the historic purchase of the three pastels from Mañach, Weill had just opened her first gallery at 25 rue Victor-Massé—to the horror of Degas, who lived a few steps away. Degas was outraged by the presence of a Jewish dealer in the neighbourhood and glared at the door whenever he passed. Weill, who had learned the trade working for an antique dealer, had started by peddling Daumier and Lautrec prints, which she displayed pegged like laundry on clotheslines. It was Mañach who persuaded her to show modern, especially Spanish, painters—Picasso being one of the first—and it was he who helped her hang the walls of her new gallery with fabric, do the carpentry and (his family trade) install the locks. '*Place aux jeunes!*' (Make way for the young!) was Weill's battle cry. She exhibited and, what is more, sold Matisse as early as 1902; and befriended Dufy, who baptized her 'La Merveille'. Among other artists this homely Jewish spinster with spectacles thick as goldfish bowls helped discover were Derain, van Dongen, Metzinger, Modigliani, Marquet, Manguin and Maurice Utrillo.

Weill was so scrupulous that she refused to buy from Utrillo when he was drunk for fear of taking advantage of him; so protective of her artists that she allowed herself to be dragged off by the police rather than unhang one of Modigliani's supposedly indecent nudes; and so disdainful of commerce that she would not do business with anyone who had a *sale tête*. No wonder this prickly, peppery schoolmarm of a woman, who prided herself on telling people what she thought of them and had the invective with which to do so, never made enough money to build up a stock (in 1909 she let a van Gogh go for sixty francs) or sign up any of the artists she discovered, let alone set herself up in any comfort. She cooked

Picasso. *Old Woman*. Barcelona or Paris, 1900. Gouache on varnished paper ('fried' drawing), 12.6×11.7 cm. Museu Picasso, Barcelona. Inscribed to Pere Mañach.

most of her food on the gallery stove and used her bedroom for storage. Weill's scruples were her undoing. Like all the major artists she had discovered, Picasso ceased selling through her the moment he began to be successful (1905–06). 'He was dead right,' she agreed. He had 'had enough of this Montmartre pauper.'[18] D.-H. Kahnweiler, who would become Picasso's first serious dealer, was contemptuous of '*braves amateurs*' like Weill. But Picasso remembered her with exasperated affection. He did a no-nonsense portrait of her in 1918, which served as a frontispiece for her lively memoirs, *Pan! Dans l'Œil* (1933). When she died, in 1951, aged eighty-six, *la petite mère Weill* was living on charity, despite owning a small but fine collection of early drawings and watercolours, which she kept as a nest egg for her heirs.

Picasso. *Portrait of Berthe Weill.* Paris, 1920. Black chalk on paper. Private collection.

On the strength of Weill's success with the three pastels, Mañach offered Picasso a contract of a hundred and fifty francs a month. He immediately accepted. Because this arrangement foundered a year later, Mañach has fared badly with the artist's biographers, one of whom dismissed him as 'the black sheep of a respectable family'.[19] This is true only to the extent that Mañach had been banished by his autocratic father for being unconventional. But he had an instinctive feeling for modern painting and had reason to see himself as an idealistic and progressive promoter of young Spanish artists (he had dealt at one time or another with Canals, Junyent and Pichot, and developed contacts with Weill and the other more go-ahead dealers in Paris). Ambroise Vollard, who gave Picasso his first show, mentions Mañach favourably in his memoirs and describes a visit, some years later, to the safe-and-lock factory in Barcelona: 'At the entrance to the workshops a lamp was burning before the statue of a saint. "The workmen pay for the oil," [Mañach] said to me. "So long as the little lamp is burning, I am safe from a strike."'[20] Evidently a calculating man. But even after returning to Barcelona on his father's death and settling down to a conventional life of marriage and commerce, Mañach never ceased to support modern art. The showroom that he commissioned Josep Maria Jujol to design on the Carrer Ferran (now demolished) in 1911 boasted decoration that was far more advanced than anything in Paris, Vienna or London. Jujol (who had collaborated with Gaudí on some of the tiles for the Parc Güell) frescoed the ceilings and walls of the principal gallery with freeform arabesques, curlicues and polka dots, which predict Miró's work of the thirties.

As well as paying Picasso a stipend, Mañach directed friends in search of portraits, and collectors, to his studio. Emmanuel Virenque, the Spanish consul, bought the flashy *Blue Dancer* (Pierrot and Columbine, who is wearing a shiny satin dress that evokes memories of *preciosismo*, the nineteenth-century Spanish preoccupation with glittering surfaces). The discriminating Conseiller d'Etat and art patron Olivier Sainsère acquired 'an enchanting painting of a child in a symphony in whites',[21] and would go on buying Picassos until 1906, while also providing the artist with very necessary official protection. (Fernande Olivier recalls Sainsère arriving unannounced at the Bateau Lavoir studio a few years later, and catching the artist in his nightshirt. She begged Picasso, 'who was never in the least embarrassed by his state of undress, to put on some trousers.'[22]) Picasso is also alleged to have made money by selling views of Montmartre to tourists who had come to see the Exposition,[23] but there is

Picasso. *The Blue Dancer.* Paris, 1900. Oil on canvas, 38×46cm. Private collection.

Entrance to the Moulin de la Galette and the new Dance Hall there, 1898. Photos: Bibliothèque Nationale, Paris.

Opposite:
Top left: Renoir. *Ball at Moulin de la Galette*. 1876. Oil on canvas, 131×175cm. Musée d'Orsay, Paris.

Top right: Toulouse-Lautrec. *At the Moulin Rouge: The Dance*. 1890. Oil on canvas, 116×150cm. Philadelphia Museum of Art, The Henry P. McIlhenny Collection in Memory of Frances P. McIlhenny.

Bottom: Picasso. *Moulin de la Galette*. Paris, 1900. Oil on canvas, 90.2×117cm. The Solomon R. Guggenheim Museum, New York.

no evidence for this improbable story. The black chalk drawings often brightened with pastel—café or cabaret interiors, details of fashionable dress and local types glimpsed in the street—that fill sketchbooks of the period were certainly not intended for the delectation of tourists. These jottings are in the nature of snapshots: mementos of Paris for Picasso to take home and savour, as he would every scrap of Parisiana, even the dust on his shoes.

The earliest and most important of Picasso's Paris paintings is his highly charged scene of dancers at the Moulin de la Galette. This dance hall, above which Rusiñol, Utrillo and Casas had once had an apartment, was a hallowed haunt of Catalan expatriates. Picasso would already have been familiar with the look of the place from the unprepossessing view that Casas had painted ten years earlier and Rusiñol had acquired for Cau Ferrat. Casas portrayed the dance hall in daytime as a desultory place that catered to a working-class clientele. Picasso saw the Moulin in a more glamorous, if lurid, spirit. The floor is crowded with a mob of dolled-up cocottes and their top-hatted clients doing one of the new South American dances. The garlands of lights and the hard, bright colours of the women's dresses are rendered with utmost effulgence, but it is typical of Picasso that he has conceived the composition in terms of *modernista* shadows rather than impressionist light.

Van Gogh. *Dance Hall at Arles*. 1889. Oil on canvas, 65×81cm. Musée du Louvre, Paris.

Picasso's *Moulin de la Galette* also challenged two artists who were far more formidable than Casas: Renoir and Toulouse-Lautrec, each of whom had devoted major works to this very subject. Picasso would have known Renoir's sparkling view of the outdoor dance floor from visits to the Musée du Luxembourg, which had just been enriched with this impressionist masterpiece and countless others from the collection of Gustave Caillebotte. He would also have known Toulouse-Lautrec's lower-key but no less masterly indoor view of the music hall, from reproduction, if not at first hand. That someone so new to French art should have pitted himself against these masters at the top of their form is a measure of Picasso's confidence and daring. He did not have the easy victory over Renoir and Toulouse-Lautrec that he had had over Casas. Nevertheless, Picasso's *Moulin de la Galette* shows that within weeks of arriving in Paris the nineteen-year-old Spaniard had established his right to a place in the modern French tradition; what is more, without making any concessions to impressionism or neo-impressionism. Unlike Renoir, who uses colour to generate an all-over sparkle of light, Picasso takes refuge in Spanish chiaroscuro—darkness lit up with incandescent splashes of crimson and yellow. Unlike Toulouse-Lautrec, whose sense of the reality always transcends his *fin-de-siècle* stylizations, Picasso evokes an erotic ambiance all the more exciting for being faintly menacing. It is as if he saw the cocottes through Casagemas's eyes with a little help from van Gogh (*Dance Hall at Arles*). And then, what a sense of the new century Picasso has already developed. Whereas Toulouse-Lautrec's gas-lit dancers embody the ta-ra-ra-boom-de-ay of the 1890s, Picasso's tarts with their mascara and lipstick, their cheek-to-cheek smooching, project a sexuality that is distinctly twentieth century. They have abandoned the raunchy cancan for the more sophisticated Argentine tango and Brazilian maxixe (for which the Moulin de la Galette was famous).[24] The girls fondling each other in the foreground are more svelte, more heavily made up.

Casas. *Dance at the Moulin de la Galette*. Paris, 1890. Oil on canvas, 100×81.5cm. Museu Cau Ferrat, Sitges.

Picasso. *Morphine Addicts*. Paris, 1900. Oil and pastel on board, 57×46cm. Private collection.

Whereas Lautrec confronts us with very matter-of-fact lesbians *dans l'intimité*, Picasso cannot resist portraying them—he was, after all, only nineteen—as *osé* and titillating.

As soon as it was painted, the *Moulin de la Galette* was sold through Berthe Weill for 250 francs to one of the most progressive collectors of the day, Arthur Huc, publisher of *La Depèche de Toulouse*, an important provincial newspaper. Huc had commissioned posters from Toulouse-Lautrec and Maurice Denis and hung his offices with works by Bonnard and Vuillard, Sérusier and Vallotton. His house in Toulouse had doors decorated by Denis and walls hung with paintings that were the scandal of the local bourgeoisie.[25] And there in Huc's prestigious living room hung the *Moulin de la Galette*—the first Picasso painting to enter a French collection. Later it was bought by Justin Thannhauser, the Berlin dealer, who settled in New York and, shortly before he died, presented this and the rest of his collection to the Guggenheim Museum.

That raw sexuality could be harnessed to art was one of the major revelations of Paris. Accustomed as he was to Spanish constraint, Picasso was surprised to see couples not only embracing in public but depicted doing this and more in the works of artists like Steinlen. He was also surprised by the lack of shame shown by Parisian artists, who set up their easels in the street and painted away while people watched. He had always chosen the relative privacy of a park or cloister. In Barcelona, people did not publicly display sexual attraction for one another outside the Barri Xino. In Paris they did so all over the place. All of a sudden Picasso's work abounds with embracing couples. A case in point is the series of black chalk drawings, pastels and paintings of a working-class man and woman locked in such a close embrace that they melt into a single mass. This image has been taken more or less straight from scenes of street life by Steinlen—an illustrator whose work was very popular with Barcelona artists. On this trip to Paris Picasso would fall heavily under the influence of his radical imagery. Munch's *Kiss* (Picasso could have seen a reproduction of the first version, which dates from 1896) might also be a source for these meshing profiles and mouths, which will reappear time and again in Picasso's work. These proletarian lovers are first seen out of doors, by day as well as by night, with the Butte de Montmartre in the background. Finally Picasso brings them indoors, into a sordid Zola-esque bedroom. Here the woman's compliance gives way to panic, and she wrenches herself away from the brute who is grabbing her. The relish that has gone into this rape scene prepares us for the ferocious lechery of later work. A whimsical touch is the black cat crouched eerily on the bed: a dig at Manet's *Olympia*. Otherwise the scene is gutter verismo—far more powerful than the idylls that lead up to it.

Picasso. *Man in a Spanish Cloak*. Paris, 1900. Oil on canvas, 80.5×50cm. Wuppertal, Von der Heydt-Museum.

Picasso also tried his hand at local colour: a Montmartre fair, street scenes, a café interior, cancan dancers (inspired by Toulouse-Lautrec's lithograph *Troupe de Mademoiselle Eglantine*). Like the *Moulin de la Galette*, these works reveal that Picasso had put *modernisme* behind him and was becoming a painter of modern French life in a modern French manner. At Mañach's behest, he churned out some portraits, including a fashionably veiled woman in an embroidered pelisse; a pastel of a nice-looking, genteel girl whose lack of character has defeated the artist; and a large dull oil of a painter with big feet, dressed in a cloak, long violet

Steinlen. Illustration for *L'Honneur aux champs* by Camille de Sainte-Croix on the cover of *Gil Blas,* June 1, 1900. Bibliothèque Nationale, Paris.

Picasso. *The Kiss*. Paris, 1900. Pastel on paper, 59×35 cm. Museu Picasso, Barcelona. Inscribed to Lluís Vilaró.

Picasso. *Frenzy*. Paris, 1900. Pastel on paper, 47.5×38.5 cm. Galerie Beyeler, Basel.

scarf and voluminous Basque beret. He was probably one of the *bande Basque*—almost as large an ethnic group in Paris as the *bande Catalane*—but there are no other clues to his identity. Picasso also amused himself decorating the walls of the rue Gabrielle studio with a frieze of the Temptation of St Antony—a subject that he returned to a year or two later, when he and Pichot painted the walls of their favourite haunt, Le Zut. Like all Picasso's early murals, the rue Gabrielle frieze has disappeared without a trace—no sketches, no photographs, not even a verbal description. A pity, because the legend of St Antony fascinated Picasso: each time it surfaces in his work, it has a peculiar relevance to his circumstances. As Picasso would have known from his training in sacred art, St Anthony was thought to protect the faithful from the devil and the plague. He was also a healer, particularly of St Antony's fire, which is usually identified with genital herpes or syphilis. Picasso certainly knew about the various temptations to which St Antony was subjected by the devil disguised as a woman—a woman from whom the saint shrinks in fear and fascination. The tormented Casagemas springs to mind. Like Cézanne in his *Bathers*,[26] Picasso would draw upon these temptresses in *Les Demoiselles d'Avignon*; and again in 1909, when he envisages a major composition on the theme.

Joaquim Sunyer in Paris, *c.*1900. Jaume Sunyer collection.

* * *

Because he spoke very little French, Picasso kept as close as possible to his fellow expatriates. Some of these were old friends from Barcelona. Among his new friends was the Basque Francisco Iturrino, who would share an exhibition with him at Vollard's the following year; there was also an ambitious Catalan, Joaquim Sunyer Mirò. In Barcelona Picasso had barely known Sunyer, who seldom returned home after moving to Paris in 1894. For all his gifts as a painter, he was not very popular—more like a Spanish guitarist than a painter, someone complained, forever looking at himself in a mirror. He was a hard worker, dedicated to self-promotion. When he was not badgering the illustrators Steinlen and Willette to get him commissions, he was toadying celebrities who frequented the Chat Noir. His blandishments worked with Jehan Rictus,[27] who allowed Sunyer to illustrate his *Soliloques du Pauvre*, despite Steinlen's having already done so. And it must be admitted that Sunyer's plates are beautifully engraved—a consequence of his friendship with Delâtre, the greatest printer of his day. True, too, they foreshadow some of the melancholy spirit and themes of the Blue period, especially one of an old guitarist that Picasso would certainly have known. Sunyer's paintings of contemporary life, faintly Nabi in flavour, are far more expressive than similar works by Canals. If Picasso had not overshadowed him, Sunyer might have made a greater name for himself. Instead he returned to Catalonia and developed a chip-on-the-shoulder attitude towards his infinitely more gifted rival.

There would be a further cause for Sunyer's envy. Shortly after Fernande Olivier met Picasso in 1904, Sunyer picked her up in the street and started an affair with her. To his rage, she ultimately moved in with Picasso. In later years (mid-1930s) relations are said to have deteriorated further. Sabartès spread a story that he had caught Sunyer erasing his

Sunyer. *Guitarist.* Illustration for *Les Soliloques du Pauvre* by Jehan Rictus, 1897. Private collection.

Sunyer. *Woman at her Toilette*. Paris, c.1900. Pastel, pencil and wash on cardboard, 26.7×27.9cm, with Picasso's signature added. Museum of Fine Arts, Houston. John A. and Audrey Jones Beck Collection.

Picasso. *Pompeu Gener*. Barcelona, 1900. Pen and wash on paper, 8.4×7.8cm. Museu Picasso, Barcelona.

Casas. *Jaume Brossa*. c.1906. Charcoal and pastel on paper, 56.5×44cm. Museu d'Art Modern, Barcelona.

signature from a pastel of a nude washing herself and replacing it with an accomplished facsimile, 'Picasso'. On the strength of this story Sunyer has been assumed to be one of the many Picasso fakers (the envious Opisso was another suspect) operating out of Barcelona. However, Sabartès bore many grudges, including one against Sunyer. This story should therefore be treated as an invention.[28]

In addition to his fellow painters, Picasso was in contact with two Catalan intellectuals, Pompeu Gener, an old friend from Barcelona, and Jaume Brossa Roger, a new friend who had been living in exile since 1896. Both held themselves aloof from the less-committed members of the *bande Catalane*. They were ardent anarchists, ardent Nietzscheans, ardent devotees of new developments in the theatre. Gener, whose imposing appearance had inspired Casagemas's caricature of him as Velázquez's Count-Duke of Olivares, had given up scientific studies to become a drama critic and literary journalist—in Paris as well as Barcelona. Brossa, who had just completed an Ibsen-like play, *Els Sepulcres Blancs* (1900), was more of an activist: he had been exiled from Spain for distributing anti-military pamphlets in the wake of the anarchist bombing of the Corpus Christi procession in 1896. His anarchist exhortations in *L'Avenç* apparently led to the suppression of the paper. Over the years, however, Brossa's political ideas underwent a considerable change. Always a Nietzschean, he drifted more and more to the right. By 1903, if not before, Brossa had converted to the right-wing Mediterraneanism inspired by the Action Française.[29]

Thanks largely to Casagemas, Picasso had come round to Nietzsche, above all to his exalted view of the artist as '*superhombre*', genius, '*Yo el Rey*'. Some of Brossa's Nietzschean observations—'the wonderful image of the world that lies deep in the camera obscura of the ME [that is] compensation for disgust with life'[30]—could almost have been formulated by Picasso. Likewise Brossa's call for 'courageous anti-snobbery in art and life' and his concept of 'a negative spirit [joining] a positive spirit reconstructing and renewing lost force' might well have inspired Picasso's famous dictum that his works are 'a summary of destructions'.[31]

Casagemas, not Picasso, was the one who had been an anarchist sympathizer and friend of Brossa's; he and Gener would have brought Brossa and Picasso together in Paris. After Casagemas's death, there seems to have been no further contact between Brossa and Picasso until 1917, when the former attended a reception honouring the latter's return to Spain. If Picasso is to be seen as an anarchist,[32] we must be careful to understand the nature of his anarchy. It was an instinctive feeling that had its roots deep in his *alma española*. It even shows up in successive analyses of his handwriting.[33] And it will show up repeatedly in his work, not least in *Les Demoiselles d'Avignon*. But Picasso's anarchy did not, above all at this early period, reflect a political stance. He was adamant on this point. As Kahnweiler, who was sympathetic to radicalist views, maintained, the young Picasso was 'the most apolitical man I ever met'.[34]

When Picasso went to Paris in 1900, the *bande Catalane* included a number of anarchists. The fact that they were Utopian sympathizers rather than hard-core activists did not stop the French authorities from suspecting them, as they did virtually every young Spanish artist or writer, of subversive activity. According to Picasso, the police once threatened

Olivier Sainsère, c.1900. Wood engraving after a photograph. Bibliothèque Nationale, Paris.

him with an *enquête* on the grounds of his associations—an ordeal from which he was saved by his powerful patron Olivier Sainsère.[35] As a result, Picasso, who was terrified of the police—the French police especially—and of the threat of surveillance, would have been exceedingly wary of any anarchist involvement. It was one thing to sign a protest against the draft in a Catalan newspaper, as he and many of his friends did.[36] In the climate of terrorism prevailing at the time, it was quite another thing to risk being branded as a subversive alien. In art Picasso was a hero, less so in life. An obsessive concern with self-preservation was one of his most consistent characteristics. Given the colossal courage he devoted to his work, there was little left over for other causes, however noble. Had he been a politicized anarchist, he would surely have boasted of it in later years, when it would have been to his credit. He never did, not even to Roland Penrose, a lifelong anarchist, who would have had every reason to make the most of this affiliation in his biography, instead of taking the line that, so far as the young Picasso was concerned, 'politics . . . belonged to another sphere, and the language of politicians was as foreign to him as the speech of distant tribes.'[37] Nor for that matter did Picasso ever lay claim—even at his most *engagé* phase—to any political commitment prior to his espousal of the leftist cause at the time of the Spanish Civil War, beyond professing a lifelong sympathy with the downtrodden, the victims of war or tyranny or want.

* * *

On this trip to Paris, Picasso saw a lot of old friends from Barcelona—among them Casas, Utrillo and Pichot—who had hurried up to visit the Exposition Universelle before it closed. We know this from a couple of drawings that show Picasso and a group of cronies jubilantly leaving the exhibition arm in arm. How jubilant Picasso felt about his own contribution we can only guess. *Last Moments* had been hung much too high, and its tenebrism must have seemed turgid and immature compared with the Parisian sophistication of his latest work. And yet, if the preparatory sketches are any guide, the artist had reason to feel a certain pride: there must have been more reality and intensity to *Last Moments* than to the other exhibits in the Spanish pavilion. However, it was not in Picasso's nature to look back. His main concern on this trip was to establish a foothold in the Parisian art world and give himself a crash course in modern French painting so that he could come back and eventually settle in Paris. He gorged on the Exposition's huge official show of French art. This included a very strong 'modern' section: David, Delacroix, Ingres, Daumier, Corot, Courbet, Manet (*Le Déjeuner sur l'herbe*) and the impressionists. Picasso also spent a great deal of time at the Louvre and the Luxembourg, where nineteenth-century French painting, including the impressionists, was housed. At the same time he did the rounds of commercial galleries, above all the more progressive ones on the rue Laffitte—Durand-Ruel, Le Barc de Bouteville, Bernheim-Jeune and Vollard. As to what impressed him, the only record we have is the mirror of his work. There is no trace of the impressionists, nor of Cézanne, Seurat, Gauguin or the Nabis, in any of the paintings done on this first trip to Paris. Picasso seems to have been drawn to Degas, Toulouse-Lautrec and van Gogh,

Picasso. *Leaving the Exposition Universelle* (left to right: Odette, Picasso, Pichot, Utrillo, Casagemas, Germaine). Paris, 1900. Charcoal, coloured chalks and pencil on paper, 47.8×61 cm. Private collection.

but it is the influence of illustrators rather than *artistes-peintres* that pervades Picasso's first Parisian scenes: Steinlen above all, whom he had admired for at least two years, and whom he is said to have met—probably through Sunyer. His verismo subjects—those brutal proletarian embraces—are taken straight from Steinlen, as is the journalistic drama and no less journalistic compassion. But, unlike Steinlen (or Steinlen's great precursor, Daumier), Picasso is more interested in registering the throb of physical passion—he is never critical of lust—than in making a social comment. On the authority of Kahnweiler Picasso was also drawn to the work of another illustrator, Bottini.[38] Who, the reader may well ask, is Bottini?

This forgotten painter—dubbed 'the Montmartre Goya' and 'the Guys of our time' (Arsène Alexandre)—was almost certainly an acquaintance of Picasso's. The son of a Parisian barber, George Alfred Bottini was born in 1874. After studying under Cormon, he settled in a Montmartre garret and devoted the rest of his short life to portraying the prostitutes and inverts of Pigalle. That he was an admirer and friend of Toulouse-Lautrec and the self-styled 'Pornocrates' Félicien Rops comes as no surprise. Their unabashed approach to sexually explicit (in Rops's case, pornographic) subjects paved the way for Bottini's first exhibition (1897), *Bars et Maisons Closes*, which had a *succès de scandale* with such risqué subjects as *Lesbiennes*, *Insexués* and *Pierrreuses*. Bottini's best work glows with a fine, *fin-de-siècle* phosphorescence, but at its less than best, which is frequently, the effect is not so much pungent as precious. He, too, often deserves Jean Lorrain's comment: 'Inspired by Forain [he] paints like a Degas who draws badly.'[39] Nevertheless his whores in their livid makeup and huge hats, glowing incandescently against murky peacock-coloured backgrounds, left a perceptible shadow on Picasso's early Paris work, not least on the masterpiece of the period, the *Moulin de la Galette*. For all his unevenness, Bottini was known for 'mixing his materials like an alchemist'.[40] A favourite trick was to age his work by using poor-quality paper which he would discolour by ironing; when the gouache or watercolour was done, he would apply the iron once again to give the surface a shine—a variation on the *dibujo frito* technique that Nonell passed on to Picasso. This kinship can also be detected in the hard-faced, overdressed 'Diamond Lils' who dominate Picasso's work for the next year or so. Bottini's lithographs and woodcuts of absinthe drinkers and the like (1897–98) look ahead even further and predict, albeit feebly, the outcasts of the Blue period[41]—outcasts among whom Bottini himself deserved a place. All too soon, tertiary syphilis would destroy his physical and mental health and his fragile talent. After dinner one evening in 1907, he went mad and knifed his mother. Incarcerated in the Villejuif asylum, he died a few months later in a straitjacket.[42]

Steinlen. Illustration for *Le Regard vers l'amour inconnu* by Guy de Téramond on the cover of *Gil Blas,* December 7, 1900. Bibliothèque Nationale, Paris.

George Bottini. *At the Theatre.* 1902. Watercolour over pencil on paper, 41.7×28.7cm. Private collection.

* * *

After almost two months of intense and incessant work, Picasso and Casagemas returned to Barcelona. The main reason for going home, Picasso said, was the deterioration in Casagemas's state of mind. The sexually voracious Germaine made no secret of her frustration with this weird man who insisted on regarding her as his 'fiancée' but never

Picasso. *Spanish Dancer*. Málaga, 1900. Charcoal and pastel on paper pasted on cardboard, 35.7×20.7cm. Kröller-Müller Rijksmuseum, Otterlo.

consummated the relationship. For all the satisfaction to be obtained from this lover, she might as well go back to the arms of her husband, the mysterious Monsieur Florentin. And what a worry Casagemas was becoming. Once, when Germaine had taunted him, he had threatened suicide. Picasso, who had promised his family he would be home for Christmas, insisted that Casagemas accompany him. Pallarès was left behind in the rue Gabrielle studio, but he found the place too big; besides, he was afraid of the local apaches. And so he moved to 130*ter* Boulevard de Clichy, where Signac also had a studio. Picasso and Casagemas returned to Barcelona a day or two before Christmas and spent a week or so with their families. And then they took off for Málaga.

This trip to his birthplace, Picasso maintained, was intended to divert Casagemas and cure him of *chagrin d'amour*. Sabartès suggests another, more personal, motive: Picasso's 'need to come to terms with his Andalusian roots, to determine where he stood in relation to Málaga, Madrid and Barcelona.'[43] There was a practical reason for the visit: Picasso had recently turned nineteen and was liable for military service. This could be avoided by paying a fine of 1,200 pesetas. Who except rich Uncle Salvador could come up with this sum? To wheedle the money out of Uncle Salvador, Picasso would have been obliged to visit Málaga. However, he was much too proud and resentful to play up to the censorious doctor. Egged on, I suspect, by Casagemas, he could not resist the urge to behave outrageously.

The two young men arrived in Málaga on New Year's Day, 1901, wearing the same corduroy suits they had lived in for the last two months. Around Picasso's neck was a locket containing a stuffed beetle instead of the accustomed lock of a loved one's hair. Casagemas was drunk all the time and possibly on drugs. So scruffy did they look that the landlady of the inn, the Tres Naciones on Calle de Casas Quemadas, refused them a room. Fortunately Picasso's cousin, Antonio Padrón Ruiz, lived next door and vouched for them. The pious Dr Salvador was appalled by the appearance of the two *decadentes*—and how dare Pablo not wear mourning for the recently deceased Aunt Pepa? He threw his nephew's bohemian headgear into a dustbin and packed him off to a barber for a haircut and to a tailor for some suitable clothes.

Instead of mending his ways, Picasso fuelled his uncle's disapproval further by refusing to make a round of family visits. He and Casagemas hung around low bars, gypsy dives and whorehouses, including that of Lola la Chata, the brothel his father used to patronize. Inevitably very little painting was done; and nothing much has survived from this trip except a drawing of Murillo Carreras, who taught art at the Escuela, and some sketches of flamenco dancers, whorehouse interiors and local types. Casagemas did a few drawings of similar subjects in sepia or sanguine. However, their way of life was not conducive to work or, for that matter, rest. Far from distracting Casagemas, the constant visits to brothels must have increased his feelings of inadequacy: whether there was a showdown we do not know. All we do know is that after ten days or so Picasso's solicitude and patience gave out; he could no longer handle his friend's problems: not just his drunkenness—a failing Picasso very seldom shared—but his excessive dependence on him, his excessive demands on his precious energy. Picasso seems finally to have realized the ambivalence, the parasitic nature of Casagemas's feelings for him; realized that he must abandon his subservient friend and get away at all costs. He invoked Uncle Salvador's influence with a local shipping line and put his cracked-up friend on a boat for Barcelona. It was the last Picasso saw of Casagemas; it may also have been the last he saw of his birthplace. At the same time he finally dropped the use of the family name and signed his pictures 'P.R.Picasso' and eventually 'Picasso'. The next step was to give Madrid another try. And so he took a train to the capital.

Casagemas. *Old Couple*. Málaga, 1900. Pen and chalks on paper. Private collection.

-MADRID-
NOTAS D ARTE
POR FRANCISCO de A. Soler
Y-Pablo Ruiz Picasso-

12

Madrid 1901

Picasso. Cover of *Arte Joven,* no.3, Madrid, May 3, 1901. Museu Picasso, Barcelona.

Opposite: Picasso. *Madrid – Notas de Arte.* Advertisement for book Picasso planned with Francisco de Asís Soler. Madrid, 1901. Charcoal on paper. Private collection.

PICASSO'S DEPARTURE FOR MADRID was not as impulsive as it appeared to his family. There was a good reason for giving the capital he had so disliked a second chance. A seemingly prosperous young Catalan, Francisco de Asís Soler, who had formerly directed a *modernista* magazine called *Luz,* had suggested that he collaborate with him on a magazine, just as Utrillo and Casas had done on *Pèl & Ploma.* Soler would edit and Picasso illustrate a new periodical, to be called *Arte Joven.* This would be a cultural bridge between the capital and Catalonia. The two men must already have been acquainted. Before moving to Madrid, Soler had frequented Els Quatre Gats, and presumably discussed the project with Picasso the previous year in Barcelona.

Picasso's drawings of Soler reveal an elegant amateur; his articles in *Luz* and *Arte Joven* appear to confirm this. In fact he was a pretentious littérateur of little talent, who had disdained his native Catalan for the more classic Castilian. If he edited magazines, it was to get his Castilian effusions into print. Once again the Soler family came up with enough money to launch a new venture—not enough to sustain it. Their fortune, such as it was, came from an electric abdominal belt—advertised as a panacea for intestinal problems and impotence—which the older Soler had invented back in Barcelona and the younger was now promoting in Madrid. In the aftermath of Picasso's flight from Málaga, his abandonment of Casagemas, Soler's offer seemed a godsend. With luck *Arte Joven* could earn him some badly needed money, enhance his reputation as an illustrator, enable him to sample the cultural life of the capital, go back to talking and thinking in Castilian instead of Catalan, and provide a pretext for easing Casagemas out of his life. It would also, Picasso hoped, leave him enough time to fulfil the terms of the contract he had signed with Mañach.

When he arrived, around the middle of January, Picasso moved into a pension on the Calle Caballero de Gracia—'with fried eggs and all that'.[1] Soler must have recommended these lodgings, as they were on the same street as the electric-belt business. The petty rules and regulations of boarding-house life were not at all to Picasso's taste; and as soon as possible he found an attic apartment—'a great barn of a place'—at 28 Calle Zurbano, and on February 4 he signed a lease for a year, an indication that he meant to settle in Madrid. Calle Zurbano was a decent address, but the apartment was spartan: no heat except a brazier, no light except a candle stuck in a bottle, no furniture except a folding bed, a straw mattress, a pine table and a chair. But the attic was spacious enough to serve as an editorial office and storage area as well as a studio. Since their inaugural number was due to appear on March 11, the two editors had little more than two months in which to edit, print and distribute it. One of Picasso's first editorial acts was to write to Utrillo (probably towards the end of February). *Arte Joven* proposed 'to dedicate almost all the second issue to Rusiñol'; would Utrillo send him some of the plates of Rusiñol's garden paintings from *Pèl & Ploma*.[2] This project came to nothing beyond the publication of Rusiñol's story 'El Patio Azul', accompanied by a Picasso portrait.

Toledo (the Cuesta de San Justo) at the beginning of the century. Photo: Mas.

Hardly had he arrived than Picasso took off for Toledo (forty-eight miles away by train) and a neighbouring village, whose name he could not remember. Despite the imminent deadline, he decided to take another look at El Greco, whose work was easier to study in Toledo than anywhere else. What he saw took longer than usual to digest. More than a year would go by before he began to draw on his memories of the Toledo altarpieces, but once he started, he reverted to them again and again. He was also in search of subjects with which to illustrate episodes in Pío Baroja's picaresque novel, *Aventuras, inventos, y mixtificaciones de Silvestre Paradox*, which Soler had obtained for publication. The 'Orgía Macabre' section—a sacrilegious fantasy about the Pope being chased out of Rome and ending up disguised as an old beggar outside Toledo cathedral—was not the one that Picasso finally illustrated, but it inspired some marvellous drawings of sinister-looking ruffians in big Toledano hats and capes (the beggar-pope?). The most striking one was used for the cover of the first issue of *Arte Joven*. In the margin of one of these drawings a brothel is listed: 'Calle Grava—Casa d'amor'. This 'Casa d'amor' was presumably the setting for the many whorehouse sketches that date from this trip. The Toledano village he visited seems to have inspired some paintings of a church with a belfry, which hark back to Nonell; so do a couple of paintings of peasant gatherings.[3] Though probably executed from memory or notes back in Madrid, these Hispagnolist potboilers were done with Mañach's clients in mind. The dealer did not let Picasso forget that he was expected to provide a constant supply of saleable paintings in exchange for his monthly remittance.

In Madrid, Picasso threw himself into the production of the magazine. But this new responsibility bored him. If he had indeed gone to Madrid 'in further quest of himself',[4] he must have realized that he was wasting his time: doing the wrong job in the wrong place. What had induced him to identify with a magazine whose avowed aim was to promote *modernisme*? After his trip to Paris, *modernisme* must have seemed irredeemably provincial. It had had its day. And why waste time doing illustrations for an amateurish magazine when he should have been concentrating on drawing and painting for the Paris exhibition that Mañach had promised him? And why indeed stay on in Madrid: a city that he disliked, a city that he found less geared to modern art than Barcelona? Maybe he should go back to being a Catalan, or take the daunting step of settling in Paris.[5] Sabartès, who knew Picasso as well as anybody at the time, sees the seemingly assured young prodigy a prey to all kinds of confusions and doubts, despite the ferocity of his ego.

* * *

Above: Picasso. *Spanish Woman.* Toledo or Madrid, 1901. Charcoal and crayon on sketchbook page, 16×24cm. Marina Picasso collection.

Picasso. *Old Man with Toledano Hat.* Toledo, 1901. Charcoal and crayon on sketchbook page, 16×24cm. Marina Picasso collection.

Picasso. *Couple in a Garden.* Madrid, 1901. Charcoal and watercolour on paper, 31.8× 26.7cm. Private collection.

Picasso's confusion was compounded and in the long run resolved by terrible if not altogether unexpected news from 'Cinto' Reventós: on February 17, Casagemas had committed suicide in Paris. After being shipped out of Málaga, Casagemas had returned to his family in Barcelona, where he had spent the next month or so pining for Germaine. At least twice a day he had written her passionate love letters begging her to marry him. Finally, around the middle of the month, both Germaine and Pallarès had received identical postcards, announcing Casagemas's imminent arrival in Paris. Would they meet him at the Gare d'Orsay? While waiting for the train, Germaine complained to Pallarès about her admirer's desperate letters and sexual problems. Her husband served her needs well enough, she said. 'I'm going to tell Carles that if he likes we can still be good friends, but nothing else.'

Finally the train drew in. Casagemas was elegantly dressed in a suit of olive-coloured velvet. No, they could not live together, announced Germaine, who had taken the precaution of moving back with her complaisant husband. Casagemas agreed to stay with Pallarès, who had by now rented a smaller, safer apartment (130*ter* Boulevard de Clichy). The only problem was that the Catalan sculptor Manolo Hugué (always known as Manolo)—soon to become one of Picasso's closest friends—had just arrived in Paris in order to evade military service and had cadged a bed off Pallarès. And so the three of them would be uncomfortably squashed. The next few days were very tense. On the sixteenth, Germaine must have broken the news to Casagemas that she would never marry him, for on the morning of Sunday the seventeenth, Casagemas told Pallarès that he intended to return home forthwith. To celebrate his departure he invited everyone—Germaine, Odette, Pallarès, Manolo, Riera, the Catalan collector, who had arrived from Barcelona that very morning, and Pujulà i Vallès (the critic who had written so favourably about Picasso's Quatre Gats show)[6]—to a farewell dinner. He chose a neighbouring restaurant called L'Hippodrome, which Picasso painted some months later.[7] *Pneumatiques* were sent summoning the girls. Meanwhile the four male guests departed to spend the day at the Louvre, leaving Casagemas behind: he had letters to write, he said—suicide notes.

Casagemas. *Germaine at a Café*. Paris, 1900. Pen and wash on paper. Private collection.

That evening, the seven friends had a good dinner, washed down by several bottles of wine. Casagemas, who had hitherto seemed very depressed, was ominously elated. Germaine guessed that something was up, but became seriously worried only when, around nine o'clock, Casagemas stood up to make a speech—in French, presumably in deference to Odette. As he did so, Germaine noticed that the pockets of his elegant velvet suit bulged with letters and a gun. According to the police report, Casagemas handed the letters to Germaine, asking her to read them. When she saw that the top one was addressed to the chief of police and simultaneously realized that Casagemas, who was on her immediate left, was reaching in his pocket for the revolver, she dived to the floor, crawled under the table and took shelter behind Pallarès, who was sitting opposite. Seeing a revolver pointed at him, Pallarès barely had time to duck and deflect the barrel before Casagemas yelled at Germaine, '*Voilà pour toi!*' and fired. Thanks to Pallarès's intervention, the bullet missed, but the explosion knocked Germaine to the ground. Concluding that he had killed the woman he loved, Casagemas put the gun to his head, and crying out '*Et voilà pour moi!*,' shot himself in the right temple. Germaine got to her feet and, weeping hysterically, embraced Pallarès, begging forgiveness for having used him as a shield. Manolo, who was notoriously allergic to firearms (also to the truth), claimed that he had grabbed the much taller Casagemas from the back and rammed his head forcefully against his shoulder, which triggered the second shot. Casagemas had then fallen dead in Manolo's arms; 'his face like a crushed strawberry was all blood. I lost consciousness. . . .'[8]

The moment shots rang out, the restaurant emptied, but the clients were soon back with the police. The French have a traditionally tolerant view of *crime passionel*, which this evidently was, and the first concern of the police was to rush Casagemas, who was still alive, to Dajou's pharmacy nearby for first aid; then to the Hôpital Bichot, where he died shortly afterward (11:30 P.M.). Meanwhile Germaine and Odette took Pallarès to the same or another pharmacy for treatment of an eye which had been temporarily blinded by the blast, and then back to Odette's house (11 rue Chappe), where they settled him into an enormous bed.

Riera and Pujulà i Vallès must have disappeared in the mêlée, as their names are missing from the official account.[9] Manolo stayed around and gave a statement to the police. He took advantage of the situation and made Germaine his mistress. Later in the year she would have an affair with Picasso, then a more permanent one with Ramon Pichot, whom she would ultimately marry.

The morning after Casagemas's suicide, Manolo says, he 'went to meet Jaume Brossa, whom Torres Fuster [another Catalan painter] had contacted to arrange Casagemas's affairs. . . . Because the family was supposed to take care of the body, Brossa had terrible problems with the authorities. . . . They didn't know what to do and Brossa wanted to stall so that he could wait for the family to arrive and arrange for the corpse to be transported to Barcelona. Finally, the family came and took care of everything.'[10] Manolo may be correct about problems with the authorities but he is in error about the other details. Brossa arranged for the funeral to take place at the Cimetière Montmartre a few days later. A memorial service was subsequently held at Santa Madrona in Barcelona. At Els Quatre Gats, where he had been especially popular, there was much grief. Manolo's claim that Casagemas's mother dropped dead on hearing of her beloved son's suicide is nonsense.[11] According to Vidal Ventosa, she was told he had died of natural causes.[12]

Picasso. *Head of Casagemas*. Published in *Catalunya Artística*, February 28, 1901. Museu Picasso, Barcelona.

Picasso did not go to Barcelona for the memorial service, but he contributed a drawing of Casagemas to Marquina's obituary in *Catalunya Artística* (February 28). In this likeness of Casagemas and others executed over the next two years there is an eerie development: hitherto Picasso had usually portrayed Casagemas's left profile; henceforth he always portrayed the right profile, the side through which he shot himself. Whether or not Picasso bore any blame for abandoning his friend, the guilt he felt towards Casagemas, like the guilt he felt towards his dead sister and (in fantasy at any rate) towards the father he wanted to kill, would provide his art with just the catharsis it required. In the course of time this inspirational guilt would call for many more sacrifices.

* * *

Picasso. *Prostitute in a Doorway.* Published in *Arte Joven,* preliminary number, March 10, 1901. Museu Picasso, Barcelona.

Picasso. *Head of Cornuti* and study for *The Dressing Room.* Madrid, 1901. Black conté crayon on paper, 14×22cm. The Baltimore Museum of Art, Bequest of Philip B. Perlman.

Casagemas's suicide literally coloured Picasso's work. 'It was thinking about Casagemas's death that started me painting in blue,' Picasso told Daix,[13] but he did not start doing so for another six months. For the time being his work remains surprisingly festive. Apart from Nonellish drawings of low life for *Arte Joven*—like the one of a harlot crouched in a doorway numbered 69—Madrid manifests itself mostly in a series of bravura paintings and pastels. These are oddly Parisian in feeling: hard-faced cocottes in crinolines so bouffant that the wearer takes up an entire sofa. A boudoir or a box or dressing room at the theatre provide appropriate settings. The degenerate-looking fop in white tie, tail coat and kid gloves who is ogling one of these girls was identified by Vidal Ventosa as Alfonso XIII (later a great supporter of Diaghilev and an admirer of Picasso's décors). Since the monarch would have been fifteen years old at the time, this is out of the question.

The largest and most ambitious of these courtesans is the *Lady in Blue*, which portrays a hieratic dominatrix, heavily made up like the *Moulin de la Galette* women, dressed in a late nineteenth-century version of an eighteenth-century costume: an enormous hat, an enormous butterfly bow and an enormous white crinoline embroidered in silver swags. A bizarre pastiche of Velázquez and Goya (e.g. the state portrait of Queen María Luisa in the Prado), Aubrey Beardsley and Bottini, with vestiges of *modernisme* thrown in. Though he no longer attached much importance to large juried exhibitions, Picasso submitted this set piece to Madrid's Exposición General de Bellas Artes. It was accepted and figured as number 963 in the catalogue. In the same exhibition Mir's showy Mallorca landscape *Red Mountains* and Rusiñol's group of romantic garden scenes attracted considerable attention; not, however, Picasso's dazzling *Lady in Blue.* Disappointment might explain why he abandoned this hetaera, so might lack of money for shipping or other costs. Despite his acute need of large canvases, he never claimed this work back from the exhibition, and it ended up in Madrid's Museo de Arte Contemporáneo by default.

The Madrid courtesan pictures are an exception to the general rule that Picasso's style and subject matter reflect his way of life. There was not much of a gilded demimonde in Madrid (people went to Paris for that), but even if there had been, Picasso would not have had access to it. He drew partly on fantasy, partly on the vision of other artists (e.g., Lautrec, Steinlen and Bottini) and partly on his memories of *la vie parisienne*—not least the magazine of that name that celebrated the charms of the *grandes cocottes.* The impact of Goya is also apparent, above all in the more grotesque paintings: the *Old Harlot* and the *Dwarf Dancer.* No matter whether these works were done in Madrid or Barcelona or Paris, or, as I believe, started in Madrid and finished in Paris (spring–early summer 1901), they are the first manifestations of the combination of compassion and grotesquerie, and the notion of conventional beauty as a sham that Picasso derived from Goya. How often he would echo Goya's dictum 'Ugliness is beautiful'.

In his early days '*le petit Goya*' was wary of falling under the spell of '*le grand Goya*'.[14] However, as the *Lady in Blue* and other viragos in huge crinolines reveal, Picasso could not entirely escape the looming shadow of this Saturn who had a dangerous habit of devouring his artistic progeny. Later he would discover how to profit from Goya without

Picasso. *The Dressing Room*. Madrid, 1901. Pastel on paper, 32×40 cm. Private collection.

Picasso. *Lady in Blue*. Madrid, 1901. Oil on canvas, 133.5×101 cm. Museo Español de Arte Contemporáneo, Madrid.

Goya. *Pygmalion and Galatea.* 1815–20. Brush and sepia wash on paper, 20.5×14.1 cm. The J. Paul Getty Museum, Malibu.

Above: Picasso. *Dwarf Dancer.* Madrid, 1901. Oil on canvas, 102×60 cm. Museu Picasso, Barcelona.

Left: Picasso. *Old Harlot.* Madrid, 1901. Oil on cardboard, 67.4×52 cm. Philadelphia Museum of Art, Louise and Walter Arensberg Collection.

appearing to do so. He learned how farce and tragedy can be played off against each other to subversive effect; how pictorial puns, especially erotic and scatalogical ones, can endow an image with a different set of meanings and connotations;[15] and how certain symbols—keys and locks, for instance—can be used as a secret language that can be interpreted sexually, metaphysically or, in the case of Goya, politically.[16] The puns on sculptor's utensils as sexual organs in Goya's *Pygmalion and Galatea* anticipate similar puns in Picasso's late paintings, where an artist 'has' a model with his brush. And in his great mural for the Palais de l'Unesco in 1958—the vast and vastly underrated *Fall of Icarus*—there is an unmistakable quotation from Goya: Icarus is a pun on the flying sleepwalker in Goya's *Capricho* no. 61, *'Volaverunt'*. It is only when Picasso sets out to paint war that he displays a certain wary ambivalence towards Goya. In *Guernica* he contrives to keep a safe distance between his and his great predecessor's visions of war-torn Spain. But in his *Massacre in Korea* (1951) he makes the mistake of trying to ginger up a trite image with magic fire from Goya's *Third of May*. In his later prints Picasso finally comes to terms with Goya and institutes a wonderfully assured and spirited dialogue with him across the darkness of the centuries. And the black, death-haunted paintings that the aged and increasingly deaf Picasso shut himself away at Notre-Dame-de-Vie to paint are a fitting response to the black, death-haunted paintings that the aged and almost totally deaf Goya came up with in his no less idyllic retreat, the Quinta del Sordo.

Picasso. *Self-Portrait*. Madrid, 1901. Charcoal on paper, 46×31 cm. Private collection.

In old age Picasso would admit to being very conscious of old masters breathing down his neck. Far from being bothered by this, he was so secure in his genius that he conjured master after master into the heart of his work and had his way with them. However, as a nineteen-year-old in Madrid—albeit a supremely gifted one—Picasso must have been daunted by the sheer weight not just of Goya but of Velázquez and the other masters of Spain's Golden Age that he saw in the Prado. If he left Madrid sooner than he originally intended, it was partly, I suspect, because he felt in danger of being overwhelmed. The splendours of Spain's past compounded the miseries of Spain's present. In order to fulfil himself as a modern painter he had to get out of this city without hope.

There were other reasons for resenting the capital—not least the cold that chilled Picasso's Andalusian bones just as it had three winters earlier. Self-portraits show us a pale skinny waif wrapped in an overcoat, warming his hands against the miserable weather. Even worse was the chill from which the warmth of Els Quatre Gats had hitherto shielded him: the chill of bourgeois disdain. He found the Madrileños glacial. They felt about Catalans the way Catalans felt about Andalusians. The young writers who were associated with *Arte Joven*—Unamuno, Pío Baroja and his brother, Ricardo (an indifferent painter), the French poet Cornuti and the sculptor-poet Alberto Lozano—were welcoming, but the casual camaraderie of Els Quatre Gats was missing. None of them became long-term friends.

Picasso. *Alberto Lozano*. Madrid, 1901. Crayon on paper, 21.3×12.5 cm. Private collection.

Picasso expresses his feelings about Madrileño snobbery in a bitter drawing of a suave, top-hatted patron fastidiously pulling on his gloves while a shaggy, pipe-smoking artist looks on quizzically—evidently there has been no sale and no rapport. Another drawing of a shabby clown in undershirt and braces (an illustration to one of Soler's *Crónicas*) makes

Picasso. *Clown.* Published in *Arte Joven,* preliminary number, March 10, 1901. Museu Picasso, Barcelona.

Picasso. *Soler in a Frock Coat.* Published in *Arte Joven,* no.4, June 1, 1901. Museu Picasso, Barcelona.

a similar point: it attacks bad actors and the like who dress up in frock coats and top hats and are interested only in appearances. Soler wanted to suggest that the editors of *Arte Joven* were more like poor clowns who wanted 'to sweep away pretension and hypocrisy.' Picasso portrays the poor clown in his own image, but characteristically gives the lie to Soler's protestations by depicting him in another drawing as a top-hatted, frock-coated, cane-carrying man-about-town—everything Soler professed to despise.

Arte Joven also reflected the nihilism of the '*Noventayochistas*' (the 'Generation of 1898')—the literary movement that a group of Madrileño writers had ironically named in 'honour' of the year in which the last vestiges of the Spanish empire had been lost. Defeat in the Cuban War had devastated Spain morally and economically, as well as politically, and it had caused a violent reaction against the bigotry and backwardness—the '*retraso*'—that afflicted the rickety kingdom. The 'Generation of '98' capitalized on this mood of demoralization and despair (much as the German dadaists would, after an even more disastrous defeat two decades later). Hence the mixture of mockery and tragedy, irony and idealism that characterizes their writing—particularly that of Pío Baroja, the principal novelist of the movement.[17] Hence, too, their fascination with anarchism. However, to quote the hero of Baroja's anarchistic novel (*Red Dawn*): 'Anarchism! Literature! Manuel felt that there was a certain affinity between these things, but he could not say what it was.'[18]

Like most other progressive magazines of the day, *Arte Joven* published some uncompromisingly anarchist articles, but it was no more or less committed to this or any other political cause than the editors were. The contributions were eclectic, but in the light of future developments, one contribution to the first issue in particular bears the unmistakable stamp of Picasso's approval: Nicolas María López's 'La Psicologia de la guitarra'. López describes a woman and a guitar in terms of each other. 'Its pegbox, the head, is like a woman's . . . its neck rectilinear as the Venus de Milo's. The box has the elegant curve of shoulders, the sensuousness of hips.' Like a woman, the guitar prostitutes itself, falls into the wrong hands, accompanies lewd songs at an orgy, becomes intoxicated. Like a woman, the guitar is the passive instrument on which a man plays. Like a woman, a guitar makes a show of rebellion and then 'submits like a slave'. This misogynistic story stayed in Picasso's mind; it would be mirrored in the anthropomorphic still lifes with guitars and mandolines that he painted twenty-five or thirty years later, especially the ones in which he conceals the presence of a mistress from his wife by encoding her as an object or cipher.

For all the trouble that Picasso and Soler lavished on *Arte Joven*, it was too sophisticated and precious to be a success. Sad, because the idea of reconciling Madrid's 'Generation of '98', which was primarily literary, with Barcelona's *modernisme*, which was artistic as well as literary, was not a bad one. (Twenty years later Salvador Dalí also tried, and failed, to build a similar bridge between the avant garde of these two cities with the handsome art magazine he edited in Sitges, *L'Amic de les Arts.*)

The main trouble was that *Arte Joven* was underfinanced and understaffed. Besides Picasso and Soler there was only Camilo Bargiela to help out in Madrid and Jacint Reventós in Barcelona. Advertisements failed to materialize, except ones for Soler's 'Cintura Eléctrica', Els Quatre Gats (both probably gratis) and a Madrid publisher's list of anarchist literature. Picasso even appealed to Uncle Salvador for financial help—failing that, a subscription—but naively or provocatively (one can never be sure with Picasso), he sent him a copy of the preliminary issue. A barrage of abuse was the only reply: 'What are you thinking of? What's the world coming to? Who do you take me for? This is not what we expected of you. What an idea! And what friends! Just keep going the way you're going now and you will see. . . .'[19] Responses such as this explain the editorial in a subsequent issue announcing that 'the gilded youth of Madrid and the illustrious ladies of the aristocracy do not like *Arte Joven*! This pleases us greatly.'

Arte Joven was shocking only to the extent that it was anti-Establishment, anti-Catholic and, as its name signified, pro-youth. To demonstrate his simplistic concept of 'the young of all ages', Soler thought up an absurd pantheon of the 'eternally young', including 'Virgil, Homer, Dante, Goethe, Velázquez, Ribera, El Greco, Mozart, Beethoven, Wagner'. The format of the magazine was based on *Pèl & Ploma*, except that its illustrations were all in black and white instead of colour.

Ricardo Baroja. *José Martínez Ruiz (Azorín)*. Published in *Arte Joven*, no.4, June 1, 1901. Museu Picasso, Barcelona.

Two further contributions to *Arte Joven* manifest the morbid stigma of Picasso's taste of the period. One is a short story, 'The Last Sensation', by Soler (published in the third issue, May 3, 1901), that describes the mental processes of a suicide. In drawing heavily on Picasso's knowledge of the Casagemas case, it constitutes a memorial to him. The other is the story (originally written in Catalan) that Picasso had been promised by his friend Rusiñol. 'El Patio Azul' reads a bit like a Blue period painting. Despite overtones of Maeterlinck, the story evidently derives from Oscar Wilde: it concerns the metamorphic power of art over life—a concept with which Picasso had no problem in identifying. Rusiñol relates how an artist finds his portrait of a beautiful woman fading away just as the flowers in her blue patio are fading away. As she dies, her beauty and the floral beauty of her patio merge in the blueness of the painting. So much for the symbolism: now for the irony. After her death, the lady's heirs want to buy the painting from the artist, not for its magical qualities or memories but to impress prospective buyers of the house. In the end the heirs ask the artist to paint the lady out of the blue patio. The languorous, hallucinatory mood is characteristically *fin-de-siècle*, and hints at the morphine addiction from which Rusiñol had nearly died a few months earlier.

Some of the most interesting contributions to *Arte Joven* were made by Azorín (José Martínez Ruiz), a lively essayist, remembered as much for his evocations of the Castilian countryside as for his polemical writings. In the April 15 issue he published 'La Vida', an anarchist tract that advocates boycotting elections and abolishing the law. Art should be the key to life, Azorín wrote, and the world one great bohemia. Azorín's Utopianism would have appealed to Picasso; so would his nihilistic stories—for instance, the one called 'The Emotion of Nothingness', about the funeral of a young girl, whose delicacy is contrasted with her black grave with its 'decayed boards and shreds of clothing and blackened bones'—shades of *Last Moments* and Conchita's funeral.[20]

Of the *Arte Joven* writers, Pío Baroja is the one with whom Picasso seems to have had the most ambivalent relationship. In 1900 this morbidly truculent and retiring Basque, who would eventually become the foremost Spanish novelist of his day, had abandoned being a country doctor to run a bakery belonging to his brother (likewise a novelist as well as a painter). As he baked away in a Madrid slum, Baroja came to identify with the poorest of the poor, and to write about them. His experience of low life inspired his remorselessly realistic trilogy, *The Struggle for Life* (1904), which is written in short, sharply focused scenes of film-like immediacy. The third volume of this trilogy depicts the vicissitudes of a group of anarchists to whose ideas Baroja is sympathetic, although he never actually became an anarchist. For all his sympathies and antipathies (he was a fervent racist), the novelist refrained from any political commitment ('except for a few months in 1910, when I belonged to the Republican party'[21]) until 1937. At this ominous moment he published an article in the Buenos Aires *Nación*, condemning the Spanish Republic and declaring that although he had always been 'a man of liberal tendencies who believes that everything of value' emanates from the masses, he put his hopes for the future in a fascist dictatorship—'the lesser of two evils'.[22]

Picasso. *Pío Baroja*. Published in *Arte Joven*, no.4, June 1, 1901. Museu Picasso, Barcelona.

This pro-fascist stance could well explain why Picasso eventually turned against Baroja. For he had originally warmed to the black humour and anti-clericalism of his novel *Silvestre Paradox*. The drawings he did for the 'Orgía Macabre' section catch the dark nastiness of Baroja's vision to perfection. Two or three years later, there are even more striking parallels between them: Baroja also went through what might be described as a Blue period. He focuses on the same victims of society as Picasso, though from a very different angle. His brutal realism takes no account of art; Picasso's symbolism is highly aesthetic. In *Weeds*, the second volume of *The Struggle for Life*, there is even a character, Alejo, who sculpts seemingly Blue period groups: 'aged hags huddled together with arms . . . that reached almost to their ankles: men that looked like vultures.'[23] Baroja despises Alejo: he cares little for resemblance and is therefore no 'master of his art'. Yet another possible reason for Picasso's dislike of the novelist is the description of himself in Baroja's *Memorias* (written fifty years later and, in Picasso's view, far from reliable) as 'a violent little friend of mystification and hyperbole' who had more 'literary talent' (he presumably means literary discrimination) than his contemporaries.[24] Was Baroja being wise after the event, or had he spotted a quality—Picasso's instinctive literary judgement—that is usually thought of as a later manifestation, one that was evoked by French, not Spanish, writers?

In old age, Picasso waxed 'tenderly nostalgic' about *Arte Joven*.[25] The contributors he specifically recalled were not the stars like Baroja and Unamuno, nor the anarchists, but the lesser figures: Pedro Barrantes (the author of 'Angeles Sánchez Plaza', an ode to a blind girl); Camilo Bargiela (the editorial assistant who wrote occasional essays); Alberto Lozano (the scarecrow-like sculptor and mystic poet, whose ugliness endeared him to Picasso); and Enrique (*sic*) Cornuti, who did not actually write for *Arte Joven*, because he 'was French from Béziers and spoke awful Spanish. But he was the one who taught all those people in Madrid what they needed to know about French poetry and a lot of other things besides. He was a real nut. He went to a cemetery with me one night—one of those mad stunts we indulged in during those days—and he proceeded

Picasso. *Contributors to 'Arte Joven'* (left to right: Unidentified man, Cornuti, Soler, Picasso, Lozano). Madrid, 1901. Crayon on paper, 24×31.7 cm. Private collection. Published in *Arte Joven*, no.2, April 15, 1901.

to spout reams of poetry at the tombstones.'[26] Cornuti, a hanger-on of Verlaine, reappears in Paris: the epitome of a *poète maudit*, as Picasso would record in an eerie Blue period portrait (see illustration, p. 259).

The memories of *Arte Joven* days recorded by Baroja's painter brother Ricardo tell us all too little. The group apparently met at the Café de Madrid or Horchatería de Candelas to drink *horchata* (a summer drink made from an almond-flavoured root). 'Picasso would observe our group and then later from memory draw the fantastic silhouettes of Cornuti, Urbano and Camilo Bargiela, illuminated by the wavering light of a street-lamp. He was a boy whose eyes twinkled and in front of them a lock of hair constantly danced.'[27] These portraits do not seem to have survived. A pity, because little information about this Madrid period has come to light. However, passages in the brother's novels evoke the marginal life that Picasso would have led and the disillusioned bohemian friends he would have made: young men who throng bowling alleys, music halls and fritter shops, even in a Cinecromovideograph,[28] talking, talking, talking, always out of work and out of money. It is an all-male world; the girls, whether good or bad, whores or seamstresses, are ciphers. The more enterprising anarchists go in for bombings and on occasion blow themselves up, saving women and children from the consequences of their handiwork. In the background there is sometimes a public execution and an organ-grinder playing a tango.

Picasso. *Madrid Café*. Madrid, 1901. Charcoal on paper, 30×42 cm. Private collection. Published in *Arte Joven*, preliminary number, March 10, 1901, as one of the illustrations due to appear in *Madrid—Notas de Arte*.

Picasso's striking advertisement for Soler and himself in the first number of *Arte Joven* had announced another publication, to be called *Madrid —Notas de Arte*, but nothing came of this. On the contrary, far from embarking on a new project, Soler was obliged to close down *Arte Joven* after only five issues for lack of a following as well as of funds (the last issue was dated June 1, 1901).[29] Soler did not give up on his literary career; his next job was editor-in-chief of *La Música Ilustrada*, and he continued to write: a collection of short stories, which came out in 1901, and some dramatic sketches. He died suddenly in August 1903, while on holiday in Tenerife.

Even if *Arte Joven* had kept going, it is unlikely that Picasso would have stayed on in Madrid, as he had originally planned. Apart from his disenchantment with the city and the way things had turned out, he was coming under pressure from Mañach. The dealer was fed up with sending a monthly remittance and receiving little or nothing in return, especially as he had succeeded in persuading Vollard—the most enterprising young dealer in Paris—to put on an exhibition of Picasso's work early that summer. Faced with Mañach's recriminations, Picasso decided to take his work to Paris in person rather than ship it: 'too complicated to . . . devote himself to "export" when all his time was taken up with "production",' Sabartès said.[30] Another reason for leaving Madrid was that Picasso had been invited—through the good offices of Utrillo—to share a show with Casas at the Sala Parés, the latter's gallery in Barcelona, at the beginning of June. Utrillo was not entirely disinterested. He had devised the show as a promotion for the newly revamped *Pèl & Ploma*; it may also have been a ploy to discourage the wunderkind's defection from Els Quatre Gats. By granting Picasso parity with the local *chef d'école*, Utrillo may have hoped to tempt his 'petit Goya' to settle once more in Barcelona and succeed Casas as *'el Rey'*.

Picasso. *Bullfight*. Barcelona, 1901. Oil on canvas, 46×47.8cm. Private collection.

The ploy, if such it was, failed. After abandoning the Madrid apartment he had leased for a year, Picasso returned to Barcelona early in May. But he did not even wait for the exhibition at the Sala Parés to open on May 15; he left instead for Paris, to prepare for the show at Vollard's that was scheduled for June 24. There was time for only a week or two in Barcelona. After shutting himself away for a few days' rest in the family apartment, he returned to his old haunts and his old friends. They found him much changed. Two months in Paris, followed by four months in Madrid, had transformed Picasso into a self-assured man of the world. 'We listened to him open-mouthed,' says Sabartès, 'but his stay was so brief that we didn't have time to grasp what he was telling us; we plied him with questions and had hardly begun to realize that he was among us when he was gone.'[31] Sabartès fails to add that Picasso found time to paint a prodigious number of canvases during this two-week visit—canvases that he hoped would attract French buyers. Last time he had gone to Paris, his bullfight scenes had been the first to sell; and so he did some corridas—heavily encrusted paintings as opposed to pastels—and not all of them set in the Barcelona bullring. At least one is based on sketches he had made of a village bullfight near Toledo. There were also cabaret scenes, a group of surprisingly Monet-like seascapes (the artist probably made a trip along the Catalan coast with Pichot), a portrait of his sister and a Mother and Child in a landscape that seems to derive from the Flemish Madonnas he had seen in the Prado. An eclectic group, considering the paintings were started, if not entirely finished, in less than two weeks. The thick impasto is a new development: partly the consequence of recycling old canvases.

No catalogue was prepared for the Sala Parés show, and no checklist has survived, so we have to guess at the contents, which were apparently limited to pastels and drawings. Since Picasso was always eager to exhibit his latest work, the exhibition would have included some of the courtesans in crinolines, one or two portraits and cabaret scenes, and a few of the vignettes of low life that he had done in Toledo and Madrid for *Arte Joven*. As for Casas, he exhibited a portrait of Picasso—a further honour—with the skyline of the Butte de Montmartre in the background. The setting indicates either that the drawing had been executed the previous year, when he and Picasso were both in Paris, or that Casas preferred to visualize his redoubtable rival having a success away from Barcelona. Casas was seen at less than his best: his contribution consisted mainly of the facile drawings he had churned out to promote the new *Pèl & Ploma*. Each new subscriber for a year had been promised one of these, 'assigned by lottery to avoid the embarrassment of choosing'. This show spells the end of Casas as a *modernista*. Henceforth he would devote himself to society portraits, as did Carolus Duran's other famous student, John Singer Sargent, then at the height of his fame. But Casas's likenesses of mid-western matrons never achieve Sargent's rich satin gleam.

Picasso. *Rocky Shore*. Barcelona, 1901. Oil on panel, 30×20cm. Jan Krugier Gallery, New York.

The story that Picasso refused to attend the opening of the Sala Parés show in a fit of pique brought on by Utrillo's inclusion of Casas cannot be substantiated.[32] He may well have been disappointed at finding himself involved in a promotional stunt for *Pèl & Ploma*. If, on his side, Utrillo was upset at Picasso's leaving Barcelona on the very eve of the vernissage (around May 31), he put a good face on it. As a fervent Francophile, he was hardly in a position to criticize anyone for choosing to pursue a career in Paris rather than in Barcelona. That he bore no grudge is confirmed by the very favourable review of the show that he wrote in the June issue of *Pèl & Ploma* under his pen name, 'Pincell'. The article is valedictory in tone. It conjures up an artist 'who speaks Castilian with a Barcelona accent (as was noted in the only issue of the Madrid magazine, *Mercurio*)',[33] an artist who was saved from 'sun-drenched Málaga [by] his move to Barcelona', only to be dazzled by the glamour of the Parisian art scene. Just when Picasso was beginning to enjoy success, Utrillo sees him abandoning Paris for the south of Spain, to judge how his memories measured up to his new ideas; and then moving on to Madrid, where, Utrillo says mysteriously, Picasso 'experienced what happens to many artists sooner or later, [but] Paris with its bad reputation and feverish lifestyle seduced him once again.' Utrillo ends by consigning Picasso to 'that centre where all the arts bloom more profusely'. He attributes his nickname for him, 'le petit Goya', to 'French friends', and concludes by hoping that Picasso, not yet twenty, will live up to his bohemian allure: with his big *pavero* (turkey-breeder's hat) that had got so faded in the Montmartre rain, his notoriously avant-garde scarves, not to speak of his *mirada fuerte* eyes. 'We trust that his outward appearance will be misleading; in our hearts we know we will turn out to be right.'[34]

Casas. *Picasso in Montmartre.* 1901. Charcoal and conté crayon with pastel on paper, 69×44.5cm. Museu d'Art Modern, Barcelona. Published in *Pèl & Ploma,* June 1901.

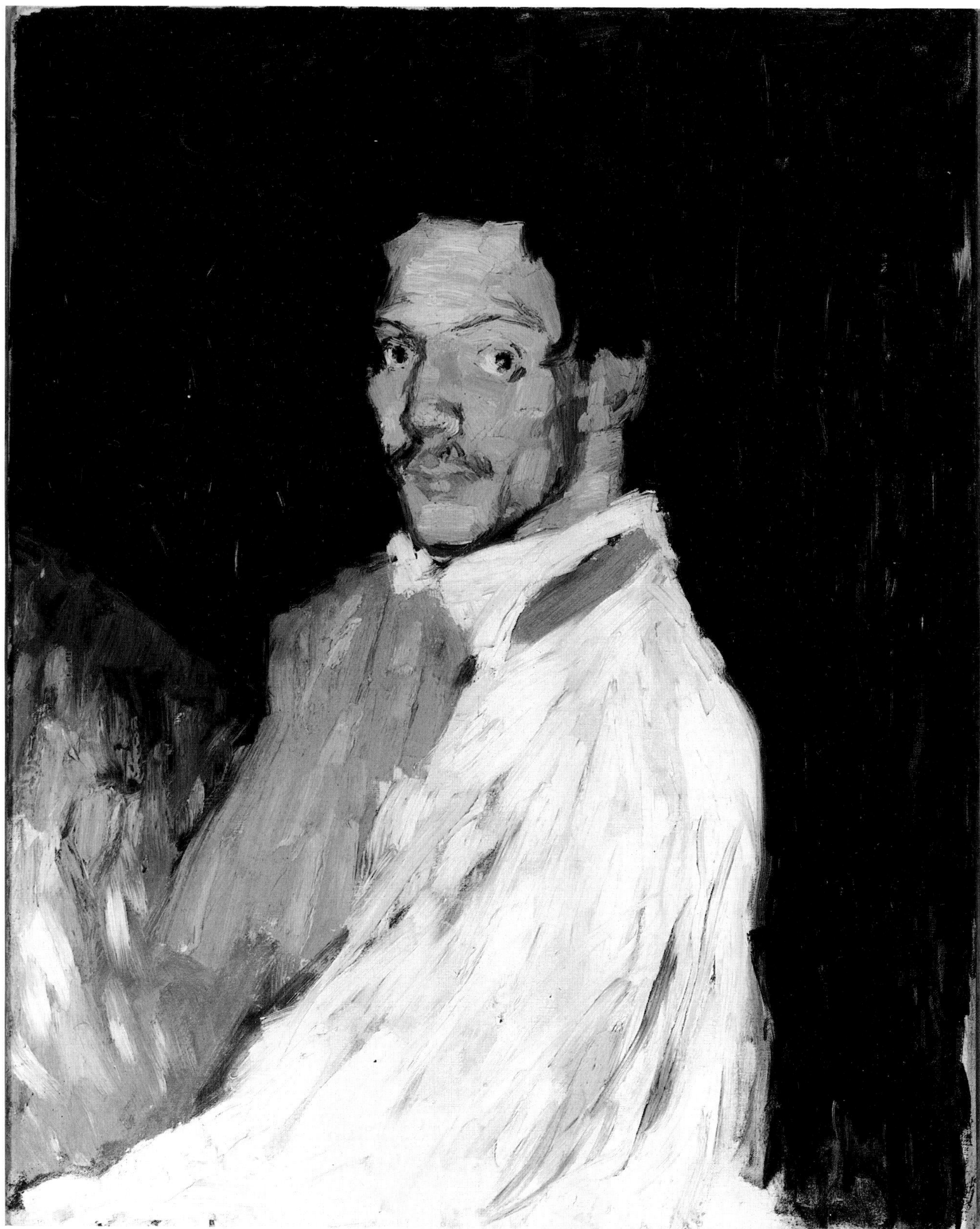

13

Success at Vollard's

Picasso. *Self-Portrait with Jaume Andreu Bonsons.* Paris, 1901. Crayon on paper, 31×37 cm. Private collection.

Opposite: Picasso. *Self-Portrait 'Yo Picasso'.* Paris, 1901. Oil on canvas, 73.7×59 cm. Private collection.

For the second trip to Paris, none of Picasso's closest friends was free to accompany him: Casagemas was dead, Pallarès back in Horta, and Sabartès not yet ready to leave Barcelona. And as he disliked travelling alone, he had to look around for a new companion, preferably one with means. In Jaume Andreu Bonsons—a friend of Casagemas's and an habitué of Els Quatre Gats—he found someone more or less suitable. Prosperous parents were paying for young Andreu to go to Paris and study art. A sketch that Picasso did immediately after their arrival shows Andreu, hearty, bearded, pipe-smoking, clutching a Gladstone bag; Picasso defiant-looking in his big black turkey-breeder's hat, muffled up against apparently unseasonable weather—it was mid-May (not March, as Sabartès says)—carrying a portfolio. In yet another drawing done around the same time he depicts himself as others would have seen him—weighed down with even more impedimenta: easel, palette, paintbox, and canvas—all set to work on his forthcoming exhibition. He already shows uncanny detachment about himself.

Andreu went off to find lodgings, while Picasso headed for 130*ter* Boulevard de Clichy,[1] the apartment where Casagemas had spent the last few nights of his life. After the suicide, Pallarès had stayed on for a few months, and then returned to Horta for the summer with his family. Since he was not coming back to Paris, he had stored his odds and ends of furniture with Torres Fuster and allowed another Catalan friend, a sculptor called Niell, to use the apartment until Picasso arrived. Little knowing that an artist is ill-advised to have his dealer as landlord or roommate, Picasso had rashly arranged to share it with Mañach. He got the larger of the two rooms as a studio/bedroom; the dealer got the smaller one. Primitive washing and toilet facilities existed on a communal landing. Mañach was of course stuck with the rent; whether or not this was the original arrangement, it would eventually make for problems.

Although he had brought some fifteen to twenty-five paintings and a quantity of drawings and pastels with him from Spain, Picasso still had nothing like enough for his show. This was due to open on June 24, just over a month after he arrived in Paris, so he had to work fast. Gustave Coquiot, who wrote the preface to the catalogue, claimed that he painted at the rate of ten pictures a day, which is nonsense. The more reliable Félicien Fagus, writing at the time of the show, thought three pictures a day—a figure confirmed by the artist, who said that 'this was probably

Picasso. *Self-Portrait in front of the Moulin Rouge* (with Andreu Bonsons at bottom right). Paris, 1901. Ink and crayon on paper, 18×11.5cm. Private collection.

Renoir. *Portrait of Ambroise Vollard*, *c.*1911–12. Oil on panel, 30×25cm. Musée du Petit Palais, Paris.

true of certain days.'[2] He was not exaggerating. When the exhibition opened, it included at least sixty-four paintings, pastels and watercolours and an unknown number of drawings. Since the gallery was small and another artist was sharing the space, these were hung floor to ceiling. Haste is reflected in the execution, which is on the whole wonderfully vigorous, if a bit slapdash. There is no denying the brilliance, energy, and originality of the best paintings: for instance *Old Harlot, Harlot with Hand on Her Shoulder,* or *Dwarf Dancer* (since these look back at van Gogh and Signac and ahead to Vlaminck and Derain, they are sometimes described as 'proto-Fauve'). Equally, there is no denying that some of the works were far from resolved.

To spur him on, a professional model, Jeanne or Jeanneton, was hired, but Picasso was never at ease with these girls, even if, as he said, he usually slept with them. The two paintings of Jeanne—one naked on a bed, the other dressed up in a feathered hat—lack the sparkle that sex generates in his work. Mañach must have had a hand in the choice of subjects, since these included such popular genres as flower pieces, racecourse scenes and evocations of childhood, which had never figured in Picasso's repertory before, and seldom would again. Besides being saleable, these subjects would have provided an antidote to the low-life scenes, which might otherwise have swamped the show. As Coquiot said many years later, the exhibition was 'juvenile and diverse';[3] there was an '*embarras de choix*—everyone could find a subject he liked'.

Within days of setting up house together, Mañach took Picasso to see Ambroise Vollard in his small gallery on the rue Laffitte, where the exhibition was to take place. Mañach could hardly have done better for his unknown protégé. Vollard was already establishing a reputation as the wiliest, most enterprising young dealer in Paris. He was a Creole from La Réunion (a French colony in the Indian Ocean) and, as the eldest of ten children of an attorney, had been sent to study law in France. But he was compulsively acquisitive; once he had passed his exams, he renounced his legal career to devote himself to the sale-rooms and the *bouquinistes* beside the Seine, ferreting out drawings and prints by Daumier, Forain, Guys and Rops. To pay for his finds he had to limit his diet to sea biscuits, but even when he started to make a small profit, Vollard continued to lead an austere life, except for the gastronomic splurges for which he was famous. In 1890 he opened a small gallery on the rue Laffitte. The only way to succeed, Vollard realized, was to establish a close personal rapport with the painters he admired. Thanks to pushiness and persistence and refusal to accept no for an answer, he was soon on the best of terms with most of the impressionist and post-impressionist masters, and on the worst of terms with other dealers. Few of his confrères loathed Vollard more than Berthe Weill, who is so critical of him in her memoirs that she is obliged to disguise him as 'Dolikhos'. Weill claims that he would beat her down to 'a rock-bottom price on an Odilon Redon and then tell the artist that he should not sell her any more work: she was ruining his prices by asking too little.'[4] Kahnweiler, however, regarded Vollard as the most brilliant dealer of his day, except for Durand-Ruel. '*Mes seuls vrais maîtres*,' he said.[5] The inspiration for Kahnweiler's gallery on the rue Vignon came from Vollard's on the rue Laffitte, also from Vollard's precept that 'art-dealing was about selling paintings not buying them'.

Picasso, Mañach and Torres Fuster in front of Picasso's portrait of Iturrino in the Boulevard de Clichy studio, 1901. Musée Picasso, Paris. Below the flower piece on the back wall are pages from *Arte Joven* and what appears to be a lost sketch for the *Moulin de la Galette*.

Henri Evenepoel. *The Spaniard in Paris* (Iturrino). 1899. Oil on canvas, 218×150 cm. Museum voor Schone Kunsten, Gent.

One of the first artists into whose good graces Vollard had managed to insinuate himself was Renoir, who would paint flattering portraits of him, as well as of his mistress, Madame de Galéa. Vollard also established rapports with Degas, Sisley and Pissarro (a Creole like himself). However, it was above all his support of Cézanne's underrated genius, his clever exploitation of the artist's enormous accumulation of his own work (major exhibitions in 1895 and 1899), followed by his no less canny manipulation of Gauguin's charismatic legend, that enabled Vollard to lure progressive collectors from all over France, Germany, Russia and Scandinavia, not to speak of America, to his gallery. Later he would invest heavily in the Nabis and the Fauves; he also became a fervent promoter of Rouault and Maillol. But that is as far as his commitment to modern art would go.

It was not only his manner that was uncouth; young Vollard also suffered from an uncouth appearance: he was undeniably ape-like. With his serendipitous gift for *objets trouvés*, Picasso once held up a slice of cold tongue in the middle of lunch and announced it was a portrait of Vollard. The meaty part approximated the dome of his head and the lingual root caricatured his simian features. According to Picasso, Vollard was never as quick off the mark as Kahnweiler would be a decade later. Nevertheless he developed an amazing flair for nurturing and promoting, if rarely spotting, genius, and not only in painting. He became so obsessed with the writer Alfred Jarry that he wrote a sequel to the Ubu plays (it is not as if the original ones are entirely by Jarry). The illustrated books he published are perhaps his most creative achievement.

Thanks largely to Mañach's persuasiveness, Vollard had developed a taste for young Spanish artists. He had given Nonell a show in 1899; and now there was this gifted youth from Barcelona. Why not try him out? In his unreliable *Recollections of a Picture Dealer*, Vollard tells all too little about his first meetings with Picasso, except that he was, surprisingly, 'dressed with the most studied elegance . . . [and] though only eighteen [he was nineteen], had finished about a hundred paintings, which he was bringing me with a view to an exhibition. This exhibition was not a success.'[6] Vollard's memory played him false; or, more likely, he deliberately falsified the record. The exhibition was a success, but to his eternal discredit, he failed to follow it up with a second show and left Picasso's career to founder. For all his pretensions to being a patron of progressive young artists, for all his vaunted discrimination, Vollard had no faith in the saleability of the melancholy blue paintings Picasso embarked on a few months after the show. He much preferred the cheerful work of Picasso's co-exhibitor Francisco Iturrino, a Basque—some ten years older than Picasso—who had already made a modest reputation with Hispagnolist scenes: picturesque peasants doing picturesque folkloric things. If this artist is remembered today, it is largely for his connection with Picasso, and also with Matisse, whom he took to Andalusia in 1911.[7] He is remembered, too, for his dramatic Spanish looks—ascetic as one of Zurbarán's monks—which are commemorated in a striking portrait by Evenepoel and an even more striking one by Derain. There was also a huge portrait by Picasso, done for their joint exhibition, which failed to sell and was painted over sometime after the show.[8]

In order to promote Picasso's first Paris exhibition, Mañach and Vollard invoked the help of Gustave Coquiot, a writer of risqué *feuilletons*,

Right: Picasso. *Bibi La Purée.* Paris, 1901. Oil on panel, 49×39cm. Private collection.

Above: Picasso. *Boulevard de Clichy.* Paris, 1901. Oil on canvas, 61.5×46.5cm. Private collection.

Right: Picasso. *Les Blondes Chevelures.* Paris, 1901. Oil on cardboard, 56.5×38cm. Private collection.

Below: Picasso. *Races at Auteuil.* Paris, 1901. Oil on cardboard, 46×61cm. The Joseph H. Hazen collection, New York.

Below right: Picasso. *Child with a Doll ('Le Roi Soleil').* Paris, 1901. Oil on cardboard, 52×34cm. Private collection.

Left: Picasso. *Woman with a Cape (Jeanne)*. Paris, 1901. Oil on canvas, 73×50 cm. The Cleveland Museum of Art. Bequest of Leonard C. Hanna, Jr.

Above: Picasso. *French Cancan*. Paris, 1901. Oil on canvas, 46×61 cm. Private collection.

Below left: Picasso. *Nude with Stockings*. Paris, 1901. Oil on canvas, 66.5×52. Private collection.

Below: Picasso. *Le Divan Japonais*. Paris, 1901. Oil on cardboard, 70×53.5 cm. Private collection.

chronicler of the social and theatrical worlds and art critic (author of the first monograph on Toulouse-Lautrec). In exchange for a fee or payment in kind—in Picasso's case a portrait—he would put his lively pen at the disposal of dealers in need of a preface or a favourable review. Coquiot probably came up with most of the titles of Picasso's paintings, since so many sound contrived: for instance, *Le Roi Soleil* (a flamboyant Lord Fauntleroy), *La Fille du Roi d'Egypte* (slang for 'gypsy girl'), *Les Blondes Chevelures* (three girls at play), and numerous euphemisms for the word 'whore' (*Morphinomane*, *L'Absinthe*, and the like). These fanciful titles —so untypical of Picasso—have complicated the identification of specific paintings. However, between them, Palau and Daix have identified most of the exhibits with reasonable certainty.[9]

D. O. Widhopff. *Gustave Coquiot*. *c*.1910. Pencil and charcoal on paper. Bibliothèque Nátionale, Paris.

Coquiot's principal job was to drum up support for the unknown artist by writing an elegant puff of a preface and arranging to have it reprinted in a newspaper (*Le Journal*, June 17, 1901) a week before the exhibition opened. His appreciation of Picasso is enthusiastic but glib. He sees him in a would-be Baudelairean light as a painter of modern life—primarily of women, 'of every kind of courtesan', from the *poule de luxe* to the murderous slut, 'pursuing her prey, the man she then fleeces in her sordid garret'; of dancers 'performing frenzied high-kick cancans' at the Moulin Rouge; 'exultant young girls, possessed by the devil, in a desperate swirl of skirts'; and of smartly dressed women seen at the racetrack 'against finely bedecked grandstands and the carefully tended turf of the course'. Since women's sexuality was Coquiot's favourite theme, he inevitably envisioned Picasso's work in its glow.

For all that he was an opportunist and an operator, Coquiot would be tireless in his efforts to help Picasso make some badly needed money. He and his wife, Gabrielle, took him into their comfortable bourgeois home, and though they may not have treated him like their child, as they subsequently claimed to have done, they were certainly hospitable. After Coquiot became a dealer, around 1917, he evoked these old favours, but Picasso did not respond to repeated overtures. Had he not rewarded him in 1901 for his preface and favourable review with a large and handsome portrait, albeit a curious hybrid? (Picasso has applied van Gogh's heavily loaded brush to a van Dongen-like image of Coquiot as an urbane Mephistopheles in white tie against a livid *fin-de-siècle* background.)

In addition to Coquiot's preface, an appreciative if wordy critique appeared in the prestigious *Revue Blanche*. It was entitled 'The Spanish Invasion'.[10] The author was Félicien Fagus (pseudonym of Georges Faillet). This 'small, bearded, sort of a blond Mallarmé, enveloped in a hooded cape',[11] was a minor employee of the Préfecture at a Paris *mairie* by day; by night he came into his own as a convivial anarchist. Early in the century Fagus abandoned anarchy for the royalist cause; the next step was devout Catholicism. Since one of his functions was to keep the register of births and deaths at the *mairie*, much of his versifying (a blend of Villon and Verlaine) was written on the back of death certificates. Many of these poems were published in *Testament de ma vie première*, a copy of which Fagus gave Picasso and which the latter passed on (along with a copy of Claudel's *L'Arbre*) to André Salmon on the occasion of their first meeting three years later.[12] Fagus's *Revue Blanche* article (July 15, 1901) places

Picasso. *Portrait of Gustave Coquiot*. Paris, 1901. Oil on canvas, 100×80 cm. Musée National d'Art Moderne, Paris.

Picasso in the forefront of an artistic invasion of Paris from beyond the Pyrenees, an invasion that is characterized by

> a harsh imagination, sombre, corrosive, sometimes magnificent, but a . . . consciously lugubrious magnificence. . . . All these artists . . . follow their great ancestors . . . particularly Goya, the bitter, mournful genius. His influence is seen in Picasso, the brilliant newcomer. He is the painter, utterly and beautifully the painter; he has the power of divining the essence of things. . . . Like all pure painters he adores colour for its own sake . . . he is enamoured of all subjects, and every subject is his. . . . Besides the great ancestral masters, many likely influences can be distinguished—Delacroix, Manet (everything points to him, whose painting is a little Spanish), Monet, Van Gogh, Pissarro, Toulouse-Lautrec, Degas, Forain, Rops. . . . Each one a passing phase, taking flight as soon as caught. . . . Picasso's passionate surge forwards has not yet left him the leisure to forge a personal style; his personality is embodied in this hastiness, this youthful impetuous spontaneity. . . . The danger lies in this very impetuosity, which could easily lead to facile virtuosity and easy success. . . . That would be profoundly regrettable since we are in the presence of such brilliant virility.

Casas. *Portrait of Pere Coll.* Barcelona, 1899. Charcoal and pastel with yellow powdered ground on paper, 57×23.3cm. Museu d'Art Modern, Barcelona.

Fagus was supposedly a man of impregnable integrity, but he too was rewarded with a handsome work, *Les Blondes Chevelures*. Vollard and Mañach obliged Picasso to give a painting to each of the three critics who wrote enthusiastically about his show: Coquiot, Fagus and the Catalan Pere Coll.[13] Coll's piece in *La Veu de Catalunya*, and François Charles's brief mention in *L'Ermitage* are alike in being divided between praise for Picasso's 'éclat' and 'genius' and reservations about his excessive diversity and productivity. The perspicacity of these critics does them credit. For, along with indisputable artistry, the paintings did show signs of indisputable haste—something that Picasso did not as yet know how to turn to his advantage. And all those influential painters listed by Fagus did not as yet equip the artist with a synthetic style; they provided him with an ad hoc compendium of contemporary trends.

Nevertheless, the Vollard exhibit was a stunning bravura performance for a neophyte, and it included some brilliant *tours de force*. Mañach's insistence on saleability paid off: the show was not only a *succès d'estime*; it was, in a modest way, a financial success. Well over half the items sold. '[The Vollard show] went very well,' Picasso said many years later. 'It pleased a lot of people. It was only later, when I set about doing blue paintings, that things went really badly. This lasted for years. It's always been like this with me. Very good and then suddenly very bad. The acrobats pleased. What I did after that didn't please any more!'[14] Vollard was the man whom the acrobats would please. He would re-establish himself as Picasso's principal dealer in 1906—he found the Rose period more saleable than the Blue—but would drop Picasso a year or so later. Vollard was utterly defeated by the onset of cubism; however, he had developed such a power-base in the art world that he kept Picasso's friendship until his death.

Picasso. *Portrait of Ambroise Vollard.* Paris, 1901. Oil on cardboard, 46×38cm. E. G. Bührle collection, Zurich.

One small mystery involving Picasso and Vollard needs clearing up: whether or not, in 1901, the artist did a portrait of him, as he did of the two other men involved in this exhibition. No question about it, he did. The trouble is that the painting of Vollard has traditionally been identified as a second portrait of Coquiot, despite the fact that it depicts someone

Picasso. *Harlot with Hand on Her Shoulder* (also known as *Margot*). Paris, 1901. Oil on cardboard, 69.5×57cm. Museu Picasso, Barcelona.

very different from the extravagantly bearded and moustachioed figure we know from Picasso's famous portrait—the one of him wearing a white tie with a frieze of dancing girls in the background. The other portrait represents a less flamboyant, less hirsute, less Mephistophelian figure. (Coquiot could not have changed that much in a matter of weeks.) It not only resembles Vollard physically; it also evokes his messy gallery on the rue Laffitte, hung from floor to ceiling with his stock. What more likely than that this vain monkey of a man, who had posed for Cézanne and Renoir, should have sat to the young Picasso? Given the nobility of the Cézanne and the fantasy of the Renoirs (he appears in one portrait as a torero), is it not also likely that Vollard would have refused to acknowledge this clumsy portrait by a nineteen-year-old nobody that makes him look like a junk dealer? Moreover, it is not very interestingly characterized. Even when, in 1911, Picasso painted a cubist masterpiece of him, Vollard was not particularly pleased and sold it off two years later to Morozov, the Russian collector, for 3000 francs.

Picasso was delighted with the exhibition. 'I really had a lot of money but it didn't last long,' he said.[15] The future looked so promising, there was no need to save. Mañach, too, was pleased. His investment had paid off and left him with several items for stock. Picasso took back a number of paintings, some of which he would in due course recycle.[16] Two seascapes and a portrait of Germaine were among the few unsold works that he failed to paint over. Since some of the buyers are named in the catalogue as an enticement to others, Vollard—or more likely Mañach—had evidently made a few sales before the show opened. Two of these collectors are already known to us: Olivier Sainsère, who bought the paintings entitled *Danseuses* and *Madrileña* (possibly a portrait of the artist's sister); and Emmanuel Virenque, the Spanish consul, who is listed as owning *Le Divan Japonais*.[17] (When friends complained about the subject—a weary-looking whore with cancan girls in the background—Virenque exchanged it for a racecourse scene.) Other collectors listed in the catalogue are Madame Besnard, the wife of Picasso's colour merchant; Maurice Fabre of Narbonne, a client of Vollard's who already owned a number of fine Gauguins, including the great *Pastorale Tahitienne*, now in the Tate Gallery; a Monsieur Ackermann, thought to have been a dealer; Eugène Blot, who took pride in his reputation as a *dénicheur* (literally a bird's-nester, that is to say a small-time speculator in modern art) and bought a number of Cézannes from Vollard;[18] a Monsieur Personas, who must have been A. Personnaz, a collector friend of Sainsère and Blot; and, most interesting of all, 'Madame K. Kollwitz, *artiste peintre à Berlin*', who bought *La Bête*. This can only have been the pastel of a rape, done on Picasso's first trip to Paris—the most 'difficult' subject in the exhibition (see illustration, p. 169). Since Kollwitz's early work is so close in spirit to Nonell's *Cretins de Bohí*, it is not surprising that she should have been the first artist outside Spain to acquire a Picasso.[19]

Picasso. *Old Man in Toledano Hat*. Toledo, 1901. Pencil and wash on paper, 20.4×12.4cm. Musée des Beaux-Arts, Reims. Inscribed to Berthe Weill.

As for works sold after (as opposed to before) the show opened, no records have survived. Whether an early collector like Arthur Huc acquired anything, we do not know. An inscription on a drawing records that within a day or two of his arrival Picasso had a visit from Berthe Weill (June 3, 1901). She presumably wanted to have first pick of the things he had brought from Spain. Some of the other more progressive *dénicheurs* must also have made purchases. And Vollard, most retentive of dealers, would have kept items back for himself. Likewise Mañach retained a few things for stock; he was forever thinking ahead to future sales, although, to his credit, he never sold Picasso's large, bold portrait of him. This portrait —partly inspired by Toulouse-Lautrec's poster of Aristide Bruant, partly by Casas's poster-like portrait of Pere Romeu—was one of the most arresting works in the show. Mañach would also have made a few sales to Catalans, e.g., the magnificent Fauvish *Harlot with Hand on Her Shoulder* that Lluís Plandiura, the pioneer Barcelona collector, acquired very early on. And if Palau and Daix are correct that the painfully picturesque *Portrait of Bibi La Purée*—a bedraggled homosexual actor who had known Verlaine and haunted the cafés of the Quartier Latin[20]—corresponds to one or other of the '*Portrait*' entries in the catalogue (numbers 7 and 25), we can identify yet another buyer: Monsieur Gompel, a rich cousin of Picasso's new friend and admirer Max Jacob, who must have set up this sale.

On the strength of the Vollard show, Picasso was asked to do posters and magazine illustrations. He was not anxious to compromise his status as a serious *artiste-peintre*, but Coquiot persuaded him to accept. After all, Toulouse-Lautrec and Steinlen did not disdain such work. Josep Oller, the Catalan impresario of the Moulin Rouge, was also interested in helping his compatriot: he asked Picasso to design a poster (never printed) —a Lautrec-like quartet of dancers—to publicize one of his other establishments, Le Jardin de Paris. The maquette for this poster was signed 'Picasso'; not so the illustrations of cabaret performers Picasso did for a magazine that lived up to its silly title: *Frou-Frou*. As a form of disguise, Picasso made a point of using a name and a '*rubrica*' (monogram)—'Ruiz' in a *modernista* circle—that he had abandoned a year earlier. Reverting to his real name as a pseudonym for hackwork would have appealed to his sense of irony. In one case he even erased his original signature and substituted 'Ruiz' for it.[21] The *Frou-Frou* drawings, entitled '*Appâts pour hommes*' (Lures for Men) and '*Beuglant et Chahut*' (Catcalls and Capers), are facile and eye-catching, seemingly worked up from sketches done from life in theatres or cabarets or café-concerts. The first to appear (on August 31, 1901) depicts an unnamed cancan dancer. Two weeks later *Frou-Frou* published a page of four drawings, including two of Toulouse-Lautrec's favourite subjects, Jane Avril and Grille d'Egout ('Sewer Grating'), as well as Marie-Louise Derval, the well-known actress, and Polaire, the gamine singer so admired by Colette. Polaire may well have slept with Picasso, for when he returned to Paris in 1902, he did some erotic drawings—one of a girl masturbating, another with a gigantic vagina on the wall behind her—which are unmistakably of this cat-faced girl.

Coquiot also asked Picasso to do a series of portrait drawings of entertainers and demimondaines for an album of professional beauties that he proposed to publish.[22] The subjects were to include Jeanne Bloch, Jane Thylda, La Teresina, Anna Thibaud, Rose Demag, Jane Avril, Liane de Pougy and 'her rival in whoredom and diamonds',[23] La Belle Otéro. None of the above seems to have been drawn until 1902; however, I suspect that the two paintings of a bedizened and bejewelled courtesan entitled *Woman with a Necklace*, done shortly after the Vollard show (i.e. summer 1901), were inspired by La Belle Otéro.

Picasso. *Portrait of Pere Mañach*. Paris, 1901. Oil on canvas, 100.5×67.5cm. National Gallery of Art, Washington, D.C., Chester Dale Collection.

Appâts pour hommes

Picasso. *Lures for Men*. Reproduced in *Frou-Frou*, August 31, 1901. Bibliothèque de l'Arsenal, Paris.

820

Beuglant et Chahut

POLAIRE

GRILLE D'ÉGOUT

LA DERVAL

JEANNE AVRIL

(Dessins de Ruiz.)

Top left: Picasso. *Catcalls and Capers.* Reproduced in *Frou-Frou,* September 14, 1901. Bibliothèque de l'Arsenal, Paris.

Left: Picasso. *Sada Yacco.* Paris, 1901. Ink and gouache on paper, 40×31 cm. Heirs of the artist.

Top: Picasso. *Woman with a Necklace.* Paris, 1901. Oil on canvas, 65.3×54.5 cm. Private collection.

Above: Picasso. *Nude on a Bed.* Paris, 1902. Ink on paper, 23.1×33.8 cm. Museu Picasso, Barcelona.

Photographs of Polaire (*top*), Sada Yacco (*centre*) and La Belle Otéro. Bibliothèque Nationale, Paris. Polaire's is inscribed to Colette's husband, Willy, 'whom I hate with all my sick heart'.

Picasso was less successful in his portrayals of another popular performer of the day, Yvette Guilbert, who appeared at the Olympia music-hall in the summer and autumn of 1901. His pastels fail to transcend Toulouse-Lautrec's iconic image. Nor did Picasso have much luck with the exotic Japanese dancer Sada Yacco. To promote her appearance at the Théâtre de l'Athénée in late September 1901 on the same bill as Loïe Fuller, she commissioned Picasso to do a poster of her *à la japonaise*. Like all the artist's early projects for posters, this one came to nothing: his heart does not seem to have been in it. Far from taking any interest in a genre of art that was still having an enormous impact on the modern movement, Picasso failed to understand what anyone saw in Japanese prints (as he told Gertrude Stein on the occasion of their first meeting). If he assimilated anything of their influence, it would have been largely by osmosis, via Toulouse-Lautrec, Gauguin, van Gogh or the Nabis. The seemingly Japanese silhouettes Picasso devised for the fashionable women in feathered hats, big as parasols, and fishtail trains that he had observed in the paddock at Chantilly or Auteuil, are more likely to derive from Bonnard than, say, Utamaro. Picasso's drawings of Sada Yacco in action have a tension that is lacking from the design for the actual poster with its spoof Japanese characters: a feeble exercise in japonaiserie. Although Picasso subsequently acquired some Japanese prints, erotic ones, mostly, it was not until *Guernica* that he succeeded, albeit briefly, in exploiting the idiom in some studies of a pretty little mouth open in an unpretty little scream. 'I loathe exoticism,' he told Apollinaire. 'I have never liked Chinese, Japanese or Persian art.'[24]

* * *

One of the happiest and most lasting consequences of the Vollard show was Picasso's friendship with Max Jacob. This originated with an admiring note that the aspiring poet had left at the gallery. The pale, thin gnome with strange, piercing eyes almost immediately assumed the role of mentor in Picasso's life. Here at last was a Frenchman—brilliant, quirkish, perverse—with whom he found instant rapport, even if at first they had no language in common except mime and were in so many respects unalike. Jacob was Jewish and homosexual ('*sodomite sans joie . . . mais avec ardeur*')[25] and deeply insecure ('*Cher Max! Il était toujours sur la défensive*,' as Cocteau wrote); although five years older than Picasso, he had yet to fulfil his early promise. However, he was infinitely perceptive about art as well as literature and an encyclopedia of erudition—as at home in the arcane depths of mysticism as in the shallows of *l'art populaire*. He was also very, very funny. Jacob had been a brilliant student of philosophy (especially Bergson) at Quimper (Brittany), where his father had a successful tailor's business—hence 'the back of the shop smell' that Cocteau, ever the envious admirer, detected in his work. After quarrelling with his family he went to Paris (1894) to study at the Faculté de Droit and the Ecole Coloniale. Although a diligent student, and a lifelong advocate of diligence in his numerous protégés, Jacob ultimately dropped out to become a journalist and art critic for the *Moniteur des Arts* (1898–99). A sudden loss of faith in his writing decided him to abandon journalism and study art. This venture, too, was ill fated. At the Académie Jullian, where he enrolled, the desperately shy young pauper from the provinces had a humiliating time; an elegant student once asked superciliously whether he was the pencil-seller. And the academic teachers, J. P. Laurens and Benjamin Constant, found his drawings inept. They were not wrong. However, Jacob's facile gouaches (Christian Dior opened his art gallery with a show of them in 1936) would provide him with a better livelihood than his far from facile writing.

To earn enough money to live, Jacob was obliged to sweep out shops, work as a lawyer's clerk, tutor (or, as he said, 'nanny') and '*secrétaire, secrétaire, secrétaire, secrétaire*'. His only half-way decent job was helping to lay out the illustrated pages of *Le Sourire*, when Alphonse Allais was editor-in-chief. This magazine published his first (not very good) poems. When Jacob met Picasso, he was living in extreme poverty on the Quai aux Fleurs in an attic, where the floor gleamed like a skating rink. Jacob was maniacally tidy: 'It's I who do the housework,' he used to say, rubbing together delicate hands that were as well kept as the floors.[26] The poet has described his first encounter with Picasso in some detail, though he omits to say that he fell in love with the artist.

Drawing of Max Jacob, 'made in a café in 1894 by an itinerant artist when [he] was a student at the Ecole Coloniale'. Pencil on paper. Bibliothèque Doucet, Paris.

> At the time of his great and first exhibition, I, as a professional art critic [not strictly true], had been so struck with wonder at [Picasso's] production that I left a word of admiration with Ambroise Vollard. And the same day I received from M. Mañach, who looked after [Picasso's] interests, an invitation to visit him. Already this first day we felt a great sympathy for each other.
>
> Picasso had a magnificent top hat which he later gave me; for although he always had a taste for cheap clothes, bought in workmen's stores, this was the last touch of refinement; he is very fastidious and matches his underpants to his socks with as much love as he does a painting. . . .
>
> Picasso spoke no more French than I did Spanish, but we looked at each other and shook hands enthusiastically. This took place in a large studio in the place Clichy, with some Spaniards sitting on the floor, eating and conversing gaily. . . . They came the following morning to my place, where Picasso took a huge canvas, which has since been lost or covered over, and painted my portrait seated on the floor among my books and in front of a large fire.
>
> I remember giving him a Dürer woodcut, which he still has. He also admired my *images d'Epinal* [popular woodcuts of historic events], which I think I was the only person collecting at that time, and all my Daumier lithographs; I gave him everything, but I think he has lost it all. That night all the Spaniards went away, except for Mañach, who went to sleep in an armchair, while Picasso and I spoke in sign language until morning.[27]

When the two first met, both had reached a critical point in their lives: Jacob had been too slow off the mark; Picasso, if anything, too quick. Over the next three or four years, they would see each other through a great deal of poverty. The 1903 comic strip in which Picasso visualized Jacob's eventual triumph (see illustration, p. 267) applied to both of them. The goddess of Fame proffered not only a laurel wreath but a ham. These two short men with big heads—hence their penchant for top hats, which made up for lack of height—were like two sides of the same coin. Painting turned out to be Jacob's *violon d'Ingres* (avocation), and poetry Picasso's. Both owned to having a black streak; both believed implicitly in the magic function of art. But Jacob was more of a giver—Pygmalion to a series of male Galateas—and Picasso more of a taker. And Jacob was always ready to share the treasures of his well-stocked mind, his poetic imagination, his mystical obsessions and his high camp sense of fun with anyone who was worthy, as well as with quite a few—the thieving Maurice Sachs, for instance—who were not. Michel Leiris, who worshipped Jacob, confessed in *L'Age d'Homme*, that masterpiece of terse eloquence, 'I might have gone so far as to share his vice if that would have been the means of acquiring his genius.'[28] Not that this was an obligatory quid pro quo: Jacob's relationships with his Galateas were usually platonic, and his love for Picasso was no less intense for having no sexual outlet. It would be surpassed only by his homo-erotic cult of Christ, who appeared to Jacob after the artist ceased being his next-door neighbour and he needed a new god.

Until Jacob came into his life, Picasso had found nobody, apart from Cornuti in Madrid and a few of the more literate Catalans in Barcelona, to guide his steps through the maze of French culture. Now he had hit upon the most beguiling cicerone it was possible to find. Just as well that Jacob was also very patient. 'Picasso spoke awful French,' Berthe Weill said 'and it was hilarious to hear Max yelling his head off in the baboo language . . . one uses on a foreigner or a child.'[29] If Picasso eventually learned to speak French that was idiomatic and witty, and on occasion eloquent (despite a heavy Spanish accent), it was almost entirely due to the poet's tuition.

Picasso. *Self-Portrait in a Top Hat*. Paris, 1901. Oil on paper, 50×33cm. Mr and Mrs Sven Salén, Stockholm.

Jacob's place in Picasso's life would be usurped but never left unfilled. For the next sixty years or so the artist would always have his own poet laureate—preferably someone with the advantage of a painterly as well as a poetic sensibility, the better to cross-fertilize his imagination. Max Jacob was the first in a line that would later include Apollinaire, Cocteau, Breton and Eluard (some might add Gertrude Stein), each of whom influenced Picasso's life as well as his work. Jacob opened up Picasso's mind to the beauty of the French language by putting him through an intensive course in French literature. His gifts as a performer brought new life to poets that Picasso had known only in translation: Racine, Corneille, Baudelaire, above all Verlaine. Jacob's dislikes should also be taken into consideration. He dismissed Mallarmé as a stilted obscurantist and a transcendental artificer of Japanese bibelots; and he accused Rimbaud of standing for disorder, which he abhorred. (Jacob's successor, Apollinaire, would be the one to convert Picasso to the view that 'there are no other poets. Rimbaud is the only one.')

Sabartès has described a typical evening in Picasso's studio when lack of funds obliged the group to stay at home, and Jacob would provide the entertainment:

> Max would begin to read Verlaine, slowly and softly at first, suddenly he would get agitated, start gesticulating, wildly turning the pages of the book. Each time he began a new poem, he would raise his voice, and make more and more emphatic movements with his arms to mark a pause, emphasize a word, or accentuate a rhyme. And then in utter darkness, as if extracting the verses from the very depths of memory, he would begin to read *Un grand Sommeil noir*. He must have known it by heart. He would recite it slowly in a hollow voice, stretching out the cadences with breaks and pauses. . . . Sometimes he seemed to leave the verse suspended in mid-air. At the end of the last stanza, he would clothe the words '*silence . . . silence*' in a sigh, and then collapse, flat out on the floor.[30]

As Fernande Olivier (soon to be Picasso's mistress) describes in her memoirs, Jacob also loved to make people laugh:

> He was a singer, a singing-teacher, a pianist, a comedian if called upon to be, and the life-and-soul of all our parties. He used to improvise little plays, in which he was always the main actor. I must have seen him do his imitation of a barefoot dancer a hundred times, and each time I enjoyed it more. His trousers were rolled up to his knees to reveal two hairy legs. In shirt-sleeves, his collar wide-open to expose a chest forested with curly black hair, with his bare-bald head and his pince-nez, he would dance with tiny steps and pointed toe, doing his best to be graceful and making us rock with laughter. . . . There was the gay songstress, which he did with a lady's hat on his head and a translucent veil swathed about him, singing in a heady soprano which was in tune but somehow totally ridiculous. . . .
>
> He used to sing the *Langouste atmosphérique* by Offenbach and *Sur les rives de l'Adour*. These and dozens of other songs used to delight us evening after evening . . . he knew all the operettas, all the operas, all the tragedies—Racine and Corneille—and all the comedies by heart. He used to do the scene from *Horace*, which begins: '*Qu'il mourût* . . . ' acting all the parts, endlessly changing position and coming in on his own cues. He and Olin used to do an elocution class, with the pupil stammering so badly that the teacher finds himself stammering too.[31]

Jacob was such an accomplished mimic that he managed to convert the poet Reverdy to Catholicism by acting out each of the Stations of the Cross in turn, as they sat drinking in a café. His mimicry, his capricious yet scholarly mind and his slavish infatuation entranced Picasso, who became more and more dependent on his company, more and more immune to his perverse side. When Jacob was drinking heavily or on drugs, the saintly clown in the top hat and monocle revealed less attractive aspects of his protean nature. Sweetness and generosity would give way to paranoia. The poet would turn into a porcupine who would shoot quills of malice at anyone he suspected of slighting him. His gaffes were many and never unintentional. And he fuelled his misogyny—a source of constant amusement to Picasso—by cultivating women who confirmed him in this view, women who inspired contemptuous amusement in his friends: malicious 'models', sly old concierges, whose gossip he treasured, or *monstres sacrés* like his great friend the former courtesan Liane de Pougy, whom Picasso was supposed to draw for Coquiot's book. Torn as she was between the roles of born-again Catholic and procuress (her husband, Prince Georges Ghyka, preferred two girls to one), this penitent Magdalen was a perfect match for the born-again Jacob. She shrewdly diagnosed his dichotomy: 'a mixture of genius and ridiculousness, love and hate, sweetness and rage, kindness and cruelty, and yet so generous . . . '[32]

Rightly or wrongly, Jacob blamed his problems on his parents. Life at home had been so miserable, he claimed, that at the age of seventeen he had tried to hang himself with his tie just before dinner. His father had upbraided him: 'Aren't you ashamed to play the fool as though you were still a child?' 'There's always time to kill oneself,' the mother said. Like so many of Jacob's stories, this was almost certainly a fabrication. Prudence Jacob and her son were both too self-centred for comfort. 'We are very alike,' she told Liane de Pougy. 'After three days together we can't stand each other.' When he finally tried a heterosexual relationship (late 1902) he picked on a coarse but motherly woman. Although forever after he vaunted the idyllic nature of this romance, Jacob soon extricated himself from it. Fernande Olivier, one of the few women Jacob really liked, maintained that this affair 'disgusted him with women forever. [He] saw himself as perpetually persecuted, particularly by the wives of friends, even those who loved him best. He could show such hostility and suspicion when talking to a woman that the conversation occasionally ended in violence. Then he would vanish . . . but we knew how to deal with him and were always delighted to have him back.'[33]

Besides forming Picasso's literary tastes, Jacob interested him in the occult—a source for much of the mystery in his work. Jacob was obsessed by every aspect of magic. He had delved into the Cabala, both Jewish and Christian; he had also made a study of astrology, palmistry and other forms of divination. He claimed to have lectured on the subject; claimed, indeed, to have so scandalized 'a proletarian audience' with a talk on 'the scientific origins of the occult sciences' that an enraged mob had chased him into the Bois de Boulogne, crying, 'He's poisoned the minds of the people. . . . We'll get him.'[34] Whether or not this happened, there is no doubt that Jacob was actively involved in occult practices. Later in his life, his 'magus' would be a little jeweller from the Boulevard du Temple, who had a rendezvous every Sunday morning in the Forêt de Saint-Germain with 'a female faun' and whose supernatural powers were embodied—at least so Jacob later told a group of lay-brothers at Saint-Benoît—in the foulness of his breath. After his conversion to Catholicism in 1909, he continued to believe in astrology, though not in astrologers. He never ceased casting horoscopes and reading the Tarot cards and hands—a skill that earned him the occasional fee, the entrée to fashionable houses and the gratitude of young men who attracted him. He always filed his friends' correspondence by astral signs divided into decans. Jacob may well have made other divinatory projections for his new friend, but the only one to have survived is a chart of Picasso's hand (see illustration, p.267)—probably done when the artist returned to Paris in 1902. This chart is stronger in poetic insight than prophetic powers. However, Jacob's influence as a palmist is of far less consequence than his influence as a seer. That mysticism and poetry begin to illuminate Picasso's work just as Jacob begins to illuminate his life is no coincidence. Years later, Jacob would refer to himself as the 'homunculus' who inspired Faust.[35]

Max Jacob. *Picasso in the Square*. Paris, *c*.1901. Crayon and wash on paper, 34×26cm. Petit Palais Musée, Geneva.

=PARIS=
LUCHA TERIBLE
en casa PEIX entre
JAUMEANDREU y
MANACH
-LA JOLIE
FAGUETTE-
la Odette se indigna
¡¡Escribe y mande el
"Pel y Ploma"
Adios
-Picasso-

14

Painter of Human Misery

'You forget that I am Spanish and love sadness.'
(Picasso to his second wife, Jacqueline)[1]

The popular singer Louise Fagette performing in *Le Danger de l'autre.* Cover of *Paris Qui Chante,* June 7, 1903.

Opposite: Picasso. *Alleluia* in a letter to Utrillo: (front, top right) 'Manolo jealous', (centre left) 'Terrible fight in the fish house between Jaume Andreu and Mañach', (centre right) 'Manolo is thrown out of the room by the police'; (reverse, left) 'Odette gets angry',' (right) 'La Jolie Faguette [*sic*]'. Paris, 1901. Pen and crayon on paper, 17.5×23cm. Private collection.

On his return to Paris in 1901 Picasso did not resume sleeping with his former mistress Odette but switched to the *femme fatale* who had provoked Casagemas's suicide, Germaine. Odette was furious, and so was Manolo; he had been carrying on an affair with Germaine ever since the shooting. To Picasso their jealousy was a source of boyish pride. He promptly sent off an *alleluia*—a comic strip—to Utrillo in Barcelona, picturing the dramas that had ensued. Typical of the nineteen-year-old pasha to boast of his conquests and make fools of his friends. Manolo is portrayed being evicted from Picasso's apartment by the police for making a jealous scene: Andreu and Mañach are having '*una lucha terrible en Casa Peix*' (presumably a fish house).[2] Picasso could not remember what Mañach was fighting about. Although Manolo had every reason to be jealous, he said, they were soon reconciled. Henceforth he and Manolo would be the closest of friends, until they drifted apart at the beginning of the war.

Picasso had endless picaresque stories about Manolo—a scoundrel of overwhelming charm and spirit, he said. Unfortunately his temperament does not come across in his work and his qualities as a neo-classical sculptor—a lesser Maillol—have been upstaged by his legend. Fernande Olivier has described Manolo as 'the quintessential Spaniard, small with the blackest possible eyes set in a black face beneath the blackest of black hair. He was ironic, gay, sensitive, lazy, and very excitable.'[3] He was also a great liar, pickpocket, practical joker, con man. He was the illegitimate son of a general, who is said to have turned him out of his house for insolence. Thereafter he lived by his wits. Picasso liked to recount how, after some outrageous escapade, the general had ordered the police to bring his son before him to be disciplined. When his father had finished his admonishments, Manolo burst into crocodile tears and asked permission to embrace him. In the process he stole his watch. And then there was the daughter of the Barcelona dairywoman, whom he adored because she let him sculpt goddesses and animals in butter. 'If they tried to shoot Manolo,' Picasso said when riots broke out in Catalonia, 'his executioners would be sure to miss because he would make them helpless with laughter.'[4] Different friends had different explanations as to why Manolo settled in France and could never return to Spain. Brassaï says that when he was drafted into the military, he had opted for the cavalry. Issued with a horse, he had ridden it across the Pyrenees,

Manolo. *Self-Portrait.* Paris, 1901. Conté crayon on paper, 29.5×19cm. Museu Picasso, Barcelona.

Manolo. *Maternity. c.*1900. Plaster, ht: 27cm. Museu Cau Ferrat, Sitges.

and sold it and its accoutrements to the French for enough money to get him to Paris.[5] Manolo's biographer gives a less dramatic account. The collector Riera had invited him to Paris; thanks to a loan from Rusiñol's wife, the sculptor simply took the train and, to avoid military service, stayed on in France.[6] Manolo was not allowed back into Spain until there was an amnesty for deserters in 1927. Whereupon he and his wife, Totote, went to live at Caldes de Montbui, a spa in Spanish Catalonia. He stayed there until he died in 1945. His last words (to his wife), were in character: '*Je m'en vais . . . tu viens?*' ('I'm off . . . are you coming?')[7]

Picasso and Manolo were much alike: small and dark, intense and energetic. They shared a sense of humour and mischief that was black and sardonic, nonetheless childish; a sense of braggadocio that masked all manner of fears. They also shared a distaste, rare among their friends, for getting drunk. But this did not stop them from spending wild nights on the town. Picasso, who was ten years younger than Manolo, had once again found a companion who was fatherly and protective and utterly amoral. 'Little Pablo', as Manolo called him, listened to him more than to anyone else. He was probably the only person Picasso permitted to mock him, criticize him, contradict him. Manolo even got away with the diabolical joke of introducing the youthful-looking 'Little Pablo'—condemned to silence by his ignorance of French—as his daughter. Picasso's indignant protests were drowned in a chorus of laughter and applause.[8] Manolo was not alone in divining a certain girlishness in Picasso: the French Catalan sculptor Maillol, whose studio Picasso visited about this time, gives a description of him: 'he was thin; he had a slight build; he was very like a young girl. He made a special trip to see me at Villeneuve-Saint-Georges [a Parisian suburb]. He sang me a Catalan song. He was very sweet.'[9]

For all his gifts, Manolo preferred to live by expedients, even petty larcenies, rather than make an honest living. One morning, when Max Jacob was still in bed, Manolo stole his only pair of trousers. A few hours later, he brought them back. It was not, as Jacob first thought, a sudden attack of conscience: none of the old-clothes dealers would take anything so shabby. He played the same trick on Léon-Paul Fargue—'borrowed' a suit from him that Fargue never saw again. And when his friend the Spanish sculptor Paco Durrio rashly lent him his studio, he came back from Spain to find that Manolo had sold his magnificent Gauguin collection to Vollard. 'I was dying of hunger,' the thief told Durrio. 'I didn't have any choice: it was my death or your Gauguins. I chose your Gauguins.' (Terrified that he might be accused of receiving stolen property, Vollard returned the paintings to the owner.)[10] To raise money, Manolo would periodically organize raffles of his sculpture, but these affairs were always rigged. Sometimes all the tickets had the same number. 'I'm too generous,' he would say. 'I don't want to make anyone jealous.' The day of the drawing seldom arrived, for he would usually have sold the prize, or bartered it. Antics such as this were a constant delight to Picasso, but in the summer of 1901 there was a darker tinge to their friendship. The fact that Manolo had been a witness to Casagemas's suicide and that both he and Picasso had posthumously cuckolded their friend constituted a morbid link—one from which the artist would squeeze every last drop of guilt, so that he could set about exorcising this death in his work. Where better—or, for that matter, worse—to embark on this process of exorcism than the very apartment where Casagemas had spent his last days, a few steps from the restaurant where he took his life? And to heighten the *frisson*, what better, or worse mistress to take than the explicit cause of Casagemas's suicide, Germaine herself?

Picasso. *Head of the Dead Casagemas*. Paris, 1901. Oil on panel, 27×35cm. Musée Picasso, Paris.

Picking away at the scab of his guilt stimulated Picasso into painting a strangely varied series of *memento mori*. Some are anguished, others mocking. The earliest reference to the tragedy may have been unintentional: a colourful, innocent-looking painting of two women (Germaine and Odette?) being served dinner by a waiter. The setting was traditionally taken to be the Café de la Rotonde, until Picasso said that it depicted the terrace at L'Hippodrome, the restaurant where Casagemas met his end.[11] We should not, however, attach too much significance to the location of this scene. Picasso would have been in a rush to finish it for his show, and the choice of the Hippodrome could have been dictated as much by its proximity as its associations. The artist did not address the Casagemas tragedy directly for at least six months after the event, when he executed the first of three paintings of Casagemas on his deathbed. Two of the macabre heads have bullet holes in them. Picasso showed these agonized works to very few friends, and then stashed them away, only divulging them at the end of his life. The heads differ considerably in style—from Fauve expressionism to Blue period pathos—and were presumably done over several months (between July and October or November 1901) at moments of acute stress, to judge by their raw pain. The thick impasto and bright colour in the earliest of the three paintings derive from the work of that other victim of a self-inflicted bullet, van Gogh. Picasso had not arrived in time for the exhibition that established the artist's reputation: the great retrospective held in Paris that spring. But the reverberations were still being felt and, like the Fauves, Picasso could not escape his violent wake. Van Gogh helped him to unlearn all accepted notions of artistic decorum and pour his heart and guts, spleen and libido onto canvas—not just at this moment but at other times, especially towards the end of his life, when he set out to make angst palpable in paint. What, for instance, could be more van Gogh-like than the huge symbolic candle flame—an incandescent vagina—whose sunburst of rays illuminates Casagemas's ravaged face with a strip of St Elmo's golden fire?

Picasso. *Head of the Dead Casagemas*. Paris, 1901. Oil on cardboard, 52×34cm. Heirs of the artist.

The second and sketchier version of these *memento mori* has the incoherence of a sob. The head is the more disturbing for being portrayed upright as if alive, but with eyes closed as in death, and a gash of black paint where the bullet entered. It brings to mind the lines about death in Lorca's *Duende* essay: 'In Spain, the dead are more alive than the dead of any other country . . . their profile wounds like the edge of a barber's razor.'[12] The third and most finished version is less painful than the other two: Picasso has distilled raw horror into a blue essence. This is one of the first two paintings that can be described as 'Blue period'. The other is the idealized portrait of Sabartès known as *The Poet Sabartès* (see illustration, p.216). There is an eerie resemblance between these two paintings. Since the two men could hardly have been less alike in physiognomy or character, one can only wonder whether the grafting of Sabartès's profile, with its baroque scroll of a lip and baroque volute of a chin, onto

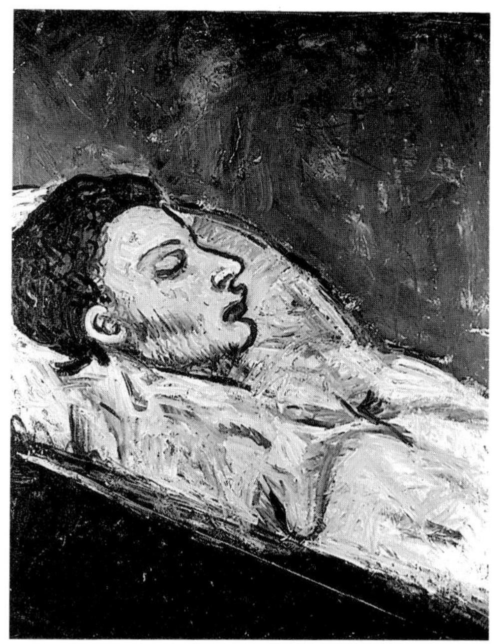

Picasso. *Casagemas in his Coffin*. Paris, 1901. Oil on cardboard, 72.5×57.8cm. Private collection.

Picasso. *The Burial of Casagemas (Evocation)*. Paris, 1901. Oil on canvas, 146×89cm. Musée d'Art Moderne de la Ville de Paris.

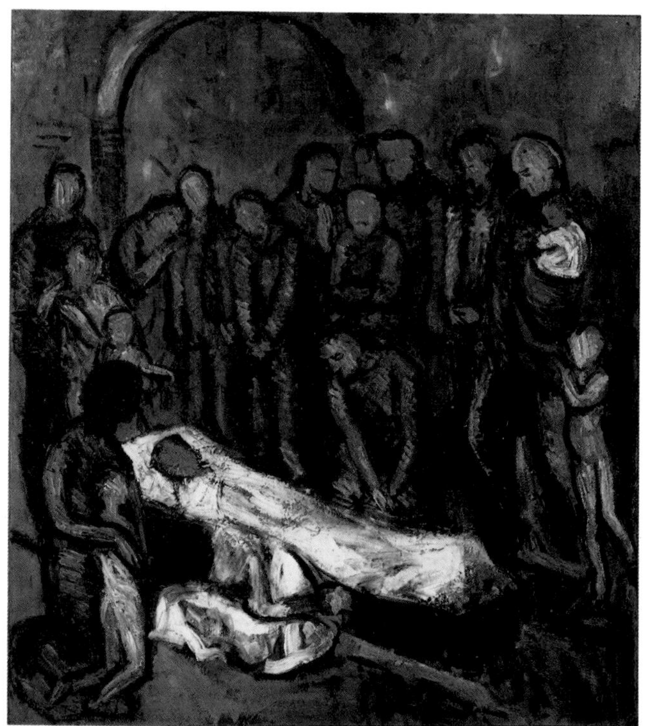

Picasso. *The Mourners*. Paris, 1901. Oil on canvas, 100×90.2cm. Private collection.

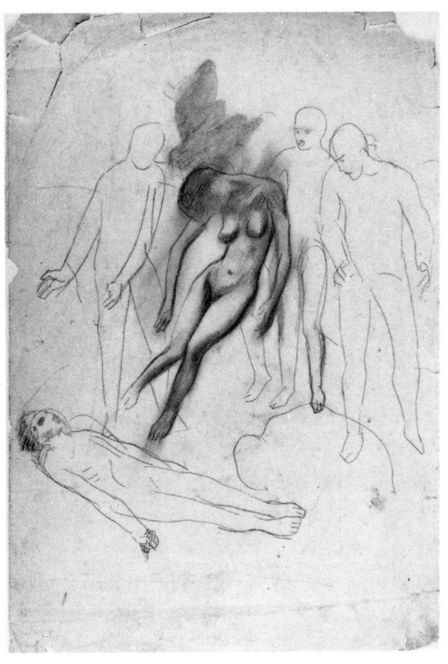

Picasso. Study for *Evocation*. Paris, 1901. Black chalk on paper, 24×31cm. Musée Picasso, Paris.

the chinless Casagemas reflects a desire on Picasso's part to fuse the identities of these two friends, who were so antithetical.

For the next two mementos of death, Picasso switched to allegory. It has been suggested that his original idea was to portray Casagemas 'wearing a hat, with a staff, a pipe and two little angel's wings on his shoulders presenting himself before St Peter at the gates of heaven'.[13] If this whimsical conceit ever crossed Picasso's mind, he rejected it. Nonetheless he drew on his training in sacred art, also on memories of the El Grecos at Toledo, and came up with two largish mock altarpieces. The first, *The Mourners*, is appropriately sombre and religious; the second, *The Burial of Casagemas* (also known as *Evocation*), is both sacred and blasphemous—a Goyesque combination that Picasso would make his own. Since these allegories (for which there are a number of sketches) look backward to the Golden Age of Spanish art and forward to the high style of the later Blue period and memorialize the most traumatic event of the artist's young life, they have attracted much art-historical attention. In fact, neither work succeeds in commemorating the tragedy anything like as effectively as the horrendous death heads. The process of catharsis still has another two years to go; not until he paints his Blue period masterpiece, *La Vie*, will Picasso finally exorcise Casagemas. Even then the psychic scar would never quite heal. Other deaths would reopen it.

Casagemas looked like a debauched El Greco saint; so it is only fitting that *The Mourners* derives from this artist, whose influence culminates but by no means ends with *Les Demoiselles d'Avignon*. The naked child on the right of the mourners has been taken from the naked John the Baptist child on the right of El Greco's *Holy Family with St Anne and St John* in the Prado. The throng of sorrowing outcasts parodies the noblemen in *The Burial of Count Orgaz*, the painting that Picasso had gone to see around the time Casagemas killed himself. The mourners' blank, featureless faces tend to confirm the story that as a student Picasso had substituted caricatures of his teachers for those in the El Greco. They also look ahead to the new identities he gives El Greco's figures in his so-called play, *El Entierro del Conde de Orgaz* (1957–58), and sacrilegious print (1970) on the same subject (see illustration, p.93).

El Greco. *Holy Family with St Anne and St John*. c.1595. Oil on canvas, 107×69cm. Museo del Prado, Madrid.

For the second, larger, painting, *Evocation*, Picasso once again draws on El Greco: *The Dream of Philip II*, as well as *Count Orgaz*. The lower part of *Evocation* roughly corresponds to *The Mourners*: a group of stylized figures in blue-black robes hover over a blank-faced corpse enveloped in a white shroud. The top half is a total contrast: a farcical *Ascension* (with a nod to Odilon Redon's *Phaeton*). Casagemas receives a last embrace from a nude woman (Germaine?) before being carried off on a white horse to Paradise. A group of whores, naked except for gartered stockings, wave the heaven-bound hero on his way. Looking on is the draped mother figure—accompanied by the children Casagemas could never have had—who haunts Blue period paintings and plays a leading role in *La Vie*.

Picasso presumably intended *Evocation* to be an ironical commemoration of an ironical man. But the symbolical whores and the symbolical mother of symbolical children bidding a farcical farewell to a man who had failed to live up to her sexual demands fail to do justice either to Picasso's corrosive sense of guilt or to his corrosive sense of humour.

This art-school facetiousness reminds us of something we are apt to forget: the artist was still only nineteen. To judge by Sabartès's descriptions, the Picasso's early murals must have followed the same pattern. These lost works poked the same sardonic fun at the temptations of St Antony that *Evocation* pokes at the tribulations of Casagemas. *Evocation* seems the more hollow for failing to draw upon those very elements—irony and pathos, blasphemy and faith—that Picasso would play off against one another to such disturbing effect in years to come, not least in the *Crucifixion* of 1930, where he distils his private fears and dilemmas and tatters of faith into a terrifying parable of public malaise.

Picasso. *The Greedy Child*. Paris, 1901. Oil on canvas, 92.8×68.3cm. National Gallery of Art, Washington, D.C., Chester Dale Collection.

Although Picasso had affairs with other girls, Germaine, who is so intrinsic to these mementos of death, remained part of his entourage until she went to live with Pichot. After her marriage to Pichot in 1906 or 1907,[14] they settled in a small Montmartre house called La Maison Rose—and there, apart from trips back to Barcelona, they remained until 1918, when Pichot returned to Spain for good. After his death on a trip to Paris in 1925, Germaine fell chronically sick. Picasso helped her financially until she died in 1948. She was fortunate in having a devoted coterie. Gertrude Stein says that friends 'used to carry her in her armchair to the nearest cinema . . . regularly once a week. I imagine they are still [1933] doing it.'[15] Over the years Picasso contrived for the onus of Casagemas's death to pass from his shoulders onto Germaine's. Françoise Gilot, his mistress in the 1940s, relates that, shortly after World War II, he took her to the Maison Rose to see this pathetic relic, who was about the same age as himself but seemed infinitely older. The wretched Germaine has been downgraded from 'model' to 'laundress'.

> We made our way up the hill . . . [and] found the rue des Saules. We went into a small house. [Picasso] knocked at a door and then walked inside without waiting for an answer. I saw a little old lady, toothless and sick, lying in bed. . . . Pablo talked quietly with her. After a few minutes he laid some money on her night table. She thanked him profusely and we went out again. Pablo didn't say anything as we walked down the street. I asked him why he had brought me to see the woman.
>
> 'I want you to learn about life,' he said quietly. But why especially that old woman? I asked him. 'That woman's name is Germaine Pichot. She's old and toothless and poor and unfortunate now,' he said. 'But when she was young she was very pretty and made a painter friend of mine suffer so much that he committed suicide. She was a young laundress when I first came to Paris. The first people we looked up, this friend of mine and I, were this woman and friends of hers with whom she was living. We had been given their names by friends in Spain and they used to have us come eat with them from time to time. She turned a lot of heads. Now look at her.'[16]

It was 'a little like showing someone a skull to encourage him to meditate on the vanity of human existence,' Gilot says.[17] She evidently had no idea of the irony of the situation, no idea that Picasso, like Bluebeard, was giving her a key to perhaps the darkest area of his past.

* * *

Sometime in October Sabartès announced that he was ready to make his long-awaited first trip to Paris. His messiah had beckoned: 'I had to follow him,' Sabartès writes, 'this passion for Paris was like a contagious disease.'[18] When 'the poet' stepped from the train early one morning at the Gare d'Orsay, Picasso and Mateu de Soto (who had arrived two or three days earlier) were there to meet him. Sabartès was 'stupefied' at the honour. Picasso was a notoriously late riser; on the other hand, he was always—even in old age—punctilious where old friends were concerned. A hotel room with two beds had been booked, a few steps from his studio; the other bed was for Mateu who had been sleeping on Picasso's floor. After lunch the three of them repaired to the studio. Sabartès was horrified by the novelty of the recent work. The only example he gives is the *Portrait of Coquiot* (if it was still in the studio, the sitter had presumably asked for a few changes), but he presumably had in mind such simplified images as the *Woman with a Necklace* (see illustration, p.202), the *Seated Harlequin*, the *Child Holding a Dove* and *The Greedy Child*. What apparently shocked him was the playing-card crudity and motley colours of recent works.

Picasso. *Seated Harlequin*. Paris, 1901. Oil on canvas, 80×60.3cm. The Metropolitan Museum of Art, New York, Gift of Mr and Mrs John L. Loeb, 1960.

Sabartès explains that he was dismayed because Picasso had dared to make these radical changes in his absence. Several links in the evolutionary chain, he says, were missing. This brought on a feeling of vertigo, of being 'on the brink of an abyss'. As Picasso showed him the canvases stacked against the wall, mercilessly scrutinizing his face for his reactions, paranoia compounded Sabartès's vertigo. It was not just the changes in style that disturbed him; changes in the attitudes of his two best friends disturbed him even more.

> Soto had known all this for only two or three days, yet already he was making common cause with Picasso to frighten me.
>
> 'What do you think of it?'
>
> 'I'll get used to it.'[19]

Later, Picasso took Sabartès and Mateu to the Musée du Luxembourg. Instead of describing Picasso's reactions to the museum's great collection of nineteenth-century French art, Sabartès rhapsodizes smugly about the charms of the neighbourhood: 'its atmosphere harmonized better with my spirit, and I decided to leave the room in Montmartre' (for the Latin Quarter).[20] He and Mateu moved to the Hôtel des Ecoles on the rue Champolion, round the corner from the Musée de Cluny. Was Sabartès, one wonders, out to establish a certain independence of Picasso? It would seem so, for he tried to form a *tertulia* in the nearby Café La Lorraine, a bohemian establishment that reminded him of Els Quatre Gats. Besides Soto, Manolo and Fontbona, the group probably included Iturrino, Juli González and Josep Dalmau, the painter and avant-garde dealer from Barcelona. Sometimes Picasso would come down from Montmartre at noon, and they would lunch together in a Turkish restaurant on the Place de la Sorbonne. Otherwise he would appear after dinner and they would spend the evening in the café. Sabartès has described one of these evenings in the Café La Lorraine, when his *tertulia* had failed once again to materialize. He had ordered a glass of beer and was sitting alone, dreadfully bored, waiting for Picasso to appear. From time to time he would peer across the smoke-filled room in the hope of catching sight of his

Picasso. *Child Holding a Dove*. Paris, 1901. Oil on canvas, 73×54cm. Private collection, London.

friends, but he was too myopic to see more than a few feet ahead of him. The buzz of conversation, the click of billiard balls, made him feel all the more lonely and dejected. And then, suddenly, salvation! Picasso and his friends had arrived. Picasso was ahead of the rest, eyes blazing voraciously as he drank in the spectacle of his pitiful friend. Unwittingly, Sabartès had inspired one of the first and finest manifestations of what came to be called the Blue period. 'Thinking I was alone,' he writes, 'I had fallen into the trap of Picasso's stare.' It was a sensation that all the artist's friends would sooner or later experience.

When Sabartès went to the studio a day or two later, Picasso picked a canvas[21] off the floor and put it on the easel: 'I was astonished to see myself just as he had surprised me in the café, caught at a fugitive moment on my journey through life. . . . I understood what had inspired my friend . . . the spectre of my solitude.' His myopic eyes had expressed so clearly what was in his mind: 'thought and gaze unite and are lost in the void.'[22]

Picasso. *The Poet Sabartès* (also known as *Le Bock*). Paris, 1901. Oil on canvas, 82×66cm. Pushkin Museum, Moscow.

Sabartès thus came to see himself as the progenitor of Blue period blueness. But symbolist Paris had been in the throes of a bluish obsession ever since the early 1890s. Art nouveau artefacts are pervasively blue—peacock blue, Madonna blue, ice blue. To take but one example: Emile Gallé had exhibited a glass bowl entitled *Blue Melancholia* at the 1892 Salon. It was engraved with a verse by the symbolist poet Maurice Rollinat: 'How many times a languid / Memory shows the heart / Its blue and melancholy flower.'[23] Sabartès, however, was incapable of seeing Picasso's new style in anything but a personal context: 'Regarding myself for the first time in that marvellous blue mirror . . . like a vast lake whose waters contain something of myself . . . I perceived a new aspect of Picasso's art . . . a glimmer of a new horizon. . . . Henceforth, my soul communed with the "blue" doctrine of a pictorial dream.' Poor besotted Sabartès does not see that 'the marvellous blue mirror' mocks as well as flatters. By portraying the myopic poetaster as a soulful *fin-de-siècle* visionary, and by insisting (most unusually for him) that this portrait be called *The Poet Sabartès*—a title that mocks and flatters Sabartès's dilettantism—the artist endows this sentimental image of his toady with a teasing touch of irony. By envisaging Sabartès and Casagemas in the likeness of each other (the shared profile), Picasso, who already saw painting as a magic act, gives the knife a further twist. He resurrects the dead in the guise of the living and hints that Sabartès should step into the suicide's shoes—shoes for whose owner the poet had felt nothing but abhorrence. This portrait commemorates the first phase in Sabartès's ultimately total sacrifice of his identity to Picasso. Many years later, when Picasso obliged him to put his own interests ahead of any personal commitments, including those to his wife, Sabartès cravenly complied.

'A few weeks after having joined the family created by Picasso,' Sabartès wrote an article about his Blue period work 'from the point of view of its content.' The article was never published and is presumed lost, but he gives a résumé of it in his memoir. While no longer 'shocked by Picasso's shrieking colours,' Sabartès says, he still had difficulty assimilating the flatness and simplifications of works done earlier in the year, because they were painted when he was not around. Since he had been in at the birth of the Blue period, he had no problem accepting it. 'My spirit fused with it . . . it gradually possessed me.' There was a no less egotistical reason for Sabartès's acceptance of this morbid, monochromatic new style: it stemmed from the morbid, monochromatic tenebrism (e.g., *Last Moments*, *Poor Geniuses*, etc.) that had preoccupied Picasso a year or so before—the last time Sabartès and Picasso had seen each other every day.

Sabartès was more privy to his friend's gloomy thoughts than anyone else, and his account of 'Picasso's ideas at the beginning of the Blue period [as exemplified by] conversations with him at the time' is the more valuable for having the artist's imprimatur. According to Sabartès, Picasso was dominated by the idea that

> art emanates from Sadness and Pain. . . . Sadness lends itself to meditation . . . grief is at the basis of life. We are passing through . . . a period of uncertainty that everyone regards from the viewpoint of his own misery . . . a period of grief, of sadness and of misery. Life with all its torments is at the core of [Picasso's] theory of art. If we demand sincerity of the artist, we must remember that sincerity is not to be found outside the realm of grief.[24]

Picasso. *Self-Portrait.* Paris, 1900. Pen and sepia on paper, 20.5×12.6cm. Private collection. Inscribed '*Pictor e-n Misere Humane* [*sic*]'.

Sabartès does not account for all this misery. He does not see it stemming from developments in Picasso's life, nor does he relate it to any specific social ills, except some vague *maladie du siècle*. Besides the notion of life as a vale of tears, Sabartès goes on to credit Picasso with another basic notion: art as an instinctive form of self-expression—a channel for all those blue, blue tears. The true artist must forget everything he has been taught, Sabartès paraphrases Picasso. Knowledge is a hindrance, because it obstructs our vision and impedes spontaneity. Art schools are inefficient, thwarting, harmful. Rigid rules and academic methods are absolute barriers to the development of a personality. Expression can be 'pure' only when it stems directly from the artist; not when the artist is a medium for the transmission of other people's ideas. An artist should harness his work to his intuition, as primitive painters do. Artifice has not contaminated the innocence of their vision. Sabartès does not specify the painters, but they presumably included the Italian primitives Picasso had seen in the Louvre, the Catalan primitives he knew through Vidal Ventosa. He must also have had in mind the synthetic primitivism of Gauguin. Traces of the Gauguins Picasso had seen in Vollard's stock were already showing up in his work: for instance, the exotic floral frieze, the stylized gestures, above all, the flat areas of colour ('the playing-card look' that had so shocked Sabartès) of the *Seated Harlequin* with the white face and ruff of Pierrot.

There was apparently a lot more in Sabartès's article about 'the relationship between colour and feeling', about 'an anti-theoretical theory' and other vague *modernista* notions that, recapitulated from memory forty years later, make little or no sense. More prescient is Sabartès's reference 'to the bluish whiteness of a moonbeam slanting through the window in a painting of a woman in a prison cell . . . the caress of the pale light . . . making her shrunken shoulders look still chillier. . . .'[25] There was also a passage about hands: 'nightmare of all artists . . . hands . . . [that] seek each other's warmth . . . that denote fear and throb with anxiety; some timid, others freezing with cold, others astir as if to banish solitude . . . The painter has been able to give form to a sigh, to make inert bodies breathe, to infuse life into the dead.'[26]

Picasso. *Saint-Lazare Woman by Moonlight.* Paris, 1901. Oil on canvas, 100×69.2cm. Detroit Institute of Arts. Bequest of Robert H. Tannahill.

Steinlen. Cover of *Le Mirliton,* March 1892, with a verse of Aristide Bruant's song '*A Saint-Lazare*'. Bibliothèque Nationale. Paris.

Toulouse-Lautrec. *A Saint-Lazare.* 1886. Cover for *Le Mirliton* reprinted as the cover of *La Plume,* February 1, 1891.

The evening the article was finished, Sabartès called on Picasso to discuss it with him. Some English journalists from *The Studio* were already there. To avoid being interviewed, the artist told Sabartès to read them his essay, which was in Castilian—'a language they won't understand', Sabartès objected. 'What of it?' Picasso replied. After the first page the English journalists nodded off. When the reading ended, 'they arose, gave thanks effusively, and departed.' 'If it hadn't been for [you] we'd not have got rid of them,' Picasso could never resist teasing Sabartès. 'And you! Telling me they wouldn't understand!'[27]

* * *

Sabartès's evocation of a woman prisoner—chilled, shrunken-shouldered and bathed in moonlight—refers to one of several paintings that resulted from Picasso's visits to the women's prison of Saint-Lazare in the late summer or early autumn of 1901. He had gone there to paint the inmates, many of whom were whores. 'Thanks to the good offices of Dr Louis Julien [*sic*: Jullien],' Picasso later claimed, 'he obtained permission to visit Saint-Lazare where [a "Phrygian" bonnet] was worn by the women who were set apart from the others because they had venereal diseases.'[28] Dr Jullien was a venereologist, so Picasso may have been one of his patients—how else would he have known him? After all, he had frequented the lowest whorehouses since the age of puberty; and, according to Françoise Gilot, he admitted in the late 1940s to having caught a venereal disease early in life.[29] Given the depression that descended on Picasso around the time of his Saint-Lazare visits, he may have found that he was infected. This might explain the change in the mood of his work. So might the fear of becoming infected, especially as he was about to embark on another love affair—with a mysterious girl called Blanche.

Picasso maintained that he had applied to visit Saint-Lazare because the models there cost him nothing. This was common knowledge in Montmartre. The prison was even the subject of a famous song, '*A Saint-Lazare*', which was performed night after night in Aristide Bruant's cabaret—one of the *boîtes* Picasso and Casagemas had visited on their first trip to Paris. Picasso would have seen the great Saint-Lazare drawing (1886) that Toulouse-Lautrec did for the cover of Bruant's magazine, *Le Mirliton* (first published August 1887); it hung on the cabaret walls. Lautrec portrays one of the whores in her syphilitic bonnet writing an abjectly adoring letter to the pimp who exploits and maltreats her. The drawing echoes the wry, sentimental mood of Bruant's ballad. Here is the last verse of this ballad (prototype of the ballads Edith Piaf would sing fifty years later):

I end my letter with a kiss
So long, man of mine,
Though you're not affectionate
Oh, how I adore you like
I used to adore God, and Papa,
When I was a little girl
And used to go to communion
At Saint'-Marguerite.

Jean Béraud. *La Salle des Filles à Saint-Lazare*. 1886. Oil on canvas, 144×110.5cm. Private Collection.

A. Morand. *Entrance to the Infirmary at Saint-Lazare*. Charcoal on paper. *c*.1900. Musée Carnavalet, Paris.

Saint-Lazare prison. *c*.1900. Bibliothèque Nationale, Paris.

Toulouse-Lautrec was not the only artist to portray a Saint-Lazare girl. Two years later, Jean Béraud—best known for fashionable genre scenes—had executed a large, uncharacteristically earnest painting, *La Salle des Filles à Saint-Lazare*, that depicts the institution in a sanctimonious light. If the modish Béraud addressed this highly charged subject, other artists of the period certainly followed suit. Dr Jullien was very proud of a macabre painting, which had a place of honour in the vestibule. All newly arrived prisoners were obliged to pass in front of this admonitory image: the funeral cortège of an inmate flanked by gaolers and nuns. This 'conjunction of *memento mori*, prostitutes and venereal disease' has even been said to have fired Picasso's morbid imagination.[30]

The availability of free models was only part of the lure of Saint-Lazare. What primarily drew this 'painter of human misery' to the place was the opportunity of demonstrating how art could function as 'the child of sadness and pain'. Where else would he find models that exemplified his equivocal view of sex as ecstatic and tender, but also guilt-inducing and bound up with suffering, even death? The dog-Latin inscription '*Pictor en misere humane*' that he had added to a self-portrait the year before was prophetic. This is how Picasso now came to see himself.

Saint-Lazare was unique in being a penal institution run by nuns.[31] The severe seventeenth-century building on the corner of the Boulevard Magenta and the rue du Faubourg Saint-Denis stood on the site of a medieval leper-house. As Dr Jullien would have told Picasso, it had been a famous place of penitence ever since its foundation by St Vincent de Paul in the seventeenth century. Sinners were sent there '*pour se faire blanchir l'âme*' (to cleanse the soul). Everyone—prince of the church, venal official or subversive playwright (i.e. Beaumarchais)—was obliged to start his penance with a severe whipping.[32] Powerful families could have mad or uncooperative relatives incarcerated there. During the Revolution, the Saint-Lazare became a state prison: at first a *prison de luxe*, as we know from the scenes that Hubert Robert (briefly an inmate) painted of the interior. The aristocracy could bring in furniture and musical instruments, even servants. Under the Jacobins, it changed into a place of utmost terror. André Chenier spent his last days there. The Marquis de Sade was luckier: he survived for another twenty years. In 1824 it became a women's gaol. The administration was entrusted to the Sisters of St Joseph; about a hundred of them were put in charge, their blue and black habits distinguishing them from lay helpers. The institution held almost a thousand prisoners. Criminals and prostitutes were allowed to bring babies as long as they were still being nursed.

Some of the inmates had actually arranged to be arrested in time to give birth in the relative security of the prison. Compared with conditions at other prisons, the living conditions at Saint-Lazare were supposedly 'unique in their quiet, clean, truly beautiful way', to quote a description of the place published in 1890.[33] The Saint-Lazare was 'a strange city, in which a many-faceted world lived in sorrow, in blasphemy, in remorse, in prayer, in self-sacrifice and in laborious activity; a religious order, a hospital . . . a store, even a central laundry and bakery for the prisoners of the [department of the] Seine.'[34] Picasso's friend Francis Carco has a different story to tell. He was overwhelmed by the gloom and the smell: a combination of 'the convent, the bedroom, the soup-kitchen and the

Left: X-ray of Picasso's *Portrait of Sabartès* (see illustration, p. 226): *Saint-Lazare Inmate*. Paris, 1901. Museu Picasso, Barcelona.

Right: Picasso. *Absinthe Drinker*. Paris, 1901. Oil on canvas, 73×54cm. State Hermitage Museum, Leningrad.

Picasso. *Women at the Prison Fountain*. Paris, 1901. Oil on canvas, 81×65cm. Private collection.

Picasso. *Mateu de Soto and a Saint-Lazare Prostitute*. Paris, 1901. Pen on paper, 30.8×20cm. Albright-Knox Art Gallery, Buffalo, New York, Gift of ACG Trust, 1970.

Gauguin. *At the Café (Madame Ginoux)* (detail). Arles, 1888. Oil on canvas, 73×52cm. Pushkin Museum, Moscow.

Gauguin. *Head of a Breton Woman*. *c*.1894. Gouache on cardboard, 27×36cm. Private collection.

pharmacy'.[35] Floors, windows and domestic utensils were kept spotlessly clean, but the nuns regarded any attempt at personal hygiene on the part of the inmates as an '*outrage à la pudeur*' (offence against modesty). There were no showers, washbasins or towels. If the girls complained, they were condemned to solitary confinement—not entirely solitary: there were rats.

Further information about the prison is to be found in an article by a journalist intent on abolishing the draconian police system of confining prostitutes to specific houses and districts and subjecting them to enforced medical examinations for syphilis, '*le péril vénérien*'.[36] Hoche, who visited the prison under the auspices of Dr Jullien, says that 'visits to the venereal patients . . . took place across two sets of bars separated by . . . 1.5 to 1 metres.' Visitors accompanied by staff members would presumably have been spared this obstacle. Picasso did not limit his encounters with these sick women to the actual gaol. After he had washed his hands in disinfectant and made his way through the locked gates, he would go to a nearby café frequented by the outpatients. There he would observe the girls in a more congenial setting. Since Picasso seldom moved without a sketchbook, it is surprising that, apart from the outstanding one of a 'puta de Saint-Lazare' with Mateu de Soto, virtually no prison drawings have come to light. There must have been studies for the dejected-looking whores seated at café tables, whom he portrays more frequently than the prisoners. For stylistic inspiration Picasso evidently looked elsewhere. Several of the women who lean their elbows on the table, heads held hopelessly in bony, attentuated hands, have been modelled on Madame Ginoux, the Arlesian brothel-keeper whom Gauguin painted (1888) in front of a soda syphon at a café table (a painting that van Gogh had admired to the extent of copying it). Picasso would have seen this work at Vollard's. If the pose and stylizations of these whores and the harlequin who sometimes keeps them company stem from Gauguin, the mannerist elongations of limbs and hands stem from both El Greco and Gothic sculpture.

Picasso was fascinated by the so-called Phrygian bonnet that the prostitutes wore.[37] In reality it was not at all Phrygian. The authorities would hardly have defiled the sacrosanct emblem of the Revolution and the republic—Marianne's allegorical headgear—by designating it as the badge of a syphilitic whore. Moreover, a Phrygian bonnet is red and helmet-shaped; the Lazaristes' '*bonnet d'ordonnance*' was either brown or white (white if the inmate was syphilitic), and tied under the chin; it derives from the sort of coif that working women wore in the previous century. In making a special feature of this bonnet, Picasso seems once again to be following in Gauguin's footsteps. Although the first of his prison paintings—the tentative head of a bonneted girl—has unfortunately disappeared under yet another portrait of Sabartès, enough shows up in an x-ray to reveal how she derives from Gauguin's strikingly similar head of a Breton girl that Picasso had often seen on Paco Durrio's walls. Even the *Women at the Prison Fountain*—two rough-looking whores, one clutching a baby, seated by the fountain in the prison laundry—have a Breton or Arlesian look. Gauguin's brooding peasants helped Picasso arrive at a mythic image that would beautify and dignify his whores and enshrine them in a wider, more romantic context than a prison laundry.

Picasso. *Mother and Child.* Paris, 1901. Oil on canvas, 112.3×97.5 cm. Fogg Art Museum, Harvard University, Bequest of Collection of Maurice Wertheim. Class of 1906.

Picasso. *Woman Ironing.* Paris, 1901. Oil on canvas, 49.5×25.7 cm. The Metropolitan Museum of Art, New York, The Alfred Stieglitz Collection, 1949. Inscribed to Sabartès.

Like most visitors, Picasso was appalled by the presence of children in the prison; hence so many Saint-Lazare images have to do with motherhood. It did not take Picasso long to idealize and stylize these sullen-looking women into mannerist Madonnas of exquisite sensibility and serenity, whose faces and hands and babies are all of extreme attenuation. The bonnet is transformed into a becoming cowl; the hideous hospital jackets (of black-and-blue striped drugget) into elegant, dark blue El Greco-like habits; and the grim archways of the Saint-Lazare building are replaced by curtains or a suggestion of undefined space that belie incarceration. In their timeless clothes these harlot Madonnas exist in a blue limbo—'*El Patio Azul*'—which corresponds far more to the etherealized melancholy of *modernisme* than the grim realities of prison.[38] These mothers are as prettified in their way as the peasant Madonnas that sanctified poverty in seventeenth-century Spain and Italy.

Blue period paintings make sorrow acceptable to bourgeois taste by sentimentalizing and sanitizing it. As André Salmon (soon to be one of Picasso's closest friends) rhapsodized in a 'Blue period' poem: drunkenness was '*douce et romantique*'.[39] Far from triggering feelings of outrage, the '*douce et romantique*' paintings of the Blue period tend to allay the public's (and conceivably the artist's) guilt. Why else, when he ultimately became politically involved, did Picasso come to disparage the Blue period?[40] In those early days, he later joked, the principal victim of society, as far as he was concerned, was himself.

That the Saint-Lazare women were victims of society nobody would deny, but they are also to some extent Picasso's victims. There is a hint of eroticism, even sadism, to their portrayal. Over the next two or three years the desirability of Blue period women tends to be proportionate to their despair. The laundresses, for example: the first ones, seemingly done from life, are raw-boned harridans who look more than equal to their task. A few months later Picasso did an oil sketch (inscribed to Sabartès) of an exhausted but far more appealing woman bowed over her ironing board. Three years later, he would paint a larger version of the same subject, the famous *Woman Ironing*, now in the Guggenheim Museum. Mannerist exaggeration has softened the impact of the original image, and the laundress looks not so much syphilitic as touchingly, vulnerably tubercular. Hollow eyes and cheeks have been rendered with such sensuousness that she comes across as a spectre of sick sex appeal. Years later Picasso would describe women with some relish as 'suffering machines'. There is more romantic agony than social criticism to Blue period imagery.

The most important of the Saint-Lazare paintings is *The Two Sisters*. Although executed a year or so after the first prison visits, and in Barcelona, not Paris, it belongs with the rest of the prison group. Picasso took enormous trouble over this work. There are a number of major drawings for it: mostly in a hybrid style that combines elements from Egyptian, Greek, Romanesque and Gothic art, inspired by visits to the Louvre. He even wrote a letter about it to Max Jacob (July 1902; see illustration, p.249): 'I want to do a painting of the drawing I am sending you, *The Two Sisters*. It's a picture I am doing of a Saint-Lazare whore and a mother.'[41] By transcribing this letter incorrectly when he first published it and writing '*sœur*' instead of '*mère*', Sabartès has caused confusion. He opened

El Greco. *Visitation*. Painted for the Capilla Oballe in San Vicente, Toledo, 1607–14. Oil on canvas, 97×71 cm. Dumbarton Oaks Research Library and Collection, Washington, D.C.

Picasso. Drawing for *The Two Sisters*. Barcelona, 1902. Pencil on paper, 45×32 cm. Musée Picasso, Paris.

Picasso. *The Two Sisters*. Barcelona, 1902. Oil on panel, 152×100 cm. State Hermitage Museum, Leningrad.

the door to the mistaken identification of the figure on the right, who is holding a baby, as a nun or nursing sister,[42] and the interpretation of the painting as a Visitation (relevant only insofar as it resembles El Greco's little *Visitation* in composition, colour and mystery). *The Two Sisters* has also been seen as an allegory of sacred and profane love.[43] This makes sense to the extent that it embodies the harlot-Madonna concept of the earlier Saint-Lazare paintings. And it fits in with yet another of Picasso's paradoxes: the view of woman as goddess and doormat, heroine and victim. But *The Two Sisters* transcends these cut-and-dried concepts; it can be read, like all Picasso's major works, on more than one level, and be seen in more than one light. Instead of insisting on one meaning at the expense of another, we should accept the painting's essentially ambivalent nature: ambivalent in its overtones of prison and cloister, Eros and Thanatos, its secular subject matter and quasi-sacred power; ambivalent also in its modernity and medievalism, its sophistication and primitivism, its flatness and relief.

While *The Two Sisters* looks back at Saint-Lazare, it looks ahead to *La Vie*—the great cathartic painting of 1903 that would supposedly lay Casagemas's ghost. Both are about life and death; both involve seemingly ominous confrontations. The resolute look and stance of the 'sister' with the baby on the right anticipates that of the mother in *La Vie*, who stands for life, whereas the whore-sister on the left of *The Two Sisters* is portrayed as if close to death: she is wrapped in a shroud-like robe, her shoulders are bowed, eyes closed. The very nature, scale and bas-relief look of the panel—*The Two Sisters* is not on canvas—suggest an altarpiece: one of those painted ones peculiar to seventeenth-century Spain that simulate a carved (and therefore more costly) altarpiece. There may also be faint echoes of the two altarpieces Picasso did for the Barcelona convent, both of which seem to have portrayed a miraculous confrontation, one with Christ, one with the Virgin. If Picasso now drew on his apprenticeship as a devotional painter—his iconographical knowledge of such subjects as the Visitation and Annunciation—it was not in a devotional spirit; it was because he wanted to use a traditionally hallowed image, subliminally, as it were, to endow his whores with an air of universal relevance and mystic power.

* * *

By the autumn of 1901, Picasso's life, like his work, had settled into a classic bohemian pattern, limited by the confines of Montmartre, limited, too, by poverty. Odette had faded from the picture: Germaine was with Pichot and so was now a friend rather than a mistress. The artist's new girl was called Blanche; nothing is known about her. Drawings in an unpublished sketchbook confirm that she was elegant as well as pretty—probably a *midinette*, like Germaine. Her reign was short. By the end of the year, if not before, she seems to have been out of Picasso's life. As for relaxation, the artist and his entourage would meet of an evening at one or another of their favourite cafés and then, funds permitting, go on to a cabaret, almost always in Montmartre. Since Rodolphe de Salis's death, the Chat Noir, which had inspired Utrillo and Rusiñol to found Els Quatre Gats, had declined. And the Moulin Rouge had become touristy and expensive

Picasso. *Portrait of Blanche*. Paris, 1901. Charcoal and coloured crayons on sketchbook page, 20×12cm. Private collection.

—worth visiting only if the Catalan proprietor, Oller, was handing out free passes to his compatriots. Most evenings the group went to a sordid hole, 'Le Zut', on the Place Ravignan—in those days a dangerous neighbourhood frequented by apaches, who were still rumoured to scalp their victims (like their Indian prototypes). Sabartès has described Le Zut: there were two rooms, filthy, dark and vermin-ridden, furnished with benches and barrels. Frédé, the guitar-playing owner, had kept the smaller room for the exclusive use of the Spaniards: Picasso, Manolo, Soto, Sabartès, Pichot (and Germaine), Durrio and Fontbona. The larger space—known as the 'stalactite' room, because of the strips of coloured paper that hung from the blackened rafters—catered for a more varied clientele: neighbourhood artists and poets, models and mistresses, whores and pimps; occasionally there would be a knifing; occasionally a pistol shot would cause a sudden silence, and a body would be carried out. 'Don't worry, friends, it doesn't happen every day. Have another drink,' Frédé would reassure them. The Spaniards kept to themselves, afraid of going into the big hall—'We would not have known how to behave in that company.'[44]

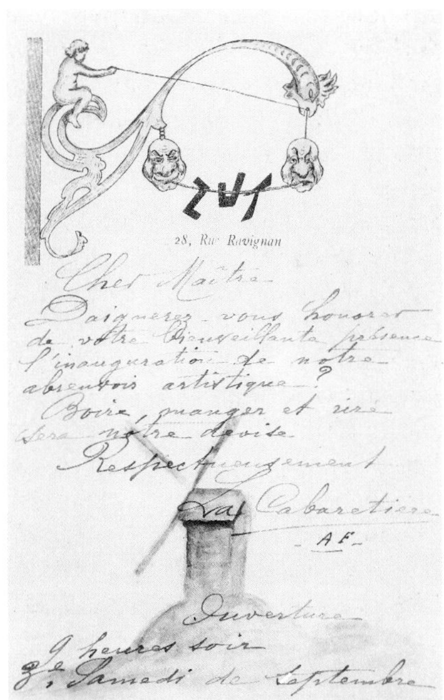
ZUT
28, Rue Ravignan

Cher Maître
Daignerez-vous honorer de votre bienveillante présence l'inauguration de notre abreuvoir artistique?
Boire, manger et rire sera notre devise.
Respectueusement
La Cabaretière
– A F –
Ouverture
9 heures soir
3e Samedi de Septembre

Invitation to the opening of Le Zut. Musée de Montmartre, Paris.

Sabartès persuaded Frédé to clean up 'the wretched room we called ours': scour the soot-blackened lamp, whitewash the dingy walls and disinfect the verminous furniture. Picasso and Pichot decided to fresco the place. The night before they embarked on this undertaking, Sabartès and Mateu de Soto slept on the floor of Picasso's studio. It was freezing. First thing in the morning they all left for Le Zut, picking up a young girl en route to help with the spring-cleaning. Sabartès and Soto made paper chains. Picasso began to paint:

> With the tip of the brush dipped in blue, he drew a few female nudes in one stroke. Then, in a blank area . . . he drew a hermit. As soon as one of us shouted: 'Temptation of St Antony,' he stopped. . . . As far as he was concerned, this was enough, but more than half the wall was still unpainted . . . [this] he tackled without uttering a word, without lifting his brush except to load it with more colour. It was as if he did not hear us talking, as if he were unaware of our presence. . . . His lines sprang from the wall . . . as if hypnotized . . . they obeyed the mandate of his will. Next to the group of nudes was a portrait of me, from the waist up, larger than life, in a declamatory attitude, with a paper in my hand. Over my head a bat unfolded its wings, as in the coat of arms of my native city.
>
> Pichot contented himself with a small bit of wall in a corner . . . on which he painted an Eiffel Tower with Santos Dumont's dirigible flying above it.
>
> Of my portrait there remains no trace, not even a photograph. . . . It disappeared with the Zut. . . .
>
> That evening our whole group gathered in the Zut. . . . Frédé placed a group of tiny glasses on the top of the barrel: there was no beer, because Frédé had had no money to settle his brewer's bill.[45]

After this transformation, Picasso and his friends spent even more time at Le Zut, seldom leaving until dawn. The artist would then return to his studio and sleep until noon. We know how his room looked from that familiar painting *Le Tub*. Above the bed hangs Toulouse-Lautrec's poster of May Milton and one of the Catalan seascapes that had failed to sell at Vollard's. The cosiness and neatness of the room and the inclusion of a vase of flowers—all very unlike Picasso—bespeaks the presence of a woman. And, sure enough, there is a naked girl—Blanche, to judge by a study for a red-headed girl in the same pose enveloped in a towel, sponging herself in a hip-bath. (When not in use, the bath served as a container for Picasso's library, including works by Claudel and Fagus.) The strangely small scale of the nude—she looks like a piece of sculpture—in proportion to the setting is an indication of the liberties Picasso now felt free to take. This is a historic painting, the first manifestation of a subject that will come to obsess Picasso: a specific model in a specific studio at a specific time—descriptive as a diary entry, but allegorical in its implications.

Picasso. *Le Tub (The Blue Room)*. Paris, 1901. Oil on canvas, 50.4×61.5cm. The Phillips Collection, Washington, D.C.

Sabartès describes the rest of the studio: 'the first thing one saw was . . . the *Burial of Casagemas* [he means *Evocation*, not the *Mourners*] which hung, I know not . . . how, as if it were a screen used to conceal something which it were better to keep out of sight.'[46] And, come to think of it, *Evocation* lends itself to this role. Between the studio and Mañach's room there was a fireplace with a mirror above it—the mirror in which Picasso looked long and deep in search of an image; few artists in history have been so preoccupied by their appearance or painted themselves in so many different guises. Besides the bed there was an easel, a wickerwork armchair, a couple of other chairs, a table that was covered with newspaper when used for dining, also a couple of huge dictionaries which friends used as pillows, if, as often happened, they stayed late and slept on a strip of carpet on the floor. Against the wall were ever-mounting accumulations of odds and ends—an ad hoc form of storage which, in one form or another, would take over room after room in one after another of Picasso's studios and houses. Sabartès, who did not like Mañach, does not bother to describe how he lived—very much on his own, it would seem. Picasso cannot have been a considerate roommate. When he was working, he wanted peace and quiet and solitude; when he was not working, he wanted the opposite and would come to life rowdily and gregariously. Max Jacob's recitals and comic turns were noisy; noisier still were the Spaniards with their shouting and singing and guitar-playing. Mañach would not have minded if the work was selling, but Vollard, to name only one potential buyer, disdained the Blue period until it found favour with the Steins. Picasso would derive cynical amusement from the way the public at first rejected these paintings and then took them to its heart in preference to the rest of his work.

Picasso. *Portrait of Jaime Sabartès*. Paris, 1901. Oil on canvas, 46×38cm. Painted over the head of a Saint-Lazare inmate (see illustration, p.220). Museu Picasso, Barcelona.

One gloomy winter afternoon Sabartès found Picasso in the studio alone, bored and frustrated: 'Today I haven't done a thing. . . . If you stay quiet a minute, I'll paint you.'[47] And he took the most tentative of the Saint-Lazare studies (seemingly the first) and transformed it into another portrait of Sabartès: bluer even than *The Poet Sabartès*, but less idealized. The blubber-lipped face with the pince-nez requires only a beard and bowler hat to resemble Toulouse-Lautrec. Sabartès has described the artist awkwardly at work:

> . . . seated on a dilapidated chair, perhaps lower than an ordinary chair, because discomfort does not bother him . . . he delighted in self-mortification and enjoyed subjecting his spirit to tortures so long as they spurred him on. The canvas was placed on the lowest part of the easel, and this compelled him to paint in an almost kneeling position.

Picasso. *Portrait of Mateu de Soto.* Paris, 1901. Oil on canvas, 63×46cm. Oskar Reinhart Collection, Winterthur.

> As a rule the palette was on the floor. . . . I do not recall ever having seen Picasso hold [it] in his hand. He assures me that sometimes he does, just like everyone else . . . but I have always seen him mixing his colours by leaning over a table, chair, or the floor. . . . He surrenders body and soul to this activity . . . as if . . . bewitched. So absorbed, so wrapped up in silence is Picasso . . . that whoever sees him . . . understands and keeps quiet . . . the silence [is] scarcely broken by the creaking of his chair . . . caused by all his creative fever . . . [by] the sound of . . . the brush attacking the canvas.[48]

What Sabartès calls 'self-mortification' is Picasso's habit of making things difficult for himself. Now that he could solve all the usual technical problems, it was all the more imperative to renounce the easy way. Hence a lifelong preference for awkward expedients and improvisation. Picasso would never have much use for elaborate studio paraphernalia, except for a sturdy old printing press. Nor would he care much for fancy materials, except at the time of cubism when, thanks to Braque, he took to using canvas as fine as linen. Although he had a passion for very good paper—seventeenth- or eighteenth-century for preference—he tended to use standard issue from his colour merchant. Throughout his life, he abhorred anything that evoked the pompous image of '*le maître*', and always preferred to paint, as Sabartès points out, on 'a table, chair or floor'.

*　　　*　　　*

Picasso. *Portrait of Mateu de Soto.* Paris, 1901. Oil on canvas, 46×38cm. Heirs of the artist.

Early in the winter, Mateu de Soto moved out of the hotel room that he shared with Sabartès in the Latin Quarter, back into Picasso's studio. Since space was limited, the penniless Soto must have been more desperate than usual, or Picasso had broken with Blanche, or needed someone to help him cope with Mañach, who was becoming increasingly tiresome. The cool and reserved Mateu would have proved a supportive ally. Picasso executed portraits of his new roommate just as he had of Sabartès. Until he found himself a permanent, live-in mistress, his portraits would continue to be almost exclusively of men (Catalan for preference); virtually all the women in his work are *midinettes* or whores, idealized though some of them are. If Picasso saw women as harlot-Madonnas, he saw men as El Greco saints. After doing a literal likeness of the clean-shaven Soto at work on a minute piece of sculpture, with *Evocation* on the wall behind him, Picasso embarked on a second, more deeply felt, portrait of him. He has projected so much of his own *duende* into this second Mateu that it reads like a rehearsal for the great blue self-portrait he was about to execute. Or is it simply that Picasso and Soto have both grown identical beards and moustaches? The Soto portrait is one of the few Blue period paintings that Picasso kept all his life.[49]

Without Soto to share his room in the Latin Quarter, Sabartès lost interest in the Café La Lorraine and the *tertulia* he had tried to establish there. Except for the hours between dawn and noon, when, like Picasso, he slept, Sabartès spent all his time in Montmartre. At the end of the evening Picasso and Mateu would accompany Sabartès part of the way home: 'We'll leave you around here,' one would say. 'Most of the time we would part near the Place de l'Opéra, but if our conversation had not reached a conclusion . . . I did not mind retracing my steps, and my friends . . . would accompany me back [to Montmartre] once again. Sometimes we repeated these comings and goings until we were exhausted, separating finally near the Trinité or the Place de la Comédie Française.'[50] Fed up with these peregrinations up and down a steep hill, Sabartès finally decided to leave the Latin Quarter for a hotel in Montmartre—probably just before Christmas.

For all the camaraderie of the Catalans and the diversions arranged by Max Jacob, Picasso was becoming increasingly nervous and fidgety. By the beginning of December (1901), he had taken to disappearing when his friends least expected it. He had more or less given up work and always seemed preoccupied, but never vouchsafed any explanation. Sabartès provides no real answer. He is too discreet to mention the disappointment Picasso must have felt after the Vollard show; too discreet to go into the problems Picasso was having with Mañach, who seems to have held the artist responsible for the way his work was failing to sell; too discreet to let us know whether Picasso was suffering from some disease or having problems with Blanche. As well as all this there was the artist's old enemy the cold, compounded by poverty and homesickness (his French was still rudimentary). Above all, there were the pressures and isolation imposed by the ever-growing consciousness of his awesome potential.

Three successive self-portraits provide insights into the artist's diminishing peace of mind over the seven months he spent in Paris on this trip. Compared with the one painted immediately after his arrival in June, the one painted just before he left at the end of the year demonstrates how rapidly and deeply his view of himself as well as the world had changed. The images are as different as masks of the comic and tragic muse. The first self-portrait (no. 1 in the Vollard show; see illustration, p. 192) is a brilliantly theatrical—one might say operatic—performance. Suitably enough, it ended up in the collection of Hugo von Hofmannsthal (bought in 1913 with his first royalties from *Rosenkavalier*). Picasso portrays himself with all the panache of a society painter of the *belle époque*—elegantly moustachioed and arrogantly assured in his bouffant white smock and vermillion *lavallière*. As a self-portrait, it is a consummate bravura painting; it is also a masquerade. This is the first time Picasso capitalizes on his amazing eyes: the area of white above and below the pupil is no exaggeration. The charismatic *mirada fuerte* and the defiant inscription, '*Yo Picasso*' ('I, Picasso'), dare us to question his right to be the new messiah of art. To bolster the authority of the image, Picasso has had recourse to a great old master, Nicolas Poussin: one to whom he will return more than once in future years. He has glanced back at that artist's self-portrait in the Louvre. ('Picasso does not redo Poussin. He is Poussin in 1901.'[51]) '*Yo Picasso*' also looks forward: to Fauvism. Years later Picasso boasted that his green shadow anticipated the green stripe down the forehead and nose in Matisse's famous Fauve portrait of his wife (1906; see illustration, p. 413)—'How about that!' he proudly exclaimed in front of a reproduction of the work.[52]

The second of the three self-portrait paintings, done a month or two later, is also self-dramatizing, also inscribed with an emphatic '*Yo*'. But in its black gloom, this baleful, Munch-like image—evidently done by lamplight—is in total contrast to its meretricious predecessor. The expressionistic fervour and intensity is very close to that of the Casagemas

Picasso. *Self-Portrait*. Paris, 1901. Oil on cardboard, 51.5×31.7 cm. Mrs John Hay Whitney Collection, New York.

death heads, and can be attributed to the same source: van Gogh. Thanks partly to van Gogh, the eager boy wonder of the Vollard show has all of a sudden turned into a visionary old beyond his years, whose burning gaze defies the world with ferocious Nietzschean authority.

The most remarkable of all is the Blue period self-portrait that Picasso painted some five months later, shortly before returning to Barcelona. The devils have quieted down and Picasso sees himself as an alienated expatriate devoured by self-pity, chilled by more than the cold. Stylistically it harks back to the Golden Age of Spain. This time the self-dramatization involves seeing himself as he has just portrayed Soto, in the guise of an El Greco monk, an other-worldly ascetic. In the delicacy and subtlety of the drawing (the features have been *drawn* with a very fine brush dipped in Prussian blue), this is probably Picasso's most beautifully wrought painting to date. There is as much play-acting to this romantic image of the 'poor genius' as there is to its predecessors. This is confirmed by a drawing that resembles the painting, except that it presents us with a totally different character. By adding a starched collar and an elegantly striped cravat, Picasso has transformed himself, on paper at least, into a respectable young man of means. Yes, 'play-acting', but there is more to these self-portraits than that. Each masquerade reflects a different aspect of the truth. The first one portrays the artist whom Braque would in later years call 'a talented virtuoso'; the second portrays the driven genius who would ultimately paint *Les Demoiselles d'Avignon*; the third portrays the romantic symbolist of the Blue period.

Picasso. *Self-Portrait*. Paris, 1901. Oil on canvas, 81×60cm. Musée Picasso, Paris.

Doubts as to domicile as well as identity began to plague Picasso. In Madrid he had yearned for Paris; once settled in Paris, he yearned for Barcelona; back in Barcelona, he would yearn for Paris again. Now that he had abandoned French eclecticism for a new form of Spanish tenebrism, he might as well return to the security of Barcelona instead of staying on in misery and poverty in Paris. There was another pressing problem: the relationship with Mañach had broken down. The details are far from clear. Sabartès, who was a witness to the denouement, gives a very circumspect account. It all came down to money. Where Picasso's paranoid attitude to what Sabartès calls 'economic devices' (i.e. money) is concerned, the secretary is always fanatically discreet. Indeed his discretion has led some biographers to conclude that Sabartès was covering up an unrequited passion for Picasso on the part of Mañach.[53] Such evidence as we have points in a very different direction.

If Picasso is recorded as being distraught, it was because the contract with Mañach that had come into force the previous January was due to expire in a matter of days. Given the lack of enthusiasm for the new blue paintings on the part of collectors, it is likely that Mañach proposed to lower the monthly stipend he was paying, or receive more in return for it; and that he insisted on a say in the choice of subjects. Picasso, on the other hand, probably owed Mañach work or money or both, and wanted to retain certain paintings for himself. Then there was the shared apartment. Whatever reimbursement Mañach wanted for the rent would have compounded the other problems. The artist was so destitute, Mañach seems to have reckoned, that his only option would be to accept whatever he was offered. This was to leave out of account Picasso's pride and obstinacy. He decided to break with Mañach, even at the risk of breaking with his collaborators, Vollard and Berthe Weill. Meanwhile he had stopped painting. Why build up Mañach's stock? Loath though he was to throw himself on his family's mercy, he wired his father for enough money to cover his train fare back to Barcelona. Mañach probably knew this and dreaded the arrival of the funds that would release this valuable, if not yet saleable, artist from his clutches.

For some reason Picasso did not tell Sabartès or Mateu de Soto about his plan to leave. They learned the truth one evening at the end of 1901 or beginning of 1902, when they paid a visit to a fellow Spaniard, Paco Durrio, the sculptor, ceramist and jeweller. Durrio lived a few doors away from Le Zut, in the Bateau Lavoir studio that would ultimately become Picasso's. Friends could not resist confiding in him.

Gauguin. *The Guitar Player* (Paco Durrio). 1902. Oil on canvas, 90×72cm. Private collection.

> [He] was very small, very plump and inquisitive [Fernande Olivier wrote in her memoirs]. He had a sound and original temperament . . . sincere and dedicated; a man with real human warmth. . . . [He] had two heroes: Gauguin and Picasso. . . . He used to help his friends with infinite tact. One day, when he was completely broke, Picasso found a tin of sardines, a loaf and a bottle of wine on his doorstep; they had been left there by Durrio.[54]

Durrio owned a great many works by Gauguin—the famous collection that had been stolen by Manolo, sold to Vollard and returned to him—and Picasso enjoyed studying them and listening to Durrio describe Gauguin's charismatic behaviour on his return from Tahiti to Paris (1893–95) and the ongoing problems with his finances. Of current concern was the saga of his sale of Gauguin's masterpiece *D'où venons-nous? Que sommes-nous? Où allons-nous?* to a Spanish collector friend of Durrio's (Virenque?)—a sale that had been sabotaged by Vollard. Over the next few years Durrio would come to admire Picasso more and more and would ultimately see him as the only artist worthy of inheriting his hero's sacred mantle. To further this prospect, he encouraged Picasso to follow Gauguin's example and try his hand at ceramic sculpture.

In his memoirs Sabartès has given an account of this evening with Durrio.

> [Picasso] showed such interest in what Paco was doing that one might have thought he had just discovered his sculpture. There was much talk about Gauguin, Tahiti, the poem *Noa Noa*, about Charles Morice and a thousand other such things. Picasso put so much enthusiasm into the conversation that he seemed to have forgotten the reason for his melancholy . . . suddenly in the heat of the discussion, he began to recount what till then he had been so obstinately keeping to himself . . . Picasso had made up his mind to leave us immediately. Now quite coolly he explained his plan, as if forgetting that he had wished to conceal it. We left Durrio's studio very early [in the morning] for Picasso wanted to get home to see his mail. We went up in single file, like children afraid to face the dangers we imagined ahead. But when Picasso opened the door, fear vanished, the letter [from don José] was on the floor. On the bed, fully dressed, Mañach was lying on his stomach, talking to himself, as if delirious:
>
> 'The letter! The letter!'
>
> Picasso gave him an ugly look, made a scornful grimace, and let us into the studio without uttering a word. What for? The three of us were surely thinking the same thing. His eyes surveyed the walls, the floor, the ceiling, and we all went out again into the street. Doubtless he could not work there any longer. He needed a change of environment.[55]

It is on the strength of this admittedly reticent account (Sabartès is always reticent where business is concerned) that Mañach has been accused of being 'a would-be seducer . . . less interested in Picasso's genius than his body'. Sabartès 'hints [this] strongly'.[56] He hints at nothing of the sort. Elsewhere, he gives a rational explanation for the row:

> [Picasso's] Catalan friends were always coming to see him. Mañach was not at all happy that Picasso should have them to lunch in the studio. Moreover, business was not going as well as he had hoped. Hence Mañach was fed up with having to lay out more than he could afford. Perhaps one of the reasons for the lack of sales was the change in Picasso's style. The fact that his earlier work had pleased the public was enough to put him against it.[57]

Picasso in the studio on Boulevard de Clichy, with Mañach (right) and Fuentes Torres and his wife, 1901. Musée Picasso, Paris.

So far as we know, Mañach, who subsequently married, never showed any sign of homosexuality. He was fearful of losing Picasso because he had come to have a very clear idea of his potential. On his side, Picasso resented Mañach because he was a hard bargainer—something that the artist would forever hold against the dealers who exploited his early poverty. Although Mañach saw himself as an idealist, always ready to promote the cause of contemporary Spanish art, he was also a businessman and obliged to be miserly if sales were slow. Picasso would never forgive him. When, in 1923, Jacint Salvadó—the Catalan painter who modelled for some of the neo-classical harlequins—called on Picasso with a letter of introduction from Mañach, he was at first refused entry to the studio.

A day or two after the confrontation with Mañach—that is to say early in January—Picasso returned once again to Barcelona: to his old room in his parents' apartment. Under the terms of his contract, most of his recent work remained in Mañach's hands, but if his portfolio was empty except for a few sketchbooks and portraits of himself and friends, his head was filled with ideas for paintings—mostly inspired by memories of Saint-Lazare.

-Picasso-

15

Barcelona 1902

Nonell in his studio with two gypsies, *c.*1906. Photo: Mas.

Once again the New Year brought about an unexpected change in Picasso's circumstances. Eight months earlier, in May, he had left Barcelona headed for Parisian glory. Now he was back without a penny, reduced to living off his parents at 3 Carrer de la Mercè. And there he stayed, content for once to let his mother fuss over him, feed him and restore him to health. At the same time he arranged to share a large studio at 10 Carrer Nou de la Rambla, next door to the Eden Concert. Angel de Soto had rented this space so that he could have somewhere to sleep and their mutual friend, Josep Rocarol, somewhere to work.[1] It was a large room on the roof, with a terrace. Visitors were soon complaining of the squalor.

Among the few paintings that Picasso had been able to bring from Paris were the portraits of himself, Sabartès and Soto. Mañach had no claim on these. Picasso had promised the second of his Sabartès portraits (the one painted over the Saint-Lazare girl) to the sitter, who had asked for it to be taken back and deposited with his family. As soon as he returned, Picasso set about fulfilling his promise, but since he did not know the Sabartèses, he felt disinclined to face the comments and criticism that a visit would inevitably involve. And so he stopped en route at Els Quatre Gats and left the painting with Pere Romeu for safe-keeping. Romeu stuck it in a gilt frame—an oval one, to judge by the ring of nail-holes around the head—and hung it on the wall. And there it stayed until the tavern went out of business. Romeu's widow subsequently sold the portrait (also one of herself with the same tell-tale signs of oval framing) for next to nothing to Angel de Soto, from whom Picasso later bought it. It remained in his possession until it was donated to the Museu Picasso in Barcelona.

If, as seems likely, Picasso arrived home before January 17, he would have been able to visit Nonell's show at the Sala Parés. The show included fifteen paintings, mostly of the gypsies who were encamped in a shantytown on the outskirts of Barcelona. To soften the impact of these acrid subjects, the Sala Parés had thrown in a group of saccharine works by Baldomer Gili i Roig. These did not appease the local public. They were scandalized by the show, the more so when the January number of *Pèl & Ploma*, devoted mostly to Nonell, ran a pseudonymous attack signed 'Pincell' (Utrillo) on Catalan philistinism. *Pèl & Ploma* also included a grotesque fantasy by Eugeni d'Ors, entitled 'The End of Nonell',[2]

Opposite: Picasso. *Blue House*. Barcelona, 1902. Oil on canvas, 51.7×41.5cm. Private collection.

Above: Picasso. *Crouching Woman.* Barcelona, 1902. Pen on paper, 8.9×9cm. Musée Picasso, Paris.

Above right: Picasso. *Crouching Woman.* Barcelona, 1902. Oil on canvas, 63.5×50cm. Private collection.

Right: Nonell. *Gypsy.* 1904. Oil on canvas, 120×120cm. Museu d'Art Modern, Barcelona.

whose windy rodomontade represented everything that Picasso had come to despise in *modernisme*. There was, however, something prophetic about d'Ors's conceit (seemingly inspired by black Goyas rather than blue Nonells) of: 'the foul slime of city sewers; those wasted by . . . disease, vice and degeneration . . . wanderers without family or homeland, vagrants and tramps and beggars; outlawed races . . . their heads crawling with lice . . . dark spirits at the mercy of animal instincts . . . hooligans, whores, bawds, cretins, madmen, thieves and hired assassins'[3] rising up and killing Nonell for having exposed their plight to the world. It was prophetic in that Nonell died young, of typhoid contracted when he was off with the gypsies. Prophetic, too, about the mob: a month later there was a general strike followed by riots in which many were killed, many more wounded.

Picasso. *Portrait of a Man*. Barcelona, 1902. Oil on canvas, 93×78cm. Musée Picasso, Paris.

In the past Nonell had depicted the plight of the sick and the destitute with a fervour that could be termed Goyesque if the concept and style were less journalistic. His new work was different. Nonell was abandoning social criticism for a more picturesque approach. Instead of harping on the misery of his vagrants and gypsies, he tended to make their plight romantically acceptable. But despite his efforts, Nonell's gypsies found no more favour in Barcelona than Picasso's outcasts would. Within a very few years, however, the Catalans would change their tune and take chauvinistic pride in his romantic renderings of gypsy themes, as appealing in their way as Granados's arrangements of *cante jondo*. So much pride, indeed, that patriotic Catalans would come to believe that Nonell had exerted a major influence on Picasso's Blue period.[4] This claim does not hold up. Some of Nonell's Goyesque darkness seeped into Picasso's tenebrist work of 1899, and many of the Blue period dramatis personae —vagabonds, beggars, whores—make a prior, though much less poignant appearance in Nonell's work. At their period of greatest affinity (1902–03), however, neither artist would have much inkling of the other's progress. When Picasso was in Paris, Nonell was in Barcelona, and vice versa. In the end, Nonell took far more from Picasso—colour, facture, drama— than Picasso ever took from Nonell. Despite rumours to the contrary, there was very little animosity on either side, just an occasional touch of envy on the part of Nonell, who at one point lived in the Bateau Lavoir (probably in Canals's studio). That was dispelled when Picasso moved on to cubism, leaving Nonell in undisputed charge of gypsy territory.

* * *

Any major move from studio to studio, house to house, city to city usually makes itself felt in subtle adjustments to the atmosphere of Picasso's work. This was not the case when he returned to Barcelona in January 1902. The first paintings done in the Carrer Nou de la Rambla studio carry straight on from the ones he had been doing in Paris. So we cannot always ascribe a particular work to one place or the other, to late 1901 or early 1902. Picasso was not always prepared to clarify these finicky points. When Daix asked whether the painting of a soulful-looking young man with a beard was painted in Paris or Barcelona, the artist explained that 'he was a kind of madman who roamed the streets . . . models stay, but artists travel'.[5] Barcelona is in fact the answer.

Back in Barcelona, Saint-Lazare continued to cast its blue shadow on Picasso's work. In the Barri Xino, where the artist often ended his evenings, many of the same conditions prevailed. Syphilitic whores were as plentiful as in Paris. So were many other victims of society, war and the forces of law and order. Social unrest, which had already boiled over in 1901, when soldiers with machine guns opened fire on striking workers, boiled over again just after Picasso's return. A demand on the part of the metalworkers for a reduction of their working day from twelve to nine hours resulted in a general strike that lasted from February 17 to 24. The civil governor of Barcelona panicked and turned his authority over to the military governor. He called in the hated General Weyler, the butcher of Cuba, whose massacres and concentration camps had so horrified the Americans that they had intervened on the side of the insurgents. Weyler stamped out the strike with his habitual cruelty, triggering a week of strife that left at least ten dead and a great many workers and students incarcerated in the fortress of Montjuich. Amidst accusations that *agents provocateurs* had been used and that the military had resorted to the techniques of the Inquisition to induce confessions, the government fell. When order was restored, the poor were even poorer and angrier than before. And far from subsiding, troubles between left and right, Madrid and Barcelona, Catalanists and Nationalists continued to fester. There would be a further strike in 1903; and then in 1909 a catastrophic uprising: the Setmana Trágica. The savagery of the reprisals left all too many scores unsettled. Civil war was unavoidable, even if it would take another twenty-five years.

Striking workers in Barcelona on May Day, 1901. Drawing from *La Campana de Gracia*, August 18, 1901. Institut Municipal d'Història, Barcelona.

The fact that Barcelona was the most politically troubled city in western Europe impinged less on Picasso's life and work than one might think (or even hope), especially given his pro-Communist stance in later years. Like most of the Catalan intelligentsia—those associated with Els Quatre Gats in particular—he was on the side of the downtrodden.[6] And the dismal conditions in the slums and shantytowns of Barcelona evoked in him the same somewhat predatory compassion that the Saint-Lazare hospital had done. But in Barcelona as in Paris, it was primarily the women, above all the whores, who engaged his sympathy—the victims of social conditions that had been endemic in Spain since long before the Golden Age—rather than the victims of the current industrial or agricultural system.

Sketchbooks of the period include several drawings of beggars and down-and-outs, but virtually none refer to the riots in Barcelona. The only seemingly polemical work of this period is characteristically sardonic: a drawing, possibly the first idea for a magazine illustration, of a bearded speaker haranguing the world from a mound: 'I speak to you [reads the caption] of very important things, of God, of art . . . ' 'Yes, yes, but my children are starving,' replies a poor man who stands by with his wife and children—the quintessential Blue period group. The drawing, sarcastically captioned '*Muy importante*,' indicates that the artist's sympathies lay with this needy couple rather than with the rabble-rouser. That Picasso's only overt social comment at this troubled moment in Spanish history is directed at idealistic cant rather than political persecution, capitalist exploitation or reactionary clericalism is a measure of his fundamentally apolitical stance. 'In Spain there is a king,' the artist who saw himself as 'Yo el rey' once told Kahnweiler, 'therefore I am a royalist.'[7]

Picasso. *'Muy importante'*. Barcelona, 1902. Pen on paper, 13.5×21.2cm. Museu Picasso, Barcelona.

Insofar as Picasso had any ideology at all in these early days, it was compounded of sentimental liberal sympathies flavoured with a dash of Els Quatre Gats *anarquismo*, an attitude that radicals held in contempt. The members of the Quatre Gats group, Jaume Brossa said, were 'neurotic dilettanti, concerned only with being different from the philistines and the bourgeois'.[8] This was a far cry from the activist views of the workers, who formed the hard core of Catalan anarchism. Thirty years later, Picasso would come out and sympathize with the Front Populaire in France, but it was not until Civil War broke out in 1936 that his unfocused leftism hardened into serious political commitment. Even then, he did not actually join the Communist party; he waited until the end of World War II. Thenceforth Picasso would always be happy to serve the party on appropriate occasions as a figurehead, but he was the reverse of militant. Jacqueline told me that he was very clear as to what he was against—fascism, war and want—but then, so was virtually anyone of goodwill or intelligence, Marxist or not. He was far less clear as to what, as a good Communist, he was really for. Allowances must also be made for Picasso's love of paradox, his perversity, his dislike of orthodoxy in any form. We can no more tie him down to a consistent set of views or values at the beginning than at the end of his life. Every belief had to have a verso—several versos—as well as a recto; it had to work upside-down as well as the right way up. As he used to say in his early days, 'I'd like to live like a pauper with lots of money.'[9]

Picasso. *Germaine in a Headscarf.* Barcelona, 1902. Oil on canvas, 46×40.8cm. Private collection.

* * *

In Barcelona the Blue period began in earnest. Picasso's memories of Saint-Lazare manifest themselves in a steamy portrait of Germaine Pichot. She is portrayed, eyes aglitter, mouth half open, lips suggestively curled, wearing a headscarf very like the 'Phrygian' bonnet, and posed in front of the archway which, time and again, stands in for the Escorial-like galleries of the women's prison. Was this a private joke—a veiled way of accusing Germaine of whorishness or, conceivably, of having syphilis? Her past history and future invalidism make this a possibility. Or was Picasso making an ironical observation on the end of her affair with him and the start of another with his old friend Ramon Pichot? Whatever point it was intended to make, this painting exemplifies Picasso's habit—more pronounced in later years—of charging the portraits of the women in his life with hidden messages and manipulative devices: sometimes calculated to warn or punish or tease; sometimes to seduce or entrap.

In a further quest for morbid inspiration, Picasso had his friend Dr Jacint Reventós take him to see the morgue at the Hospital de Santa Creu i Sant Pau, where he worked as an intern. 'There I saw a dead woman,' Picasso reminisced fifty years later, 'who had undergone a gynaecological operation; her face made a great impression on me, and when I went home I painted her from memory.'[10] He subsequently gave the painting to Jacint. The image is curiously unmoving; in order to generate pathos, Picasso required the stimulus of a subject who was alive to pain or grief or degradation. Besides this work and *The Two Sisters*, discussed in the previous chapter, Picasso executed some eight or ten paintings of seated or crouching prostitutes or beggar women which hark back in spirit

Picasso. *Head of a Dead Woman.* Barcelona, 1902. Oil on canvas, 44.5×34cm. Museu Picasso, Barcelona.

to the Saint-Lazare.[11] Conditions in Barcelona were even worse than in Paris. At least the Saint-Lazare women had a roof over their heads. Their Catalan sisters and brothers were street people.

Over the next two years Picasso's victims would get thinner and sicker and sadder; some would be mad; many blind. The artist, however, thrived. As long as he remained in Spain, his energy and gusto would never falter. Depression would set in only if his work went badly or if the crassness of his Catalan cronies got on his nerves. '*Misere humane*' was for his subjects, not for him. 'People seem to think I'm tragic,' Picasso remarked in one of those volte-faces that are so typical of him, 'when they come to see me they have funereal airs and talk about catastrophes. But I like to laugh.'[12]

The bluer Picasso's paintings become, the more they are permeated by the sea. Picasso had grown up in a succession of seaports, and when he lived in Barcelona he liked to prowl the beach of Barceloneta, behind the harbour, where the homeless subjects of his work were to be found; or he would go on expeditions up and down the coast with Pichot in his boat, or to the family's beach house at Cadaquès, or Ramon's shack at Punt del Sortell. Picasso had a way of using the sea to amplify the mood of a subject: in these early years to enhance the melancholy; later, to very different ends. On his honeymoon in 1918 the beach stands for *joie de vivre*; in the late twenties and thirties it becomes an arena for sexual acts of Dionysian intensity; and, in the late forties, a place for classic idylls. For Picasso of the Blue period, beaches had the advantage of no specific associations; they were outside time and place—a blue limbo. In the course of 1902, the sea takes over as a backdrop for a series of romantically destitute mothers and children (fathers do not impinge until the following year) wandering sadly and silently on the beach. Like the Saint-Lazare women, these figures stand for the problems rather than the joys of motherhood. Why did they bring these waifs into this sad blue world? How to feed them and clothe them? How to love rather than resent them? The artist may have released these women from prison, but is the beach any better? They have certainly not shaken off their air of incarceration and alienation. And the ominous boat (shades of Puvis de Chavannes) that awaits them in the background of some of these compositions surely signifies death.

Marià Pidelaserra. *Portrait of Emili Fontbona*. 1901. Oil on canvas. Private Collection.

The most evocative of these mothers by the sea—the one holding a flower in one hand, a baby in the other—bears an inscription to Dr Josep Fontbona, whom Picasso knew through his sculptor brother, Emili. The painting could have been a quid pro quo for services rendered: quite considerable services, given its importance. Since Fontbona was a gynaecologist,[13] Picasso probably required his attentions for a girlfriend. The flower, in the nineteenth and early twentieth centuries, also had a specific connotation. Worn by a prostitute, it was, according to Freud (who cites Dumas's *La Dame aux Camélias*),[14] a traditional warning of menstruation or illness. There is an even more overt reference to menstruation to be found in a work of 1902: a watercolour of a whore gazing down at her bloodied bidet.

Around the time he gave Josep the *Woman on the Seashore*, Picasso consulted Emili Fontbona on a very different matter. He wanted to find out how to model in clay. Emili was technically adept and therefore a

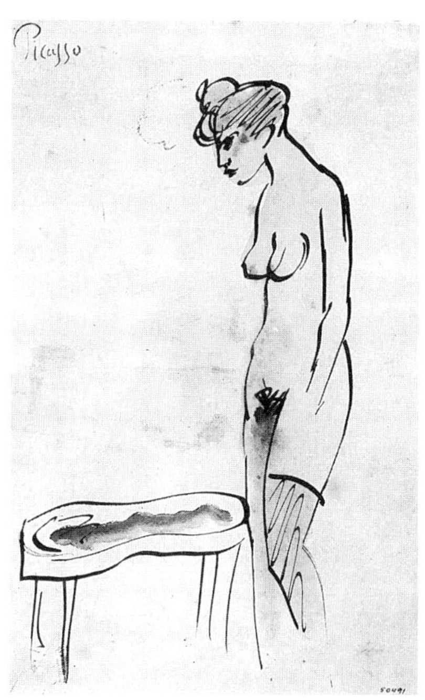

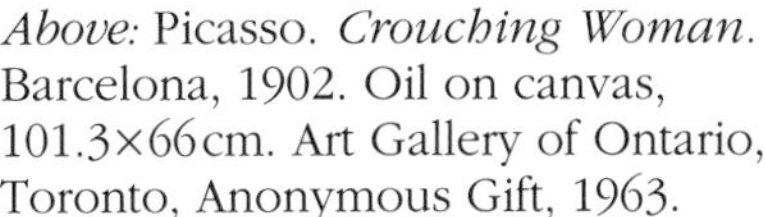

Above: Picasso. *Crouching Woman.* Barcelona, 1902. Oil on canvas, 101.3×66cm. Art Gallery of Ontario, Toronto, Anonymous Gift, 1963.

Top right: Picasso. *Woman at a Bidet.* Barcelona, 1902. Pen and watercolour on paper, 19.8×13cm. Museu Picasso, Barcelona.

Right: Picasso. *Woman by the Sea.* Barcelona, 1902. Oil on canvas, 83×60cm. Inscribed to Dr Josep Fontbona. Private collection.

Above: Gauguin. *Vahine no te miti.* 1892. Oil on canvas, 93×74.5 cm. Museo Nacional de Bellas Artes, Buenos Aires.

Left: Picasso. *Two Women at a Bar.* Barcelona, 1902. Oil on canvas, 80×91.5 cm. Private collection, Japan.

Above: Picasso. *Crouching Nude* (known as *Blue Nude*). Barcelona, 1902. Oil on canvas, 46×40 cm. Private collection. (At the upper left are vestiges of a boat as in *Woman by the Sea;* see previous page.)

Left: Picasso. *Seated Woman.* Barcelona, 1902. Bronze, ht: 15 cm. Musée Picasso, Paris.

sensible choice. But he was something of a crank: a fervent supporter of *modernisme* and yet a sworn enemy of art nouveau; an advocate of primitivism and yet an admirer of Rodin (and later one of Gaudí's assistants on the Sagrada Família). Picasso's first attempt at modelling was made at the Fontbona family's large villa in the Sant Gervasi district. His *Seated Woman* is very assured, not very original: it harks back to the Rodins he had so much admired on his first trip to Paris. The Rodinesque conception of this *Seated Woman*—its undulating surface but cohesive mass—suggests that many an early Blue period painting derives from the same sculptural source. A portrait drawing of Fontbona bears a remarkable likeness to the idealistic orator (see illustration, p.236), who is depicted with mysterious little busts at his feet, also to a figure who appears in a preparatory study for *La Vie* (see illustration, p.273). Picasso seems to have been intrigued by his air of madness, which was far from feigned. Under the delusion that his 'intelligence was being annihilated', Fontbona would suffer a serious nervous collapse in the winter of 1904–05, from which he would never fully recover. This coincided with an attempt by Junyent to build Fontbona into a major figure. To the delight of Sabartès, the failed sculptor, who favoured Fontbona's rival, Mateu de Soto, the attempt came to nothing.

Picasso. *Emili Fontbona*. Barcelona, 1902. Pen on paper, 45.5×31.7cm. Museu Picasso, Barcelona.

Despite this initial success, Picasso did not sculpt again for another two years. All the same, Rodin remained in his thoughts. When, in 1903,[15] he again turned his attention to modelling and produced two more pieces, the *Blind Singer* and the *Picador*, that had been carefully worked out on paper beforehand, the results were still heavily indebted to Rodin (the *Blind Singer* especially; it owes everything to the *Man with the Broken Nose*). It was only when Picasso moved to Paris and resumed sculpting under the auspices of Paco Durrio that Gauguin would replace Rodin as an exemplar. Thanks to Rodin, Picasso gave more thought to the backs, as opposed to the fronts, of the figures in his paintings. In the course of 1902, naked shoulder blades took over from draped breasts. The vulnerability of a girl's back seems to have had an irresistible appeal for him. The passivity with which heads are bowed and napes of necks are proffered implies an invitation, above all to an Andalusian brought up on the principle that man commands and woman submits. Sculpture revealed that a woman's back can express as much grief and pain, as much sexual attraction, as her front; and for Picasso it obviated the problem of depicting a girl's breasts persuasively as attributes of want.

Emili Fontbona. *Woman of Amposta*. *c*.1904. Terracotta. Whereabouts unknown.

Gauguin likewise opened Picasso's eyes to the expressive possibilities of backs. The pose of the so-called *Blue Nude* is one that occurs time and again in Tahitian Gauguins. This new preoccupation is best exemplified by the stylized back view of two prostitutes seated at a bar. Picasso has carried Gauguin's simplifications to an extreme point: dresses are reduced to sarong-like sheaths; arms melt into torsos;[16] anecdotal detail is suppressed except for a single empty glass. There is no recession; everything happens on the picture surface. The *Two Women at a Bar* is a strange hybrid: *fin-de-siècle* symbolism crossed with twentieth-century experimentation. On the one hand it is eerily erotic and *modernista* in subject and mood; on the other, it adumbrates a new kind of pictorial notation that looks ahead to cubism. Had Picasso stayed on in Paris, the stimulus of the avant garde might have encouraged him to continue along this promising path. In Barcelona such stimulus was confined to architecture and the decorative arts. There was no one with whom Picasso could discuss modern art except González, but he, too, was set on moving to Paris. And so, instead of extending his frontiers even further, he lapsed back into a relatively conventional idiom. We have only to compare the back of the girl on the right of the *Bar* painting with the very similar back of the acrobat in the *Young Acrobat on a Ball* of 1905 (see illustration, p.347) to see that, although his technique and ideas continued to develop, three years would pass before he resumed his modernist momentum.

Picasso. *Portrait of Corina Romeu*. Barcelona, 1902. Oil on canvas, 60×50cm. Musée d'Art Moderne, Céret.

In Barcelona Picasso continued to do portraits of friends—mostly drawings and caricatures. An exception is the conventional painting of Corina Romeu, wife of the proprietor of Els Quatre Gats. Evidently done to please an old friend, it is closer to the spirit of nineteenth-century Spanish portraiture than that of the Blue period. This portrait may have been done to celebrate the birth of the Romeus' baby (May 12, 1902), as was a drawing of this child, which Romeu had printed on cards announcing the baptism (Picasso was paid twenty-five pesetas). Far more interesting—stylistically and technically—is the delicate watercolour portrait of Juli González seated on top of Tibidabo (the 'mountain' behind Barcelona, which had recently been made more accessible by the construction of a funicular).[17] Why, one wonders, would Picasso, who usually liked to portray his friends in oil paint on canvas in his studio, take it into his head to pose González on a mountain top? Why, too, the unfamiliar style and exceptional finesse of this watercolour? The oddly oriental air cannot be attributed to Picasso's friend the Japanese dancer Sada Yacco, who had recently (May 9 and 10, 1902) shocked the Catalan bourgeoisie and delighted Els Quatre Gats (just as she had delighted Paul Klee, nine months earlier in Rome) with performances of her spectacle, *Geisha*. The influence turns out to be Persian rather than Japanese. Picasso told me that a Persian painter of his acquaintance, whose name he could not recall, had taught him the rudiments of Moghul painting and given him an exquisitely fine brush ('fine as any pen') contrived from a quail's feather. Hence the faintly Moghul look of this portrait and an equally delicate watercolour of a whore in gartered stockings. This Moghul look seems not to have outlasted the Moghul brush.

Picasso. *Portrait of Juli González*. Barcelona, 1902. Watercolour and ink on paper, 29×24cm. Didier Imbert Fine Art, Paris.

Picasso also did several more self-portraits: some in front of a mirror, some from memory, and some in profile, as others would have seen him. And then there are fantasies like the one of him in a toga by the sea, holding a palette, just as thirty years later he would visualize himself as a classical sculptor; there are also some of him making love. Rather more puzzling are two allegorical drawings, one of which includes a self-portrait. Both of them feature a colossal deity—a voluptuous earth-mother, and a wreathed and bearded Jupiter, whose outstretched arms present the beholder with the naked artist about to embrace a naked mistress. These allegories are more likely to have been ideas for the light-hearted murals with which Picasso liked to decorate studio walls than projects for easel paintings. A generic resemblance to the Lovers card suggests that they may have been inspired by the Tarot, which Max Jacob had brought to the artist's attention.

* * *

Sabartès does not say why he stayed on in Paris for three or four months after Picasso left. Maybe he thought Paris would transform him into the poet he still aspired to be; maybe he wanted to see if he could break away from the man who exerted such a hold over him. At all events he returned, early one spring morning, to Barcelona. After cleaning up, he had his long hair chopped off—in Barcelona the emblem of his vocation might be mistaken for a sign of anarchist affiliation—and went to the apartment of Picasso's parents to surprise his young god in bed. It was Sabartès who was surprised; Picasso now rose earlier and went immediately to work in his studio. This, Sabartès discovered, was a vast room surrounded by a terrace, with blazing sunlight coming in through the windows and beating down on the roof. Rocarol, whom Sabartès had not hitherto met, painted at one end of the room; Picasso at the other. Sabartès was relieved to find that the artist had not changed his style but was still faithful to the mannerisms of the new blue phase that he saw as a joint creation—the embodiment of the months they had spent, side by side, in Paris. Had he found Picasso 'following another road', Sabartès says, he would have considered this as stylistic infidelity: a deliberate attempt 'to detach himself from what had recently united us'.[18] Absurd as this attitude is, we should remember that the poet's concept of the Blue period as a joint venture, with himself as a brotherly muse, had the artist's blessing. It is a leitmotif of the memoirs, which were written at Picasso's behest and with his collaboration. The thought of his secretary basking in his blue shadow would have appealed to his twisted humour. There had to be some return for Sabartès's Faustian sacrifice of his identity to the artist's ravening ego.

Picasso. *Allegory*. Barcelona, May 1902. Pencil on paper, 28×22.5 cm. Museu Picasso, Barcelona.

Sabartès describes how he and Picasso immediately fell back into their Parisian habit of daily meetings. 'Henceforth, every day was the same. At times I left [Picasso] at the foot of the stairs [leading to the studio]; at others, if he insisted, I went up with him. If he asked me to stay, I stayed . . . once he began to work, he was more at ease than if he were alone, for with me by his side, he did not need to think about me.'[19] For all this talk of togetherness, the memoirs hint at resentment. Sabartès no longer had the artist to himself. During the poet's absence in Paris, Picasso had come to rely on other friends: notably the Junyer Vidal brothers (see pp. 281–2), who would become his inseparable companions. Dislike of friends like the Junyer Vidals accounts for Sabartès's claim that 'as a matter of principle Picasso does not criticize people because that does not interest him, but he is not averse to hearing the opinions of others no matter how derogatory.'[20] This is a roundabout way of letting us know that the artist liked Sabartès to denigrate other members of his entourage, just as he liked them to denigrate Sabartès. Picasso was already turning into an absolute monarch who divided and ruled, and enjoyed playing off his courtiers (and later his women) one against another.

The secretive Sabartès passes over Picasso's whorehouse life in silence but describes how he loved to visit the music-halls on the Gran Via, where beauties like La Belle Otéro would perform. Picasso had a special passion for 'La Bella Chelito', a saucy-looking girl who sang suggestive songs. Towards the end of the summer he did a series of drawings of this star in her most famous turn, '*La Pulga*' ('The Flea'), which involved a coy striptease in search of a flea. Sabartès has given an ecstatic description of

La Bella Chelito. One of the series of photographs that belonged to Picasso. Musée Picasso, Paris.

these sketches, some of which may be identified in sketchbooks:[21] 'delicate, graceful, exquisite . . . impressions . . . dashed off at one stroke . . . the essence of an idea jotted down with flowing pen . . . so as not to miss the minutest aspect of a gesture, the smallest detail . . . of this female body, ardent and supple, undulant, voluptuous. . . .'[22] Picasso also acquired a set of photographs of 'La Bella Chelito'—some of her posing in the bath—which testifies to his passion. Sabartès derived a vicarious thrill from Picasso's infatuations, but only so long as they were temporary. And temporary they seem to have been in 1902. True, an attractive nude girl with long black hair appears in several drawings done in the course of the summer. But she is so bland and generalized that she is more likely to have been a fantasy figure than a real girl. The inscription on one of these drawings—'*Quando tengas ganas de joder, jode!*' ('When you feel like fucking, fuck!')—sums up Picasso's sexual creed.

* * *

In the course of 1902 Picasso's work settled into a very definite pattern; so did his personal style, his look. As with the art, there was a slight air of contrivance to the way he dressed: his high-buttoned corduroy jackets, peg-top trousers that tapered at the ankle, broad-brimmed turkey-farmer's hat, and red scarf. Like most other young men of the period, he carried a stick, but for Picasso it was a surrogate sword, and he was forever parrying and thrusting with it, fencing with trees and lampposts. Later on he exchanged paintings for articles of clothing with the tailor, Benet Soler Vidal, alias '*Retalls*' ('Cuttings') and sported the fancy waistcoats then in fashion, which he remodeled and often embellished in accordance with his taste. Some of these outfits were found in a trunk at Notre-Dame-de-Vie after Picasso's death. By virtue of being worn by him and, by extension, part of him, his clothes became sacrosanct. When, many years later, Picasso put on a dinner jacket he had bought in 1919 for a Diaghilev opening, it was as if he had donned a magician's cloak. Nothing was ever thrown—let alone given—away once it had been worn: someone else might appropriate the power that had rubbed off onto it from the artist. When he found (circa 1949) that Françoise had given one of his jackets to the gardener, he raged at her: 'I will be transformed into that ugly old man. It's dreadful. It's monstrous.' She was reduced to burning his old clothes.[23] By the same token, he would sometimes 'steal' his son's clothes, even his toys, in the hope of absorbing the youthfulness that might still cling to them.[24]

'Everything immediately becomes a habit with Picasso,' Sabartès writes. In his youth, as in his old age, he hated any disruption in his daily routine. And so the pattern of his Barcelona life hardly varied. Although he had taken to rising earlier, he would always be among the last to leave the cafés. He would continue conversing with anyone who cared to keep him company, for despite his need to be alone when working, he was infinitely gregarious when idling. He would see a friend to his door and then wander up and down the ever lively Ramblas, or dally with acquaintances he had met in the street or in the café at the corner of the Plaza de Cataluña. When finally alone, Picasso would go off and play the slot machines and, thanks to an extraordinary system he had devised,

Picasso. *Nude with Mirror*. Barcelona, 1902. Crayon and gouache on paper, 38×26cm. Lefevre Gallery, London.

usually win a handful of coins. Returning home, this most nocturnal of men would not go to bed immediately; he would unwind by covering sheets of paper with his ideas; finally he would get into bed and read for hours.[25]

If Picasso was seldom able to relax outside the studio, it was because part of his mind was forever focused on his work. He was apt to become abstracted in the middle of a conversation and leave wherever he was without saying goodbye. On these occasions he had to get away from people, Sabartès says; otherwise he would lash out, sometimes quite venomously. Not at Sabartès, of course—he seems to have been the only person allowed to dog the artist's footsteps: 'knowing that I understood his state of mind, and confident that . . . I would not poke my nose into his inner conflicts . . . each of us was a perfect example of solitude in companionship.'[26]

Picasso. *Flyer for Els Quatre Gats* (left to right: Romeu, Picasso, Rocarol, Fontbona, Angel de Soto, Sabartès). Barcelona, 1902. Pen on paper, 31×34 cm. Private collection.

Apart from chronic poverty, one of the reasons for Picasso's bouts of temper was his increasing impatience with Barcelona and everything it stood for: his truculent father, his nice but irredeemably second-rate friends. To Picasso, fresh from the artistic and intellectual stimulus to be found in Montmartre and the Latin Quarter, the bohemianism of Els Quatre Gats that had formerly diverted him now seemed excessively provincial, the more so since most of its brighter habitués had moved to Paris. The tavern was no longer the focal point of Picasso's social life. Nevertheless, he still felt well enough disposed towards the scene of his debut to do a flyer for the place—a drawing of himself, Romeu, Rocarol, Fontbona, Angel de Soto and Sabartès[27]—headed 'Food and drink served at all times'. The flyer was part of a campaign to polish up the tavern's tarnished image. During Picasso's eighteen-month absence in Madrid and Paris, Els Quatre Gats had gone downhill. Of the three original proprietors, only Romeu, the manager, was still identified with the place; and he lacked the imagination and flair that the job required. Casas and Rusiñol had lost interest, and Utrillo devoted most of his time to editing *Pèl & Ploma* and, after 1903, the art-historical journal *Forma*. Apart from loyalty to the ineffectual Pere Romeu, the only reason to frequent the tavern was the existence of a friendly waiter—perhaps the waiter commemorated in the drawing for the menu[28]—who allowed clients to run up bills. This was important: Picasso was earning no money and living off family and friends.

*   *   *

Picasso. *Portrait of Joan Vidal Ventosa*. Barcelona, 1900. Charcoal and watercolour mixed with coffee on paper, 47×27 cm. Museu Picasso, Barcelona.

Pere Romeu's place in Picasso's life was now taken by another good friend, Joan Vidal Ventosa. This genial young man had studied art, particularly sculpture, at La Llotja. He later worked as a restorer (of Gothic altarpieces in particular) and photographer of ancient monuments, ultimately becoming official photographer to the Barcelona museums. Vidal's passion for Catalan Romanesque stemmed from the fact that his father was sacristan of the famous Isglesia del Pi (Church of the Pine). In the early days of their friendship Picasso and Sabartès often used to meet in the family's little house on the corner of the square. When the weather was fine, Vidal Ventosa, Picasso and other friends would take chairs and sit outside in the sun. After the sacristan's son was through with Mass on Sunday, they would buy *tortells* at the pastry shop and then visit the latest exhibition at the Sala Parés. These get-togethers earned the studio on the Plaça del Pi—the room that may have inspired *Poor Geniuses*—the nickname 'El Guayaba' (the story goes that an artist's model mispronounced the German *Valhalla*, but El Guayaba means the guava fruit). The informal discussion group soon developed into a club with its own premises.[29]

More than anyone else, Vidal Ventosa opened Picasso's eyes to the hieratic drama of Catalan Romanesque. He may well have taken the artist along on expeditions to photograph ecclesiastical buildings, altarpieces, frescoes and sculptures in the backwoods of Catalonia: for instance to the remote Valley of Bohí—home of Nonell's goitrous cretins—where some of the finest Romanesque churches (Santa María and St Clement of Tahull) are to be found. *The Two Sisters*—the masterpiece of the artist's Guayaba days—may derive in large part from El Greco, but the air of primitive sanctity owes much to early Catalan sculpture. Picasso was also familiar with the illuminated manuscripts which are among the glories of Catalan art; however these did not exert an influence on his work until much later.

Romanesque Christ in the collegiate church in Manresa, shown in 1902 in the exhibition of Ancient Art in Barcelona.

Sabartès would see to it that Picasso never forgot his debt to Vidal Ventosa, their greatest mutual friend. When he became the artist's secretary, he would arrange for Vidal Ventosa to earn occasional fees by sending Picasso photographs of the undocumented works that were always surfacing in Barcelona. These needed to be authenticated or, more often, denounced as forgeries. On Picasso's last visit to Spain (August–September 1934), Vidal Ventosa accompanied the artist to the newly installed galleries of Romanesque painting in the Museum of Catalan Art. They did not see each other for another twenty years. In November 1955, Sabartès arranged for this old friend to visit Cannes. Picasso met him at the station; they had an emotional reunion. And then in 1965, when the old photographer needed money, Sabartès suggested that Picasso give him a drawing; he also arranged for it to be sold. A year later Vidal Ventosa died.

Picasso's enthusiasm for the early art and architecture of Catalonia was reinforced by the great exhibition of Ancient Art that opened at Barcelona's Palace of Fine Arts in the autumn of 1902. The show, which included El Grecos and Zurbaráns but focused on Catalan Romanesque and Gothic, was hailed with patriotic fervour. It was the first major reappraisal of a field of art that had been all but forgotten since the Dark Ages. Village churches, monasteries and convents were scoured for unrecorded treasures. It was hoped that this manifestation of Catalan piety would assuage separatist passions. These had been provoked earlier in the year, when the Madrileño authorities had decreed that the flag of Spain, instead of the flag of Catalonia, should fly over the 'Floral Games' (the annual festival of Catalan culture). On the Spanish flag being brought into the hall, the booing and whistling had been so deafening that the May 4 opening ceremony had to be abandoned. No such unpleasantness marred the opening of the Ancient Art exhibition. After the savage suppression of the riots earlier in the year, Catalanist circles were more militant than ever. Waves of self-congratulatory patriotism enhanced the art-historical importance of the occasion. Henceforth a taste for Catalan primitivism would be obligatory for the bourgeois intelligentsia. Collectors and dealers in local art sprang up all over Catalonia. The Junyer Vidal brothers were not the only Catalan 'connoisseurs' to put their antiquarian knowledge

'Gegants' in the Corpus Christi procession, June 1902, in front of the Town Hall in Barcelona. Photo: Mas.

and skills to financial advantage by rescuing, overrestoring and, if need be, faking the relics of their cultural heritage.

More of this Catalanist fervour rubbed off on Picasso than one might have expected. For all the reservations he had come to have about the state of contemporary art in Barcelona, he was still fanatically loyal to his Catalan friends and their cause. By identifying with them and playing the role of *Catalanista*, he could feel less Andalusian. Rocarol has described how the death of the revered Father Jacint Verdaguer—the poet-priest who personified the spirit of Catalanism and yet was singled out by Lorca for his *duende*—enabled Picasso and his inner circle to manifest their fervour:

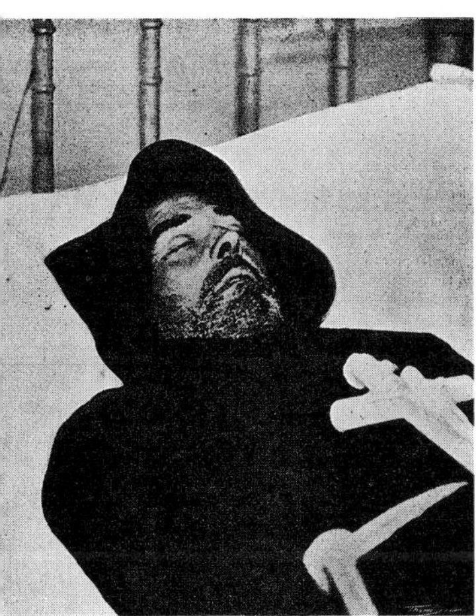

Father Jacint Verdaguer on his deathbed. Photograph published in *Joventut,* June 19, 1902.

> On the night of his death [June 10, 1902] Angel de Soto, Picasso, Sabartès, and I left Els Quatre Gats and walked all the way to Villa Joana [Verdaguer's house]. There we waited at the door from the early morning for his funeral cortège to leave. When the coffin appeared, we strewed it with wild flowers we had picked along the way. Then it was placed on an extremely shabby old hearse, accompanied by a few journalists. [En route] they left the dead man unattended outside a tavern and all of them went in to have breakfast. Since we were still young and idealistic and had great admiration and respect for the poet, this made us very indignant. . . . An editor on *La Vanguardia*—came out . . . with oily traces of sardines on his beard, and asked us who we were. We told him to go to hell. When this shameful cortège arrived at the Josepets church in Gràcia, it was reorganized with tremendous pomp and ceremony. . . .[30]

Around the time of the Ancient Art exhibition, the Junyer Vidal brothers commissioned Picasso to record another manifestation of Catalanism—the feast of the Mercè (Our Lady of Ransom)—for the front page of their newspaper, *El Liberal.* Thanks to ever-mounting local patriotism, the 1902 procession was much larger than usual. So many floats and deputations poured in from all over the province that the feast had to be postponed from the usual day, September 24, until October 5. Art students were recruited to decorate the floats and construct the papier-mâché giants that figure in the drawing. Despite smudgy printing, the *El Liberal* illustration is not without interest. The stereotypical Blue period mother and child make their first public appearance; and the procession includes a prophetic detail: the youthful Dionysos (complete with wreath and thyrsus) with whom Picasso will later identify. Although averse to doing commercial work, Picasso could not refuse his generous new friends. Around the same time, he did a flyer, inappropriately decorated with Pierrot and Columbine, for a patent medicine called Lecitina Agell, said to cure lymphatic conditions and bone disease. He was once again obsessed with returning to Paris and urgently needed money for the trip. Apart from the Junyer Vidals' handouts, all Picasso and Angel de Soto had to live on was a share of the pittance that Rocarol earned doing illustrations for a perfumery catalogue.

Picasso. Cover of *El Liberal,* October 5, 1902. Museu Picasso, Barcelona.

* * *

Picasso's poverty was the more galling in view of the money that the hated Mañach continued to make out of his earlier, more saleable work. Since their split-up at the beginning of the year, the dealer had followed

Picasso. Advertisement for the Agell cure for neurasthenia. Barcelona, 1902.

up the success at Vollard's with an exhibition (April 1–15, 1902) at Berthe Weill's. A minor painter, Louis-Bernard Lemaire, was also included in the show. The little-known Adrien Farge wrote the catalogue preface; its only interest is that it enables us to identify some of the works left in Mañach's stock, notably *Le Tub*. Picasso would not have relished Farge's praise for Mañach's discrimination: 'already amateurs are making the pilgrimage to the little gallery on the rue Victor-Massé.' The most eye-catching exhibit seems to have been a large *Virgin with Golden Hair*, apparently Picasso's only work in the *cloisonniste* style (a style involving the separation of areas of colour, as in enamelling) that he had tried out the previous summer. This mysterious painting has disappeared,[31] but an article by Félicien Fagus (the poet who wrote art criticism for the *Revue Blanche*) about young Spanish painters (Zuloaga, Nonell, Iturrino and Losada, as well as Picasso) includes an intriguing description:

> . . . this very young girl lying on her belly, head raised staring out at nothing, suspiciously inhaling and sniffing with the snub little snout of an animal; here is the insensate creature who would attain divinity; here is the sphinx. All this conceived in flat areas of matt colour enclosed by studiously elaborate and emphatic outlines; this simplification emphasizes . . . the stained glass impression.[32]

Fagus ends his article with a challenge that Picasso would have found impossible to resist:

> All these [Spanish] painters have temperament, race and individuality . . . They do not yet have their great man, the conqueror . . . from whom everything will start anew, who will give shape to a limitless universe. They remember . . . Goya, Zurbarán, Herrera; they are stimulated by Manet, Monet, Degas, Carrière, our Impressionists. Which one—the time is ripe—will become their Greco?[33]

Picasso. *Portrait of Sebastià Junyer Vidal*. Published in *El Liberal*, October 16, 1902.

Since he was no longer under contract to Mañach, Picasso made no money out of the Berthe Weill show, but he would have heard that his work was selling. He would also have read Fagus's review and taken to heart the question of who was to be the next El Greco. The news that Weill was organizing yet another exhibition in November finally convinced him to go to Paris. This time he would not have to contend with Mañach, who had returned to Barcelona, following his father's death, to take over the family business. Picasso felt sure that he could make some badly needed money by consigning some of his more recent works—the desolate mothers on the beach, the Catalan versions of the Saint-Lazare women—to the Weill show. He could set about finding a serious Paris dealer who would guarantee him a regular income; and he could take up Fagus's challenge and show the world who would be the next El Greco. He would consult the enterprising mind of his admirer Max Jacob. As he had written to the poet in July (in the letter describing *The Two Sisters*), he felt out of sympathy with his Barcelona colleagues. 'I show the local artists what I do but they think there is too much soul but no form it is very amusing you know talking to people like that but they write very bad books and they paint idiotic pictures—that's life.'[34] No doubt about it, Paris was the place to be.

Picasso may well have had another motive for making this trip. He was going to be twenty-one on October 25; this meant that he once more faced the threat of military service. For some time there had been an understanding that Uncle Salvador would pay the requisite 1,200 pesetas to buy the artist out of conscription. But the good doctor had been so horrified by his nephew's provocative behaviour in Málaga, eighteen months earlier, that he was no longer keen to help. Worse, the parrot cry familiar to artistic sons of philistine parents—the army will knock some sense into you—was taken up by don José. In his increasing bitterness, he inclined to agree with his brother that military service might do Pablo a lot of good. Picasso was kept in suspense. Did he threaten to take refuge from conscription in France—an act that would have meant following Manolo into permanent exile? Very possibly. In the end it seems to have been the ever-supportive doña Maria who persuaded Uncle Salvador to come up with the money. Rocarol has described how Picasso accompanied him to the military board, when he (Rocarol) bought himself out with the money provided by his mother.[35] Thanks to the last-minute arrival of funds from Málaga, Picasso was soon able to do the same. Within a matter of days the two friends left for Paris, as we know from the October 20 edition of *El Liberal*. 'The celebrated artist, Pablo Ruiz Picasso, left for Paris on yesterday's express,' the social column announced. 'He was accompanied by the distinguished artists Juli González and Josep Rocarol. Picasso intends to make a long stay in Paris.' As things turned out, his stay was not long; it was disastrous.

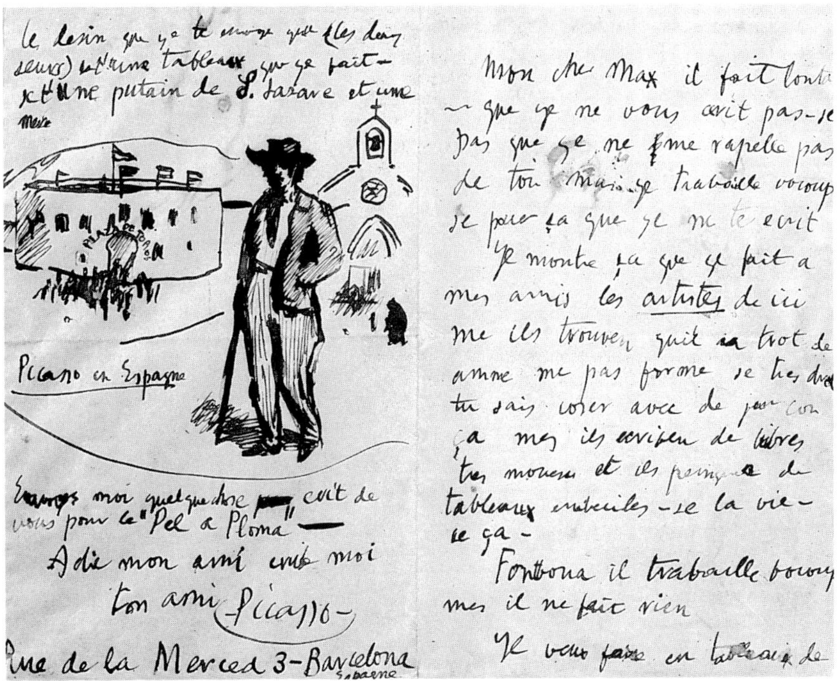

Mon cher Max il fait lont[illegible]
que je ne vous ecrit pas - se
pas que je ne me rapelle pas
de toi mais je travaille boucoup
se pour ça que je ne te ecrit
Je montre ça que je fait a
mes amis les artistes de ici
me ils trouven quil a trot de
amme me pas forme se tres dro[illegible]
tu sais coser avec de pour con
ça mes ils ecriven de libres
tres mouvais et ils peingen de
tableaux imbeciles - se la vie -
se ça -
Fontbona il travaille boucoup
mes il ne fait rien
Je veux faire un tableau de

le desin que je te envoye [illegible] (les deux
[illegible]) [illegible] tableaux que je fait -
[illegible] une putain de S. Lazare et une
mere

Picasso en Espagne

Envoye moi quelque chose [illegible] ecrit de
vous pour le "Pel & Ploma" —
Adie mon ami ecrit moi
ton ami -Picasso-
Rue de la Merced 3 - Barcelona
Espagne

Picasso. Letter to Max Jacob with a self-portrait in front of the Barceloneta bullring. He writes that he is enclosing a drawing of 'a Saint-Lazare whore and a mother'. Barcelona, July 1902. Pen on paper, 20×26 cm. Private collection.

16

Third Trip to Paris

Picasso. *Head of a Spanish Girl.* Paris, 1902. Crayon and charcoal on paper, 37.5×28cm. Marina Picasso collection.

Opposite: Picasso. *Upraised Head.* Paris, December 1902. Charcoal on paper, 31×23.5cm. Marina Picasso collection.

PICASSO CHOSE TO VEIL HIS CATASTROPHIC third trip to Paris in forgetfulness and legend. Sabartès, who was not in Paris this time, confuses the record by stating that Picasso was accompanied by Sebastià Junyer Vidal. (Sebastià went along on the next trip; his exhibition of Mallorcan landscapes had just opened in Barcelona—at the Sala Parés on October 12—so this time he stayed behind.) The announcement in *El Liberal* was correct: Picasso's companions on the 1902 trip were Juli González and Rocarol, even if in later years Picasso recalled the presence of González but not Rocarol; and Rocarol failed to remember González. Picasso may have come to resent the critical attitude that Rocarol developed towards him, and expunged him from memory. Rocarol's memoirs record that the journey started most inauspiciously; he had all of thirty-five pesetas in his pocket; Picasso felt sure of making some sales and so brought virtually nothing.[1] Lack of money would not have mattered if the affluent Sebastià had accompanied them.

After they arrived in Paris on October 29, González went his own way. Picasso forsook Montmartre and, at Rocarol's suggestion, headed for Montparnasse. There they took a small room in a cheap hotel for a week. Rocarol was paying; he slept mostly on the bed, Picasso mostly on the floor. So desperate was the artist to find a dealer that he went, the very first day, to show his work to the impresario of impressionism, Durand-Ruel. But Durand-Ruel's eye for modern art was long past its zenith; nothing came of this visit. Did Picasso call on Vollard, whose gallery in those days was next door? Probably, in the hope of raising some money. But thanks to Mañach, he may not have had a good reception. From the rue Laffitte, Rocarol tells us, they went on to Montmartre to call on Mateu de Soto, now living in a studio on the rue Cauchois with a girl from Málaga, who had presented him with a son. Mateu was almost as poor as his visitors, but he helped Rocarol, whose money ran out at the end of the first week, by letting him sleep in the studio. If he took in Rocarol rather than Picasso, it was because Rocarol was a far older friend of the Soto family than Picasso. On his side, Picasso would have preferred to give the Catalan coterie, to which Mateu belonged, a wide berth. His success eighteen months earlier had made him an object of envy; and he would not have wanted any of the Catalans to exult over his lapse into destitution.

Had his luck improved, Picasso would have contacted the *bande Catalane.* Instead, things steadily deteriorated. Pride obliged him to avoid

Top left: Picasso. *Portrait of Jane Avril.* Paris, 1902–03. Pastel and charcoal on paper, 30.5×23cm. Private collection.

Top right: Picasso. *Portrait of Anna Thibaud.* Paris, 1903. Conté crayon on paper. Whereabouts unknown.

Left: Picasso. *Portrait of Mlle Teresina.* Paris, January 1903. Conté crayon on paper, 32.5×25cm. Museu Picasso, Barcelona.

Picasso. *Jeanne Bloch.* Paris, 1902–03. Ink and watercolour on paper, 15.5×10.5cm. Lionel Prejger collection, Paris.

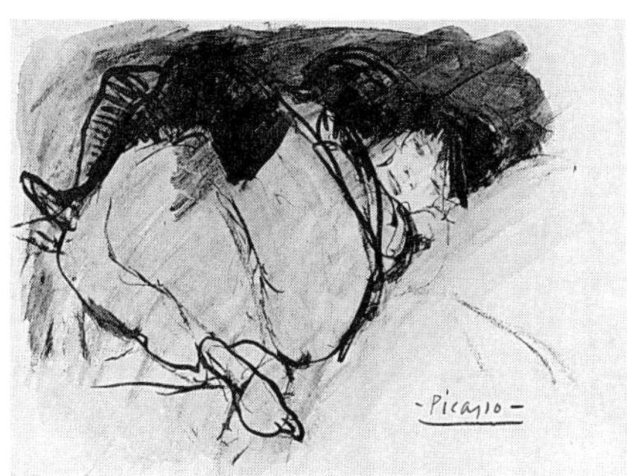

Picasso. *Couple Making Love.* Paris, 1902–03. Ink and coloured wash on paper, 25.5×36.4cm. Musée Picasso, Paris.

Montmartre and stay on the Left Bank, where he had few contacts and did not feel at home. No more evenings at Le Zut, let alone more fancy establishments. Max Jacob was one of the few supportive friends he saw, but all Jacob could do was commiserate: his circumstances were almost as parlous as Picasso's. As for girlfriends, we know virtually nothing. Blanche seems to have disappeared. However, the existence of an album of watercolours of a young man, seemingly the artist, making love to a girl —an album Picasso 'vaguely' remembered having inscribed 'to Louise'[2] —would indicate that he did not lack for sexual partners. There are also some powerful drawings of a Spanish girl, once with a tortoiseshell comb in her hair and a gypsy's kiss curl. But her eyes are so huge and ravenous that she might well be a figment of Picasso's erotic imagination. Hunger aroused his ardour. Many other drawings done at this lowest point of his early life are charged with a desperate sexuality; but then, as he said, sex was the only appetite he could afford to indulge.

On their second day in Paris, Picasso and his travelling companion went to the Louvre; Rocarol complained about all the walking and seeing nothing, 'since there was so much to see'.[3] However, he was delighted to meet Berthe Weill. After first refusing to buy anything and then haggling, she purchased a small work by Rocarol for twenty francs. What happened between Weill and Picasso we do not know. He presumably handed over whatever paintings and drawings he had brought from Spain to be included in her forthcoming show and sold on consignment. He also seems to have checked in with Coquiot, who commissioned a series of black chalk drawings of vedettes and demimondaines for an album of well-known beauties. These were to include such stars as Jane Thylda, the mime from the Olympia music-hall (later Princesse Auguste de Broglie-Revel); Teresina, the Spanish dancer (mistress of the poet and occultist Fernand Divoire); Rose Demag; Anna Thibaud; and, most celebrated of all, Jane Avril. Many of these stars were impossibly spoiled and vain, and after successive rebuffs, Picasso said, he lost patience and abandoned the project.[4] However, he must have earned something by way of reimbursement; there were hardly any other commissions or sales on this trip.

Anna Thibaud performing the '*Rondeau du Baiser*'. Photograph in *Paris Qui Chante,* September 13, 1903.

The only one of these women Picasso actually liked and felt privileged to have drawn was Jane Avril. The two surviving portraits of her (handsome black chalk drawings, one of them heightened with pastel) reveal that Picasso was determined to come up with a new image for the face that Toulouse-Lautrec's posters had made into an icon. He succeeded. He found Jane Avril far more sympathetic than the other vedettes he drew, Picasso said. For one thing, she had started life as an equestrienne in a circus. This endeared her to him. For another, this slender, neurasthenic woman, who danced all alone 'like a delirious orchid',[5] was more artistically perceptive than her rivals. She not only adored Toulouse-Lautrec but understood the finer points of his work and enjoyed discussing them with Picasso. 'It was all a bit sad, since she knew he was dying.' (He died in October.)

Ludovic Galice. Poster for Jeanne Bloch at La Scala. 1890s. Musée des Arts Décoratifs, Paris.

*   *   *

After Rocarol abandoned his hotel room, Picasso moved to Sabartès's old haunt in the Latin Quarter, the Hôtel des Écoles on the rue Champolion.

In a desperate attempt to raise money, he resorted to producing what he confessed was a crowd-pleaser. He chose a subject that was the reverse of his own circumstances: an unthreatening pastel of two young mothers tending their children in a cosy bourgeois interior, complete with the vase of flowers that so often, in these early days, betokens hackwork. 'I rolled it up and took it to Berthe Weill,' Picasso said. 'She lived in Montmartre at the other end of Paris. It was snowing. And me with my pastel under my arm. She had no money so I went away . . . and left her the pastel.'[6] Without a penny left, he had to leave the Hôtel des Ecoles. Someone suggested that he move in with a sculptor called Agero (nicknamed Sisket), whom he hardly knew. Agero was prepared to share his poky attic room—five francs a week it cost—in the Hôtel du Maroc (now the Hôtel Louis XV) on the rue de Seine. 'A very beautiful man' is how Gertrude Stein described Agero. 'He looks like a Greco, I [Toklas] said in english. Picasso caught the name, a false Greco, he said.'[7]

Picasso. *Two Mothers with Children.* Paris, 1902. Pastel on paper, 37×46cm. Private collection.

Agero's attic had a sloping ceiling; most of the space was taken up by a large iron bedstead, on which one of the lodgers had to lie if the other needed to move around. The mess must have been appalling, since Picasso, who was notoriously untidy, often used the sculptor's name as 'a byword for disorder'.[8] Very little light filtered through the minute *œil-de-bœuf* window; still, Picasso managed to produce a formidable body of work—mostly drawings that have a dark, smouldering power. As if the labels of the artist's early phases were not misleading enough, Palau has dubbed these three miserable months in Paris 'the dirty period', on the grounds that the artist was 'probably neither washing nor changing his linen as often as he would have liked'.[9]

More to the point than Picasso's cleanliness or lack of it (he was, in fact, obsessively clean) was his lack of means. He could not afford to buy proper materials or candles or oil for a lamp, and was obliged to improvise on odd scraps of paper and do without much light. Hence the murkiness of these intensely felt drawings. It recalls the 'tenebrism' of 1900, except that this time Picasso had far more to be gloomy about. The dark old-masterish look of these compositions resulted from his frequent visits to the relative warmth of the Louvre just across the river from his hotel. He went there to study; also probably to draw—at least the galleries were warmer and better lit than his hotel room. Many of these heavily inked drawings, including one that represents the corpse of an old man, appear to be studies for an ambitious *prix de Rome*-like composition with a tragic theme. Once again this failed to materialize, presumably for want of canvas. Picasso seems to have envisaged a *Last Moments* scene involving, significantly, a dead father (as opposed to a poor genius or a young woman) on a bed in the background; a mother in the foreground raising her arms to heaven—in the manner of a seventeeth-century Niobe —while her two children, one holding a baby, try to comfort her. A group of superb heads in profile, mouths open in fear or anguish, relate to this composition. There is no mistaking their Poussin-esque provenance: the *Massacre of the Innocents* at Chantilly and the *Rape of the Sabines* in the Louvre. These paintings would be a recurrent source of inspiration at times of private or public stress. Other drawings in the series envisage an even more ambitious but less overtly tragic family scene: a group on the seashore, including two boys wrestling, and a group in a

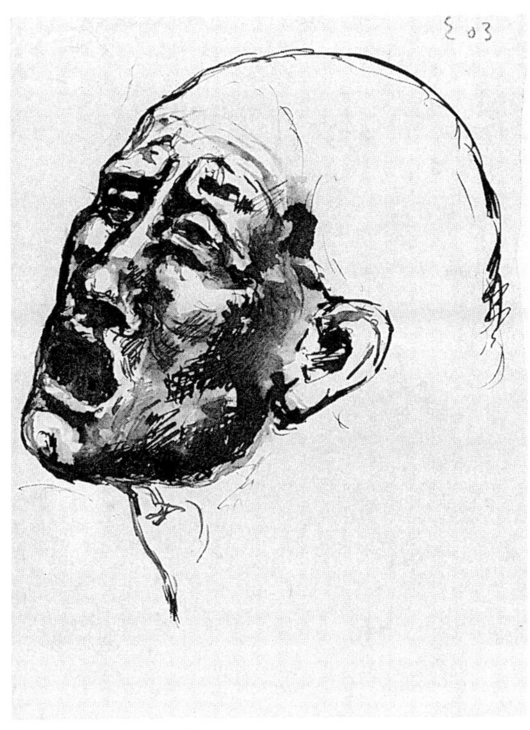

Picasso. *Head of a Crying Woman*. Paris, January 1903. Pen, sepia and black ink on paper, 23×18.1 cm. Musée Picasso, Paris.

Picasso. *Deathbed Scene*. Paris, December, 1902. Pastel on paper, 23.5×21 cm. Heirs of the artist.

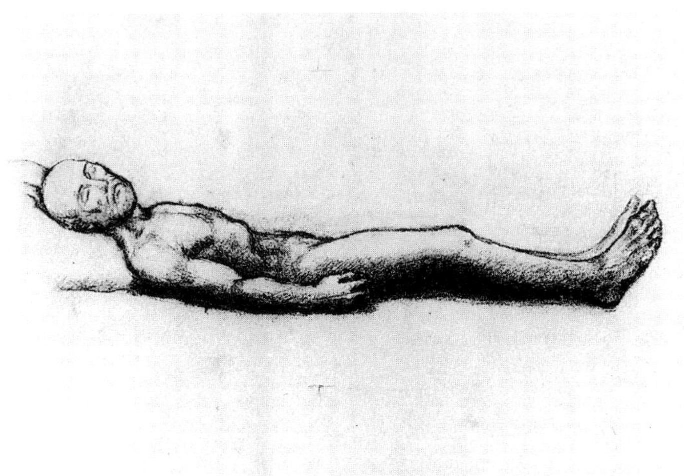

Picasso. *Dead Man*. Paris, 1902. Crayon on paper, 17×31 cm. Heirs of the artist.

Picasso. *Mother with Upraised Arms*. Paris, 1902. Pen and black ink on beige paper, 26.1×18.7 cm. Musée Picasso, Paris. Annotations refer to a complete edition of Alfred de Vigny's poems.

Picasso. *The Golden Age*. Paris, December 1902. Pen and watercolour on paper, 26.1×40 cm. Museu Picasso, Barcelona.

Picasso. *Boat Putting out to Sea*. Paris, January 1903. Pen and sepia on paper, 23.5×31 cm. Musée Picasso, Paris.

Above: Picasso. *La Soupe*. Paris, 1902. Oil on canvas, 38.5×46 cm. Art Gallery of Ontario, Toronto, Gift of Margaret Dunlap Crang, 1983.

Above right: Puvis de Chavannes. *St Geneviève Provisioning Paris* (detail of left panel). *c*.1897. Oil on canvas, 64×140 cm. Musée du Louvre, Paris.

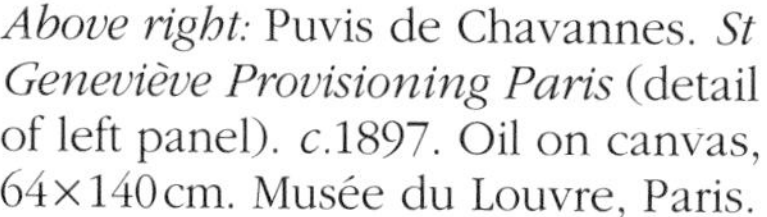

Right: Picasso. Notes on Puvis de Chavanne's 'painting of hunger'. Paris, January 1903. Pen on paper, 14.6×18.1 cm. Museu Picasso, Barcelona.

boat to whom the mother hands one of her children (doña María consigning Conchita to death's boatman, Charon?). There is also a group of pastoral scenes, some of which include the figure of a man with a lamb, that anticipates the great sculpture of 1943.

These anguished fisherfolk and shepherds also have a more up-to-date derivation than Poussin: Puvis de Chavannes, an artist whose influence on Picasso will come and go over the next four years and briefly recur during the so-called neo-classical phase.[10] Santiago Rusiñol, who revered Puvis as a modern equivalent of El Greco, was originally responsible for Picasso's interest in this painter. He had taken such pride in having attended a banquet in Puvis's honour in 1895 that he had written about him as 'the most universal genius of the art of our time.'[11] For his pains, Rusiñol had been made an associate of the Société Nationale des Beaux Arts—an accolade that inspired Picasso to do a caricature entitled *Lo que el Rusiñol le pensaba* ('What Rusiñol was thinking'). Rusiñol is portrayed being crowned with a wreath marked '*Associé*' by a flying muse of Puvis-like decorum. Picasso dutifully went to the Panthéon to see Puvis's great frescoes, completed five years earlier. And he admired a scene from the life of St Geneviève (the saint feeding starving Parisians) sufficiently to copy it. The scene he chose—an old woman dying of hunger being helped by a young woman and a man of the people—was relevant to his own predicament; and he inscribed his copy, '*De Puvis en el Panteon / el cuadro de la hambre*' ('From Puvis in the pantheon / a picture of famine'). He also took another figure in the same fresco, stripped him of his clothes and gave him a sack to carry instead of a jug.[12] These acrid drawings transcend the *fin-de-siècle* sentimentality of the originals. Puvis's amalgam of neo-classicism and romanticism, which had had such an influence on Gauguin's work a few years earlier, would henceforth be a major ingredient of the Blue period style.

Picasso. *Lo que el Rusiñol le pensaba.* Paris, 1903. Pen on trade card, 13.3×8.8cm. Perls Galleries, New York.

Though seemingly destined for a major composition, the heavily inked drawings inspired by Puvis and Poussin resulted in only one small painting, *La Soupe*, which Picasso would not do until he had returned to Barcelona. The earliest studies for this work (Paris, December 1902) depict a man or woman proffering bread or soup to a beggar woman or some children, as in the Puvis fresco. Subsequent studies hint at trouble: the collapse of the beggar; the outbreak of a fight. After all this *Sturm und Drang*, the subject is painlessly resolved back home (Picasso was no longer starving): pared down to a Saint-Lazare mother in Tanagra draperies handing a steaming bowl of soup to a stylized little girl (seemingly the prototype of Balthus's stylized little girls). *La Soupe* looks back to *The Two Sisters* in that it resembles a bas-relief—a Roman rather than a Romanesque one. For all its modest size, the painting is perfectly resolved; repeating it on a larger scale would have been pointless. Given the shock of his Parisian deprivations, charity, or the lack of it, was much on Picasso's mind. The theme of most future Blue period paintings is charity withheld. *The Soup* is exceptional: it celebrates the act of giving.

Picasso. Copy after part of Eugène Carrière's *Family Group*. Paris, 1903. Conté crayon on paper, 32.5×21.5cm. Private collection. Engraved by another hand and published in *El Liberal,* August 10, 1903.

During this trip to Paris, Picasso fell under the spell of another *fin-de-siècle* French artist, Eugène Carrière, whose paintings of his wife and one or other of his numerous children peering out wanly from a penumbra of sepia fog were greatly admired by Rodin and Degas. Carrière was also an especial favourite with the Catalan painters. Rusiñol, Casas and Utrillo had all had their work 'corrected' by him when they were students; Sunyer, too, studied at the academy that Carrière had opened in 1900. Given these connections, Picasso may well have visited Carrière's studio. At least he was sufficiently impressed to copy his large family group of the late nineties (National Gallery of Canada) of himself, his wife, Sophie, and his youngest son. The drawing, with the self-portrait omitted, was published in *El Liberal* alongside Picasso's Puvis copy and his not very brilliant drawing of Rodin's bust of Dalou. Carrière's influence on the Blue period did not last very long or go very deep. It merely confirmed Picasso in his addiction to monochrome and motherhood subjects (e.g., the group of mother-and-child pastels that he did after returning to Barcelona). Carrière's combination of mother-love and sfumato—'some brute's been smoking in the nursery,' Degas is supposed to have said—was too fuzzy and genteel for an artist as graphic and anti-bourgeois as Picasso.

Hôtel du Maroc (the second hotel on the right) at the turn of the century. Photo: Bibliothèque Nationale, Paris.

* * *

Picasso later described his weeks at the Hôtel du Maroc as the lowest period of his entire existence. The behaviour of some mysterious Spaniards staying in the hotel reinforced the misery and degradation of his life there. 'I become sad when I think with disgust of those Spaniards of the rue de Seine,' he wrote to Max Jacob the following year.[13] Who they were and what they did we do not know. Sabartès says only that Picasso could not 'stomach some grotesque incidents and the pettiness of persons known to him and Max. Picasso refused to speak about this matter and the vile and repugnant egoism of the individuals concerned, preferring not to stir the mud with which he was besmirched . . . at the Hôtel du Maroc.'[14]

Why all this mystification? Manolo mentions preventing a sculptor called Polvora from committing suicide in this hotel,[15] but this does not seem to be relevant. Nor was the 'false Greco', Agero, apparently to blame. 'Poor fellow, he took me in,' Picasso said when questioned about the Hôtel du Maroc episode.[16] Palau speculates that the 'vile and repugnant' Spaniards wandered from room to room with the aim of organizing some sort of orgy.[17] If this theory is correct, the culprits could only have been men: Picasso is unlikely to have minded girls invading his attic. A further clue is the fact that the only painting on canvas of this period represents the cherubic artist lying back being fellated by a girl. This unpublished work came to light recently when it was left to the Metropolitan Museum by Scofield Thayer (the eccentric editor of *The Dial* and a collector of erotica, who had bought it in the early 1920s before he went mad). It is a feeble daub, lacking any of the relish that usually characterizes the artist's sexual images. Why then did the penniless Picasso expend his one and only canvas on it? The most likely explanation is that the 'vile and repugnant' Spaniards supplied the desperate artist with materials on condition that he paint erotica for them. This would fit with the work's subsequent appearance at an exhibition of Blue period painting organized in Barcelona (March 1912) by Josep Dalmau, a former Quatre Gats painter who was living in Paris in 1902.[18]

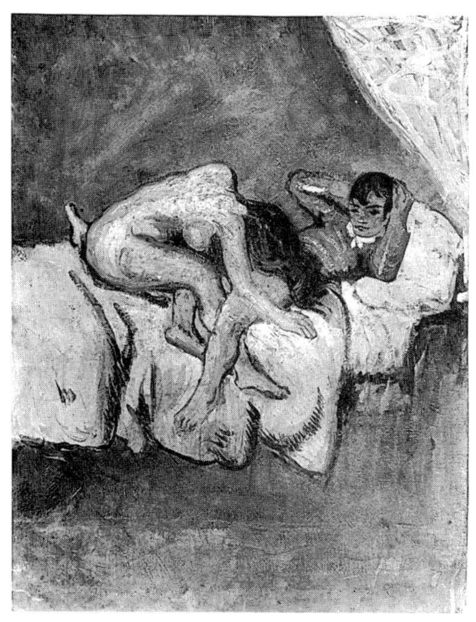
Picasso. *Portrait of the Artist Making Love*. Paris, 1903. Oil on canvas. Metropolitan Museum of Art, New York, Bequest of Scofield Thayer, 1984. Photo: Mas (taken at Picasso's exhibition at Dalmau's gallery, 1912).

So poor was the artist that he was reduced to stealing from Rocarol, by this time installed in a room of his own (at a cost of two francs a day).

Rocarol reports meeting Picasso in the street one winter evening. 'I've just been to your studio,' he said, 'the door was open. I found some bread on the table. I ate it. I found some coins too, and I took them.'[19] To the rescue came Max Jacob, who was working as a 'nanny' (his word for tutor) to a boy of good family. One day he brought his pupil to the Hôtel du Maroc to see how Picasso was faring. He was appalled at the deprivation and squalor. 'For the rest of his life this nice gentleman will remember having seen misery coupled with genius,' Jacob said of his former pupil.[20] Although almost as hard up as the artist, this charitable man went out and bought Picasso some *pommes frites*, and then proposed that he move in with him. He had a room on the fifth floor of 137 Boulevard Voltaire, in an unattractive industrial quarter of Paris. It was bleak but spacious and, until Picasso arrived, meticulously tidy.

Picasso. *Simian Self-Portrait.* Paris, January 1, 1903. Pen on paper, 11.8×10.7 cm. Museu Picasso, Barcelona.

Jacob's subsequent recollections of the weeks spent sharing his room with Picasso suffer from poetic licence and lapses of memory. Hence confusion on the part of biographers.[21] When Picasso installed himself on the Boulevard Voltaire, Jacob is assumed to have had a job nearby at the Paris-France department store. This was run by his rich cousin, Gustave Gompel (the man who had bought Picasso's portrait of Bibi la Purée at the Vollard show in 1901). However, according to the firm's records,[22] Jacob did not officially start work there until February 5, 1903, about three weeks after Picasso returned to Barcelona. He must still have been employed as a 'nanny'. The story that Jacob was already putting in a long day's work at the department store may well have had its origins in the need to foster the notion of an unshared bed—a bed in which Picasso slept by day and Jacob by night. Since both men were notoriously nocturnal, this arrangement could not always have worked. However, it made for propriety. The boyish-looking Picasso had yet to cultivate the requisite degree of Andalusian machismo and he would have dreaded anyone thinking that he shared a bed with a known homosexual, least of all one who was in love with him. For the besotted Jacob the frustrations must have been even more distressing.

Picasso. *Cornuti and a Companion.* Paris, 1903. Watercolour on paper, 31×23.5 cm. Private collection.

When his morale was low, Picasso was apt to turn, as now, to self-portraits. Most of these portray him full-length and naked, sometimes with hair parted to the left or in the centre; arms in various hieratic positions. An exception is a caricature of himself as an unkempt monkey with a scruffy moustache and paintbrushes sticking out like antennae from behind his ears. Instead of looking soulful, he is prancing around having a good scratch and grinning devilishly, in ironic celebration of New Year's Day, 1903. The drawing is inscribed: '*Picasso par lui-même.*' The only friend of whom there is any pictorial record at this period is Cornuti, Picasso's colleague from *Arte Joven* days, who was also a friend of Jacob. The artist did a haunting portrait of this satyr poet, seated with a midinette in front of a glass of absinthe—his nemesis.[23]

Out of pride and penury and, I suspect, nervousness that his relationship with Jacob might be misconstrued, Picasso avoided his old friends in Montmartre. Instead he kept to the depressing 11th *arrondissement* and made do with the bounty and fantasy of Jacob's mind instead of Le Zut. Jacob was an insomniac, and he livened the long cold nights by expounding on the glories of French literature and the secrets of mysticism, doing everything in his power to stimulate and beguile his roommate.

Back from tutoring, Jacob would busy himself with the housekeeping and prepare whatever food he could afford—on good days, omelettes, beans, Brie and *pommes frites*; on bad days, nothing. Years later, Jacob still harped on their first meal, eaten out of doors on the rue de la Roquette: a putrid fish and a rotten sausage that contained nothing but gas. Many of Picasso's stories of these early days likewise end with this gaseous sausage that exploded when cooked.[24] It even survives in some of the later poems.

* * *

Around the time Picasso moved in with him, Jacob surprised his friends (and, one suspects, himself) by taking on a mistress—for the first and last time. Her first name has been variously given as Cécile, Geneviève or Germaine; her surname as Pfeipfer, Peifer or Acker.[25] Jacob had met her in a workers' bistro he frequented. When one of the habitués accused him of making advances to his wife—a tall, skinny woman he had never even noticed—Jacob made a point of apologizing to this unknown female for unwittingly causing her trouble. Whereupon she told him the saga of her life: a brute of a husband, thirteen lovers and so forth. They took to going out together and embarked on an improbable courtship. One day she announced her intention of leaving her husband and moving in with Jacob. She told him that she would cost him nothing. She was used to work. She knitted dolls' dresses.[26] He was twenty-seven; she was twenty.

Picasso may well have pushed Jacob into this heterosexual escapade: at least it deflected some of the poet's adoration away from him. Over half a century later, he could not resist a dig at Jacob's preferences, when he illustrated a posthumous edition (1956) of his *Chronique des temps héroïques* with four prints, three of them portraits, the other of Jacob's naked back and buttocks. Yes, he had steered the poet in the right direction, Picasso said, when I showed him a photograph of a then unpublished drawing inscribed 'Genoveva' (*sic*). 'A portrait of Max Jacob's one and only mistress,' he declared, and gleefully annotated the photograph, '*Geneviève, amie de Max Jacob, vers 1903*'. He conveyed the impression—an impression that the bare-breasted woman in the drawing helps to confirm—that the dolls' dressmaker had slept with him as well as Jacob.

After Picasso's return to Spain in the middle of January 1903, Jacob left the Boulevard Voltaire for a one-room apartment on the Boulevard Barbès; Cécile moved in with him. For a time he claimed to have been idyllically happy: the two greatest moments of his life, he said, were 'the first night with my first love and [the] first vision of God six years later'.[27] Jacob's grim drawing of her, looking middle-aged and dowdy in hat and veil, belies the inscription, '*Cécile, la seule passion violente de ma vie*'. Picasso's brooding Geneviève is much more attractive than Jacob's frump. If Picasso had not been so adamant about his identification, we might wonder whether they were really one and the same.

After eight months, Cécile's intellectual limitations and incessant knitting of tiny garments reawakened Jacob's distrust of motherly women, and he went back to young men. His account of the end of the affair is too self-serving to carry conviction: he was fired, he claims, in November 1903,

Picasso. Lithograph (Vallauris, September 23, 1953) and drypoint (Cannes, September 7, 1956) published in Max Jacob's *Chronique des temps héroïques*, 1956. Musée Picasso, Paris.

Picasso. *Portrait of Geneviève* (Max Jacob's mistress). Paris, 1903. Pastel on paper. Whereabouts unknown.

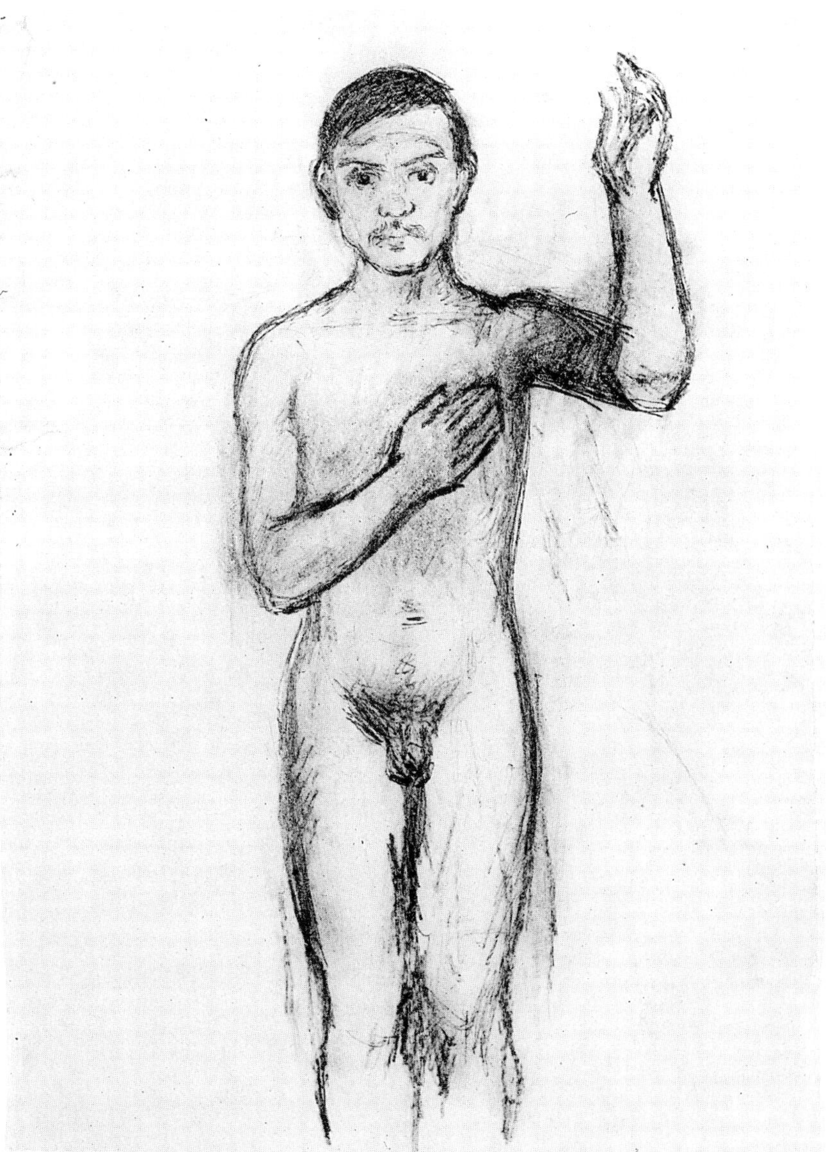

Picasso. *Nude Self-Portrait*. Paris, 1902–03. Pencil on paper, 27.5×20.5cm. Private collection.

Max Jacob. *Portrait of Cécile* (also known as Geneviève), 'the only violent passion in my life'. 1904. Pen on paper. Nicole Rousset-Altounian collection.

Max Jacob. *Portrait of Picasso*. Paris, 1903. Pen on paper, 26×17.5cm. Musée Picasso, Paris.

for living in sin with Cécile. He could not bear to put her through the misery of his joblessness (Jacob wrote to a friend in 1943), so, after emptying all the money he had into her handbag, he tearfully sent her back to her husband. 'She, too, was weeping. For years and years my eyes sought her out in the street, and when I exhibited for the one and only time at the Salon des Indépendants, it was in the hope that she would come and see my works [1907].'[28] His wish was granted: she appeared at the vernissage, and Picasso and Braque are said—if we can believe Jacob—to have commented on her beauty. Twelve years later, by which time Cécile/Geneviève had married 'a quite well-known comic writer and cartoonist' (who has not been identified), her 'beauty' had disappeared. A friend recalled: 'a summer's day in 1919, a whole gang of us—Max, Gris, Reverdy, etc.—were seated on the terrace of the Café des Pierrots . . . when Max turned pale and buried his nose in a glass of beer, murmuring, Cécile! A huge lady in a red tailor-made was advancing down the rue Houdon.'[29]

For publishing a highly coloured account of their early association in his *Le Roi de Béotie* (1921) and recycling it a few years later in one of the first numbers of *Cahiers d'Art*,[30] Jacob was taken to task by Picasso. The two of them had contemplated suicide, Jacob hinted: 'Picasso may perhaps remember the day we gazed from the height of our balcony down to the ground and the poems of Alfred de Vigny that made us weep.'[31] Picasso was not at all pleased: such a thought had never entered his head, he claimed. But Jacob was right about de Vigny. On two separate occasions Picasso noted down details of de Vigny's collected works in his sketchbooks. He was the right poet to assuage feelings of spiritual loneliness, of oppressed and unrecognized genius. Eventually Jacob's mythmaking about their penniless days, his alternations of obsessive piety and chip-on-the-shoulder malice, his successive sales of the drawings and memorabilia he had been given (he was always broke), would take their toll. 'Picasso has been my friend for sixteen years,' Jacob wrote to Tristan Tzara in 1916. 'We have hated each other and done each other as much harm as good, but he is indispensable to my life.'[32] In the end it was more than mutual resentment that came between the two old friends, it was politics. On January 1, 1937, Picasso drove down from Paris with his son and 'a pretty Etruscan lady (Rose period)' to see Max Jacob at the Abbey of Saint-Benoît. Although they laughed and cried, he could not resist needling the poet. 'Isn't the shadow of the basilica too black for Max?' the artist asked a mutual friend. As Picasso veered to the left, Jacob veered to the right, and became a royalist and supporter of Catholic fascist causes.[33] These political differences, coupled with Picasso's deep-rooted fear of authority, should be borne in mind by anyone who wonders why the artist would always acknowledge his enormous debt to Jacob and yet do nothing to help him in 1943, when he was arrested by the Germans and sent to Drancy concentration camp. Ironically, it was the collaborationist Cocteau who was the hero of the occasion: he telephoned Gerhardt Heller of the *Propaganda Staffel* and had Sacha Guitry intervene with Abetz to set Jacob free. But it was too late. 'Saint-Matorel' had died of pneumonia the day before, on March 5, 1944.

* * *

Berthe Weill's exhibit (November 15–December 15) featured three other painters besides Picasso: Ramon Pichot, Launay, about whom little is known, and Girieud, a popular Montmartre figure known as 'L'Abbé', who failed to sustain his early promise. Picasso's hopes that it would solve his financial problems, at least temporarily, were dashed. Nothing sold. This is the more puzzling since the exhibits—besides the six paintings, three pastels and drawings listed in the catalogue, there were numerous addenda—were not confined to the Blue period, which the public had yet to appreciate. Some were Parisian scenes left over from the Vollard show and should therefore have found favour. Thilda Harlor's catalogue preface gives an idea of the mixture: 'three studies of women . . . dedicated to misery, solitude and exhaustion,' also 'a theatre box and some studies of Paris, the enclosure at Auteuil with its kaleidoscope of light-coloured dresses; and girls of the sort whose faces beneath outsize hats are brazenly painted with rouge for nights on the street.'[34]

Picasso. *Couple at a Music-Hall.* Paris, 1902. Pastel on cardboard, 30.5×38.7 cm. Private collection. The work described in Charles Morice's review.

That none of the works he had brought from Barcelona (e.g., the great pastel of *Mother and Child on the Shore*) and given to Weill on consignment found a buyer reduced Picasso to despair. There was a small consolation: the symbolist poet and theorist Charles Morice, one of the more influential and progressive critics of the day, wrote a serious and on the whole favourable review (*Mercure de France*, December 1902). While expressing reservations about the gloom of the Blue period paintings, he pays tribute to the young painter's mastery. As usual Morice was sententious but perceptive:

> Extraordinary what sterile sadness weighs down the entire work of this very young man. His oeuvre is already uncountable. Picasso is someone who painted before learning to read, someone who has been commissioned to express by means of his brush everything in existence. One might say a young god out to do over the world. But he is a dark, unsmiling god. The hundreds of faces that he paints grimace—never grin. His own world would be no more habitable than his leprous shacks. As for the painting itself, it is sick—whether incurably so I know not. But sure enough he has the strength, the gift, the talent. What drawing! A crouching nude is little short of a miracle. What composition! A man and woman in a music-hall, turning away from the stage in the background, where a dancer performs in a blaze of light, is as disturbing and provocative as one of the *Fleurs du mal.* People of indeterminate sex, 'mundane demons' with woebegone eyes, heads bowed, brows dark with desperation or thoughts of crime. . . . Should one in the last resort want this painting to regain its health? Isn't this child with his terrible precocity destined to consecrate masterpieces to a negative sense of life, to a sickness from which he more than anyone else suffers? . . .[35]

Louis Trillat. *Portrait of Charles Morice.* Published in *La Plume,* July 15, 1889.

Morice's praise for Picasso's work would have been the more welcome, coming as it did from an intimate friend of Verlaine and Mallarmé, as well as a close associate of Gauguin (despite embezzling money due to Gauguin while he was off in the South Seas). For helping to edit and partly rewrite the artist's *Noa Noa*, Morice had been taken back into favour, as Paco Durrio would have told Picasso that fraught evening a year earlier. Indeed it was probably Durrio who had brought Picasso's work to Morice's attention and arranged a meeting between the two men. This meeting had one propitious consequence: Morice gave Picasso a copy of

67

Chapitre IV –

Le Conteur parle –

Mes voisins sont devenus pour moi presque des amis. Je m'habille, je mange comme eux. Quand je ne travaille pas je partage leur vie d'indolence et de joie, avec de brusques passages de gravité. Le soir, au pied des buissons touffus que domine la tête échevelée des cocotiers, on se réunit par groupes, – hommes, femmes et enfants. Les uns sont de Tahiti, les autres des Tongas, puis des Arouai, des Marquises. Les tons mats de leur corps font une belle harmonie avec le velours du feuillage, et de leurs poitrines cuivrées sortent de vibrantes mélodies qui s'atténuent en s'y

Gauguin. Page of the illustrated manuscript of *Noa Noa* prepared in collaboration with Charles Morice, 1893–97. Musée du Louvre, Paris.

Picasso. *Standing Nude*. Barcelona, December 1902. Charcoal on paper, 24×16cm. Private collection. Signed 'Paul Picasso'.

Noa Noa, the miscellany of folklore, fable and reminiscence (marred only by the addition of Morice's orotund commentaries and poems) that Gauguin hoped would make his painting more comprehensible in symbolist circles. No one would reap greater benefit from *Noa Noa* than Picasso. It would be the main conduit for the primitive power and mystery and drama that he appropriated from Gauguin. Picasso could not resist embellishing his copy with drawings of his own. Unfortunately this book, which never left the artist's possession in his lifetime, vanished after his death. The artist's son, Claude Picasso, remembered seeing it as a child and being amazed that his father had had it bound in an ornate golden cover set with jewels.[36] Cooper, who claimed to have examined it, saw it as a 'talisman'.

In the absence of this seminal copy of *Noa Noa*, we need only turn to Picasso's work to discover the depth and intensity of his identification with Gauguin. One of the most revealing examples is a drawing dating from early 1903—a portrait of the artist fondling the buttocks of a recumbent nude—which is taken directly from Gauguin's *Manao Tupapau* (*The Spectre Watches over Her*). Picasso would have been very familiar with this painting, not just from having read the extensive explanation of it in *Noa Noa*, but from having actually seen it at Vollard's at the time of his 1901 show. Gauguin claims that this painting has nothing to do with sex: it is about fear—'the spirit of a living girl linked with the spirit of Death. Night and day. Otherwise the picture would simply be a study of a Polynesian nude.'[37] Picasso has thus knowingly portrayed himself as the spirit of the dead, who watches over and terrifies the girl. Another striking example of Picasso's identification with Gauguin is the signature on a Gauguin-esque drawing of a nude (executed in December 1902, although it has been mistakenly dated December 1903). For the one and only time in his life the artist signed himself 'Paul Picasso'—in deference to Gauguin, who would die a few months later (May 1903).[38] This fits in with Picasso's predatory attitude to other artists' signatures, and his dawning instinct that Gauguin was the pathfinder to follow through the sacred wood.

* * *

The misery of Picasso's 1902 Parisian Christmas emerges in two sentimental studies of a skinny old man and skinny little boy, both blue with cold, selling mistletoe. Like Dickens, Picasso could make mawkishness work for him, but there is more to these gouaches than that. Once again Picasso has borrowed from El Greco: not only the stylizations and the composition, but also the theme of El Greco's great altarpiece of St Joseph clutching the Christ Child that he knew well from his visits to the Chapel of San José in Toledo. Looked at in the light of the Greco, the *Mistletoe Seller* allegorizes Picasso's messianic relationship to his father. Like don José, the seedy old man, who stands in for St Joseph, is obliging his son to market a sacred emblem—the pathetic clump of mistletoe that is a wistful echo of Greco's avalanche of flowers. Ironically, the larger and more important *Mistletoe Seller* ended up in the collection of Max Pellequer. This banker, who accumulated a fine collection of Picasso's work in the course of acting as his *homme d'affaires*, made a number of acquisitions

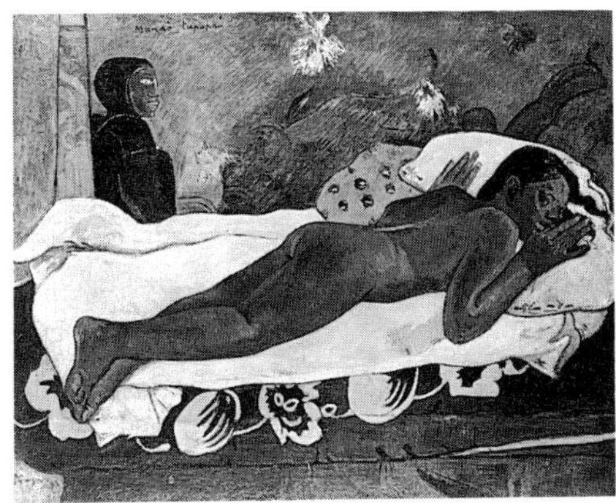

Above: Gauguin. *Manao Tupapau (The Spectre Watches over Her).* 1892. Oil on burlap, 72.5×92.5cm. Albright-Knox Art Gallery, Buffalo, New York, A. Conger Goodyear Collection, 1965.

Right: El Greco. *St Joseph and the Child Christ.* 1597–99. Oil on canvas, 289×147cm. Toledo, Museo San Vicente, from the Chapel of San José.

Above: Picasso. *Self-Portrait with Reclining Nude.* Paris, 1903. Ink and watercolour on paper, 17.6× 23.2cm. Museu Picasso, Barcelona.

Right: Picasso. *Mistletoe Seller.* Paris, 1903. Gouache on paper, 37.5×27cm. Private collection.

directly from the artist. And it would have been typical of Picasso to give (or exchange for services rendered) this Christmas card-like evocation of poverty to the man who looked after his money.

If Picasso's first three visits to Paris all ended shortly before or after Christmas, this can be attributed to his Andalusian loathing of the cold. Why go on freezing and starving when he could return home to Barcelona and the relative comfort of his parents' apartment? The main problem in January 1903 was money for the ticket home. Picasso was not going to apply to his family as he had done last time. Berthe Weill claimed to be broke, so Picasso threw himself on the mercy of Madame Besnard, the wife of his colour merchant, who already had a small collection of his work. Madame Besnard was persuaded to pay two hundred francs for the superb pastel *Mother and Child on the Shore* that he had brought with him from Barcelona to sell at the December show. To have something to live on back in Spain, Picasso tried to unload all the work he had with him for a further two hundred francs. There were no takers. And so, before leaving Paris, he rolled up everything that was left and asked Ramon Pichot to store it for him. A year or so later, when Picasso returned to take possession of this cache, it was found to have vanished from the top of the cupboard where it had supposedly been stashed. In the end, Pichot discovered it hidden under the cupboard.[39] 'If [this cache] had been lost,' Picasso joked many years later, 'there would have been no Blue period, as everything I had hitherto painted was in that roll.'[40]

Picasso. *Mother and Child on the Shore*. Paris, 1903. Pastel on paper, 46×31 cm. Whereabouts unknown. Probably the pastel Picasso sold to Madame Besnard to pay for his ticket home to Barcelona.

Most biographers end their account of this unhappy stay in Paris with a legend that the artist reiterated to one biographer after another—a legend that everyone but Daix, who dismisses it as a 'metaphor', seems to have believed. He felt so cold, Picasso said, that he was obliged to burn a mass of drawings. Sheer fantasy! The room he shared with Jacob was equipped with a stove almost as tall as himself (1 metre, 45 cm., as is recorded in a sketch of it). Drawings would not possibly have kept it going. Besides, there was far more readily available fuel—crates and suchlike—to be picked up in the street. This picturesque story derives from *La Bohème*, Puccini's recent (1896) opera that had been enjoying enormous success: the moment in the first act when the freezing hero, Rodolfo, consigns the opening of his tragedy to the stove in order to warm himself. Years later, Picasso told Geneviève Laporte that Jacob used to drag him (no opera-lover) to see *La Bohème* (also, I believe, *I Pagliacci*), and that 'it made Max weep each time we went to it'.[41] Picasso would have had every reason to identify with the 'poor geniuses' of Puccini's verismo opera, but he was a fanatic about preserving his work and would never have burned or otherwise destroyed drawings, unless they were beyond salvaging.

Picasso. *Stove in the Boulevard Voltaire Apartment*. Paris, 1902–03. Pen on trade card, 11.7×7.6 cm. Museu Picasso, Barcelona.

During his weeks at the Boulevard Voltaire, Picasso would have been exposed to Jacob's addiction to ether and henbane—drugs that stimulated his powers as a 'Pythia'. So far as we know, Jacob did not initiate Picasso into drugs, but he certainly initiated him into the Tarot and taught him about palmistry. Two sheets of paper survive (both bearing an outline of Picasso's left hand), in which Jacob gives a reading of his friend's hand. To judge by a sketch of Jacob on the sheet in which the poet sets out to explain the science of palmistry, these undated charts probably date from this Paris period. On the other sheet Jacob analyses Picasso's

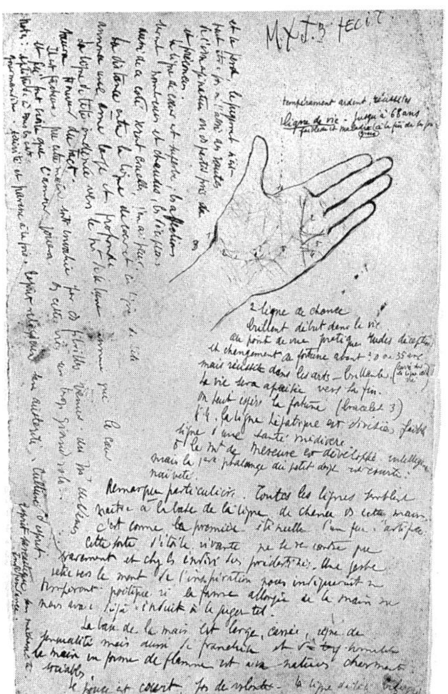

Max Jacob. Chart of Picasso's left palm. Paris, 1902. Pen and conté crayon on paper, 29×18.9 cm. Museu Picasso, Barcelona.

hand. An 'ardent temperament', he says. All the lines stem from the base of the fate line, 'like the first spark of a firework'—a most unusual phenomenon seen only in the hands of 'predestined individuals.' Jacob is remarkably unprescient: 'Weakness and illness up to the age of sixty-eight. . . . Life will grow more peaceful toward the end. Wealth can be hoped for.' Nor is he much more illuminating when he speaks from experience: 'The line of the heart is magnificent, love affairs will be numerous and warm . . . disappointments will be cruel—they alarm me . . . love will play too large a role in [Picasso's] life. Notes: aptitude for all the arts—greed—energetic and lazy at one and the same time—religious spirit without austerity—a cultivated mind—sarcastic wit without malice—Independence.'

Many years later, Jacob collaborated with Claude Valence on an astrological handbook, *Miroir de l'Astrologie*. Jacob wrote a section on each of the astral signs: the Cancer section is a self-portrait, the Scorpio section is based on Picasso. Thanks to hindsight, Jacob's analysis of the artist's birth sign is more revealing than that of his hand. Besides making the obvious connection between seminal energy, predatory sexuality and the scorpion's poisonous sting, Jacob cites less familiar symbols connected with the sign: the eagle and the dove; the first stands for the flight of thought (which remains inaccessible), the second for the Holy Ghost. 'The Scorpion is a principle of life and death; its dispositions are extreme and contradictory. The spirit is revolutionary.'[42]

Before leaving Paris, Picasso drew a wishful-thinking *alleluia* (entitled *Histoire claire et simple de Max Jacob*). Dated January 13, 1903, this comic strip shows Jacob writing a book, reading it to a publisher, earning enough money to dine at Maxim's, being honoured as a poet by Greek deities drawn after Puvis de Chavannes, and having his statue carved by Rodin in the Champs Elysées. In time this wishful thinking would come true for both the poet and the artist. But no amount of recognition, no amount of gold, would ever heal the wounds that Picasso suffered during these hellishly humiliating three months. Henceforth his deprivations and degradations would entitle him to take an even blacker view of life than before. He would feel he had the right to avenge himself on the world, and behave on occasion like a hurt and imperious child, who makes others suffer because he has suffered. Forevermore, his attitude to money would oscillate betwen extremes of generosity and stinginess. His loathing of poverty was equalled only by his distrust of riches. To his credit, Picasso did not become disenchanted with Paris. After returning to Barcelona around the middle of January, he remained for well over a year, but this would be his last prolonged stay on Spanish soil. Defeat had made him more than ever determined to go back to Paris and prevail. Where else could a modern artist get a measure of his own powers?

Picasso. *Histoire claire et simple de Max Jacob*. Paris, January 1903. Pen and ink on paper, 19×28 cm. Musée Picasso, Paris.

17

La Vie

Picasso. *Interior of the Artist's Studio*. Barcelona, 1902. Pen on paper, 15×12.2cm. Museu Picasso, Barcelona.

Opposite: Picasso. *La Vie*. Barcelona, 1903. Oil on canvas, 197×127.3cm. The Cleveland Museum of Art, Gift of Hanna Fund.

BACK HOME PICASSO PINED FOR PARIS, despite the misery he had endured there. The evening he returned to Barcelona, he made straight for the family apartment on the Carrer Mercè, and went to bed in his old room. The following morning, while he was still asleep, his mother took his filthy clothes away, brushed them, and polished his shoes. When he awoke and discovered what she had done, he flew into such a rage that this usually resilient woman was reduced to tears. Her crime? She had deprived him of his 'Parisian dust', he told his mistress Geneviève Laporte some forty years later.[1] He soon recovered from his tantrum. For all that he missed his Parisian dust, Picasso resolved for the time being to make do with the Catalan variety. Barcelona was bereft of artistic challenge, but there were advantages: a measure of security, a supportive mother, '*qu'il adorait*', as he told Max Jacob,[2] a lively sister, a circle of admiring friends; and not least the nearness of the Mediterranean, which would always have a regenerative effect on him.

For the next fifteen months Picasso set about perfecting the synthesis towards which he had been working ever since the Vollard show eighteen months earlier. Catalan primitives, El Greco, Morales, Poussin, Puvis de Chavannes, Carrière, above all Gauguin, are only some of the sources that he pillaged for elements that he could transform—Picassify. And within a very few months he had arrived at a romantically agonized view of life and a style that was appropriately eloquent, mannered and, for all its derivations, original. In the course of the next year Picasso proceeded to exploit this new synthesis in a succession of spectacular *tours de force*. At their best, these paintings have a solemn presence and air of compassion; at their less than best, the virtuosity is disconcertingly pat, the concept trite, the blues shrill and maudlin. This bitter-sweet blend of technical prowess and manipulative sentiment found surprisingly little favour outside the artist's immediate circle. Over the years, however, the paintings of this so-called Blue period have become popular favourites. Very rich people consistently pay higher prices for them than for any other examples of twentieth-century art. These distillations of suffering and want either exorcise the guilt of mammon or else make it the more enjoyable.

For all his ambivalence toward his father, Picasso continued to sleep under the parental roof. As usual he had no difficulty finding a studio; he simply moved in with the obliging Angel de Soto, who had taken over the studio apartment on the Riera Sant Joan that Picasso had formerly shared with Casagemas. Since the walls were still daubed with the decorations Picasso and Casagemas had executed three years earlier, the place must have conjured up, especially to someone as superstitious as Picasso, the direst of memories. Or was this a challenge he welcomed? Just as the apartment on the Boulevard de Clichy, where Casagemas had spent his last days, had done two years earlier, the Riera Sant Joan studio would once more inspire Picasso to raise the artist's troubled spirit on canvas.

What had become of this studio between Casagemas's death in February 1901 and Picasso's return there almost two years later we do not know. Did the family keep it shut up until the lease ran out, when de Soto took over? Or had de Soto been allowed to use it all along? For Picasso a welcome dividend would have been the large canvas of *Last Moments*, which had been stored there ever since its return from the Paris exhibition of 1900. Given the strides he had made in the last three years, the *modernista* concept of *Last Moments* would have seemed outmoded—not worth preserving. After being reduced to working on scraps of grubby paper, Picasso found the painting a godsend. The canvas that had embodied his bid for international success in 1900 could once more be put to the same use. He would scrape it down and show the Catalans as well as Félicien Fagus who would be El Greco's heir.

* * *

La Vie, the great set piece that Picasso began planning in the spring of 1903, has given rise to more mystification than any other early work by the artist. Since mystery is intrinsic to the painting's power, we should respect it instead of trying to dispel it. Here we would do well to remember that Picasso had recently spent several weeks cooped up with a man who was a part-time fortune-teller; and that this fortune-teller had taught him the rudiments of astrology, chiromancy and the Tarot.[3] Thirty years later Picasso would still draw on the Tarot in his writing as well as his painting. The fact that certain puzzling works done in the spring and summer of 1903 require to be 'read' by the light of the Tarot suggests that Jacob gave him a pack to take back to Barcelona. The mystical drawings of Christ on the cross, surrounded by embracing couples of female nudes, and a hieratic Pythia or priestess in a mandala derive from both the Wheel of Fortune and the World cards.[4] The World card, which stands for completion, perfection and synthesis—something that was much on Picasso's mind—is usually represented by a more or less naked woman in a mandala surrounded by the symbols of the four Evangelists,[5] in the same way that the allegorical figures in these drawings are surrounded by a mandala of saints and fornicating lovers.

Besides the Wheel of Fortune and the World cards, Picasso invokes one other, the Popess card. She stands for wisdom and good judgement, also impatience and coldness as exemplified by the virgin goddess Diana, and Hecate, protectress of warlocks and witches. The Popess surely inspired the mysterious Pythia in her long flowing robes (the Tarot emblem of the stream of consciousness), who sits between a writhing female nude and a bearded Greco-esque saint playing a stringed instrument. These allegories hint at the dualities inherent in Picasso's nature—sacred and profane, demonic and angelic, mystic and matter-of-fact. But they

World and Popess cards from a traditional Marseilles Tarot pack. Private collection.

Picasso. *Woman in a Mandala of Figures*. Barcelona, 1903. Pen and sepia on paper, 33.6×23.1 cm. Musée Picasso, Paris.

Picasso. *Crucifixion and Embracing Couples*. Barcelona, 1903. Pencil and blue crayon on paper, 31.8×21.9 cm. Musée Picasso, Paris.

Picasso. *Man Striking a Woman.* Barcelona, 1903. Blue crayon on paper, 23×18.2cm. Museu Picasso, Barcelona.

Picasso. *Man and Pregnant Woman.* Barcelona, 1903. Conté crayon on paper, 23×17.8cm. Museu Picasso, Barcelona.

Picasso. *Embrace.* Barcelona, 1903. Pastel on paper, 98×57cm. Collection Walter–Guillaume, Musée de l'Orangerie, Paris.

also reveal the artist's curiosity in seeing how magic could heighten the drama and mystery of his work. Just as years later Picasso would shuffle pieces of cut paper before locking them into a revelatory pattern, he now sets about shuffling his pack of images and laying them out in a manner that can best be described as divinatory. Once *La Vie* is seen in the light of this procedure, the element of mystery turns out to be essential to our understanding.

Picasso very seldom gave names to his paintings and usually hated the titles that dealers, critics or art historians invented. A rare exception is *La Vie*. This ambitious, not to say pretentious, title is first recorded within a week or so of the work's completion, so it was thought up by the artist himself, or at least had his approval. Given a group of related drawings (spring 1903) depicting a man's reaction to a woman's pregnancy, the title probably antedated the finished work. Picasso proposes four different scenarios: the man on his knees begs the woman for forgiveness; he throws his hands in the air denying responsibility, while she lays her head on his chest; he points accusingly at the tearful woman's belly; he chastizes her. Did the artist or one of his close friends find himself in a similar situation? More than likely. Picasso's subjects usually have their origins in everyday life. And life—hence also birth and death—is what Picasso's major new composition proposed to address. The bearded man,[6] who appears here and in many other works of this period, is a generic type: an alienated 'poor genius' figure on whom the artist projects his own doubt and frustration, anger and fear. Picasso resolves this domestic situation in more finished drawings of the now contrite couple locked in each other's arms. In the culminant *Embrace*, a highly finished pastel with a bed in the background, they embrace and the man presses the penis that caused all the trouble against the woman's pregnant belly with a warmth and affection that is foreign to most Blue period work.

Picasso. Preparatory drawing for *La Vie*. Barcelona, 1903. Conté crayon on paper, 14.5×9.5cm. Museu Picasso, Barcelona.

Paradoxically, *La Vie*—the painting that this *Embrace* engendered—is often said to allegorize impotence rather than fertility. Picasso hints at this, we are told,[7] by the equivocal pose of his two central figures—by the way Germaine presses her far-from-pregnant stomach fruitlessly against Casagemas's unpromising *cache-sexe*. This view of *La Vie* as a reference to Casagemas's supposed impotence has also been questioned.[8] For one thing, the earliest preparatory drawings for *La Vie*[9] reveal that Picasso, not Casagemas, was originally the central figure. The tall, androgynous-looking mother on the right, with her huge feet, who stares balefully at the preoccupied couple, was at first a stooped, older-looking man—a cross between Picasso's eccentric sculptor friend Fontbona and don José. These different combinations of figures represent desperate attempts on the artist's part to come up with an allegory that would have some measure of personal relevance and yet be universal enough to do justice to his demanding title.

In another of these early sketches, the Picasso figure makes a hieratic gesture that derives directly from the Tarot (in his use of the Tarot, Picasso has something in common with contemporary composers and choreographers who consult the *I Ching*). The right hand points upwards; the left hand, forefinger outstretched, makes an admonitory, downward gesture. Because the gesture is not repeated in the painting, little attention has been paid to the right hand in this drawing. However, it is the clue to

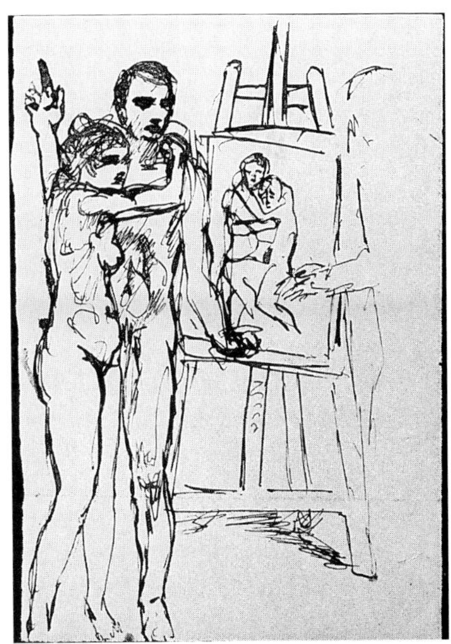

Picasso. Preparatory drawing for *La Vie*. Barcelona, 1903. Pen and sepia on paper, 15.9×11cm. Musée Picasso, Paris.

the meaning of the mysterious left forefinger that has kept historians guessing:[10] Only Alfred Barr nobly admits defeat: 'Obviously allegory is intended.'[11] Anyone familiar with occult iconography will recognize this upward and downward gesture.[12] It symbolizes the most famous of all mystical axioms, contained in the *Tabula Smaragdina* ('The Emerald Tablet'), attributed to the legendary Hermes Trismegistus: 'Whatsoever is below is like that which is above as all things are made from one.' The uplifted right hand symbolizes power from above, while the down-pointing left hand symbolizes the passage of power to a plane below. (Further confirmation of this gesture's meaning is to be found in a sheet of five studies done two years later of a cloaked harlequin with his hands in a sequence of similar positions.) Cartomancers identify this gesture with the first card in the Tarot pack, the Magician: the card that stands for willpower, skill, originality, creativity and guile. The Magician also relates to Hermes Trismegistus, with whom, I suspect, Jacob had already identified Picasso—hence Picasso's adoption of the above/below gesture. It is no coincidence that Guillaume Apollinaire,[13] another student of the occult and the Tarot, would soon come up with a similar identification in a poem that apostrophizes the artist as '*Harlequin Trismégiste*'. In *La Vie* Picasso shuffles his pack of images and lays out a hand, just as, night after night on the Boulevard Voltaire, Jacob had shuffled the Tarot and laid out a hand to see what was in store for the two of them.

Picasso. *Harlequins with Raised Hands*. Paris, 1905. Pen on paper, 24.5×17 cm. Private collection.

X-rays reveal that the central figure in *La Vie* was originally Picasso, as in the preliminary drawings. He had intended a self-portrait and replaced it with the portrait of a friend, the artist told Penrose.[14] So much for the idea that *La Vie* was conceived as an apotheosis of Casagemas, or an allegory of his impotence and suicide. Nor does the substitution of Casagemas's head for Picasso's automatically turn it into one. That is far too limited a reading. As for the suppression of the 'that which is above' gesture, Picasso would have had little choice: an upraised right hand would no longer have fitted into the composition. On its own, the downward gesture heightens the mystery—and, yes, the theatricality—of the painting, and it could apply equally to Picasso's or Casagemas's circumstances. Like all the major arcana in the Tarot, it has a positive or a negative meaning—strength or weakness of will, decisiveness or indecisiveness—according to which direction the card faces when dealt. Perfect for an artist who wanted to endow an image with ambivalent or antithetical meanings.

Magician card from a traditional Marseilles Tarot pack. Private collection.

The mother plays a supporting role. She appears to be an afterthought, an interloper. In comparison with the high finish of the central group, she is painted somewhat sketchily. (The don José figure, who occupied this spot in some of the preparatory drawings, does not show up in any of the x-rays.) By now this draped mother and child is such a cliché in Picasso's work that her appearance constitutes something of an imaginative lapse. However, if we accept the Tarot analysis, she could well signify the sixth card in the pack: the Lovers, whose multiple meanings correspond to elements in *La Vie*. Like *La Vie*, this card usually depicts three figures: a naked Adam and Eve in the company of an angel or cupid. In one of the standard interpretations, the Adam figure has to choose between the angel and Eve—between, as it might be, sacred and profane love, or between submitting to the passions or conquering them. There is also an element of frustration and opposition in this card: echoes of the expulsion

Gauguin. *D'où venons-nous? Que sommes-nous? Où allons-nous?* (detail). 1897. Oil on canvas, 139.1×374.6 cm. Museum of Fine Arts, Boston, Tomkins Collection.

Lovers card from a traditional Marseilles Tarot pack. Private collection.

of Adam and Eve from paradise—the subject of one of the two Gauguinesque easel paintings in the background. These are also set out like cards waiting to be read—especially the lower one, in which part of a second image—a *Noa Noa* woman enveloped by a large bird—can be dimly discerned in the underpainting of the crouching figures. Since the figures in these background 'paintings' seem to have stepped out of Gauguin's *D'où venons-nous? Que sommes-nous? Où allons-nous?* (which Picasso knew from Vollard's), there is a case for seeing *La Vie* as a response to Gauguin's masterpiece. It certainly poses the same nebulous and unanswerable questions.[15]

The advantage of the Tarot hypothesis is that it does not explain away *La Vie*'s disquieting power, and it fits with what Picasso told Antonina Vallentin: '"I certainly did not intend to paint symbols; I simply painted images that arose in front of my eyes; it's for others to find a hidden meaning in them. A painting, for me, speaks by itself, what good does it do, after all, to impart explanations? A painter has only one language, as for the rest . . ." And his sentence ended with a shrug of the shoulders.'[16]

Burying *Last Moments* underneath *La Vie* has been interpreted as a symbolic act—a replacement of a deathbed scene with a painting concerned with rebirth and redemption—instead of another example of an impoverished artist's recycling process. It would be easier to accept this romantic interpretation if Picasso had had other options. He did not. The link in subject matter is coincidental. The substitution of one image for another resembles the aleatory act of a cartomancer, who has no choice in the cards he lays on top of one another. I am reminded of T. S. Eliot's Madame Sosotris, 'the wisest woman in Europe, / With a wicked pack of cards', who intones:

> Here is Belladonna, the Lady of the Rocks,
> The lady of situations. . . .
> And here is the one-eyed merchant, and this card,
> Which is blank, is something he carries on his back,
> Which I am forbidden to see. . . . [17]

In the case of *La Vie*, the card we are forbidden to see is not so much *Last Moments* as the figure of Picasso that lurks under that of Casagemas. By substituting the image of the suicide for a self-portrait, Picasso memorializes himself in the guise of his dead friend. This has the ring of exorcism. The artist confessed to André Malraux that exorcism was one of the motivating forces behind *Les Demoiselles d'Avignon*: 'my first exorcism picture . . . absolutely.'[18] Exorcism is indubitably one of the principal themes of Picasso's work, but surely *La Vie* is the first major manifestation of it. *La Vie* is also the first metaphysical manifestation of the studio theme that time and again will dominate the work: the theme of 'Theatrum Mundi'[19] —an arena where art becomes inextricably entwined with life. We have only to envisage the artist at work on *La Vie*, painting Casagemas in and himself out, against the bizarre trompe-l'oeil décor, to see the origins of this concept. In his last decade Picasso will lay the ghosts and resurrect the memories and images of a lifetime in a studio that is a microcosm of his universe.

Since one of the preparatory drawings is dated May 2, and the finished work is known to have been sold by June 4, *La Vie* was presumably

CRÓNICAS DE ARTE

PICASSO Y SU "OBRA,,

¡Pablo Ruiz Picasso! He ahí un nombre que para muchos es poco menos que desconocido, pues entiéndase bien que hasta la mayor parte de los que le «conocen», no le conocen lo suficiente para entenderle y juzgarle.

Picasso. *Self-Portrait,* published in *El Liberal,* March 24, 1904.

painted in the course of May. A promotional article in the June 4 issue of *El Liberal,* probably written by Carles Junyer Vidal, announced the sale:

> Pablo Ruiz Picasso, the well-known Spanish artist, who has had so many triumphs in Paris, has recently sold one of his latest works for a respectable price to the Parisian collector M. Jean Saint-Gaudens. This belongs to the new series that the brilliant Spanish artist has been painting and to which we will soon devote the attention that it deserves.
>
> The painting . . . entitled *La Vie,* is one of those works which can at a stroke establish an artist's name and reputation. The subject is interesting and provocative, and the conception is of such strength and intensity that it is without a doubt one of the few truly impressive works to have been created in Spain for some time.

La Vie is said to have established Picasso's name and reputation and 'vastly increased his fame in the Barcelona art world'.[20] But since there is no record of its being exhibited or published, and since it was apparently sold within a few days of completion, 'vast' local fame could only have accrued if the new owner had left the painting in the artist's studio for retouching or varnishing. This turns out to have been a possibility: Picasso said he remembered working on *La Vie* in the Carrer del Comerç studio,[21] but he did not occupy these premises until late 1903, so it may well have remained in the artist's hands for some months after being sold. Picasso's ever-growing throng of friends and admirers would thus have been able to take a look at it. Odd that apart from the *El Liberal* writers and Sebastià Junyent's portrait of the artist in front of *La Vie,* nobody in Barcelona—not even Sabartès, who claims to have seen Picasso every day—left any record of the artist's most important painting to date. Even the 'Parisian collector M. Jean Saint-Gaudens' has vanished without trace. Which of Picasso's friends introduced this buyer? Was it, as I suspect, Junyent, who occasionally acted as the artist's agent? This might explain why he painted Picasso in front of *La Vie.* Apart from the fact that it ended up with Vollard, the painting's early provenance is veiled in mystery.

The money for *La Vie* cannot have lasted long, or perhaps it was paid in instalments, for on August 6 Picasso wrote to Max Jacob:

Picasso. *La Jota.* Tiana, 1903. Watercolour on paper, 25.3×34.3cm. Private collection.

> I'm working insofar as I can, but I don't have enough 'dough' ['*galette*'] to do the things I'd like to do. I spend days without being able to work, that's very annoying . . . I'm thinking of doing a painting of three metres of some sailors in a small boat . . . but I have to have the money first. You can't imagine how fed up I've been for some days . . . as well I'm all on my own. Perhaps I'll go to Mallorca '*l'ile dorée*' they say it's very pretty.[22]

Nothing came of the sailors in the boat, and Picasso did not in the end go to Mallorca. Judging by a group of delicate drawings and watercolours of Catalan peasants in local costume—wining, dining, dancing the *jota,* playing the guitar, herding sheep—he went instead to stay with the Reventóses on their country property at Tiana, some seventeen kilometres north of Barcelona. (Whenever Picasso's name came up, Ramon Reventós used to say that 'the ochres of his harlequins were stolen from the golden colour of the vineyards at Tiana in the autumn'.[23]) Hitherto the drawings he did there have been catalogued as 'Evocations of Horta de Ebro'. In view of Picasso's habit (at least at this early phase) of working from life, this is most unlikely. These charming rustic scenes (especially the interior with a bowed peasant woman serving soup—a quotation from his painting of the year before) suggest that he once again contemplated doing some Hispagnolist subjects to sell in Paris. There was still a demand for them.

Luis de Morales. *Pietà*. Late 16th century. Oil on panel, 71×49cm. Málaga Cathedral.

* * *

If Carles Junyer Vidal (or whoever wrote the piece about *La Vie* in *El Liberal*) described the latest paintings as a 'new series', that is how Picasso envisaged the latterday martyrdoms—*The Blind Man's Meal, The Ascetic, The Old Guitarist, Tragedy,* and *The Blind Beggar*—with which he followed up *La Vie*. These images of destitution, old age and blindness exemplify much the same spirit as the writing of the 'Generation of 1898', the same despair, compassion and exasperation over the wretched condition of Spain. But despite Picasso's youth (he would be twenty-two in October 1903), they have more intensity and depth than Pío Baroja's raw chunks of low life. And how expertly he dramatizes things: sharpens the focus and heightens the pathos. This sense of drama has its origins in Spanish religious painting: Picasso's Blue period subjects could only have been conceived by someone who had been brought up on the agonized martyrs, lachrymose Magdalens and flagellated Christs—waxen faces stained with tears, livid bodies streaked with blood—to be found in Andalusian churches, above all in the dolorous works of Luis de Morales, such as the *Pietà* in Málaga Cathedral.

Just as Picasso had represented purity and sanctity by its opposite—the Madonna by the whore—he now concentrated on allegories of the senses in reverse. Sight is represented by a blind man; taste by a starving man staring at an empty plate; hearing by an old guitarist who is not only blind but seemingly deaf to the world; and touch by a blind man groping for a crust of bread.[24] Although the figures in most of these paintings are blue with cold, they were executed in the heat of a Mediterranean summer. Years later Picasso dismissed his Blue period works as 'nothing but sentiment'. He was especially hard on *La Vie*: 'That picture is awful. The rest can be said to be not too bad!'[25] Shame masked a measure of pride. These disclaimers were a form of self-defence, intended to disarm criticism. Then again, his sense of pity towards himself as well as others was ambivalent, not to say warped. A hint of gratification can be detected (as it was at Saint-Lazare) in the relish with which he portrays subjects more pitiable than himself on that last trip to Paris. Although he wrote self-pityingly to Max Jacob, recalling the days of misery they had shared,[26] those days of misery engendered some of the most popular icons of the century.

Picasso. *The Blind Beggar*. Barcelona, 1903. Watercolour on paper, 53.9×35.8cm. Fogg Art Museum, Harvard University, Bequest of Collection of Maurice Wertheim, Class of 1906.

To the themes of cold, hunger, imprisonment and disease is now added blindness. Was Picasso, hypochondriacal at the best of times, afraid of going blind? This fear has been attributed to the threat (real or imagined) of syphilis and its aftermath, also to castration fantasies.[27] But a more immediate cause was the progressive deterioration of his father's sight, which now threatened his ability to teach at La Llotja. Picasso's reaction was nothing if not Oedipal. One of his most memorable images of blindness, *The Old Jew*, portrays a saintly-looking old beggar, not unlike don José.

Picasso. *The Ascetic*. Barcelona, 1903. Oil on canvas, 130×97 cm. Barnes Foundation, Merion Station, Pa.

Picasso. *The Old Jew*. Barcelona, 1903. Oil on canvas, 125×92 cm. Pushkin Museum, Moscow.

Picasso. *The Blind Man's Meal*. Barcelona, 1903. Oil on canvas, 95.3×94.6 cm. The Metropolitan Museum of Art, New York.

Right: Picasso. *The Old Guitarist*. Barcelona, 1903. Oil on panel, 122.9×82.6 cm. The Art Institute of Chicago.

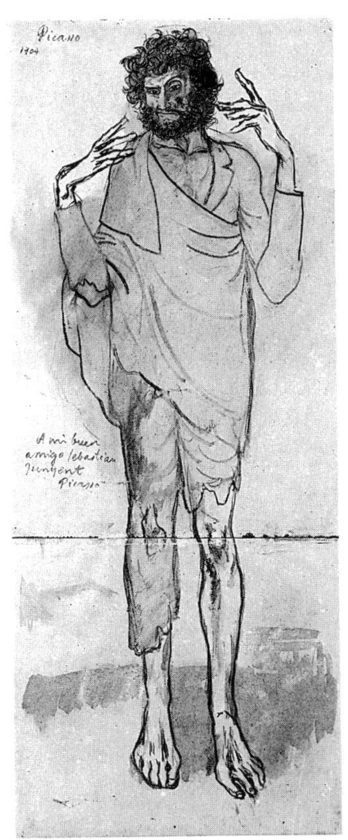

Picasso. *El Loco (The Madman)*. Barcelona, 1904. Watercolour on paper, 85×35cm. Museu Picasso, Barcelona.

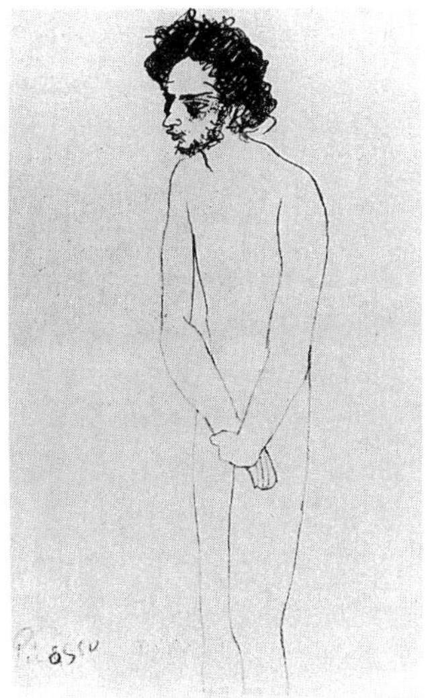

Picasso. *Casagemas Naked*. Barcelona, 1903–04. Pen and blue crayon on trade card, 13.3×9cm. Private collection.

Beside him is seated a youth, not unlike the artist as a boy, who serves as his father's eyes. This painting went through many metamorphoses: the original setting was a fishing boat, and the old Jew held a mandolin.[28] Instead of painting *The Old Jew* in the studio he shared with Soto, Picasso set up his easel in his parents' apartment on the Carrer de la Mercè, where his father's failing eyes would have been upon him. He has inscribed the back of the canvas with the Ruizes' full address, as if to register that this symbolic blinding took place in the family home. Picasso also inscribed the front of this canvas with the date: 'D. 1903' (that is to say, December 1903), but he subsequently painted this over.[29]

Picasso said many enigmatic things about blindness, none more enigmatic than this often-quoted observation: 'There is in fact only love that matters. Whatever it may be. And they should put out the eyes of painters as they do of bullfinches to make them sing better.'[30] Penrose, to whom this was said, interprets it allegorically: 'The allegory of the blinded man has pursued Picasso throughout life like a shadow as though reproaching him for his unique gift of vision. It is a paradox that a man who lives . . . by his eyes should consider even for a moment the advantages of blindness.'[31] On the other hand, if the obsessively superstitious artist invoked the prospect of what he most feared in life, was not this a way of protecting himself against it? Then again, Picasso's eye functioned as a surrogate sexual organ: the removal of vision might thus enhance sexuality, might prove that 'only love . . . matters'.[32] The equation of vision and sexuality is inherent in the *mirada fuerte*. Thus, when Picasso turns his malign gaze on himself at a time of psychic stress, he ends up as a blind Minotaur; and when he and his model exchange Medusa stares in the late paintings, they paralyse each other.

The Old Jew and the other mendicant paintings are all intensely blue, relieved only by livid yellowish highlights and cadaverous flesh tones, the better to set off heavy blue shadows. But one painting, *The Ascetic*, is even bluer than the rest—bluer than is generally realized, for it has been hidden away in the Barnes Collection outside Philadelphia for some sixty years and never loaned or reproduced in colour. The original comes as a shock. The cerulean is painfully shrill—another example of Picasso's use of bright mannerist colours to excruciatingly sour effect. *The Ascetic* represents an extreme point in the artist's addiction to blues. Over the next six months he will gradually abandon monochrome and allow warmer colours to prevail.

The lack of preparatory drawings suggests that neither *The Old Jew* nor any of its numerous kin were done from life. The only exception is a ragged lunatic with crooked eyes set in a crooked face, shaggy whiskers and shaggy locks—a familiar sight in the streets of Barcelona—who fascinated Picasso and inspired a number of sketches and watercolours.[33] Picasso also had the diabolical idea of doing a portrait drawing of Casagemas in the guise of this wild-eyed character, depicted naked so that the artist can have him clasp his hands shamefacedly in front of his genitals. Andalusians traditionally use mockery as a form of exorcism; and this brutal little drawing exorcises Picasso/Casagemas almost as effectively as that solemn riddle *La Vie*.

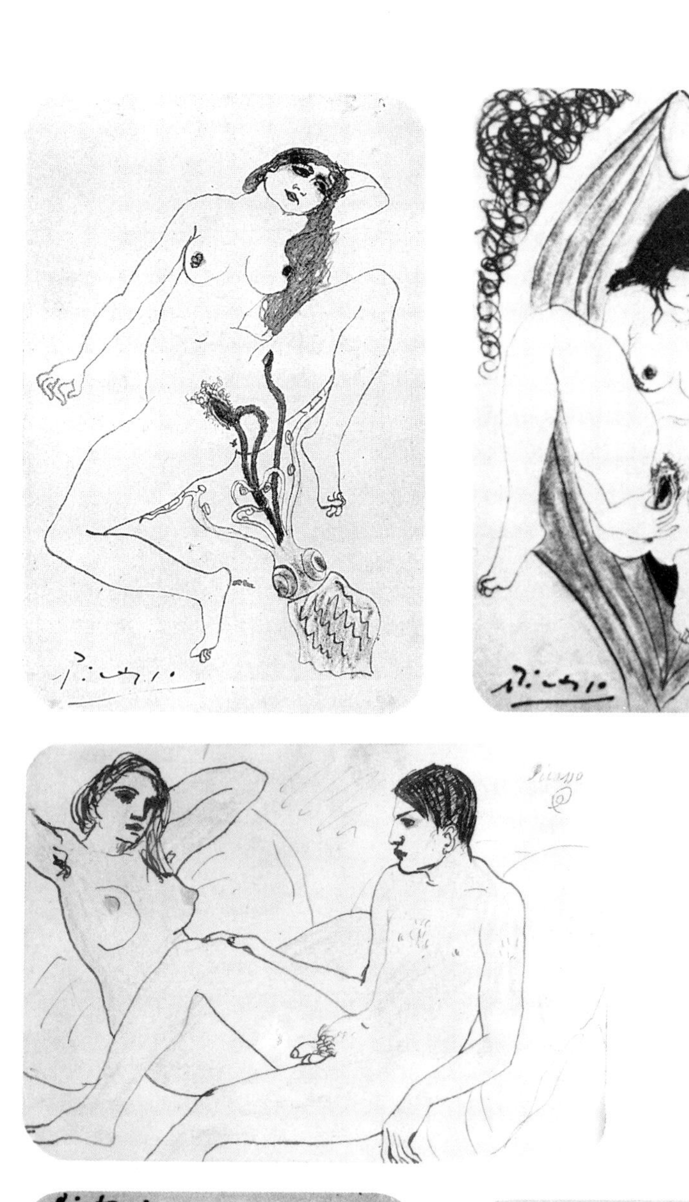

18

Farewell to Barcelona

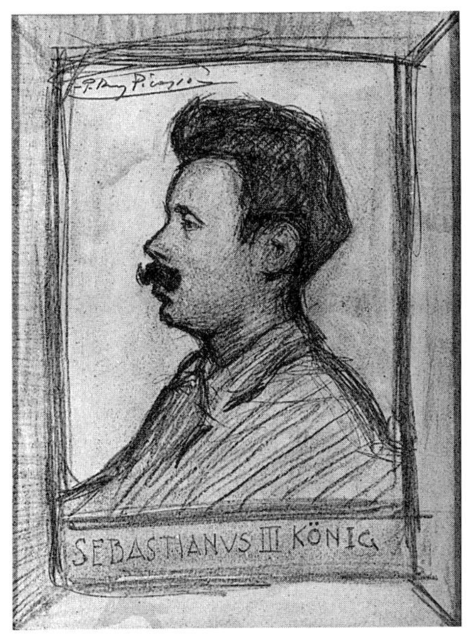

Picasso. *Sebastianus III König* (Sebastià Junyer Vidal). Barcelona, 1900. Pencil, coloured crayon and watercolour on paper, varnished, 21×16cm. Museu Picasso, Barcelona.

Opposite: Picasso. Erotic drawings on trade cards. Barcelona, 1903. Pen, sepia and wax crayons on card, each 13.3×9cm. Private collections.

BACK IN BARCELONA, PICASSO HAD RESUMED his old habit of surrounding himself with a supportive band of friends. Sabartès was a fixture, but he spent much of his time with the Junyer Vidal brothers, Sebastià and Carles, not entirely to the delight of his former companions. The Junyer Vidals were well off—they had recently inherited a prosperous yarn and stocking shop from an uncle. In return for their hospitality and occasional financial help, Picasso supplied them with paintings and drawings. Since Picasso was still chronically broke, he welcomed the brothers as patrons. He would spend hours at a time in the Junyer Vidals' shop, gossiping with the proprietors and drawing on large sheets of wrapping paper or the back of small trade cards. Many of these have survived. One group provides a microcosm of Picasso's sexual fantasies: some have a graffiti-like directness; others an adolescent prurience; the most revealing manifest a perversity and misogyny that anticipate the artist's surrealist chimeras of the 1930s. Bending over a squirming girl is an ageing boulevardier, whose bald pate opens up into a vagina. Even more premonitory (specifically, of the biomorphic studies for sculpture that date from 1927) is a drawing of a bearded deity in the form of an erect penis with a woebegone woman trapped in its scrotum. Another group consists of caricatures of Sebastià, the elder of the Junyer Vidal brothers; these are sometimes allegorical (parodies of Puvis de Chavannes) and usually bawdy (Sebastià in the company of a procuress or whore, or in a toga holding a lyre dreaming of Mallorca, where the rocks sprout copulating couples and the caves are huge vaginas). With his frizzy hair and Kaiser Wilhelm moustache (e.g., the comic portait of Sebastià ironically inscribed, 'Sebastianus III König'), Sebastià was eminently caricaturable. A bit of a clown, it would seem. As a painter, he had some success with the Mallorcan landscapes (1900–04) he exhibited at the Sala Parés (where, in poorer days, he had worked as a salesman). Later his painting petered out.

The direction of the Junyer Vidals' aspirations had been changed by their inheritance. Egged on by his younger brother, Carles, an art and drama critic of no great distinction, Sebastià gradually abandoned painting to help his sibling edit *El Liberal*, the newspaper he had founded. This journal was no more than its name suggests:[1] mildly liberal in its views and of little interest except insofar as it published one of the first favourable appraisals of Picasso's work.[2] Although this was probably written by Carles, the literary Junyer Vidal, Sebastià continued to be the brother Picasso

Sebastià Junyer Vidal, *c.*1900.

Picasso. Sketch for unexecuted poster for *El Liberal*. Barcelona, 1900. Conté crayon on paper, 33.7×36.3cm. Museu Picasso, Barcelona.

preferred. There are no portraits, not even a caricature, of Carles. Sebastià, however, is portrayed in over twenty sketches and a large slipshod painting that does not deserve to be as frequently reproduced as it is. He is seen seated at a café table beside a scrawny prostitute with a telltale red flower in her hair. Besides enjoying his largesse and his company, Picasso had become so intrigued by Sebastià's endearing ugliness that the portrayal of it developed into a compulsion. Sebastià continues to haunt Picasso's work until their trip to Paris together in 1904. After briefly sharing a studio, he returned to Barcelona and faded from Picasso's life. Like other Catalan artists who had the misfortune to work in Picasso's shadow, Sebastià eventually gave up painting. He devoted himself instead to the 'collection' that he kept in his museum-like house at Vallcarca, not far from Rusiñol's Cau Ferrat at Sitges. The Junyer Vidal brothers eventually took to collecting Catalan primitives and sculpture—often damaged works that the frustrated artist would over-restore and sell for large sums to American museums (not least the Cloisters in New York).[3] Despite being a vociferous keeper of the artist's flame, Sebastià has fallen under suspicion of faking Picasso's early works—and with good reason: a suspicious number of fakes have a Junyer Vidal provenance. And, ironically, a number of authentic drawings from the collection have been questioned because the grasping brothers embellished them with fake signatures in the hope of getting better prices.

The brothers Oleguer and Sebastià Junyent, whose father owned the Filantropia Diverso, are often confused with the Junyer Vidals. They not only had a similar name; they were also comfortably off, dabbled in the arts and were supportive friends of Picasso. Sebastià Junyent was a Llotja-trained painter who wrote art criticism (including a major essay on Ruskin in 1903) for *Joventut*. He also arranged for some of Picasso's drawings to be published in this magazine.[4] Junyent's ardent support of the artist was apt to take the form of high-flown hectoring. This antagonized Sabartès, who would make merciless fun of Junyent's pretentious notions and once even proposed that a spoof monument be erected to this *modernista* proselytizer outside the offices of *Joventut*. Junyent was one of the artist's first collectors, though he seldom held on to his acquisitions for long. In 1903, he and Picasso cemented their friendship by doing portraits of each other. For all its qualities, the one by Picasso is unusually conventional; the one by Junyent is redeemed by being posed in front of *La Vie*. Junyent is said to have acquired the Blue period masterpiece *The Old Jew* for 500 pesetas. Whether this painting was in fact sold or was collateral for a loan from Junyent is hard to say. Certainly the price is astonishingly low (a third of what don José had asked for his son's *First Communion* in 1896). And no sooner had Sebastià acquired this major work than he relinquished it for exhibition and, in due course, sale in Paris—a service that Picasso rewarded in September 1904 with one of the first prints that he pulled of *The Frugal Repast*.

Another friend who helped Picasso out at this period is the tailor, Benet Soler Vidal ('*Retalls*'), who fancied himself a patron of artists and writers. Picasso, who had already done a couple of drawings of him two years earlier, now embarked on a large portrait of Soler, his wife and four children (Mercè, Antonita, Carles and Montserrat) having a picnic. The Soler daughter who is standing at the centre of the family group recalled

Right: Sebastià Junyent. *Portrait of Picasso in front of 'La Vie'*. Barcelona, 1903. Oil on canvas. Reproduced in *Forma,* 1904.

Far right: Picasso. *Portrait of Sebastià Junyent*. Barcelona, 1903. Oil on canvas, 73×60cm. Museu Picasso, Barcelona.

Picasso. *Manet's 'Olympia' Attended by Sebastià Junyer Vidal and Picasso*. Barcelona, 1903. Pen and coloured crayons on paper, 15×23cm. Private collection.

Picasso. *Sebastià Junyer Vidal and a Woman in a Café*. Barcelona, June 1903. Oil on canvas, 126.4×94cm. Los Angeles County Museum of Art, Bequest of David E. Bright. Inscribed to Junyer Vidal.

Far left: Picasso. *Portrait of Señora Soler.* Barcelona, 1903. Oil on canvas, 100×73cm. Bayerische Staatsgemäldesammlungen, Munich.

Left: Picasso. *Portrait of Benet Soler.* Barcelona, 1903. Oil on canvas, 100×70cm. State Hermitage Museum, Leningrad.

Below: Picasso. *The Soler Family* (background painted by Sebastià Junyer Vidal). Barcelona, 1903. Oil on canvas, 150×200cm. Musée des Beaux Arts, Liège. This photograph shows the painting before the background had been painted out by Picasso.

that Picasso amused himself carving away with a needle at the tailor's chalks her father used,[5] but he remembered no such thing, and none of these incised chalks have survived. Despite the inclusion of a dead hare, a gun and other shooting paraphernalia, which is supposed to identify the occasion as a shooting picnic, it is all too evident that the group posed indoors. There are also separate portraits of Benet and his wife, Montserrat, who would frequently have Picasso to lunch and dinner at their apartment round the corner from Els Quatre Gats. These meals and a new wardrobe were the quid pro quo for these portraits. Half a century later the artist took nostalgic delight in reviving this system of barter. 'Just like the old days in Barcelona,' he would say, as he exchanged drawings for outrageously patterned jackets and trousers with Sapone, an Italian tailor who lived in Nice, 'except that now it would be so much cheaper to pay in cash.'

Manet. *Le Déjeuner sur l'herbe.* 1863. Oil on canvas, 208×264cm. Musée d'Orsay, Paris.

The ambitious group of the Solers is no masterpiece. Picasso based his composition on Manet's *Le Déjeuner sur l'herbe*, the painting that he had so much admired in the Luxembourg on his first visit to Paris, and that he would obsessively replicate many years later (1959–60). Besides appropriating Manet's sensuous facture, Picasso helps himself to his innovative lighting: hence the shadowless, alienated faces, which are such a striking feature of this otherwise banal scene. For all that he has come up with lively portraits of these well-intentioned bourgeois, the project failed to engage his sympathy or interest; and he left the picnic unfinished. To Soler's dismay, Picasso had insisted on posing the family against a plain blue, cycloramalike background instead of a conventional landscape setting. Since the artist would not yield on this point, Soler prevailed upon Sebastià Junyer Vidal, who agreed (with Picasso's permission) to sketch in a woodland scene like an old-fashioned photographer's backdrop. Ten years later, when Soler sold all three family portraits through Kahnweiler, Picasso insisted on painting out Junyer Vidal's landscape. He is said to have experimented with a cubist setting[6]—an attempt to contrast disjunctive methods of notation?—but reverted to his original concept of a plain background. Only then did he allow his dealer to sell this conversation piece to the Wallraf-Richartz Museum in Cologne.[7] Of the individual Soler portraits the one of the wife is the more accomplished. Unfortunately, the blue light in which Picasso has bathed Señora Soler gives her a bilious rather than romantic air.

*　　　*　　　*

The portraits that Picasso did of his closest friends, Angel de Soto and Sabartès, in the course of his last months in Barcelona delve far more deeply into character and take far greater liberties than the Soler ones. The deformations in the Soto portrait—the jug ear, skewed mouth, prognathous chin—seem caricatural, but the image transcends caricature. By this time Picasso had learned how to exploit his inherent gift for caricature in depth as a means of dramatizing psychological as well as physiognomical traits. Whereas the average caricaturist externalizes things and comes up with an image that is slick and trite—an instant cliché—Picasso internalizes things and comes up with an enhanced characterization of his subject.[8] Picasso enlarges Angel's heavy-lidded eyes out of all proportion

Picasso. *Portrait of Angel de Soto.* Barcelona, 1903. Oil on canvas, 69.7×55.2cm. Mrs Donald S. Stralem collection, New York.

and endows them with his own obsidian stare. Among his immediate predecessors, only van Gogh had this ability to galvanize a portrait with his own psychic energy. Even the mocking portrait of Sabartès that dates from the following spring (his last appearance in Picasso's work for thirty years or more) takes us aback with its pitiless assessment. The pink fleshy lips, the huge myopic eyes behind pince-nez, the supercilious eyebrows, the provincial dandyism (starched collar, silk cravat, velvet-collared over-coat): what a sardonic, twistedly affectionate portrayal of provincial pretentiousness it is. Picasso subtly mocks the poetaster—Jacobus Sabartès, as he had taken to calling himself—who had given a reading of his work a year earlier (March 1903) in the large room at Els Quatre Gats—a reading that the reviewer of *La Vanguardia* had characterized as 'deficient; his diction made his long-winded prose seem erratic . . . boring . . . monotonous.'

Picasso. *Portrait of Sabartès.* Barcelona, 1904. Oil on canvas, 49.5×38cm. Private collection.

Sabartès unwittingly explains the ambivalence of this portrait. The two friends had spent an evening in a café with 'imbecile' companions, who had pestered Picasso for advice on their work. On the way home, the artist was bored, grumpy, monosyllabic. Back in the studio, he harnessed his ill humour to yet another portrait of the poet: little by little he sublimated his irritation into paint.

> [Picasso] began to observe me from different angles. He took a piece of canvas, put it on the easel and got ready to paint.
> 'I'm going to paint you,' he said. 'Do you want me to?'
> 'All right. But at least you'll give it to me?'
> 'Of course . . . '[9] Thus he found a pretext for keeping me by his side without having to talk. . . . I stood motionless not far from his easel. His eyes went from the canvas to me and from me to the canvas; when it was covered he talked to me again:
> 'Say something . . . Anyone might think you were in a bad mood.'
> After this he put away his brushes, because by now he felt relieved. . . .
> 'Tomorrow we'll continue,' he said lightly.
> He was no longer the man of an hour ago. Were he now to meet the 'imbeciles', he would converse with them . . . would even find them sympathetic.
> 'This is nothing yet. I'll have to do some more work on it. Shall we go out for a walk? The fresh air will do you good.'
> He was ready to talk about no matter what. Now everything seemed the greatest fun . . . Next day he finished the portrait in a very brief session . . . all he had to do was go over a brushstroke, strengthen the background, colour the lips. [And then] suddenly he stopped, for his present vision differed from the first . . . he could no longer see me as he had the day before.[10]

Picasso had portrayed Sabartès as the quintessence of an 'imbecile', a scapegoat for the shortcomings of all the other members of his Catalan coterie.

Sabartès discerns 'greater skill' in Picasso's handling of his flesh tones than ever before, and sees the golden glitter of his tie-pin and the pink of his lips as 'harbingers of a new manner'.

> [Picasso] had learned what he could do with blue, and now he wanted to discover to what extent he could dispense with it. Evidently he was on the eve of a revolutionary development. But for this he must change his environment, breathe different air, speak another tongue, converse on other

> subjects, compare his ideas with those of others, see new faces and adopt a new way of life; begin all over again . . . he must return to Paris; and this time for good.[11]

Just as he boasted that an earlier portrait of him had set off the Blue period, Sabartès implies that his rosy lips set off the Rose period.

Before leaving Barcelona, Picasso did yet another favour for Sabartès, who had rented a two-room apartment at the top of a dilapidated medieval building on the Carrer del Consolat. Much as he and Casagemas had done in the Riera Sant Joan studio, Picasso decorated the walls with a succession of bawdy images. Dominating everything was an *œil-de-bœuf* window, which he transformed into a wide-open disembodied eye. This source of light 'seemed to be watching what was going on', just like the all-seeing light bulb, with its shade of sun-ray eyelashes, that illuminates *Guernica*. The focus of the eye's gaze was a group of recumbent, seemingly amorous, figures and a portentous inscription: 'Although separated from me the hairs of my beard are gods just as much as I am.' This inscription has inevitably given rise to all kinds of biblical and mystical explanations.[12] However, Sabartès specifically claims that its origin was literary. If so, it can only have been inspired by a memorable passage in Lautréamont's *Chants de Maldoror*, the black bible of the surrealists that Jacob knew well. The narrator describes going to a whorehouse and looking through a grille into a room clotted with blood and bits of dried meat. There he sees an enormous blond hair coiling and uncoiling and moaning that it has been abandoned after a night of wild sex ('a long voyage over the reefs of ether') by its master, who is no less than God. When God returns to recover the missing fragment of his divinity, 'the hair and its master hugged one another close like two friends who meet after a long absence.' For Picasso, who saw himself as God, Sabartès might well have been a fragment of his divinity.

Sabartès seated with members of the Guayaba group, including (also seated) Quim Borralleras, *c*.1903. Musée Picasso, Paris.

On the wall next to the studio window the artist 'imprisoned a rigid nude of huge proportions in the manner of Assyrian bas-reliefs'.[13] These murals were of course all in blue. On the wall facing the window he painted the half-naked body of a Moor with an erection, suspended from a tree. This figure also has an arcane literary source: the celebrated pornographic novel *Gamiani*[14]—celebrated because the depravity of the action is in total contrast with the high romanticism of the prose —which describes, among other perversities, a hanging that triggers orgasm.

> The feet were very rigid but slightly projecting: one was bare; from the tip of the other dangled a babouche at a right angle to the sole of the foot. This miracle of equilibrium, which gave a faint semblance of life to the lower part of the Moor's body . . . caught the eye and directed it towards the ground, where a young couple, totally naked, delivered themselves in the hanged man's presence, to the passionate game of love.
>
> As he withdrew his brush, Picasso glanced away from the wall and told me, as he had at the Zut: 'Some day I'll come back and we'll continue.'[15]

He never did. And like the rest of the early wall decorations, these were soon destroyed. No drawings for them exist and no photographs were ever taken. Without Sabartès's description of the Moor's terminal orgasm, we would be in the dark about this association of Eros and

Thanatos in Picasso's art—not the first and certainly not the last but the most bizarre.[16]

The fact that Sabartès's windows looked directly across at La Llotja, the Stock Exchange building that housed the art school, has been suggested as an explanation for Picasso's perverse flights of fancy. The thought of his father giving drawing lessons to naive young students across the street from this morbid mural might well have titillated him. So would the thought of Sabartès confronted day after day with the orgasmic death throes of the slippered Moor. The artist's memory played him an odd trick. Despite almost total visual recall, he expunged all record of the Moor from memory. The only detail of the Sabartès murals that he could ever remember was the eye.

* * *

Picasso's most ambitious and highly finished portrait of this period in Barcelona is the famous one of a wall-eyed procuress, *La Celestina*. While it is central to the Blue period, it also looks ahead to the late work. From the mid-1950s onwards, Celestina will reappear in Picasso's work as a symbol of the bawdy Spain that he left as a young man but often returned to in imagination, as death approached.[17] She epitomizes the spirit of the Barri Xino; but since old women are traditionally held to signify death in the Spanish countryside (in many small towns an old woman used to walk the streets like a town crier, announcing deaths), Celestina can also be seen to stand for mortality. And her reappearance in some of the last engravings is ominous.

Celestina was a famous fictional character: villainess of Fernando de Rojas's *La Tragicomédia de Calisto y Melibea*. First published in 1499, this novel in the form of a play has always been enormously popular in Spain, so much so that the name Celestina is still applied to any go-between or procuress, such as the model for this painting. Picasso knew Rojas's book from adolescence, if not before. In later life he collected various editions, the earliest dating from 1601. An *olla podrida* of sentimental romance, bawdy comedy and high tragedy, the story was always dear to his heart. Money, love and betrayal are the themes. In the hope of earning a fat fee, crafty old Celestina acts as a go-between in the romance of Calisto and Melibea. At first things go right, then very wrong. The plot ends in tragedy: Calisto's accidental death and Melibea's dishonour and consequent suicide. Celestina and her fellow conspirators likewise perish. At the end of his life Picasso fantasized that he was a painter/novelist; and he set about 'rewriting' Rojas's story in a sequence of prints (part of the so-called *Suite 347*). These bizarre variations on the fifteenth-century narrative include, among much else, the transformation of the aged voyeuristic Celestina into the aged voyeuristic Picasso.

Picasso. Aquatint from *Suite 347*. Mougins, October 1, 1968. 22.5×32.5cm. Bibliothèque Nationale, Paris.

The original Celestina was surprisingly versatile. As one of her accomplices in the novel describes her, 'she had six trades in all. She was a seamstress, a perfumer, a past master at making up cosmetics and patching maidenheads, a procuress and a bit of a witch.' In an early reference to Celestina—a drawing of 1903—Picasso depicts her in the company of a girl plying the first and the fifth of these trades, knitting and procuring. 'Celestina often gained entry into well-to-do households by selling yarn,

Picasso. *La Celestina*. Barcelona, March 1904. Oil on canvas, 81×60 cm. Musée Picasso, Paris.

Picasso. *Self-Portrait Painting 'La Celestina'*. Barcelona, 1904. Conté crayon and coloured crayons on paper. Whereabouts unknown.

Picasso. *Celestina Knitting*. Barcelona, *c*.1903. Pen on paper, 23×23 cm. Private collection.

which symbolized the way in which she would weave together the lives of her young lovers.'[18] In 1968, Picasso would make a series of references to her other callings: as a cosmetician in engravings of her painting the face of a prostitute; as a witch in a poem that mentions her 'magic powders'; as a patcher of maidenheads in portrayals of her clutching rosary beads. Rojas's Celestina used rosary beads as an abacus to count up the membranes she had to repair, the girls she had to procure, the money she stood to make. Picasso probably borrowed this attribute of Celestina's profession from Goya, who did as many as thirty drawings of an old Celestina-like procuress, including some with a rosary.[19] The Blue period Celestina harks back to the Golden Age of Spanish art. A black mantilla and cloak endow the old bawd with an air of timeless dignity, more in keeping with a seventeenth-century prioress than a twentieth-century procuress. A *grande dame* of the gutter. Characteristically, Picasso gives her a more than passing resemblance to his pious aunt Pepa, whose portrait he had done eight years earlier (see illustration, p.59).

The model for Picasso's 'Celestina' was Carlota Valdivia, and she plied her trade at 12–4° Conde de Asalto (now Carrer Nou de la Rambla), a few doors away from his studio. This is the address of the Eden Concert, the music-hall that Picasso had frequented when he first explored Barcelona's nightlife. An inscription on the stretcher indicates that Carlota Valdivia operated out of a room on the '*escalera interior*' (inside staircase). The inscription also includes a date, March 1904. However, the painting looks as if it had been started earlier—towards the end of 1903. Over half a century later, Picasso's memory of his real-life Celestina had not faded. When in 1959 I told him I was going to Barcelona to do some research on his early portraits, he insisted on writing down the name and address of this long-dead procuress in my diary: 'She could always fix you up,' he said, as if she were still in business.

Despite the wall-eye, Carlota was better looking than the crone described by Rojas, who was not only wrinkled but heavily scarred. None of that is to be found in Picasso's painting. Even the hint of whiskers is not necessarily a blemish; in nineteenth-century Spain facial hair on women was much admired. For a change, we are spared Blue period sentimentality and mannerist exaggerations. The gravity of the image, the virtuosity of the handling, suggest that Picasso derived some of his inspiration from Velázquez. He has ennobled Celestina with some of that master's painterly eloquence, just as a year or two later he would ennoble his Rose period portraits—the one of Benedetta Canals and the *Woman with a Fan* in particular—with elements taken from the same source (Velázquez's *Woman with a Fan* in the Wallace Collection). As a rule, Picasso tended to steer clear of Velázquez's shadow. It would be another fifty years before he was ready to measure himself against *Las Meninas*—and what a titanic combat that would prove. Meanwhile, Picasso's principal Spanish inspiration would continue to be the infinitely less respectable Cretan interloper, El Greco.

Picasso's obsession with El Greco dated back to 1897, when he had gone to study in Madrid, and been impressed by his 'magnificent heads'—the ones he had copied (deny it though he might) in the Prado. As early as 1899 he had filled page after page of a sketchbook with caricatures of Greco-like portraits, and the wishful-thinking inscription: '*Yo El*

Picasso. Sheet of drawings inscribed '*Yo El Greco*.' Barcelona, *c*.1899. Pen on paper, 31.5×21.8cm. Museu Picasso, Barcelona.

Picasso. *Angel de Soto with a Whore*. Barcelona, 1902–03. Ink and watercolour on paper, 21×15.2cm. Museu Picasso, Barcelona.

Greco, yo Greco'. Picasso's identification derived further encouragement from his friends Rusiñol and Utrillo, who, with Manuel Cossío, author of the 1908 *catalogue raisonné*, pioneered the artist's rehabilitation as a great master. The fact that most of the Spanish art establishment (including don José) continued to regard El Greco as a freak and a madman endeared him all the more to Picasso. Meanwhile Félicien Fagus's challenge in the 1901 *Revue Blanche* as to who would be the next El Greco still rang in his ears. By dint of collecting dubious examples of El Greco's work, Ignacio Zuloaga may have felt that he fitted this bill, but the paintings Picasso did in Barcelona in the course of 1903 proved that he was the only serious contender. In Paris, post-impressionism had lured Picasso into the mainstream of the modern movement; in Spain, El Greco tugged him in another direction. It was a retrogressive step, as the secular martyrs of the Blue period confirm. They reveal that as yet Picasso had appropriated little but externals: obvious mannerisms such as the attenuated limbs, elongated and skeletal fingers, thin ascetic faces. In due course the influence of El Greco the offbeat mannerist would give way to that of El Greco the mystic,[20] the apocalyptic visionary who was both an outsider and (albeit by adoption) a great Spanish artist. Picasso would set about stealing El Greco's sacred thunder; we will hear it rumbling away in the background of *Les Demoiselles d'Avignon* until it is drowned out by tribal drums.

* * *

By the end of 1903 Picasso was once more restless and confused. Although Barcelona had proved to be a good place to work—he told Jacob that he proposed to spend the winter there 'to get something done'—he was determined to have another try at establishing himself in Paris. But no sooner had he decided to leave Barcelona than he changed his mind and moved to another studio. He had to get away from his distracting roommate, Angel de Soto. Every evening after he left his job, Angel would fill the studio with friends. If Picasso's work had gone well, the friends might amuse him; if it had gone badly, they would irritate him, and he would ensure that everyone else felt as angry and frustrated as he did. Towards the end of the year he arranged to sublet a studio at 28 Carrer del Commerç from a young student of sculpture, Pablo Gargallo, who had been awarded a travelling scholarship by La Llotja and was leaving to study in Paris.[21] Besides being opposite the studio of Nonell, the only local artist he respected,[22] 28 Carrer del Commerç lay in the shadow of the Palace of Fine Arts in the Ciutadella Park. Having painted two ghostly nocturnes of Barcelona as a city of the dead from the roof of his Riera Sant Joan studio earlier that year, he now tried his hand at a bold autumnal view of the Palace. The touches of red in the roof and trees come as a relief after so much blue. Like the pink in Sabartès's lips, these touches of colour are the first intimations of dawn after the long blue night.

As winter set in, Picasso became ever more of a loner. He insisted on keeping his own hours, working hard when the mood was on him, wandering off by himself to desolate city beaches, gypsy camps, whorehouses. He needed peace. He needed to be on his own. Once again he decided to execute a great definitive work and asked his father to prepare a large panel for him. But when it was ready, he was at a loss for a subject and nonchalantly dashed off a group of figures. 'His need of a studio to himself,' Sabartès says, 'of a panel specially prepared, as if for an altarpiece, and his thirst for solitude were manifestations of extreme restlessness.'[23]

What became of the large panel? Only two major paintings of this period have a wooden support: the magnificent *Old Guitarist* in the Art Institute, Chicago, and the slapdash *Tragedy (Poor People on the Seashore)* in the National Gallery, Washington. The latter must be the large sketchy group described by Sabartès: it is glib and sentimental—awash in self-pity. (The preparatory sketches, one painting and three or four drawings, are much more sensitively handled than the large panel.) Barefoot and in rags, the family is depicted literally blue with cold, standing on blue sand against a blue sky and bluer sea. A small boy huddles up to his father (much as he does in the sentimental *Mistletoe Seller*, done the previous Christmas) opposite his becomingly draped Tanagra-like mother who looks glumly downward. There is all the usual alienation, but little of the tension that we find in the first manifestations of this subject. Picasso had evidently tired of his own cliché. A few months earlier or a few months later, he would have put this panel to much more effective use; he might even have come up with the 'altarpiece', the definitive work that don José was still so anxious for him to do, so anxious that, despite his disapproval of the path his son was following, he had been ready to fashion the support for it. Picasso was all too evidently bored with Barcelona: there was no stimulus, no challenge left. In imagination he was already back in Paris.

Picasso. *Tragedy*. Barcelona, 1903. Oil on panel, 105.4×69cm. The National Gallery of Art, Washington, D.C., Chester Dale Collection.

During his last months in Barcelona, Picasso felt a mounting exasperation with his band of friends. *Modernisme* was finally disintegrating. Most of the more gifted or sympathetic members of the movement had moved to Paris; only the ungifted or unenterprising ones stayed behind. And yet, much as he despised his provincial cronies, he had become dependent on their love, loyalty and jealousy of one another over him, as well as on their uncomprehending praise. He could neither live with them nor do without them. He had come to feel the same way about Els Quatre Gats, and was both relieved and annoyed when the establishment closed its doors in July 1903. El Guayaba was a poor substitute: the premises were inadequate, and the local piety stifling. Picasso's all-male world required a focal point, and the only other alternative was his former studio on the Riera Sant Joan. When funds permitted, Angel and Picasso would arrange picnic dinners:

> The provisions came up from the patio in the bucket used for drawing water from the well, and accompanying the meal would be the bill:
>
> 'To the Gentlemen Painters:
> for sausages—so much
> for string beans—so much
> for bread—so much
> etc.
> Total 1 peseta 20 centimos.'[24]

As for girlfriends, there is no sign in any of the paintings or drawings of 1903 that Picasso had a steady mistress. But then, apart from Rosita del Oro (whom he still saw from time to time), he never carried on regular affairs in Barcelona. Paris was for mistresses, Barcelona was for whores.

For all his reclusiveness, Picasso remained on excellent terms with his mother and sister. His father was becoming more and more of a problem. Failing eyesight, melancholia and a lack of sympathy with his incomprehensible son had exacerbated don José's bitterness. And so, as Sabartès puts it, 'his family fades into the distance'.[25] When, at the beginning of April, Picasso finally made plans to leave for Paris for the fourth time, he did not admit that he was emigrating for good. He arranged for *El Liberal* to publish announcements two days running (April 11 and 12) that 'The artists Messrs Sebastià Junyer Vidal and Pablo Ruiz Picasso are leaving Barcelona on today's express for Paris, in which city they propose to hold an exhibition of their latest works.' Since there was no prospect of an imminent exhibition in Paris for either Picasso or Sebastià, these announcements were presumably intended to mislead his parents. They left when they did for the good reason that a Montmartre studio had become available. Paco Durrio was abandoning the Bateau Lavoir for a larger space (with room for a pottery kiln) in the *zone du maquis*—a neigbourhood wasteland that was being reclaimed from the apaches. At last Picasso could count on a permanent Parisian base.

José Llopart. Caricature of Pere Romeu with his puppets and four cats, satirizing the decline of Els Quatre Gats, which closed in July 1903. Published in *La Esquella de la Torratxa,* 1902.

19

Montmartre and the Bateau Lavoir

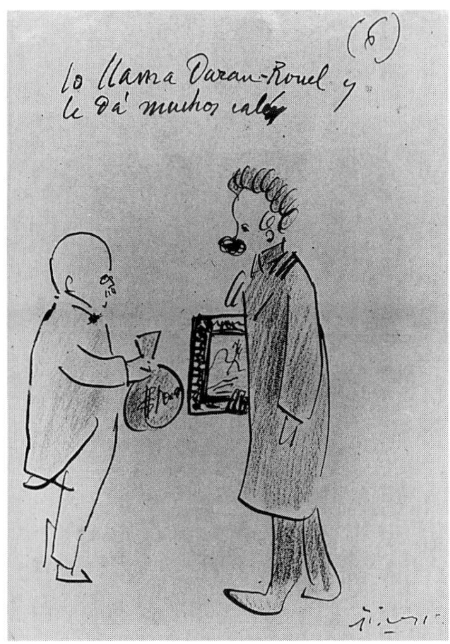

Picasso. *Sebastià Junyer Vidal Selling a Painting to Durand-Ruel.* Paris, 1904. Ink and coloured crayons on paper, 22×16cm. Museu Picasso, Barcelona.

Opposite: Picasso on the Place Ravignan, 1904. Musée Picasso, Paris.

PICASSO'S FOURTH VISIT TO PARIS ended far more happily than his third: he at last succeeded in establishing a foothold in the city whose very dust he revered. For the rest of his life he would settle in France and would come to be regarded as a French artist: a luminary of the School of Paris. However, he remained a Spaniard at heart, a man of the Mediterranean. Although he would only once (summer to autumn, 1917) return for more than a few weeks to his own country, his work would never lose its Spanish intonation, its Andalusian sensuousness and resilience. And although he liked to grumble about his adopted country, Picasso was the first to admit that it was far and away the best place for a modern artist to live. Spanish friends detected a French tinge to him, he said. Not the French: somehow they always made him feel more of a Spaniard.

* * *

Sebastià paid the rent of the Bateau Lavoir studio (fifteen francs a month), which was one of the reasons Picasso chose him as a travelling companion. Picasso's *alleluia* recording their journey suggests that Sebastià hoped to make a career in Paris. This wishful-thinking comic strip culminates in a caricature of Sebastià selling the frock-coated dealer Durand-Rouel (*sic*) a painting for a bag of gold. Despite a moderate art-school competence (to judge by a landscape drawing on the back of one of Picasso's portraits of him), Sebastià's resolve faltered, and after a few weeks he returned to family responsibilities in Barcelona and the occasional painting expedition to Mallorca. Unlike some of Picasso's other Catalan courtiers, Sebastià never again played more than a marginal role in his life, although in old age he encouraged gullible people to believe that he had launched the artist's career.

Picasso left a vast quantity of juvenilia—paintings, drawings and sketchbooks—behind in Barcelona[1] but had all the works he valued shipped to Paris. He could never bear to be without a dog, so he took along Gat, the mongrel that Utrillo had given him. As soon as he had settled in, he would acquire two more dogs, Feo and Frika. Don José and doña María had recommended their son to a Spanish priest, Father Santol—related to one of their friends—who had settled in Paris and opened a shelter for the homeless at 40 Avenue La Motte-Piquet. Father Santol later claimed that he had provided Picasso with a bed for the first days of his stay in

Picasso. *Father Santol.* Paris, 1904. Pen on paper, 27.5×21.3cm. Heirs of the artist.

Picasso. *Feo and Gat.* Paris, 1904–05. Pen on paper. Reproduced in André Salmon's *Manuscrit trouvé dans un chapeau.*

Paris. A portrait of the priest confirms that there was cause for gratitude; however, Picasso insisted that he had done the drawing in return for a loan—an explanation conceivably dictated by *amour-propre* rather than veracity. Much as he might deny it, Picasso would have been in need of Father Santol's charity, for Paco Durrio had removed what little furniture there had been in the Bateau Lavoir studio. All that remained was a bed, which Junyer Vidal claimed, as he was paying the rent. Durrio had also left behind a guest, a gypsy, with whom Picasso was expected to share a rug on the floor. The gypsy, Fabián de Castro, turned out to be 'the most heart-rending guitarist in all of Spain',[2] and he became such an admirer of Picasso that he, too, decided to be a painter. He was not ungifted. In no time he was turning out portraits, signed 'El Gyptano', which would be highly praised by André Salmon.[3] Fabián is presumably the gypsy painter with whom Picasso is supposed to have had an affair.[4] True, El Gyptano developed a fixation about Picasso and therefore fills the role of lover better than the ten-year-old muleteer at Horta; true again, they both slept on the floor, but there is no evidence or likelihood of a sexual relationship.

Long before the Bateau Lavoir became what Max Jacob was to call 'the Acropolis of cubism', it had acquired a certain notoriety, much of it legendary. For instance, its former nickname, '*La Maison du trappeur*' —still current when Picasso moved in—was said to have derived from a Canadian trapper or fur trader who had lived there. Romantic fantasy! The wooden shack merely corresponded to the popular notion of a log cabin. In fact it had started life as a piano factory; it then became a locksmith's workshop, until 1889, when the landlord converted it into studios. Thanks to the architect's negligence or fancy, the place abounded in mysterious *oubliettes*—gaps and spaces serving no conceivable purpose—which gave it a seedy allure. Because of the neighbourhood's notoriety, rents were low, and the studios soon found occupants. In the early nineties tenants included a number of anarchists, who made converts among the layabouts on the Place Ravignan: 'artists and young students who claimed to be philosophers because they were neither painters, sculptors nor poets'.[5] All this anarchistic activity attracted the attention of the police. Eventually there was a raid, whereupon the more faint-hearted tenants departed, along with the anarchists. The *Maison du trappeur* then became a nest of symbolists. They, too, were proselytizers. Gauguin was a frequent visitor (1893–95) after his return from his first visit to Tahiti. In the course of calling on his friends Maxime Maufra and Paco Durrio, he would go from studio to studio, spreading the good word: '*Tu seras symboliste.*' And the dramatist Paul Fort, who is said to have lived there, recruited some of the tenants to help paint décors for his symbolist productions at the Théâtre de l'Œuvre, across the Place. Durrio attracted impoverished Spaniards to the building: Canals and Sunyer, who arrived around 1901, Picasso in 1904 and Juan Gris in 1906. Before Picasso moved out in 1909 (he held on to his studio until 1912), several painters, among them van Dongen, Herbin and, briefly, Modigliani, would reside there. The writers included Picasso's old friend Max Jacob, who had previously lived a few doors away, and his new friends André Salmon and Pierre MacOrlan, who would later live off their memories of the Place Ravignan. Both Jacob and Salmon have been credited with inventing the nickname Bateau Lavoir (as the laundry boats moored in the Seine were called) that

Back of the Bateau Lavoir on rue Garreau. Photo: André Fage.

Front of the Bateau Lavoir.

made this wretched building famous: Jacob, because of all the washing he saw hanging outside on his first visit; Salmon, because of its hollow boathouse resonance.

Anyone entering the Bateau Lavoir through the main door on what was then called rue Ravignan (later Place Ravignan and later still Place Emile Goudeau) was confronted by a one-storey building. But in fact this stack of shacks clung precariously to the side of the Montmartre hill, and the back section gave onto the rue Garreau, three floors below. Picasso's studio was on the ground floor (that is to say, on the rue Ravignan level) at the end of the passage on the right. It was quite large and well lit by a row of windows. The only distinctive feature was a series of large blackened beams. The place was so jerry-built that the walls oozed moisture —'glacial in winter and a Turkish bath in summer'[6]—hence a prevailing smell of mildew, as well as cat piss and drains. The place was grubby, as were many of the people who lived there (not Picasso: he was compulsively clean). On a basement landing was the one and only toilet, a dark and filthy hole with an unlockable door that banged in the wind, and, next to it, the one and only tap. This provided water for some thirty studios; the alternative was the fountain in the middle of the Place Ravignan. There was no gas or electricity. Accidents were frequent, especially in winter, when the studios were so cold that water would freeze in a glass. Picasso recalled a German artist climbing onto the roof to clear snow off a skylight and falling to his death down an unsuspected ventilation shaft—an *oubliette* that claimed many a drunk, he asserted. Another tenant would have died of asphyxiation if he had not managed to throw a malfunctioning stove out of an upstairs window. And then there was a local flower girl, who met a fate implicit in many a Blue period painting: she froze to death on the little square.

Roofs of the Bateau Lavoir, annotated by Picasso to show the windows of his studio. Bibliothèque Nationale, Paris.

Not all the tenants of the Bateau Lavoir were artists. André Salmon devotes a chapter of his *Manuscrit trouvé dans un chapeau* to an old peasant whose name and profession, SORIEUL CULTIVATEUR, were spelt out in large white enamel letters on the padlocked door of one of the cellars.[7] In the summer Sorieul's musty *cave* was stacked with bundles of asparagus and carrots and garlands of onions; in the winter with sacks of mussels that he would fish heaven knows where, clean under the tap in the corridor, and feebly try to sell, crying '*à la moule, à la moule*'. Sorieul had no idea that his 'best friends' (Picasso, Derain, Vlaminck, Max Jacob, etc.) were anything special. That his son should become a *monsieur*, a success, was his only concern. But Sorieul *fils* was a drunk and had difficulty holding down a job as a sandwich man—a métier whose pictorial possibilities fascinated Picasso (this fascination comes to light in many a late cubist image and in the Managers' costumes in *Parade*). After too much to drink the sandwich man would rail at the world in a cracked voice; whereupon the *bande à Picasso*, fortified by quantities of *anis del mono*, would retaliate by chanting 'Sorieul! Sorieul! Sorieul!' to the tune of a Neapolitan serenade. The walls of the Bateau Lavoir were as little protection against noise as they were against cold and damp. At night the yells of lovers' fights would give way to the moans of conciliatory embraces. 'Picasso's big dogs would pull on their chains and bark furiously; van Dongen's little girl, burst into tears; the Italian tenor, break into song; and old Sorieul, cough until dawn.'[8]

Picasso. *The Artist with his Dog Feo.* Paris, 1904. Pen on paper. Private collection.

The squalor may have made for discomfort and rows, but there was also a degree of camaraderie that Picasso would always remember in a heroic light. In retrospect even the concierge, Madame Coudray, became a legendary character. Towards the end of World War II, Picasso took Françoise Gilot to see the building. Her account of the visit concludes: '[The Bateau Lavoir] represented the golden age, when everything was fresh and untarnished, before [Picasso] had conquered the world and then discovered that . . . the world had conquered him.'[9] 'Famous, of course I'm famous,' Picasso said to Malraux when he was in his late eighties, but it was at the Bateau Lavoir he claimed to have experienced the only kind of fame that mattered to him. 'When [Wilhelm] Uhde came from the heart of Germany to see my paintings, when young painters from all over the world brought me what they were doing, asked me for advice, when I never had a sou. Then I was famous. I was a painter not a freak [*une bête curieuse*].'[10] At their last meeting, Malraux promised Picasso that, as Minister of Culture, he was going to declare the Bateau Lavoir a historical monument; and he duly did so on December 1, 1969. 'If only we had been told that when we were living there,' the artist commented.[11] Five months later the ramshackle wooden building went up in flames.[12]

Furniture was a luxury at the Bateau Lavoir. MacOrlan said the reason so many tenants used *L'Intransigeant* as a mattress was that it had six more pages than other newspapers.[13] Picasso did not have too much of a problem. The constant *va-et-vient* of Spanish artists meant that basic household necessities were handed on from friend to friend. Pablo Gargallo, the sculptor whose Barcelona studio Picasso had rented earlier in the year, was returning to Catalonia. He sold the contents of his room on the rue Vercingétorix—a truckle bed, mattress, chair, table, footbath—for eight francs, as well as a drawing of an old beggar (to judge from Picasso's inscription to Gargallo and the date, May 6, 1904). Junyer Vidal soon returned to Mallorca to spend the summer painting. Picasso settled in for good. Once he had the studio to himself, he called on Manolo and a starving Spanish waif to move Gargallo's stuff on a handcart from Montparnasse up the hill to Montmartre. The effort almost killed the waif; worse, Picasso refused to give him the promised five francs—it was all he had; instead it was spent on dinner for the three of them.

The biggest and most eye-catching painting that Picasso executed in the first few months at the Bateau Lavoir, *Beggar with Basket of Flowers*, has disappeared, most likely under a Rose period harlequinade, *Acrobat and Young Harlequin* of the following year, in the Barnes Collection.[14] From Fernande Olivier's description of its impact the first time Picasso lured her into his studio, this painting was yet another spectre of Catalan misery:

> . . . a cripple leaning on his crutch and carrying a basket of flowers on his back. The man, the background, everything in the picture, was blue, except the flowers, which were painted in fresh, brilliant colours. The man was haggard, gaunt and miserable, and his expression told of his hopeless resignation. The effect was strange, tender and infinitely sad, suggesting total hopelessness, an agonized appeal to the compassion of mankind.[15]

Picasso. *Beggar with a Crutch*. Barcelona or Paris, 1904. Pen and wash on paper, 36×24.8cm. Private collection.

Fernande also recalled that Picasso was working 'on an etching, which has become famous since: it is of a man and a woman sitting at a table in a wine-shop. There is the most intense feeling of poverty and alcoholism

Picasso. Book jacket design for *Hôtel de l'Ouest, Chambre 22*. Paris, 1904. Watercolour and crayon on paper, 55×44cm. Private collection.

Odilon Redon. *Portrait of Olivier Sainsère*. 1905. Red chalk on paper, 44.9×36.2cm. Ian Woodner Family Collection, New York.

and a startling realism in the figures of this wretched, starving couple.'[16] She refers of course to *The Frugal Repast*, the quintessential Blue period image—the one that links Picasso's Spanish past with his French future, conceived as it was in Barcelona and executed under the supervision of Canals in Paris. Picasso engraved *The Frugal Repast* on a zinc plate that had already been etched by Joan González (the sculptor's brother, who had been working in Paris since 1901).[17] González, or possibly Canals, who helped Picasso prepare the plate, had left traces of a landscape on it. *The Frugal Repast* was Picasso's first major engraving: the progenitor of what is arguably the greatest graphic oeuvre in the history of art.[18] But, to my mind at least, it is a technical *tour de force* rather than a masterpiece. For all the dexterity, it rings a bit hollow. Fernande put her finger on this failing: these Blue period works, she came to realize, were 'intellectual in conception'. She is right. *The Frugal Repast* is a bit too manipulative. Picasso had high hopes of making some money out of this print, so he sent two copies to Junyent in time for Christmas, 1904. One was a gift that Junyent was supposed to pass on to don José (Picasso had to write twice before this was actually done). The other copy (inscribed to Junyent) was evidently intended to be shown around in the hope that sales would be forthcoming. Picasso promised to send another one to Sabartès, who had just set up as a trader in Guatemala.

One of the first friends Picasso contacted on arriving in Paris was the good-natured journalist Gustave Coquiot, who was always ready with some scheme or other. This time it was a book jacket and a theatre poster. On July 13, Coquiot wrote to Picasso, telling him to see Monsieur Pierre Valdagneat at the Librairie Ollendorf about doing the cover for his play *Hôtel de l'Ouest, Chambre 22*, which he had written with Jean Lorrain (the over-jewelled, over-*maquillé* novelist with whom Proust had fought a duel). Picasso's idea for this book jacket—the melodrama had opened at the Grand Guignol on May 28, 1904—never advanced beyond the maquette stage. A similar fate befell the poster that Picasso was asked to design later in the year for the next Coquiot-Lorrain play, *Sainte Roulette* (which was first performed on October 10, 1904). It was turned down by the manager of the Théâtre Molière. For all his sense of drama, Picasso was evidently not cut out to be a designer of theatrical posters. Coquiot also wanted the artist to do some portraits—of whom, we do not know: possibly his wife and daughter, who later professed to have been very attracted to Picasso. Coquiot promised to provide the necessary canvas and paint if the artist came and dined, so the subjects are likely to have been family members.

Besides Coquiot, who tried to help out with commissions, and Olivier Sainsère, the Conseiller d'Etat who helped out with a *permis de séjour*, and various dealers—Weill, Sagot, Soulié—who paid derisory prices for the odd painting and drawing, almost the only Frenchman Picasso saw on a regular basis was Max Jacob, who continued in the roles of acolyte and tutor. Otherwise most of his friends were Spanish: the Pichots, who were always ready to give him a meal; Canals, who helped him with engraving; Paco Durrio, who saw Picasso as another Gauguin; Manolo, whose buffoonery kept him amused; Zuloaga, whose hospitality compensated for the *grand maître* manner he cultivated; Sunyer, who was Picasso's rival for the favours of Fernande; and many more who divided their time between

Picasso. *Old Beggar*. Paris, 1904.
Pen on paper, 29×22 cm. Ian Woodner Family Collection, New York. Inscribed to Gargallo.

Picasso. *The Frugal Repast*. Paris, 1904.
Etching, 46.3×37.7 cm. Private collection. Inscribed to Junyent.

Paris and Barcelona. Picasso's French was still far from fluent, still very heavily accented and high-pitched, as Andalusian French is apt to be. Self-consciousness about his accent combined with shyness—something he never really lost and subsequently camouflaged with horseplay—made him seem more taciturn than he really was. Hence Picasso's constant need for the company of his Spanish friends. With Manolo, for instance, he could behave as freely and outrageously as he liked. And if Fabián de Castro was around with his guitar, the Place Ravignan would reverberate with flamenco and the yells and drumming of feet that accompany it. Picasso would clap his hands and launch into one of his raunchy flamenco dances.

Picasso. *Woman with a Raven*. Paris, 1904. Charcoal, pastel and watercolour on paper, 64.8×49.5cm. The Toledo Museum of Art, Gift of Edward Drummond Libbey.

Little by little the blue light that had permeated Picasso's paintings for the last two years began to lose its chill. Certain pictures are still excessively, exclusively blue. But even that quintessential image of the Blue period, the scrawny, sulky, sexy alley-cat known as the *Woman with Helmet of Hair*, with her indigo chignon and ice-blue skin, has lips of palest pink. Flesh tones become ruddier, and by the middle of the summer there are even reddish backgrounds. While a new sense of colour slowly develops, the mannerisms associated with the Blue period become even more pronounced. For the next six months or so, extremities, fingers especially, are attenuated to the point of appearing triple-jointed. Shoulders are as wide and skeletal as clothes-hangers, from which torsos seem to droop like flimsy garments. And, as mannerists do, the artist makes rather too much of the neck muscle. The two versions of the *Woman with a Raven* done in the summer of 1904, represent an extreme point in these idiosyncrasies. And then, just as he had managed to rid his palette of blue, Picasso purged his style of these other excesses.

If during the summer of 1904 Picasso's work was afflicted with false starts and backward looks, it could have been because he was prone, as émigrés often are, to bouts of anguish, insecurity and loneliness. His immediate prospects were bleak; he was still chronically poor and, like most young Spaniards, automatically suspected by the authorities of being an anarchist or terrorist, something that would always paralyse him with fear. On one occasion he was obliged to invoke the help of Olivier Sainsère in order to stop a police inquiry into his connections with people suspected of anarchist sympathies.[19] Fortunately the twenty-three-year-old Picasso had developed resilience and, so long as his work went well, could usually switch from black gloom to ecstatic joy, from childish fun to intense concentration, in a matter of minutes. Fortunately, too, he had managed to develop a certain manipulative cunning in his dealings with the world: wheedling or, if need be, browbeating everybody (except dealers, who almost always got the better of him) into doing his bidding. Freeloading became a way of life. Disarming charm, youthful charisma and ruthlessness, coupled with demonic energy and fanatical drive, would see him through to glory.

Picasso. *Portrait of Madeleine*. Paris, 1904. Pastel and gouache on cardboard, 67×51.5cm. Musée Picasso, Paris.

* * *

A new face in his work reveals that Picasso had found a new mistress. Madeleine she was called; all we know is that she was a model. To judge by a very literal portrait in profile (this re-emerged only in 1968, when

Picasso. *Woman with Helmet of Hair*. Paris, 1904. Gouache on board, 41.6×29.9 cm. The Art Institute of Chicago, Bequest of Kate L. Brewster.

Picasso. *Woman Ironing*. Paris, 1904. Oil on canvas, 116.2×73 cm. Solomon R. Guggenheim Museum, New York, Gift of Justin K. Thannhauser, 1978.

Picasso. *Woman in a Chemise*. Paris, 1904. Oil on canvas, 72.5×60 cm. Tate Gallery, London.

the artist discovered that its cardboard support had been used to back a frame)[20] and a large black chalk drawing of Madeleine squatting cross-legged on the floor, she was pretty in a delicate, bird-like way (her nose and forehead formed a straight line). Madeleine's thick hair, loosely drawn back into a chignon, and her boyishly lean body recur in a number of works done over the next six or nine months—works that mirror the blurring of the Blue into the Rose period. Two idealized versions of her chart this process: the bluish *Woman in a Chemise* and the very similar but pinkish *Seated Nude* (in the Musée d'Art Moderne, Paris) done a month or two later. Madeleine's bone structure also inspired the *Woman with Helmet of Hair*, the skeletal *Woman Ironing* and the no less skeletal girl in *The Frugal Repast*. Picasso would always take pleasure in the fact that the skinny allure he contrived for his Blue period girls predicted a look that fashionable women would cultivate decades later.

Madeleine also figures in two overtly lesbian compositions: a gouache of two intensely blue nude look-alikes with their arms round each other's shoulders; and an Ingresque watercolour of a naked Madeleine—easily distinguishable by her hawk-like profile—advancing meaningfully on a nude blonde lying back on a bed with her legs invitingly open. 'I don't know whether Madeleine went in for feminine attachments,' says Daix, 'or whether Picasso's curiosity or jealousy was the point.'[21] Enjoyment, more likely. Picasso's penchant for lesbianism emerges in a group of gouaches and watercolours of two girls having sex, the most important of which he gave to Apollinaire. The poet kept it by his bed, 'being as greedy for such spectacles as Picasso'.[22] Verlaine's six Sapphic sonnets, *Les Amies* (1867) may have inspired these subjects,[23] but a more likely source is George Bottini, who had executed some similarly stylized and delicate watercolours of lesbians a few years earlier. Picasso probably knew these, for his early patron Olivier Sainsère had acquired some of them. He would also have seen Toulouse-Lautrec's paintings of girls in bed together. But whereas Lautrec depicts women having sex as matter-of-factly as if they were doing laundry, Picasso is unashamedly prurient. Lesbian subjects had a practical as well as an erotic attraction for him. Short of deriving inspiration from classical myth or allegory, what more natural or up-to-date pretext for confrontations between two female nudes could he find? It was not until sunbathing became a cult after World War I that Picasso was able to portray two nude women lying unequivocally together on a beach. He would later use this subject as a means of pitting rival women in his life against one another and weaving them into his personal mythology.

Picasso. *Madeleine Crouching*. Paris, 1904. Pencil and charcoal on canvas, 100×81.5 cm. Musée d'Art Moderne, Saint-Etienne.

At the height of the summer, Madeleine found herself pregnant. Whereupon, with Picasso's approval, she had an abortion. 'Can you imagine me with a son sixty-four years old?' he would say to friends whenever he showed them the newly discovered portrait of Madeleine. Around the time Madeleine realized she was pregnant, the artist embarked on an on-again, off-again affair with another model—one who lived conveniently close: in the Bateau Lavoir. This girl went under many different names but is best known as Fernande Olivier. Another possible reason, one suspects, for Madeleine's abortion. Fernande's memoirs omit any mention of her rival, but the two girls overlapped. Although Picasso first met Fernande in August 1904, it is Madeleine's skinny beauty that continues to haunt

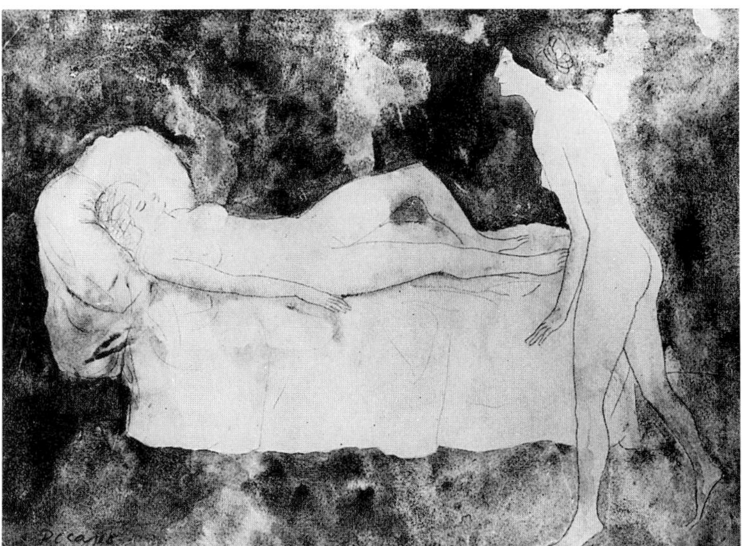

Left: Picasso. *Les Amies*. Paris, 1904. Gouache on paper, 55×38 cm. Private collection.

Above: Picasso. *The Two Friends.* Paris, 1904. Pencil and watercolour on paper, 27×37 cm. Private collection.

Below: Picasso. *The Embrace,* Paris, 1905. Oil on cardboard, 63×90 cm. Private collection. Inscribed to Apollinaire.

Picasso. *Mother and Child*. Paris, 1904. Black crayon on paper, 33.8×26.7cm. Fogg Art Museum, Harvard University, Bequest of Meta and Paul J. Sachs.

the work—at least until spring 1905. One need look no further than the tender images of a Madeleine-like mother and child of late 1904 and early 1905. The fact that these paintings date from the time when Madeleine would have given birth and that one of them depicts an unusually tender and seraphic Virgin and Child suggests that they may have been done not so much in expiation of guilt over the abortion as in the spirit of what-might-have-been. Picasso would always be torn between longing to have children and exasperation at the responsibilities involved.

Besides Madeleine, Picasso was seeing two other girls at this time, and their exotic features also contributed to the anorexic look that characterizes the girls of the intermediary Blue-into-Rose period. There was the gothically skeletal Marguerite (known as Margot) Luc, stepdaughter of Frédé Gérard, who had taken over Le Zut and now operated its successor, Le Lapin Agile. Margot, who subsequently married Pierre MacOrlan, is portrayed in the height of *fin-de-siècle* mannerism kissing the raven she had trained and stroking him with grotesquely long, thin fingers. This is the bird that hopped about the Lapin Agile, pecking at crumbs and uttering ominous croaks. Picasso may not have slept with Margot, but he certainly had a brief affair with another girlfriend of the period, Alice, whom he nicknamed '*la vièrge*'. According to Gertrude Stein, this beauty 'was the daughter of a workingman and had the brutal thumbs that . . . were a characteristic of workingmen. . . . She had a certain wild quality that perhaps had to do with her brutal thumbs and was curiously in accord with her madonna face.'[24] Since adolescence Alice had been the mistress of Maurice Princet, a disagreeable if gifted mathematician who worked as a government actuary and made some extra money on the side selling the occasional Picasso (one of them to the eminent collector of Gauguin and van Gogh, Gustave Fayet of Béziers). Alice was notoriously unfaithful to this implacably bitter man: 'thin with a face eaten into by a wiry red beard and expressing nothing but malevolent mockery'.[25] She much preferred lusty young Spanish painters, above all Picasso, who once found her so titillated by his copy of Rétif de la Bretonne's pornographic *L'Anti-Justine* that he insisted on drawing her while reading it. (According to Daix, her excitement explains the exclamation point after the inscription: '*A Alice!*')

Despite her infidelities, Princet finally decided to marry Alice.[26] 'It is wonderful to long for a woman for seven years and possess her at last,' Max Jacob said sententiously. Picasso was more realistic: 'Why should they marry simply in order to divorce?' Why, indeed? Not long after the ceremony—towards the end of 1905—Alice met André Derain, whose reputation as a Fauve was second only to Matisse's. They fell passionately in love. Some months later, Alice left Princet for Derain, and in due course (1907) they were married. Picasso could not remember when he first met Derain.[27] Their paths are said to have crossed at Azon's restaurant as early as the winter of 1904.[28] But even if they did not actually meet, they knew about each other through mutual friends. Since Derain was seldom in Paris (he spent the summers of 1905 and 1906 on the Mediterranean, the intervening winter and spring in London), he and Picasso did not become close friends until the autumn of 1906. 'The result of this closeness', Apollinaire maintained, 'was the almost immediate birth of cubism.'[29] This is not at all how it happened.

Picasso. *Virgin and Child*. Paris, 1904. Gouache on paper, 63×48cm. Private collection.

Although Alice is the subject of a very few drawings and a sculpture, her Madonna-like looks left their mark on Picasso's work. He grafted her features onto those of Madeleine and Margot and came up with the skeletal image that characterizes the final phase of the Blue period—a foretaste of how he would later juggle and integrate the physiognomies and identities of his various mistresses. During the next year or so he would also blur sexual characteristics. Alice's pout—her *bouderie*—which figures on the faces of many other girls, will look equally at home on the sulky faces of Rose period youths. Hence increasing confusion as to the gender of Picasso's figures. This trend towards unisexuality ceases only when Fernande Olivier finally emerges in all her voluptuousness, an event that will not occur until the beginning of 1906.

Picasso. *Alice Derain*. Paris, 1905. Sepia on paper, 36×26.6cm. Galerie Rosengart, Lucerne. Inscribed to the sitter.

Agosto 1904
Picasso

20

La Belle Fernande

Staircase at the Bateau Lavoir. Photo: André Fage.

FERNANDE OLIVIER, PICASSO'S FIRST GREAT love, came from the same bohemian milieu as did the models he had slept with on earlier visits to Paris, but she had more allure, sophistication and polish. She told Gertrude Stein that Evelyn Thaw (who had been much in the news because of her husband's murder of Stanford White) was her ideal: 'So blonde, so pale, so nothing'[1]—so utterly unlike herself. Fernande's lively memoirs, *Picasso and His Friends*, describes how the affair started in the summer of 1904. Since she also lived in the Bateau Lavoir, she was always bumping into Picasso. 'Why does he spend all his time on the Place Ravignan?' she remembered thinking. 'Whenever does he work?' Later she learned that he preferred painting at night, so as not to be disturbed. Fernande says their first meeting took place one thundery evening. She was on her way home. He was chatting to Ricard Canals on the Place Ravignan. As she passed, he held out a tiny kitten to her, 'laughing and blocking my path. . . . I laughed too and he took me to see his studio.'[2]

On the basis of weather reports, Palau concludes that this encounter must have occurred on August 4, a particularly stormy day. At first the affair was of the most casual kind: Picasso was still involved with Madeleine; Fernande was living with a sculptor, also having an affair with Joaquim Sunyer. Picasso, according to Fernande, never stopped cajoling her to come and live with him, and from time to time she would spend a few days, once a few weeks, in his studio. But a year would pass before she would move permanently into the studio that she has evocatively described.

On her first visit Fernande was astonished by the sadness of Picasso's work and the mess in which he lived:

> Huge, unfinished canvases stood all over the studio and everything there suggested work: but, my God, what chaos!
>
> There was a mattress on four legs in one corner. A little iron stove, covered in rust; on top a yellow earthenware bowl for washing; beside it on a whitewood table was a towel and a minute stub of soap. In another corner a pathetic little black-painted trunk made a pretty uncomfortable seat. A cane chair, easels, canvases of every size and tubes of paint were scattered all over the floor with brushes, oil cans and a bowl for etching fluid. There were no curtains. In the table drawer Picasso kept a pet white mouse which he tenderly cared for and showed to everybody.

Opposite: Picasso. *The Lovers.* Paris, August 1904. Ink, watercolour and charcoal on paper, 37.2×26.9 cm. Musée Picasso, Paris.

> . . . the studio was a furnace in summer, and it was not unusual for Picasso and his friends to strip completely. They would receive visitors half-naked, if not totally so; with just a scarf tied round the waist.
>
> Anyway, Picasso liked wearing no clothes, and the beauty of his limbs was no secret. He had small hands and was very proud of his Andalusian feet and legs, which were well-shaped though a little short. His shoulders were broad and he was rather stocky. He always regretted the lack of those few inches, which would have made him ideally proportioned.
>
> In winter the studio was so cold that the dregs of tea left in cups from the day before were frozen by morning. But the cold did not prevent Picasso from working without respite.[3]

Fernande had a mass of reddish hair, green, almond-shaped eyes and long prehensile fingers like a monkey—'midwife's hands', her foster mother said. For all that she was indolent, self-indulgent and promiscuous, she was also beguiling, easy-going and affectionate. Her real name was Amélie Lang; and she had been born out of wedlock in Paris on June 6, 1881, to one Clara Lang and a remote gentleman in a top hat. The remote gentleman gave his half sister, Madame Belvallé, enough money to bring up Fernande in petit-bourgeois comfort. The adoptive family was probably Jewish; Belvallé could well be a gallicization of Schoenfeld.[4] Monsieur Belvallé lived above the workrooms where he manufactured silk flowers, feather ornaments and artificial plants in pots. He was a nice enough man, but his wife was a virago: as cruel and contemptuous to her ward as she was loving and indulgent to her own daughter. When at the age of eighteen Fernande was seduced by a brutal young shop assistant, Madame Belvallé forced her to marry the culprit; otherwise 'she would be packed off to a reformatory'. And so on August 8, 1899, Fernande became the wife of Paul-Emile Percheron, who tried and failed to beat and rape her into submission. After a miscarriage the following winter, which left her unable to bear children, she ran away. To believe Fernande (which is usually but not always possible), she was picked up that same spring day by a young sculptor called Laurent Debienne, who installed her in his studio and launched her on a career as a model. She boasted of posing for Cormon, Carolus Duran, Boldini, Henner, Rochegrosse and, very briefly (if at all), Degas. Mostly academic artists, she complained; which meant that she had to keep very still for hours on end. She also grumbled that Debienne pocketed her earnings. Fernande enjoyed a succession of affairs on the side, notably one with Sunyer, but they remained together in one of the Bateau Lavoir studios from 1901 until September 1905, when she moved in with Picasso.

Francis Picabia. *Model in Cormon's Studio.* 1906. Oil on canvas, 81×60cm. Private collection.

Most of what we know about Fernande—and for that matter about Picasso in these early years—comes from her memoirs, above all the delightfully evocative *Picasso and His Friends.* So vivid is the writing, one can only assume that Paul Léautaud (who wrote the preface) or her other literary friend, Max Jacob, lent a hand. When this book came out, in 1933, Picasso was outraged by the invasion of his privacy and, prompted by his even more outraged wife, tried to stop publication. However, he later admitted that, despite inaccuracies and errors of omission, Fernande had provided the most authentic picture of the period.

More than twenty years after she died in 1966, another book by Fernande, *Souvenirs intimes* (1988) appeared, edited by her godson Gilbert

Krill. These memoirs, which fizzle out in 1911, are said to be based on a diary that Fernande started to keep on her fifteenth birthday. She had already used much of the material as a basis for the first book. The second time round, she changes her tune, with the intention of playing on Picasso's feelings. 'I am going to tell you the story of my life,' she says, rather ominously, in a preface written sometime in the mid-fifties:

> Perhaps you will then be able to understand me better. You have always doubted me [and] my love . . . [but] those years I lived by your side were the only happy period of my life. Now that time has whitened the hair that you once loved, gnarled the hands that you once loved, silenced the laughter that you also loved, though not always, I feel an urge to tell you what my life was like before you, after you.[5]

From previous experience Fernande knew all too well that the prospect of yet another book of indiscreet memoirs would cause Picasso maximum annoyance and anguish. *Souvenirs intimes* must therefore be regarded as more in the nature of a threat than a love token, especially in view of the author's contention that 'since it is necessary to eat in order to live, it is likewise necessary to use all the means at one's disposal to improve one's material circumstances.'[6] In other words the *Souvenirs* were a genteel form of blackmail on the part of the impoverished Fernande. Her pious old friend Marcelle Braque, who had come to resent Picasso, allowed herself to be used as the go-between in this delicate matter. The moment Fernande received a million old francs from the lover she had not seen for almost fifty years, the manuscript went back into her little basketwork valise.

The new book fails to answer some of the questions it raises. Fernande's sculptor lover, for instance, Laurent Debienne. Was that his real name? Picasso told Daix that Fernande's previous lover had been called Gaston de la Baume. Since Fernande sometimes signed herself 'la Baume', and since there was someone by that name (but no Debienne) listed as living at the Bateau Lavoir,[7] were they one and the same person? Also the pseudonym Fernande Olivier. Why did this twenty-three-year-old girl have to invent yet another name when she already had so many to choose from: Lang, Belvallé (or Belvalet, as she sometimes spelt it), Percheron, not to speak of Debienne and de la Baume? And what are we now to make of Fernande's previous claim that she was introduced into the world of art by 'one of my close relations, who was married to a painter'?[8] The second book makes no further reference to this 'close relation', who is sometimes identified as Fernande's sister (adoptive sister presumably), the mistress, not the wife, of Othon Friesz. And it is as unforthcoming about the end of the affair with Picasso as her earlier publication.

Nevertheless, these *Souvenirs* are useful in that they clear up most of the mystery in which Fernande had previously shrouded her early years. They tell us more about her painting—something she barely touched upon before, except to describe the gaffe that Paul Poiret, the couturier, made on his first visit to Picasso's studio:

> Dressed with a carefulness which could not be accused of erring on the side of fastidiousness and moderation . . . he came in and fell back stunned, before a small gouache—a portrait of a woman.
>
> 'Oh! Remarkable! Delightful! Admirable! A portrait of Madame?' he inquired, indicating the painter's companion.

Fernande Olivier. *Self-Portrait.* 1936. Pastel on paper, 42×33cm. Private collection.

Fernande Olivier. *Self-Portrait; Portrait of Picasso.* Reproduced in *Picasso et ses amis,* 1933.

'Yes,' Picasso answered, grinning derisively. 'It's a portrait of Madame . . . by Madame.'[9]

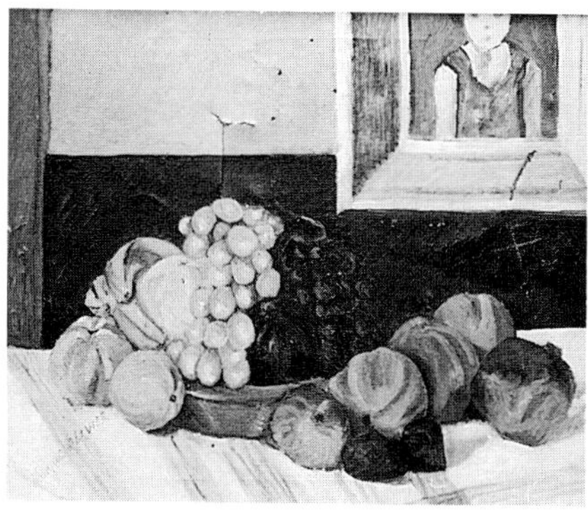

Fernande Olivier. *Still Life.* Oil on canvas, 48×57 cm. Private collection.

The line drawings that illustrate her original book—a self-portrait and a portrait of Picasso—are the only published evidence of Fernande's gifts. 'For a long time I tried my hand at painting,' Fernande says in her *Souvenirs.* 'I was gifted; I would like to have been directed, to have received some guidance from Pablo, who refused to be of help. "Have fun," he told me, "that's all you need, what you're doing is much more interesting than what you would do if you followed someone else's advice."'[10] Some fifty years later, Picasso made much the same comment when he showed some friends (including myself) a portfolio which, he claimed, contained the entire oeuvre of Fernande. The work was all the better for not trying to be Picasso, he said, and went on to comment that Dora Maar had had the sense to go her own way, as opposed to others who made the mistake of copying him. He was right; in their expressionistic boldness, Fernande's surprisingly large and dramatic heads owed more to van Dongen than Picasso; they were as stylized as Marie Laurencin's, only more primitive and mask-like—somewhat Fauve. Too bad, these far from negligible works are said to have disappeared from Picasso's estate. They entitle us to take Fernande's artistic credentials more seriously than we otherwise might. And they provide a possible explanation for the presence in certain sketchbooks of drawings that do not appear to be by Picasso.

The *Souvenirs* also clear up the mystery surrounding Fernande's affair with Sunyer, which she omitted from her previous book. Shortly after she met Picasso in 1904 and was being courted by him, Sunyer tried to pick her up in the street. He followed her back to Canals's studio, where she was staying, and arranged to be introduced. The promiscuous Fernande soon succumbed to Sunyer's advances, but she claims that their relationship was purely physical. Aside from '*cela*' (her euphemism for sex), he did not please her: 'He had the character of an intelligent peasant: shrewd, shy and a little pretentious.'[11] However, he was an ardent lover: 'He has opened up a side of life to me that I know nothing about. It's wonderful and exciting, but my heart remains closed to him. After it's over my only desire is to get as far away from his arms as possible, back to my solitary bed.'[12] Sunyer wanted Fernande to move in with him; she briefly did. But he gave her no money; and then one day, when he appeared with a parcel of expensive clothes—silk shirts, underwear and socks—she realized that he was being kept by a rich older woman.[13] And so she left him for Picasso.

Fernande Olivier. *Vase of Flowers.* Oil on canvas, 47×39 cm. Private collection.

The most startling revelation of these posthumous memoirs is the role that opium played in Picasso's seduction of Fernande. Her previous book implied that Picasso did not try the drug until 1908: he smoked 'two or three times a week for a period of some months, until the death of Wiegels [in June 1908] put an abrupt end to these practices.'[14] Now we learn that Picasso had started smoking opium four years earlier, in the summer of 1904. He was going to buy a pipe, he told Fernande shortly after they met, and teach her to smoke. They were soon doing so on a regular basis. Fernande claims that the drug changed her attitude to life and love and sex. 'Everything suddenly seemed beautiful, clear, good.

Fernande Olivier and Benedetta Canals in Canals's studio, 1904. Private collection.

Picasso. *Portrait of Benedetta Canals.* Paris, 1905. Oil on canvas, 88×68 cm. Museu Picasso, Barcelona.

Canals in his studio at the Bateau Lavoir. Photograph by Picasso, 1904. Musée Picasso, Paris. The photo on the mantlepiece is of Benedetta.

Canals. *At the Bullfight* (detail). 1904. Oil on canvas, 157×257 cm. Private collection. The painting, commissioned by the Catalan banker Ivo Bosch, was exhibited in Paris in 1904.

Opium has perhaps enabled me to understand the real meaning of the word "love". . . . I discovered that I knew Picasso at last, that I "experienced" him better. It seemed that he was the one I had always waited for.'[15] Thanks to opium, Fernande finally felt as one with Picasso and decided to move in with him:

> I have spent three days with Pablo [she writes in the late summer of 1905], I love to smoke opium, I love Pablo, he is tender, kind, amorous, he pleases me. How can I have been blind for so long? . . . I no longer think of getting up in the middle of the night and going off to find Sunyer . . . whose caresses used to give me so much pleasure. I am happy in the arms of Pablo, much fuller of happiness than I ever was with Sunyer. I love him. I'm going to love him so much. He doesn't want me to go on posing—a problem since Cormon and Sicard have embarked on *grandes machines* with me as a model. [Pablo] wants me to go and live with him. What should I do? I am going to try and gain a week's respite by seeming to hesitate, but my mind's made up. However I am frightened of his jealousy. He can be violent.[16]

Sunyer. *At the Circus* (detail showing Fernande Olivier). 1905. Pastel on paper, 31×48cm. Private collection.

The *Souvenirs* inform us that Fernande finally moved in with Picasso one very hot Sunday—the day the statue of the Chevalier de la Barre was inaugurated on the Butte de Montmartre, behind the Sacré Coeur: i.e. September 3, 1905. After a drowsy afternoon lolling on a divan, she had suddenly decided around five o'clock to summon Picasso, who lived on another floor of the Bateau Lavoir, to carry her little wooden trunk over to his studio. 'With one leap you were outside lugging my trunk'—in her book the old lady wags an arch finger at the lover she has not seen for almost fifty years—'with another leap you were back home, where you shut me and the trunk up with you while your arms enclosed me.'[17] One thing had changed since her earlier visits to the studio. The little alcove with its rotting floor off the main studio—'oratory, junkroom, mortuary what you will' (Salmon would nickname it 'the maid's room')—had been transformed into a 'chapel' dedicated to Fernande—an anomaly in the Bateau Lavoir, but less so in a Spanish house, where dead relations (one thinks of Conchita) were frequently commemorated in this way. The 'altar' consisted of a packing case covered in the white lawn blouse she had worn on their first meeting and a pair of cerulean blue Louis-Philippe vases filled with artificial flowers, 'like Cézanne must have had'.[18] Hanging on the wall was a pen-and-ink drawing of Fernande (subsequently stolen) done to celebrate their first encounter; it was mounted on stuff from a blue chemise that she had abandoned in the studio. What sort of feelings, Fernande asks, would have inspired this fetish-hung altar? Amorous mysticism, irony, self-mockery? Fernande's diagnosis is correct: eroticism, irony, shreds and tatters of faith, would always be inextricably mingled in Picasso's work; so would the trivial personal things that reminded him of the loved one.

Besides titillating Picasso, the lesbianism that is hinted at in the *Souvenirs* seems to have attracted Gertrude Stein. Stein used elements of Fernande for her character Melanctha, the sexually attractive black girl in *Three Lives*. And when her new girlfriend, Alice Toklas, took French lessons from Fernande in 1907, she too developed a certain *tendresse* for her:

> Fernande spoke a very elegant french, some lapses of course into montmartrois that I found difficult to follow. . . . To have a lesson in french one has to converse and Fernande had three subjects, hats, we had not much

Picasso. Study for *The Actor* with heads of Fernande. Paris, late 1904. Pencil on paper, 47×31.5cm. Private collection.

> more to say about hats, perfumes, we had something to say about perfumes. Perfumes were Fernande's really great extravagance, she was the scandal of Montmartre because she had once bought a bottle of perfume named Smoke and had paid eighty francs for it at that time sixteen dollars and it had no scent but such wonderful colour, like real bottled liquid smoke. Her third subject was the categories of furs.[19]

Toklas, or rather Stein (the confusion arises from Stein's having written her memoirs in the guise of her companion), is correct: Fernande's passion for perfume was such that anyone who wanted to track Picasso down in a crowd had only to follow her scent.[20] Correct, too, in that Fernande's tastes ran to finery rather than domesticity. Even if she had wanted to, she was not allowed to do anything about the mess and disorder of Picasso's studio, for he insisted on taking care of the housework and shopping himself. He did not trust the very loving but not very faithful Fernande to leave the house alone, so he kept her locked up, like the oriental odalisque that friends remember her resembling. He also kept her without shoes—only an old pair of espadrilles. At first Fernande enjoyed the role of love object, but after a year or two she began to resent Picasso's Andalusian jealousy and possessiveness; she would run away and set up on her own. On these occasions Gertrude Stein would ask Alice Toklas to check whether Fernande was wearing her earrings. If she was not, it meant they were in pawn—a sure sign that her money was running out. Soon she would have to return to her master.

During the first year or so of their relationship, Fernande seldom appears in drawings and paintings—partly because Picasso was still seeing Madeleine; partly out of discretion. Discretion was called for, Picasso said, because Fernande had not yet divorced her crazy husband (nor did she ever do so); in addition, she had two jealous ex-lovers to contend with. An even more likely explanation is that Fernande's voluptuous looks did not correspond to the etiolated aesthetic of the Blue period. Apart from a drawing of a girl who looks like Fernande having sex with a young man who could well be the artist (dated August 1904, so possibly executed on the occasion of their first sexual encounter) and the lost portrait around which the studio altar was arranged, the first identifiable portrayals of Fernande, with her almond eyes and full mouth, are two sketches on the same sheet as a preparatory drawing for the large painting, *The Actor*, done at the end of 1904. These are very literal images; they are as yet unredeemed by the air of feline sensuality that the artist would contrive for her, and there is also no attempt to gloss over Fernande's incipient double chin. In an engraving done in January 1905, Picasso does his best to whittle her face down to Blue period proportions. But the engraving of a skeletal beauty in profile done around the same time suggests that he could not get Madeleine's delicate bone structure out of his mind. This mingling of features was a means of reconciling a new love with an old one, playing one off against the other.

Picasso. *Head of Fernande*. Paris, January 1905. Etching, 12.1×9cm. Musée Picasso, Paris.

Of these early Fernandes, the most revelatory are two remarkable watercolours that date from the winter of 1904–05. They are identical in size, style, conception and subject. Both portray Fernande asleep; in one she is watched over by Picasso; in the other by a *farouche*-looking man with a shaggy mane of hair. The time-honoured theme of the sleeper watched, which first manifests itself in the 1901 drawing of the artist in the role of

Above: Picasso. *Debienne Watching Fernande Asleep.* Paris, 1904. Pen and watercolour on paper, 36×26 cm. Whereabouts unknown.

Above right: Picasso. *The Artist Watching Fernande Asleep (Meditation).* Paris, 1904. Pen and watercolour on paper, 36.8×27 cm. Private collection.

Picasso. *Faun Unveiling a Sleeping Woman.* Paris, 1936. Etching and aquatint, 31.7×41.7 cm. Musée Picasso, Paris.

Gauguin's spirit of the dead contemplating a recumbent girl, will recur time and again in Picasso's later work. It will inspire all sorts of ingenious interpretations on the part of art historians.[21] All the more reason, then, to establish what the earliest manifestations of this theme are about. As he will often do when a woman enters or leaves his life, Picasso encodes a message to her in his work. Hitherto we could only guess at the message. Now we can be reasonably certain as to its gist. The suggestion that the *farouche*-looking man might be Fernande's sculptor lover can at last be confirmed.[22] Fernande's recently published *Souvenirs* include a detailed description of Debienne (de la Baume?) when she first met him (1899); and this corresponds in every respect (except the beard) to the crazy-looking figure in Picasso's watercolour. 'Large black eyes were the only good features in a sombre face already marked by wrinkles . . . a nose that jutted out too much from scrawny cheeks covered by a beard . . . a beautiful head of hair on a head too big for the small, skinny body, a long thin neck with an emphatic Adam's apple.'[23] These two watercolours can thus be seen to spell out the alternatives confronting Fernande: the danger of remaining with her vindictive, uncaring lover contrasted with the safety of life with her 'tender, kind, amorous Pablo'—especially now that their love potion, opium, had brought them so close.

Picasso, 1904. Inscribed to his musician friends Suzanne and Henri Bloch. Musée Picasso, Paris.

Once again Picasso's eyes seem to exert a strange power: the *mirada fuerte* power to conjure Fernande from the bed of the weak watcher into the arms of the strong watcher. In middle age the manipulative artist, disguised as a faun, will once again portray himself watching a sleeping girl. This time Picasso is the one with the options: two mistresses to choose between. As he explained, some years later to Françoise Gilot, the faun is studying his mistress, trying to read her thoughts, trying to decide whether 'she loves him because he is a monster'.[24] Picasso made a no less revealing comment on this theme to yet another mistress, Geneviève Laporte. While showing her a prized possession, a large amethyst in which a drop of water was imprisoned like a tear, he invoked the theme of Psyche, the barrier that sleep represents—the nearness and farness of the sleeper. 'When a man watches a woman asleep, he tries to understand,' he said; 'when a woman watches a man asleep, she wonders what sauce she's going to eat him with.' This was not a joke.[25]

Similar ambiguities are to be found in many other works of the period: the watercolour of Madeleine advancing on a recumbent nude, for instance. This could refer to Madeleine's sexual tastes; it could explain why Picasso left her, or she left him. It could be an erotic fantasy, or wishful thinking, as in the case of the two drawings, known as *The Christ of Montmartre*, of a naked man throwing himself off a parapet onto the roofs of Paris. These are said to have been inspired by the suicide of the so-called Christ of Montmartre, but, as Picasso pointed out to Daix, this man hanged himself in his studio, whereas in the drawing, 'he's throwing himself out of the window'.[26] Picasso omitted to say that he has given the suicide Debienne's features. One of the drawings is even dominated by a mean-looking self-portrait. Shamanism!

Picasso. *The Christ of Montmartre*. Paris, 1904. Pen and watercolour on paper, 36×26cm. Foundation Prince M., Zurich.

* * *

During Picasso's first months at the Bateau Lavoir Max Jacob continued to be his principal French mentor, but the two of them would never re-establish the degree of intimacy that they had shared on the Boulevard Voltaire. Jacob was jealous of the artist's mistresses, particularly Fernande, who has described how 'ambiguous, biting and flattering' he was on the occasion of their first meeting; how ironically low he bowed, hat in hand.[27] This meeting must have taken place late in the summer of 1904, for Fernande was still working as a model—for a sculptor, hence all the plaster dust on her clothes. She tried to cut short Jacob's facetious greetings so that she could go home and change her dress. 'But why?' he said. 'The mess doesn't show in the sun.'[28] Despite his initial malice, Jacob realized that if Fernande was to be enthroned as Picasso's mistress, he had better cultivate her as an ally. He set about charming her and soon became her devoted friend. They went on commiserating with each other long after Picasso had dropped them.

Max Jacob. *Portrait of Manolo*. 1903. Pencil, purple ink and crayons on paper, 23×15.8cm. Musée Picasso, Paris.

In fact, as Jacob would soon realize, he had less cause to be jealous of the new women in Picasso's life than of the new poets. After six months in Paris, the artist's friends were no longer limited to his *tertulia* of Spanish cronies. Manolo, who was better at promoting other people than himself, had introduced Picasso to a couple of young *littérateurs*, André Salmon and Guillaume Apollinaire. Jacob's reaction to these new luminaries was ambivalent—enthusiastic yet resentful, especially of Apollinaire. He resented Apollinaire for filling Picasso's head with too much symbolist cant, for praising Rimbaud at the expense of Verlaine. He also resented his heterosexual bonding with Picasso, from which he was excluded. However, Jacob put a deceptively good face on things. If he mocked Apollinaire, it was usually behind his back. For instance, he put Picasso and Salmon up to making merciless fun of Apollinaire's effusive way of signing his letters: '*la main amie* [the friendly hand] *de Guillaume Apollinaire*.' One snowy night Salmon returned home to find a fur glove dangling from his doorknob; inside was a note in Jacob's writing: '*Snow-glove, la main sanglante* [the bleeding hand] *de Guillaume Apollinaire*.' Later there would be bitter quarrels, but on the whole the poets soon settled into a well-regulated pattern, revolving around Picasso like planets around the sun, corresponding with each other, if unable to meet, in verse.[29] This camaraderie lasted until Apollinaire died (1918). Later on, Jacob was eased out of Picasso's life at the behest of the artist's wife, Olga, who did not think him respectable. By that time, however, Jacob had been discovered by *le tout Paris*. Salmon would also be banished.

The first of Salmon's three volumes of memoirs—it covers the period from 1903 to 1908—is a principal source of information (and misinformation) about Picasso's *bande* at the Bateau Lavoir. Its title, *Souvenirs sans fin*, is a warning the reader does well to heed. There are many evocative vignettes, but on the whole these are not as perceptive or sharply focused as Fernande Olivier's amateurish recollections. Salmon is a typical veteran campaigner—garrulous, self-promoting, diffuse. For all that he was in at the birth of the Rose period, that he came up with the title of *Les Demoiselles d'Avignon*, that he was one of the closest observers of cubism, he lets us down time and again by telling us everything except what we need to know. There is a reason for these omissions. During the Spanish Civil War Salmon sided with Franco; and during

André Salmon, *c*.1900. Bibliothèque Nationale, Paris.

World War II he worked for a collaborationist newspaper. His memoirs —written between 1945 and 1955—have to be read in the light of his former friend's resentment and disapproval.[30] Where Picasso was concerned, Salmon had to tread very carefully indeed. He could not check facts and dates with him. The date of his first meeting with Picasso, for instance, is out by a year. Salmon says 1903; it actually took place early in October 1904, and was masterminded by Manolo. '*Yo te présente Salmon*,' Manolo said to Picasso (both spoke terrible French) as they entered the studio, '*en pleine époque bleue*.' Manolo had hoped that Salmon would be sufficiently impressed to write about the work. He was indeed overwhelmed, but no article came of the meeting. Salmon's first impression of Picasso is often quoted: the famous lock of hair falling over 'the black-currant eyes'; the blue mechanic's jacket worn over the white shirt, the fringed Spanish cummerbund wound tightly round the slim waist. On a Napoleon III *guéridon* stood an oil lamp which provided the large studio with a modicum of light. When Picasso showed Salmon his paintings, he was obliged to hold up a candle, which threw a faint glimmer onto 'the suprareal world of the *misère bleue*.' 'What didn't we discuss that night?' Salmon tantalizes us with this question that he does not—out of forgetfulness or fear—attempt to answer. 'We didn't break up until dawn, and then only to see each other again almost immediately.'[31] Salmon soon moved into the Bateau Lavoir, and for the next two or three years Picasso would see more of him than of any other friend.

Salmon was three weeks older than Picasso. Although born in Paris, he had grown up in St Petersburg, where his father worked as an engraver, making prints after old masters. Around the turn of the century the father had returned to Paris, leaving his son in Russia. For a year or two Salmon *fils* worked in a junior capacity at the French embassy in St Petersburg, before being called back for military service in France. That over, he embarked on a career as a poet and literary journalist. When he met Picasso, he was already working on Apollinaire's short-lived magazine *Le Festin d'Esope* and writing for the humorous journal *L'Assiette au Beurre*. In 1906 he published a book of thirty-two symbolist poems with a frontispiece of *Two Saltimbanques* by Picasso. The closeness of imagery between these poems and Rose period paintings is hardly surprising since the poet and painter had become such near neighbours.[32] The poems were dedicated to Mallarmé, Moréas and Jacob, as well as Picasso, and were published by *Vers et Prose*, Paul Fort's new magazine, of which Salmon was editorial secretary. *Vers et Prose* planned to give a last chance to the new generation of symbolist writers. The first number came out in March 1905; it included contributions by Gide, Maeterlinck, Verhaeren and Henri de Régnier among others. Later the same year it published Apollinaire's great poem, '*L'Emigrant de Landor Road*'; and in 1906 a chapter of Jarry's autobiographical novel *La Dragonne*. Its stylistic diversity reflects the breakup of the symbolist movement into new constellations.

Paul Fort in his apartment with issues of *Vers et Prose* stacked behind him. Jeanne Fort-Severini collection.

When he met Picasso, Salmon was the epitome of a romantic young poet: tall, lantern-jawed, saturnine, often garbed in a 'carrick'—one of those all-enveloping overcoats with tiers of capes favoured by English coachmen. By all accounts he was a charming man, loved and admired by Picasso and, above all, Apollinaire, who wrote a delightful epithalamium in a bus on his way to Salmon's wedding (July 13, 1909—hence the line 'Paris is decked with bunting because . . . my friend André Salmon is being married'[33]). Apollinaire thought very highly of Salmon and collaborated with him on three plays, none of which ever came to anything. Too much of his brilliance evaporated in talk, as Fernande recalls:

> The more scabrous the story, the more exquisitely was it told. Unlike his friends Guillaume Apollinaire and Max Jacob, Salmon got his effects through a kind of wit which was delicate, as a poet he was perhaps more sentimental than the others. A dreamer with an alert sensibility, he was tall, thin, distinguished, with intelligent eyes in a very pale face, and he looked very young. Nor has he changed since then. His long fine hands held the wooden pipe, which he always smoked, in a way which was characteristically his. His gestures were a little gauche and clumsy: a mark of his shyness.[34]

Gertrude Stein is less enthusiastic: 'Salmon was very lithe and alive, but Gertrude Stein never found him particularly interesting'[35] (her feelings were reciprocated). The writing that Apollinaire praised for its 'languorous elegance' would not have pleased her, even if she had bothered to read it. It is everything she dislikes: quirkish, aphoristic, dandified, 'truffled' (Apollinaire's word) with pungent asides and passages of mandarin virtuosity. How deftly Salmon captures those eye- and mind-fooling visions that shine so brightly in the dark night of drugs but usually evaporate when exposed to the harsh light of morning. Later, it is true, Salmon's imagination would burn out, his style tarnish; and Cocteau would appropriate not only his poppy fields but his concept of *Le Secret professionel*, title and all. In the *exalté* atmosphere of the Bateau Lavoir, however, his writing flourished. And if drugs played an increasingly important role in the activities of the *bande à Picasso*, it was thanks to Salmon as much as Jacob.

Then, as now, drugs were a way of life. Ether, excessive use of which hastened Alfred Jarry's death, could be legally bought at any pharmacy for thirty centimes a dram. Jacob was likewise so addicted to this drug that he was obliged to conceal the smell by burning incense in his Bateau Lavoir studio. This made matters worse. In the belief that the combination of incense and ether could only signify a Black Mass, neighbourhood gossips attributed the poet's visions of Christ and the Virgin Mary to Satanic practices. Above all there was opium. There were several *fumeries* in Montmartre. Picasso is said to have frequented the fake 'Baron' Pigeard's. This painter, yachtsman and boat-builder had founded the Union Marine de la Butte Montmartre, which included such an improbable mariner as Max Jacob. Members were taught sea shanties, swimming (*à sec*, on camp stools), how to chew tobacco and spit straight. But what Pigeard most liked was to introduce his friends to opium. At night his studio became Montmartre's leading opium den. There was also one that Modigliani, already a hashish addict when he settled in Montmartre in 1906, used to attend. It was organized by his patron, Dr Paul Alexandre. A firm believer in the power of opium and hashish to stimulate the imagination, Dr Alexandre had set up an artists' commune in a tumbledown *pavillon* on the rue du Delta. Whether or not Picasso attended Dr Alexandre's parties we do not know. He was certainly acquainted with the doctor, who was one of the first Montmartrois to buy a major painting

Picasso. *The Artist Smoking a Pipe,* Paris, 1904. Pencil on paper, 20.9×13.1 cm. National Museum, Stockholm. Inscribed to Max Jacob.

by him: the Gauguin-esque *Greedy Child* in the National Gallery, Washington (see illustration, p.214). And Picasso could hardly avoid seeing his protégé, Modigliani, when he lived at the Hôtel du Poirier on the Place Ravignan and briefly rented a Bateau Lavoir studio in 1906. Moreover, Modigliani was the first painter of note to fall under Picasso's influence. To an admirer of one of his early portraits (it depicted a young actress who recited poetry at the Lapin Agile) Modigliani replied: 'It's nothing of the sort! It's still a Picasso, but a failed one. Picasso would put his foot through a daub like that.'[36] Despite Modigliani's admiration, Picasso kept aloof from him: when drugged or drunk he was a menace. However, Max Jacob and Apollinaire became his close friends; likewise Salmon, who wrote the book (1926) about Modigliani that created the legend of the *peintre maudit* whose genius was liberated by drugs.

In the '*Nuit d'opium*' section of *Le Manuscrit trouvé dans un chapeau* Salmon evokes the drowsy, erotic atmosphere of these trips to *paradis artificiels*—trips that inspired Picasso, years later, to confess that opium had 'the most intelligent of smells'. Salmon could be describing an evening at Pigeard's or Alexandre's, or chez Paulette, whose opium-clouded gatherings on the rue de Douai he and Apollinaire attended. Hopping over the recumbent guests like an acrobatic dancer, a man in a crimson dressing-gown serves tea, while a thin blonde in black silk stockings and a faded kimono twiddles the 'pellet of poison' over a lamp; her lover, 'a pretty sailor' given to cracking his joints, enumerates the enchantments of an endless voyage: '*Aden . . . Djibouti . . . La Barbade . . . Ceylan. . . Marseille . . . Singapoor . . . O'Thaïti . . . la mer intérieure! . .*'[37] And then the sailor grabs the blonde in a wrestler's grip. The scene reminds Salmon of an alchemist's hideaway, a witches' coven, a gypsy encampment—terrain towards which Picasso was edging.

Fernande's memoirs describe a similar evening at the Bateau Lavoir; Salmon was a permanent fixture:

> Picasso and his friends had got to know a couple of opium smokers [presumably Pigeard and a girlfriend] at the Closerie. Always intrigued by novelty, [he] tried the drug: the first time he smoked was at this couple's house, later on they came to his studio. He got hold of the little lamp and the marvellous amber-coloured bamboo pipe with the penetrating smell, and twice or three times a week, for a period of some months [four years, as Fernande admits in her posthumous *Souvenirs*], he would experience that wonderful oblivion, when all sense of time and of oneself is lost.
>
> Friends—the number varied, but there were always some—would sit on straw mats and spend many delightful hours in an atmosphere of heightened intelligence and subtlety. There would be cold lemon tea, conversation and delicious contentment. Everything seemed to take on a special beauty and nobility; we felt affection for all mankind in that skilfully muted light from the big oil lamp, the only light in the house. Sometimes, if the light went out, there was only the flicker of the opium lamp to shed its furtive rays on a few tired faces. . . . The nights would slip away in a warm, close intimacy, stripped of all suspect emotions and desires. There would be discussions on painting and literature, which seemed to be coloured by a new and rarefied sensitivity.
>
> Friendship would lower its guard, grow tender and indulgent. When we woke up the next day this communion was forgotten, and quarrels and bickering started up again. There never was a group of artists more given to mockery and the unkind and intentionally wounding word.[38]

Picasso. *Head of Fernande.* Paris, 1905. 1905. Engraving, 16.3×11.9 cm. Musée Picasso, Paris.

Wiegels (left) drawing Jules Pascin on the terrace of the Café du Dôme, *c.*1906.

Pascin. Caricature of Wiegels. *c.*1906. Whereabouts unknown.

For Picasso and Fernande these evenings would eventually come to an abrupt end, but not until June 1908, when the bizarre young German painter G. Wiegels, who had moved into the Bateau Lavoir in 1905 or 1906, committed suicide. Hitherto Wiegels has been a man of mystery. Picasso was too traumatized by his suicide—for which he was unfairly blamed—to want to discuss him. Even Fernande is ambivalent: 'This unhappy little painter of strange habits and equivocal appearance—a smooth, bald head, a young face with the tough, over-accentuated features of a Prussian, and a hard penetrating expression . . . turned out to be a person of great gentleness, with a delicate and appealing sensibility, [but] he was rather too highly strung.'[39] 'Highly strung' is a euphemism for homosexual. The only known photograph of Wiegels portrays a dandified young man in a curly-brimmed bowler doing a drawing of Pascin on the terrace of the Dôme.[40] The only known portrait of him—a drawing by Pascin—is even more revealing: an elf-like figure with a doll, dressed in a skirt (or kilt?), a redingote and the inevitable bowler. Further corroboration of Wiegel's sexual orientation comes from Hans Purrmann (one of Matisse's gifted German pupils). He devotes a chapter of his memoirs to Rudolf Levy, who also studied under Matisse. Levy 'was always accompanied by a devoted and admiring young man. One of these was Wiegels from Düsseldorf, with whom Levy shared a studio near the Place Clichy in Montmartre.'[41]

Poor Wiegels! His mother and a group of art-loving ladies from Düsseldorf had clubbed together to finance his studies in Paris. But instead of fulfilling his promise, he succumbed to drugs and rapidly went to pieces. Wiegels's self-destructive, childlike charm endeared him to the more motherly girls of the Butte, also to other homosexuals, such as his compatriot Wilhelm Uhde, who introduced him to Picasso. The chemistry worked. Wiegels's slavish capacity for hero worship, his sexual problems and inadequate gifts, must have been all too fatally reminiscent of Casagemas. When his roommate, Levy, left Montmartre for Montparnasse and set himself up as the leading light of the expatriate Germans at the Dôme, Wiegels was encouraged by Picasso to move into the Bateau Lavoir. With his bald, or more likely shaven, pate, this eager victim is a likely source for the attenuated skinheads and androgynes who haunt the wastelands of the Rose period.

Henceforth Wiegels would play a curiously evanescent role in Bateau Lavoir life. 'In his ingenuous way he attached himself to us,' Salmon says.[42] Besides being taken up by Picasso, he had 'the redoubtable luck of getting to know Matisse, Braque, Derain, Jacob and Apollinaire . . . but he never became part of our society. None of us indoctrinated him. He looked and listened without ever understanding anything, except that he managed to convince himself that his professors in Munich had led him astray, that he was not on the right track.' Salmon also confesses to 'having often wondered whether we were not all partly responsible for Wiegels's suicide.'[43] Indeed, this is how some of the young man's fellow expatriates, rightly or wrongly, would perceive the *bande à Picasso*. In the Café Dôme Picasso was thought to have been a Svengali, who mesmerized Wiegels into abandoning the timid impressionism that he originally favoured for Picassoism. But if *The Bathers*—one of this artist's few known works—is any guide, this accusation is as unfounded as the

Above: Picasso. *Sheet of caricatures:* including Apollinaire (bottom, second from left smoking cigar), Fort (below eagle's head), Moréas (to the right of Fort and again above), Salmon (below the larger head of Moréas), Fernande (below Moréas), Henri Delormel (bottom left, wearing collar) and others. Paris, 1905. Pen, sepia and pencil on paper, 25.5×32.7 cm. Musée Picasso, Paris.

Right: G. Wiegels. *The Bathers.* 1906. Oil on canvas. Formerly Municipal Collections, Düsseldorf.

story that Picasso caused Wiegels's suicide by telling him his painting was so bad that suicide would be his only option. Purrmann repeats this story, but only to contradict it. Drugs were entirely to blame, he says. Shortly before killing himself, Wiegels complained to friends of hallucinations: he was convinced he had turned into 'a horse on the street or some kind of animal'.[44] This and constant threats of suicide induced Manolo to move into his studio and watch over him. As soon as Manolo's back was turned, Wiegels took a massive dose of opium, ether or hashish (accounts differ) and hanged himself. He left a note for his mother and the Düsseldorf ladies, who had shown such faith in him, saying that he had been unworthy of their charity. He was killing himself, he claimed, because he had spent the last instalments of their bounty on that classic alibi for compromising situations, '*filles de joie*'.[45] Salmon confirms that there was nothing to this story. Pennilessness was endemic at the Bateau Lavoir; so 'these tiresome problems could always be settled in our little republic'. What *is* true is that the suicide was discovered the following morning by the postman who had come to deliver a money order from Germany. He gave the alarm, whereupon Picasso, who was painting a full-length nude on a cupboard door, rushed to Wiegels's studio and found his body hanging in the window.[46]

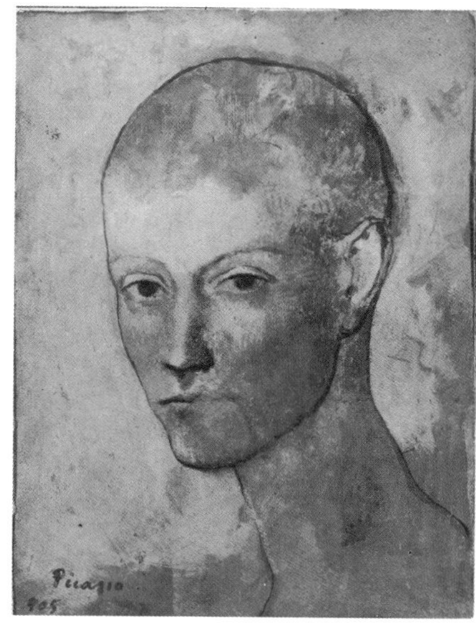

Picasso. *Head of a Boy.* Paris, 1905. Gouache on cardboard, 31×24cm. The Cleveland Museum of Art, Gift of Leonard C. Hanna, Jr.

Such was the shock of Wiegels's death, Fernande tells us, that 'nobody ever smoked a single pipe of opium again'.[47] By 'nobody' she means herself and Picasso, who went into shock after seeing the body. Salmon, Jacob and other members of the group continued to indulge. At Wiegels's tatterdemalion funeral—more like a fancy dress ball, according to Dorgelès[48]—the painter Denèfle shared an open carriage with a girl in a scarlet dress who had ingested far too much hashish. Under the illusion that this was Mardi Gras or her wedding procession, she scandalized the onlookers by blowing kisses and pelting them with funeral flowers. If the coachman had not whipped up the horses, the entire cortège would have been arrested.

* * *

In later years Picasso did not like to be questioned about drugs,[49] least of all about their relevance to developments in his work. However, on March 14, 1953, he unburdened himself to Cocteau. 'Yesterday Picasso talked about opium,' he noted in his diary, 'he says that "apart from the wheel it is man's only discovery". He regrets that one cannot smoke freely and asks if I still smoke. I tell him that I don't and regret this as much as he does. "Opium", he adds, "promotes benevolence, witness the smoker's lack of greed. He wants everyone else to smoke."'[50] Between the summer of 1904, when Picasso met Fernande, and the summer of 1908, when Wiegels died, drugs cannot be left out of account. The more one studies the evidence, the more one realizes that they played more of a role at the Bateau Lavoir than is usually thought. For most of his years there, Picasso, his mistress and closest friends—Jacob, Salmon, the mathematician Princet, Mollet and on occasion Apollinaire—were all opium smokers (Jacob, Wiegels, MacOrlan and others in the *bande à Picasso* also experimented with ether, hashish and morphine). Besides facilitating the conquest of Fernande, opium flavours the themes and the mood of many late Blue and early Rose period works; and it may well have engendered some of the hallucinatory frenzy of *Les Demoiselles d'Avignon*. We should, however, be wary of overemphasizing its importance. Picasso regarded his work as sacrosanct and always kept his physical and mental energies tuned to the highest pitch. Work, sex and tobacco were his only addictions. *Le dérèglement de tous les sens* was fine for a *peintre* or *poète maudit*—for Modigliani or Jarry, who could not function without powerful stimulants—not for him. Besides, according to Picasso, *poètes maudits* had to remain *poètes maudits*; if they reformed they were no longer any good. For Picasso such a prospect was unthinkable.

As to how drugs affected Picasso, Fernande is our only witness: 'At a time when we were eager to experience new and different sensations . . . we had gathered at Princet's . . . taking hashish, Princet, Max, Apollinaire and Picasso expanded in ways which revealed a great deal about them.'[51] Princet simply wept about his wife, who had just left him; Apollinaire shouted with delight and fantasized that he was in a brothel; Max Jacob, an old hand at these experiences, sat in a corner beatifically happy, while Picasso, in a state of nervous ecstasy, hallucinated that he had invented photography and might as well kill himself as he had nothing left to learn. 'He appeared to have had a revelation [Fernande writes] that one day he would be prevented from developing. He would come to the end and find a wall which would impede all progress. No longer would he be able to learn, or discover, or understand, or penetrate little by little into the secrets of an art which he wanted to make new and fresh.'[52] Drugs threatened to make things too easy.

Picasso. *Two Saltimbanques*. Paris, March 1905. Drypoint, 12.2×9.1 cm. Private collection. Used as the frontispiece to Salmon's *Poèmes*, published in 1905.

Besides causing the drowsiness that pervades the watercolour of the artist contemplating the sleeping Fernande, opium could also account for the inward, trancelike expression on the faces of the waifs that Picasso portrayed wandering catatonically about the wastelands of Montmartre, even on the faces of such icons of the Rose period as the *Boy with a Pipe* and the *Woman with a Fan* that date from the time when he was plying Fernande with opium. No wonder those two impenitent opium smokers Jean Cocteau and Christian Bérard drew on Picasso's *saltimbanques* for the physical types, those tough but androgynous roustabouts and sailors, that they launched on the fashionable world in the 1920s. These figments of *opiomane* fantasy reflect a ray of smoky light back onto the works that inspired them. The languid magic and beauty of Picasso's work between 1904 and 1906 may stem from symbolist poets and painters, but the callowness and lack of psychic tension that afflicts the more Wiegels-like of the *saltimbanques* can be attributed, at least in part, to the 'black blood of the poppy'.

21

The Apollinaire Period

Picasso. *Apollinaire Smoking a Pipe.* Paris, 1905–06. Pen on paper, 16×11 cm. Private collection.

Opposite: Picasso. *Apollinaire as an Academician.* Paris, 1905. Pen, ink and wash on paper, 22×12 cm. Musée Picasso, Paris.

'YOU'VE HEARD OF LA FONTAINE AND Molière and Racine,' Max Jacob announced to the *bande à Picasso*, 'well now that's us.' The third of the new trio was of course Guillaume Apollinaire, who entered Picasso's life at the same time as Salmon. When and where did Picasso and Apollinaire actually meet? Salmon said 1903; Picasso 1904; Apollinaire and Max Jacob 1905. Picasso was right. Although a summer's evening is usually mentioned, the meeting occurred a few days before his twenty-third birthday (October 25, 1904) and the opening of a group show that included Picasso at Berthe Weill's gallery.[1] Salmon further confuses things when he claims in his memoirs to have been present at this momentous confrontation.[2] He was not; he was, however, present when Picasso introduced Max Jacob to Apollinaire a day or two later.[3] Further confirmation of the October date is the postcard that Jacob sent Salmon within hours of their first meeting. It includes two postscripts: one conveying greetings in Picasso's hand, the other confirming that the show would open the following Monday—'*à 2 1/2 précises*'.[4]

As to the exact location of the meeting, there are two possibilities: the Criterion or Austen's Railway Restaurant (more familiarly known as Fox's bar), both on the rue d'Amsterdam, a short distance from the Gare Saint-Lazare; both home to Apollinaire, who as yet had no apartment of his own; both English-owned. Years later, apropos the Englishness of Ionesco's play *The Bald Soprano*, Picasso rhapsodized about the Englishness of these bars: 'Picture to yourself an English bar. Everything was English. The proprietor and his wife were English. The bar was very long, made of very nice wood, perhaps mahogany, but English mahogany. The beer was English. . . . all the drinks were English.' And Picasso went on to evoke Apollinaire entering one of these dens of Englishness—'Ionesco's bar'—'with a woman wearing a hat big as an umbrella'.[5] He described how Apollinaire hung round these bars until he had summoned up enough Dutch courage to take the train back home to the rented villa in the suburb of Le Vesinet. There he would have to face his drunken virago of a mother, who lived with a younger lover and a macaque monkey and organized private gambling parties. 'Which one of you debauched the other?' she once asked Salmon when he accompanied Apollinaire home after a night on the town. She still treated her 'Wilhelm' as if he were an incorrigible child and would beat him, as she would her lover.

Both the Criterion and Fox's bar catered primarily to a racetrack crowd —touts, jockeys, grooms—from training establishments at Maisons Laffitte, a few stops down the line from the Gare Saint-Lazare. But they also attracted the *gens louches*, riffraff, who gravitate to railway stations, as well as writers with a penchant for local colour. The Criterion is where Huysmans ended his aborted trip to England;[6] also where Alphonse Allais, the humorist, would be found dead in 1905. Austen's, or Fox's bar, would later become celebrated as '*le rendez-vous des cubistes*'—as witness Braque's great engraving of a still life (1911) with the word 'FOX' inscribed on a mirror, window or wall in the background. Since these two 'English' bars were virtually interchangeable, Apollinaire, who considered himself a connoisseur of such places, would have taken his guests to both; it hardly matters which he chose for the initial drink. In retrospect Mollet plumped for Fox's, Apollinaire for the Criterion.[7]

George Bottini. *Bar anglais, avenue de la Grande-Armée.* 1902. Whereabouts unknown.

On Apollinaire's side, the credit for setting up this momentous meeting belongs primarily to the legendary 'Baron' Jean Mollet—the poet's secretary, one might say his Figaro. A former pupil of the Jesuits at Amiens, Mollet had been so captivated when he heard Apollinaire recite his poems at the April 25, 1903, Soirée de la Plume (a Saturday-night function at which young writers could present their work), and Apollinaire had been so taken with Mollet's idiosyncratic wit and style that they became instant friends. Apollinaire had dubbed him 'Baron' and set him and André Salmon to work for his magazine *Le Festin d'Esope*. Later, when Apollinaire was able to afford a place of his own, Mollet would take time off from his brother-in-law's electroplating business to look after the poet's apartment. He would do the shopping, polish the furniture and floors —always impeccably monocled and dressed in gleaming yellow gloves. Mollet sometimes fixed Apollinaire up with girls: one was the accommodating Paulette, who dispensed opium on the rue de Douai. He also rounded up interesting new talent for him. A rare find had been the mischievous Manolo, but rarer by far were the two men that Manolo now produced: Picasso and Max Jacob. They would be much to Apollinaire's taste, Mollet realized; and at the earliest opportunity he escorted the artist down from the heights of Montmartre and served him up to the poet, as a chef might serve up the first truffle of the season. At this point Mollet usually vanishes from Picasso's biographies, but in fact he became a valued member of the *bande à Picasso* and forty years later would still be a regular visitor to the studio.

Maurice Raynal. *Portrait of Jean Mollet.* 1913. Pen on paper. Private collection.

In an article written in 1947 Mollet recalled that on the occasion of the famous meeting with Picasso on the rue Amsterdam in October 1904, Apollinaire 'was in the company of a short, fat, red-haired Englishman (said to have been a Mr Frip) flanked by two black women whose eye-catching outfits and gigantic plumed hats intrigued Picasso. Without interrupting his discourse on the relative merits of English and German beers, Apollinaire gave the new arrivals a knowing wink.'[8] Mollet's instincts had been right; Apollinaire and Picasso immediately became fast friends; and in the years to come they would serve as each other's catalyst to an extent unparalleled in the history of art and literature. A few days later, as Picasso was about to take Max Jacob to meet his new friend at Austen's bar, Salmon appeared at the Bateau Lavoir. He had not as yet met Jacob. So he, too, came along—a fact that Jacob overlooks in his account of the meeting:

> Apollinaire was smoking a short-stemmed pipe and expatiating on Petronius and Nero to some rather vulgar-looking people . . . jobbers . . . or travelling salesmen. He was wearing a stained, light-coloured suit, and a tiny straw hat was perched atop his famous pear-shaped head. He had hazel eyes, terrible and gleaming, a bit of curly blond hair fell over his forehead, his mouth looked like a small pimento, he had strong limbs, a broad chest looped across by a platinum watch-chain, and a ruby on his finger. The poor boy was always being taken for a rich man because his mother—an adventuress, to put it politely—clothed him from head to toe. She never gave him anything else. He was a clerk in a bank on the rue Lepeletier. Without interrupting his talk he stretched out a hand that was like a tiger's paw over the marble-topped table. He stayed in his seat until he was finished. Then the three of us went out, and we began that life of three-cornered friendship which lasted almost until the war never leaving one another whether for work, meals or fun.[9]

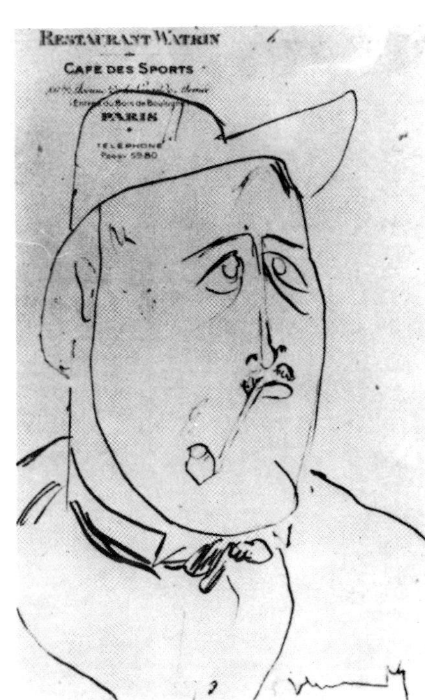

Vlaminck. *Portrait of Apollinaire.* 1905. Pen on paper. Private collection.

Apollinaire's experience of contemporary art had hitherto been limited to a few convivial meetings with the Fauve painters Derain and Vlaminck, who lived near his mother. However, he was a voracious learner, and thanks to the guidance of Picasso as well as Max Jacob, he soon became a leading pundit, and later an erratic apologist for cubism, futurism, not to speak of other lesser movements. Picasso had exhausted Max Jacob's repertory of literary vaudeville; he was all too familiar with his curiosity shop of a mind; and he was finding Jacob's adoration—'You are what I love most in the world after God and the saints,' Jacob once told Picasso[10] —an obstacle to friendship. He needed another brilliant poet to cannibalize, someone preferably of the same sexual orientation. And in Apollinaire, who was as iconoclastic as himself, Picasso found the ideal counterpart. Despite differences of temperament—Apollinaire was more urbane, more of an operator—there were many parallels between the two of them. Both had reached a comparable stage in their development: both were in the throes of extricating themselves from a love-hate dependence on symbolism; both were out to destroy old canons and establish new ones. Both were secretive, generous with everything except money and protean to the point of genius (a point just short of madness). Both could be tender and charming, but on occasion cutting and cruel—devotees of the Marquis de Sade as well as Nietzsche. Both were innately polymorphous, not just in libido but in style, taste, ideology. Both revelled in the dark side of their natures and would exploit this in their work. Both came of families that had achieved distinction in the Church, and although they claimed to have lost their faith, Catholicism left its stamp on their lives. And just as both were sometimes tempted to identify with Christ, both were sometimes tempted to identify with the devil.

* * *

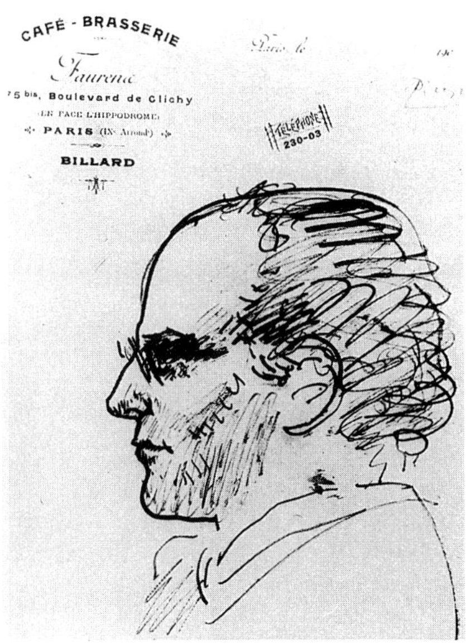

Picasso. *Portrait of Max Jacob.* Paris, 1904–05. Pen on paper, 25.8×20.8cm. Private collection.

Picasso was always fascinated by the mystery surrounding Apollinaire's birth; he even went so far as to spread the story that he was the illegitimate son of a bishop, citing his ecclesiastical mien as evidence. The poet was indeed born out of wedlock in Rome (baptismal name: Wilhelm Albert Wladimir Alexandre Apollinaire de Kostrowitzky), on August 26, 1880. His mother, Angelica de Kostrowitzky, was the daughter of a minor

Angelica (Olga) de Kostrowitzky. Private collection.

member of the Polish nobility who had settled in Rome and become a papal chamberlain. She was a wilful and attractive child who grew into a wilful and attractive woman, notorious for flying into rages and swearing like a whore in several languages. The identity of Apollinaire's father is not known for certain, but he was probably Francesco Flugi d'Aspermont, born in 1835 to a noble family from St Moritz.[11] After serving on the staff of the last King of the Two Sicilies, the good-looking Francesco wandered Europe, womanizing and running up gambling debts, but usually returning to Rome, where his eldest brother was head of the Black Benedictines. During one of his Roman sojourns Francesco took up with Angelica. Marriage with such a woman was out of the question, so for the next few years the two of them gambled their way from one casino to another. The birth of Guillaume and a younger brother, Albert, made little difference to their way of life. The children were farmed out.

Regardless of its credibility, another, rather more romantic, version of the poet's birth deserves consideration—one that was known to Apollinaire and encouraged him in certain fantasies. Early in the nineteenth century a member of a collateral branch of Angelica's family, Melanie de Kostrowitzky, had gone to live in Vienna, where she supposedly had a son by Napoleon's heir, the *roi de Rome*, known as L'Aiglon (the eaglet). This boy had been entrusted to the care of Vatican prelates, through whom he eventually met his beautiful cousin Angelica. He slept with her and supposedly fathered Guillaume, who would thus have been Napoleon's great-grandson. Support for this far-fetched thesis takes the form of a horror story, '*La Chasse à l'Aigle*' (incorporated in *Le Poète assassiné*), which tells how an old man—an illegitimate son of L'Aiglon, condemned for reasons of state to wear the mask of an eagle—escapes from the palace of Schönbrunn. Before the eyes of the Apollinaire-like narrator, the creature is pursued, unmasked and killed by guards. This vengeful fantasy of an illegitimate son about an illegitimate father of royal birth whom he watches being unmasked and killed may not have much bearing on the poet's paternity, but, like the stories that Picasso came to believe about himself and his father, it casts light on the way family legends can colour a creative imagination. Apollinaire appears to have agreed with Picasso: 'In art one has to kill one's father.'

Picasso. *Apollinaire as a Pope*. Paris, 1905. Pen on paper. Private collection.

Apollinaire was brought up by his disreputable mother in Monte Carlo, where he attended the Collège Saint Charles. Like Picasso, he underwent a brief phase of adolescent devoutness, followed by a loss of faith, followed (some years later) by sacrilegious exploitation of his former piety. Again like the adolescent Picasso, Apollinaire wrote, drew and edited his own newspapers, *Le Vengeur* and *Le Transigeant*, but compared with the childish ones Picasso had produced a year or two earlier, Guillaume's are infinitely precocious —'anarcho-symbolist', he claimed, and filled with the latest literary and social gossip. Apollinaire's first poems are signed 'Guillaume Macabre'. One of them, '*Mardi Gras*' (1898–99), looks ahead to the imagery of the Rose period—a period that would in some respects be a joint venture with Picasso. This poem evokes the carnival at Nice, but its 'pierrots wreathed in roses / pale ghosts who prowl at night', its 'Harlequins, Columbines and Punchinellos with crooked noses' flitting through deserted streets, will soon be flitting in and out of Picasso's compositions.

Apollinaire was nineteen when he wrote '*Mardi Gras*'; the same year that his mother (now known as Olga) and her lover, a professional gambler called Jules Weil, were obliged by the authorities to leave Monte Carlo. They next tried their luck in Belgium. But Olga's reputation as an *entraineuse* (a woman who earns commission on the money she persuades men to spend in restaurants and nightclubs) was such that she was refused admission to the casinos of Spa and Ostend. So she and Weil moved on, leaving her two sons masquerading as 'young Russian counts' in a pension at Stavelot in the Ardennes. His charm and courtesy ensured the penniless Guillaume infinite credit. He spent the next three months rambling over the peat bogs of the Fagne, courting a local girl, communing with elves and filling notebooks with ideas that ended up as his Arthurian hotchpotch, *L'Enchanteur pourrissant. Le Poète assassiné* (finally published in 1916), which opens with a poet's conception on a road two leagues from Spa, was likewise begun at this time. At Stavelot he developed an obsession with medieval legend and magic rituals; he took to signing his poems with a cabalistic swastika. His most prized possession was a mildewed book on demonology, from which he read aloud as if already a magus. In later years Apollinaire would continue to draw on his knowledge of magic and ritual, as would Max Jacob. Strange that the two poets who were closest to Picasso and exerted the greatest influence on his early development—Apollinaire and Jacob—should both have seen themselves as magi.

Apollinaire, *c*.1899. Private collection.

When the brothers finally heard from their mother, she sent them just enough money for train fares. To avoid paying the rent they owed, she told them to '*filer à la cloche du bois*', make a midnight escape and join her in Paris. Guillaume and Albert were easily traced and hauled into court for bilking the Belgian pension. On grounds of poverty, Olga got the case dismissed. Guillaume would have liked to spend his time writing, or roaming the streets and educating himself in libraries and bookshops, but his mother made him work as a post clerk. The poems he wrote in his spare time and submitted to the *Revue Blanche* and other magazines were never accepted; so he was reduced to hiring himself out as a ghost, or drawing on his already extensive knowledge of eighteenth-century erotica and becoming a hack pornographer—an apprenticeship that later stood him in good stead. His life finally improved in August 1901, when Kostro, as his friends then called him, was engaged to tutor the daughter of the German heiress Elinor, Vicomtesse de Milhau. While working for her in Germany, he fell unhappily in love with a genteel English governess, Annie Playden. *Chagrin d'amour* inspired the poem '*La Chanson du mal aimé*', which would establish him once and for all as a great poet. Kahnweiler, who never ceased to denounce Apollinaire's art criticism, came to admire '*La Chanson du mal aimé*' so fervently that he and his wife learned it by heart.[12] Picasso would identify more closely with Apollinaire's later masterpiece '*Zone*' (1912), particularly its last lines, which allude to his exploitation of tribal gods as opposed to Christian ones:

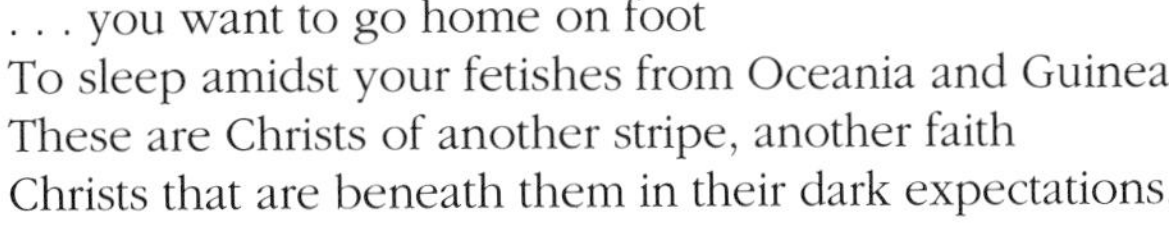
. . . you want to go home on foot
To sleep amidst your fetishes from Oceania and Guinea
These are Christs of another stripe, another faith
Christs that are beneath them in their dark expectations.

On his return to Paris in 1902, Apollinaire's incessant bombardment of little reviews with samples of his verse and prose was finally rewarded. He even achieved his ambition of appearing in the *Revue Blanche*. But it was not until Paul-Napoléon Roinard—a minor poet on the fringes of symbolism, but a shrewd judge of writing—brought his work to the notice of *La Plume* that Apollinaire's perseverance paid off. At the historic Soirée de la Plume (April 25, 1903) he suddenly emerged in the forefront of the avant garde. These soirées, formerly presided over by Verlaine, '*prince des poètes*', in a haze of absinthe, had originated in 1889, when the magazine of the same name (the inspiration of the Quatre Gats' *Pèl & Ploma*) had been founded. By the time Verlaine died, in 1896, they had petered out. But they were revived in 1902 by Karl Boes, the new editor of *La Plume*, in the same premises: a cellar on the Place Saint Michel, once called the Café de l'Avenir, then Soleil d'Or, and now Café du Départ—an unwelcoming name, Apollinaire said, designed to hasten you on your way. Salmon, who made his debut that same night, describes Apollinaire, with 'a wisp of moustache half hiding an almost feminine pout',[13] leaning against the piano in front of an absurd moonlit backdrop. He declaimed some of the Rhenish poems he had written in Germany, ending with '*Schinderhannes*', a ballad about a highwayman and his hiccupping followers. 'Tonight I must hie myself to the Rhine / To find a rich Jew to murder . . . ' Apollinaire bellowed this out to considerable applause. A new luminary was born. Jean Mollet and André Salmon rushed up to congratulate him and became instant disciples. Karl Boes insisted he contribute to *La Plume*; Apollinaire's long symbolist poem '*Le Larron*' ('The Thief'), with its poignant autobiographical line '*Ton père fut un sphinx et ta mère une nuit*', was accepted for the August issue of the magazine.

A few Saturdays later, Apollinaire met Alfred Jarry, whose iconoclastic ideas would soon exert a formative influence on him and later, through him, on Picasso. Over numerous glasses of stout, the two poets discovered a great deal of common ground in each other's manic fantasy, anarchic wit and taste for the absurd. Jarry recited some of his poems 'with their metallic ring', and after watching some of their friends do a cakewalk so frenetic that the girls' hair came unpinned, they spent the rest of the night pacing the streets of Saint-Germain-des-Près. At one point, Jarry pointed his revolver—the famous revolver that would become Picasso's talisman—at a passer-by who had the presumption to ask the way. They mostly complained about the increasing stagnation of the soirées. And it is from this night that their revolt against the old guard of the symbolists began to gather force; so did their friendship. Apollinaire embarked on a Jarry-esque pastiche, '*Le Jim-Jim des Capussins*', which has not survived. (At the same time Max Jacob started his Jarry-esque novel, *Le Phanérogame*, 1903–07, about an American who propels himself through the air by rotating his thighs, and who ends up in a lunatic asylum for 'advanced degenerates'—i.e. poets and painters.)[14] At Jarry's instigation, Apollinaire played a variety of tricks on the adherents of *La Plume* (dressing up like a tramp, foisting spoof guests on their meetings), but the more he struggled to escape the tendrils of symbolism, the more they clung. He was not alone in this dilemma. When the *Revue Blanche*—the most prestigious of contemporary magazines—collapsed in 1903, Apollinaire saw his chance and launched *Le Festin d'Esope*, a magazine

F. A. Cazals. *Alfred Jarry*. December 1897. Lithograph. Bibliothèque Nationale, Paris.

Picasso. *Apollinaire*. Paris, *c.*1905. Pencil on paper. Whereabouts unknown.

that would capitalize on the crosscurrents churned up in the wake of symbolism. Although he had a full-time job bringing out a dubious new financial journal, *Le Guide du Rentier: Moniteur des petits capitalistes*, for a dubious new banker called Meunier (whose forehead had been badly scarred by a bullet fired at point-blank range by an indignant client), Apollinaire contrived to be an attentive as well as imaginative editor of *Le Festin*. He insisted that the magazine should not cater to this or that coterie or reader. To this end he published writers of the most divergent views. Apollinaire was seconded by Mollet as business manager; Salmon was secretary and landlord (his small apartment overlooking the Lapin Agile constituted the office); Jarry acted as subversive muse.

In its handsome brick-red cover *Le Festin* prospered—at least at first. Apollinaire was good at drumming up advertising (he even sold space to boys' magazines like *The School-Fellow* and *Der Schulfreund*). But 'his aim was to have no aim',[15] and the magazine failed in the summer of 1904, as much for lack of focus as for lack of funds. As Salmon said, it took the same time to die as a man takes to be born. Apart from an act of Jarry's comic operetta, *L'Objet aimé*, most of the best things in *Le Festin d'Esope* were written by the editor: notably first drafts of numerous poems and his gossipy *Notes du mois*, and questionable stockmarket tips signed 'Fortunio'. In presenting so much of his verse and prose to the public, the magazine launched Apollinaire as a poet, also as an editor and a budding impresario. When Apollinaire first met Picasso, he was already planning another magazine, *La Revue immoraliste*, which lasted only one issue, but this included Apollinaire's review of the artist's 1905 show. Next came *Les Lettres modernes*, which was no more successful: one issue appeared. Seven more years would pass before Apollinaire became editor of a review that was worthy of him, *Soirées de Paris* (1912). But even this defiantly avant-garde publication lasted a mere two years—closed down after twenty-seven issues by the war. If *Soirées de Paris* had such an impact on cultural history, it was because Picasso and his followers had provided Apollinaire with a platform from which the poet could rally recruits to whatever new movement in art or letters had taken his erratic fancy.

* * *

Reassured by the whiff of brimstone and brilliance they detected in each other, Picasso and Apollinaire became the best of friends. Henceforth Apollinaire would abandon his old haunts on the rue d'Amsterdam, abandon his *bande à Guillaume* and take to climbing the hill to Montmartre, where he joined the *bande à Picasso*. And henceforth a blue chalk sign would hang on Picasso's studio door: RENDEZ-VOUS DES POÈTES. Salmon declared that the pen would defend and explain the canvas; and the brush would colour the poem. However, if Picasso's brush had had to rely on Salmon's, Apollinaire's or Jacob's pen, it would have acquired little in the way of lustre. There was nothing promotional about the '*rendez-vous des poètes*'; it was more in the nature of Picasso's 'think tank'. It enabled the artist to become vicariously a poet—a poet in paint, not yet a poet in words. Significantly, Picasso's first attempt at poetry consists of a few fumbled words in French[16] to thank Max Jacob for a drawing he had given him. If Picasso later became a poet—a considerable poet, as we can see now that his writings have been published—it is thanks as much to Max Jacob and Apollinaire as to the surrealists.

Until he died, fourteen years after they met, Apollinaire would be a constant solace, a constant goad to Picasso. He opened up his imagination to a vast new range of intellectual stimuli: to new concepts of black humour, to the pagan past and the wilder shores of sex. Apollinaire, who was already obsessed by the works of the Marquis de Sade—'the freest spirit that has ever existed', he wrote[17]—had no difficulty converting Picasso to the cult of the Divine Marquis, not just his pornography but his philosophy, his definition of art as 'the perpetual immoral subversion of the existing order'.[18] Apollinaire encouraged Picasso to exorcise the last vestiges of the blues and leaven his Andalusian *duende* with a transfusion of Parisian *vie en rose*. He encouraged him to picture himself in different roles: the self-dramatizing role of a *saltimbanque*, strolling player or circus performer, the picturesque outcast at odds with conventional society; or the more equivocal role of harlequin, the player of tricks that alarm and mystify as well as entertain. After a year or so of friendship, Apollinaire, who claimed to have learnt about magic from the elves of the Fagne, held a mirror, in the form of a poem, up to Picasso and showed him his reflection as Harlequin Trismegistus, a demonic magician. The poet knew the old Walloon legends about 'her-lequin'—a soul escaped from hell.

Apollinaire exerted an immeasurable influence on Picasso's imagination and intellect, but the only time he left any overt imprint on his subject matter was when they were both preoccupied with harlequins—that is to say, during the first eighteen months or so of their relationship. So similar is their imagery that it sometimes seems as if the painter and the poet had access to the same imagination. Indeed the Rose period (as the next eighteen months have come to be called) could as well be renamed the Apollinaire period. Although there is no evidence that any collaboration was envisaged, the series of thirteen engravings—mostly *saltimbanque* subjects—that Picasso began towards the end of 1904 look as if they were intended as illustrations to Apollinaire's poems of the period.[19] The *Salomé* drypoint echoes the mocking mood of Apollinaire's lines on the same subject: 'Weep not, pretty jester to the king / Take this head instead of cap and bells and dance.' Picasso gave Apollinaire a copy of the drypoint which the poet evokes in one of his first two articles on the artist's work: 'Fatherhood has transformed harlequin; his wife bathes in cold water and admires her figure, as frail and slim as that of her husband, the puppet.'[20] Even when Apollinaire later develops into a defiantly modern poet with his quasi-cubist techniques of '*découpage poétique*,' simultaneism and slogans taken from posters and newspapers, he continues to see the artist as Harlequin Trismegistus. The ghosts that crop up in the famous *Calligramme* portrait of the artist, '*Voyez ce peintre*' (1917), are familiar old friends from 1905: 'the acrobat on horseback the moustachioed poet a dead bird and so many tearless children.'

Picasso. *Salomé*. Paris, 1905. Drypoint, 40×34.8cm. Musée Picasso, Paris.

* * *

Left: Picasso. *The Saltimbanques*. Paris, 1905. Drypoint, 32.7×40.3cm. Musée Picasso, Paris.

Above: Picasso. *Mother Arranging Her Hair*. Paris, 1905. Etching, 23.5×17.6cm. Musée Picasso, Paris.

Right: Picasso. *The Bath*. Paris, 1905. Drypoint, 34.4×28.9cm. Musée Picasso, Paris.

For all the stimulus of a poet's imagery, Picasso's eye would also require the stimulus of a visual experience. This was very much the case with the *saltimbanques*. There had been a revival of interest in tumblers ever since the successful run of Louis Ganne's operetta, *Les Saltimbanques*, which opened at the Théâtre de la Gaité in December 1899. Picasso might well have seen this boisterous yet touching romance of circus life, but we cannot be sure. Asked about the origin of his *saltimbanques*, he was specific.[21] After visiting his family's friend Father Santol at his hostel for down-and-outs on the Avenue La Motte-Picquet (presumably in order to borrow or repay money), he was walking home through the Esplanade des Invalides when he came upon a troupe of acrobats. Whether they were performing or simply milling around between turns, as they are usually portrayed, he did not specify, but they stayed in his memory. Palau thinks this happened around Christmas 1904. But the summer is also likely; possibly around the *quatorze juillet*. This is the traditional time for street fairs to be set up in the city, as Apollinaire conflrms in '*Un fantôme de nuées*' ('A ghost of a cloud'), a poem written in 1909 but still redolent of Rose period imagery:

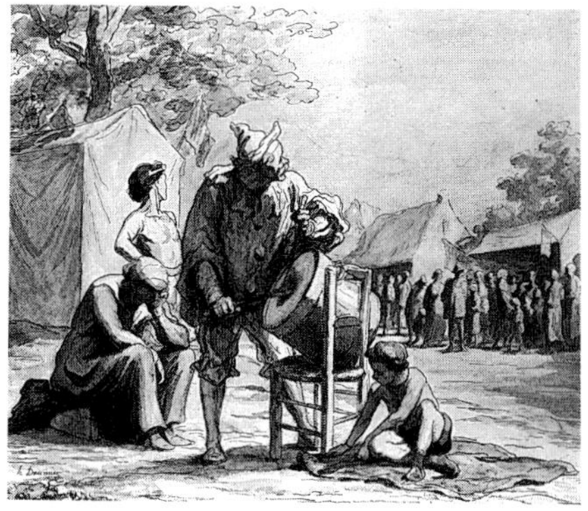

Above: Daumier. *Saltimbanques*. *c*.1855–60. Pen and watercolour, 33×40cm. Victoria and Albert Museum, London, Courtesy of the Board of Trustees.

> As it was the eve of the *quatorze juillet*
> Around four in the afternoon
> I went out in the street to watch the *saltimbanques*
>
> These folk who perform in the open air
> Are becoming rare in Paris
> In my youth one saw more of them than one does today
> They've almost all left for the provinces
>
> I took the boulevard Saint-Germain
> And on a little *place* between Saint-Germain-des-Près and the
> statue of Danton
> I found the *saltimbanques*
>
> . . .
>
> Dirty rugs were spread on the ground
> Rugs with creases that will never come out
> Rugs that are virtually the colour of dust
> With stains of yellow and green obdurate
> As a tune that sticks in one's head
>
> . . .
>
> The *saltimbanques* didn't make a move
> The oldest wore tights of that purplish pink one finds
> On the cheeks of certain fresh young girls close to death
>
> A pink that often nestles in dimples near the mouth
> Or around the nostrils
> A pink full of betrayal
>
> It was as if this man wore
> The livid colour of his lungs on his back . . .

Below: Edgar Chahine. *Weightlifting: Boulevard de Clichy* (detail). 1902. Etching, aquatint and drypoint, 16.5×45.5cm. Bibliothèque Nationale, Paris.

A description that Rainer Maria Rilke wrote (1907) of a family of strolling players in the Paris streets is also dated '*le quatorze juillet*'. Rilke, who would later base the fifth of his *Duino Elegies* on Picasso's *Saltimbanques*, had been following the activities of a specific troupe 'for at

Paula Modersohn-Becker. *Portrait of Rainer Maria Rilke.* 1904. Oil on cardboard, 34×26cm. Private collection.

least two years and probably longer'.[22] Since they could well have been the same acrobats that Picasso had seen on the Esplanade des Invalides, his words are worth quoting:

> In front of the Luxembourg Gardens, near the Panthéon, Père Rollin and his troupe have spread themselves out again. The same carpet is lying there, the same coats, thick winter overcoats, taken off and piled on top of a chair, leaving just enough room for the little boy, the old man's grandson, to come and sit down now and then between breaks. . . . But look, Père Rollin, who is so famous at the fairs, doesn't 'work' any more. He doesn't lift the huge weights any more, and though he was once the most eloquent of all, he says nothing now. He has been transferred to beating the drum. . . . But there, his daughter is speaking to him; quick-witted and strong, and with more brains than any of the others. She is the one who holds things together, it's a joy to see her in action. . . . '*Musique*,' she shouts. And the old man drums away like fourteen drummers. 'Père Rollin, hey Père Rollin,' calls one of the spectators, and steps right up, recognizing him. But the old man only incidentally nods in response; it is a point of honour, his drumming, and he takes it seriously.[23]

Ten years later Rilke's preoccupation with strolling players would develop into a fixation on Picasso's great *Saltimbanques* composition. Hertha Koenig, then owner of the painting, had lent Rilke the Munich apartment where it hung. As he sat day after day meditating on this canvas, which epitomized the Paris he loved and thus helped him to forget the war, Rilke embarked on one of his most engaging elegies. Just as Apollinaire draws on Picasso's vision and his own recollections for his *saltimbanque* poems, Rilke grafts his memories of Père Rollin and his troupe onto his reactions to Picasso's elegiac set piece. The result was the fifth of his *Duino Elegies*, the one that starts:

> But tell me, who *are* they, these wanderers, even more
> transient than we ourselves, who from their earliest days
> are savagely wrung out
> by a never-satisfied will (for *whose* sake)? Yet it wrings them,
> bends them, twists them, swings them and flings them
> and catches them again; and falling as if through oiled
> slippery air, they land
> on the threadbare carpet, worn constantly thinner
> by their perpetual leaping, this carpet that is lost
> in infinite space.[24]

Through Picasso's German friend Wilhelm Uhde, Rilke had met Picasso when he lived in Paris,[25] and he had seen through the picturesque sweetness of the Rose period to the coldness and alienation at its core.

The origin of the harlequins is more of a problem than that of the *saltimbanques*. Harlequins were virtually extinct, except in pantomimes, fancy-dress balls or Mardi Gras parades. They survived mostly in popular imagery. One possible source for the harlequin theme is suggested by the painting traditionally entitled *The Actor*: a tall, gaunt, white-faced figure dressed in a commedia dell'arte costume leaning out across the footlights at an unseen audience. At his feet two hands emerge from a prompter's box—a fixture in theatres and opera houses but an anomaly on the sort of stage used by strolling players. Although Picasso already knew a number of gifted actors—Harry Baur, Charles Dullin and Marcel

Picasso. *The Actor*. Paris, 1904. Oil on canvas, 194×112 cm. Metropolitan Museum of Art, New York, Gift of Thelma Chrysler Foy, 1952.

Olin among them—he did not, in these early years at least, enjoy the French theatre. 'He found it boring,' Fernande says. His French was not up to it. Later in life, he would love the classic French drama and remember passages from Molière's *L'Ecole des femmes* and *Les Femmes savantes* by heart, although he was too self-conscious about his accent to recite them.[26] In 1905 the only other references to the theatre are caricatural drawings of a doublet-and-hose drama. Nor did he have much time for classical music: he preferred *cante jondo* or popular hits. We do, however, know that Max Jacob dragged him more than once to the opera, so the so-called *Actor* could have been an opera singer. The artful way he holds his hand in front of his open mouth as if to project his voice into the darkness of the auditorium corroborates this. And given his commedia dell'arte finery, he might conceivably have been inspired by Canio, the tragic anti-hero of *I Pagliacci*. Or, if not by any specific character, at least by the aria '*Vesti la giubba*' ('On with the motley'), which is famous as much for its tear-jerking message—the buffoon must make his audience laugh while his heart breaks—as for its tear-jerking melody.

Through Max Jacob Picasso had made friends with two professional musicians: a brother and sister, Henri and Suzanne Bloch. He was a violinist, she a Wagnerian opera singer. Henri, who was not the only one of the artist's early friends to realize that money could be made out of his work, arranged for a major portrait (for which there are preparatory drawings) to be painted of his sister—a larger, coarser version of Fernande. He also wheedled Picasso into giving him the melancholy head of a Barcelona prostitute with a kerchief tied round her neck. (According to Podoksik, the inscription to Bloch has been painted over,[27] presumably when the work was put on the market a few years later.) In exchange, the Blochs gave Picasso and Max tickets for musical events—an Enesco concert, for instance, and very likely for Caruso's season of *verismo* opera at the Théâtre Sarah Bernhardt in the summer of 1905.[28]

Since its first performance in 1892, *I Pagliacci* had been a hit the world over, not least in Paris, where it had its debut in 1902. Jacob, who had a passion for *verismo* opera, loved it and moreover identified with it: 'How many times have I not seen Max Jacob play the buffoon, his eyes haggard with desperation!' an intimate friend once said.[29] Since he had already taken Picasso to see *La Bohème* in 1902 (hence the legend of the burnt drawings), Jacob would certainly have encouraged him to see *I Pagliacci*. The cast of characters recalls Rusiñol's play about strolling players, *L'Alegria que passa*, which Picasso knew from Barcelona.[30] True, Leoncavallo's plot (said to have been based on a murder case that the composer's father, a judge, had once tried) is melodramatic, whereas Rusiñol's is ironically sad. But both works are concerned with the impact of commedia dell'arte players on the inhabitants of a country village, the impact of fantasy on reality.

Chromolithograph of the first production of *I Pagliacci* in Milan, 1892.

The remorseless Calabrese story of adulterous passion and vengeful murder would have gone straight to Picasso's suspicious Andalusian heart, especially at a time when he was jealous of the none-too-faithful Fernande. Not that the theme of the opera ever surfaces in *The Actor* or any other painting. What Picasso may have appropriated is the self-pitying, self-dramatizing message of '*Vesti la giubba*', as well as Leoncavallo's ingenious grafting of commedia dell'arte onto *verismo*. If a modern composer could introduce Harlequin, Pierrot and Columbine into a scene of contemporary life, why not a modern painter?

There are of course countless literary precedents for Picasso's harlequins, many of them known to Picasso through Apollinaire or Jacob.[31] Symbolist writers had rescued Harlequin, Pierrot and Columbine from the tops of chocolate boxes, postcards and the like, and given them a new dimension of ineffable *tristesse*: for example Laforgue's play *Pierrot fumiste* and Verlaine's eerie poem '*Pierrot*'. Verlaine's Pierrot 'is no longer a moonstruck dreamer, or unrequited lover, but a character of tragic proportions':[32]

> See, in the terror of the lightning flash
> his pale blouse, on the cold wind, has the shape
> of a long winding-sheet, his mouth's agape
> and seems to howl while the worms gnaw his flesh. . . .
> His eyes are holes of phosphorescent light,
> and the flour makes more awful the bloodless face
> with the pointed nose of one about to die.

If Verlaine was the first French poet for whom Picasso developed a taste, it was largely Jacob's doing. Even when Apollinaire converted him to the rival cult of Rimbaud, Picasso never abandoned his first enthusiasm. He went so far as to copy out Verlaine's '*Cortège*' into one of the sketchbooks he took to Holland in 1905. A surprising choice: this poem is as ornately decadent and perverse as one of Beardsley's rococo pastiches. '*Cortège*' is about an eighteenth-century beauty, attended by a black page who holds up her sumptuous skirts higher than he need, and by a monkey in a brocaded waistcoat, who gambols on ahead of her. The little boy and the monkey are both aroused by the lady's charms, but she goes her way quite unconscious of the insolent admiration of what the ethnically insensitive poet describes as her 'familiar animals'. The only echo of this poem to be found in the artist's work is the famous gouache of a harlequin family (the first Picasso to be bought by the Steins), which includes a large anthropomorphic ape. Unlike the amorous pet in Verlaine's poem, Picasso's primate regards its human companions with family pride rather than desire. But then, as Apollinaire would observe, Rose period animals look very human; the sexes, too, are often indistinguishable—especially the sex of the harlequins. 'Some of them match the splendour of the women, whom they resemble being neither male nor female.'[33]

Picasso. *Acrobat and Young Harlequin*. Paris, 1905. Oil on canvas, 190×108 cm. Barnes Foundation, Merion Station, Pa.

The androgyny that afflicts many of Picasso's figures until well into 1906 is no sudden aberration. Suppression of sexual characteristics, male as well as female, is typical of the *fin-de-siècle* aesthetic—typical above all of notions popularized by the preposterous Sâr Péladan. Occultist, novelist, aesthete, archaeologist, art critic, philosopher, playwright, impresario of the Salon de la Rose+Croix, Péladan left a more perceptible mark on the art and literature of his time than is usually realized.[34] Although people scoffed at Péladan's egomaniacal pretensions and ridiculous vestments, neither Jarry, Jacob, Apollinaire,[35] nor for that matter Picasso, entirely escaped the stigma of his occult ideas concerning the Apocalypse, cabalism, androgyny and the mystical nature of sex. Two fixations peculiar to *fin-de-siècle* artists stem from Péladan: the notion of 'man possessed by

Marcellin Desboutin. *Portrait of Sâr Joséphin Péladan.* 1891. Oil on canvas, 120.5×81.5 cm. Angers, Musée des Beaux-Arts.

woman; woman possessed by the devil'; and the notion that 'the androgyne is the plastic ideal'—'the aesthetic experience of the highest metaphysic'.[36] In the light of these theories it is hardly surprising that the soothsayer was nicknamed the 'Sâr Pédalant'. In fact, he seems to have had no pederastic inclinations. Except insofar as Wiegels's equivocal appearance may have helped inspire them, the androgynes who haunt Picasso's work of 1905–06 should be seen not as ephebes but as a reflection of *fin-de-siècle* notions of ideal beauty. Figures of ambivalent sex and identity, unconnected to any time or place or station in life, were very much in the air.

Phenomena that interested Gauguin usually interested Picasso; for instance the androgynous 'Mahus'—effeminate males whom Tahitians raised from childhood as women—that Gauguin wrote about in *Noa Noa.* For Gauguin, Mahus symbolized the enigma of male sexuality; androgynes were figures of magical power. Hence Picasso's boys and girls have been shorn of hair like priestly initiates. Their timeless, unisex costumes (tights, cloaks and ruffs) and unisex headgear (tricornes, crowns and wreaths) further blur the difference between the sexes. What is the destination of these ambivalent ghosts: a carnival, a wake, or Limbo?

One of the most poetic Rose period images is the *Boy with a Pipe.* It conjures up Verlaine's poem '*Crimen Amoris*', about a palace in Ecbatana where 'adolescent Satans' neglect the five senses for the seven deadly sins, except for 'the most handsome of all these evil angels, who is sixteen years old under his wreath of flowers . . . and who dreams away, his eyes full of fire and tears.' The poem may actually have inspired the painting. Late one night, the *bande à Picasso* was deep in discussion, when something occurred—could Jacob have been reciting '*Crimen Amoris*'?—which prompted the artist to leave wherever they were gathered and rush back to his studio. There he crowned the portrait of 'the young artisan' that he had been unable to resolve with a wreath of roses. 'By a sublime stroke of caprice he had turned the picture into a masterpiece.'[37] The model for this painting is likely to have been an 'evil angel' called 'p'tit Louis', whom Picasso described fifty years later. 'P'tit Louis' was the most regular of the Bateau Lavoir's visitors: 'local types, actors, ladies, gentlemen, delinquents'. 'He stayed there, sometimes the whole day. He watched me work. He loved that.'[38] And he died in the prime of his delinquent life.

The female equivalent of 'p'tit Louis' was 'Linda la Bouquetière', a teenage flower seller from the Place du Tertre, who sold her body as well as her roses outside the Moulin Rouge. Later a model for van Dongen and Modigliani, she posed for the famous *Girl with a Basket of Flowers*, the so-called *Fleur du Pavé* (the second Picasso to enter the Stein collection). It was her mother's fault she had become a whore, Max Jacob felt; and he vainly tried to reform Linda, by enrolling her in a Catholic youth organization called the Children of Mary.[39] Years later (1944), this painting took on a new significance for Picasso. Fifteen-year-old Geneviève Laporte had asked to interview him for her school magazine. Picasso agreed to do so: she bore such a striking resemblance to the little flower seller who had modelled for him and doubtless slept with him forty years before. In due course Geneviève became his mistress, and he took her to see the painting. He told her how he had originally wanted to paint the little prostitute

Gauguin. *Marquesan Man in a Red Cape*. 1902. Oil on canvas, 92×73cm. Musée d'Art Moderne, Liège.

Picasso. *Boy with a Pipe*. Paris, 1905. Oil on canvas, 100×81.3cm. Mrs John Hay Whitney Collection, New York.

Picasso. *Geneviève Laporte as a Bride*. August 2, 1951. Pencil on paper. Private collection.

Picasso. *Redheaded Girl*. Paris, 1905. Coloured crayons on sketchbook page, 14.5×9cm. Marina Picasso collection.

Picasso. *Girl with a Basket of Flowers*. Paris, 1905. Oil on canvas, 155×66cm. Private collection.

dressed for her first communion but had finally done her in the nude. With Geneviève he proceeded to do the reverse. 'I missed you so much last night,' he told her one morning (1951), 'that I imagined you naked . . . but one doesn't always get one's way with one's pencil.' The drawing he gave Geneviève depicts her veiled in white, holding a bouquet—dressed not as a *première communiante* but as a bride. For once in Picasso's work, the girl is smiling. 'You see, as a bride, you have a Mona Lisa smile.' He turned his wishful-thinking fantasy into a joke.[40]

An entry in Fernande's diary (undated, but presumably written in 1905–06) records a less savoury model than Linda:

> Pablo has brought back to the studio a young girl found I don't know where whom he is going to do as Joan of Arc. Bizarre-looking rather than beautiful with bright red hair and large, rather coarse but good features. She started posing two days ago. But last night I realized she must have been crawling with lice, as both of us have caught them.[41]

A medicated shampoo effected a cure. When the girl reappeared Fernande paid her and told her not to return until she, too, had deloused herself. She never did, and Picasso's Joan of Arc never materialized. Except possibly for the redhead who appears on page 11 of the *saltimbanques* sketchbook, none of these sketches has come to light.

Picasso. *Harlequin's Family*. Paris, 1905. Crayons and wash on paper, 16.5×12.4 cm. Private collection. Inscribed to Fernande.

Besides painting sulky-looking gamins, Picasso turned once more to the theme of motherhood. These images of harlequin families at home reflect the artist's newfound domestic happiness. But why the baby? The appearance of an infant usually means that Picasso's wife or mistress or someone close to him has given birth. So far as we know, nobody in his entourage had done so. These *maternités* are more likely to be about motherhood denied rather than motherhood granted. The artist would always enjoy relaying messages to his women through his work. And just as he had chided Madeleine for the non-birth of his child in a series of Madonnas, he now implicitly chides Fernande for her inability to have children in a succession of harlequinades that include the image of a wife nursing a baby. The only surviving drawing that the artist inscribed to Fernande makes this point: it portrays a Picasso-like jester playing an accordion while a Fernande-like companion changes her baby's clothes. By now the artist must have known that this was something his mistress would never be in a position to do. Hardly surprising, then, that she should have sold this guilt-inducing souvenir to Sarah Stein (Gertrude's sister-in-law), after she broke with Picasso in 1911.[42]

On the other hand, the gift of one of these drawings to Apollinaire was anything but reproachful: it would have been a tribute to his participation in Picasso's harlequinade. Ten years later he likewise aimed to give pleasure rather than pain when he presented yet another of these works to Gaby Lespinasse, the girl he was then desperate to marry. He wanted to foster an image of himself as ineffably innocent and affectionate, and promote the prospect of a marriage that would be blissfully bohemian.

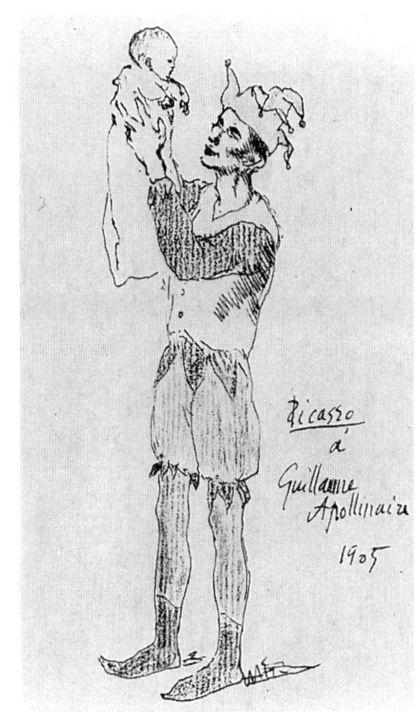

Picasso. *Jester Holding a Child*. Paris, 1905. Ink and crayons on paper, 17×10 cm. Private collection. Inscribed to Apollinaire.

* * *

Picasso. Study for the *Circus Family*. Schoorl, 1905. Pen on sketchbook page, 16×12cm. Heirs of the artist.

Picasso. *Circus Family*. Paris, 1905. Watercolour and pen on paper, 24×30.5cm. The Baltimore Museum of Art, Cone Collection.

The first of the strolling-player paintings to be started and the last to be finished was the huge *Saltimbanques*. 'There was first of all one large canvas, a group of acrobats on a plain,' Fernande writes, 'some of them resting, the others working. A child trying to balance on a ball. This canvas, if memory does not deceive me, was transformed several times.'[43] The sheer size of the original canvas (at 225×235cm, later cropped to 212×229cm, a few centimetres smaller than *Les Demoiselles d'Avignon*) indicates that the artist was more than ever determined to come up with a major composition that would once and for all establish his reputation. Picasso embarked on this vast canvas toward the end of 1904. Besides being the largest, it was by far the most ambitious project he had ever tackled. There were numerous preliminary studies—drawings, watercolours and engravings—and two or three, maybe even more, total repaintings. An x-ray analysis of the work has revealed five separate states; these kept the artist busy for much of the next year.[44] To judge by a watercolour in the Baltimore Museum and a unique state of a related engraving (which has been lightly scored with horizontal and vertical lines, as if to square it up for subsequent enlargement),[45] the composition, as originally conceived, was more idyllic than its Blue period predecessors. It was also relatively free of allegorical overtones. There was not as yet a heroic self-portrait at the centre to imply a parallel between bohemian *saltimbanques* and bohemian artists, nor was there any glimmer of the foreboding that pervades the final version (see illustration, p.384).

Fernande's 'acrobats on a plain' were in fact mostly women engaged in domestic chores, gathering firewood, washing dishes and looking after children. One of the two babies in the foreground of the Baltimore watercolour is white, the other black—a conceit that Picasso recalled over half a century later, when a white guitarist and a black flautist came to sit on the beach beside him and play their instruments.[46] But the main focus of the composition is not so much the mother and grandmother as the nimble child—at first a boy, later a girl—who is being trained by a harlequin to do a balancing act on a ball. X-rays reveal that the original tonality of the painting was bluish, though emphatically less than before. It has been suggested that this switch from blue to rose was inspired by the peach-coloured awning of the Médrano circus.[47] This may have been a contributing factor, but more to the point was the improvement in Picasso's fortunes (a beautiful mistress, enthusiastic patrons), the switch from gloomy Spain to *la ville lumière*, as well as boredom with the colour blue. Not that a gamut of pinks necessarily implies joy; pink could have had the same morbid associations for Picasso that it had for Apollinaire in some of his *saltimbanque* poems. In these he evokes 'pulmonary pink'; 'the livid colour of his lungs' worn on an old acrobat's back; or the tubercular flush 'on the cheeks of certain fresh young girls near to death'. In this respect the Rose period is the Blue period turned inside out.

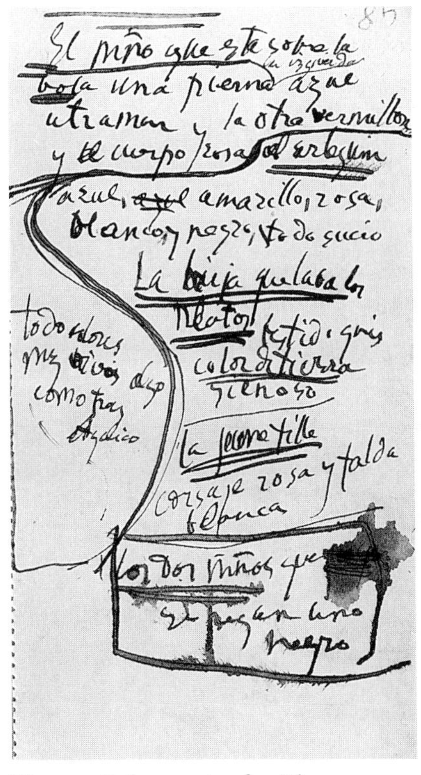

Picasso. Colour notes for *The Saltimbanques*. Paris, 1905. Pen on sketchbook page, 14.5×9cm. Marina Picasso collection.

In the course of repainting the *Saltimbanques*, Picasso decided against using the central group of the harlequin and the girl on the ball. Since the image of the girl was too promising to waste, and since her prowess may well have been a metaphor for his own dexterity, he went ahead and incorporated her into another major composition, *Young Acrobat on a Ball*, this time contrasting her lithe dynamism with the muscle-bound immobility of the circus strongman. He had recently laid out so much money on materials for *The Saltimbanques* that he was in no position to buy another large canvas. Instead he recycled his 1901 portrait of Iturrino. In the distance, looking out toward the high sierra, there is a woman holding a baby; there is also another child, a dog and a white horse. These minuscule figures could be said to stand for Spain, the big ones in the foreground for Paris. Given the sculptural air of the *Young Acrobat on a Ball*, it comes as no surprise to discover that Picasso borrowed the concept of the girl from a bronze, *Boy Balancing on a Ball* (1888), by a minor German sculptor, Johannes Goetz—something he had probably seen illustrated in an art magazine.[48] Not even a trained acrobat could have held the pose for more than a few seconds. For the seated strongman Picasso seems to have used one of his friends from the Cirque Médrano. The box on which he sits is a studio prop that recurs again and again in works of the period, notably in drawings of a potbellied buffoon, usually dressed in red tights, a ruff and jester's cap and bells, who also worked at the circus (Picasso has for once recorded the model's name—'*El tío Pepe, don José, à 40 ans*'—probably because it is the same as his father's). El tío Pepe will reappear in the final version of *The Saltimbanques*, where he seems, like Rilke's Père Rollin, to be the father of the troupe.

Picasso. *Tío Pepe Seated.* Paris, 1905. Pen and watercolour on sketchbook page, 14.5×9cm. Marina Picasso collection.

During the nine months or so that Picasso spent working on *The Saltimbanques*, Apollinaire was an almost daily visitor to the Bateau Lavoir. Some of the changes in theme and mood may well have originated with him. Clues to the close rapport between poet and painter are to be found in (the already quoted) '*Un fantôme de nuées*'. This purports to describe a specific event on a specific day, but it also incorporates memories of the *Young Acrobat on a Ball*, not to speak of *The Saltimbanques*, where the little tumbler was originally a boy, as here, and not a girl.

> You should have seen this thin wild-looking character
> His gray beard a cloud of ancestral ash
> Heredity worn as it were on his face
> He seemed to dream about the future
> As he mechanically churned his hurdy-gurdy
> Into a sublimely slow lament
> Gurgles, squawks and heavy groans.
>
> . . .
>
> From under the hurdy-gurdy stepped a little tumbler
>   dressed in pulmonary pink
> With bits of fur at wrists and ankles
> He let out some peremptory yells
> Arms elegantly spread he bowed
>
> With one leg backwards as if genuflecting
> He made a salutation to the four cardinal points
> And when he balanced on the ball
> His thin body turned into music so sheer that none of the
>   spectators could resist the sight of him
> His musicality of form
> Put the hurdy-gurdy to shame
>
> . . .

Johannes Goetz. *Boy Balancing on a Ball*. 1888. Bronze, ht: 24.6 cm. National Gallery of Art, Washington, D.C., Gift of Dieter Erich Meyer, 1976.

Picasso. *Young Acrobat on a Ball*. Paris, 1905. Oil on canvas, 147×95 cm. Pushkin Museum, Moscow.

Above: Picasso. *Head of a Jester*. Paris, 1905. Bronze, ht: 41.5 cm. Musée Picasso, Paris.

Above: Picasso. *Hurdy-Gurdy Man and Young Harlequin*. Paris, 1905. Gouache on cardboard, 100.5×70.5 cm. Kunsthaus, Zurich.

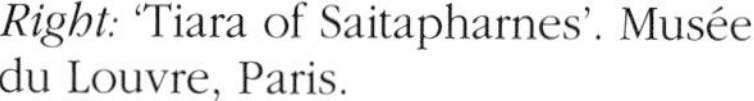

Right: 'Tiara of Saitapharnes'. Musée du Louvre, Paris.

Far right: Picasso. *Old Man Wearing a Diadem*. Paris, 1905. Pen and watercolour on paper, 17×10 cm. Pushkin Museum, Moscow.

Picasso. *Ex-Libris for Apollinaire.* Paris, 1905. Pen and watercolour on paper, 19×12cm. Ex-Douglas Cooper collection.

The little tumbler did a catherine-wheel
So harmoniously
That the hurdy-gurdy stopped playing
And the organ-grinder hid his face in his hands . . .
Renewed redskin cries
Angelic music of trees
And the child made off

The inclusion of a hurdy-gurdy player in Apollinaire's poem raises questions about a similar figure who appears again and again in Picasso's work. This bearded old phantom in a jester's cap and bells seems to have been inspired by a similarly costumed character in a play or operetta with a commedia dell'arte theme that Picasso sketched during an actual performance sometime in 1905. Studies of this aged figure transposed to a wasteland setting hint that the artist contemplated including him in place of the girl in a straw hat in *The Saltimbanques.* Picasso subjects the hurdy-gurdy man to successive changes of identity. The cap and bells suggested a Slavic diadem,[49] so he is turned into a sinister Ivan the Terrible figure, his diadem engraved with writhing lovers. It likewise suggested a crown: hence a satanic-looking monarch. Picasso also dresses him up in ermine, sets him down to dinner, equips him with an Apollinairean sneer, and serves him up to the poet as a bookplate in mocking homage to his qualities as trencherman, roué and jester, as well as a monarch like himself.

The cap and bells also crowns the artist's other laureate-cum-jester, Max Jacob. After leaving the Cirque Médrano with Jacob one evening, Picasso decided to use some clay he had in the studio to do a head of his friend. Inspiration could well have come from the large Rodin retrospective at the Luxembourg—according to Charles Morice, the biggest event of the spring 1905 season. Since there were no facilities for modelling at the Bateau Lavoir, they probably went to Durrio's. The clay rapidly took on the appearance of Jacob, the artist remembered, but the next day he continued to work on it and only the lower part of the face retained its likeness. The jester's cap was added as the head changed its character.[50] Sooner or later most of Picasso's entourage would be subjected to this process of metamorphosis—into an image that was comic or, as here, allegorical. The artist regarded Jacob as a jester. Very well, he should be portrayed as one. Picasso went further with Apollinaire. He transformed him into a sailor in a rowing boat, a full-bellied coffeepot, a torero ('don Guillermo Apollinaire'), an up-to-date pope wearing a new-fangled wristwatch as well as the triple tiara, an Academician with a cocked hat and a pipe stuck in his ear, an artilleryman brandishing a sabre, and a naked bodybuilder. He never lets us forget Apollinaire's versatile nature and mysterious ancestry.

PICASSO

22

Dealers and *Dénicheurs*

Picasso. *Henri Delormel (Louis Libaude)*. Paris, 1905. Ink wash on paper, 29×22.8cm. Musée Picasso, Paris.

THE DEPRIVATIONS OF HIS EARLY years in Paris left Picasso incorrigibly bitter. During his first year there, he was reduced time and again to requesting financial help from his friends back in Barcelona. Sometimes he came out and asked directly; sometimes he wrote letters harping on his poverty. Rusiñol refused him the 'pension' that he solicited. Junyent said he would consider letting him have some money, but in exchange for paintings. Sabartès sent him some rubbings of Guatemalan coins, 'in case you are in need'. Sebastià Junyer Vidal said he was short of cash but promised to mail him something if his circumstances improved. In short, nobody came to his rescue. Picasso's revenge would be to help his Barcelona friends out when one by one they applied to him for financial aid in the years to come.

Picasso would never lose his bitterness, but he did not—surprisingly—blame his sufferings so much on reactionary social forces or establishment blindness as on the dealers who had preyed upon him in his youth. Apropos his 1930 *Crucifixion*, he said, not entirely in jest, that the centurions throwing dice for Christ's raiment reminded him of dealers. His resentment of the men and women who trade in the sacred stuff of art went deep—more especially since he had once been so dependent on them. Kahnweiler would eventually rescue him from the hyenas of Montmartre and the rue Laffitte, but this former banker's straightforward business-like methods never entirely assuaged the artist's sense of paranoia where dealers were concerned.

Until Apollinaire persuaded Vollard to renew his interest in Picasso's work and buy twenty of his early paintings (April 1906), the artist was obliged to rely on a few small-time dealers, who took advantage of his pennilessness. Apart from the maddeningly unbusinesslike but relentlessly honest Berthe Weill, there was only one exception: Léon ('le père') Angély, who was not so much a dealer as a *dénicheur*. Picasso was fascinated by Angély: he was blind. A retired legal clerk of limited means, he spent his days going from one Montmartre atelier to another, led around by a little girl, who would describe the works he was being 'shown'. His 'stupendous flair' is hard to credit.[1] Maybe it was the girl who had it. At all events Angély's inspired speculation went unrewarded. World War I inflation forced him to unload his Picassos, Modiglianis, Utrillos and much else before prices took off. By the time he died (1921), he had nothing left. The little that Fernande tells us about le père Angély's visits

Opposite: Picasso. *Vase of Flowers*. Paris, 1901. Oil on canvas, 65×49cm. Tate Gallery, London. Bought from Picasso by le père Soulié and later owned by Delormel.

Picasso. *Delormel at a Brothel.* Paris, 1905. Pen on paper, 26.7×21.6cm. Private collection (ex-Apollinaire collection).

to the Bateau Lavoir suggests that Picasso may have drawn on memories of the sightless art lover and his child guide when (1934) he depicted a blind minotaur being led around by a little girl.

The most obnoxious of these *dénicheurs* was Louis Libaude—'a hyena that preyed on carrion'[2] and a sanctimonious hypocrite to boot. Libaude led a double life. As Henri Delormel, he was a seemingly respectable literary man: author of numerous essays and a satirical book about Polaire (the music-hall star whom Picasso drew and Colette immortalized); sometimes referred to as head and sole member of the Bohemianist school, whatever that was; and founder of *L'Art littéraire* (1892–94), a 'revuette', as it was known, to which Rémy de Gourmont, Mallarmé, Gide and Jarry contributed. Indeed Delormel was the first editor to print Jarry's work, including some major early texts. When his magazine failed, the editor quarrelled with his tempestuous young contributor—presumably about money. To avenge himself, Delormel published (1897) a story viciously lampooning Jarry and his close friend Léon-Paul Fargue as homosexuals; he depicted them recognizably as 'Death Head' and 'Androgyne'. A year later Jarry got his revenge in a section (Book 3, chapter XII) of his *Exploits and Opinions of Doctor Faustroll*, which he published in the *Mercure de France* (May 1898). This was dedicated to 'Louis Lermoul', so that readers could identify the subject: a putrefying monster feeding on its own excrement (a reference to the 'putrefying' doctrines of symbolism and Catholicism)[3]: '*non pas un homme mais une île*', Jarry says—'the isle of Cack in the sea of Shit'.

Picasso is likely to have known of Delormel's role in Jarry's life. This awareness could well explain his caricatures of him—literally as a 'prick', with a phallic knob of a face emerging from a high starched collar. Picasso would have met Delormel at the *Vers et Prose* evenings, probably through Apollinaire, whose magazine *La Revue immoraliste* (subsequently *Les Lettres modernes*) he backed to the extent of two issues. Picasso also got to know Delormel in his Dr Jekyll guise, as Libaude (his real name), a Dickensian villain who had swindled so many local artists that when he did the rounds of the studios on the Butte, he slunk along in the shadow of buildings and carried a revolver for fear of attack. A former auctioneer of horses, Libaude was up to every trick of the art trade. Too stingy to pay for a dealer's licence, he pretended that he was a private collector who sold on a friendly basis to other collectors. Because of his reputation as a bloodsucker, he was obliged to hide behind small-time dealers like Soulié. Fernande had once overheard him saying that he bought Picassos because they were going to be worth a lot of money, not because he liked them.[4] Ambulance-chasing was one of Libaude's specialities. When he heard that Modigliani was dying in hospital, he combed the dealers and cornered the market at very little cost to himself, and, the moment the artist's death was announced, went from café to café boasting of his coup. After Libaude died, his daughter sold a hundred 'White' Utrillos—a small part of his collection—for a million francs.[5] A number of Picassos are recorded as having a Libaude provenance, but if he is remembered, it is largely thanks to the artist's caricatures of 'le gros Lolo'.

The two dealers with whom Picasso did most of his business after moving into the Bateau Lavoir were le père Soulié and Clovis Sagot. Both were as canny as the infamous Libaude but not quite so cold-blooded.

The burly Eugène Soulié could have stepped out of a Daumier lithograph. He had started life as a wrestler in a fairground—the sort who issues challenges to all comers—and ended up selling mattress ticking and bedding on the rue des Martyrs, just opposite the Cirque Médrano. Soulié became an art dealer because many of his clients were poor painters reduced to bartering their canvases for the necessities of life. If an artist's work found buyers, Soulié would come up with money instead of goods. Since he was drunk most of the time—he is said to have averaged fifty aperitifs a day—it was sometimes possible to get the better of him, but nothing would ever induce him to give more than a hundred francs for a painting. Soulié stored bedding inside his shop and stacked paintings out on the pavement at the mercy of dogs, cats, thieves and the elements. Picasso would have recourse to the drunken *matelassier* only when all other alternatives had failed—that is to say quite often. He would send Max Jacob over with an assortment of works on paper, for which Soulié is reputed to have paid as little as three francs a gouache and ten centimes a drawing, but at least he would pay in cash. And for the next day or two there would be enough money to buy food, paint and canvas, oil for the lamp and coal for the stove.

Picasso. *Le Père Soulié*. Pen on paper. Whereabouts unknown.

In time Soulié attracted a clientele: *dénicheurs* and dealers in search of a bargain, like Libaude (for whom he acted as a cover). When one of these asked Soulié to find him a flower piece in a hurry, he rushed over and commissioned it from Picasso. The only problem: there was no white paint and no money to buy any. But since the artist desperately needed Soulié's twenty francs, he contrived to work round this shortage and come up with an acceptable bouquet. Picasso seldom painted flowers out of choice; most of the early flower pieces were done in the hope of raising money. They still fulfil this purpose: Picasso's flower pieces fetch ever higher prices. These early commissions may have given the artist a distaste for the genre. Later in life he would make a point of exorcising the prettiness of floral arrangements. Bouquets from admirers would be put in a vase without water. 'They don't need it,' he used to say. 'They're going to die anyway!' and he would leave them around as a *vanitas*. This association of flowers with mortality could account for the menace of the late flower pieces.

Besides selling to Soulié, Picasso later bought from him his first Douanier Rousseau, a portrait thought to be of Yadwigha, the Polish schoolmistress who modelled for *Le Rêve*. He told Florent Fels that he had spotted the portrait of a woman 'with a hard look' sticking out of one of Soulié's stacks; he was fascinated, he said, by its 'French penetration, clarity, decision. A huge canvas. I asked the price. "Five francs," said the dealer, "you can paint over it." It is one of the most revealing French psychological portraits.'[6] Picasso purchased the Rousseau in 1908—that is to say, towards the end of Soulié's life, when aperitifs and absinthe were taking their toll, and there were recurrent problems with the police. He was arraigned for illegal betting, also a murky *affaire de mœurs*. It was all too much for Soulié, who went into a deep depression and was taken off to hospital. He died in April 1909, missed but not greatly mourned by a whole generation of painters—Modigliani, Metzinger, Dufy, Friesz, as well as Picasso—whose indigence was the source of his fame.

Henri Rousseau. *Portrait of Yadwigha*. 1895. Oil on canvas, 160×105cm. Musée Picasso, Paris.

* * *

Clovis Sagot was more serious than the feckless Soulié, more assiduous in his exploitation of Picasso and other Montmartre painters. 'He was a hard man,' Picasso later recalled, 'very hard, almost a usurer.'[7] To mitigate this impression, Sagot made much of having worked as a clown and a baker, as if these professions guaranteed his geniality. In fact, he had learned the métier helping out his stuffy older brother, Edmond, a well-known print-dealer on the rue de Châteaudun.[8] If he chose to set up on his own, it was not out of clownish whim but because he was bored with print-dealing, bored with his brother and eager to strike out in the modern field. Clovis Sagot (known as 'le frère Sagot', to differentiate him from Edmond) established his Galerie du Vingtième Siècle in a former pharmacy at 46 rue Laffitte, a few doors from Vollard. His only charity was to treat needy artists with patent medicines left over from his predecessor's stock. The remedy did not necessarily fit the malady, according to Fernande, who says that Sagot once claimed to have the perfect cure for a heavy chest cold she had caught; the medicine turned out to be for diabetes.[9] Gertrude Stein's brother Leo attributes two obsessions to Sagot: modern art and a brand of liquorice called Zan, 'that had the properties of a life-preserver. He would put a bit of Zan between his teeth and commend its virtues; then we were back again on the latest show, the latest artistic scandal, the prospects for the future.'[10]

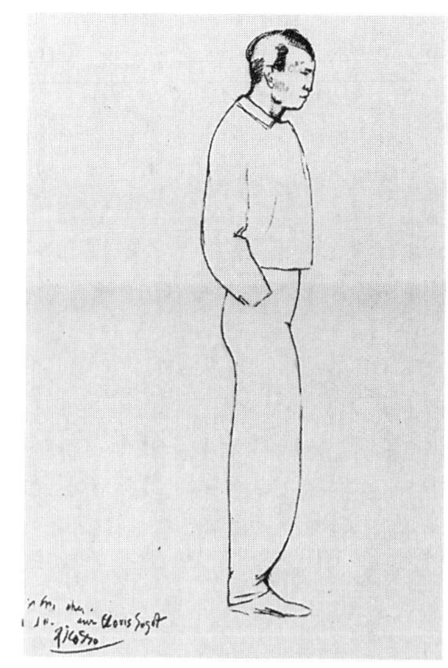

Picasso. *A Spaniard.* Barcelona, *c.*1903. Pen on paper, 36×25cm. Whereabouts unknown. Inscribed to Clovis Sagot.

Sagot 'twinkled with enthusiasm whatever . . . the subject,' says Leo Stein, but then Stein was a big buyer whom the dealer was intent on charming.[11] Picasso had a very different story to tell. Sagot, he said, was a past master at assessing the exact degree of an artist's desperation and squeezing maximum benefit from it. After his return from Holland in the late summer of 1905, when he was even more penniless than usual, Picasso asked Sagot to come and look at his work. The dealer picked out three things, the *Girl with a Basket of Flowers* and two of the Dutch gouaches, and offered seven hundred francs for them. Picasso refused this offer but a few days later concluded that he had better accept. No luck. Sagot had reduced the offer to five hundred francs. Outraged, Picasso turned this down. By the time he realized he had to give in or starve, the offer had shrunk to three hundred francs. Fernande accuses Sagot of being 'a sly fox without scruples or compassion'; he was not only a Shylock, he was a thief. When she caught him slipping extra drawings in with ones he had bought, he merely gave her a clownish grin. And she complains of his brazen cheek: arriving at the Bateau Lavoir with an armful of flowers from his country garden, 'so that [Picasso] can do a study of them and then give it to me'.[12] Sagot was one of the main reasons for Picasso's lifelong distrust of dealers. It is to the artist's credit that much later, when he could have got his own back, he would always be scrupulously fair. Teasing the trade was his only revenge. In the 1950s he loved to make the pompous print-dealer Baron Petiet grovel by repeatedly putting off appointments to sign one of his many sets of the 'Vollard' engravings. Even Kahnweiler would be kept on tenterhooks for days, sometimes weeks, not knowing for sure whether he would get delivery of the works Picasso had *said* he would sell.

Picasso. *Portrait of Clovis Sagot.* Paris, 1909. Oil on canvas, 82×66cm. Kunsthalle, Hamburg.

Although Picasso rarely said anything good of Sagot, he paid him the rare compliment of a major cubist portrait. A surprisingly gentle character with a faint look of Cézanne is revealed. One realizes why Kahnweiler, who saw his first Picasso as well as Juan Grises in this man's gallery, had a certain wary respect for him, and why Sagot was credited with spotting the best work in any exhibition or studio. By the time he died (1913), Sagot had lost most of his former artists to more generous or more professional dealers, above all Kahnweiler. His widow's attempts to carry on the business were not successful. In a touching obituary Apollinaire compared him with Père Tanguy,[13] although Tanguy was more liberal to the impressionists than Sagot was to the cubists. He also recalled Sagot's pawning his watch chain to raise enough money to buy some paintings from Picasso. 'I do not know whether he ever redeemed it, but I do know that he never wore it again. Poor Clovis Sagot! He died just at the moment when the works he had defended so persistently were beginning to become famous.' 'Among the painters who will miss him', Apollinaire cites Picasso, Herbin, Gris, Laurencin, Utrillo, Valadon, Metzinger, Gleizes and Léger. If Picasso put up with Sagot, it was because, for all his stinginess, he was blessed with a genuinely avant-garde eye; he was one of the few people around who had an instinctive idea of what the cubists were trying to do. Sagot was also fierce in his promotion of 'his' artists, as we know from Leo Stein, who gave him full credit for bringing Picasso's work to his and Gertrude's attention.

Sagot seldom held exhibitions in his gallery; he usually hung a selection of works from stock on his walls. Berthe Weill's 'group shows' were organized along similar ad hoc lines. Since Picasso had no regular dealer, it was difficult for anyone who was not a habitué of the studio to keep up with his development. When Parisians finally had the opportunity of seeing a largish group of recent work, the sponsor was not any of his usual dealers but the critic Charles Morice. He arranged for the exhibition to take place at the Galeries Serrurier on the Boulevard Haussmann. This locale had no previous or subsequent association with Picasso, and little seems to be known about it beyond the name of the director, a Monsieur Dulong. As usual the artist was desperate for money. 'One has to eat,' he wrote to his old friend Jacint Reventós in Barcelona (February 22, 1905).

> If it were only that! When you have to make arrangements with other people . . . it's such a terrible waste of time, scrounging the last peseta to pay for the studio or restaurant—and believe me all the struggle and trouble isn't worth it. . . . It only teaches the same . . . idiotic lesson one learned at the hands of the bourgeois in Barcelona. Anyway I continue working and in a few days am going to have a small exhibition. God willing, people will like it and I'll sell everything I'm showing. Charles Morice is in charge of organizing it. He tries to write about whatever he's sponsored in the *Mercure de France*—we'll see what happens. Another day I'll write you more.[14]

Picasso. *Young Acrobat with a Monkey* (personal invitation to Max Jacob for Picasso's 1905 exhibition). Paris, 1905. Pen, wash and watercolour on paper, 21.7×12.5cm. Private collection.

This 'small exhibition' opened on February 25 and lasted a mere nine days. Morice included two other artists, Auguste Gérardin and the fascinating Swiss Rosicrucian Albert Trachsel,[15] and, as Picasso had hoped, he wrote a preface to the catalogue and an appreciative article in the *Mercure de France* (March 15). Nothing is known about the arrangements Picasso made with the proprietors of the gallery. Nor is there any record of sales. The catalogue lists thirty paintings and gouaches plus three engravings and an album of drawings.[16] Most of the exhibits were probably on consignment either from the artist himself or from Sagot, who had visited the Bateau Lavoir on February 19 and purchased several works, including two little harlequins ('*sur fond rouge*'), the *Harlequin with a Dog* and a watercolour entitled *Fleur du pavé*. Picasso does not seem to have made more than a marginal sum out of the Serrurier exhibition—barely enough to keep him in materials, rent and food over the next few months—for he was penniless by June. If at this time he earned a reputation for cadging off friends, he can hardly be blamed. He knew his worth and was in no doubt as to where his first duty lay: to himself. His progress could not be allowed to falter for want of a few francs. That the world owed him a living became an article of faith.

Picasso. *Charles Morice's Daughter*. Paris, 1905. Pencil on paper. Whereabouts unknown.

The Serrurier exhibition may not have earned much money but in its modest way it was a *succès d'estime*. The sponsorship of Charles Morice, who had written excitedly, though not very perceptively, about the 1902 show, was considered an honour. Since the critic had been able to discuss the recent work with the artist and since the latter had done a charming drawing of the critic's daughter, his preface took a more sympathetic, less censorious line than he had taken before.[17] However, Morice was too hidebound a symbolist to give youth the benefit of the doubt. And, sure enough, in the *Mercure de France*, where he was the regular art critic, he could not resist using the new works to knock earlier ones, a few of which were included in the show: 'sterile melancholy', 'a taste for the sad and ugly for their own sake', 'premature twilight of spleen', etc.

Morice's reservations gave Apollinaire a pretext for his first panegyric to Picasso. Without naming Morice, he chided him for his retrovision. 'It is said that Picasso's work reveals a precocious disenchantment. I think the opposite' is how he started his review in *La Revue immoraliste*, his own magazine. However, polemics were not as yet Apollinaire's forte, and since this was his first attempt at art criticism, he reverted to what he did best—a prose poem:

> Underneath the tawdry costumes of these slender *saltimbanques*, one senses the presence of typical working-class boys, fickle, cunning, clever, poor and deceitful. Picasso's young mothers wring those fragile hands that young working-class mothers so often have . . . his naked women are adorned with the escutcheon of a fleece—the shield of Western modesty—that conventional painters scorn.[18]

Picasso. *Harlequin's Family*. Paris, 1905. Gouache, pen and collage on cardboard, 60.6×45.2cm. Private collection.

Had Picasso, one wonders, confided in Apollinaire his childhood fantasy that women's bodies were covered in pubic hair? The poet wrote no less lyrically but at greater length in the more widely read *La Plume*. What is more, the article included five illustrations that had probably been picked by Picasso: *Woman with a Raven, The Two Friends, Seated Harlequin, Acrobat and Young Harlequin* and *Two Acrobats with a Dog*. Apollinaire evokes Picasso's harlequins and tumblers with such insight and empathy that he could almost have had a hand in their genesis:

> . . . children who have strayed away without learning their catechism. It has stopped raining and they have come to a halt. 'Look, people actually live in those hovels, how shabbily dressed.' They are not to be caressed, these children who know so much. 'Mama, love me to death!' They know how to leap in the air and perform acrobatic feats like ingenious hypotheses. . . . Old men wait around enveloped in freezing mist, not a thought in their heads . . . it is only children who meditate.
>
> For a year Picasso's painting emanated from the azure depths of an abyss, blue with pity. . . . Pity made Picasso harsher. . . . A nearby stove

Picasso. *Two Acrobats with a Dog*. Paris, 1905. Gouache on cardboard, 105.4×74.9 cm. The Museum of Modern Art, New York, Gift of Mr and Mrs William A. M. Burden. Illustrated with Apollinaire's article in *La Plume*.

> warms the gypsy caravan. Singers break into song, and farther off soldiers pass by cursing their fate. . . . Too young to have reached puberty, girls suffer the anxieties of innocence; animals instruct them in religious mysteries. In their finery, some of the harlequins are a match for the women, whom they, being neither male nor female, resemble. Colours are as matt as frescoes; contours are firm. Situated on the frontiers of creation, animals are human, sexes indistinguishable. . . . You cannot confuse these *saltimbanques* with actors. Look upon them with piety, for they are celebrating their silent rites with utmost attention. Notwithstanding certain similarities in drawing, this is what distinguishes [Picasso] from Greek vase painters. There, the terracotta surface is decorated with bearded priests, babbling away as they sacrifice animals resigned to their fate. Here, virility may be beardless; but it manifests itself in thin, sinewy arms and the flat planes of a face; there is also a mystery to the animals.

The essay ends on an unexpected Hispano-Mauresque note:

> More than any other poet, sculptor or painter, this Spaniard sears us like a sudden blast. His meditations are unveiled in silence. [Picasso] comes from afar, from the compositional opulence and brutal ornamentation of seventeenth-century Spain. Those who are acquainted with him will recall that the manifestations of his ferocity transcend mere experiment. The quest for beauty dictates his course. He has discovered himself to be more of a Latin in morality, more of an Arab in rhythm.[19]

After the Serrurier show, Picasso virtually ceased to exhibit in Paris. This was not a sudden, arbitrary decision. It was an attitude that he came gradually to adopt—an attitude that would be fanned by a growing interest on the part of collectors in his work. Why court further misery at the hands of indigent or unscrupulous dealers when he could sell directly to collectors himself? And then, although he was more than ever confident of his powers, Picasso did not want to pit himself publicly against the emergent forces of Matisse and the Fauves until he felt sure that he had the upper hand. So no more participation in group shows or official exhibitions in France. Outside France was another matter. Zuloaga arranged for Picasso to send a painting—*Acrobat and Young Harlequin*—to the 1905 Biennale in Venice. The painting was collected and shipped in March, but it cannot have met with the committee's approval, for it was sent back to the Bateau Lavoir. Picasso was very disappointed, but this setback did not prevent him from actively pursuing his career (1908–14) by exhibiting in every major European city—except Paris.

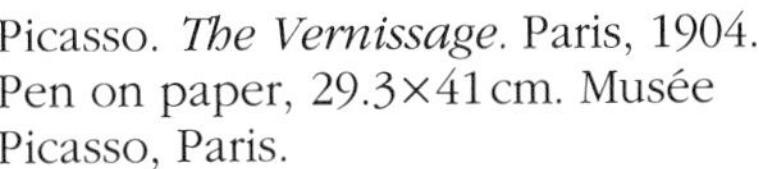

Picasso. *The Vernissage*. Paris, 1904. Pen on paper, 29.3×41 cm. Musée Picasso, Paris.

à alfred Jarry

23

The Absence of Jarry

Alfred Jarry. Programme cover for *Ubu Roi* at the Théâtre des Pantins. Lithograph, 1897. Collège du Pataphysique, France.

BY THE BEGINNING OF 1905 PICASSO and his *bande* had settled into a communal way of life that had not outwardly changed much since the days of Murger's *Scènes de la vie de bohème* fifty years earlier. Cooking facilities at the Bateau Lavoir were very primitive, so the group usually ate at one or another of the Montmartre bistros that gave credit. A facetious (unpublished) sonnet that Princet gave Picasso conveys an idea of the hearty horseplay that must have been one of the more depressing aspects of these places. It describes how a carafe was thrown across the bistro at him and knocked his hat off into a bowl of *fromage à la crème*. The most amenable of the local restaurateurs was an Auvergnat called Vernin, whose malodorous premises were conveniently situated next to the pawnshop on the rue Cavalotti. Fernande recounts how bored they became with the food; however Vernin had 'a lamentable memory' and sometimes forgot about the debts he allowed clients to accumulate. The alternative to Vernin was Azon's bistro, Aux enfants de la Butte, on the rue des Trois Frères. The food was just as bad, but Azon would sometimes take pity on deserving cases and wipe a slate clean of debt. At one time or another, Derain, Modigliani, Utrillo and Vlaminck, as well as the *bande à Picasso* were habitués of the place. If Vernin and Azon refused credit, Picasso was obliged to trek across Paris to Montparnasse to the Avenue du Maine,[1] where he had found another indulgent *patron*. On the long walk back to Montmartre he would ransack the dustbins for food for his cat and dogs.

When none of the *bande à Picasso* had any money, they would keep to the Bateau Lavoir and entertain each other. Max Jacob would get things going, which was not difficult since the group included some bright young actors, the Spaniards were always ready to sing and dance, and the poets needed no prodding to recite. With luck, someone would have a bottle of *anis del mono* or some hashish. On Tuesdays Salmon would walk Picasso and Fernande half-way across Paris to the rowdy soirées that he and his fellow editors of *Vers et Prose* organized at the Closerie des Lilas, a café-restaurant which was (indeed still is) on the borderline between the old Latin Quarter and the up-and-coming artist's section of Montparnasse. So well attended were these gatherings that they soon superseded the symbolist Soirées de la Plume. It was Els Quatre Gats all over again. Picasso enjoyed these occasions and drew caricatures of the habitués, just as he had of his *tertulia* in Barcelona. 'What life,

Opposite: Hermann-Paul. *Alfred Jarry*. 1901–05. Pencil, ink, crayon and gouache on paper, 53×34cm. Musée Picasso, Paris.
This portrait was owned by Picasso.

what uproar, what madness,' Fernande wrote of these drunken events.[2] Besides Paul Fort, who would be declared *'Prince des poètes'* in 1912, the presiding spirit was Gauguin's friend Jean Moréas (born Iannis Pappadiamontopoulis), '*le Ronsard du Symbolisme*'. This flamboyant but grubby dandy—made grubbier by the cheap black dye that rubbed off his hair and moustache onto his monocle and gold-ringed fingers—would welcome arriving guests, women and Jews especially, with facetious insults. Picasso would always be greeted with heavy-handed questions as to whether Lope de Vega or Velázquez had any talent. 'What's so boring about painting is all the paraphernalia you need . . . easels, tubes of paint, brushes, studios . . . models,' Moréas would say. 'I compose my [poems] in my head walking about in the rain.'[3] If Picasso held Moréas in sufficient awe to put up with his jeers and pretensions ('*Je suis un Baudelaire avec plus de couleur*'), it was because Apollinaire thought well of him and Manolo had become a devoted disciple and an adherent of his Ecole Romane.[4]

Picasso. Caricatures of Paul Fort, Henri Delormel and André Salmon. Paris, 1905. Pencil on one of Fort's visiting cards, 5.6×8.8cm. Musée Picasso, Paris.

Among the many new friends Picasso made at the *Vers et Prose* evenings were two young writers, Maurice Raynal and Henri-Pierre Roché, who would introduce him to the Steins. Raynal was in the process of squandering most of a recent inheritance on backing the *Vers et Prose* magazine. With some justice he would hold the loss of his fortune against Fort and Salmon; however, he remained a lifetime friend of Picasso and later (1921) wrote the first monograph on his work and numerous other studies. For many years, under the pseudonym '*Les Deux Aveugles*' (The Two Blind Men), Raynal and the Greek editor E. Tériade would write a progressive column on modern art for the far-from-progressive *L'Intransigeant*, the Paris evening paper. Raynal was one of the friends whose names Picasso had a habit of mentally ticking off—a compulsive litany to ward off death—every day of his life. When he heard that Raynal had died (1954), he told a friend that he felt very guilty: that day he had left Raynal's name off the list. 'But that doesn't mean you killed him,' said his friend. 'To be forgotten is worse than to be dead,' he replied.[5]

Maurice Raynal, 1903.

The Closerie des Lilas evenings enabled Picasso to meet artists and writers from all over the world, among them Italians like Soffici, Marinetti and Severini (who married Paul Fort's daughter), Americans like Leo Stein and Stuart Merrill, the English artist Augustus John ('the best bad painter in Britain,' Picasso called him),[6] as well as assorted Germans, Dutch and Scandinavians, and last but not least a young Greek student, Christian Zervos, who many years later would compile Picasso's *catalogue raisonné* and edit *Cahiers d'Art*. The *Vers et Prose* writer who would exert the greatest influence on Picasso was a *poète maudit*, only eight years his senior, whose rocket-like career was already nearing its end: Alfred Jarry. Jarry was friendly with Jacob, Apollinaire and Salmon; he has also been claimed by one biographer after another as a great friend of Picasso's. This friendship is a collective fantasy. The two men never met.[7] This did not stop Picasso from identifying more deeply with Jarry than with any other writer, including Apollinaire. Although the two iconoclasts never knew each other, they knew all about each other. When Jarry died, it was as if Picasso took possession of his demon as it departed his body. Jarry's sexual ferocity, his cult of the ridiculous and the absurd, his chameleon-like powers of stylistic mimicry and parody, his exploitation

Picasso. *Moréas Fat*. Paris, 1904. Pen on paper, 31.5×24cm. Heirs of the artist. Inscribed to Christian Zervos.

of the primitive and what we now call 'pop', his droll miscegenation of blasphemy and Christian dogma: these are just some of the weapons that Picasso appropriated from Jarry's armoury.

* * *

Jarry was born on September 8, 1873, in Laval, a sleepy town on the borders of Brittany. He despised his 'insignificant little bugger' of a father[8] but adored his mother, a strong-willed, slightly cracked woman who boasted of descent from one of William the Conqueror's knights and raised her brilliant son to be passionately pro-Breton and Catholic. It was at the Lycée at Rennes, in an atmosphere of adolescent smut and nihilism, that he laid the foundations of his career, helping schoolfriends concoct scabrous plays about their physics master. These plays were the raw material for *Ubu Roi*,[9] whose first line, '*Merdre!*,' (the additional *r* made the word even more subversive), when uttered on the first night (December 10, 1896), proved to be the password that opened up the French theatre to the avant garde. In Jarry's outrageous, high-camp hands puerile nastiness took on the force of an anti-personnel bomb. Although his fame is primarily identified with these schoolboy farces, they are little more than an overture to his masterpiece, the dauntingly dense *Exploits and Opinions of Doctor Faustroll.*

Jarry on his racing bicycle, *c.*1898. Collège du Pataphysique, France.

Partly to publicize *Ubu*, Jarry cultivated an outrageous *m'as tu vu* persona—'like a jack-in-the-box that had just popped up,' said Henri de Régnier. 'There was something mechanical and articulated about him.'[10] Jarry compensated for his small physique by body-building; he would canoe up and down the Seine or ride round Paris on a racing bicycle dressed for the Tour de France. This maniacal *sportif* also loved to fence and shoot, hence the carbine on his shoulder, the revolvers in his belt. On more formal occasions he would wear a shirt contrived out of paper with a trompe-l'oeil tie inked onto it (a precedent Apollinaire would follow; also Picasso, who would make paper ties and crowns for friends called upon to wear 'formal attire'). His bizarre appearance and the robotic diction that he had developed to brilliant comic effect prompted André Gide to compare Jarry to Kobold, the plaster-faced clown at the Cirque Médrano.

Jarry eventually installed himself in a legendary room on the rue Cassette. The landlord had doubled the storeys in the building by cutting each one in half horizontally. The tiny room—'*notre grande chasublerie*' Jarry called it—was on floor two-and-a-half. Apollinaire, who tried and failed to take Picasso there, has left a vivid description:

> Jarry's place was filled with reductions. This half-floor room was the reduction of an apartment in which its occupant was quite comfortable standing up. But being taller than he, I had to stay in a stoop. The bed was the reduction of a bed; that is to say, a mere pallet. Jarry said that low beds were coming back into fashion. The writing table was the reduction of a table, for Jarry wrote flat on his stomach on the floor. The furniture was the reduction of furniture—there was only the bed. On the wall hung the reduction of a picture. It was a portrait [of Jarry by the Douanier Rousseau], most of which he had burned away, leaving only the head. . . . The library was the reduction of a library, and that is saying a lot for it . . . a cheap

> edition of Rabelais and two or three volumes of the *Bibliothèque rose*. On the mantel stood a large stone phallus, a gift from Félicien Rops. Jarry kept this member, which was considerably larger than life size, always covered with a violet skullcap of velvet, ever since the day the exotic monolith had frightened a certain literary lady who was out of breath from climbing three and a half floors.
>
> 'Is that a cast?' the lady asked.
>
> 'No,' said Jarry. 'It's a reduction.'[11]

The assumption that Picasso knew this room and its occupant intimately is the fault of Max Jacob. When Jarry's name came up in conversation, the artist would try to correct this misapprehension, but people persisted in believing otherwise. Fortunately Hélène Parmelin reports Picasso as saying, sometime in the mid-fifties, that 'he regretted not having known Jarry; that he went to see him one day with Apollinaire, but Jarry was out, "*et puis c'est fini*"'[12]—Jarry died. This negates Jacob's often-cited description of the writer giving the artist a rusty Browning revolver from his arsenal in the course of dinner. Max was notorious for his *blagues*, his hoaxes:

> At the end of a supper, Alfred Jarry gave up his revolver to Picasso and made a gift of it to him.
>
> . . . At that time it was recognized:
>
> 1. that the tiara of the psychic Pope Jarry was loaded in [the] revolver, [the] new distinguishing mark of [the] papacy.
>
> 2. that the gift of this emblem was the enthronement of the new psychic Picasso.
>
> 3. that the revolver sought its natural owner.
>
> 4. that the revolver was really the harbinger comet of the century.[13]

The mock solemnity does not make for credibility. Yet this spoof account has always been taken at its face value. No other witness confirmed Jacob's story. On the contrary, Fernande's casual remark 'I got to know [Jarry] very slightly a few months before his death',[14] that is to say in the summer or fall of 1907, supports the artist's assertion that he never knew him. She and Picasso were separated at this period: hence her use of 'I' and not 'we'. Jarry evidently did not frequent the Bateau Lavoir. But he and Picasso had so many mutual friends—Apollinaire, Jacob, Salmon, the writer Maurice Cremnitz—and were always attending gatherings like the *Vers et Prose* meetings at the Closerie des Lilas, that their paths must have come close to crossing. The symbolic gift of the revolver was probably arranged by proxy through Jacob, or as a result of Apollinaire's confiscation of it at the end of Jarry's life.

If the painter and the poet never met, it was because Picasso established himself in Paris around the time that Jarry's excesses began to take their toll. More often than not Jarry was in a state of collapse from alcohol or drugs or was away from Paris. Poverty compounded his problems: he could no longer afford absinthe (which he is said to have diluted with red ink) and so had fallen back on ether. Without money for food or heat, Jarry had barely survived the winter of 1905–06. Once again he fell desperately ill, and his sister took him back home to Laval to recover. By the end of May he was so weak that he received extreme unction; however, he rallied and hung on for another seventeen months. Successive crises

Jarry and Alfred Vallette, 1898. Collège du Pataphysique, France.

were followed by periods of convalescence at Laval, or he would stay with the publisher Alfred Vallette and his wife, Rachilde, a novelist, or next door to them at Le Tripode, his often-flooded Seine-side shack.

Jarry returned to Paris in April 1907 but had another relapse that kept him in bed until July. Overwhelmed by debt, he tried to recoup by publishing *Le Moutardier du pape*, a farcical operetta set in ninth-century Avignon.[15] This sold less well than expected; and if it had not been for the charity of friends, Jarry would have been thrown out of his '*chasublerie*'. He paid one last visit to Laval in the summer of 1907 and returned to Paris in the autumn. When he disappeared from his usual haunts towards the end of October, worried friends forced the door of his garret. Finding Jarry semi-conscious and half-paralysed, they took him to the Hôpital de la Charité. He would die on All Saints' Day (November 1), he told the man in the next bed. Sure enough he did—not, however, of his excesses but of tubercular meningitis.

Jarry received the last rites around the same time that the *Demoiselles* was receiving the last touches. The breakthrough that this painting constitutes has yet to be seen in the light of the breakthrough that Jarry had made ten years before when he crashed the barrier between fantasy and reality, and established his parodic science of 'pataphysics', which would detonate all traditional canons of beauty, good taste and propriety. To prime himself for his campaign, Jarry had embarked on a systematic *dérèglement de tous les sens* through drink and drugs and self-destructiveness of every kind. The master plan succeeded all too well. Jarry was dead at thirty-four, leaving Picasso to reap the rewards of his martyrdom without having to pay the price of addiction.

The lack of personal contact between the donor and recipient of this rusty old Browning—the weapon that armed its owner with Nietzschean powers of destruction—enables us to see this transaction in the Jarry-esque light of a relay race. One runner drops out: another takes over. The baton, in this case the pistol, is the metaphorical link between these two undersized supermen who took it upon themselves to revolutionize our perception of reality. Jarry's hold on Picasso's imagination was the more palpable for being vested in something as menacing as a gun, especially one that the writer had carried around with him and fondled, brandished and frequently fired.

Picasso would have heard time and again how Jarry had fired a blank cartridge at the stuttering Belgian poet Christian Beck during a *Mercure de France* banquet in 1897 (an incident that inspired the banquet scene in Gide's novel *The Counterfeiters*, where Jarry appears as himself and fires a blank shot at another poet); likewise how, in April 1905, Jarry had shot at Manolo for being so sober and *bien pensant* at a drunken dinner given by Maurice Raynal; whereupon three pregnant women are supposed to have fainted ('It came off as literature, didn't it?' Jarry said to Apollinaire, who confiscated the revolver); and how, much to Apollinaire's delight, Jarry had caused a fracas at the Cirque Bostock by threatening to shoot Menelick, one of the lions, because its trainer lacked the authority to control 'this prince of the desert'.[16]

Picasso did Jarry's 'pataphysical' weapon proud; he claimed that he constantly used it to scare off bores and morons. There was the evening at the Lapin Agile when he fired a fusillade of shots after three earnest young Germans had exasperated him with questions about his aesthetic theories; they fled into the night just as Manolo had done. No less Jarry-esque was the time when Picasso and Manolo (on the right end of the revolver this time) found themselves sharing a cab with yet another boring German, who insisted on reciting his poems. Such was the tedium that Picasso fired through the cab's roof and left the German to be locked up by the police. Anyone who spoke ill of Cézanne would be silenced with the famous weapon and the threat 'One more word and I fire'. And the revolver came in useful when Picasso returned to Horta de Ebro in 1909 with Fernande. On discovering that the 'Picassos' were not married, two scandalized village women threw stones at their window. Not to be outdone, the artist emerged on the balcony, swearing and brandishing a gun.[17]

Jarry. *Ubu*. 1896. Woodcut, 7.4×11.3cm. Collège du Pataphysique, France.

If Picasso instinctively identified with Jarry, it was because he was not only a most imaginative writer but a most original draughtsman and illustrator and the possessor of an exceptionally discriminating eye. Most of Jarry's graffiti-like images take the form of woodcuts, but he did a few paintings and bas-reliefs, one of them in Picasso's collection. 'It isn't always easy to guess [what it represents],' Picasso said. 'This one is a man with an owl at his feet. . . . Did you know that Jarry always had a live owl in his home? His owls are the ancestors of mine.'[18] Picasso also admired the gross Ku Klux Klan-like figure with a cone-shaped head that Jarry devised to represent the character of Ubu. As early as 1905 he did variations after this figure, one of them holding a ceramic, on a sheet of sketches of Paco Durrio. In 1937 he again drew on this classic incarnation of crassness when looking for a suitably buffoon-like image to represent General Franco in his anti-Fascist *Dream and Lie of Franco*. (The Ubu-like caudillo on a tightrope balancing a banner of the Virgin on the end of his penis is particularly Jarry-esque.) Likewise, in 1953, when he needed an image of chemical warfare for his mural *La Guerre*, Picasso had recourse to the bag of black bugs that figures in the satanic frontispiece to Jarry's *César Antechrist*. Even Picasso's famous *Head of a Bull* (1942) made of bicycle parts, which hangs on the wall like a Crucifix, may derive from Jarry's sacrilegious essay 'The Passion Considered as an Uphill Bicycle Race' ('There are fourteen turns in the difficult Golgotha course. Jesus took his first spill at the third turn . . . Veronica, a girl reporter, got a good shot of him with her Kodak'). Jarry makes a point of confusing the bicycle's cross frame 'with that other cross, the straight handlebar'.

Jarry's iconoclastic example was the more valuable to Picasso at a moment when he, too, was extricating himself from the toils of symbolism. Jarry was far more successful than Apollinaire in turning his back on nineteenth-century romanticism and envisioning subversive new concepts. Years before the word 'cubist' was applied to Braque's painting, Jarry applied it to his so-called physick-stick, part heraldic emblem, part mathematical cipher, part phallic symbol: 'uprooted phallus, DON'T JUMP AROUND SO! . . . Demi-cubist creature, on the pole of your axis and your id.'[19] The Haldernablou section of *Les Minutes de sable mémorial* likewise provides a foretaste of cubism in such geometrical descriptions as an 'isosceles skull', 'the trapezium of an open book', 'a hexagonal face engraved with the circles of two eyes', 'the hypotenuse of his chest', and much else in the same vein. Elsewhere Jarry's spokesman, Ubu, proclaims,

Picasso. Drawings of Ubu, Paco Durrio holding a vase and a woman with a dog (Renée Péron). Paris, 1905. Pencil and coloured crayon on paper, 26.5×32.5cm. Musée Picasso, Paris.

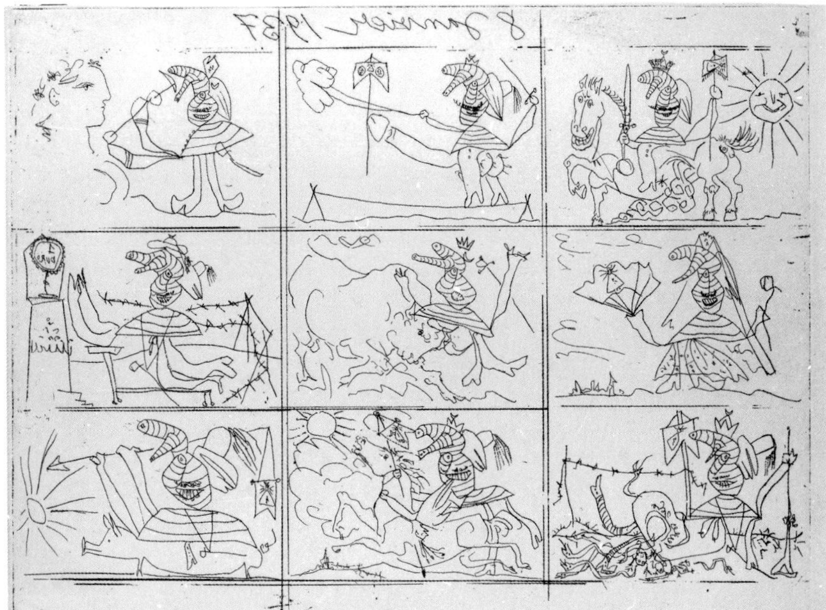

Picasso. *The Dream and Lie of Franco I.* Paris, January 8, 1937. Etching and aquatint, 31.7×42.2cm. Musée Picasso, Paris.

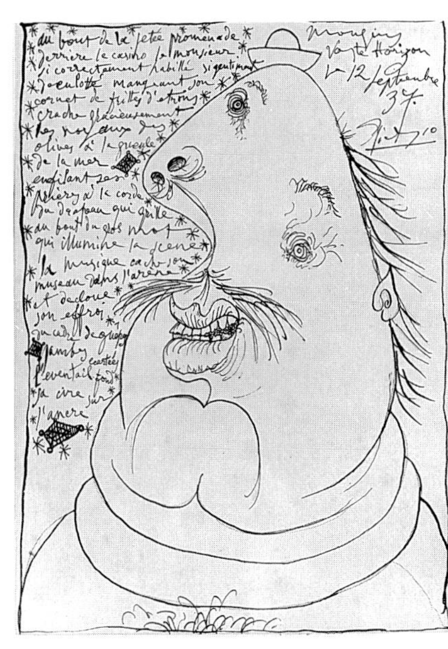

Picasso. *At the End of the Jetty.* Mougins, 1937. Pen on paper, 28.5×21cm. Mr and Mrs Lee V. Eastman collection, New York.

'I no longer do paintings . . . I make geometry.'[20] And 'God's sacred phallus' that rampages through the temples of Sodom and Gomorrah dealing death and destruction to those who go in for 'the sharps and flats of Eros' rather than 'banal plainchant': does not this anticipate Picasso's biomorphic projects for sculpture in the 1920s?

Jarry foretold other aspects of cubism when he came to define 'pataphysics' in *The Exploits and Opinions of Doctor Faustroll* (completed, as Jarry facetiously put it, when the twentieth century was minus two years old, i.e. 1898, but not published until 1911). Pataphysics, this 'neo-scientific novel' claims, is 'the science of imaginary solutions, which symbolically attributes the properties of objects, described by their virtuality, to their lineaments.' To illustrate this, Jarry argues that

> to claim that the shape of a watch is round [is] a manifestly false proposition—since it appears in profile as a narrow rectangular construction, elliptical on three sides; and why the devil would one only have noticed its shape at the moment of looking at the time? . . . But a child who draws a watch as a circle will also draw a house as a square, as a façade, without any justification, of course; because . . . he will rarely have seen an isolated building, and even in a street the façades have the appearance of very oblique trapezoids.[21]

Jarry. *César Antechrist*. 1894. Lithograph, 19×16.5cm. Collège du Pataphysique, France.

Even more striking is the way that the most opaque of Jarry's poetic dramas, *César Antechrist*—it draws on the Apocalypse, Renan's *L'Antichrist* and above all *Le Latin mystique*, Rémy de Gourmont's treasury of medieval legend and symbolism—anticipates, and at the same time elucidates a problem at the very heart of Picasso's work: his contradictory use of symbols. Again and again (sometimes in the same work) the very same symbol is made to stand for principles or ideas that are totally antithetical. This perverse procedure, which has made the interpretation of the *Demoiselles, Guernica* and much else so confusing, may well have had its source in Jarry, who sets up a symbol, knocks it down, upends it, reverses it, conflates it with other symbols in other contexts. 'The identity of opposites' is how Jarry explains this phenomenon. 'Not only are the signs plus and minus identical but so too, ultimately, are the concepts of day and night, light and darkness, good and evil, Christ and Antichrist.'[22] It is a theory by which Picasso would always live and paint, and, much later in life, write. 'I remember,' Paulo Picasso told his father, 'that I used to hear you repeat again and again, "Truth is a lie."'[23]

In the days of the Bateau Lavoir Picasso was not a great reader, or so Fernande maintained, least of all of arcane metaphysical texts in a language he had yet to master, so he is more likely to have absorbed Jarry's essence through Apollinaire or Jacob, Salmon or Cremnitz, than at first hand. Apollinaire, whose debt to the author of *Ubu* was prodigious, is likely to have been the principal conduit for his ideas—a conduit rather than a catalyst. Since Apollinaire would have risked forfeiting some of his power over Picasso by introducing him to someone who was infinitely more sensitive to new trends in art than he was, he may, consciously or not, have kept them apart. It is a tragic irony that Jarry never actually saw *Les Demoiselles d'Avignon*, the painting that embodies so many of his theories and fantasies—the more so since Apollinaire, by then Picasso's closest friend, utterly failed to appreciate its qualities.

Thirty years later, when Picasso temporarily abandoned painting for writing, he would turn again to Jarry. His poetry of the late thirties bubbles with Jarry-esque images, but it is Picasso's plays, above all *Le Désir attrapé par la queue* (January 1941)—a farce about wartime preoccupations with hunger, cold and sex—that carry on Jarry's tradition of scatology and slapstick. Picasso did not conceal the source of his inspiration. After the first reading of *Le Désir* in the spring of 1944, he asked the 'cast' back to his studio and extracted a draft of Jarry's *Ubu Cocu* from the cupboard where he kept the manuscripts of his poet friends, often annotated and illustrated by himself. While the Leirises, Sartres and Aubiers inspected the yellowing pages, Picasso recited Jarry's lines from memory. Ten years or so later, Tristan Tzara brought a manuscript of *Doctor Faustroll* to show Picasso. Would he do a cover for it? Inspired by Jarry's incendiarism of Rousseau's portrait, he heated a poker until it was red-hot ('I just might set fire to the house,' he threatened) and burned the poet's portrait into the cover of the manuscript. Picasso had an instinctive flair for the right gesture.[24]

Picasso. *Bathers: Design for a Monument.* Dinard, July 8, 1928. Pen and tinted wash on sketchbook page, 30.2×22cm. Musée Picasso, Paris.

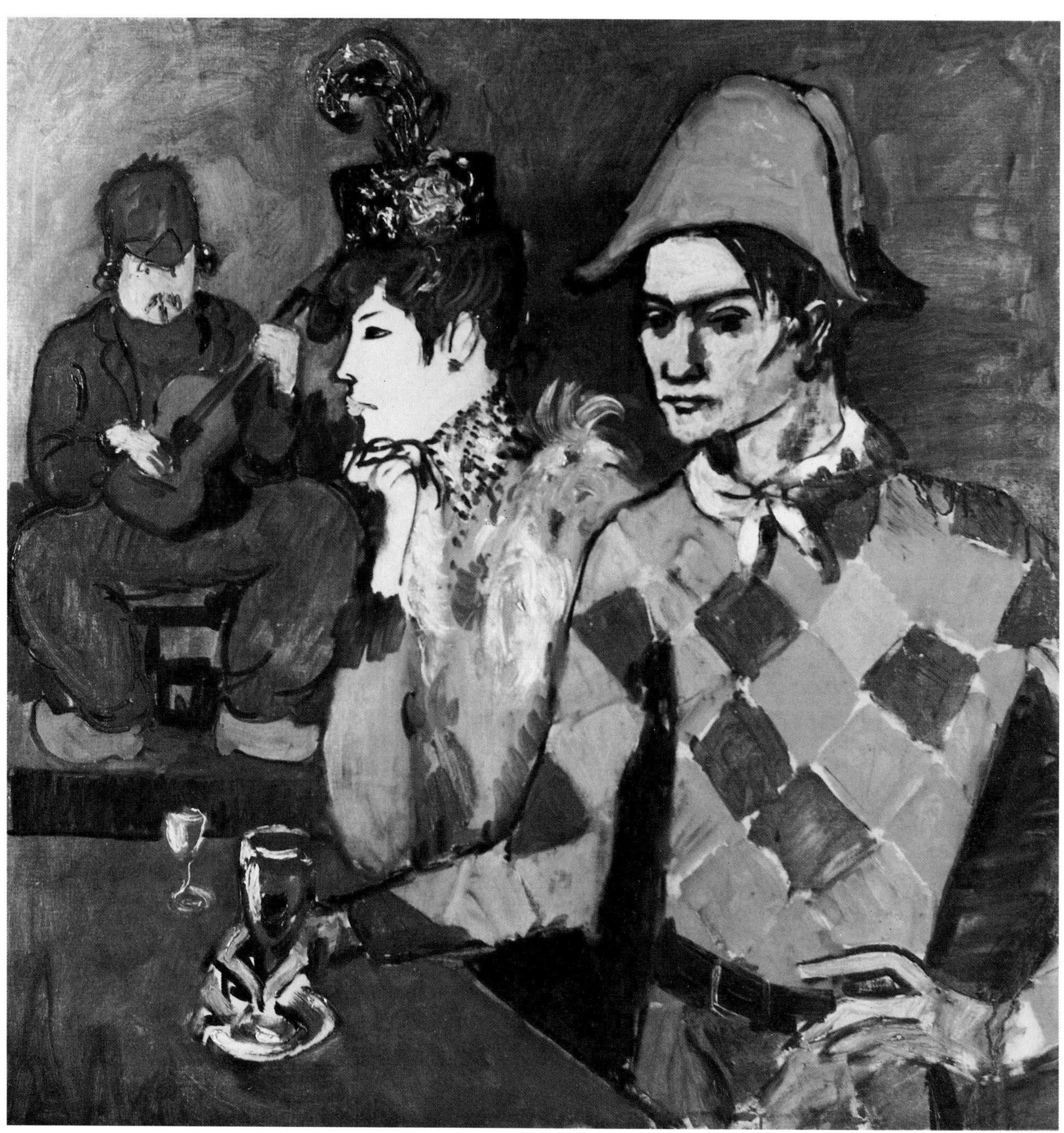

24

Au Lapin Agile

Kees van Dongen *The Clown*. c.1905–07. Oil on canvas, 100×81cm. Private collection.

Opposite: Picasso. *Au Lapin Agile*. Paris, 1904–05. Oil on canvas, 99×100.3cm. Private collection.

WHENEVER THEY COULD AFFORD IT, the *bande à Picasso* went to prizefights or the circus. 'Picasso would have been proud to make friends with a boxer,' Fernande says.[1] And years later he boasted that he and his friends 'were greatly respected in Montmartre for our tough airs and our biceps. We were taken for boxers. Sometimes cabdrivers wouldn't charge us.'[2] As for the circus, ever since his adolescent affair with Rosita del Oro, it had been his favourite form of entertainment, after the bullring. Moreover the Cirque Médrano—only a few streets away from the Bateau Lavoir—had just launched a major new attraction: the great clown Grock, who made his debut in December 1904. 'I was really under the spell of the circus,' Picasso later recalled. 'I liked the clowns best of all. . . . Did you know that it was here at the Médrano that clowns first began to abandon their classic costumes and dress in a more burlesque fashion? It was a real revelation. They could invent their own outfits, their own characters, do anything they fancied.'[3] Fernande confirms this: 'Grock was a revelation, and there were tornadoes of laughter and hysteria. . . . I never saw Picasso laugh so happily as at the Médrano. He was like a child.'[4]

Picasso's circus scenes make no specific references to Grock or Antonet or Jarry's lookalike, Kobold, or 'Caoutchouc' (the india-rubber man) whom van Dongen painted during his 1905 stint at Médrano. The poetic style of the Rose period precluded knockabout humour. Also Picasso was too narcissistic to identify with anyone less romantic or appealing than a harlequin or *saltimbanque*. Fifty years would go by before he could portray himself as a stunted Grock, ancient and childish, mocked and mocking as a court dwarf.[5] Even the one major work of the Rose period that portrays circus performers, *Young Acrobat on a Ball*, was not, strictly speaking, a circus painting. The circus involved movement, and Picasso always preferred static to dynamic subjects; hence the hesitant look of his sketchbook drawings of acrobats in action. Far more masterly are the gouaches that he worked up back in the studio: the little equestrienne cavorting on a huge carthorse, or the slip of a girl being hoisted aloft by an acrobat with biceps larger than her waist. Picasso never shows us the circus ring or the audience, as Degas, Lautrec and Seurat do, nor are we given a look upwards at the trapezists (for this we have to wait until 1933, when a visit to Médrano inspired paintings of acrobats swooping about in the spotlights like swallows). As a rule Picasso prefers to focus on a single figure or couple—an image that is compact and static rather than

Left: Cirque Médrano in Montmartre, *c.*1910.

Far left: Marthe and Juliette Vesque. *The Equestrienne Wally Slezak at the Cirque Médrano.* September 4, 1904. Watercolour on paper. Musée des Arts et Traditions Populaires, Paris.

Left: Picasso. *Equestrienne* (detail). Paris, 1905. Charcoal on paper, 27×21cm. Marina Picasso collection, Galerie Jan Krugier.

Below left: Marthe and Juliette Vesque. *Brick and Grock at the Cirque Médrano.* December 4, 1904. Watercolour on paper. Musée des Arts et Traditions Populaires, Paris.

Picasso. *Equestrienne.* Paris, 1905. Gouache on cardboard, 60×79cm. Private collection.

random and mobile. So he concentrates on backstage subjects—subjects with humanity or pathos. As Fernande describes, Picasso

> would spend all his time at the bar, which was always thick with the hot, slightly nauseating smell seeping up from the stables. He would stay there all evening . . . talking to the clowns. He enjoyed their oddness, their speech, their jokes; though these were usually pretty feeble when they weren't actually performing. He admired them and had real sympathy for them.
>
> He knew Ilès and Antonio, Alex and Rico. Once he invited a Dutch clown and his wife, who was a Polish equestrienne, to dinner. They were both—particularly the man—the coarsest people imaginable.[6]

For all their coarseness, they struck Picasso as true artists, like himself: wanderers who led a picturesquely marginal existence when they were not, like him, performing feats of prodigious skill. His trio of poets were likewise addicted to the circus; for them, however, it was a light-hearted metaphor for the world at large, and as such it figures in their poems.

Picasso. *The Athlete,* Paris, 1905. Gouache on cardboard, 54×44cm. Private collection. Inscribed to Paul Fort.

* * *

Whether or not they went to Médrano or the Cirque Bostock on Place Clichy, Picasso and his gang would usually end up at Le Lapin Agile (the successor to Le Zut) on the rue des Saules. Originally known as the Cabaret des Assassins—after the portraits of famous murderers that hung on its walls—it had subsequently been sold to André Gill, the famous illustrator, and was known as Le Lapin à Gill, hence Le Lapin Agile (the agile rabbit) and the inn sign Gill had painted of a rabbit leaping out of a casserole. The next proprietor was a truculent woman called Adèle, who had once partnered La Goulue in her famous quadrille and counted Toulouse-Lautrec among her clients. She sold out to the enterprising Frédé, who wanted to rise above the squalor of Le Zut and give up his other métier: selling fish off the back of a donkey, while playing a clarinet to attract customers. The Lapin Agile was especially attractive in summer. Picasso would bring his dogs and sit on the rustic terrace in the shade of the acacia tree in whose branches the proprietor's monkey would play, while Lolo, his artistic donkey, ate everything in sight. There was also a tame raven that belonged to the proprietor's stepdaughter, Margot—the subject, as we have seen, of two remarkable portraits. Before Fernande moved in with him, Picasso would occasionally have other girls on his arm: Germaine, for one, who was no more faithful to Pichot (whom she had yet to marry) than she had been to Casagemas. Germaine shared Picasso's passion for the circus—in her case for the 'carneys' who became her lovers, rather than for the actual spectacle.[7]

Flyer for the Lapin Agile in the 1890s. Musée de Montmartre, Paris.

Since Picasso had painted the walls of Le Zut with a Temptation of St Antony three years earlier, it was only natural that he should be asked by Frédé to come up with an apotheosis of his new establishment—this time on canvas. Picasso assigns Frédé to the background and portrays himself in harlequin costume in the foreground.[8] Next to him is Germaine, wearing a boa and a hat sprouting an elegant tuft of feathers. The contrast between his timeless motley and her fashionable finery makes for ambivalence. Why, in view of his ardent courting of Fernande, did he

At the Lapin Agile. *c.*1872. Bibliothèque Nationale, Paris.

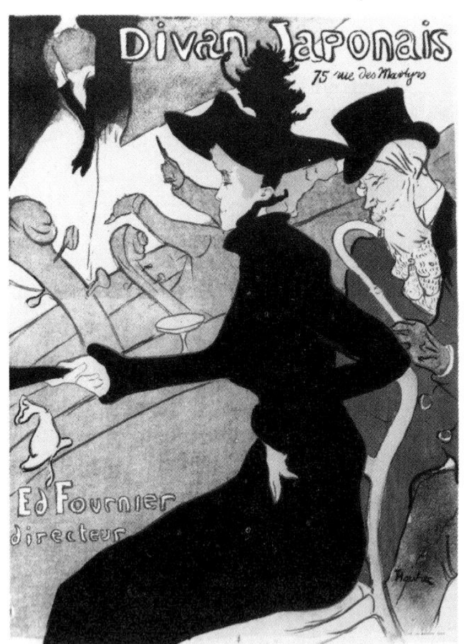

Toulouse-Lautrec. *Le Divan Japonais.* 1893. Lithographic poster, 80.8×60.8cm. Musée des Arts Décoratifs, Paris.

Picasso. *Harlequin.* Paris, 1905. Pen on notebook page, 14.3×9.2cm. The Metropolitan Museum of Art, New York, The Alfred Stieglitz Collection, 1949. Drawn on the back of a page on which Picasso had listed names and addresses in Paris, including those of the artists Durrio, Canals and González.

include Germaine? She was just a stand-in, Picasso said.[9] Since Fernande was still married to Percheron and living with Debienne/de la Baume, she could not have allowed herself to be *affiché* on the wall of a bohemian cabaret, above all in the company of yet another lover.

Au Lapin Agile is the only work of this period to have been executed for a specific purpose and a specific place: to embellish the tavern's dark and dingy *grande salle.* This room was dominated by a huge cast of Apollo with a lyre, a plaster relief from Java and a life-size *Crucifixion* by Walsey ('a Christ of the cabarets, comrade Jesus in the socialist spirit of the period,' according to Salmon).[10] Like the Valadons, Poulbots, Girieuds and other works by little-known artists that hung alongside it, Picasso's painting was done in exchange for credit; nonetheless he took the commission seriously—the more so since collectors and dealers made a point of visiting the tavern. The famous old *chansonnier populaire* Aristide Bruant had backed Frédé and appointed him his successor, so Picasso took his cue from Bruant's image-maker, Toulouse-Lautrec. Four years earlier, he had based his portrait of Mañach on one of the Bruant posters; this time he drew instead on Lautrec's no less famous poster of Jane Avril for Le Divan Japonais. Germaine's chalk-white profile is strikingly like that of Lautrec's Jane Avril (whom Picasso had also portrayed); her hat even sports a similar feather. Since Picasso's painting had to register across a large, crowded, smoky room lit by lamps 'shaded with red silk scarves',[11] this poster-like conception served a practical purpose. The necessarily broad brushwork—a contrast to most of Picasso's recent work—recalls Manet's easy, eloquent facture rather than Lautrec's. There is also something of Manet about the cool, alienated air of the figures. Picasso shows himself to be, albeit briefly, 'a painter of contemporary life', such as Baudelaire had postulated.

A scene in a novel by Eugène Marsan, published in 1906, gives an idea of the impact of *Au Lapin Agile* and the reputation that Picasso was beginning to make. Sandricourt, the hero (and ostensible author) of the novel, and his creator are discussing the cabaret and its colourful owner and clientele:

> M. Sandricourt pointed out an eye-catching picture done in flat, burned-out colours: 'This Harlequin and Colombine are famished (notice the eyes), for they are penniless and, for want of anything to eat, they drink. They don't pay the slightest attention to each other; but I can tell that they are in love. The young artist who painted that in two hours will become a genius, if Paris does not destroy him.'
>
> I objected, for I had instantly recognized the hand that had painted the yellow, red, green lozenges of their tights onto the skinny bodies of Harlequin and Colombine.
>
> 'The painter of this Harlequin', I said, 'already has a reputation. . . . He is an Andalusian, and one who paints, as only a Spaniard can, that look and those tatters. You could call him . . . the Callot of the *saltimbanques*, but be sure to remember his name: Picasso.'[12]

An even larger, more loosely painted canvas, executed around the same time and entitled, though not by Picasso, the *Marriage of Pierrette*,[13] may also have been intended as a decoration for the Lapin Agile. It was originally conceived as a theatrical scene with a commedia dell'arte flavour, based on a series of drawings that seem to have been done in the course

Left: Picasso. *Marriage of Pierrette.* Paris, 1905. Oil on canvas, 115×195cm. Private collection.

Below: Interior of the Lapin Agile, c.1905, with Frédé playing his guitar.

of a performance. One of these portrays Harlequin, Columbine, Pierrot and various attendants, and is inscribed: 'the harlequin black blue and pink perhaps yellow instead of pink . . . and the woman in blue and white (with a plate of fruit) dressed in vermilion and green / carmine. A green meadow would not be a bad idea.' En route from sketchbook to canvas, the setting changed from theatre to cabaret (the Lapin Agile?). The harlequin is not exactly a self-portrait; however, this figure, who has his hand behind his back as if clutching a bunch of flowers, and who bows and blows a kiss to some revellers—a pretty girl with a fan, wearing a headscarf (as Fernande often did), a slightly sinister-looking sugar daddy in a top hat (seemingly a portrait: there are other drawings of him) and three wan guests—is evidently self-referential. Farewell, the Harlequin/Picasso figure seems to be saying, but to whom or what? The theme is no more resolved than the execution.

Picasso. Study for *Marriage of Pierrette*. Paris, 1905. Conté crayon on paper, 25×33.5cm. Heirs of the artist.

* * *

Picasso's life came to revolve round the Lapin Agile much as it had revolved round Els Quatre Gats. But Frédé, whom we see in the background of the painting, dressed as an *opera buffa* bandit in a heavy brown corduroy suit, trapper's fur hat and peasant sabots, was no Pere Romeu. The picture of '*le brave Frédé*' that emerges from the more nostalgic memoirs of the period—singing his famous repertory of street songs, playing the cello, clarinet and guitar by ear (he never learned to read music), baking pottery in his kiln, helping his Burgundian wife, '*la brave Berthe*', serve up appetizing dinners (wine included) for two francs a head and being a supportive father-figure to one and all—is too good to be true. 'Frédé was a ruffian,' Picasso said.[14] And if Montmartre eventually (around 1912) turned into a tourist trap, Frédé was partly to blame. He and his awful son shocked their original clientele by declaring some of them undesirable and catering instead to sightseers in search of local colour. In their greed for money, they replaced the Picasso painting, which had never been framed but simply nailed to the wall, with picture-postcard daubs of the Butte and sold it (in 1912) to the Berlin dealer Flechtheim, for what, Picasso said, seemed a fortune to Frédé, but was in fact next to nothing.

Isolated from the rest of Paris by its exclusion from Baron Haussmann's replanning, Montmartre had hitherto remained a village that was part bohemian, part working-class, part den of whores and thieves. In its early days the Lapin Agile was, as Salmon said, '*l'auberge du village*'. Besides Picasso and his original *bande*, the habitués would soon (1907–08) include Braque, Derain, Vlaminck, Valadon, van Dongen, Modigliani, Gris, Herbin, Marcoussis, Utrillo and Marie Laurencin; even the unbohemian Matisse paid an occasional visit. The tavern also catered to local people as well as artists, and to the apaches who made Montmartre their fief. Occasionally some of them would force their way into the bar brandishing razors, sometimes to hold up the place, more often to get back a girl who had gone off with an artist. One of Frédé's sons, Victor—a notorious rogue who was always having fights over women—was shot dead at the cash register. But by and large a 'kind of understanding comradeship existed between the poets and the gangsters'.[15]

Less welcome than the apaches were the bourgeois, who were refused entry unless introduced by a familiar of the place. In its heyday the Lapin Agile was almost as difficult to get into as the Jockey Club. The first time the elegantly dressed poet Francis Carco appeared, he was regarded with suspicion until he grabbed Frédé's guitar and belted out bawdy ballads in a Marseillais accent.[16] Working people were never turned away. The chronicler of Montmartre, Roland Dorgelès, recalls a wretched-looking waif getting up to recite: the room fell quiet as he gave 'the most heart-rending' reading of poems by Villon, Baudelaire and Verlaine anyone had ever heard.[17] Afterwards a friend came round with a hat but there was barely enough 'take' to pay for a bed. And so Charles Dullin—the future creator of avant-garde theatre—was reduced to doing his tempestuous declamations in a lion's cage at the Foire de Neuilly, before being discovered and launched on his spectacular career.[18] By and large, however, the young performers were not up to much. Most of the leading lights belonged to the *bande à Picasso*, and had a room to themselves. Apart from the irrepressible Max Jacob ('I was the dancingest little clown on earth,' he boasted to Tristan Tzara),[19] none of the *bande* deigned to perform in public.

Later (1910) Roland Dorgelès would bring the Lapin Agile its greatest notoriety. This philistine journalist decided to poke fun at modern art, and who better to take on than Picasso and Apollinaire? It all started when Dorgelès asked Apollinaire whether, if his mother died, he would commission Picasso to do a deathbed portrait of her. In the face of the poet's disdainful dismissal, Dorgelès set about concocting a spoof manifesto, which he signed 'Joachim Raphael Boronali' (an anagram of '*aliboron*', jackass). He borrowed Frédé's famous donkey, Lolo, and, in the presence of a photographer and a bailiff, tied Lolo's tail to a brush, which was dipped in one paint pot after another and applied to three canvases. The results were entitled *And the Sun Went to Sleep, On the Adriatic*, and *Seascape*. Dorgelès had these 'Boronalis' hung at the un-juried Salon des Indépendants, and arranged for *Le Matin* to publish the manifesto, photographs and affidavit.

Frédé's donkey executing a work by Boronali, 1910. Bibliothèque Nationale, Paris.

Apollinaire took all this in good part: 'a pleasant joke and not at all excessive,' he wrote in his review of the Salon.[20] The show was immediately mobbed with modern-art haters, likewise—not entirely to Frédé's displeasure—the Lapin Agile. As Dorgelès boasted, Boronali has since been listed in Bénézit's *Dictionnaire des peintres*. As he also boasted, many years later, when the French ambassador recounted the story to Hitler, the latter hooted with delight, '*Ein Esel! Wie komisch!*'[21] The donkey, Picasso thought, was really Dorgelès.

Stunts like this turned Picasso against Montmartre. And by 1912 he and most of his friends had left La Butte for Montparnasse, the other side of Paris. It was not until 1936 that he went back to the Lapin Agile. After spending a morning working at his printer Lacourière's Montmartre studio, he and Sabartès took a nostalgic stroll on the Butte, 'to get a breath of fresh air and refresh our memories'.[22] On seeing Frédé on the terrace of the Lapin Agile, they sat down and talked to him. Picasso could not resist returning on two or three subsequent occasions. A few months later Frédé was dead. In old age the artist would revert in memory more often to the Lapin Agile and the Bateau Lavoir than to any of his other haunts. All Picasso's subsequent studios, Kahnweiler said, evoked the atmosphere of the Bateau Lavoir.[23] When the nostalgia wore off, friends would often glimpse a certain residual bitterness.

*   *   *

During the winter of 1904–05 Picasso made friends with some Dutch artists who congregated at the Lapin Agile. His first contact was Otto van Rees, a pupil of Jan Toorop, who had arrived in October 1904. He and his common-law wife, Adya Dutilh, likewise a painter, had moved in with a convivial young journalist named Tom Schilperoort. The van Reeses needed their own place—Adya was expecting a baby—so Picasso arranged for them to take a vacant studio above his own in the Bateau Lavoir. And there they stayed for the next year or so. Van Rees, who later went to Switzerland and became a very minor Dadaist, never warmed to Picasso: 'He was a dreadful, crazy Spaniard,' he later told an interviewer. 'He may have been a wonderfully gifted and imaginative artist, but he was always out for his own ends. All of us were poor as church mice and helped each other with loans of materials or food or small sums of money. Picasso was the only one who never paid anybody back.'[24]

Kees and Guus van Dongen with Dolly, 1906. Private collection.

Through the van Reeses Picasso met the painter Kees van Dongen and his wife, and he arranged for them to take a studio at the Bateau Lavoir in December 1905. The red-bearded giant of a husband had done well as an illustrator for the satirical magazine *L'Assiette au Beurre*. Why didn't Picasso do the same? Much as he needed the 800 francs that van Dongen induced the paper to offer for a set of drawings, Picasso refused. He was determined to resist the easy lure of commercial work. Van Dongen's wife, Guus,[25] had recently given birth to a daughter, Dolly. Picasso played with this child by the hour—'Tablo' she called him—and in doing so became ever more friendly with her congenial parents, also with Kees's brother Jean, a potter who had settled in Montmartre and married a singer at the Lapin Agile.[26] The van Dongens kept open house, which made life much easier for Fernande—a good but lazy cook. Although she had given up modelling, Fernande posed more than once for van Dongen, clothed as well as naked. Picasso would never have allowed her to pose in the nude, so she must have done this when he was away in the course of summer 1905.

Van Dongen stayed at the Bateau Lavoir little over a year. As soon as his Fauve paintings began to sell, he moved out (Juan Gris took his place) to a more comfortable studio on the rue Lamarck behind the Folies Bergère. But he continued to spend evenings sketching away in the dance halls and cafés of Montmartre. Fernande criticizes his preference for garish scenes, but the garishness of his boss-eyed dancer or uproarious transvestite (the so-called *Soprano Singer*) is surely preferable to the modish blend of art deco and flashy Fauvism that van Dongen later adopted.

In May or early June 1905 the van Dongens, or the van Reeses, introduced Picasso to their former roommate Tom Schilperoort.[27] They became instant friends. The tall Dutchman, only a few months younger than Picasso, was already earning a reputation for himself in Paris as a cabaret '*conférencier*' and impromptu musician; he also worked as Paris correspondent, covering art, entertainment and sport for some of

Adya van Rees. *Portrait of Otto van Rees. c.*1902. Pencil on paper. Whereabouts unknown.

Van Dongen. *Modjesko, Soprano Singer*. Paris, 1908. Oil on canvas, 100×81 cm. The Museum of Modern Art, New York, Gift of Mr and Mrs Peter A. Rübel.

Van Dongen. *Portrait of Fernande Olivier*. Paris, 1905. Oil on canvas, 100×81 cm. Samir Traboulsi Collection.

Tom Schilperoort, *c.*1915. Regional Archive, Alkmaar.

his home-town (Rotterdam) newspapers. Not only was he one of Kees van Dongen's earliest reviewers, he also succeeded in publishing an interview with the dancer Mata Hari.[28] Schilperoort had recently inherited 10,000 francs and was compulsively running through it. In some respects he was not unlike Casagemas—wild, self-destructive, unfocused and generous enough to pay for everyone's drinks. By the time Picasso met him, Schilperoort was eager to return to Holland, where he planned to spend the summer with a girlfriend called Nelly.[29] Why didn't Picasso join him? he asked. He had taken a house at Schoorl, an unspoiled village in Northern Holland, picturesquely situated at the foot of gigantic sand dunes, which stretch for three bleak miles to the North Sea. It was an excessively hot summer and the penniless Picasso quickly agreed to spend June and July working in Tom and Nelly's cottage on the outskirts of the village.

The only expense was the fare. 'Max Jacob didn't have any more [money] than I did,' Picasso said. 'He went to the concierge and returned with twenty francs. I had a satchel (here Picasso mimed the fitting of the strap over his shoulder) and I'd put my paints in, but my brushes wouldn't fit. So I broke them in half and was on my way.' Picasso left his studio in the care of Salmon (who is caricatured in one of the Dutch sketchbooks) and other friends. 'Before I went I'd done a drawing of a lawyer pointing his finger, just like Daumier, and I'd signed it "H. Daumier". When I came back from Holland, I found they'd sold the drawing as a Daumier. Now whenever I go to a museum, I'm a little nervous about running into my drawing.'[30]

Picasso with Schilperoort and his girlfriend Nelly at Schoorl, 1905.

Two sketchbooks have survived from this trip. In one of them, dated '*Junio et Julio* 1905', Picasso copied down a train schedule with the note 'change trains at Haarlem.' En route he passed through Amsterdam (where Apollinaire would also spend a holiday that summer) but could not afford to stop and see the Rijksmuseum. Picasso also visited nearby Alkmaar, where he had to change from a train to a barge, and the small inland port of Hoorn (half an hour by train from Alkmaar), where he sketched what used to be the St John's guesthouse.[31] North Holland must have seemed very foreign. The 1905 Baedeker describes the square in front of the weigh house at Alkmaar, 'covered with huge piles of red and yellow cheeses, while the streets are full of the gaily painted wagons of the neighbouring peasantry'. In those days the area was seldom visited by tourists. To quote Baedeker again:

> The inhabitants are more primitive in their habits than those of Southern Holland, and adhere more tenaciously to the picturesque costumes of their ancestors. The head-dress of the women is often curious . . . a broad band of silver-gilt in the shape of a horseshoe across the forehead . . . decorated at the sides with large rosettes or oval plates of gold. Above this is worn a cap or veil of rich lace, with wings hanging down to the neck.

'Klein Zwitserland', Schoorl, at the turn of the century, with summer houses below the sand dunes.

Picasso did several studies of these coifs and some high-crowned straw hats that were also peculiar to the region. Short-sleeved bodices, voluminous skirts, clogs and little baskets completed the costume of the plump local girls, whom the artist portrayed with Rubensian relish and in one case as the three Graces in attitudes that recall the Rubens of this subject in the Prado.

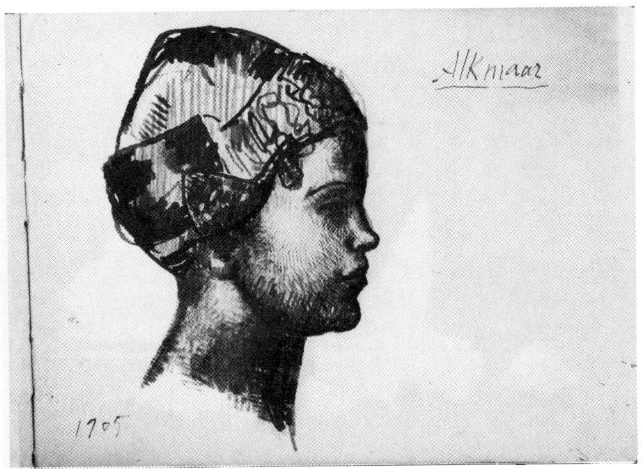

Top left: Picasso. *Head of a Dutch Girl.* Alkmaar, 1905. Pen and watercolour on sketchbook page, 12×16cm. Musée Picasso, Paris.

Above: Picasso. *Canal Scene.* Alkmaar, 1905. Watercolour on sketchbook page, 12×16cm. Musée Picasso, Paris.

House at Schoorl, *c.*1900, with traditional pyramidal roof covered with a pattern of tiles and thatch. The tiles are generally arranged in a step pattern, as here, or with curved edges, as depicted by Picasso.

Picasso. *Three Dutch Girls.* Schoorl, 1905. Gouache on paper, 77×67cm. Musée National d'Art Moderne, Paris.

Right: Picasso. *View on the North Holland Canal.* Schoorl, 1905. Pen and watercolour on sketchbook page, 12.5×18.5cm. Musée Picasso, Paris.

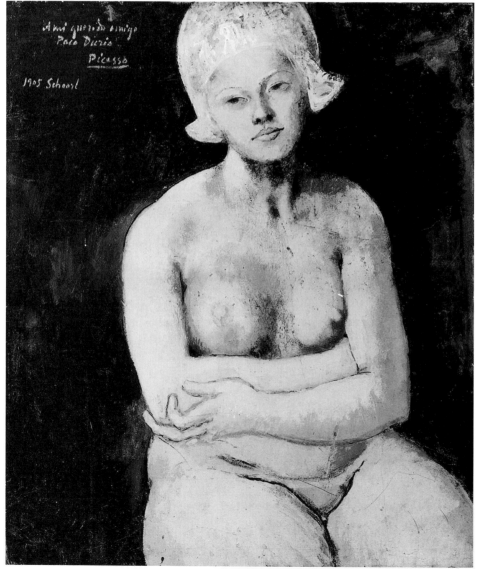

Picasso. *La Belle Hollandaise.* Schoorl, 1905. Gouache on cardboard, 77×66.3cm. Queensland Art Gallery, Brisbane, S. H. Ervin Gift, 1965. Inscribed to Paco Durrio.

The girls of Schoorl had a decisive influence on Picasso's work. We need only compare these fleshy milkmaids reared on local cheese with the skinny denizens of Montmartre living on ether and absinthe to see that the artist was developing a taste for earthier, heftier women. Fernande claimed that Picasso did not enjoy Holland, 'because it was too cloudy for one who loved sunshine, as Picasso did' (untrue: the weather is recorded as being exceptionally fine); and because the girls, 'who towered head and shoulders above him, kissing him and sitting on his knee', made him feel ridiculous.[32] Untrue again: Fernande resented being left behind in Paris. 'She was a married woman and had obligations' is the reason Picasso gave for not taking her to Holland.[33] In any case this sudden respect for morality is not convincing. Lack of funds is a more likely reason for leaving her behind. Whatever the explanation, Fernande aroused Picasso's jealousy by posing for van Dongen in his absence; and he aroused hers by showing her the nude studies he brought back from Holland—'schoolgirls like guardsmen', he said. There must have been recriminations and a reconciliation. She moved in with him for good a few weeks later.

The village café, 'De Roode Leeuw', at Schoorl at the beginning of the century.

Little is known about Picasso's life at Schoorl. Schilperoort turned out to have a wild streak. He had replaced his door knocker with a rattle made of bones, and when the postman shook this fetish, Schilperoort would make gruesome noises and jump out on him from an upper window.[34] It was difficult for Picasso to work in Tom and Nelly's small house, so after a week or two he moved out and installed himself in a pension, presumably at Schilperoort's expense. The pension overlooked the main canal at Schoorldam and was run by the unmarried daughter of the postman, Diewertje de Geus. Next door was a bargees' hang-out, a café called 's-lands Welvaren (near the present Café de Band), where Picasso would 'chat' with the locals (even when there was no language in common, he had an extraordinary gift for communicating with people), before going to paint in the attic. Picasso returned to Paris early in July;[35] so eventually did Schilperoort, to spend the rest of his inheritance. Fernande's assertion that he ended up 'the most bohemian of bohemians' is quite untrue.[36]

Thanks to the arabesques of thatch on thatch, and thatch on tile, which are typical of local architecture, many of the steep-roofed houses that figure in Picasso's sketchbooks can still be identified. McCully, who has pieced together the artist's life at Schoorl, believes that the range of sand dunes—tree-covered where they slope down to the village, Alpine in scale and Saharan in bareness nearer the sea—may have inspired the desert-like setting for the large *Saltimbanques*, which Picasso would repaint on his return to Paris.[37] The masterpiece of this brief Dutch period is *La Belle Hollandaise*. With Schilperoort's help, Picasso had found a girl who was prepared to pose naked—to the scandal of the village; some of the locals believe it was Diewertje de Geus, the thirty-year-old woman whose house he was living in, described by a neighbour as 'an adventuress, who liked to dress up in men's clothes'.[38] The result is a largish nude (gouache, chalks and oil on cardboard) that looks ahead to the hefty nudes of the following year and the giantesses of the neo-classical period. When he subsequently gave this work to Paco Durrio to hang alongside his Gauguins (a measure of his pride in it), Picasso commented that 'the most beautiful women's breasts were those that gave the most milk'[39]—a remark that

Picasso. *Nude with Dutch Bonnet*. Schoorl, 1905. Gouache on cardboard, 75.5×60 cm. Whereabouts unknown.

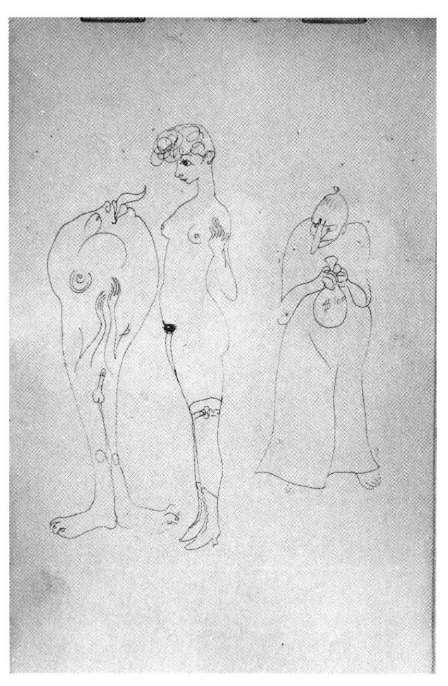

Picasso. *Man in a Brothel.* Alkmaar or Hoorn, 1905. Pen on sketchbook page, 18.5×12.5cm. Musée Picasso, Paris.

could have been made to provoke or humiliate Fernande. *La Belle Hollandaise* may have been a nursing mother (there is a related drawing of a mother and child) or the postman's daughter; Picasso may also have found models in the local whorehouses, either in Alkmaar or Hoorn, which his sketchbooks record his visiting. In one drawing a fat old man with an erection makes love to a nude girl while a procuress (shades of Celestina) runs off with a sack labelled '$100'. It has also been suggested that a huge portrait of Schilperoort's acquaintance Mata Hari as a Hindu snake-charmer might be by Picasso. There is no possibility of this whatsoever.[40]

When later asked what had become of all the drawings he had done in Holland, Picasso replied mysteriously, 'Perhaps nobody has ever seen them. They must be in some folder, tucked away in a corner somewhere.'[41] So far no material has turned up other than the two Dutch sketchbooks.[42] These reveal that besides depicting the local scene, Picasso was much preoccupied with the projects he had left unfinished in Paris. He was evidently anxious to return to Paris and wrestle once more with his *Saltimbanques*.

* * *

Back in Paris in July, Picasso resumed work on his big painting. At some point he had become dissatisfied with the original concept, which held together as a sketch but failed to work on a much larger scale. X-rays show that Picasso first reduced the extended family group to two acrobats with a dog, as in the highly finished gouache he had shown at the Galeries Serrurier. However, this would have left the vast canvas too empty, so he tried another solution: figures crammed together as tightly as football players in a team photograph. The characters, all of whom had already been portrayed individually or in twos or threes, were to be posed around the portly figure of El tío Pepe; Picasso never developed this frontal idea beyond the drawing stage. He also tried out some more complex solutions: a foreground frieze of *saltimbanques* set off against a circus ring with a girl training a cavorting horse; and tío Pepe surrounded by girls, one of whom looks at us through a spotted veil she holds up to the light. But these, too, were abandoned. After his return from Holland, Picasso repainted the *Saltimbanques* once, or possibly twice; it is impossible to establish the nature of these successive stages with any degree of accuracy.[43]

In the most worked-up sketch for the final composition there is a surprising development: the background is taken up by a racetrack scene in the manner of Degas. The speeding horses would have made a dynamic contrast with the static *saltimbanques*, but, as the circus drawings confirm, movement was not Picasso's forte, and the effect would have been distracting. He ultimately settled for a minimal setting that is much more telling. The troupe has struck camp and is about to move on—from the world of genre into the world of allegory. The figures are *gens du voyage* —wafted hither and thither, just as Picasso had been over the last five years. The tight-knit composition that he finally chose has an unusual derivation: it stems from the artist's own hand, as we know from a drawing of his palm, each finger of which represents a different figure in the central group. Even the little girl with the basket can be seen as a thumb. Picasso has also twisted the hand of the self-portrait around behind him,

Left: Picasso. *El Tío Pepe and Saltimbanque Family*. Paris, 1905. Pen, watercolour and charcoal on paper, 20.2×31.2cm. Musée Picasso, Paris.

Below: Picasso. *Saltimbanque Family* (with racetrack). Paris, 1905. Gouache and charcoal on cardboard, 51.2×61.2cm. Pushkin Museum, Moscow.

Picasso. *The Saltimbanques*. Paris, 1905. Oil on canvas, 212.8×229.6cm. National Gallery of Art, Washington, D.C., Chester Dale Collection.

as if to echo this conceit. Besides palmistry, there is a touch of the Tarot. Some of the figures have a hieratic, playing-card look. The air of fatality likewise recalls *La Vie*. Once again Picasso asks the cosmic questions that he had asked in his earlier allegory, the very same questions that his mentor, Gauguin, had formulated eight years earlier: *D'où venons-nous? Que sommes-nous? Où allons-nous?* The strength of Gauguin's masterpiece is that it itemizes the cosmos and charts the course of life; Picasso's figures seem at a loss for answers.

In addition to Gauguin, *The Saltimbanques* has other French antecedents, starting with those seventeenth-century French painters the Le Nain brothers, whom Picasso would always admire (for their 'silence', he once said) to the extent that he later bought two works formerly attributed to them.[44] Picasso also harks back to Watteau, whose Gilles and commedia dell'arte characters seem as alienated as these strolling players; and Daumier, whose gnarled old tumblers and vagabonds had captivated Picasso when he first saw them at the great retrospective in 1901. The harlequins that are to be found in works by Cézanne, Degas and Seurat have been cited as precedents for Picasso's,[45] but these serve a very different purpose. Apart from Gauguin and Puvis de Chavannes, the only late nineteenth-century master whose work exerted any deep influence at this period was Manet, whose early masterpiece *The Old Musician* (exhibited at the 1905 Salon d'Automne) looks back at Velázquez as much as it looks ahead to Picasso. Since *The Old Musician* and *The Saltimbanques* belong to the National Gallery in Washington (both bequeathed by Chester Dale), it is easy to go from one to the other and see the analogies in the light of both artists' dependence on poets: Picasso on Apollinaire; Manet on Baudelaire. Like Manet, Picasso has appropriated Baudelaire's metaphor of vagabonds as artists; and he has set his wanderers in a metaphysical wasteland, where they confront each other, not to speak of ourselves, with the coolness that Manet (primed by Baudelaire) used to such telling effect. There are also stylistic similarities: compositions that are the more redolent of real-life randomness for their seeming awkwardness; deadpan lighting that throws minimal shadows; compositions whose figures seem to belong in different perspectival contexts. The spatial disjunction between the old musician and the top-hatted ragpicker in the Manet is as striking as that between the girl with the hat and the central group in the Picasso. The latter does not belong with the Parisian *saltimbanques*; the famous sketch of her in a cone-shaped hat hung with a *rebocillo* of white muslin is usually thought to identify her as an interloper, a native of Mallorca.[46] (Picasso may have copied her from a picture postcard, sent by Junyer Vidal, who summered on the island.) There is, however, another possible source for this figure. A sketchbook page that includes croquis of a Tanagra figure, swathed in draperies, wearing a cone-shaped hat, suggests that the inspiration was in fact Hellenistic.[47] Here we should remember that Tanagra figures had become very fashionable in Paris. Twenty years later (thanks in part to Picasso), their place would be taken by tribal art.

Some of the *saltimbanques* have been incorrectly identified. Salmon claims that the fat buffoon (whose right leg is nowhere to be seen) stands for Apollinaire; he is of course El tío Pepe.[48] As for the suggestion that the little girl with the basket is Raymonde, the child that Picasso and Fernande would briefly adopt, but not for another two years, the model was

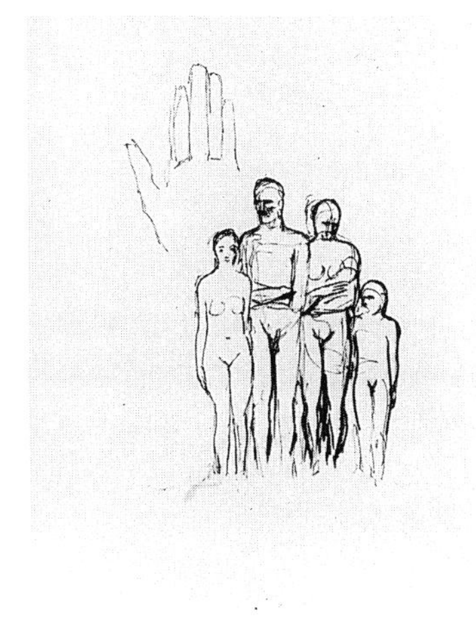

Picasso. Study for *The Saltimbanques* (based on the artist's hand). Paris, 1905. Pen on paper, 37×25cm. Heirs of the artist.

Manet. *The Old Musician*. 1862. Oil on canvas, 187.4×248.3cm. National Gallery of Art, Washington, D.C., Chester Dale Collection.

Picasso. *Girl with a Hoop.* Paris, 1905. Crayon and watercolour on sketch-book page, 14.5×9cm. Galerie Jan Krugier, Geneva.

'*un enfant du quartier*'—probably the concierge's little daughter, 'who used to play hopscotch and skip outside my windows all day long,' and 'who was so sweet I never wanted her to grow up.'[49] Picasso would always have a penchant for adolescent girls. The two youths, one of whom has a drum on his shoulder, are too cipherlike to have been intended as this or that friend.[50] Apart from El tío Pepe, the one figure that can be identified for certain is the heroic harlequin: Picasso himself, much idealized, especially as to height. In one of the sketches he actually gives himself a top hat like that of Collardet, Manet's drunken ragpicker in *The Old Musician*. But even without it, he is taller, more confident, authoritative and noble-looking than the others. And no wonder! Apollinaire had just acclaimed him as Harlequin Trismegistus (Harlequin Thrice Great), a variant on the Magician, the first card in the Tarot.

Apollinaire conferred this accolade in the last verses of two related poems, '*Spectacle*' and '*Saltimbanques*' (dated Wednesday, November 1, 1905), which he dedicated to Picasso and posted to him forthwith.[51] '*Spectacle*' contrasts the image of a female harlequin, undressing in a forest glade and gazing at her naked reflection in a pond, with her wan-faced male counterpart, wielding a star that he has plucked from the firmament. The feet of a hanged man knock three times to announce that the curtain is going up. The last verse of the final version of this poem reads:

> The blind man rocks a comely child
> The fauns trail after does
> The dwarf looks on sadly
> As thrice great Harlequin grows

The imagery of the other poem, '*Saltimbanques*', is very close to Picasso's painting of the same name. A troupe of strolling players, children and a 'wise beast' is making its way across country. One of the children dies; tomorrow he or she will be forgotten; a little *saltimbanque* blows his nose on his hand. The last verse of the poem as it was originally sent to Picasso goes:

> Suckling her newborn child
> On Lethe's milk of oblivion
> The girl has Harlequin Trismegistus
> And a sad dwarf as a minion

The waters of Lethe signify oblivion and were drunk by lost souls (as harlequins are traditionally thought to be) before reincarnation. Apollinaire may have been referring to Picasso's artistic reincarnation, for which he felt partly responsible; or the 'milk of oblivion' could be a reference to the *bande*'s indulgence in opium. One has only to imagine how the vast *Saltimbanques* canvas, which dominated the studio, must have looked at night by the faint light of an oil lamp clouded in eddies of opium smoke. How hallucinatory these life-size *saltimbanques* must have appeared as they underwent successive metamorphoses. Picasso and his friends were forever indulging in elaborate jokes and fantasies, forever pretending they were someone else, and they may well have identified with these *saltimbanques* lingering in their never-never world, their symbolist limbo.

After finishing *The Saltimbanques*, Picasso killed off Harlequin—in the very last days of 1905. Suitably enough, the large, infinitely delicate

Les saltimbanques

Dans la plaine aux calmes jardins,
Où s'éloignent les baladins,
Devant l'huis des auberges grises
Et les villages sans église,

Les plus petits s'en vont devant,
Les autres suivent en rêvant.
Chaque arbre fruitier se résigne
Quand, de très loin, ils lui font signe.

Ils ont des poids ronds ou carrés,
Des tambours, des cerceaux dorés.
L'ours et le singe, animaux sages,
Quêtent des sous, sur leur passage.

Devant l'un qui meurt en chemin
Et que l'on oubliera demain,
La main d'un petit saltimbanque
Supplée au mouchoir qui lui manque.

Et la femme donne à téter
Son lait d'oubli comme un Léthé
Au dernier-né, près du nain triste
Et de l'arlequin trismégiste.

Apollinaire
Guillaume

de mercredi, 1er novembre, 1905

Apollinaire. Manuscript of poem, '*Saltimbanques*', November 1, 1905, given to Picasso. Heirs of the artist.

Beardsley. *The Death of Pierrot.* Published in *The Savoy,* October 1896.

gouache known as *The Death of Harlequin* was acquired, shortly after it was done, by Wilhelm Uhde, a private dealer, who loaned it to Rilke (later it spent many years in the collection of Somerset Maugham). Picasso said that the subject was inspired by a suicide in the Bateau Lavoir.[52] Might he have meant someone who would subsequently commit suicide there, that is to say Wiegels, who looked like both the live and the dead harlequin in this gouache and who was very close to Uhde? It may also have derived from Aubrey Beardsley, who saw himself as Pierrot and devoted one of his finest drawings (1896) to the death of this alter ego, when he learned that he had not long to live. One of Picasso's studies for this gouache bears an annotation suggesting that the woman's hand on the pillow might be altered to place a kerchief over the dead man's face. In the end Picasso found another, no less affecting, solution. He had the corpse clasp his hands together as if in prayer, like a recumbent figure on a tomb, an effigy. Is he really dead? the two androgynous watchers seem to wonder. The trickster could well be faking. Harlequin is reincarnated again and again in Picasso's work.

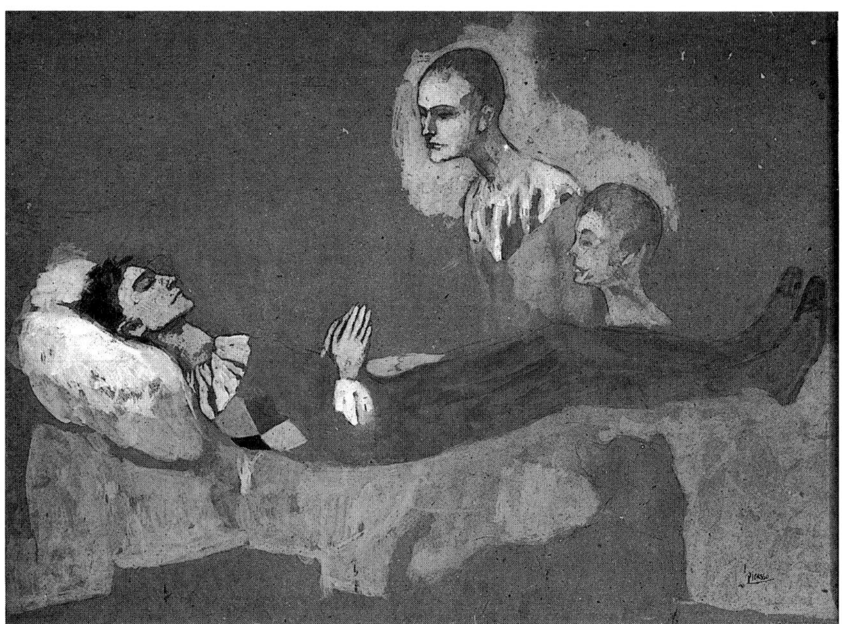

Picasso. *The Death of Harlequin.* Paris, 1906. Gouache on cardboard, 68.5×96 cm. Collection of Mr and Mrs Paul Mellon, Upperville, Virginia.

25

Collectors and Patrons

Wilhelm Uhde, 1906.

Opposite: Wall in the apartment of Gertrude and Leo Stein at 27, rue de Fleurus, *c.*1907, including six Picassos: (top) *Boy Leading a Horse* (1906), *Absinthe Drinker* (1902), *Young Acrobat on a Ball* (1905); (bottom) *Crouching Woman* (1902), *Woman with Fringed Hair* (1902), *Two Women at a Bar* (1902). Photo: The Baltimore Museum of Art, Cone Archives.

PICASSO'S RELUCTANCE TO EXHIBIT or even publish[1] his work made it difficult for people without an entrée to his studio to follow his development—difficult but not impossible. That he did not participate in any of the official Salons made little difference; he had never done so in the past; he would never do so in the future. Anyone who wanted to keep up with his increasingly meteoric progress was obliged to seek out the artist or pay regular visits to Weill, Soulié, Sagot and (after April 1906, when Picasso sold him most of his early work)[2] the devious Vollard—devious because he was averse to showing potential clients more than a sampling, seldom the best, of his treasures. After the Serrurier show in 1905, Picasso did not authorize any exhibitions in Paris until after World War I. There were a number of unauthorized ones: at an unnamed dealer's in late October or November 1905, according to Leo Stein, who was packed off to see it by Sagot. And in December 1908 Wilhelm Uhde hung three paintings by Picasso in a mixed exhibition (Braque, Derain, Dufy, Pascin, Metzinger and Sonia Delaunay were also included) in his Galerie Notre-Dame-des-Champs. The situation would change in 1908, when Kahnweiler became Picasso's principal dealer. Kahnweiler encouraged the artist in his policy of not exhibiting in Paris (there was nothing he could do about Vollard's 1910 show of Blue period work), but he usually had examples of his new work hanging on his walls or available in stock. And, between 1908 and 1914, he arranged for Picasso to be shown in most major European art centres,[3] as well as New York.

If Picasso's reputation began to spread beyond the confines of Montmartre, it was due not so much to French collectors, who bought on a very modest scale, as to a small group of competitive and persistent foreigners who came to the fore in 1905–06.[4] Wilhelm Uhde was German; Sergei Shchukin and Ivan Morozov (a later starter) were Russian; Gertrude, Leo and Michael Stein and their friends Etta and Claribel Cone were American. Picasso was fortunate in that all of them took their collecting very seriously. If they were going to invest in an artist's work, they wanted to get to know him, promote him and introduce him to other painters and critics and, less willingly, other buyers. For Picasso, who had not followed the example of Matisse and the Fauves and made his mark in the public Salons, this support was crucial. The dissemination of his work would originate in the private salons of his new collector friends.

*　　　*　　　*

Wilhelm Uhde was an enlightened Prussian aesthete who had settled in Paris in 1904, after studying art history in Germany and Italy. He liked to see himself as a missionary preaching the gospel of modern German literature and modern French art, despite the stigma of having to earn his living as a *marchand amateur* (a private dealer). His family was prosperous but puritanical (his grandfather was a pastor, his father a magistrate), and they had cut Willy off for abandoning the study of law for art history. Prussian determination and self-discipline stood him in good stead. He soon became one of the most enterprising *dénicheurs* in Paris. And he was able to set himself up in an apartment, where he could sell items from his 'collection'. Every Sunday he was 'at home' to his painter friends (besides Picasso, they would include Braque, Dufy and Delaunay), whom he would introduce to collectors and dealers. He was also the leader of a band of German artists and writers who made the Café du Dôme in Montparnasse their headquarters. They called themselves *dômiers*, and referred to their favourite café as *la cathédrale* (a pun on the German word *Dom*). In 1905, while scouring galleries and junkshops for the work of young artists, Uhde found his way to Soulié's. There for ten francs he 'bought the first work by an unknown artist that I owned', Picasso's *Le Tub* of 1901 (see illustration, p.226), the painting of a girl taking a bath in his Boulevard de Clichy studio.[5] Berthe Weill had offered this unsuccessfully to one client after another, ever since she had first exhibited it in 1902. A few nights after buying *Le Tub*, Uhde went to the Lapin Agile for the first time: 'The low-ceilinged room was filled with young painters from the rue Gabrielle and the place Ravignan. Someone was reciting Verlaine. I sat at the big table in the middle and called for wine. In the course of the evening I learned that the young man who had painted my picture was called Picasso and that he was sitting at my right.'[6] Uhde made sure that they became close friends; he paid regular visits to the Bateau Lavoir and soon acquired *The Death of Harlequin*. In due course he purchased many more Picassos; and in due course he sold most of them. But when his collection was confiscated as alien property on the outbreak of war, he still owned eleven mostly major works by the artist.

Uhde (left) with some of the *dômiers*: Walter Bondy (with moustache), Rudolf Levy (turning to the camera) and Jules Pascin. February 1910. Photo: Wil Howard.

Picasso took a strong liking to this free spirit, who had such a sharp clear eye and sharp clear mind and was so receptive to new concepts. Uhde responded with total devotion. He worked hard to understand the new language of cubism and prided himself on being one of Picasso's most loyal followers. His prissy Prussian air—immortalized in the prissy little mouth of Picasso's portrait—concealed a Nietzschean passion for art that was primitive or instinctive: Giotto, Picasso, Douanier Rousseau. In this respect he was a welcome change from the boring young Germans whom Picasso would scare off with a revolver.

Uhde was unconventional in yet another respect: he was homosexual, but far from keeping clear of Wilde's long, compromising shadow, he lived an overtly homosexual life, as did one or two of the other *dômiers*, notably Wiegels, whom he would introduce to Picasso. Even when Sonia Terck (later Delaunay's wife) persuaded 'Willy' to marry her in 1908 (the marriage was never consummated) so that she could escape from her rich Russian family, Uhde insisted that Constant, his handsome butler-lover, be included in the ménage. Gertrude Stein was much amused by Uhde: he would turn up at her Saturday soirées, 'accompanied by very tall blond good-looking young men who clicked their heels and bowed and then stood solemnly at attention. They made a very effective background to the rest of the crowd,' especially one lively evening at the Steins', when someone brought along a guitarist, and Picasso 'undertook to dance a southern Spanish dance not too respectable,' and Leo Stein imitated his old friend Isadora Duncan doing her 'dying dance'.[7]

Later Gertrude Stein would accuse Uhde—falsely—of being one of the German 'super spies'. 'Concièrge's tittletattle,' Kahnweiler said disgustedly. For him Uhde would always represent everything that was finest in the German spirit.[8] For Picasso Uhde represented something very different: he was yet another of those devoted followers (by no means all homosexual) who would provide the worship and supportive insight that the artist's ravenous ego craved. When war broke out in 1914, his German connections would prove an embarrassment to Picasso. Patriotic art-haters would misrepresent cubism as a 'Boche' manifestation. Picasso would be none too pleased at Uhde's returning after the war to Paris to collect and deal again: not cubism but the primitive painters—Bombois, Bauchant and his cook, Séraphine—who were cashing in on the success of the Douanier Rousseau. He would be even less pleased in 1928, when Uhde published a turgid book, *Picasso et la tradition Française*, which puts forward a view of the artist as the embodiment of the German and Gothic soul. This was too big a price to pay for Uhde's adulation. Picasso stopped seeing him. Later Uhde wrote another book, *From Bismarck to Picasso*. The association of these two names drove Hitler to strip Uhde of his nationality.

Picasso. *Portrait of Uhde*. Paris, 1909–10. Oil on canvas, 81×60cm. Private collection.

*   *   *

Besides the German constituency drummed up by Uhde (and later Kahnweiler), Picasso would soon attract a Russian one through Shchukin, as well as an American one through the Steins. Looking back on these early years at the end of his life, Picasso said that although most of the poets in his life and, yes, most of the girls were French, the majority of the people who kept him alive were of other nationalities. The Russians were the most lavish patrons. Before 1914, by far and away the largest accumulation of early Picassos (as well as Matisses) was to be found in Moscow, thanks to the members of two rich merchant families, the Morozovs[9] and the Shchukins, who prided themselves on being enlightened and liberal—members of the intelligentsia rather than the aristocracy.[10]

The most gifted and perceptive of the Russian collectors was Sergei Shchukin, one of six brothers, all of them fanatical collectors, but none more fanatical than this shy and unprepossessing man. Sergei's brilliant business mind had endeared him to his father—a textile magnate—who gave him a handsome eighteenth-century palace in the middle of Moscow that had belonged to the Trubetskoy family.[11] Shchukin or his father originally hung its walls with gloomy realist paintings by members of the so-called Wanderer school. And then, in 1898, in his early forties, he suddenly tired of these and, to the dismay of his wife, set about replacing them with impressionists and post-impressionists.[12]

Shchukin disdained advisers and relied on an eye that never failed to accommodate itself to successive developments in modern art. When in

Sergei Shchukin, 1900. Count Rupert de Keller collection.

1906 he visited the Salon des Indépendants, he reacted instinctively to the mastery of Matisse's Fauve paintings. He asked Vollard to introduce him to the artist, and he not only purchased but commissioned many of Matisse's early masterpieces. 'Shrewd, subtle and serious' is how Matisse described this shy little dynamo of a man with pronounced Tartar features, who would subsequently buy thirty-seven of his most challenging paintings. Shchukin's sudden receptiveness to modernism was brought about by a combination of good and bad fortune. During the revolution of 1905, he made huge profits by cornering the textile market on a hunch that the situation would soon be brought under control. Henceforth he kept substantial funds outside Russia in order to finance his wholesale acquisitions.

Dining-room of Trubetskoy Palace, Moscow, with works by Gauguin and Matisse, 1912–13. Count Rupert de Keller colection.

Retribution, however, was at hand. Returning a few months later from a grand tour of Egypt with his wife and family (including a son, Grigorii, who had been deaf from childhood), Shchukin suffered the shock of his youngest son's disappearance at the time of Cossack raids, police violence and rioting on the streets of Moscow during the 1905 revolution. Shchukin's wife would die suddenly in 1907, and his deaf son and a brother both committed suicide shortly after. The inclusion in his collection of *memento mori* by both Derain and Picasso is therefore hardly surprising.[13] Modern art was a catharsis. For this Tolstoyan ascetic and confirmed atheist collecting became a vocation.

Shchukin is usually said to have been taken to see Picasso by Matisse in 1908. The only source for this information is Fernande Olivier; and in this and other respects she is mistaken:

> One day Matisse brought an important collector from Moscow to see [Picasso]. Chukin [*sic*] was a Russian Jew [*sic*], very rich and a lover of modern art. He was a small pale, wan man with an enormous head like the mask of a pig. Afflicted with a horrible stutter, he had great difficulty expressing himself and that embarrassed him and made him look more pathetic than ever. Picasso's technique was a revelation to the Russian. He bought two canvases, paying what were very high prices for the time—one of them was the beautiful *Woman with a Fan*, and from then on he became a faithful client.[14]

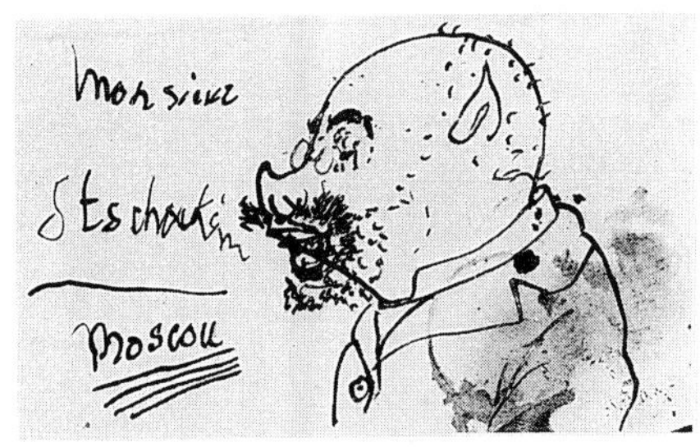

Picasso. *Monsieur Stschoukim*. Paris, 1906. Pen on paper, 17×21.5cm. Heirs of the artist.

This *Woman with a Fan* dates from 1909, so if Fernande is correct that this was his first Picasso, Shchukin could not have met Picasso until that year. However, there exists a monstrous caricature (inscribed 'Monsieur Stschoukim [*sic*] Moscou') with a pig's snout and ears such as Fernande describes. Zervos dates this 1905, but it is more likely to have been done in the spring of 1906. Further corroboration of a pre-1908 date for Picasso's meeting with Shchukin is provided by Gertrude Stein. She describes how the Russian came to visit her after seeing *Les Demoiselles d'Avignon* in Picasso's studio (seemingly in the course of 1907): 'He said almost in tears, what a loss for French art.'[15] This would imply that Shchukin already admired Picasso, even if he had not yet started to collect his work. Since he went to Paris to see the Matisse exhibition at the Galerie Druet, as well as the third Salon des Indépendants (March 20–April 30, 1906), Shchukin could already have met Picasso in the course of that visit; he could also have been shown the paintings that Vollard had just bought from Picasso. Failure to buy might explain the venomous caricature. However, Shchukin prided himself on being *au courant* with the latest developments in the artist's work, so he is likely to have acquired early works like *The Two Sisters* (1903), *The Old Jew* (1904) and *The Boy with a Dog* (1905) in 1906–07, rather than later, when his interests switched to cubism. The Russian critic Muratov's failure to mention any Picassos in his 1908 article on the Shchukin collection[16] does not necessarily rule out their inclusion. Shchukin's first love was Matisse; and his *grand salon rose* was consecrated to that artist's work. His Picassos were crammed together, frame to frame, in a far less spacious room, what Yakov Tugendhold called 'Picasso's cell'.[17] In Shchukin's opinion, 'Matisse should paint frescoes for palaces, Picasso frescoes for cathedrals.'[18]

Despite his carping remark about the *Demoiselles*, Shchukin had no problem overcoming his initial distaste and adjusting to Picasso's revolutionary new concepts. The harshness and violence of the images was in keeping with the harshness and violence of his life. And just as he had cornered cotton, he was soon cornering the key works of the artist's successive phases, except for what has come to be known as hermetic cubism (1910–11). Shchukin would buy paintings from Kahnweiler before the paint was dry and have them shipped off to Moscow. Only habitués of the artist's studio or Kahnweiler's gallery would have had an opportunity of seeing these works in Paris; in Moscow, they would be available to one and all. From 1909 onwards Shchukin opened the Trubetskoy palace to the public every Sunday morning. Young Russian artists, like Malevich, Tatlin, Larionov and Gontcharova, would be as conversant as young French artists with the latest work by Picasso and Matisse. The dissemination of the Blue and Rose periods as well as cubism thus radiated as much from Moscow as from Paris. When in 1918 the Soviets expropriated the Trubetskoy palace and collection, it included fifty-one Picassos, many of them masterpieces. At first Shchukin was kept on as curator. Among the foreign visitors he showed round were two French deputies. One of them, Mario Moutet, commented on the irony of the way 'our bourgeoisie let all these treasures go . . . while yours collected them and is being persecuted for it.'[19] Lunarcharsky was protective, so apparently was Trotsky (Picasso was his favourite modern painter). Nevertheless, Shchukin soon decided to escape to the West, where he had deposited enough money to live in modest comfort with his second wife, a pianist,[20] and even buy the occasional Dufy.

The Picasso room in the Trubetskoy Palace, Moscow, before 1917.

* * *

Leo, Gertrude, Allan, Michael and Sarah Stein. Paris, *c.*1905. Beinecke Rare Book and Manuscript Library, Yale University.

As a collector of Picasso and Matisse, Shchukin had no rivals outside Russia except the Steins: Leo, Gertrude, their brother, Michael, and his wife, Sarah. The rivalry between the Russians and the Americans was intense, but the conventions were observed. After going through the stock of one dealer after another, Shchukin would pay a call on Gertrude and compare notes. They respected each other's opinions. When Leo and Gertrude parted company in 1913, he purchased some of their finest Picassos. Although the Steins were by no means as rich as Shchukin, they had the advantage of being on the spot and on more intimate terms with the artists of their choice—Gertrude with Picasso, Michael and Sarah with Matisse. Leo originally had the most perceptive eye, but he developed a loathing for cubism, just as his sister developed a passion for it. And she continued to collect the artist's cubist work until the movement had run its course. Thereafter she never bought another thing by Picasso.[21] This did not, however, impede their relationship. 'She and Picasso were phenomenal together,' the American painter Gerald Murphy said in the 1920s. 'Each stimulated the other to such an extent that everyone felt recharged witnessing it.'[22]

Gertrude Stein, *c.*1901. Beinecke Rare Book and Manuscript Library, Yale University.

To understand Gertrude and Leo's relationship to Picasso, as well as each other, we need to consider their history. They were third-generation Americans. In 1841 their grandfather and his four sons (including Daniel, Leo and Gertrude's father) had emigrated from Bavaria to Baltimore, where they set up a prosperous textile and clothing business. Shortly after the birth (February 3, 1874) of Gertrude, the youngest of seven children, the brothers dissolved their partnership. The abrasive Daniel moved his family to Vienna, where they lived comfortably. Nevertheless, they returned to the United States in 1880.

Leo Stein described his father as a dominant, aggressive person who never read a book. Gertrude went further: 'Fathers are depressing,' she wrote. 'Mothers may not be cheering but they are not as depressing as fathers.'[23] Gertrude was delighted that her father continued to feud with the other Steins, because this meant that he took his family off to Oakland, California, where he invested in property and became vice-president of the Omnibus Cable Company. And then one morning they could not wake him. 'Leo climbed in by the window and called out to us that he was dead in his bed and he was. . . . Then our life without father began,' Gertrude exulted, 'a very pleasant one.'[24] The eldest son, Michael, served as guardian and second father to Leo and Gertrude. He sold out the family holdings and saw that his siblings were well provided for. Leo later said that he (and presumably Gertrude) had around a hundred and fifty dollars a month to spend and that this was enough to live comfortably and travel. In addition there would be occasional windfalls; for instance, late in 1904, Michael told Leo and Gertrude they had a credit of eight thousand francs. Hence their acquisition over the following years of Picassos and Matisses as well as Renoirs, Gauguins and Cézannes.

At first Leo and Gertrude were inseparable. When he went to Harvard, she enrolled at the Harvard Annexe (later named Radcliffe). She subsequently claimed to have been a favourite pupil of Leo's hero, William James, whose definition of genius—'the capacity to get into a biographical dictionary'—left a lasting impression on her. At James's behest she helped his brilliant protégé Hugo Munsterberg in a series of experiments on the workings of the mind. Since Gertrude boasted of 'never having had subconscious reactions' (and would disapprove of Picasso when he gave full rein to his subconscious in the late 1920s), she did not prove a very objective researcher.[25]

After Harvard Gertrude enrolled at Johns Hopkins School of Medicine in Baltimore. Leo joined her there to study biology, and they set up house together. But laboratory work bored Leo. 'One day I got a great idea in aesthetics—something along the lines of . . . Croce . . . and I dropped biology and decided to go to Florence for a few years.'[26] In Florence Leo met Bernard Berenson and on the strength of this new association decided to write a life of Mantegna. Nothing came of this project. Mary Berenson pronounced Leo a voluble bore, but her husband took a more charitable view. Although Leo Stein was 'always inventing the umbrella',[27] he evidently had the makings of a connoisseur. Ironically, it was Berenson —so blind as a rule to twentieth-century art—who unwittingly launched Leo's career as one of the greatest patrons of the modern movement.

With Leo off in Italy, Gertrude likewise lost interest in medical studies. The formerly brilliant student made such a botch of the model of an embryonic brain that a professor wondered whether she was quite sane. And wasn't it odd that (like Picasso, two years later) she had taken up boxing and hired a welterweight as a sparring partner? A classmate who lived below complained that the chandelier used to swing 'and the house echoed with shouts of "now give me one on the jaw. Now give me one in the kidney."'[28] Gertrude showed virtually no interest in feminism or politics; however, she took a liking to some of the emancipated women involved in the movement, especially the self-dramatizing and manipulative May Bookstaver, for whom she developed a passion. Partly to escape a relationship that was fraught with jealousy and frustrations, partly to avoid a career in medicine for which she was unsuited, partly to be reunited with her beloved Leo, Gertrudé left Baltimore for Europe. In September 1902, after staying with the Berensons in Surrey, Gertrude and Leo rented a cottage nearby, and then decided to winter in London. However, the Dickensian gloom and 'the dead weight of that fog and smoke-laden air' drove Leo to Paris and Gertrude back to New York (February 1903), where she tried to exorcise the pain of May Bookstaver's rejection in a *roman à clef* entitled *Q.E.D.*[29] She liked New York: 'It was clean and straight and meagre and hard and white and light.'[30] But after six months of it she pined once more for Europe.

Gertrude Stein with her nephew Allan, *c.*1905. Musée Picasso, Paris.

By the end of 1903 Paris had become the Stein family's preserve. Leo arrived in December 1902; Gertrude in October 1903; Michael and his wife, Sarah, who would devote themselves to promoting Matisse rather than Picasso, in December 1903. Gertrude had originally intended to return to America every winter but decided to settle permanently in France. A wise career move: acceptance at her own valuation might have been difficult in America. Leo welcomed his sister and her contribution to the expenses of his new establishment. The two of them soon became what Maurice Sterne described as 'the happiest couple on the Left Bank'.[31] Since they had last seen each other, Leo's egomania had set off yet another metamorphosis. Dining one night with the young and unknown Pablo Casals (whom the Michael Steins had befriended when he was on tour in San Francisco), he had 'felt himself growing into an artist'. Back in his hotel, he made a blazing fire, took off his clothes, and began to draw from the nude in front of the mirror. Next thing, he enrolled at an art school and devoted all his time to painting, 'but nothing came of it,' he said, 'because of a neurosis'.[32] This new vocation necessitated a studio; and thanks to a sculptor uncle, Ephraim Kaiser, Leo found the perfect place, a *pavillon* at 27 rue de Fleurus, off the Boulevard Raspail. He hung the walls with his collection of Japanese prints, the Wilson Steer he had recently bought in London and the painting of a woman in a white dress with a white dog by Raoul du Gardier, a minor marine painter.

Leo Stein at 27 rue de Fleurus, *c.*1905. The Baltimore Museum of Art, Cone Archives.

When Leo moaned about 'the dearth of art' in Paris (*embarras de richesse* should surely have been the problem), Berenson wrote and told him about Cézanne, 'so I went to Vollard's, and was launched'.[33] On his

Cézanne. *Madame Cézanne with a Fan*. 1879–82. Oil on canvas, 92.5×73cm. E. G. Bührle collection, Zurich.

next visit to Florence, Leo had further opportunity to study Cézanne. His mentor was Charles Loeser, a Macy's heir and a most eclectic collector. For fear of shocking visitors, Loeser kept his numerous Cézannes hidden in the bedroom and dressing room of an otherwise traditionally appointed villa; later he would hang them in the music room that he built for his protégés, the Lener Quartet. What Leo referred to as his 'Cézanne debauch' opened up his eyes and mind to modern art. He began to haunt the more progressive dealers, also the Salon d'Automne and Salon des Indépendants, where he bought a Vallotton and a Manguin. According to Gertrude's letter of November 1904 to her friend Mabel Weeks, 'We is doin business too we are selling Jap prints to buy a Cézanne.'[34]

Thanks to the revelation of Cézanne, Leo soon became the leading patron of the most radical regeneration in painting since the Renaissance. Encouraged by his sister-in-law, Sarah, he proceeded to buy not only the Cézanne but Matisse's Fauve masterpiece, *Woman with a Hat*, out of the 1905 Salon d'Automne.[35] He then went on to acquire much of Picasso's best recent work.[36] Between 1905 and 1907, Leo was unquestionably the most adventurous and discerning collector of twentieth-century painting in the world. Vollard liked to sell him pictures, Leo said, 'because we were the only customers who bought pictures, not because they were rich, but despite the fact that they weren't.'[37] As usual, Leo lacked momentum. Just as he had lost faith in his successive vocations—philosopher, biologist, art historian, even dancer (his imitations of Isadora Duncan were 'too beautiful to be burlesque', said a girl who wrote a poem about them)—he now lost faith in himself as a collector and an artist. His feelings for the painters he had acquired with such uncanny discrimination turned to resentment. He first took this resentment out on Picasso, giving way to spasms of mad laughter in front of *Les Demoiselles d'Avignon*; then on Matisse, whom he accused of being 'rhythmically insufficient';[38] and finally, though not for some years, he renounced his former god, Cézanne.

As Leo's self-esteem dwindled, Gertrude's grew and grew, and she assumed the one role that her chronically *manqué* brother had brilliantly, if all too briefly, filled: that of art patron. Leo never forgave her for abrogating his function; never forgave her for being able to inflate her balloon-like ego to the limit, while his burst. Leo became odder and odder. The Steins' writer friend Hutchins Hapgood depicts him at this period as obsessive to the point of mania: 'He was concentrated on the reform of his digestive apparatus. . . . He would come to lunch and Fletcherize each mouthful (chewing it exactly thirty-two times), giving us a careful account of what the probable result would be.'[39] Hapgood shrewdly diagnoses the nature of Leo's malaise:

> The slightest flaw, real or imaginary, in [Leo's] companion's statements, caused in [Leo] intellectual indignation of the most intense kind . . . something in him took it for granted that anything said by anybody except himself needed immediate denial or at least substantial modification. He seemed to need constant reinforcement of his ego. . . . Had it not been for the shadow of himself, his constant need of feeling superior to all others, he would have been a great man.[40]

Picasso. *Portrait of Leo Stein*. Paris, 1906. Gouache on cardboard, 24.8×17.2cm. The Baltimore Museum of Art, Cone Collection.

Leo's life was not made any easier when Gertrude's lover, Alice Toklas, moved in with them in 1910. She proceeded to take such total charge of

Gertrude's life that Leo complained of 'having seen trees strangled by vines in this same way'.[41] Three fraught years later, the brother and sister decided to part. In 1913, they split up the collection, selling off a few major works through Kahnweiler to Shchukin and Morozov. As they were no longer speaking, negotiations had to be arranged through Alice, who would go back and forth between Gertrude in one room and Leo in another, arranging the terms of the *partage*. Leo took the Cézannes and sixteen Renoirs and went to live in Settignano. Gertrude stayed on in Paris with most of the Picassos and Alice. She had done very well but was heartbroken at not getting a Cézanne still life. To console her, Picasso gave her a charming little watercolour of a green, Cézanne-esque apple.

* * *

Picasso. *Harlequin's Family with an Ape*. Paris, 1905. Gouache, watercolour and ink on cardboard, 104×75cm. Konstmuseum, Göteborg.

Gertrude and Leo give different versions of their first purchase of a Picasso. Gertrude misidentifies the painting. Leo is more circumstantial: shortly after buying the Matisse *Woman with a Hat*—that is to say, in late October 1905—he describes going to Sagot's:

> There was a Spaniard whose works [Sagot] lauded, and as he had done me some favors I bought a little Spanish watercolor; but when he recommended another Spaniard, I balked. 'But this is the real thing,' he said. So I went to the exhibition,[42] and in fact this was the real thing. Besides the pictures, there were some drawings for which I left an offer, since there was no one in charge of the show, but from this I heard nothing further. When, a few days later, I dropped in at Sagot's to talk about Picasso, he had a picture by him, which I bought. It was the picture of a mountebank with wife and child and an ape. The ape looked at the child so lovingly that Sagot was sure this scene was derived from life; but I knew more about apes than Sagot did, and was sure that no such baboon-like creature belonged in such a scene. Picasso told me later that the ape was his invention, and it was a proof that he was more talented as a painter than as a naturalist.[43]

As she was paying for half of them, Gertrude felt entitled to a say in the acquisitions Leo proposed, although she had as yet little or no inkling of modern art. Hitherto her only recorded purchases had been prints by Zorn and Hayden and a painting by the forgotten American artist Ernst Schilling, for which she had paid six hundred dollars. She now tried to unload it in order to buy a Manet.[44] Fortunately she was a quick learner and Leo a born pedagogue. A close friend reported that 'Leo was her mentor, dictionary and encyclopedia, supplying on demand any information she required.'[45] Inevitably they did not always agree. A few days after buying the *Harlequin's Family with an Ape*, Leo took Gertrude to Sagot's to look at another Picasso; the full-length nude of a *Girl with a Basket of Flowers*—a painting that the dealer had advertised as *La Fleur du Pavé* on the cover of *Le Courrier Français* (November 2, 1905). Gertrude hated it. She said she 'found something rather appalling in the drawing of the legs and feet, something that repelled and shocked her. She and her brother almost quarrelled about this picture. He wanted it and she did not want it in the house. Sagot gathering a little of the discussion said, but that is alright if you do not like the legs and feet it is very easy to guillotine her and only take the head. No that would not do, everybody agreed, and nothing was decided.'[46]

Gertrude took the dealer's joke too seriously; he would never have guillotined the young girl. Over his sister's objections, Leo went back to Sagot's, where, he says, he briefly met Picasso, and bought the painting for 150 francs, twice what the artist had been paid for it.

> That day I came home late to dinner [Leo continues the story], and Gertrude was already eating. When I told her I had bought the picture she threw down her knife and fork and said, 'Now you've spoiled my appetite. I hated that picture with feet like a monkey's.' Some years after, when we were offered an absurd sum for the picture and I wanted to sell it—since for that money one could get much better things—Gertrude would not agree to sell, and I believe that she always kept it.[47]

Picasso. *Leo Stein Walking*. Paris, 1905. Pen and sepia on paper, 33.5×23.5cm. Private collection.

Once again accounts differ. Despite her dislike of the painting, Gertrude claims that she arranged for Leo to meet Picasso through Henri-Pierre Roché, the peripatetic journalist who would subsequently win fame as the author of *Jules et Jim*.[48] This sharp-eyed connoisseur of art and literature was ideally placed to be a go-between with Picasso. To earn extra money he was acting as adviser and agent to collectors of modern art (the most important would be the American John Quinn), and in this capacity he would win the friendship and respect of many of the more avant-garde artists, Brancusi especially. Gertrude describes Roché as

> a very earnest, very noble, devoted, very faithful and very enthusiastic man who was a general introducer. . . . He could introduce anybody to anybody. . . . He was tall and red-headed and he never said anything but good good excellent. . . . He had done a great many things, he had gone to the austrian mountains with the austrians . . . Germany with the germans . . . Hungary with the hungarians . . . England with the english . . . As Picasso always said of him, Roché is very nice but he is only a translation.[49]

Roché became one of the most useful of the Steins' Parisian friends. Gertrude introduced him into her work as 'Vrais', a character who is always putting his stamp of approval on things. She also wrote a portrait in words about him: a tribute to the fact that he was the first and, for some years, the only Frenchman (and certainly the only member of Picasso's circle) to have an understanding—in the beginning enthusiastic, later critical—of her writing. In fact it was Leo who made friends with Roché. He became a regular visitor at 27 rue de Fleurus, where he spent long evenings, listening to Leo pontificate on art, science and psychology. Besides taking Leo to the Soirées de la Plume, where he met Moréas, Jarry and Apollinaire, Roché suggested harnessing his gifts as a writer to Leo's as a thinker. The book would be called 'Conversations with Leo Stein'. As usual nothing came of this project.[50]

Opposite: Two views of the Steins' apartment at 27 rue de Fleurus, *c.*1906. Among the works at the top are Cézanne's *Madame Cézanne with a Fan,* a painting probably by Leo Stein, Renoir's *Two Bathers,* Matisse's *Woman with a Hat,* Toulouse-Lautrec's *The Sofa,* and (below right) a portrait of Michael Stein by Leo Stein. The lower photo shows (top) Manguin's *Standing Nude,* Bonnard's *Siesta,* Picasso's *Girl with a Basket of Flowers;* (bottom) Cézanne's study for *The Smoker,* a Renoir and a Daumier, Picasso's *Head of a Boy* (1905) and Maurice Denis's *Mother in Black.* The Baltimore Museum of Art, Cone Archives.

Picasso, who had met Roché at the Closerie des Lilas, was delighted that he should bring over this new collector. Gertrude, however, sulked. She refused to meet the painter of the girl 'with feet like a monkey'. (Not that the girl's feet are the least like a monkey's: the ape in Leo's first Picasso must have played havoc with Gertrude's visual memory.) Leo was overwhelmed by his visit to the Bateau Lavoir. Forty years later, he remembered his amazement at Picasso's piercing eyes: 'When Picasso had looked at a drawing or print, I was surprised that there was anything left on the paper, so absorbing was his gaze. He spoke little and seemed neither remote nor intimate—just completely there. . . . He seemed more real than most people while doing nothing about it.'[51]

Picasso and Fernande in Montmartre, *c.*1906. Musée Picasso, Paris.

When Picasso and Fernande came to dine at the rue de Fleurus a few days later, Gertrude shed her prejudice. She was immediately attracted to this 'good-looking bootblack', as he was to this extraordinarily intense and warm yet granite-like young woman with her striking unfeminine head and 'deep temperamental life quality'.[52] In Gertrude's third-person account:

> [Picasso] was thin, dark, alive with big pools of eyes and a violent but not a rough way. He was sitting next to Gertrude Stein at dinner and she took up a piece of bread. This, said Picasso, snatching it back with violence, this piece of bread is mine. She laughed and he looked sheepish. That was the beginning of their intimacy.
>
> That evening Gertrude Stein's brother took out portfolio after portfolio of japanese prints to show Picasso . . . Picasso solemnly and obediently looked at print after print and listened to the descriptions. He said under his breath to Gertrude Stein, he is very nice, your brother, but like all americans, like Haviland, he shows you japanese prints. *Moi j'aime pas ça*, no I don't care for it. As I say Gertrude Stein and Pablo Picasso immediately understood each other.[53]

Henceforth Picasso and Gertrude would see each other on a regular basis. However, he still felt shy and awkward on social occasions, so he would bring members of his *bande* to her soirées. Salmon would complain about the hostess's prudishness and lack of humour. On the other hand, Max Jacob would do his best to please her and keep the guests amused with impromptu farces culminating in falsetto renditions of airs from operettas and saucy little pirouettes. After Picasso, Gertrude's favourite was Apollinaire. She was impressed by his ability to take an idea and elaborate it 'by his wit and fancy carrying it further than anybody . . . could have done. . . . Oddly enough generally correctly,' she smugly allowed.[54] But since he was a writer bent, like herself, upon glory, and out, like herself, to abolish punctuation and syntax, Gertrude was careful to withhold her accolade of genius. If her vivid portrait of him in the *Autobiography of Alice B. Toklas* introduced Apollinaire to a generation of American readers, it was not as a great poet but as a genial personality. It is quite possible that she never read any of his writing apart from art criticism. According to Kahnweiler, Gertrude's wilful ignorance of contemporary French literature (not only of Apollinaire and Jacob but later the surrealists, whose verse she would dimiss as 'girls' high school stuff')[55] was almost as surprising as her profound knowledge of English literature. But then Apollinaire was no less guilty of chauvinism. He spoke better English than Gertrude spoke French and yet showed as little interest in her 'aesthetic experiments' as she did in his. To judge by the only reference to the Steins in his work (1907), he regarded them as faintly comic.

> [Felix Vallotton] is exhibiting six paintings, among them a portrait of *Mlle. Stein*, that American lady who with her brother and a group of relatives constitute the most unexpected patrons of the arts in our time.
>
> *Leurs pieds nus sont chaussés de sandales delphiques,*
> *Ils lèvent vers le ciel des fronts scientifiques:*
>
> (Bare feet shod in sandals Delphic,
> Skyward they raise their brows scientific.)
>
> Those sandals have sometimes done them in. . . . Beverage peddlers are especially averse to them.

> Often when these millionaires want to relax on a café terrace . . . the waiters refuse to serve them and politely inform them that the drinks at that café are too expensive for people in sandals.
>
> But they could not care less about the ways of waiters and calmly pursue their aesthetic experiments.[56]

It was not long before other members of the Parisian avant-garde followed the *bande à Picasso* to the Steins'. Their *pavillon* was the only place in Paris where there was a permanent display of all that was best in contemporary art. By the time Gertrude and Leo went their separate ways, they had accumulated what amounted to a major retrospective of Picasso's (and Matisse's) work. Besides a magnificent sequence of Blue period, Rose period and cubist masterpieces (studies included), there were countless smaller works on panel or paper that constituted a microcosm of the artist's early development. This was eclipsed only by Shchukin's ensemble in Moscow.

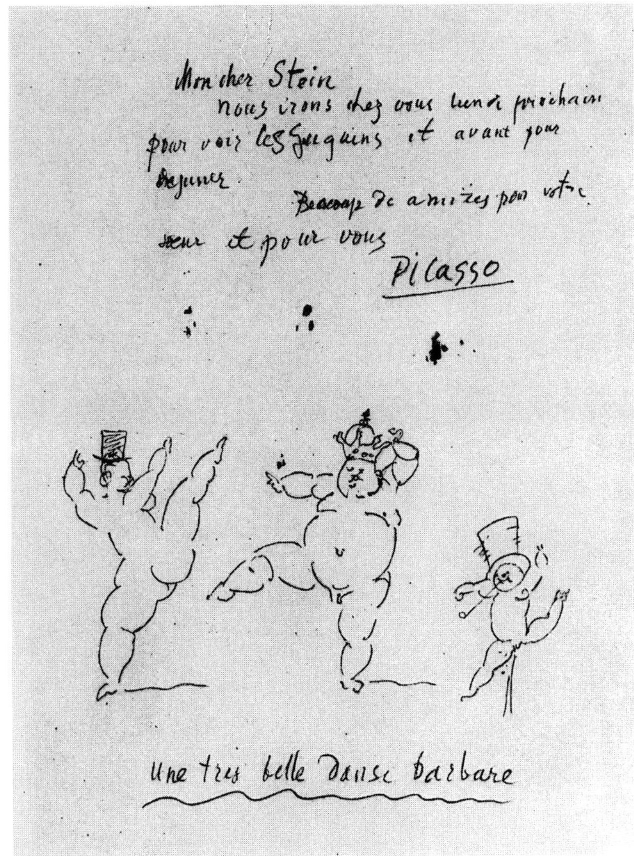

Mon cher Stein
nous irons chez vous lundi prochain
pour voir les Gauguins et avant pour
déjeuner.
Beacoup de amitiés pour votre
soeur et pour vous
Picasso

Une très belle danse barbare

Picasso. Letter to Leo Stein accepting an invitation to see the Steins' Gauguins. 1905. Private collection.

26

Two or Three Geniuses

Ingres. *Portrait of Louis-François Bertin.* 1832. Oil on canvas, 116×95cm. Musée du Louvre, Paris.

GERTRUDE STEIN'S PERSONALITY AND appearance so fascinated Picasso that shortly after their first dinner, in the autumn of 1905, he asked to paint her portrait. For the rest of the winter this would have first claim on his attention. Gertrude says she sat some ninety times. She would have us believe that nobody else had posed for Picasso since he was sixteen, although she well knew that he had never ceased using models. She and her brother had just bought one portrait, *Girl with a Basket of Flowers*, and were about to buy another. The sittings began in the depths of winter, so the rusty old Bateau Lavoir stove had to be kept stoked to the maximum for Gertrude's comfort. Next to it was a large broken armchair in which this short monolithic woman took up the same authoritative pose, only in reverse, that Ingres had devised for his portrait of the newspaper proprietor Louis-François Bertin, a painting Picasso had seen in the Louvre.[1] If Picasso's portrait was to hang alongside the two great acquisitions that the Steins had made at the Salon d'Automne, he had to come up with an authoritative image—one that would stand up to the Cézanne and overshadow Matisse's *Woman with a Hat.* Both Cézanne and Matisse had given their wives a fan to hold; however, there would be no feminine accessories for Gertrude. Picasso endowed her with Monsieur Bertin's hands, and nothing to grip but her knees.

Gertrude's memoirs evoke Picasso's studio more vividly than the actual painting of the portrait:

> There was a couch where everybody sat and slept. There was a little kitchen chair upon which Picasso sat to paint, there was a large easel: and there were many very large canvases . . . of the end of the Harlequin period when the canvases were enormous . . . there was a little fox terrier that had something the matter with it and . . . was again about to be taken to the infirmary. . . . Fernande offered to read LaFontaine's stories aloud to amuse Gertrude Stein. . . . She took her pose, Picasso sat very tight on his chair and very close to his canvas and on a very small palette which was of a uniform brown grey color, mixed some more brown grey and the painting began. . . .
>
> Toward the end of the afternoon Gertrude Stein's two brothers and her sister-in-law and Andrew Green came to see.[2] They were all excited at the beauty of the sketch and Andrew Green begged and begged that it should be left as it was. But Picasso shook his head and said, *non.* It is too bad . . . no one thought of taking a photograph of the picture as it was then and of course no one . . . that saw it then remembered at all what it looked like any more than do Picasso or Gertrude Stein.[3]

Opposite: Picasso. *Portrait of Gertrude Stein.* 1906. Oil on canvas, 100×81.3cm. The Metropolitan Museum of Art, New York, Bequest of Gertrude Stein, 1946.

At first the painting probably resembled the portrait of Gertrude's nephew, Allan, executed that same winter.

Practically every day after lunch, Gertrude took a horse-drawn omnibus across Paris from the Odéon to the Place Blanche and then had a stiff climb up to the Bateau Lavoir. After posing for most of the afternoon, she strode down the hill of Montmartre, across the Seine to the rue de Fleurus. 'Saturday evenings the Picassos walked home with her and dined.'[4] These evenings eventually developed into the Steins' weekly salon.

While Picasso was at work on the painting, Etta Cone, Gertrude Stein's old friend from Baltimore, paid frequent visits to the studio. Etta did not like the portrait, and she 'found the Picassos appalling but romantic'.[5] However, she allowed herself to be browbeaten by Gertrude into helping them out. Whenever Picasso's finances failed, Etta or her sister, Dr Claribel, were 'made to buy a hundred francs' worth of drawings.[6] After all a hundred francs in those days was twenty dollars.'[7] Gertrude tells us that Picasso used to call the two sisters 'the Miss Etta Cones', but she failed to get the pun: 'Etta Cones' means 'Hey, high heels!' in Spanish (*Eh, ¡tacones!*).

Picasso. *Portrait of Allan Stein.* Paris, 1906. Gouache on cardboard, 74×59.7 cm. The Baltimore Museum of Art, Cone Collection.

The Cone sisters came from the same prosperous Jewish background as the Steins. Etta, who was shy, somewhat artistic but very rigid in her ways, looked after the housekeeping; Dr Claribel, who was self-centred and imperious (Picasso called her 'the Empress'), did research in the pathology department at Johns Hopkins, where she would later become a professor. The sisters enjoyed a very close, very twisted relationship. When they went to the theatre, Claribel would take two good seats, one for herself and one for her impedimenta; Etta would have a seat at the back. The Cone sisters seem to have been lesbian: there was 'sex in both', Gertrude noted in her draft of the word-portrait she did of them.

The Steins' relationship with the Cones would prove fruitful. Aided and abetted by their brother Michael, Gertrude and Leo were instrumental in persuading them to collect modern art. (Etta was by far the more active.) Hence their magnificent bequest to the Baltimore Museum. Rich as it is in early Picasso, it is richer still in Matisse. The collection has its origins in the batches of drawings (they cost around two dollars apiece) that Gertrude urged the sisters to buy off the floor of the Bateau Lavoir studio. Later the Steins saw to it that they, too, would benefit from the Cones' passion for collecting. They sold them things. They also tried—and failed—to have Picasso do a portrait of one or the other of the sisters. According to Picasso, the Steins and other friends referred to the *Woman with a Fan* of 1909, which Shchukin eventually bought, as a portrait of Etta Cone, but it had not been conceived as such. Much later (July 14, 1922) the artist executed an Ingresque drawing of Claribel and was paid 1000 francs in new banknotes after the sitting. Consciously or not, he had the formidable doctor assume a pose very similar to Gertrude Stein's in her famous portrait.

Claribel Cone, Gertrude Stein and Etta Cone in Florence, 1903. The Baltimore Museum of Art, Cone Archives.

During the three months or so of Picasso's and Gertrude's daily exposure to each other's implacable regard, a powerful charge was generated between them: a deep psychic feeling that went way beyond friendship and yet was not the least amorous, often not even amicable; a feeling that would flourish, despite all manner of rows, until the mid-1930s. Gertrude came to enjoy posing, she said; 'the long still hours followed by a long dark walk intensified the concentration with which she was creating her sentences.'[8] And so, while the artist wrestled on canvas with Gertrude as if she were a sphinx whose image held the key to the future of his art, the sitter ruminated on her work in progress. 'The long still hours' enabled her to compose in her head the 'Melanctha' section of *Three Lives*—usually considered the best part. Besides observing the ever-present Fernande to see how her traits could be used to animate the character of the vulnerable black girl Melanctha, who is 'always full with mystery and subtle movements and denials and vague distrusts and complicated disillusions',[9] Gertrude also kept her obsidian look beamed on the artist. As winter wore on, the sitter set about hitching her covered wagon to Picasso's comet.

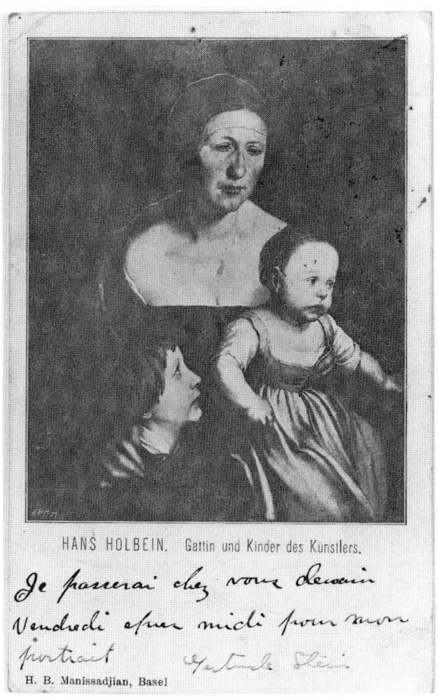

Postcard from Gertrude Stein to Picasso, confirming a sitting for her portrait, March 9, 1906. Musée Picasso, Paris.

In her determination to promote herself into a genius, if need be by osmosis, Gertrude subsequently wrote as though her *ipse dixit* were enough to transform legend—the legend of herself as Picasso's one and only muse—into fact. Her chronicles, notably *The Autobiography of Alice B. Toklas* and *Everybody's Autobiography*, have been widely read and deservedly admired except by victims of her personality cult, headed by her brother. Since Leo prided himself, with good reason, on being more perceptive about art than his sister, he resented her claiming that his discernment had been hers, even if, by abrogating his greatest gift, he had put that temptation in her way. 'God, what a liar she is!' Leo wrote to Mabel Weeks after the publication of Gertrude's Toklas book. 'Practically everything that she says of our activities before 1911 is false in both fact and implication, but one of her radical complexes (sibling rivalry) . . . made it necessary to eliminate me.'[10] Leo finally decided to tell his side of the story, but Gertrude died (1946), while *Appreciation* (1947), the bitter book that was intended to correct her myth-making, was still in galleys. Revenge was denied him.

As a collector of cubism, Gertrude proved to have a sharp eye for the pick of Picasso's studio. But before hailing her discrimination, we should examine her motives for embracing the movement, especially since her own taste ran to kitsch: 'miniature alabaster fountains with two tiny white doves poised on the brink [and] forget-me-not mosaic brooches.'[11] One of the attractions of cubism was the very fact that it proved such 'an obstacle to her brother. . . . Cubism was a game she could play without her brother.'[12] On her own admission, Gertrude had little sense of quality. A 'painting may be good, it may be bad, medium bad or very bad or very good but anyway I like to look at it.'[13] This lack of artistic judgement emerges in her two portraits of Picasso and her 1938 monograph.[14] She comes up with remarkably few insights and hides her ignorance of basic concepts behind a barrage of simplistic repetition. Her 1909 word-portrait of the artist consists of a single idea relentlessly reiterated:

> This one was always having something that was coming out of this one that was a solid thing, a charming thing, a lovely thing, a perplexing thing, a disconcerting thing, a simple thing, a clear thing, a complicated thing, an interesting thing, a disturbing thing, a repellant [*sic*] thing, a very pretty thing. This one was one certainly being one having something coming out of him . . .[15]

Picasso. *Frika, Gat malade.* Paris, 1906. Pen on paper, 32×24cm. Heirs of the artist.

This excretory notion of the creative process—surely more applicable to the writer than the artist—recurs in the 1938 monograph:

> Picasso was always obsessed by the necessity of emptying himself, of emptying himself completely, of always emptying himself . . . all this existence is the repetition of a complete emptying, he must empty himself, he can never empty himself of being Spanish, but he can empty himself of what he has created . . . he empties himself and the moment he has completed emptying himself he must recommence emptying himself, he fills himself up again so quickly.[16]

When the gist of this passage was explained to Picasso, he reacted with ironical resignation: 'She's confusing two functions.'

Leo, Gertrude and Michael Stein in the courtyard of 27 rue de Fleurus, *c.*1906. The Baltimore Museum of Art, Cone Archives.

Tossing around in the swell of Gertrude's prose are some perceptive comments about Picasso's intrinsic Spanishness and about the calligraphic quality of his work. But when (in 1936) he actually became a writer, Gertrude was fiercely competitive and dismissed his poetry as 'not poetry'. Poetry was her preserve. Picasso had better keep to painting. Therein lay their polarity. 'I was alone at this time in understanding him perhaps because I was expressing the same thing in literature perhaps because I was an American and, as I say, Spaniards and Americans have a kind of understanding of things which is the same.'[17] To believe Gertrude, her exercises in new writing— sometimes rhythmically mesmerizing, sometimes inert and shallow—are a mirror image of Picasso's cubist work. True, the writer and painter both managed to liberate themselves from traditional means of verbal and pictorial expression and come up with a new form of notation. True again, both of them had a similar way of displaying, at the same time concealing, their feelings, especially about the women in their lives, by resorting to a private code. Here Gertrude was the pioneer. But there the parallels end. Gertrude aimed to strip words of their meaning and associations and transform them into something as abstract and arbitrary as the 'music' that she idly improvised on the piano (only on the white keys, never the black ones). To the extent that she succeeded, Gertrude corresponds to certain non-figurative artists rather than to Picasso, who rejected abstractionism and liked to think that his work was if anything more, certainly not less, real than the real thing. That was one of the reasons why he represented real things—newspapers, cigarette packets—by themselves.

Differences rather than similarities emerge if Gertrude's 'Objects' from the first section of *Tender Buttons* are compared with Picasso's still lifes of the same date. They could not be more antithetical. Gertrude comes up with dissociative word patterns, hermetic jingles; Picasso, with a not-always-recognizable but nonetheless itemized configuration that provides us with clues as to the size, markings and texture of specific objects: clues to the nature of their formal and spatial relationships; clues also to the artist's paradoxical feelings about his work, his women and the world around him. Why did Gertrude persist in seeing his and her oeuvres as equivalents? Picasso asked Leo. Why did she insist that there were two geniuses in art today: 'Picasso in painting and I in literature'? Gertrude claimed to use words 'cubistically', Leo said, in a manner most people found incomprehensible. 'That sounds rather silly,' Picasso observed. 'With lines and colours one can make patterns, but if one doesn't use words according to their meaning, they aren't words at all.'[18]

Picasso was no less worried by Gertrude's obsession with the word 'genius'—a word that he was loath to use about himself; a word that was seldom off Gertrude's lips, or, ventriloquially, Alice Toklas's. If he had genius, she would see that enough of this enviable, in her eyes masculine, commodity rubbed off him to make her one too. 'Pablo and Matisse have a maleness that belongs to genius,' Gertrude wrote in one of her notebooks. '*Moi aussi* perhaps.'[19] 'Genius' would provide Gertrude with an excellent pretext for setting up her own personality cult. It would also provide her with a licence to be as repetitive and on-and-on-going as she liked. 'Genius' exempted her from the obligation to revise, sharpen, above all cut, like lesser writers. When she had covered a great many pages with her seldom-corrected scrawl, she would drop them on the floor—'the daily miracle' she called it—for Alice Toklas to pick up and type. That was that. It only remained to find a publisher.[20]

Gertrude's claim to a uniquely privileged understanding of Picasso's work was not reciprocated. The artist was amused by the *Autobiography of Alice B. Toklas* but claimed to have little understanding of her more hermetic writing. Even when it was translated or explained, he confessed that he seldom saw the point. This was unusual: Picasso had such an instinctive and well-informed sense of literary values (courtesy of his poet friends) that certain admirers used to joke that he had only to look at the cover to gauge a book's contents. When Cooper asked Picasso (circa 1955) what he felt about some of Gertrude's pronouncements on art—for instance that 'most painters are not very tall and broad, there may be exceptions but generally speaking you have to be small'—he shrugged his shoulders in mock despair. The artist remained baffled to the end. In the fifties he would still ask friends whether Gertrude's writing was any good. Since she had managed to offend so many of them—not least by her adulation of Pétain—the answer was usually no. Gertrude never succeeded in convincing Picasso that she was as great as she claimed, let alone as great as himself. He seemed to go along with Cooper's suggestion that she confused being a genius with being a celebrity, and that her significance resided as much in what she was as in what she wrote. As the composer Virgil Thomson, an old friend of Gertrude and the artist, said many years later, 'Thirsting always for the kind of celebrity . . . Picasso had achieved so early, [she] described film people as "publicity saints", and she yearned to be one of them.'[21] 'Hurrah for *gloire*' is how she unashamedly put it. Picasso put it another way. On a very small panel that was intended to be fixed to the ceiling above Gertrude's bed he painted an ironical apotheosis. A group of nudes surround a scroll inscribed with the words '*Homage* [*sic*] *à Gertrude*.' One of the nudes—not unlike Alice —proffers fruit; another—Gertrude?—blows her own distended trumpet.

Picasso. *Homage à Gertrude*. Paris, 1909. Tempera on panel, 21×27cm. Private collection.

In the early days of their relationship Picasso entertained a higher regard for Gertrude than for any other woman (except his mother and his mistress). He had good reason to feel beholden: Gertrude and Leo were not only his first serious collectors; they were his first impresarios. What is more, Gertrude would wholeheartedly support Picasso—unlike Leo and Michael, who would support Matisse—when rivalry started to build up between the two artists. But even more than gratitude for her patronage, Picasso felt some kind of visceral reverence for Gertrude. She was in some respects a throwback to the self-fertilizing goddesses and dryads of folklore, who are as fearsome and all-knowing as any male deity.[22] Besides being a hieratic earth mother, she was a new species, a kind of

Felix Vallotton. *Portrait of Gertrude Stein*. 1907. Oil on canvas, 100×81 cm. The Baltimore Museum of Art, Cone Collection.

androgyne both more feminine and more masculine than the adolescent waifs of 1905. An '*hommesse*'. As Picasso used to say of Gertrude and her group: '*Ils sont pas des hommes, ils sont pas des femmes, ils sont américains.*'[23] Gertrude thought and acted like a modern-minded man—self-assured, forthright, disarmingly jovial. Mabel Dodge Luhan compared her deep abdominal laugh to 'a beefsteak'. To an Andalusian unused to liberated American females she must have seemed refreshingly matter-of-fact. What a relief after Fernande's finicky little ways—a trait Picasso always despised in women.

'Gertrude Stein and me are just like brothers,' Hemingway would later claim.[24] Picasso's feelings for Gertrude could also be described as fraternal (and sometimes filial), especially when, to her aggravation, he started calling her 'Pard'—one of the slang words he had picked up from Westerns. At the same time there was a physical—physical as opposed to sexual—aspect to his feelings for her. Gertrude confirmed him in the taste for full-bodied women that had originated at Schoorl. Although short (at five foot two, she was slightly shorter than Picasso), Gertrude was 'sturdy as a turnip'.[25] Mabel Dodge Luhan writes of 'the pounds and pounds and pounds piled up on her skeleton—not the billowing kind, but massive, heavy fat'.[26]

She loved to take long, long walks dressed in a heavy corduroy costume. And she would 'return sweating, her face parboiled'—ruddy as one of Picasso's behemoths. When she sat down and fanned

> herself with her broad-brimmed hat . . . she exhaled a vivid steam all around her [and] . . . used to pull her clothes off from where they stuck to her great legs. Yet . . . she was not at all repulsive. On the contrary, she was positively . . . attractive in her grand *ampleur*. She always seemed to like her own fat anyway and that usually helps other people to accept it. She had none of the funny embarrassments Anglo-Saxons have about flesh. She gloried in hers.[27]

And so did Picasso. Years later, Hélène Parmelin describes her husband, Edouard Pignon, and Picasso on the beach at Golfe-Juan, in ecstasy before a group of mountainous women, savouring each monstrous fold.[28]

Perhaps because he was used to seeing Gertrude in the company of other emancipated women, Picasso portrays her lookalikes in pairs, displaying themselves to each other, or putting their arms around each other's stalwart waists. These hefty maidens are the antithesis of the fashionable beauties of the *belle époque* with their swan necks encased in pearl chokers and their hourglass waists. They project the defeminized sexuality, the controversial new image of women, that polarized popular opinion in the years preceding World War I.[29] If the concept of the '*nouvelle femme*' intrigued Picasso, it was not because this lifelong misogynist felt much sympathy for the cause of women's emancipation, it was out of a god-like compulsion to create a new image that would synthesize the sexes (along the same lines as his compulsion to synthesize a woman's back and front, her face and genitalia). Drawings of 1907–08 abound with ideas for what I can only describe as a 'phallic woman'. One sheet depicts three kneeling nudes whose buttocks form an obvious phallic pun, as well as a standing woman who appears to grasp a penis—*her* penis—in her left hand. In the end Picasso arrives at a solution that is less crude and more ingenious: he turns the female diaphragm into a monumental

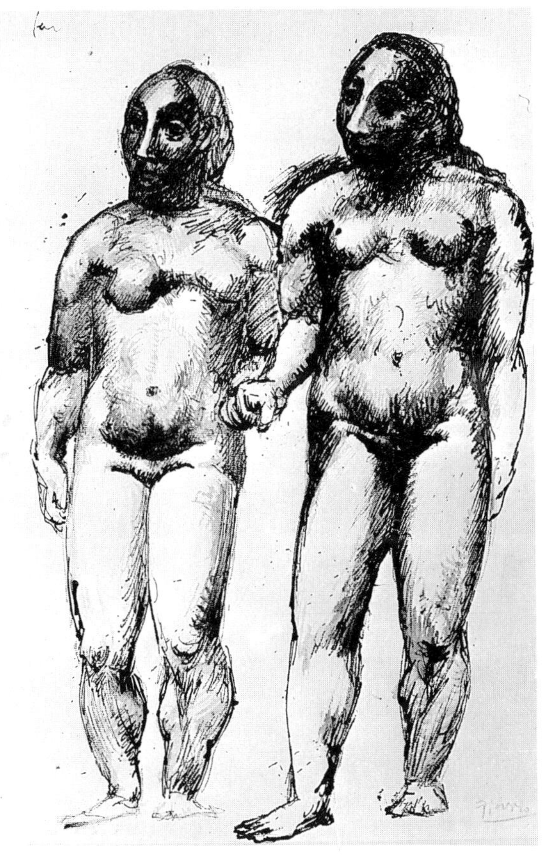

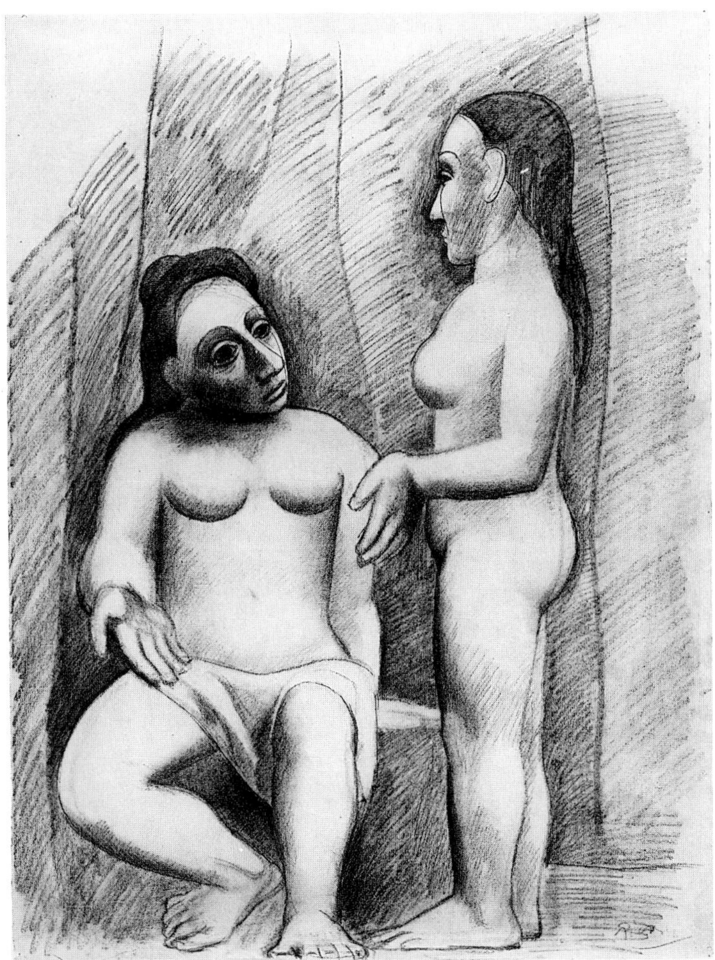

Top left: Picasso. *Two Nudes Holding Hands*. Paris, 1906. Pen and wash on paper, 48×32cm. Private collection.

Above: Picasso. *Woman Seated and Woman Standing*. Paris, 1906. Charcoal on paper, 61.5×47cm. Philadelphia Museum of Art, Louise and Walter Arensberg Collection.

Left: Picasso. Nude studies. Paris, 1907. Pen on paper, 32×25cm. Whereabouts unknown.

mandala that is both phallic and vaginal. Once again Jarry seems to hover in the background. The aggressive females—English and American for the most part—whom he unleashes on his readers have a lot in common with Picasso's Stein maidens.

The more overwhelmed Picasso felt by Gertrude's ego, the more difficulty he had in resolving her portrait. He had set himself an almost insuperable challenge: as well as coming to terms with his sitter's daunting personality, he had to reconcile Ingres and Cézanne and excel over Matisse. After more than three months of ceaseless struggle, he was obliged to admit defeat. 'Spring was coming,' Gertrude wrote, 'and the sittings were coming to an end. All of a sudden . . . Picasso painted out the whole head. I can't see you any longer when I look, he said irritably. And so the picture was left like that.'[30]

Around the time Picasso put aside her portrait, Gertrude finished *Three Lives*, some of which she had composed while sitting to Picasso. She gave the manuscript to Etta Cone to type. It was a difficult task. Gertrude's writing was almost illegible, and she had not given Etta permission to follow the sense of the words she was typing. When she was through, Etta left for Germany: she had to see a specialist about her 'bum gut' (Gertrude's phrase). While there she received a letter from Gertrude asking her to help Picasso, who had yet to sell out to Vollard and was in desperate need of money. 'Poor little Picasso', Etta commiserated. 'I'd swap all around with his health and genius were it possible.' But far from coming up with any financial help for 'poor little Picasso', Etta lent Gertrude 500 francs and, a few weeks later, wrote to ask whether she needed more: 'Don't hesitate [to say] and you needn't luxuriate in the feeling of poverty, for it's no use to.'[31] Etta's charity was evidently confined to her own ilk. Or had she been brainwashed by Sarah and Michael Stein? On January 15, 1906, these two had taken Etta to see Matisse, from whom she bought some drawings, a watercolour and a still-life painting. These acquisitions put an end to their first bout of collecting,[32] an end to the Cones' patronage of Picasso. When they resumed buying art in 1922, the sisters would concentrate on Matisse.

Picasso. *Bonjour Mlle Cone.* Paris, 1907. Pen on paper, 21×14cm. The Baltimore Museum of Art, Cone Collection.

Picasso and his sitter went their separate ways for the summer of 1906. While he set about arranging a trip to Spain, Gertrude and Leo departed for Fiesole, where they had rented a handsome hilltop house with terraced gardens, the Villa Ricci, overlooking Florence. Gertrude would spend most of the summer 'working tremendously' on her dense *roman fleuve, The Making of Americans*. There were good lending libraries in Florence, and she and Leo read and read. In the evenings they would visit the Berensons and the Loesers and entertain Etta Cone, who came to stay. Gertrude remembers receiving 'long letters [from Fernande] describing Spain and the spaniards and earthquakes'.[33] In his Pyrenean fastness Picasso was also working tremendously. Away from Gertrude's oppressive presence, he could see her clearly. Having found the key to her physiognomy, he would be able to complete the portrait from memory when he returned to Paris.

* * *

It is probably no coincidence that Picasso's dissatisfaction with the Stein portrait coincides with his first meeting with Matisse—the only other artist Picasso would ever acknowledge as a rival and ultimately accept as an equal. Even before the Steins brought them together in March 1906, Matisse must have seemed a threat. Matisse was the older by twelve years, but compared with the precocious Picasso, he was a late starter and a slow developer. By 1904, he had taken the colour theories of the neo-impressionists (above all his friends Signac and Cross) and transformed them into the explosively colourful style that came to be known as Fauvism—the last flare-up of the impressionist tradition. For all that he succeeded in shocking and dazzling the art world, Matisse was never one to let achievement impede his progress. He went on with his struggle to arrive at what he called a more lasting interpretation of reality. He would draw on Cézanne, van Gogh and Gauguin, the same sources that Picasso drew on, and come up with a totally different synthesis: as original as his rival's, but more idealized, more serene—celestial rather than demonic. There is no guilt in Matisse.

André Derain. *Portrait of Matisse.* 1905. Oil on canvas, 93×52cm. Musée Matisse, Nice.

Thanks to the Steins, Picasso and Matisse began looking apprehensively over their shoulders, accelerating their creative pace and discreetly jockeying for position. The competitiveness probably originated at the famous Salon d'Automne of 1905, when the Salle des Fauves—the gallery at the Salon devoted to Matisse and his followers: Derain, Vlaminck, Puy and briefly Rouault—was greeted with an outburst of philistine rage that had not been equalled since Manet showed his *Olympia.* Picasso was envious of all this opprobrium, envious that it should be lavished on the king of the Fauves instead of Harlequin Trismegistus. *Succès de scandale* put Matisse very much ahead. Two years later *Les Demoiselles d'Avignon* would help to redress the balance. Even if it was never exhibited, it established Picasso in his own mind and the eyes of a few followers as being in the lead. So much so that Matisse would come to fear 'his position . . . at the very heart of the School of Paris was threatened. The rival star—or dynamo—was Pablo Picasso.'[34]

The cynosure of the Fauve gallery was Matisse's magnificent *Woman with a Hat,* the painting that Leo Stein had characterized as 'the ugliest smear of paint he had ever seen', before he was coerced by his perceptive sister-in-law, Sarah, into changing his mind and buying it. Scornful artists 'sent [Matisse] a hideous woman painted with chrome oxide green stripes from forehead to chin: here was a model he would certainly want to paint.'[35] One critic compared the *Woman with a Hat* to 'the barbarous and naive sport of a child who plays with the box of colours he has just got as a Christmas present.'[36] And Camille Mauclair—who would denounce Picasso's art as 'Jewish' in the middle of World War II—revived the image Ruskin had used about Whistler: that of a pot of paint flung in the public's face.[37] Such open-minded art critics as Gustave Geffroy and Louis Vauxcelles were perplexed. André Gide, who briefly fancied himself a critic, was well disposed but condescending and misleading: 'When I heard people exclaim in front of a Matisse: "This is madness!" I felt like retorting "No, sir, quite the contrary. It is the result of theories."'[38] And Maurice Denis, the champion of Cézanne and Gauguin, who was by far the most perceptive chronicler of this historic Salon, feared that Matisse was in danger of being led astray by theory.[39] The beauty of the *Woman*

HENRI MANGUIN. — La Sieste.

M. Manguin : progrès énorme ; indépendant sorti des pochades et qui marche résolument vers le grand tableau. Trop de relents de Cézanne encore, mais la griffe d'une puissante personnalité, toutefois. De quelle lumière est baignée cette femme à demi nue qui sommeille sur un canapé d'osier !

Louis Vauxcelles, *Gil Blas*.

GEORGES ROUAULT. — Forains, Cabotins, Pitres.

Il est représenté ici par une série d'études de forains dont l'énergie d'accent et la robustesse de dessin sont extrêmes. Rouault a l'étoffe d'un maître, et je serais tenté de voir là le prélude d'une période d'affranchissement que des créations originales et des travaux définitifs marqueront.

Thiébault-Sisson, *le Temps*.

M. Rouault éclaire, mieux que l'an passé, sa lanterne de caricaturiste à la recherche des filles, forains, cabotins, pitres, etc.

Gustave Geffroy, *le Journal*.

M. Rouault... âme de rêveur catholique et misogyne.

Louis Vauxcelles, *Gil Blas*.

HENRI MATISSE. — Femme au chapeau.

ANDRÉ DERAIN. — Le séchage des voiles.

M. Derain effarouchera... Je le crois plus affichiste que peintre. Le parti pris de son imagerie virulente, la juxtaposition facile des complémentaires sembleront à certains d'un art volontiers puéril. Reconnaissons cependant que ses bateaux décoreraient heureusement le mur d'une chambre d'enfant.

Louis Vauxcelles, *Gil Blas*.

LOUIS VALTAT. — Marine.

A noter encore : ... Valtat et ses puissants bords de mer aux abruptes falaises.

Thiébault-Sisson, *le Temps*.

M. Louis Valtat montre une vraie puissance pour évoquer les rochers rouges ou violacés, selon les heures, et la mer bleue, claire ou assombrie.

Gustave Geffroy, *le Journal*.

HENRI MATISSE. — Fenêtre ouverte.

M. Matisse est l'un des plus robustement doués des peintres d'aujourd'hui. Il aurait pu obtenir de faciles bravos: il préfère s'enfoncer, errer en des recherches passionnées, demander au pointillisme plus de vibrations, de luminosité. Mais le souci de la forme souffre.

Louis Vauxcelles, *Gil Blas*.

M. Henri Matisse, si bien doué, s'est égaré comme d'autres en excentricités coloriées, dont il reviendra de lui-même, sans aucun doute.

Gustave Geffroy, *le Journal*.

JEAN PUY. — Flânerie sous les pins.

... M. Puy, de qui un nu au bord de la mer évoque le large schématisme de Cézanne, est représenté par des scènes de plein air où les volumes des choses et les êtres sont robustement établis.

Louis Vauxcelles, *Gil Blas*.

with a Hat resides in its instinctiveness; it is a triumphant demonstration of 'pure painting'. 'The courage to return to the purity of means', Matisse was later to say, is what Fauvism was all about.

The meaningless term 'Fauve' was coined by Vauxcelles, who would also coin the epithet 'cubism', which has stuck to an even greater art movement. '*Tiens! Un Donatello au milieu des fauves*' ('Look, a Donatello amidst the wild beasts') Vauxcelles had said apropos Albert Marque's pseudo-Renaissance bust of a child amidst the paintings of Matisse and his friends in the notorious Salle VII. Vauxcelles's label would not in fact become current for another two years or so. Before 1906 'incoherents' and 'invertebrates' is what the future Fauves were usually called.

We know that Picasso visited this Salon d'Automne, the third, but we can only guess at his reactions to the eight paintings and two watercolours that Matisse was showing. A measure of his envy is the fact that he would later delude himself that he had been ahead of the Fauves; that he had used green in a portrait (*Yo Picasso*) long before Matisse's famous portrait of his wife, *The Green Stripe*;[40] that he had indulged in a van Gogh-like maelstrom of brushstrokes before Vlaminck. But we need only compare Picasso's brightly hued works of 1901 with Matisse's works of 1904–05 to see that the former was exploiting bright colour schemes as a dramatic eye-catching device, whereas the latter had discovered how to juxtapose pure colours and, like God, engender light. Despite his boast that his 1901 *Self-Portrait* (see illustration, p.228) anticipated the *Woman with a Hat*, Picasso was too perceptive not to have realized that Matisse's grasp of colour was instinctive as well as analytical and in both respects way ahead of his own.

Matisse. *The Green Stripe*. 1905. Oil on canvas, 40.5×32cm. Statens Museum for Kunst, Copenhagen.

Gertrude Stein's claim that 'Matisse had never heard of Picasso and Picasso [had] never met Matisse' until she introduced them (March 1906) is only half true.[41] They knew each other's work from Berthe Weill's and Vollard's, where they had both been exhibited,[42] and they had a mutual admirer in Derain, whom Picasso had already met and with whom he would soon become very friendly. If their paths had never actually crossed, it was because Montmartre and the Latin Quarter, where Matisse lived, were two separate enclaves, and the inhabitants seldom mingled. The meeting that the three Steins (not just Gertrude, as she implied) had engineered went well. Marguerite Duthuit, Matisse's daughter, described

> the day the Steins took my father and me to the rue Ravignan. That's where we met [Picasso] for the first time. He had a big Saint Bernard dog then . . . we did not go unnoticed . . . everyone turned round and stared at us. The Steins were rather oddly dressed . . . especially Gertrude who . . . always wore dresses of heavy corduroy velvet and paid no attention to fashion. And all three of them [the third was probably Sarah] wore leather thong sandals on their bare feet, like the Romans, or like Isadora Duncan and her brother . . .[43]

Matisse. *Portrait of André Derain*. 1905. Oil on canvas, 38.5×28cm. Tate Gallery, London.

Would that we knew more about this encounter, or the return visit that the punctilious Matisse would have set up, or any of the early rapports between the two men who would soon tower over the School of Paris. Too bad Madame Duthuit remembered Picasso's great big dog and the peculiar-looking Steins rather than the artists' reactions to each other.

Picasso recalled that this meeting with Matisse coincided with the Salon des Indépendants.[44] This opened on March 20, 1906, the day after the

Opposite: Group of pictures from Salle VII (including Matisse's *Woman with a Hat*) illustrated in the survey of the 1905 Salon d'Automne in *L'Illustration*, November 1, 1905.

vernissage of Matisse's second one-man show at the Galerie Druet, which included fifty-five paintings, as well as a number of sculptures and drawings. Besides establishing Matisse as a *chef d'école*, the Druet show provided him with the financial security he had hitherto lacked. On the strength of it, Matisse departed shortly afterwards for Perpignan and Collioure in French Catalonia; after staying there for a time, he left (May 10) for a two-week trip to Biskra in Algiers—a trip that would further intensify his perception of colour and light. On his return, he went directly to Collioure and stayed there all summer. The confrontation with Picasso must therefore have taken place before rather than after he left Paris. The precise date would not matter except that, half a century later, Picasso still associated this meeting with an exhibition that signified one painting above all—'*la question du Salon*', Charles Morice called it—Matisse's great orgy of colour, *Le Bonheur de Vivre*. This magisterial figure composition constituted an even greater challenge than the *Woman with a Hat* and fired Picasso, once and for all, to go one better.

Matisse in his studio, *c*.1903.

For the last sixty years *Le Bonheur de Vivre* has been buried in the Barnes Foundation. It has never been reproduced in colour, so its seminal significance, which was widely perceived so long as it hung on the Steins' walls, is often overlooked, and as a beacon of twentieth-century art it has been outshone by *Les Demoiselles d'Avignon*. The *Demoiselles* likewise spent many years hidden away in private hands (first in the artist's studio and from 1922 in the Doucet collection), but ever since the Museum of Modern Art acquired it in 1939, it has become accepted as a principal begetter of much modern art. Like the *Demoiselles, Le Bonheur de Vivre* is a triumphant synthesis of disparate elements. This composition of bathers in a wooded glade draws on sources as different as Agostino Carracci,[45] Giorgione, Poussin and Watteau among earlier masters; Ingres, Cézanne, Gauguin and van Gogh among more recent ones; not to speak of the Abbé Breuil's drawings after prehistoric cave paintings, Greek vase decoration, Persian miniatures and Islamic motifs. Matisse has somehow succeeded in assimilating all these heterogeneous elements into a style of the utmost strength, suppleness and originality. As for the theme, Matisse turned, as Picasso had done, to symbolism, but symbolism of an earlier generation: specifically Mallarmé's *L'Après-midi d'un faune* ('*Ces nymphes, je les veux perpétuer*,' was its opening line).[46] At first even the artist's well-wishers were baffled: Signac was so upset by his principal follower's abrogation of divisionist theory and technique that he picked a fight with him after the opening. On reflection, critics came round to seeing it as a cornerstone of the modern movement.[47] Leo Stein first of all hated the painting, just as he had the *Woman with a Hat*; then he announced that it was the most important work of its time; and finally he added it to his and Gertrude's by now prestigious and highly visible collection. This acquisition must have pained Picasso. *Le Bonheur de Vivre* was much more advanced—not least in the revolutionary interaction of colour, form and line—than his conventionally depicted *Saltimbanques*. By the same token Matisse's vibrant arcadia makes Picasso's sentimental wasteland look wan and nostalgic. Now that he had been able to assess his adversary face to face, the competitive Picasso, who had recently taken up boxing, went, as it were, into training; he could no longer allow Matisse's supremacy to go unchallenged.

Matisse. *Le Bonheur de Vivre*. 1905–06. Oil on canvas, 174×238cm. Barnes Foundation, Merion Station, Pa.

Michael and Sarah Stein, Matisse, Allan Stein and Hans Purrmann in the Michael Steins' apartment at 58 rue Madame, late 1907. On the left wall is Picasso's *Saint-Lazare Woman by Moonlight* (1902; see illustration p.217). All the works on the facing wall are by Matisse. The Baltimore Museum of Art, Cone Archives.

With his carefully trimmed beard, gold spectacles and well-cut tweeds, Matisse looked more like a German professor than a painter. Picasso, on the other hand, had adopted the proletarian air of a mechanic, except in winter, when he sometimes gave the impression of wearing an acrobat's costume under his overcoat. These differences were much in evidence when the two men were seen together. This was usually at the Steins'. Gertrude and Leo were beginning to relish the power that patronage confers and, consciously or not, pitted the artists against one another at their Saturday soirées—occasions that were already reputed in social and artistic circles to be enjoyably gladiatorial. Whereas Matisse displayed 'an astonishing lucidity of mind, was precise, concise and intelligent and impressed people,' Picasso would be 'sullen and inhibited . . . he was easily irritated by people who tried to question him about his work; tried to make him explain what he was unable to explain.'[48]

Picasso was still far from fluent in French and was self-conscious about his Spanish accent, especially when Matisse was present. Leo Stein is our witness. At Durand-Ruel's exhibition (late 1906) of Manet and Redon, Stein had come upon Matisse, who claimed that Redon was vastly superior to Manet and that Picasso shared this peculiar preference. When Stein challenged Picasso on this point, he burst out angrily, 'Nonsense. Redon is an interesting painter, certainly, but Manet, Manet is a giant.' If he had agreed with Matisse, Picasso said, it was only because 'Matisse talks and talks. I can't talk, so I just said *oui, oui, oui*. But it's damned nonsense all the same.'[49]

Fernande, who admired Matisse, concludes that 'he never saw eye to eye with [Picasso]. As different as the north pole is from the south pole, [Picasso] would say, when talking about the two of them.'[50] Matisse would not necessarily have endorsed this verdict. Years later he recalled having told Max Jacob that if he were not painting the way he was, he would paint like Picasso. 'Isn't that curious?' Jacob had replied. 'Picasso said the same thing about you.'[51] A revealing story, but can we believe it? It sounds most unlike Picasso. Jacob might have invented this to make good blood between the rivals.

Leo Stein also emphasizes the contrasts between Matisse and Picasso:

> Matisse in an immaculate room, a place for everything and everything in its place, both within his head and without. Picasso—with nothing to say except the occasional firework, his work developing intuitively with no plan . . . Matisse social rather than convivial. Picasso convivial rather than social. Matisse saw himself in relation to others and Picasso stood apart, alone. He recognized others, of course, but as belonging to another system, there was no fusion. Matisse exhibited everywhere. He always wanted to learn, and believed there was no better way than to see his work alongside the work of everybody else. Picasso never showed with others.[52]

The loyal Penrose attributes Picasso's reluctance to exhibit to the fact that he 'gave away more [pictures] than he sold'.[53] This is a moot point. The truth is surely that Picasso had yet to find a dealer as serious as Matisse's Druet, and that in the face of his rival's ubiquity he preferred to remain aloof, preferred to bide his time until he felt he had the upper hand.

Picasso's persistent repainting of his huge *Saltimbanques* suggests that this work was originally intended as a *grande machine* that would make his name at the 1905 Salon d'Automne. If in the end he never exhibited the work, it was partly because the composition gave him so much trouble; it was also, I suspect, because he knew ahead of time—through the Fauve grapevine—that his *Saltimbanques* would have stiff competition from Matisse. Picasso could not submit what amounted to an advertisement for himself to a show in which Matisse participated unless he was fairly certain of coming out ahead. The alternative was to withdraw from the arena.

Matisse, Picasso realized, was already developing into one of the most inventive colourists in the history of art: one who knew how to evoke not just light but space and form and atmosphere through colour, and how to establish a whole new 'abstract' range of harmonies—in short, re-create paradise on canvas. Matisse's sense of colour was far more instinctive than Picasso's. But then a sense of colour had seldom been a Spanish painter's strongest suit. Quintessential Spaniard that he was, Picasso knew that he could extract more expression—more *duende*—out of a gamut of blacks, greys or browns than from the brighter colours in the spectrum. 'The only real colour is black,' he once said.[54] 'The Spaniards understood this. Look at Velázquez's blacks.' And again: 'If you don't know what colour to take, take black.'[55] He could also devise mannerist combinations of colour that recall Gauguin as well as El Greco in their sweetness and sourness. However, as he confessed, he added colour to compositions 'the same way one puts salt in soup'.[56] In other words, he was apt to use colour as an additive, independently of form. Hence his habit of plotting the colours of his major works diagrammatically. Picasso was very conscious of this limitation. 'I've mastered drawing and am looking for colour; you've mastered colour and are looking for drawing,' he told Matisse many years later.[57]

Picasso. Sketch for *The Saltimbanques*, with colour notations. Schoorl, 1905. Pen and crayon on sketchbook page, 16×12cm. Heirs of the artist.

At first Matisse and Picasso met regularly and subjected each other's work to intense scrutiny. As Picasso admitted over half a century later, 'If only everything that Matisse and I did at that period could be put side by side. Nobody ever looked at Matisse's work as thoroughly as I did. And he at mine.'[58] Picasso's *La Coiffure* (1906) left its mark on Matisse's treatment of the same subject (1907). And in its savage contortions Matisse's brutal *Blue Nude* (early 1907)—the last work by Matisse bought by Leo and Gertrude Stein—left even more of a mark on the *Demoiselles*.[59] In the summer of 1907 or shortly thereafter, the two artists would exchange paintings. Gertrude Stein claimed that each chose 'the picture that was undoubtedly the least interesting either of them had done.'[60] This is not true. Neither was that petty; each was careful to choose a painting from which he could learn. Picasso was emphatic on this point. Matisse picked a seemingly simplified, in fact highly equivocal still life in which the yellow concavity of the bowl is played off against the yellow convexity of the lemon. Picasso settled on a no less simplified portrait of Matisse's daughter, Marguerite (the painting with her name crudely spelt out at the top of the canvas). The reason Picasso gave me for his choice was that its bold and daring reductions stemmed from Matisse's study of drawings by his sons, Jean (born 1899) and Pierre (born 1900).[61] Picasso was very curious to see how Matisse had exploited his children's instinctive vision. The reason he gave Daix was that Marguerite is portrayed full-face, but her nose is sideways on (typical of children's drawings), as is the case with the two central figures of the *Demoiselles*.[62]

Picasso. *Pitcher, Bowl and Lemon.* Paris, 1907. Oil on panel, 64×48cm. Private collection. The painting Picasso exchanged for Matisse's portrait of his daughter, Marguerite.

Matisse. *Marguerite.* 1907. Oil on canvas, 65×54cm. Musée Picasso, Paris.

And then little by little the artists drifted apart. Picasso caught up and overtook Matisse, and the *bande à Picasso* adopted an ever more disdainful attitude towards him. Matisse, usually so cool, lost his temper and talked of 'getting even with Picasso, of making him beg for mercy'.[63] And he would make Picasso very envious when he accepted Shchukin's commission to do two large decorations for his palace in Moscow (1907–10). Picasso would later (1909) retaliate by accepting an even more ambitious commission to do nine panels for Hamilton Easter Field's library in Brooklyn.[64] This antagonism was partly the fault of the Steins; although they had brought the artists together in the first place, they had a way of projecting their own family differences onto their friends. Within a year of meeting Picasso, Gertrude had appointed herself his champion. Leo vacillated and finally opted for Matisse, but their relationship did not survive a grand tour of Italy masterminded by this exasperating cicerone, who saw himself as teacher and Matisse as pupil. Meanwhile the Michael Steins, above all the indefatigable Sarah, who helped set up Matisse's school at the end of 1907, had established themselves as that artist's leading patrons.[65] Under the auspices of the divisive Steins the north-south polarity that Fernande had perceived in the artists' relationship to each other set up the kind of tension—one thinks of Ingres and Delacroix—on which French art has traditionally thrived.

New hanging of pictures at the Steins' apartment at 27 rue de Fleurus, 1907. Picasso's portrait of Gertrude hangs above Matisse's *Woman with a Hat,* beside other Matisses, a Manet and a Renoir. On the left wall are Picasso's *Standing Nude* (1906; see illustration, p.446), *Boy with a Milk Can* (1905–06) and two *Heads* as well as a Florentine Madonna. The Baltimore Museum of Art, Cone Archives.

27

Plundering the Past

'The bad poet imitates: the good poet steals.' (T. S. Eliot)

Ingres. *Le Bain Turc*. 1862. Oil on canvas on wood, diam: 108 cm. Musée du Louvre, Paris.

Opposite: Picasso. *Woman with a Fan*. Paris, 1905. Oil on canvas, 100.3×81.2 cm. National Gallery of Art, Washington, D.C., Gift of the W. Averell Harriman Foundation in memory of Marie N. Harriman.

BESIDES THE SALLE DES FAUVES, the Salon d'Automne of 1905 included a series of exhibitions—some large, some small—that were to have a decisive effect on the course of modern art. Picasso had as yet to fall under the spell of Cézanne, so the small group of works by this master would not have absorbed him to the exclusion of other painters. Nor did the Seurat retrospective have as much of a message for him as it had for the Fauves. Picasso never regarded pointillism as much more than a device for enlivening or varying his surfaces or mocking the colour theories of the divisionists: hence a lack of luminosity when he adopts this technique. The Manet retrospective, on the other hand, was a major revelation—the beginning of Picasso's lifelong passion for the man he regarded as the first modern artist. Picasso envied the easy eloquence of Manet's brushwork, the deceptive nonchalance of his compositions and the way his figures stare back at the beholder (stares we will soon see on the faces of the *Demoiselles*). Manet's *Old Musician* in particular helped Picasso with the immediate task of finishing off *The Saltimbanques*. And his scenes of contemporary life (for instance the *Musique aux Tuileries*) may have suggested the project that Picasso contemplated early in 1907—a promenade in the Bois de Boulogne.

Even more of a revelation than the Manets was the Ingres retrospective, which included sixty-eight works. By the early years of the twentieth century Ingres had come to occupy an ambivalent position. While regarded by most modern artists as the quintessential academician, he had started to attract a following among the foes of academicism. That Degas worshipped Ingres and collected his work is less surprising than Gauguin's fervent admiration for this seemingly ultraconservative artist. 'Ingres may have died,' Gauguin wrote, 'but he was badly buried, for today he is very much alive.'[1] And Gauguin's friend Maurice Denis described Ingres as 'our most recently discovered modern master'.[2] Both Picasso and Matisse were overwhelmed by this retrospective: overwhelmed by the linear mastery of Ingres's drawings, the formal invention of his paintings, above all by his forgotten masterpiece *Le Bain Turc*. (It had been hidden away in the collection of Prince Louis-Amédée de Broglie, and earlier in that of Khalil Bey.) Matisse even went so far as to state that he preferred *Le Bain Turc* to Manet's *Olympia*, when the two paintings were hung together in the Louvre (1907).[3]

Velázquez. *Woman with a Fan*. 1638–39. Oil on canvas, 94.5×70cm. The Wallace Collection, London, reproduced by permission of the Trustees.

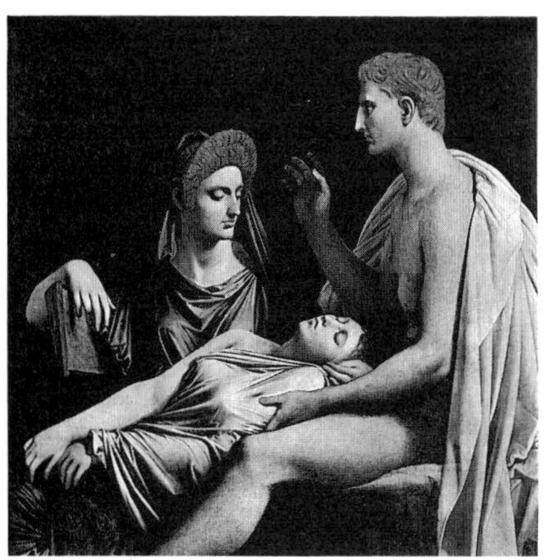

Ingres. *Tu Marcellus Eris*. 1819. Oil on canvas, 138×142cm. Musées Royaux des Beaux Arts, Brussels.

Not all young artists subscribed to this revisionist view of Ingres. Matisse may have been won over, but the younger Fauves continued to regard him as anathema; not, however, Braque, who split with them over this issue. Years later, Braque said that his eyes were opened by the unheard-of liberties that the supposedly hidebound Ingres took with appearances. Picasso likewise admired Ingres's glacial serenity, languorous eroticism and arbitrary way with anatomy; those swan-like throats, boneless arms, jointless fingers, wrap-around eyes; those shoulders, haunches, breasts piled up like satin cushions, as in some lubricious adolescent fantasy. Long before it inspired his bouts of neo-classicism, Ingres's *Le Bain Turc* would help detonate the *Demoiselles*. Despite his rejection of the *grand maître*' role, Picasso would even on occasion identify with Ingres. The musical director Ernest Ansermet recalled (1917) watching Picasso, in front of a mirror, murmur 'Monsieur Ingres' at his reflection.[4] And why not? Over the years he would salt away much of Ingres's imagery in his phenomenal visual memory.

The nature and extent of Ingres's influence on Picasso can be gauged in two of his greatest early portraits: in the cool authority of Gertrude Stein and the stillness and serenity of the *Woman with a Fan*. The model for the *Woman with a Fan* was a skinny Montmartre girl called Juliette, according to an inscription on one of the preparatory studies.[5] Picasso's idealized image of Juliette has its origins in two powerful images: Velázquez's *Woman with a Fan* and the figure of Augustus in Ingres's famous fragment *Tu Marcellus Eris*.[6] Ingres depicts Augustus with his hand raised to stop Virgil (who does not appear in this version of the painting) from continuing the story of the death by treachery of Marcellus—a story that has caused his sister, Octavia, to faint. (Octavia's son had met a similar end at the instigation of the third figure in this composition, Augustus's wife, Livia.) Ingres has frozen this moment of intense anguish into eternal stillness by portraying the three participants as classical marbles. By retaining the sculptural conception, by eliminating the two women and by endowing his Montmartre gamine with the emperor's authoritative gesture, Picasso has given the *Woman with a Fan* the hieratic air of a sphinx—the more so since, as Meyer Schapiro has observed, she appears to be in 'active communication with a partner beyond the picture field'.[7] Henceforth Picasso appropriates Ingres's sculptural concept to his own use. Just as he uses it to give monumentality to Gertrude Stein, he uses it to flesh out the Stein-like nudes of 1906. He will revert to it time and again during his various neo-classical phases, whenever he wants to enhance the palpability of his forms, to blur the distinction between sculpture and painting or do the one in terms of the other.

The *Woman with a Fan* dates from the time when Picasso was at work on Gertrude Stein's portrait; the sitter was well placed to acquire it more or less off the easel. Besides portraying what seems to have been a favourite subject of Gertrude's, this painting came to have a special significance for her. She thought it was a charm and that it would bring her luck. When in 1929 Gertrude decided to sell it so that she could finance the publication of her own work,[8] she held what she facetiously called 'a family council' to ratify this sacrifice. The 'family' council included Picasso and Toklas but no members of the Stein family apart from herself. Picasso told her that the *Woman with a Fan* had been hanging on her walls long enough, and that she could get rid of it. And so it was sold to Paul Rosenberg and bought, on the publisher Albert Skira's advice, by Mrs Averell Harriman. The decision left Alice Toklas very unhappy: 'When [Gertrude] told Picasso it made me cry. But it made it possible to publish the Plain Edition.'[9] The sale of the supposedly auspicious *Woman with a Fan* did not save the publishing venture from failure.

Picasso. Drawing for *Woman with a Fan*. Paris, 1905. Pen and ink on paper, 32×24.8cm. National Gallery of Victoria, Melbourne, Felton Bequest, 1967.

* * *

The Ingres retrospective of 1905 was only one of many sources that Picasso drew upon at this juncture. His instinctive response to Ingres coincides with an instinctive response to classical art—Greek as well as Roman, high style as well as archaic; and not just sculpture but mirror backs, Attic vases, terracottas and bronzes. Studies of a boy with a horse reveal that he had taken a good look at photographs of the Elgin marbles in 1902. But now he set about studying classical art and artefacts at first hand in the Louvre, as we know from Ardengo Soffici (the Italian futurist artist and critic who lived in Paris from 1900 until 1907). Soffici frequently encountered Picasso in the galleries of Egyptian and Phoenician, as well as Greek and Roman antiquities.[10] Picasso was not the only young artist to develop this enthusiasm. A classical revival in art and letters was sweeping through France, indeed much of southern Europe. Picasso's Greek friend Moréas had pioneered this trend in literature when he founded his Ecole Romane in the 1890s. And some of the Spanish sculptors in Paris —notably Manolo, Gargallo and Casanovas—had joined the burgeoning Mediterranean movement. So had the French Catalan sculptor Maillol; he had exhibited *La Mediterranée*—the embodiment of Ecole Romane ideals —at the Salon that included the Ingres retrospective. This was all part of a reaction against the frosty Gothic north, Pre-Raphaelitism, Celtic twilight,[11] as well as against German gods like Wagner and Nietzsche, who had held the French in thrall just as they had the Catalans of the *modernista* movement. In France the classical tradition had never really died. There had been successive attempts to rescue it from unworthy academic hands and rehabilitate it, not least by Renoir, in his *Grandes Baigneuses* of the mid-1880s (Picasso preferred the bloated pink goddesses of the artist's old age). But the most dedicated neo-classicist of all was Puvis de Chavannes, whose huge visions of a drab Arcadia dotted with groups of models in stilted poses—'Rosewater Hellenism'[12]—were enormously influential around the turn of the century.

Enric Casanovas. *Study*. c.1905. Plaster. Whereabouts unknown.

After copying Puvis's Pantheon frescoes in 1902, Picasso had found his interest confirmed by the retrospective of this artist's work (forty-three very large paintings) at the Salon d'Automne in 1904. He had also been subjected to the impassioned advocacy of his new friend Mécislas Golberg, a Polish poet, dramatist, sociologist, art critic and philosopher, who had been gaoled for his anarchist views in Poland and Germany before coming to Paris and being adopted as a guru by members of *La Plume*. A discovery of Salmon's, Golberg soon established himself as the most original and powerful thinker of the group. He was also the most politically oriented. However, as someone whom the French had once gaoled and twice expelled from the country, he had been obliged to renounce all political activity in exchange for a residence permit. Instead he focused his considerable intellect on art and aesthetics. Since he was dying of tuberculosis, Golberg had a special sympathy for those he called '*les disgrâces*'—modern 'lepers' and consumptives, victims of society who sound as if they have stepped out of a Blue period painting. Picasso thought highly of his *Morale des lignes* (written around 1905; published posthumously in 1908), which foreshadows both cubism and the later work of Matisse. Many of the theories on which Apollinaire's reputation as an art critic is based were apparently looted from the writings of Golberg, according to his great friend André Rouveyre. Rouveyre also claimed that before he died in 1907, Golberg helped draft Matisse's famous *Notes d'un peintre* (1908), '*en étroite fraternité d'esprit avec Matisse*' ('in close fraternal spirit with Matisse').[13]

Emile-Antoine Bourdelle. *Mécislas Golberg* (detail of stele). 1898–99. Bronze. Musée Bourdelle, Paris.

Golberg filled his studio with plaster casts of Greek and Roman sculpture, but he was no less obsessed with contemporary manifestations of classicism: the work of Bourdelle (who did two magnificent busts of him in 1898–99) as well as Puvis. He seems to have been largely responsible for the renewal and reinforcement of Picasso's interest in Puvis.[14] Puvis's influence can be detected in late Blue period paintings, and in some of the *saltimbanques*, but it does not become pervasive until Picasso's brief foray into classicism early in 1906. Even then Puvis impinges only for a few months and never as deeply as Ingres or Gauguin.[15] What attracted Picasso to Puvis was his would-be-modern way of classicizing things by simplifying drawing, eliminating anecdotal detail and establishing an idyllic mood in a minor key. All of this is reflected in the work of 1905–06. Picasso emulated the matt, dry surfaces that Puvis favoured—even when he was not doing frescoes[16]—also his restrained use of cool, pale colours with very little modelling or chiaroscuro. The extent of Picasso's debt to Puvis emerges in the preparatory sketches for his next project: an ambitious, never-to-be-executed composition known as *The Watering Place* (early 1906)—naked boys and wild horses on the bleak slopes familiar to us from *The Saltimbanques*.

The *Watering Place* project, which dates from the same winter as the Stein portrait, seems to have been conceived as yet another major bid for public recognition. This time Picasso envisages his breakthrough taking the form of a modern version of a classical horse-and-rider composition, such as Gauguin, another admirer of Puvis, had painted only four years earlier: the Parthenon frieze-like *Riders on the Beach*, which Picasso would have seen at Vollard's. Compared with the Gauguin, Picasso's composition is classically symmetrical: twin boys stand almost dead centre, next to twin horses that look as if they should be harnessed to a chariot on a Greek mirror back; one horse is black and one is white, like the black and white babies in the *Saltimbanques* sketch. On one side a boy rides towards us, and on the other, one rides away from us;[17] in the background is another horseman, who has been lifted from the west frieze of the Elgin marbles. Had it ever materialized, *The Watering Place* would have been better organized than *The Saltimbanques*. But by the time Picasso was ready to paint a definitive version, he had seen Matisse's *Le Bonheur de Vivre*. These Arcadian riders would hardly have qualified him for victory in the avant-garde stakes, so the project was abandoned.

Puvis de Chavannes. *Young Girls by the Sea*. 1879. Oil on canvas, 205×154cm. Musée du Louvre, Paris.

For the next six months or so, the work abounds with boys as opposed to androgynes. By stripping his harlequins or *saltimbanques* of their

Right: Gauguin. *Riders on the Beach.* 1902. Oil on canvas, 73×92cm. Private collection.

Below: Picasso. *The Watering Place.* Paris, 1906. Gouache on board, 38.1×57.8cm. The Metropolitan Museum of Art, New York, Bequest of Scofield Thayer, 1984.

El Greco. *St Martin and the Beggar.* 1597–99. Oil on canvas, 193.5×103cm. National Gallery of Art, Washington, D.C., Widener Collection. Painted for the Chapel of San José, Toledo.

Above: Picasso. *Boy Leading a Horse.* Paris, 1906. Oil on canvas, 221×130cm. Collection William S. Paley, New York.

Right: Kouros. Paros, mid-sixth century B.C. Marble, ht: 103cm. Musée du Louvre, Paris.

costumes, Picasso classicizes them. Palau has suggested that the preponderance of ephebes might denote problems with Fernande— 'some other amour' perhaps.[18] This is most unlikely. Fernande had moved in with Picasso in September, a few months before he started work on *The Watering Place* and he had seldom been happier. (Angel de Soto, who had gone to live in Málaga, had written to Picasso in April saying that he suspected Picasso of having fallen in love from the tone of his letters; Angel said he still preferred *putas*.) If Fernande makes relatively few appearances in her lover's work during her first six months of life with him, it is because Picasso had not yet been able to calibrate his style to the image of the loved one. Until he discovered how to do justice in paint to the first real passion of his life, women would be conspicuously absent from his work. Meanwhile the youths who replace the women are portrayed with no affective overtones; there is nothing to suggest that they might be objects of desire. They are classical ciphers, Péladan's 'plastic ideals'.

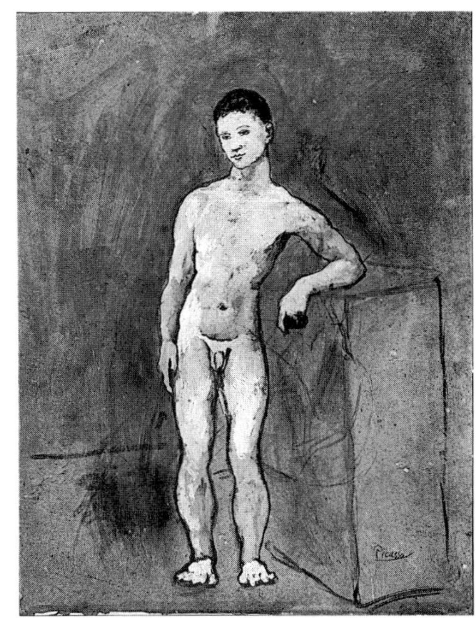

Picasso. *Ephebe*. Paris, 1906. Gouache on cardboard, 68×52cm. State Hermitage Museum, Leningrad.

Although *The Watering Place* came to nothing, it engendered one superb painting. Just as Picasso had recycled the central section of his original *Saltimbanques* composition into the *Young Acrobat on a Ball*—arguably a more successful work than its progenitor—he now utilized part of the central group of *The Watering Place* for his masterpiece of the period, *Boy Leading a Horse*. In both cases Picasso seems happier focusing on one or two figures set in a restricted vertical format than deploying a group of figures across a wide area. (A year later, he would profit from experience and cram the *Demoiselles* into a format that is a very tight fit.) Picasso worked on the *Boy Leading a Horse* and *The Watering Place* at the same time as the portrait of Gertrude Stein. His sitter resolved to buy the monumental *Boy* and persuaded Etta Cone to buy the best of the related studies. Odd, however, that although Gertrude was in the studio virtually every day of this experimental winter, she was seemingly blind to everything except her own portrait. She has nothing to say about the successive phases of Picasso's evolution through which she lived.

At first sight quintessentially Picassian, the image (221×130cm) of the *Boy Leading a Horse* turns out to be remarkably derivative. Although the idea originated in the *Watering Place* sketches, the fresco-like surface and scale stem from Puvis. Picasso was also obliged to look to El Greco for help with the bottom half of his composition: how to make six legs pictorially coherent. El Greco's *St Martin and the Beggar*, of which Picasso already had a photograph, provided the prototype; it also conferred a touch of Spanish gravity. For the figure of the boy Picasso is usually said to have adapted one of his *saltimbanques* to a kouros—an archaic statue of a naked youth given as a trophy at the Olympic games —of which there were several in the Louvre.[19] Cézanne's male bathers, which Picasso would have seen at Vollard's or the Salon d'Automne in 1904 and 1905, have also been cited.[20] Another possible prototype has never been mentioned. It was to be found on the walls of the Lapin Agile next to Picasso's harlequin painting: a large plaster cast of a figure from one of the temples in Java.[21] This figure would have confronted Picasso night after night; despite his avowed distaste for oriental art, it must have made an impression on him, for we find echoes of it in some of the standing nudes of 1906. And in stance and articulation, it provides as

Detail of cast of Javanese sculpture at the Lapin Agile (see illustration, p.373)

Picasso. *La Coiffure.* Paris or Gósol, 1906. Oil on canvas, 175×99.7cm. The Metropolitan Museum of Art, New York, Wolfe Fund, 1951.

Picasso. *Head of Fernande.* Paris, 1906. Bronze, ht:33.5cm. Norton Simon, Inc. Foundation, Los Angeles.

convincing a prototype for the *Boy Leading a Horse* as Cézanne's chunky bathers or the Louvre's rigid kouroi. One small point: the lack of a visible halter or lead-rein from the boy's evidently clutching hand has been seen as an expression of 'the unity of horse and boy . . . harmony with each other and nature'.[22] If there is no halter, it is because Picasso had taken the precaution of copying a drawing by that indefatigable portrayer of the horse, Constantin Guys, and had learned the wisdom of omitting these pictorially confusing accoutrements. If a Guys horse has reins it is almost bound to be a fake.[23]

After the *Boy Leading a Horse*, Picasso embarked on another large vertical composition, *La Coiffure*, which is painted in similar neutral colours. Once again the artist has adapted an element from an earlier composition: the theme of one girl dressing another's hair. This recurs in projects for *The Saltimbanques* as well as in drawings done in Holland of a fat woman being coiffed (so fat that she resembles the plump jester El tío Pepe). The central figure in Ingres's *Le Bain Turc*, who is having her hair perfumed (auburn, like Fernande's luxuriant chignon) may have inspired these subjects. However, a taste, amounting sometimes to a fetish, for abundant tresses afflicted almost every artist of the period, not least Munch. *Pelléas and Mélisande* had had its debut only four years earlier, and Mélisande's mesmerizing '*Mes longs cheveux*' reverberated in artistic memories. The contrast between the conventional conception and the bold execution of *La Coiffure* suggests that it was started in the neoclassical spring of 1906 and finished, like the Stein portrait, in the archaic autumn.

The sculptural look of certain Rose period paintings reflects a revival of interest in modelling in clay. Picasso followed up his conventionally conceived head of the jester with a no less conventionally conceived head of Alice Derain. Both are accomplished exercises in an unoriginal Rodin-esque manner. However, the life-size head of Fernande that Picasso modelled in clay (early in 1906 and probably in Paco Durrio's studio) is more technically assured and has a voluptuous monumentality. Desire for his model has engendered a Pygmalion-like urge to transfuse the clay with her sensuousness.

Meanwhile Picasso's awareness of sculpture had received further stimulus. The Louvre had put on view a newly acquired group of archaic Iberian sculptures (6th–5th centuries B.C.).[24] These had recently been excavated by Pierre Paris and Arthur Engel at sites in the south of Spain, notably at Cerro de los Santos (near Seville) in the artist's native Andalusia. To the non-archaeological eye these objects are of minor aesthetic interest; except for the overrefined *Woman of Elche*, they tend to be clumsy in execution, paltry in scale and low in sacred fire. Not, however, to Picasso. They were hallowed by virtue of being one of Spain's few contributions to the art of the ancient world; hallowed, too, because they represented his roots. They had been carved by people of mixed race who—like the artist's own family—had migrated to Andalusia before moving northwards. In addition to their atavistic spell, their brutality and lack of distinction commended them to someone who was anxious to demolish traditional canons of beauty. For the time being Picasso did not see how to harness their primitivism to his work. The months he was to spend in Spain in the summer would show him how to do so.

Iberian head from Cerro de los Santos. Limestone, ht: 46 cm. Musée des Antiquités Nationales, Saint-Germain-en-Laye.

El Greco, too, resurfaces. Hitherto Picasso had helped himself liberally to El Greco's mannerist conceits, but in the course of 1906 his perception of the master underwent a radical change. He saw beyond El Greco's visionary theatricality. He perceived how his adoption of an all-over play of light, which originally had a mystical connotation, could be exploited as a unifying device; and how his reconciliation of three-dimensional appearances with the two-dimensional surface of a canvas, could help solve one of the modern artist's most obsessive concerns.

The arrival in Montmartre of a masterpiece by El Greco is what had helped Picasso arrive at a deeper understanding of this artist's work. The great apocalyptic painting (once thought to have been an allegory of Sacred and Profane Love, then entitled *The Opening of the Fifth Seal*, now called *Apocalyptic Vision*) had recently been acquired by his old friend Ignacio Zuloaga. Like Rusiñol, Zuloaga had been a pioneer in the rehabilitation of El Greco; like him, he collected his work. Fernande Olivier has described the walls of Zuloaga's studio on the rue de Caulaincourt, 'covered with El Grecos and Goyas which he had managed to get from churches and convents in Spain, often in exchange for one of his works.'[25] Zuloaga had not, on the whole, been lucky with his El Grecos. Of the ten examples in his collection that Manuel Cossío (the founder of El Greco scholarship) had once accepted as authentic, eight are now thought to have been copies or workshop versions, with one *Christ on the Cross* possibly by the master's hand. However, Zuloaga had now acquired one incomparable, if badly damaged, masterpiece, the aforementioned *Apocalyptic Vision*.

Zuloaga had discovered this painting at a doctor's house in Córdoba, one of the stops on a triumphal tour of Spain he had undertaken in June 1905.[26] His companions were Rodin—known by the Spaniards as the 'Eternal Father' on account of his godlike beard—and Ivan Shchukin, an effete Russian collector of Spanish painting, not to be confused with his progressive elder brother Sergei, who was soon to become Picasso's greatest patron. Zuloaga had hoped that this carefully stage-managed trip would, on the one hand, open Rodin's eyes to the glories of El Greco and Goya (it failed to do so); and on the other, encourage Shchukin's penchant for El Greco, so that the gullible Russian could be landed with a few more dubious works by the master. When Shchukin, who was notoriously profligate, tried to fend off creditors in 1908 by selling the nine Grecos that Zuloaga had found for him, they all proved to be fakes. He poisoned himself. Retribution of an appropriate kind was in store for Zuloaga: in the next few years Russia, which had become his principal market, was flooded with fake Zuloagas.

Zuloaga, Rodin and Ivan Shchukin in Spain, June 1905.

Until the 1880s or 1890s the *Apocalyptic Vision* had belonged to Antonio Cánovas del Castillo (the prime minister, who had been assassinated in 1896), not otherwise recognized as a collector. How or why this masterpiece passed into the possession of a Córdoban doctor, Rafael Vázquez de la Plaza, we do not know. Zuloaga liked to recount how the doctor kept the painting behind an old velvet curtain for fear the sight of so many writhing nudes would shock his daughters. Rodin claimed to loathe this El Greco—predictably: in certain respects it anticipated his *Gates of Hell*. And his disapproval may explain why Zuloaga was able to steer the only great El Greco that he ever discovered into his own collection instead of the one he was forming for the ill-fated Shchukin.

Picasso. *Portrait of a Painter, after El Greco.* Vallauris, February 22, 1950. Oil on plywood, 100.5×81 cm. Angela Rosengart collection, Lucerne.

Zuloaga bought the painting for a thousand pesetas. And it was shipped forthwith to his Paris studio, where Rodin eventually came to admire it; and where Picasso saw it again and again over the next few years. It was the only major old master that Picasso would see—and see constantly at the most formative period of his career—in a friend's house rather than in a museum or dealer's gallery. And it had an incalculable influence on his style, beliefs and aspirations; it reconfirmed his faith in his *alma española* (his 'Spanish soul'); and it played a key role in the conception of *Les Demoiselles d'Avignon*, not only in its size, format and composition, but in its apocalyptic power. Months before Picasso embarked on the *Demoiselles*, the central group of the Greco is reflected in his work; for instance, the *Two Nudes* (winter 1906) who gesture at one another in front of draperies. As Picasso unequivocally proclaimed, 'Cubism is Spanish in origin, and it was I who invented Cubism. We should look for Spanish influence in Cézanne. . . . Observe El Greco's influence on him. A Venetian painter but he is Cubist in construction.'[27] This avowal dates from around 1950, when Picasso took El Greco back into his pantheon after a period of banishment. El Greco had fallen from grace by being adopted as Franco's favourite old master—thanks largely to Zuloaga, who was Franco's favourite modern painter. To make matters worse, in order to please the Caudillo, Zuloaga had taken to virulently denouncing Picasso, whose work he had been one of the first to buy. When London's New Burlington Gallery exhibited *Guernica* in 1938, it also exhibited Zuloaga's riposte to it—a melodramatic commemoration of the *Defenders of the Alcazar of Toledo.* The *Guernica* room was always full; the *Toledo* one always empty. Picasso enjoyed trouncing the fascist foe, but his regard for El Greco was temporarily tainted.

In 1950 Picasso celebrated his readoption of El Greco by doing a curiously twisted version of the master's portrait of his son, Jorge Manuel (Provincial Museum, Seville). An illustrious artist's painting of an ungifted son was a very apposite choice on the part of the illustrious son of an ungifted father. Three years later, Picasso was fascinated when Cocteau told him that the Spanish savant Dr Gregorio Marañon thought that El Greco had modelled his apostles on the lunatics in the Toledo hospice and to prove his point was getting some of the lunatics in his care to grow their beards.[28] Was Picasso reminded of how he had adopted the models he found in the Saint-Lazare hospital to his own purposes?

At the end of his life, when he reverts to his Spanish roots, Picasso will refer time and again to El Greco, just as he did in his early days. Perhaps the most bizarre reference occurs in his blasphemous parody of the *Burial of Count Orgaz* (see illustration, p.93). Besides transforming the body of Count Orgaz into a roast chicken, Picasso removes the figure known to be a self-portrait from the crowd and blows it up to fill the right-hand half of the print. In the place of El Greco he inserts a likeness of himself, sporting a beard and wearing a striped sweater. 'Yo, El Greco' again, seventy years later.[29] 'Velázquez! What does everybody see in Velázquez these days?' Picasso asked Otero in 1966. 'I prefer El Greco a thousand times more. He was really a painter.'[30] But then, unlike Velázquez, El Greco was a painter whom he evidently felt he had 'mastered'.

Zuloaga's flashy Hispagnolist painting had earned him, too, the sobriquet the 'little Goya', and in the early years of the century it had brought him considerable social and financial success. So had his flashy Hispagnolist looks: 'tall, athletic, bald even then, with a sort of classical beauty and dreamy, thoughtful eyes.'[31] Likewise his carefully orchestrated parties. Picasso and Fernande would make up for the sparseness of their fare by attending the fashionable dinners Zuloaga and his wife, Valentine, organized and richer friends, like Pichot, would underwrite. For instance, to celebrate the birth of their son on April 25, 1906, they arranged *'une petite réunion espagnole*', to which they invited Degas,[32] Rodin, Rilke, as well as such Spaniards as the composer Isaac Albéniz, the Pichot clan (including Ramon Pichot, the painter, his sister, Maria Gay, the singer, and their brother-in-law Edouard Marquina, the writer) and presumably the Pichots' friend Picasso. La Carmela danced; Llobet played the guitar; Uranga sang. . . . What more sublime background to this '*réunion espagnole*' than the *Apocalyptic Vision*? What greater challenge to Picasso? He was beginning to see how he could show the world that he was the new El Greco, but first it would be necessary to get away from Paris, to return to Spain and find some simple place where he could settle down and put everything together in a new way. Eight years before, Horta de Ebro had made a new man of Picasso; an equally primitive village in the Pyrenees, Gósol, would now make a new artist of him.

El Greco. *Apocalyptic Vision*. 1608–14. Oil on canvas, 225×193 cm. The Metropolitan Museum of Art, New York, Rogers Fund, 1956.

28

Summer at Gósol

The artist's mother, *c.*1906. Musée Picasso, Paris.

Opposite: Picasso. *Bois de Gósol* (detail). Gósol, 1906. Carved boxwood with traces of red and black paint and illegible inscriptions. Musée Picasso, Paris.

By the spring of 1906 Picasso had been away from his native land for two years—longer than ever before. Most days his mother sent him a copy of *El Noticiero* and a letter giving him the family news. She and don José regretted his move to France and were forever urging him to return, especially now that he had a *novia* they were curious to meet. Picasso had come to regard his father as insufferably reactionary and 'bourgeois, bourgeois, bourgeois'[1]—a feeling that guilt did nothing to assuage. But he never lost his love and respect for his mother: doña María grew more open-hearted, genial and gypsylike as her husband grew more bitter, crotchety and blind. Picasso's nephew Javier Vilató says that problems never daunted her. Right up to her death (aged eighty-four, in 1937), she was 'magnificent, intelligent, lively, tolerant. She never missed a day reading *La Vanguardia* and *El Noticiero*, she liked the theatre, she read a lot, she even knew how to swim at a time when it was considered eccentric.'[2] Her pride and passion was her son, but she knew him too well to make a nuisance of herself and so 'they had a good, uncomplicated relationship'.[3] He could do no wrong in her eyes. Whether or not she understood his work, she never questioned its validity. Nor, it seems, did she question his choice of women, or his abandonment of them (except in the case of his first wife, Olga, because this implied the abandonment of his son, Paulo).

Poverty and pride had hitherto prevented Picasso from returning 'home'. After his previous setbacks in Paris, he could go back to Barcelona only as a success. All of a sudden he was a success—not just critically but, in a modest way, financially. At the beginning of May Vollard had re-entered his life. Apollinaire had brought him to the studio, and for two thousand francs he had purchased twenty of his most important early paintings, excluding the big *Saltimbanques*.[4] Besides Apollinaire, Salmon and Jacob were witnesses to this transaction. Salmon remembered that Vollard carried off all the paintings and gouaches with him in the cab; they took up so much room that Vollard had to sit up front with the driver. 'Max and I gasped at this sight, the hagiographer of Saint Matorel [Max Jacob] clasped my hand without saying a word, without looking at me, utterly content, his eyes like seascapes full of tears.'[5] The disadvantage of selling to Vollard was that he stashed his treasures away and seldom showed them to anyone but favoured clients. A great many of these Picassos would not be seen again until December 1910, when

Enric Casanovas. *Dona de Gósol.* 1911. Stone. Whereabouts unknown.

the dealer organized a one-man exhibition of what Apollinaire described as 'beautiful works hitherto unknown to the public'.[6]

Two thousand francs was more money than Picasso had ever possessed —enough to get married on, except that Fernande was not divorced; enough to last a thrifty couple two or three years, except that they were not thrifty; enough to travel to Barcelona in style, which they proceeded to do. Besides wanting to prove to his parents and cronies that he had made good as an artist, Picasso was eager to show off his beautiful 'fiancée'. He also wanted to introduce Fernande to the native land that he would always love—impossible though it might be to work there— and to see it afresh through her eyes. But above all he wanted to repeat the purifying experience that he had undergone at Horta in 1898; to get away from the claustrophobic little world of the Bateau Lavoir and the Lapin Agile, of Azon and Vernin, and regenerate himself with a sojourn in the wilderness, as his great-uncle Perico, the hermit of Córdoba, had done years before.

Why Picasso decided against Horta as the setting for this retreat we do not know. He might simply have wanted to try somewhere new; or, more likely, he might have felt that the presence of a fancy French mistress would have compromised the Pallarès family. Instead he opted for the equally remote village of Gósol, five thousand feet up in the Pyrenees, near the little country of Andorra. Picasso said he had heard about Gósol 'in the usual way through friends. A sculptor in Barcelona named Casanova [*sic*] and the son of a well-known Greek prime minister [Venizelos] had been to Gósol and said it was magnificent.'[7] Picasso would also have known of the place from his old friend Jacint Reventós, who used to send his patients there for a rest cure or to convalesce: 'good air, good water, good milk and good meat'.[8]

All the arrangements for the trip were, in fact, made by Picasso's Catalan sculptor friend Enric Casanovas, who divided his time between Barcelona and Paris and sometimes spent the summer at Gósol.[9] Besides being a close friend of Manolo and Gargallo, who had lent him his rue Vercingétorix studio (source of the Bateau Lavoir furniture), Casanovas was very supportive of Picasso, always ready to help with practical arrangements or technical problems to do with sculpture. Although little known outside Barcelona, he was an infinitely more accomplished classicist than Manolo. Casanovas never joined Moréas's Ecole Romane, but he subscribed to its views; so, briefly and vaguely, did Picasso.[10] The sculptor had originally intended to accompany Picasso on the trip, but his mother fell ill, and he left Paris for Barcelona ahead of him.[11] On May 23 the artist wrote to Casanovas, this time from the Hotel Continental in Barcelona: 'Would you like to come tomorrow in the evening to the Continental so that we can arrange all the details of the journey?' Further letters written jointly by Picasso and Fernande after their arrival in Gósol confirm that Casanovas stayed behind in Barcelona but intended to follow later in the summer. He never did.[12]

Fernande has described the expedition to Spain—her first '*grand voyage*'—in some detail.[13] Accompanied by Apollinaire and Jacob, she and Picasso left the Bateau Lavoir around six in the evening to take a cab to the Gare d'Orsay. Each of them had a big basketwork valise: Picasso's was full of canvas, paints, brushes and paper; Fernande's held a smart outfit she had bought to dazzle the Catalans, as well as lots of perfume.

Enric Casanovas in his Paris studio, *c.*1904. Casanovas family collection.

Gertrude Stein says she also took along a cooking stove: 'All french women . . . when they went from country to country took along a french oil stove to cook on.'[14] If Fernande burdened herself with a 'primus', it was more likely for staving off the cold mountain air than for cooking. At the station more friends had gathered to speed them on what proved to be an arduous journey. The third-class compartment was too uncomfortable for sleep. The next day they stopped for lunch at Narbonne, and then continued to the frontier, where they changed trains. In Spain they switched to first class so as to arrive in style: Fernande was very relieved. But when they finally drew into Barcelona at seven in the evening, she was appalled by the noisy Catalan welcome in store for them. Her nerve failed her and, to Picasso's dismay, she burst into tears and begged to return home. However, after a bath and a good night's sleep, Fernande awoke 'relaxed and happy' and no longer pined for Paris. Pablo should not have taken her attack of the vapours so seriously, she said; it was 'only exhaustion and never having travelled before'.[15]

The artist's sister, Lola, *c.*1910.

Picasso and Fernande spent a busy couple of weeks in Barcelona. 'He lunched with his family and joined his friends at about three in the afternoon. Then we would go on excursions. He loved going to Tibidabo, which is a hill towering over Barcelona, with a superb view of the city.'[16] Their evenings were very social. As '*la novia de* Picasso', the beautiful Fernande in her elegant new outfit, trailing clouds of Chypre, made a sensational impression, above all on doña María. Knowing nothing about her earlier marriage, she welcomed Fernande as a potential daughter-in-law. Picasso was delighted to see his sister, Lola, who was still engaged to her long-standing fiancé, Dr Juan Vilató Gómez.[17] The artist was overjoyed at being reunited with Catalan cronies, above all the Soto and Reventós brothers, and they were no less overjoyed to have their hero back. Fernande does not mention the Junyer Vidals, but she says they saw a lot of Gargallo, who was still very poor and worked out of a slummy basement; Canals, whose wife was an old friend of Fernande's; and Casaṇovas, who was masterminding their trip. Sabartès had vanished from the Catalan scene and set himself up in trade in Guatemala City, so Fernande did not meet him. But stories about him were rife. Before leaving for South America, he was rumoured to have taken his fiancée to the opera; in the interval he had excused himself to get some matches and never returned. Sabartès had recently written to Picasso that he was about to marry a girl in Guatemala.

Fernande, Picasso and Ramon Reventós at El Guayaba, May 1906. Photo: Vidal Ventosa.

Fernande also mentions outings with Miquel Utrillo, who had just brought out his booklet on El Greco and would certainly have given a copy to Picasso (if he had not already mailed him one). This modest publication, which sold for one peseta, was limited to fifty poor-quality plates; nevertheless it was the first monograph on the neglected master. Picasso was already familiar with most of Utrillo's illustrations; he had already pillaged many of them and would do so again. For the next year or so, thanks in part to this little *aide-mémoire*, El Greco would exert an ever more insidious influence on his work. The evening before they left for Gósol (early June), Vidal Ventosa photographed Fernande, Picasso and Ramon Reventós, looking very elegant seated at a table in the Guayaba.

Now that he had established residence in France, Picasso felt more than ever drawn to Spain. 'The atmosphere of his own country was essential to him,' Fernande writes, 'and gave him . . . special inspiration. . . . The Picasso I saw in Spain was completely different from the Paris Picasso; he was gay, less wild, more brilliant and lively and able to interest himself in things in a calmer, more balanced fashion; at ease in fact. He radiated happiness and his normal character and attitudes were transformed.' She concludes that 'he would have been happier if he had lived in Spain.'[18] The improvement in Picasso's morale was already visible in Barcelona, but up in the high sierra he would come magnificently into his own.

Picasso. *Woman on a Donkey*. Gósol, 1906. Pen on paper, 17×11 cm. Private collection.

* * *

The journey to Gósol was an ordeal. The newly opened Catalan Railways took them as far as Guardiola de Berga. Gósol was only fifteen kilometres farther, but access was on muleback, over mountain tracks up gorges that were barely negotiable in summer, impassable in winter. On one side there was a 'bottomless' precipice that gave Fernande vertigo, on the other a rock wall that bruised her knees. She was terrified when the girths came loose and her saddle started to slip; the muleteer rescued her just in time. After eight hours they arrived at their destination: '*Ce fut un enchantement*,' Fernande says.[19] It still is. One of the most dramatic spots in the Pyrenees, Gósol is as unspoiled and unfrequented today as it was in 1906.

Gósol is in fact two villages. The original medieval village, built round a castle high on a hill, has been deserted for centuries. Except for the church, its ruins are barely distinguishable from the giant rocks that dot this lunar hillside. The 'new' village nestles in a valley below. It is sheltered by four separate mountain ranges: on the northwest the Serra de Cadí; on the southwest the Serra del Verd; on the southeast the Serra les Comes; on the northeast the usually snow-covered peak of Pedraforca. For all the bleakness of its surroundings, Gósol in summer is a green oasis in a landscape that is otherwise all grey except for patches of reddish earth. Local farmers had formerly concentrated on wheat, but by the end of the nineteenth century crops had given way to cattle, sheep and goats. Gósol was also known for its excellent horses, its mules—crucial for contraband—and its wily muleteers. It was not until about 1942, when a new road was built and the first cars arrived, that the village became more accessible. The result was an exodus rather than an influx. Far from being spoiled or overrun, like so many picturesque sites, Gósol has seen its population dwindle from 745 in 1910 to a pitiful 198 in 1987. Many of the young generation have taken the new road and left for a softer, more lucrative life in Barcelona. Even smuggling is no longer an alternative or an adjunct to the rough and unrewarding job of animal husbandry just below the snow line. These days such visitors to Gósol as there are tend to be pilgrims following in the footsteps of Picasso. People also come to climb mountains, hunt game and, occasionally, look for fossils. According to local legend, Picasso became an enthusiastic fossil collector while at Gósol and left with two suitcases full of his finds. Fossil-collecting on that scale would have left him little time to paint. Rather than holding fossils, the suitcases surely contained bits of wood and stone for sculptures.

A mule journey in the Pyrenees, 1904. The subject is thought to be the architect Puig i Cadafalch on an expedition to remote Romanesque churches. Photo: Mas.

Picasso. *Panorama of Gósol.* Gósol, 1906. Gouache and black chalk on paper, 47.5×61.5cm. Musée Picasso, Paris.

Picasso. *Self-Portrait*. Gósol, 1906. Charcoal on paper. Private collection.

The only inn, Cal Tampanada, had two rooms to rent. Picasso and Fernande took one of them; it was on the first floor. Down below was the main room, where meals were served at a big table flanked by benches. The innkeeper was a crusty patriarch of over ninety, Josep Fontdevila, formerly a smuggler. 'A proud old man, extraordinarily beautiful in a strange wild way he still had all his hair and teeth, which were worn down, but still brilliantly white. Mean and cantankerous with everybody, he was never in a good humour except . . . with Picasso.'[20] Fontdevila consented to be his model, and in the course of successive sittings the two men developed a profound rapport.

At first Picasso did lifelike drawings of Fontdevila's well-honed, priestly head.[21] Then, as he assimilated the old man's image, he took ever greater liberties with appearances. Most of these drawings simplify and ennoble the features, but in a related watercolour the old man's pate sprouts some scruffy hair, and his cheekbone is extended into a protuberance that will reappear on one of the *Demoiselles*. Picasso also did some nude studies of him. Would Fontdevila have posed naked? Unlikely, but two of these drawings look as if they were done from life. Picasso probably removed Fontdevila's shirt so that he could restructure his collarbone. The clavicle becomes an embryonic plinth on which he balances the chin, doing away with the neck. This device recurs again and again in the 'Iberian' self-portraits and nudes of the following winter. Studies of Fontdevila's cranial structure also enabled Picasso to devise a new configuration for the heads he would do on his return to Paris.

The artist came more and more to identify with Fontdevila. It was not just that he shaved his head to be like the old man. The drawings he did of him look like self-portraits. Did Picasso wonder how he would appear when he was ninety? Certainly the hard Pyrenean head on top of the scrawny old body looks like the artist. And then in old age Picasso kept a reproduction of one of these portraits in his living room and drew on its skull-like image for his last ominously skull-like self-portraits.[22] Except for a few views of houses—one of them a fine rose-coloured view of the village—the artist adamantly disregarded the spectacular scenery. He agreed with Gertrude Stein, who used to say: 'I like a view but I like to sit with my back to it.' He focused instead on the well-weathered planes of the old smuggler's head. Fontdevila became a metaphor for this austere region, indeed for the whole austere country. Before he left Gósol, Picasso even carved the bowl of his meerschaum pipe into the likeness of this *genius loci*,[23] who would follow him back to Paris in spirit and gradually be absorbed into his imagery.

Picasso. *Josep Fontdevila Nude*. Gósol, 1906. Conté crayon on paper, 25.7×20 cm. Private collection.

The pages of one of Picasso's sketchbooks depict a grave-looking girl with a long face—possibly a granddaughter of Fontdevila, since she is seen serving a meal in the inn. She is the inspiration for numerous drawings of peasant girls in local costume with kerchiefs tied round their heads. Her features become less specific and more generalized and Picasso gradually turns her into an El Greco. The noble beauty with which he invests the girls of Gósol, has a faint, cat-like hint of Fernande, but then, the looks of the reigning mistress are always an ingredient in Picasso's physiognomical combinations. Another sketchbook includes drawings of peasant girls carrying various loads—water jars, faggots, loaves of bread —on their heads.[24] These culminate in one of the most memorable of

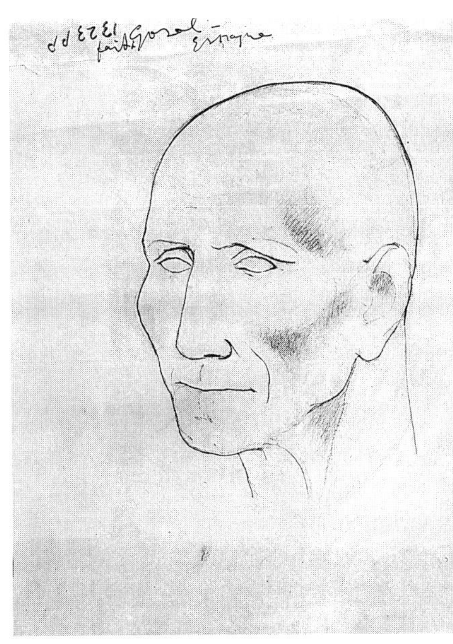

Far left: Picasso. *Head of Josep Fontdevila.* Gósol, 1906. Oil on canvas, 45.1×40.3cm. Private collection.

Left: Picasso. *Head of Josep Fontdevila.* Gósol, 1906. Pencil on paper, 43×32.5cm. Marina Picasso collection.

Below: Picasso. *Head of Josep Fontdevila.* Paris, 1907. Charcoal on paper, 63×48cm. The Menil Collection, Houston.

Below: Picasso. *Self-Portrait.* Mougins, July 1972. Pencil and white chalk on paper, 65.7×50.5cm. Private collection.

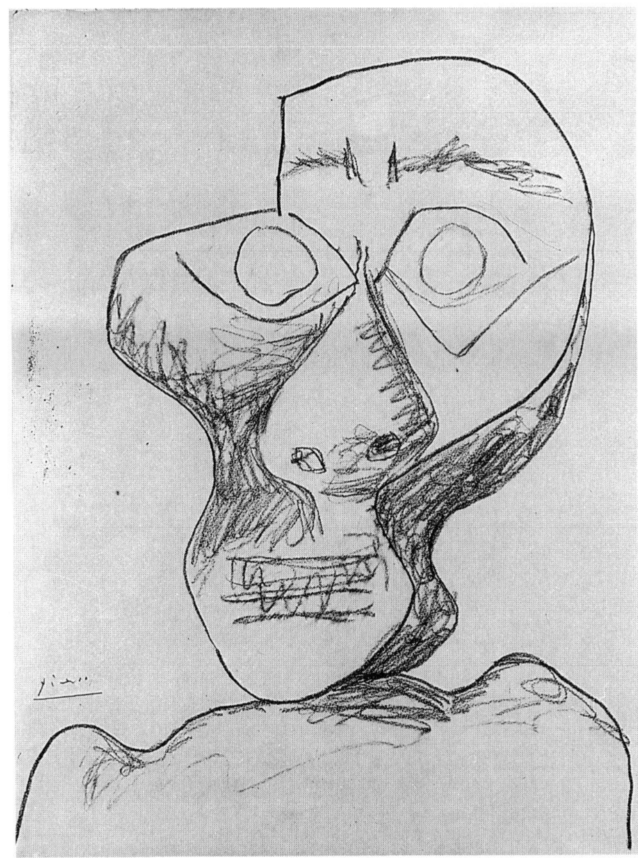

Above: Picasso. *Still Life*. Gósol, 1906. Oil on canvas, 38.5×56cm. State Hermitage Museum, Leningrad.

Above right: Gósol at the turn of the century: Cal Tampanada with villagers on the balcony.

Above: Picasso. *Houses in Gósol*. Gósol, 1906. Oil on canvas, 54×38.5cm. Statens Museum for Kunst, Copenhagen.

Right: Picasso. *Woman with Loaves*. Gósol, 1906. Oil on canvas, 100×69.8cm. Philadelphia Museum of Art, Given by Charles E. Ingersoll.

Picasso's Gósol images, the *Woman with Loaves.* Here we find the sense of sustenance and contentment that Picasso derived from renewed contact with his native soil. She is the antithesis of the street-wise gamines who stand for Montmartre, the antithesis of the images of urban want and misery that Spain formerly inspired.

The Gósol paintings confirm Picasso's joy at being back in Spain. He enjoyed speaking the Catalan he had learned eight summers before at Horta de Ebro. In the so-called *Carnet Catalan,*[25] the sketchbook that he carried with him, he noted down unfamiliar words in the local patois, also a poem in Catalan from a recently published book by Maragall. He took to using the Catalan form of his name, signing letters to Casanovas 'El Pau de Gósol'. The salubrious Pyrenees were more conducive to intense work than Paris. As well as finding ever simpler solutions to ever more complicated problems, Picasso was astoundingly prolific. During the ten weeks or so he spent in Gósol, he achieved as much as he had in the previous six months, if not more: at least seven large paintings (one of them 218.5×129.5cm), a dozen or so medium-size ones, plus countless drawings, watercolours, gouaches and carvings. He also filled two sketchbooks.[26]

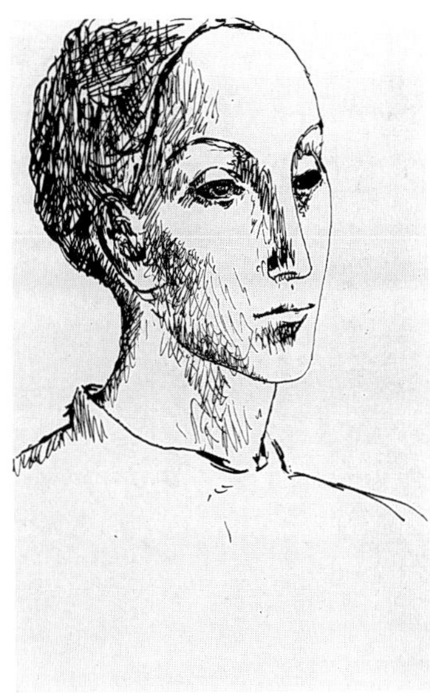

Picasso. *Head of a Woman.* Gósol, 1906. Pen on paper, 21×13.5cm. Marina Picasso collection.

Gósol prompted Picasso to branch out in new directions. Hitherto he had resorted to flower pieces only when he was desperate for money. He now addressed himself seriously to still life: a genre that he would eventually explore more exhaustively and develop more imaginatively than any other artist in history. These early efforts—clusters of opaque pots contrasted with translucent bottles, embellished with an occasional flower—are not as tentative as they seem. They look back at Redon in their pastel delicacy, ahead to Morandi in their seeming simplicity and innocence. Far from having the substance of Cézanne's coffeepots and ginger jars, Picasso's objects are insubstantial; but they are painted with a sensuousness and erotic symbolism that anticipates the sexuality of later still lifes. Everything is as terracotta or flesh-coloured as in a figure painting; and the ubiquitous *porrón* (the glass vessel from which Spaniards drink jets of wine) makes a phallic pun. The Hermitage still life, for instance, is divided into a male half (the two erect glass vessels on the left) and a female half (the two rounded pots on the right, one of which has a breast-like lid). By the same token, the erect vessels in another still life (in the Phillips Gallery, Washington, D.C.) point towards a framed print of a maja with a rose in her hair that is mysteriously inscribed *Las pregunta[s]* —'the questions'. These are the first glimmerings of Picasso's anthropomorphic concept of still life as a metaphor not just for sex but for all manner of conflicts and confrontations—a concept that will later help the artist to contrive a code that will divulge and at the same time conceal his secret desires.

Picasso. *Woman Carrying a Jar.* Gósol, 1906. Black crayon on paper, 24×19cm. The Baltimore Museum of Art, Cone Collection.

Even more impressive than the variety and quantity of work is the momentum that Picasso generated, the distance that he covered, during his nine or ten weeks at Gósol. We can follow his progress step by step. The first major paintings look back at Arcadian compositions like *The Watering Place* that he had been working on in Paris; but now that he was actually installed in mountainous, horse-breeding country, he came indoors and banishes horses from his work. Nevertheless, the focus is still on Hellenistic youth. There is an innocent zest to the naked boy who

Picasso. *Swineherd*. Gósol, 1906. Pen on paper, 17.5×11.4cm. Private collection.

gives a piggyback ride to an infant. The drum that the *saltimbanques* used to summon an audience now serves as a table, but it disappears from the second, larger (almost life-size) version, where the artist has, as it were, walked round the figure like a photographer and 'snapped' his subject from a different angle. The pose of the youth is reminiscent of the Hermes of Praxiteles (the one holding a child) at Olympia, but the subject surely derives from the mundane spectacle of a village boy charging around with another on his back.

After being raised above the youth's head one last time, the infant vanishes from the composition, but the upward gesture remains. This is a feature of a group of drawings of the prodigal son, dressed in rags and watching over a herd of swine with his crook beside him (as in Murillo's sketch in the Prado). Did Picasso identify with the prodigal son? More than once he had left his indulgent family and returned in a state of destitution. Typical of the artist to make light of the parable by having the swineherd insouciantly expose himself.[27] Other Gósol drawings reveal that Picasso envisaged a painting of this same youth set (like a Greco-Roman figure of a boy, hands above his head, that he knew from the Louvre)[28] in a niche. He ultimately opted for a large terracotta-coloured painting of the same boy in the same compact pose, but paired now, as in a frieze, with another figure seen from the back. A slight swelling of the belly, a loose tendril of hair and a vase on the head suggest that the newcomer is a girl. In an even larger painting Picasso finally took leave of male nudes. Standing on the right is a boy who is stolid and frontal as a kouros, a brother of the *Boy Leading a Horse*; seated on the left is a version of another famous classical model, the Spinario. The confrontation of these familiar prototypes is a bit pat, but the setting—local pottery (a Gósol emblem), whitewashed walls and a tiled floor—conjures up sunny Mediterranean rusticity. This redeems the composition from the plaster cast chill that is apt to afflict the work of the Ecole Romane.

Though thinly and sketchily executed, these paintings hover on the brink of sculpture. Picasso was evidently tempted to think, if not actually work, in three dimensions, like his friends Manolo and Casanovas, who had been urging him in this direction. No facilities for modelling or sculpting existed at Gósol, so Picasso opted for wood-carving—something that he had never tried. Once again Gauguin plays a part in Picasso's inspiration. *Noa Noa* describes how Gauguin and a young Tahitian went on an expedition to the mountains in search of rosewood—traditionally used for carvings of idols. It is one of the most haunting passages in the book: the innocent young savage (the androgyne again) and the old European cynic padding naked through the stillness of the jungle on their sacred quest. When they finally arrive at the rosewood grove, they chop down a tree, which gives off the rose-like scent that is called *noa noa*. As he hacks away ecstatically, Gauguin rids himself of *'mon vieux stock de civilisé'* and becomes a new man, a 'Maori'. Each time he takes his chisel to this piece of wood, he feels '*une douce quiétude . . . une victoire . . . un rajeunissement*', just as Picasso did at Gósol.

Picasso. *Youth in an Archway*. Gósol, 1906. Charcoal on paper, 59.5×42cm. The Metropolitan Museum of Art, New York, Bequest of Scofield Thayer, 1984.

Unlike Gauguin, Picasso did not have any chisels. He appealed to Casanovas, who still planned to join him, for help (June 27):

> . . . I continue working and this week they brought me a piece of wood and I'll begin something. Tell me a few days before you come so that I can

Above: Picasso. *Two Brothers.* Gósol, 1906. Gouache on cardboard, 80×59cm. Musée Picasso, Paris.

Below: Picasso. *Two Brothers.* Gósol, 1906. Oil on canvas, 142×97cm. Kunstmuseum, Basel.

Above right: Picasso. *Two Youths.* Paris, 1906. Oil on canvas, 157×117cm. Collection Walter–Guillaume, Musée de l'Orangerie, Paris.

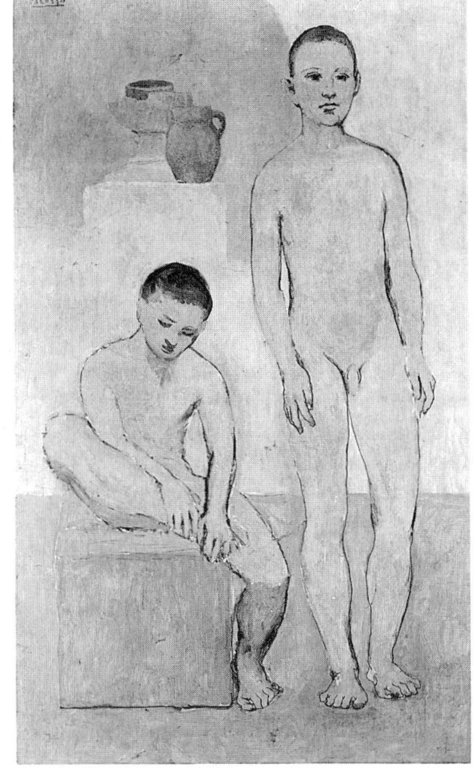

Right: Picasso. *Two Youths.* Gósol, 1906. Oil on canvas, 151.5×93.7cm. National Gallery of Art, Washington, D.C., Chester Dale Collection.

> answer you, because I may want you to bring some *eynas* [*sic*; *eines* are chisels] to work the wood. So don't forget to tell me, because it would be a nuisance to have to ask somebody else to do it and they would never arrive here or they would get lost, which is worse. So don't forget this. Manolo wrote me recently sending me many good wishes to you. . . . *Adeu* and a big hug from *Teu amic*, Pau.

Since Casanovas never got to Gósol, Picasso wrote yet again in July. Supplies were running out:

> I want you to buy or send me by mail a roll of twenty sheets of *papier Ingres* and as quickly as you can because I have finished the small stock of paper I bought in Barcelona. . . . This you can send by mail inside a cardboard tube (they sell them ready-made). And forgive me for burdening you, but you are the only one I trust for these things and I will recompense you. Tell me if you want me to send you the *cuartos* [cash] or . . . give it to you when you come. Tell me frankly. . . . Could you send me in the same package two or three small *eines* to work in wood?

Picasso. *Bois de Gósol*. Gósol, 1906. Carved boxwood, ht: 77 cm. Musée Picasso, Paris.

Whether the *eines* arrived we do not know. The three sculptures surviving from Gósol are rudimentary figures of Fernande that have been whittled with a knife—probably the famous knife from Horta that Picasso kept to his dying day—rather than professional tools. The most important is the so-called *bois de Gósol*[29] mentioned in the letters to Casanovas: a gnarled length of boxwood, manifestly anthropomorphic in form, which required very little carving to transform its protuberances into shoulders, buttocks and breasts. This carving, which has traces of polychrome and some undecipherable writing on it, was the model for a number of drawings in which Picasso visualizes Fernande's body in terms of the ship's-figurehead stiffness of the wood. A heavily annotated watercolour of Fernande with buttocks and breasts thrust out as in the *bois* reveals that Picasso contemplated doing a painting after it.[30] As usual when Picasso goes in for elaborate annotations, nothing came of this project. The *bois de Gósol* would also be the prototype for the series of sixteen carvings—skinny, elongated nudes—that Picasso did at Boisgeloup in 1930. Once again he would exploit the knots and bosses in bits of wood he picked up in the course of his walks in the park of the château.

* * *

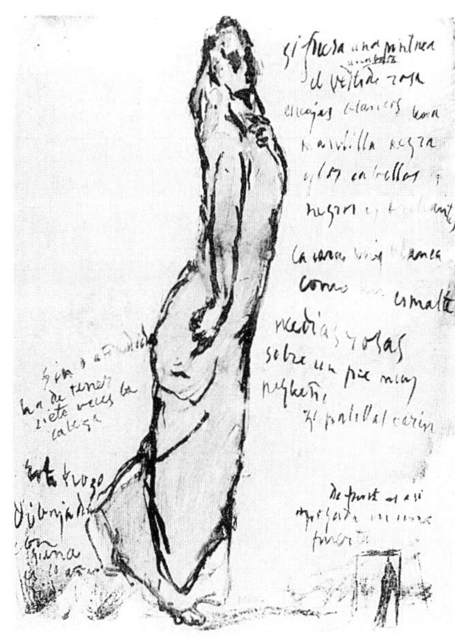

Picasso. Study after the *Bois de Gósol*, with colour notes. Gósol, 1906. Gouache on paper, 48×36 cm. Heirs of the artist.

Fernande's easygoing nature stood her in good stead at Gósol. Life cannot have been easy. Cal Tampanada was very primitive, although, unlike most of the houses in the village, it had an oven. Fernande did not mind the austerity; she did not miss the Parisian cafés and shops and friends. There was only one drawback: 'When Pablo was working I could only make myself understood in sign language.'[31] And she ran out of perfume soon after arriving; she wrote to Casanovas to ask for a bottle of *essence de Chypre*: 'a French brand if possible either Pinaud or Delettez . . . If you can't get either of these, get a good Spanish brand. Sorry to be such a bore. Would you also get two dozen postcards and the same number of 10 centime stamps.'[32] Fernande could not resist telling her friends what rapture life was, 'up there in air of incredible purity, above the clouds, surrounded by people who were amiable, hospitable and without guile . . . we found out what happiness could be like. . . . No cloud shed discord on Picasso and me, because, having no cause for jealousy, all his worries had disappeared.'[33] Never again would the two of them be as happy as they were in this Garden of Eden. For the first time a feeling of exultation irradiates Picasso's work, in particular the portraits of Fernande that celebrate her beauty, serenity and sensuality.

Fernande had lived with Picasso for almost a year and had known him for twice that long, but it is only at Gósol that her presence really makes itself felt in his work. Away from the pressures and distractions of Montmartre, not to speak of the eternal money problems, the artist recaptured his innocence and divine energy. And, as he did with one mistress after another, he fantasized that he was God creating a new Eve. Portraits of Fernande done over the next few months give off an incandescent glow. The earliest (which may have been done before leaving Paris) is the most literal. Fernande's beautiful features and crown of bouffant hair are built up out of delicate touches of pink, terracotta and vermilion. Most of the canvas has been left bare in a way that suggests a drawing by Ingres. Succeeding likenesses all stem from this feline, almond-eyed image.[34] Little by little they take on a Gauguin-esque air of mystery and gravity—a persona that Picasso evoked by showing Fernande pictorially what he wanted her to become. (This persona would survive only so long as he was around to nurture it.) Most Gauguin-esque of all is the imposing woodcut of her. Picasso hacked away at a plank to produce a rough-and-ready print as primitive and expressive as anything in *Noa Noa*. The coquettish Parisienne in her *belle époque* hat and veil who caused such a sensation in Barcelona has been stripped of her fashionable trappings. Picasso has devised a paradoxical image that is of its time yet timeless, primitive yet classical, Spanish yet French, utterly original for all its derivations. So long as they remained in Gósol, Picasso continued to see Fernande in this radiant light. Back in Paris he would be less ennobling.

Picasso. *Portrait of Fernande*. Paris or Gósol, 1906. Oil on canvas, 100×81 cm. Private collection.

The new Fernande image takes over from the classical youths. Naked girls replace naked boys. The Pygmalion-like artist has breathed life into his formerly sculptural figures. The most beautiful of the Gósol nudes is an almost life-size Fernande (bought by the Steins), for which there are many drawings. Her hands are modestly clasped in front of her. Like most of the other Gósol figures, her pale terracotta-coloured body melts into a haze of pinkish-golden light. Fernande also appears—this time fully clothed—in that mysterious painting known as *La Toilette*, where she proffers a mirror to a naked girl. Like the boys in the preceding compositions, she has her arms above her head—in her case to arrange her hair. The mirror is an appropriate emblem for Fernande: she was forever primping, hence the recurrent coiffures in the work of the next six months. The mirror also serves as a pretext for the juxtaposition of two standing women—a compositional problem for which the artist would always be finding new solutions. And it enables Picasso to play games with a mistress's identity. In *La Toilette* and numerous related studies, both figures depict Fernande. Except that her hair is anomalously black and glossy, the figure on the right looks much as she does in photographs of the period, wearing a simple 'artistic' dress wound round with a sash such as Spanish men—Picasso, for one—often wore, but not Spanish women. The nude figure on the left has Fernande's auburn hair but a very different, far less voluptuous body: this alter ego is tall, lithe and long-legged

Picasso. *Head of Fernande*. Gósol, 1906. Woodcut, 55.7×38.5 cm. Musée Picasso, Paris.

Picasso. *La Toilette.* Gósol, 1906. Oil on canvas, 151×99cm. Albright-Knox Art Gallery, Buffalo. Fellows for Life Fund.

Picasso. *Woman with Boy and Goat.* Gósol, 1906. Oil on canvas, 146×114cm. Barnes Foundation, Merion Station, Pa.

Picasso. *Standing Nude* (Fernande). Gósol, 1906. Oil on canvas, 153×94cm. Collection William S. Paley, New York.

Picasso. *The Harem.* Gósol, 1906. Oil on canvas, 154.3×109.5cm. The Cleveland Museum of Art, Bequest of Leonard C. Hanna, Jr.

Gauguin. *Bathers*. 1902. Oil on canvas, 92×73cm. Private collection.

—everything that Fernande was not. Picasso implies that his brush can enhance her beauty, just as his love can enhance her life. *La Toilette* pays tribute to the metamorphic power of art and love. Since the clothed figure is unquestionably Fernande, it is impossible to accept Schapiro's theory that she is 'beauty's servant: the painter himself'.[35] If the painter manifests himself in this work, it is off-stage. A related drawing portrays a Peeping Tom, not unlike Picasso, peering over a screen at the girl peering at herself. The angle of the mirror suggests that the girl is catching the Peeping Tom's reflection as well as her own.

In another large vertical canvas Picasso omits the dressed Fernande and places the naked girl doing her hair at the centre of the composition. On her left a putto holds a small pot on his large head; on her right a frisky white goat looks up at her.[36] Except that the positions of the child and the goat have been reversed, the composition has been taken directly from a late Gauguin *Bathers*. This girl, thinner and more elongated each time she manifests herself, has been likened to the second-century terracotta figures of flying hermaphrodites in the Louvre.[37] Their long muscular limbs, breasts and vestigial members might well have caught Picasso's eye. She is said to derive from the girl with arms above her head on the extreme left of Matisse's *Le Bonheur de Vivre*.[38] It is possible, but Picasso would hardly have wanted to be caught quoting from Matisse at this time. Surely both artists drew on Ingres: *La Source*, the dancer in the background of *Le Bain Turc*, as well as the little *Venus Anadyomene*, one of whose attendants holds a mirror up to her as she adjusts her hair.

Although Picasso's visual recall was prodigious, he probably had reproductions of Ingres in his baggage. His next set piece is a recapitulation of *Le Bain Turc*. He exploits his parodic gifts to poke fun at Ingres while also honouring him. *The Harem* is the first realization of Picasso's attempts to bring off a large-scale (154.3×109.5cm) classical figure composition. It is unresolved, but delightfully fresh and radiant—suffused with sensuous coral light and innocent eroticism. It follows the general lines of the Ingres, in that the houris (reduced from a score or more to a mere four) have been herded into the corner of a large chamber. The houris are all Fernande lookalikes: as identical in build, cipher-like prettiness and coiffure as Ingres's odalisques. But compared with Ingres's fleshy beauties Picasso's girls seem insubstantial—in danger of dissolving into the space around them. The only figure of any real substance is the naked man lounging in the right foreground—an adaptation of a similarly placed girl in *Le Bain Turc*, who is in turn an adaptation of the Vatican Ariadne. This massive muscle-builder has been variously identified as sultan and eunuch, Picasso and Apollinaire. But the substitution of a voluptuous man for a voluptuous woman in the foreground of *The Harem* is surely a pictorial pun at Ingres's expense. Nor is it the only pun in this painting. The picnic with its suggestive *porrón* and sausage and loaves is another irreverent dig.

Ingres. *Venus Anadyomene*. *c*.1858. Oil on paper, 31.5×20cm. Musée du Louvre, Paris.

A further manifestation of this blend of poetic fantasy, adolescent punning and up-to-date realism is the large gouache of two girls and a boy in an interior, *Three Nudes*. Notations reveal that Picasso meant to work this up into a large classical composition with a contemporary twist. He describes the room in some detail: 'painted pink with white curtains, and one of those worn straw-seated sofas and a purple marble fireplace with glasses and a little mirror on it.' Since Picasso shows us yet another male figure with his hand suggestively clutching a *porrón*, this time between his legs; and since he notes that the girls might 'perhaps wear gauze dresses' and should be smoking cigarettes, this is presumably a whorehouse—the first intimation of the *Demoiselles* that is likewise set in a brothel. The act of conceiving and blocking in *The Harem* brought the exploitation of Ingres to a temporary halt. It was time to return once again to the sacrosanct El Greco.

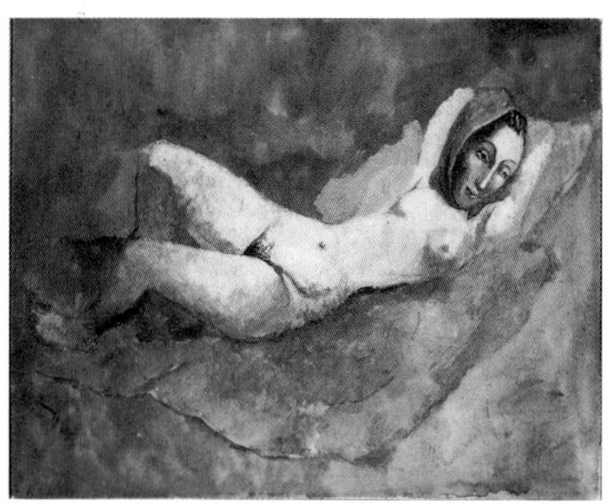

Picasso. *Reclining Nude* (Fernande). Gósol, 1906. Gouache on paper, 47.3×61.3cm. The Cleveland Museum of Art, Gift of Mr and Mrs Michael Straight.

At Gósol Picasso paid little heed to Utrillo's El Greco booklet until he had had his fill of Ingres's houris. At first he tried to reconcile the irreconcilable: to compose a hybrid out of an Ingres odalisque (the 'Ariadne' figure from *Le Bain Turc*, whose sex had been changed in *The Harem*) and the head of Fernande, as El Greco might have conceived her. The synthesis does not quite work; and Ingres fades into the background. At the same time, El Greco emerges from the Spanish shadows to tempt Picasso back to mannerist attenuations and the security of tightly knit compositions. And so the Gósol visit, which had started under Ingres's auspices, ends under El Greco's. Before leaving the mountains Picasso embarked on a major homage to El Greco. This over-life-size scene depicts a team of oxen, a blind flower seller and a seeing-eye girl. There would not have been a flower seller at Gósol; there were, however, many oxherds; and when they brought the cattle down from the mountains, they would garland the horns with flowers.[39] This composition derives from a watercolour sketch of a boy with two oxen that was probably done from life. A further source of inspiration was El Greco's St Joseph and the Christ Child being showered with flowers from heaven, which Picasso had already paraphrased in his sentimental *Mistletoe Seller* of 1902. This time the celestial bouquet fills the upper part of the painting, as if to sanctify the blind flower seller.

The Blind Flower Seller was Picasso's most experimental work to date. It gave him enormous trouble, not so much because it was conceived in Spain and repainted in France (a sketch indicates that Picasso had the idea of Gallicizing this Pyrenean scene by including the Eiffel Tower in the background), but because he had set himself an insuperable problem. He wanted to arrive at a synthesis that would embrace El Greco's mannerism, Blue period compassion, Rose period charm and what looks like Nabi decorativeness (although Picasso always claimed to loathe the Nabis, Bonnard especially). He also wanted this synthesis to involve a new form of spatial notation that would defy Renaissance perspective. *The Blind Flower Seller* is a magnificent failure. Despite their vast scale, the figures are flimsy; and the bizarre attenuations—for instance, the dwindling extremities (especially apparent in the preparatory sketches) —are not altogether successful. However, *The Blind Flower Seller* is important for what Picasso learned from it. He finally manages to make the subject of a painting project rather than recede, as traditional perspective ordained. The artist also tries out another device that looks ahead to early cubism. He uses El Greco's over-all pattern of rhythmic faceting to articulate the picture surface and give everything cohesion.

* * *

Picasso. *Three Nudes,* with inscriptions. Gósol, 1906. Gouache on paper, 61.5×47. Private collection.

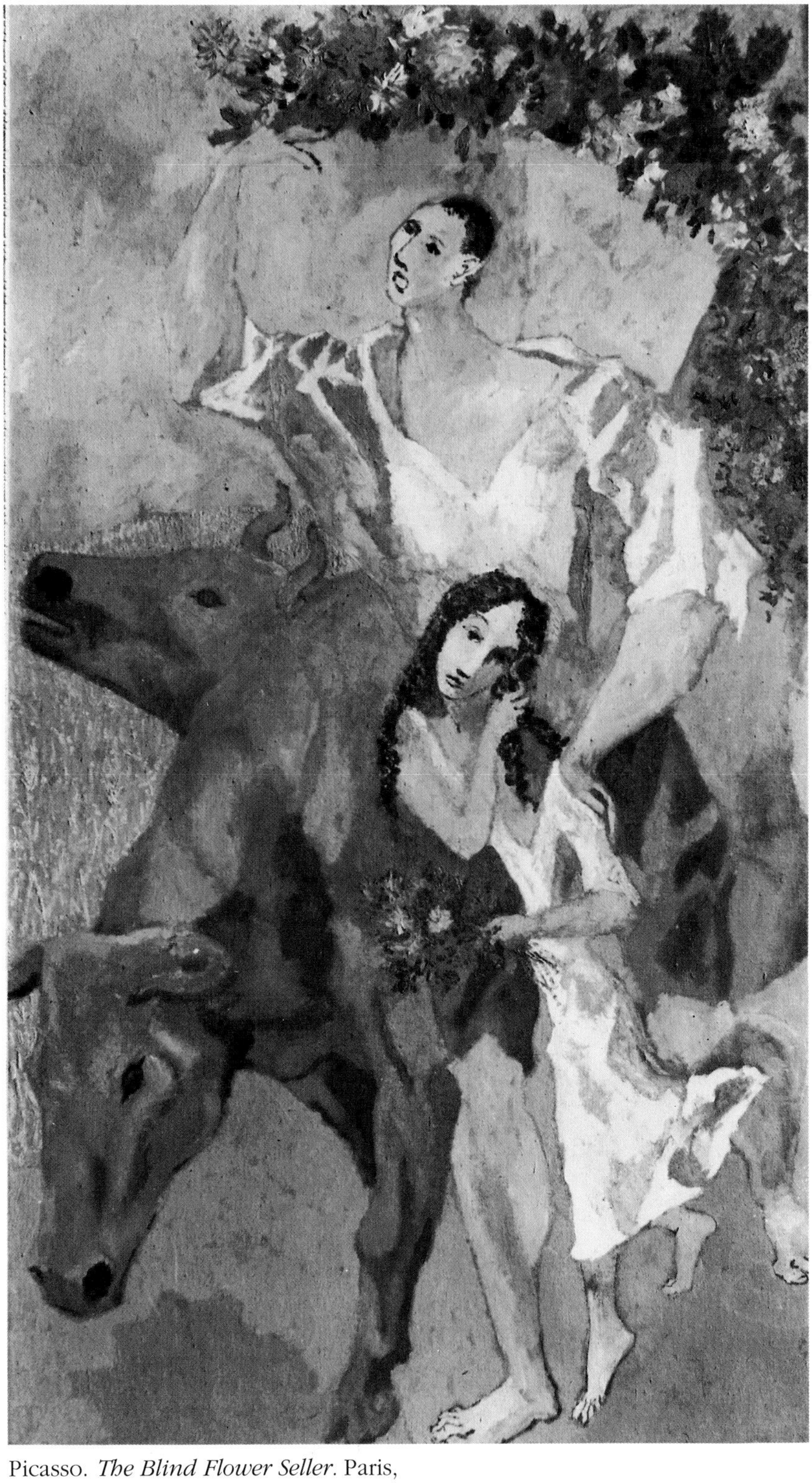

Picasso. *The Blind Flower Seller*. Paris, 1906. Oil on canvas, 218.5×129.5cm. Barnes Foundation, Merion Station, Pa.

Above: Dancing in the Square at Gósol for the Festa Major. *c.*1909.

Left: Picasso. *Dancing Couples.* Gósol, 1906. Pen on page of the *Carnet Catalan,* 7.5×12cm. Private collection.

For all its hard, scenic beauty, Gósol attracted no other visitors, no artists or poets from Barcelona (not even any of Jacint Reventós's convalescents), except for the pianist Carles Vidiella, who was renowned for lugging a piano up on muleback for his summer holiday. Picasso and Fernande presumably met this eccentric old musician. Otherwise they saw only the Fontdevila family and villagers, like the friendly farrier whose smithy was across from the inn. Given the miraculous effect on Picasso's well-being, the absence of an entourage must be counted a blessing. For all that his imagery owed a great deal to his poet friends, Picasso's phenomenal success in the solitude of Gósol confirms that he did even better without so much literary stimulus. In the clear air of the sierra the artist had become possessed of a beatific confidence and enlightenment worthy of his hermit uncle. 'A tenor who reaches a note higher than any in the score'[40] is how he describes himself in one of his Gósol sketchbooks. So elated was he, so prone to artistic visions and revelations, that he barely had time to finish wrestling with one angel before another materialized.

'The locals were enchanted by us,' Fernande writes; 'they sought out our company, brought us partridges and thrushes to vary our diet of *cocido* [bean-and-sausage stew]; and they made us play the peculiar games of the region.'[41] Picasso, who boasted of being a good shot, would also go shooting in the mountains, which abounded in deer and chamois. These expeditions were the more intriguing for being a cover for smuggling—a major local industry. Smuggling is the activity Picasso remembered most vividly about Gósol. The risk, excitement and profit; the way it pitted noble outlaws like his friend the innkeeper against the inimical forces of law and order: all this made the smuggler someone with whom he could identify—a fellow outlaw.[42]

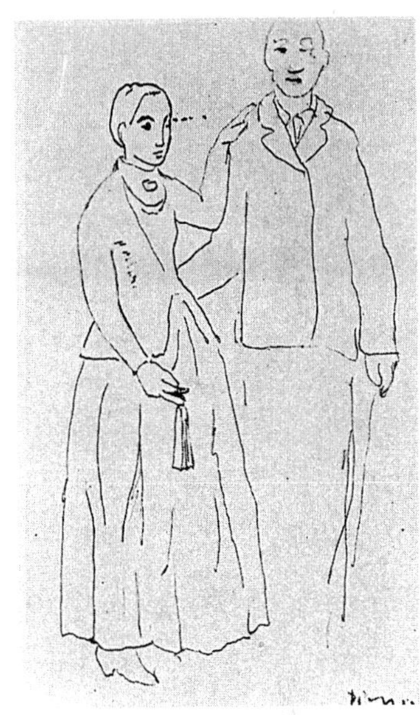

Picasso. *Gósol Couple*. Gósol, 1906. Pen on paper, 21×12.8cm. Private collection.

Religious festivals were the form of entertainment that Gósol provided. Fernande says 'there were one or two a week.'[43] In fact there were two principal ones a year, and they both took place during Picasso's visit. On St John's Eve (Midsummer's Day) villagers went up into the mountains to keep the shepherds company; they built fires and roasted goats, which they brought down to eat in the village. Next day was the Bal de la Llet (a kind of fertility ceremony that also took place at the beginning of the year); villagers (only the men) danced round a bucket of milk, and the lucky ones got their feet wet. A few weeks later, on July 20, was the feast of Santa Margarida, the patron saint of the village, after whom many of the girls were named. A mass in Gósol's handsome Romanesque church was followed by a procession, then dancing in the village square. Picasso drew the dancers and also made a rough sketch and took notes for a composition based on this fiesta. But it was another year before these ideas were transformed into a harvesting scene that is unaccountably Fauve in treatment.

According to Picasso, the primitivism in his work up to and including *Les Demoiselles d'Avignon* stemmed exclusively from Iberian sculpture,[44] and so the eventful year between spring 1906 and spring 1907 has come to be regarded as the 'Iberian period'. This is a simplification—a misleading one in that it leaves out of account the impact of Catalan sculpture. A major revelation of Gósol was the remarkable twelfth-century Madonna and Child (the Santa Maria del Castell de Gósol) that has now been

The Gósol Madonna. Twelfth century. Polychrome wood, ht: 77 cm. Museu d'Art de Catalunya, Barcelona.

removed to the Museum of Catalan Art in Barcelona. This left more of a mark on Picasso's work than is generally allowed. Friends like Rusiñol, Vidal Ventosa and others of the Guayaba group had kept Picasso informed of their efforts to rescue and record these endangered treasures. But he had not derived much inspiration from them until he found himself in Gósol, with only one work of art to hand: this Madonna. Its hieratic stylizations—the Madonna's wide-open, staring eyes and eyebrows emphatically drawn in as if by a cosmetician—will be a feature of his work for the next six months. After his return from Gósol Picasso continued to borrow from Romanesque as well as Iberian sculpture, but the influence of the former is sometimes mistaken for the latter.[45]

Picasso and Fernande had originally planned to stay at Gósol until September, when they would presumably have returned to Paris as they came, via Barcelona. But around August 12 their Pyrenean idyll was cut dramatically short; typhoid fever broke out under their very roof. The victim was Fontdevila's granddaughter, a child of ten who figures in the *Carnet Catalan*. The only available medicine was a potion made of tobacco leaves macerated in vinegar; the only doctor was hours away by mule. Picasso panicked; they must leave as soon as possible. As Fernande points out, he had a nervous terror of contagious disease.[46] Had not diphtheria killed his sister and scarlet fever nearly carried him off nine years earlier in Madrid? Someone as fearful of death as Picasso would have regarded this minor outbreak as a major menace. Worse, his flight could not be as precipitate as he would have liked. At the best of times, Gósol was far from easy to leave; this was the worst of times. The crisis had occurred just before the Festa Major (the annual festival held on August 15), when everyone in the village had a role to play. Transport might have been easier to organize if there had not been so many large canvases to be rolled for travelling. On August 13 (the letter merely says, 'Today is Monday') Picasso wrote (in Catalan) to Casanovas, telling him to forget about the various errands for Fernande

> because within a few days we are going to Paris by Puigcerdà and will take the train to Aix [*sic*, Ax] and from there to Toulouse. I never received the paper and I think it must have been lost. When you write you can tell me what I owe you and I'll send it. . . . I'll write you from Paris and would appreciate it if you wouldn't tell anyone that I'm returning there. . . . Hugs from your friend Pau.

Why the secrecy? Probably a question of *bella figura*. After his triumphant return to Barcelona in June, Picasso would hardly have wanted to reappear in frantic flight from a single case of fever. Besides, he always resented having to come up with explanations. Rather than face his solicitous family and inquisitive friends, he decided to return directly to France. This meant taking a far more circuitous route—northward over the Pyrenees—than the way he had come. Picasso jotted down the itinerary on the flyleaf of the *Carnet Catalan*: Gósol to Bellver on muleback; Bellver to Puigcerdà by coach; Puigcerdà to Ax again by coach; Ax to Paris by train.[47] Fernande describes an unexpected problem with Fontdevila: he could not bear to be separated from Picasso. The family had to fight tooth and nail to keep him in Gósol. Picasso and Fernande left at five in the morning and did not reach Bellver until five in the evening—

an hour or two late, because she drank too much white wine at lunch and had to take a nap.[48] There was also a near disaster when their mule train encountered a herd of wild mares. Some of the mules bolted, and their loads tumbled to the ground, leaving a trail of suitcases, sculpture, rolls of canvas and drawings. Miraculously nothing was lost or damaged. In no time everything was made secure, and they finished their journey safely. By the time they reached Puigcerdà, Picasso felt ill and exhausted, so they stayed there overnight. The next day he was well enough to go on to Paris.

When they reached the Bateau Lavoir their spirits sank. In the summer the studio was always an oven, but this August the heat was unbearable. Worse, hordes of mice had eaten everything in sight, including the banana-coloured taffeta cover of Fernande's favourite parasol. When Picasso and Fernande got into bed, they were attacked by bedbugs. These had even infested the divan in the studio. They had to scatter the place with saucers full of burning sulphur. Although Fontdevila had stayed behind, his spirit kept Picasso company, as a household god, a touchstone. Picasso continued to draw him as if he were still around. Indeed, he is second only to Fernande and the artist himself as a recognizable subject in the work of the next six months. If there are no drawings for the repainting of Gertrude Stein's portrait, it is because they are all of Fontdevila. The old smuggler lives on in her guise.

Picasso. *Woman with Mirror and a Peeping Tom*. Paris, 1905. Pen on paper, 25×17 cm. Heirs of the artist.

Il me semble douteux que vous puissiez parvenir à comprendre la lettre de Pablo mais je pense qu'il est préférable de laisser l'original tel qu'il est, dans ce français plus ou moins fantaisiste. Je suis vraiment désolée, miss Gertrude, de n'avoir point reçu, à Gosol, Little Jimmy mais il vous faut savoir qu'en Espagne on ne reçoit jamais de ce qui semble être utile ou pouvoir amuser les autorités postales car dans ce cas ils confisquent tout à leur profit. Quant à mon anglais!!! inutile de vous en parler.

meilleures amitiés Fernande

17 Aut 06

Mon cher ami
Stein

Je ai reçu votre letre et l'argent merci.

J'ai travaillé à Gosol et je travail ici – je vous montrerai et vous causerais de tout ça quand je

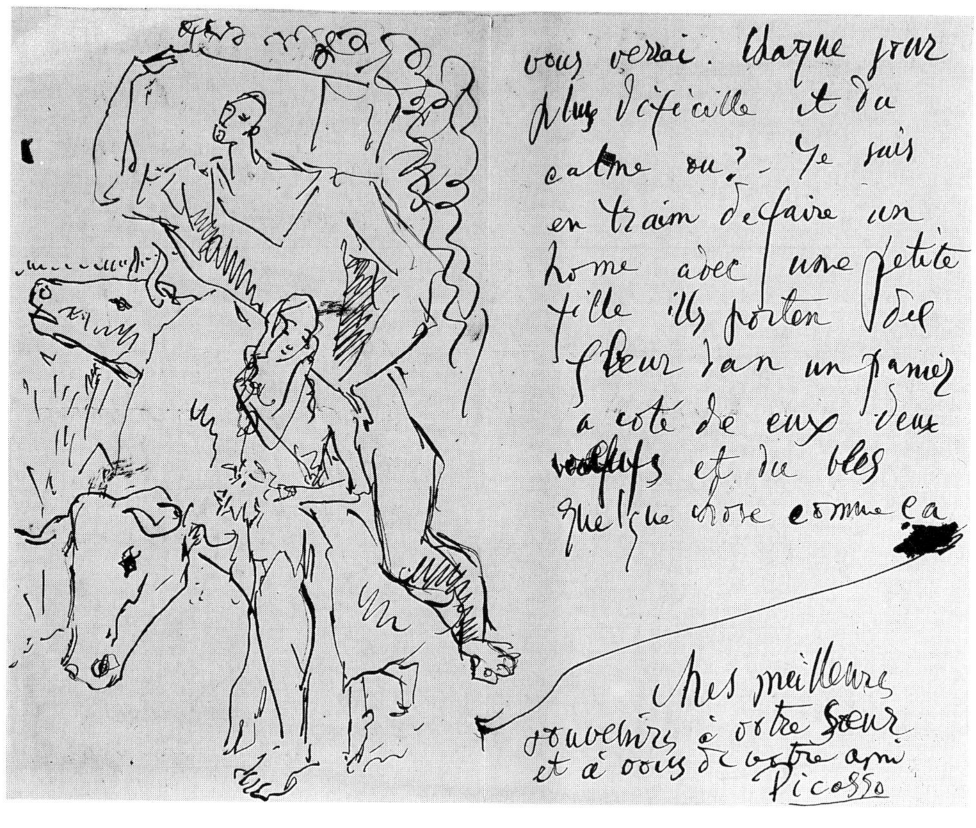

vous verrai. Chaque jour plus dificille et du calme ou? Je suis en train de faire un home avec une petite fille ills porten des fleur dan un panier a coté de eux deux voeufs et du bles quelque chose comme ça

Mes meilleurs souvenirs à votre soeur et à vous de votre ami
Picasso

29

The Mantle of Gauguin

Gauguin with his palette, *c*.1894.

'THE DAY [PICASSO] RETURNED FROM Spain,' Gertrude Stein would have us believe, 'he sat down and out of his head painted the head in without having seen Gertrude Stein again.'[1] One hesitates to contradict her, but the resolution of this masterpiece—the cornerstone of the period—cannot possibly have come about so quickly or casually. Late August or early September is a more probable date for this little area of repaint that won Gertrude recognition as one of the most familiar twentieth-century icons. '"Everybody thinks she is not at all like her portrait," Picasso said, "but never mind, in the end she will manage to look just like it." And she did.'[2] 'For me, it is I,' Gertrude asserted, 'and it is the only reproduction of me, which is always I.'[3] Picasso never corroborated Gertrude's story about the completion of the painting. On the contrary, the letter that he and Fernande wrote on August 17 to the two Steins, who were still in Fiesole, fails to mention the portrait; the artist limits his comments to *The Blind Flower Seller*, of which he includes a very rough drawing. Picasso addresses his part of the letter to Leo:

> I have received your letter and the money. Thanks.
> I worked at Gósol and am working here. I will show you and talk to you about all that when I see you. Each day is more difficult . . . I am in the course of doing a man with a little girl. They are carrying some flowers in a basket. Beside them are two oxen and some wheat . . .

Fernande addresses her part of the letter to 'Miss Gertrude'; she apologizes for Picasso's 'more or less fanciful French' and goes on to say that she never received any of the 'Little Jimmy' comics that had been mailed to Gósol.[4] 'Anything that might be useful or amusing to the postal authorities,' Fernande says, gets purloined. This, it is clear, is their first letter to the Steins since returning from Gósol. Had Picasso begun, let alone finished, repainting the Stein portrait, he would surely have informed the sitter instead of carrying on about *The Blind Flower Seller*. A stylistic comparison of the two paintings leaves one in no doubt as to which was completed first: the Gósol canvas.

In fairness to Gertrude, one should add that the legend about the artist returning from Spain and finishing her portrait in a flash of inspiration might well have originated with Picasso. This legend (insofar as it involved speed) would have catered to his view of himself as supremely quick off the mark; it would have flattered the vanity of his patron and

Opposite: Letter to Gertrude and Leo Stein from Fernande and Picasso, August 17, 1906. Beinecke Rare Book and Manuscript Library, Yale University.

helped cover up something that the sitter must never be allowed to suspect: the fact that Picasso had resolved her portrait *in absentia* by visualizing her in the guise of a ninety-year-old Spanish peasant. As a close study of the repainted area reveals, Picasso's Frankensteinian grafting of the two physiognomies cannot have come about in the casual 'Eureka' manner described by Gertrude. The reconstituted face bears witness to the most painstaking concentration. For all its apparent simplicity, the synthesis that Picasso has achieved in this portrait is very complex. It has the sheen of Ingres, the heft of Cézanne, the sharp focus of a photograph (or, given the *camaïeu* tonality, a daguerrotype) and, not least, the imperiousness of Stein. Yet its fierce intensity and uncompromising modernity are Picasso's and Picasso's alone. Gertrude's belief that all this came about in the twinkling of an eye fits in with her lazy view of genius. But then, for Gertrude that is what this painting was about: genius—her genius. It was an advertisement for herself. That is what counted; how it stood in relationship to the artist and his early development was beside the point.

Picasso. *Portrait of Gertrude Stein* (detail). 1906.

The sculptural look of the Stein portrait is usually attributed to Picasso's fascination with Iberian reliefs. I disagree. These recently discovered, recently exhibited antiquities had yet to make their full impact. The stony set of Stein's features and the emphatic hardness of her hair owe far more to the Flavian bust that Ingres devised for his Empress Livia than to the Iberian bas-relief from Osuna of a man attacked by a lion.[5] But it is above all his studies of Fontdevila that enabled Picasso to contrive the right mask for Gertrude—a mask that he would later adapt to his own head. A drawing of the old smuggler done shortly after the return to Paris reveals the artist in the throes of reconciling the two faces; and a bust executed around this time in Durrio's studio shows Picasso trying out the same trick in three dimensions. Gertrude was too vain to spot its relevance to herself.

Ingres. *Tu Marcellus Eris* (detail). 1819.

Soon after his return from Spain, Picasso had gone to see Paco Durrio. Durrio was always pressing him to try his hand at ceramic sculpture: stoneware, which permitted colour to play an organic role, as Gauguin had triumphantly demonstrated. The two of them had discussed working together earlier in the year. There might even have been some trial pieces; if so, they have disappeared. At least Picasso had been interested enough to sketch out various projects: for instance, a vase decorated with a frieze of linked nudes. In similar vein there is a drawing of three Graces on a plinth that must have been conceived as stoneware.[6] So far as we know, none of these projects materialized. Picasso's first recorded ceramic is the small bust of Fontdevila (later cast in bronze) that derives from the Gósol drawings.

Although virtually none of them can be traced,[7] Picasso's early ceramics are important in providing a direct link with Gauguin—a link forged by Paco Durrio, the previous tenant of Picasso's Bateau Lavoir studio. Even before Gauguin's death, in 1903, this beguiling little man had seen Picasso as the only artist capable of taking his hero's place. After Gauguin's death this reincarnation became a fixation. He put himself and his colossal kiln at Picasso's disposal, so that this bond could be embodied in stoneware. Gauguin had seen that stoneware could endow an artist with quasi-divine powers. What couldn't he do 'with a little clay and a little genius'?[8] If

Picasso. *Bust of Josep Fontdevila*. Paris, 1906. Bronze, ht: 17 cm. Private collection.

'God made man with a bit of clay', why couldn't an artist?[8] Gauguin, who was versed in mysticism, saw himself personifying the ancient cabalistic belief that if certain secret rituals were correctly observed, a lump of clay could be transformed into a golem. Picasso, who had learned much about such things from Jacob and Apollinaire, would adopt the same God-like approach to sculpture.

The Gauguin–Durrio connection went back to 1893, when Durrio—a Basque of French extraction, then twenty-five years old—had arrived in Paris from his native Bilbao. This exotic, dwarfish sculptor had been taken up by Gauguin, newly returned from his first trip to Tahiti. Durrio was overwhelmed by Gauguin, not least by the ceramics he was doing with Ernest Chaplet. Chaplet had broken away from the hidebound Sèvres establishment to revive the technique of stoneware.[9] And it was he who revealed to Gauguin, who revealed to Durrio, who revealed to Picasso how clay that was glazed and fired enabled an artist to be more expressive and experimental than clay that ended up cast in bronze. Knowing nothing of the large birds and beasts that the king of Saxony's master craftsman, Kändler, had sculpted at Meissen, Gauguin felt free to boast to Vollard in 1902, that he 'was the first to attempt ceramic sculpture and I believe that, although this is forgotten now, one day the world will be grateful to me. At all events I proudly maintain that nobody has ever done this before.'[10] Then, as now, Gauguin's ceramics were underrated; Durrio was virtually alone in recognizing their importance and exploring similar techniques. Given the virtuosity of his huge stoneware pieces, as well as his expertise in glazes and enamels—expertise he would share with Picasso—Durrio must have studied with Chaplet or one of his associates. (The extent to which Durrio's techniques helped Picasso revolutionize the craft of ceramics at Vallauris forty years later has yet to be taken into account.)

Picasso. *Blue Vase.* Paris, 1906. Pen and crayons on paper, 31.5×24.5cm. Ex-Galerie Suzanne Bollag, Zurich.

Before returning to Tahiti, Gauguin gave Durrio a magnificent group of paintings, drawings, prints, woodcarvings and ceramics. He also painted what has only recently come to be recognized as a portrait of Durrio playing the guitar.[11] The fifteen-year-old Judith Molard,[12] who had fallen in love with the artist, has left a touching account of Durrio's grief at Gauguin's farewell tea party (June 26, 1895). As she served tea and slices of cake out of huge mother-of-pearl shells for the last time, 'some savage whim inspired Gauguin to dance the *hupa-hupa* [*sic*] which allowed him to anticipate his real return to his real element: *Hupa-hupa Tahiti Hupa-hupa faruru He-he-he!* Meanwhile Durrio had powdered his face with flour, outlined his big soulful eyes with charcoal, got himself up in one of Judith's dresses and was pouring out his sorrow in languorous malagueñas on the guitar—malagueñas that would endear him to Picasso.

> It was like incense rising from a censer. [Durrio's] lavender-blue eyes turned to amethysts. They could not tear themselves away from Gauguin, who was standing in front of the fireplace stroking his astrakhan waistcoat, a slight quiver . . . ruffling his brow. I felt . . . I was the object of his looks.[13]

The precocious Judith ends on a confessional note: on the way to her parents' apartment on the floor below, she kissed Durrio on the mouth—not difficult, she remarks, since even in the high-heeled yellow boots he favoured, he was no taller than she was.

Federico Saenz Venturini. *Paco Durrio's Studio.* 1908. Oil on canvas, 98×78.4cm. Museo de Bellas Artes, Bilbao.

Durrio. *Head of a Man*. Glazed ceramic, ht: 30.6 cm. Museo de Bellas Artes, Bilbao.

Durrio. *Fountain (Crouching Figure)*. Glazed ceramic, ht: 58 cm. Museo de Bellas Artes, Bilbao.

Gauguin. *Oviri*. 1894. Stoneware, partly glazed, ht: 75 cm. Musée d'Orsay, Paris.

Gauguin invited Durrio to accompany him to Tahiti, but he preferred to remain in Paris and serve as a keeper of the artist's flame. He moved himself and his collection of works by Gauguin into a tumbledown Montmartre mansion on what is now the square Saint-Denis. This house, which he shared with Zuloaga and Uranga until 1901, became a principal gathering place for expatriate Basque artists (among them Iturrino, Mogronejo and Urrutia). It was only after he moved into the Bateau Lavoir in 1901 that Durrio gravitated to the more bohemian and progressive *bande Catalane*.

Durrio had originally been sent to Paris to design an ambitious mausoleum for his patrons, the Echevarrías.[14] He also made a reputation as a jeweller: art nouveau pendants in silver and enamel that are very Gauguinesque. But if Durrio is remembered for his work (as opposed to his closeness to Gauguin and Picasso), it is above all for his ceramics. When six or seven of them, all a bit taller than their creator, were first shown at Bing's Art Nouveau Gallery in 1896, Charles Morice hailed them as some of the greatest examples of art pottery ever made. Picasso, too, would speak admiringly of them. Years after they ceased to be friends, he had Kahnweiler acquire a piece for his collection. This already included a pair of anthropomorphic vases, *The Mormons*, possibly a quid pro quo for Picasso's gift of *La Belle Hollandaise* in 1905.[15]

The bust of Fontdevila, the first ceramic that Picasso fired in Durrio's kiln, lacks scale and looks somewhat tentative but is nevertheless important. Picasso learned from it not only how to sculpt in stoneware, but how to articulate the planes of Gertrude Stein's head. Around the time of its firing, Picasso's interest in stoneware was further stimulated by the examples he saw at the 1906 Gauguin retrospective at the Salon d'Automne. The most disturbing of these ceramics (one that Picasso may already have seen at Vollard's) was the gruesome *Oviri*. Until 1987, when the Musée d'Orsay acquired this little-known work (exhibited only once since 1906), it had never been recognized as the masterpiece it is, let alone recognized for its relevance to the works leading up to the *Demoiselles*.[16] Although just under thirty inches high, *Oviri* has an awesome presence, as befits a monument intended for Gauguin's grave.[17] Picasso was very struck by *Oviri*. Fifty years later he was delighted when Cooper and I told him that we had come upon this sculpture in a collection that also included the original plaster of his cubist head. Had it been a revelation, like Iberian sculpture? Picasso's shrug was grudgingly affirmative. He was always loath to admit Gauguin's role in setting him on the road to primitivism.

Besides meaning literally 'savage', *Oviri* connotes a deity that is both Eros and Thanatos. Gauguin described her as a '*Tueuse*' (a killer) and (to Mallarmé) as 'a cruel enigma'. Hence his portrayal of her as pop-eyed and 'moonstruck', stamping a wolf to bloody death. He hints at the life-giving Eros side by giving her one of the wolf's cubs to cradle against her belly, also by compacting her hideous head and voluptuous body into a phallus. One of the many *Oviri* drawings carries a mysterious inscription: 'And the monster, embracing its creation, filled her generous womb with seed and fathered Seraphitus-Seraphita.' This reference to the androgynous hero(ine) of Balzac's novel *Seraphita* ties in with the passage in *Noa Noa* that Picasso liked about going off into the forest with a young savage to hack down a tree for a carving.[18]

Picasso. Sheet of drawings: Fernande dancing and sketches of Paco Durrio. Paris, 1905. Pencil and blue crayon, 24.5×33 cm. Heirs of the artist.

Gauguin. *The Black Woman* (known as *Black Venus*). 1889. Glazed ceramic, ht: 50 cm. Nassau County Museum, Long Island.

Picasso. *Fernande Combing Her Hair.* Paris, 1906. Bronze, ht: 41.2 cm. Hirshhorn Museum and Sculpture Garden, Smithsonian Institution, Gift of Joseph H. Hirshhorn, 1972.

The 1906 exhibition of Gauguin's work left Picasso more than ever in this artist's thrall. Gauguin demonstrated that the most disparate types of art—not to speak of elements from metaphysics, ethnology, symbolism, the Bible, classical myths and much else besides—could be combined into a synthesis that was of its time yet timeless. An artist could also confound conventional notions of beauty, he demonstrated, by harnessing his demons to the dark gods (not necessarily Tahitian ones) and tapping a vital new source of divine energy. If in later years Picasso played down his debt to Gauguin, there is no doubt that between 1905 and 1907 he felt a very close kinship with this other Paul, who prided himself on Spanish genes inherited from his Peruvian grandmother.[19] Had not Picasso signed himself 'Paul' in Gauguin's honour?

Oviri also inspired a large stoneware figure of Fernande combing her all-enveloping cloak of hair. Our eyes are the mirror in which she preens. Picasso sculpted this piece in Durrio's studio under the auspices of Durrio's Gauguins (kept away from the furnace in an upstairs bedroom), and fired it in his kiln. There is a slight Iberian look to this figure, but *Oviri* and her ceramic prototypes—the sinister *Black Venus* (1889) and the one-armed *Eve* (1890)—are the main sources for Fernande's air of mystery. For the first time we get an inkling of what Picasso meant when he said that his sculptures were vials filled with his own blood.[20]

Picasso subsequently sold the Fernande ceramic and most of his other original sculptures to Vollard, who proceeded to make ten casts of each of them. He came to regret this: he always set greater store (he said) by the original, no matter what the *matière*. Bronze was too rich-looking. The advantage of ceramics was that they allowed the artist to glaze and bake colour into his forms, and to use techniques such as Chaplet's *barbotine* (a mixture of clay and coloured oxides) that enabled an artist to paint a vase as if it were a canvas and blur the distinction between painting and sculpture. Picasso did not execute more than three stoneware pieces: two heads and a nude of 1908–09. Cubism called for a less 'artistic' technique, less precious *matière*. Also Durrio permitted Picasso to continue sculpting in his studio only so long as the work remained within Gauguinesque bounds. Cubism would lie outside these bounds. For the great 1909 head of Fernande—arguably Picasso's most important cubist sculpture (as opposed to construction)—the artist used Manolo's studio.[21] Durrio was an aesthete at heart and was appalled that the artist on whom he had pinned all his hopes should have become such an iconoclast. After 1907 Picasso seldom saw Durrio again, but by that time Cézanne had all but banished Gauguin from his mind. And the revelations of tribal art had made the primitivism of *Noa Noa* seem something of a sham.

Picasso. Sheet of Drawings. Paris, 1906. Pen on paper, 30×41 cm. Private collection. Details were used to illustrate André Salmon's *Manuscrit trouvé dans un chapeau*.

Picasso
1906

30

Dionysos

'God is really another artist . . . like me.'
'I am God, I am God, I am God . . . '[1]

Picasso. *Fernande Embroidering* (detail). Paris, 1906. Pencil on paper, 31.5×48 cm. Marina Picasso collection.

Opposite: Picasso. *Self-Portrait with a Palette.* Paris, 1906. Oil on canvas, 93×73 cm. Philadelphia Museum of Art, A. E. Gallatin Collection.

THE LATE SUMMER OF 1906 WAS exceptionally hot, and the Bateau Lavoir studio, with its overpowering smell of drains and dog and paint, exceptionally stifling. Stripped to the waist, or naked, Picasso wrestled with his work, mostly with images of Fernande, likewise naked and often as not combing her hair. To judge by drawings that are one jump ahead of canvases, his brush had difficulty keeping up with his ever expanding vision. Picasso's concentration was manic, and if there were interruptions or distractions, he would explode in anarchic rage. Even when he was not working he would occasionally turn in on himself and become inaccessible, or lash out, huge eyes ablaze, at his entourage. Possessive as he was of Fernande, he would find fault with everything she did, especially her coquettish 'little ways'; these were kindling the misogyny which, sooner or later, would cripple most of his relationships with women.

Irritation exacerbated Picasso's jealousy. Given Fernande's flirtatious nature, there was some justification for it, none for his pasha-like habit of locking her in the studio when he left on an errand. The building was a tinderbox. On one occasion the studio above had actually caught fire while Fernande was locked in below. Infractions were punished. Although she had been forbidden to go to the Lapin Agile on her own, she could not resist racing over when she heard that Frédé had shot and severely wounded a marauder. Picasso had the same reaction; when he caught her there, he slapped her face in full view of a crowd of curiosity seekers. Another time, on the way home from the Lapin Agile, he upbraided Fernande for making eyes at some man in the bar. What about his behaviour with some of their women friends? Fernande counter-attacked. Had she not found him with one of them on his knee? And she rushed off in tears down the rue Lepic, pursued by Picasso. They almost came to blows before Fernande allowed herself to be dragged back to the studio. Next morning before she awoke, he went out and bought her a bottle of Chypre or Fumée, and they were reconciled. 'Dear Pablo,' she wrote in the preface to her *Souvenirs*, 'if you only knew that at that moment there was one thing in the world that made me happy—your presence—and your love.'[2]

Fernande was not always the innocent party. To get revenge, or sometimes the upper hand, she would set about exciting the jealousy she claims to have resented. One of the threats she held over Picasso's head was to resume her career as a model. She had already put this threat into

Van Dongen. *Portrait of Fernande Olivier*. 1906. Pastel on paper, 72×61 cm. Petit Palais Musée, Geneva.

practice in 1905, when she posed nude for the sexually rapacious van Dongen. And she would do so again. One cannot entirely blame Fernande for seeking her revenge. She had good grounds for complaint, not so much over this or that woman (though that, too) as over the way her lover's painting was absorbing more and more of his passion. To be the prisoner of a man who spent his time devising ever less loving and flattering images of her must have been hard to endure.

Drugs continued to play a role in Bateau Lavoir life. An entry in the Gósol sketchbook—'*opio, azafran, alcool, laudano*'[3]—suggests that such things were still on Picasso's mind. But to what extent? Apart from Fernande, the only witness we have is Alice Toklas's cousin Annette Rosenshine, a clever San Francisco girl handicapped by a cleft palate and harelip. She had arrived in Paris at the end of December 1906, to be instantly enslaved by Gertrude Stein. Every afternoon Gertrude would take her out, often to artists' studios. Annette particularly remembered going to see Picasso at the Bateau Lavoir. Fernande was lying on the bed with Picasso on one side and a second man on the other, none of them in a state to rise for guests. Recovering 'from a bohemian revelry the night before', Annette thought. More likely smoking opium or hashish, I would imagine, especially in view of the 'luminous penetrating quality of Picasso's eyes'—something Annette never forgot.[4] Could opium have helped generate the exaltation of the *Demoiselles*? I doubt it. If Picasso's indulgence in drugs was as moderate as his indulgence in liquor, opium is unlikely to have provided his imagination with much sustained stimulus.

As for the rest of the *bande à Picasso*, Wiegels was the only member whose gifts, such as they were, failed him completely. The rest were on the brink of recognition, and in some cases fame. Max Jacob, who moved (early 1907) into one of the smallest, darkest rooms in the Bateau Lavoir (a mattress raised on bricks was the principal piece of furniture), was rapidly filling a trunk with poems, which he would soon start to publish. One of the first to appear was a poem called '*Le Cheval*', which had been picked by Apollinaire to accompany his review of Picasso in the one and only number of his *Revue immoraliste*. Because it was dedicated to the artist, this poem won a degree of local fame as '*le cheval de Picasso*'.[5] It is a whimsical piece about a pensive *cheval à fiacre* (cab horse) outside the Grand Hotel. Jacob had just experienced the first of many revelations. One evening at the Cirque Bostock he had watched an acrobat climb to the very apex of the hall and hang there by his teeth, spinning parallel to the ceiling. 'That's what one should do with one's mind,' he decided.[6] He forthwith embarked on a new regime. He would leave the Bateau Lavoir every day at dawn and walk across Paris to the cascade in the Bois de Boulogne. Whenever he passed a shop that sold postcards, he would stop and note down whatever idea a specific postcard suggested. If nothing came to mind, he would force himself to remain motionless until some thought occurred to him. He would arrive back at the Bateau Lavoir in a trance of hunger and exhaustion. This, he would have us believe, was the inspiration of *Le Phanérogame*, the Jarry-esque novel that he would work on over the next two years.

Meanwhile Apollinaire had temporarily abandoned poetry for erotica: *Memoires d'un jeune Don Juan* and *Les Onze Mille Verges*, both written in 1906 and published in 1907. These were supposed to solve his financial

Fernande Olivier, *c.*1906: Musée Picasso, Paris.

problems; they were also an outlet for perverse fantasies. *Don Juan* is of little interest. *Les Onze Mille Verges*, on the other hand, is a masterpiece of its kind—a brilliant takeoff on the Marquis de Sade that is saved from horror by irony and black humour. It so delighted Picasso that Apollinaire presented him with the manuscript.[7] He was immensely proud of this treasure ('And why not, it's Guillaume's best work,' he used to say). That the *Demoiselles* came into the world around the same time as Apollinaire's heroines, Alexine and Culculine, is no coincidence. Even though pictorial imagery is inevitably less explicit and anecdotal than literary description, we can see that the poet's exhibitionistic exposure of everything that was most outrageous and violent in his libido was an example from which the painter would derive inspiration. 'To like my painting people really have to be masochists,' Picasso said.[8]

Picasso. *The Twins (Brothel Scene)*. Paris, May 1905. Pen and sepia on paper, 44×28cm. Private collection (ex-Apollinaire collection).

Apollinaire would include Picasso as a character in two of his novels: *Le Poète assassiné* (a patchwork that dates in part from 1903–04 and 1907–08 but was not assembled until 1916) and *La Femme assise* (1912–18). In the former he appears as '*L'Oiseau de Bénin*' (in earlier drafts he is also called Lain Corazo, then Paul Assot).[9] He is first seen barefoot at work on a painting of 'two nostalgic women in an icy mist'. He is last seen sculpting '*une profonde statue en rien*': a monument to the murdered poet (Croniamantal, alias Apollinaire) that takes the form of an earthwork: a ditch in the forest of Meudon. In *La Femme assise* Apollinaire originally contemplated calling the artist Paco Luis Pistratos,[10] then turned him into Pablo Canouris, a half-Spanish, half-Albanian painter with the eyes of a bird and 'hands of celestial blue'. Canouris, we are told, is a reincarnation of El Greco: 'not that Canouris imitated El Greco, but his work had been touched with the angelic violence that fills lovers of El Greco with such delightful anguish.' Picasso enjoyed being '*L'Oiseau de Bénin*'; Canouris pleased him less. Besides having his accent mocked, he was portrayed as wildly in love with an unfaithful mistress called Elvire, whom he threatens with his revolver: '*Elbirre, écoute-moi oubrre-moi jé te aime, jé te adore et si tu né m'obéis pas, jé té touerrai avec mon rébolber. . . . Oubbré-moi, Elbirre! L'amourr c'est moi.*'[11] ('Elvire, listen to me, open up, I love you, I adore you and if you don't obey me I'll kill you with my revolver. . . . Open up, Elvire! Love, that's me.') Elsewhere the Picasso character could be talking of Fernande when he says, '*Pour aboir braiment une femme, il faut l'aboir enlébée, l'enfermer à clef et l'occouper tout lé temps.*'[12] ('To have a woman properly you have to make off with her, lock her up and devote all your time to her.')

Salmon, who had established himself as a progressive if not very discriminating art critic, would also publish a *roman à clef* about Picasso and his group. *La Négresse du Sacré Cœur*, which did not appear until 1920, is all about the early Bateau Lavoir days. The silly plot concerns a small-time 'Josephine Baker' who is kept as a slave by a man called Médéric Buthor in a 'plantation house' on the Butte de Montmartre. Picasso is thinly disguised as a painter of many different periods called Sorgue. At one time Sorgue envisages humanity as 'lame, leprous and suppliant'; he also passes through what Salmon calls '*l'époque des Graces*' —a sort of Rose period. However, Sorgue never comes to life as vividly as Apollinaire's Canouris. In the *Négresse*, Jacob, MacOrlan, Uhde, Frédé, Linda la Bouquetière, p'tit Louis and many more are all recognizable, likewise the bistros and cabarets. Fact and fantasy are deftly mingled, so the novel should convey something of the texture and atmosphere of Picasso's Montmartre life. If it ultimately fails to do so, it is probably because Salmon was afraid of giving offence to his by now exceedingly formidable old friend, and so he takes refuge in wryness.

For all their faults, Salmon's *Souvenirs* are more evocative of Bateau Lavoir life than the *Négresse*: for instance, his description of the game the *bande à Picasso* loved to play—'pretending to be Degas'. It was a game after Picasso's mimetic heart. 'Who's going to be Degas today?' someone would ask, and after a lot of horseplay, 'one of us would be Degas, the illustrious curmudgeon, visiting Pablo and judging his work. But Degas did not always have to be Degas. He could as well be Puvis de Chavannes, or Bonnat, or Bouguereau, or Courbet, or even Baudelaire working up one of his Salon articles. Picasso laughed to hear himself being ridiculed, but in those good old days nobody gave a damn what they said.'[13] Memories of these studio games bore fruit over half a century later in a series of engravings that Picasso did at the end of his life (1971). These hold Degas up to mockery as a voyeuristic old man (whose likeness to don José has already been pointed out) on a visit to a whorehouse—a metaphor for Picasso's studio. Degas's contact with the whores who parade in front of him is strictly ocular—so much so that his eyes are connected to one of the girls by lines.[14]

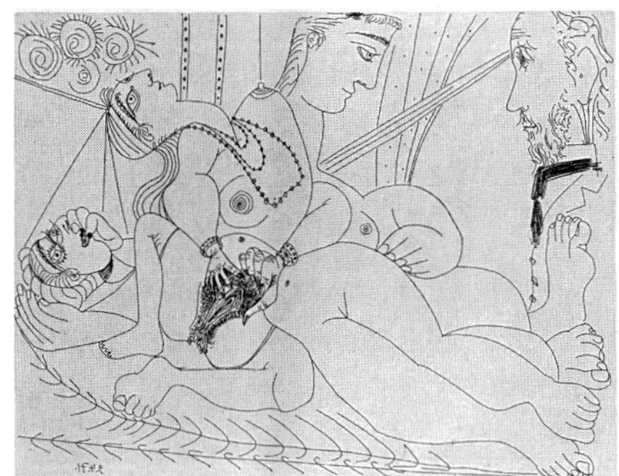

Picasso. Etching. Mougins, April 9, 1971. 37×50cm. Galerie Louise Leiris, Paris.

Another Bateau Lavoir ritual: someone would tell Picasso that a certain painting 'was still much too Lautrec!'—a criticism that had not applied to his work in years. The ensuing discussion would trigger an endless battle of wits. According to Fernande, 'There never was a group of artists more given to mockery and the unkind and intentionally wounding word.'[15] Another provocative cry—one that Max Jacob liked to 'hurl', with some justification, at Salmon and Apollinaire—was, 'Still much too symbolist!' Even in its death throes, symbolism continued to be a divisive issue, not least at the *rendez-vous des poètes*, where reverence for the movement's heroes—Verlaine, Mallarmé, Rimbaud—made it difficult to avoid their shadows. Such was the din of battle that warring adherents were known as 'cymbalists'. Rimbaud was always being fought over. As a champion of Verlaine, Jacob was irked by the way Apollinaire and Salmon incessantly praised this 'adorable monster'; he was even more irked by their successful conversion of Picasso to their cause. Picasso, need it be said, had no problem identifying with this satanic wunderkind. In no time he was insisting, *'Il n'y a que Rimbaud.'* Jarry may have exerted more of an influence on Picasso, but Rimbaud was probably his favourite French poet. He took to heart a line from the last section of *Une Saison en enfer: 'il faut être absolument moderne'*— easier said than done, he once commented.[16]

* * *

Towards the end of 1906, the image of *la belle Fernande* underwent a radical metamorphosis. From being a Gauguin-esque Ondine erotically engulfed in her own tresses, she turns into a flat-footed, bull-necked, banana-fingered earth mother. The *fines attaches*—delicate wrists and ankles—on which Fernande prided herself have disappeared like armatures into flesh as firm as india rubber. Her fine features have likewise

Picasso. *Woman Combing her Hair.* Paris, 1906. Oil on canvas, 126×91cm. Private collection.

Picasso. *Bust of Fernande,* Paris, 1906. Charcoal and red and white crayons on paper, 108×84 cm. Private collection. Given by Picasso to van Dongen.

Picasso. *Seated Nude*. Paris, 1906. Oil on canvas, 151×100 cm. Národní Galerie, Prague.

Picasso. *Nude Seen from the Back*. Paris, 1906. Crayon on paper, 62×47 cm. Private collection.

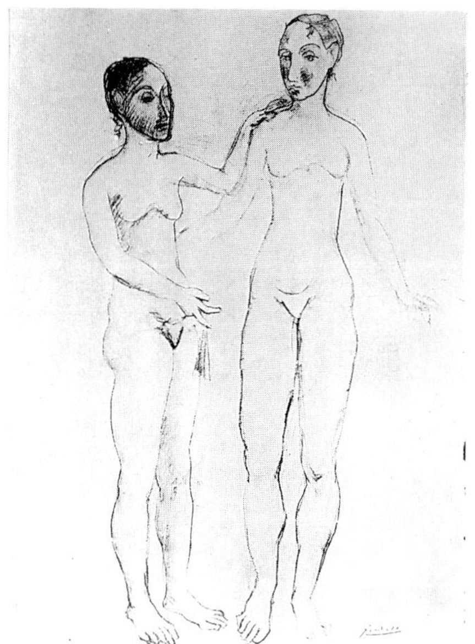

Picasso. *Two Nudes*. Gósol, 1906. Pencil on paper, 64×47 cm. Galerie Louise Leiris, Paris.

Picasso. *Two Nudes*. Paris, 1906. Oil on canvas, 151.3×93 cm. The Museum of Modern Art, New York, Gift of G. David Thompson in honour of Alfred H. Barr, Jr.

thickened into a stylized mask taken more or less directly from an Iberian relief. There are also lesbian overtones: another hefty woman appears, who holds Fernande's hand or puts an arm round her waist or shoulders. Gradually the girlfriends cease to look at us and focus on each other. Finally in the *Two Nudes*, the culminant painting of the series, one of these brick-coloured nudes ushers the other towards an opening in the background draperies into some inner sanctum. One woman is seen *en profil perdu*; the other bears a resemblance to Fernande; but the bodies —the uncorseted girth and columnar legs—have surely been modelled on Stein's. Likewise the nature of their rapport (Gertrude was currently involved with a French woman).

Cézanne. *Three Bathers*. *c*.1881–82. Oil on canvas, 50×50cm. Musée du Petit Palais, Paris. Formerly owned by Matisse.

The pictorial relationship between these two large women, whom we will meet again and again in Picasso's later work (e.g., the galumphing bathers that were used for the *Train Bleu* ballet curtain in 1922), should be seen in a broader context than this Steinian one. We can read as much or as little as we want into the arcane hand-signals by means of which they communicate: devices concerned with heightening the mystery and drama. As to whether there is any deep significance in the duality of these more or less identical figures,[17] we should bear in mind that between 1906 and 1908 Picasso sketched out a number of ambitious Cézannesque 'Bather' compositions that include several figures (drawings for the *Two Nudes* reveal that the group had originally included three or even four women). These are usually whittled down to two (the great *Three Women* of 1908 is a notable exception). The artist, who was very aware of this tendency, confessed that he did not know why; it just happened that way. He was presumably happier with tightly organized compositions. So often, Picasso would say, people come up with complicated metaphysical explanations for something that resulted from an accident or some purely pictorial consideration beyond his control. The brush does not always obey the brain. It's like a dinner: you invite six people, but only two turn up.[18]

The *Two Nudes* is an enormous advance on the Gósol girls. By restructuring and reupholstering the mammoth flank of the woman on the right and centring her left breast on her torso, Picasso shows us partial back and front views as well as a side view. For all that the pictorial space is as shallow as a bas-relief, we are able to experience his behemoths in the round more fully than ever before. The sheer heft of these figures is a measure of Picasso's increased awareness of Cézanne. Ten of Cézanne's works had been hung at the Salon d'Automne in 1905, ten more the following year, in commemoration of the artist's death that October. Picasso would also have seen many more paintings at Vollard's. But he would not experience the full impact of Cézanne until the great retrospective at the Salon d'Automne in 1907. Within a year Picasso would acknowledge the master of Aix as 'the father of us all'.

Cézanne. *Five Bathers*. *c*.1877–78. Oil on canvas, 45.8×55.7cm. Musée Picasso, Paris. Formerly owned by Picasso.

Besides seeing Cézanne's works in public exhibitions Picasso had had the opportunity of studying two paintings again and again in the intimate surroundings he preferred: one was the Steins' portrait of Cézanne's wife, to which his portrait of Gertrude served as a pendant; the other was the magnificent *Three Bathers* that Matisse had bought from Vollard in 1899 —a painting of magic power by virtue of its influence on its owner.[19] Picasso learned a lot from the *Bathers*. He learned how to give his figures

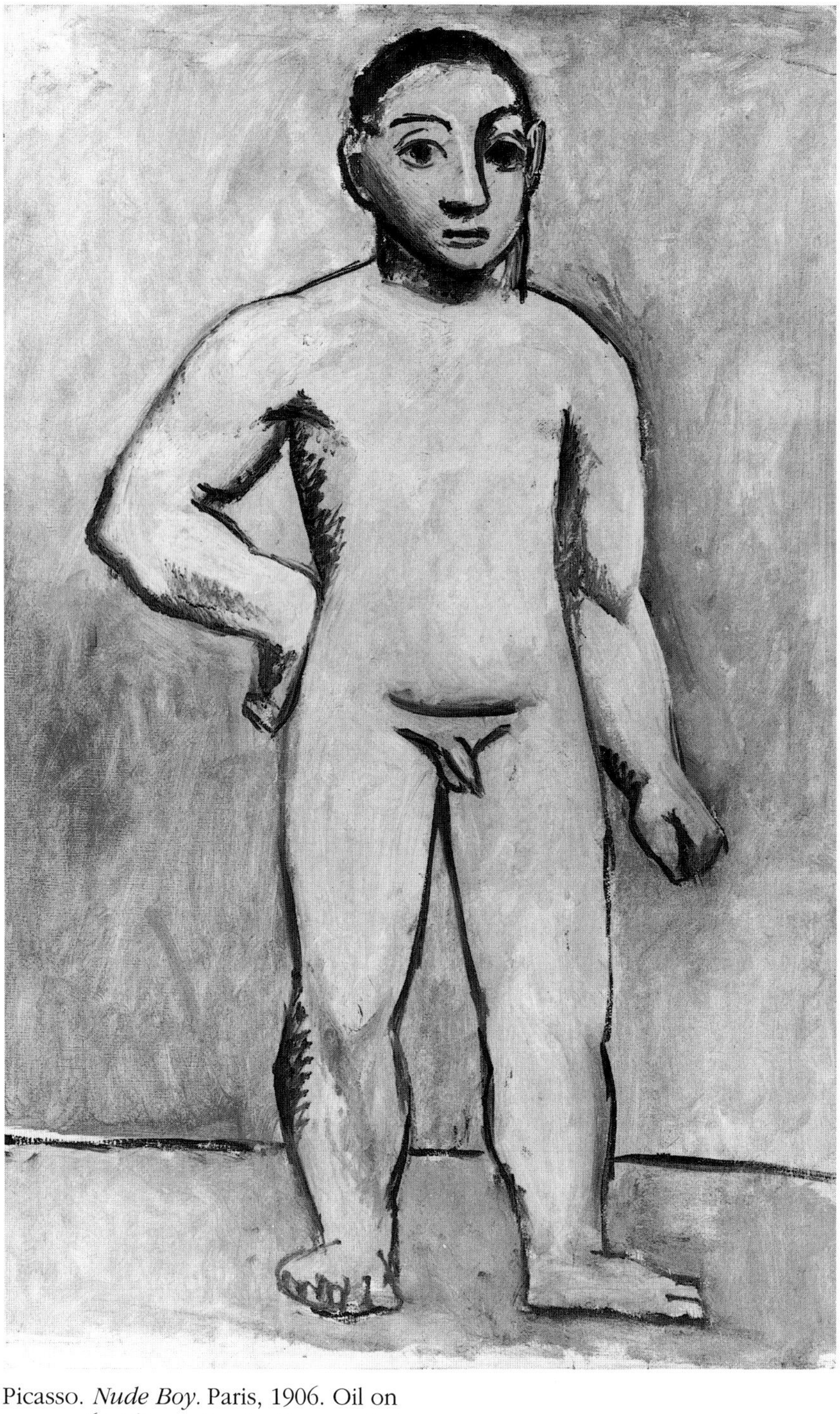

Picasso. *Bacchus*. Paris, 1906. Ink on paper, 19×15.5cm. Stolen from the Douglas Cooper collection.

Picasso. *Nude Boy*. Paris, 1906. Oil on canvas, 67×43cm. Musée Picasso, Paris.

the tension of flying buttresses; how to provide his compositions with the inner structure they had tended to lack; how to profit from Cézanne's maxim: 'When colour is at its richest, form is at its fullest.'[20] It was largely through Matisse that Picasso first learnt the lesson of Cézanne. If later on there were hard feelings, it was partly because Picasso, abetted by Matisse's former follower Braque, would carry Cézanne's ideas to such triumphant fruition.

The Gertrude Stein-like nudes were the main vehicle for the breakthrough in the winter of 1906–07. Men played a lesser role in this process. Except for Fontdevila, who still makes sporadic appearances, Picasso in one guise or another is the only man to materialize on paper or canvas. Self-portraits or not, the male figures are all self-referential. One of the more revealing of these self-referential images is a small drawing of utmost delicacy, inscribed 'Bacchus'—a drawing that the artist was delighted to rediscover in Douglas Cooper's collection.[21] Picasso has not identified himself with a bibulous old lecher astride a wine barrel but with the god's alter ego, the youthful Dionysos: the eternally reborn free spirit, the antithesis (like himself) of Apollonian rationalism. Picasso portrays Bacchus in the traditional manner as a naked youth crowned with a wreath of ivy and bunches of grapes, holding a *thyrsos* (a wand of fertility tipped with a pine cone) in one hand, and a *kantharos* (a two-handled goblet) in the other. The attributes are accurately depicted, but then this was not the first time Picasso had drawn this deity.[22] Nor the last. Dionysos reappears in a similar guise at the end of Picasso's life in an aquatint that includes his wife, Jacqueline, and a Rembrandtian painter.[23] The inscription on the drawing enables us to identify the paintings of Picasso-like boys—an otherwise puzzling feature of this period—as young Bacchuses. What more appropriate Dionysiac role for the artist to have chosen at this moment of radical renewal? Moreover, if these youths are Bacchuses, should not their female counterparts be seen as Bacchantes—those violent women who tore Orpheus apart, at Dionysos's behest, for worshipping the rival god, Apollo? This interpretation would have appealed to Picasso's admirer Federico García Lorca, who saw the cult of Dionysos as the source of Andalusian *duende*—and of *cante jondo*, its purest expression.[24] *Duende*, Lorca believed, 'had rebounded from the mystery-minded Greeks to the dancers of Cádiz or the Dionysian cry of . . . *Siguiriya*.'[25] *Siguiriya*: this cry will re-echo throughout Picasso's work.

Picasso. *Self-Portrait*. Paris, 1906. Pen on paper, 30.5×22.8cm. Private collection.

A triumphant group of self-portrait drawings and paintings bears witness to Picasso's Dionysiac exaltation at this time. In style, even looks, they take off from the Stein portrait as well as the Iberian and Romanesque heads he had come to admire. To emblazon these self-portraits with the words '*Yo Picasso*' would have been redundant. The supreme confidence of the image as well as the execution says it all. These portraits can be seen to constitute a manifesto; they propose an alternative to Fauvism; an alternative to Matisse's leadership of the avant garde. The finest of Picasso's 1906 self-portraits—the one with the palette—could well have had the effect of persuading Derain and Braque to come over to his side. It is a far more revolutionary image than Matisse's Fauve self-portrait done a month or two earlier. Instead of dazzling us with brilliant light effects or lashings of Fauve colour, the Picasso is pared down to essentials: flatly painted, minimal in colour and modelling. It is all the more

Matisse. *Self-Portrait.* 1906. Oil on canvas, 55×46cm. Statens Museum for Kunst, Copenhagen.

effective for being laconic—deadpan. Matisse's self-portrait, by contrast, demands to be admired for its bravado, its Manet-like brushwork, its van Gogh-like expressionism: what the artist called '*le coup de foudre*' (by which he meant 'love at first sight'). The painting confirms Matisse's contention (1911): 'Our school is in the direct line of Impressionism and is, in a sense, an extension of that movement.'[26] This is a simplification, but it points up the nature of his fundamental divergence from Picasso. Picasso made fun of his rival's famous 1908 statement (the one that Mécislas Golberg is supposed to have drafted): 'What I dream of is an art of balance, of purity and serenity devoid of troubling or depressing subject-matter, an art which might be for every mental worker, be he businessman or writer, like an appeasing influence, like a mental soother, something like a good armchair in which to rest from physical fatigue.'[27] Matisse wanted to soothe, comfort and delight, whereas Picasso wanted to challenge, excite and shock. Hence the latter's switch to primitivism. Hence the way clumsy Iberian reliefs take the place of glacial Roman marbles. In keeping with his emerging primitivism, Picasso has portrayed himself as tougher than he actually was, otherwise much as he liked to look—a working man in an undershirt. He has also switched his gaze away from the beholder, to demonstrate that this is no mirror image, but a detached view of himself. '*Je est un autre*,' as Rimbaud put it.

Studies for the charismatic *Self-Portrait with a Palette* differ from the final version in one significant respect. The drawings portray the artist holding a brush, but in the painting the brush has vanished: Picasso is making a fist. And in order to give this image of himself maximum impact, he resurrects the striking poster-like silhouette (borrowed from Lautrec) that he had used for his portrait of Mañach five years earlier. The image is Jarry-esque, that is to say athletic, even pugilistic: the artist as a new champion ready to take on all comers. 'He was not aggressive, but felt the right to be aggressive,' Leo Stein wrote of Picasso at this time, and went on to describe his rage at having to keep his place and not push to the head of a bus queue. 'This is not the way it ought to be,' Picasso said. 'The strong should go ahead and take what they want.'[28] Push to the head of the queue as if by right is what this Nietzschean Dionysos proceeded to do. *Le petit Goya* had developed into *le grand Picasso.*

*　　*　　*

By the beginning of 1907, Picasso was three months into his twenty-sixth year. A less driven, less exigent artist would have had every right to feel enormous satisfaction. In less than ten years, the young man who set so much store by speed and productivity had assembled an oeuvre that was larger, more accomplished and varied in style and technique, than the lifetime achievement of many another reputed master. He had proved—to his satisfaction at least—that he was not only the new Greco, the new Goya and on his way to being the new Gauguin; he was also one of the most (if not *the* most) revolutionary, inventive and disturbing artists of his generation. What is more, collectors were finally beginning to perceive his genius. However, Picasso was never satisfied. His laurels could have been a bed of thorns for all the comfort they provided. Technical virtuosity had a built-in disadvantage: facility. This had to be fought at all

Opposite top: Picasso. *Self-Portraits.* Paris, 1906. Pencil on paper, 31.5×47.5cm. Musée Picasso, Paris.

Opposite bottom: Picasso. *Self-Portraits.* Paris, 1906. Pencil on paper, 32.5×48cm. Musée Picasso, Paris.

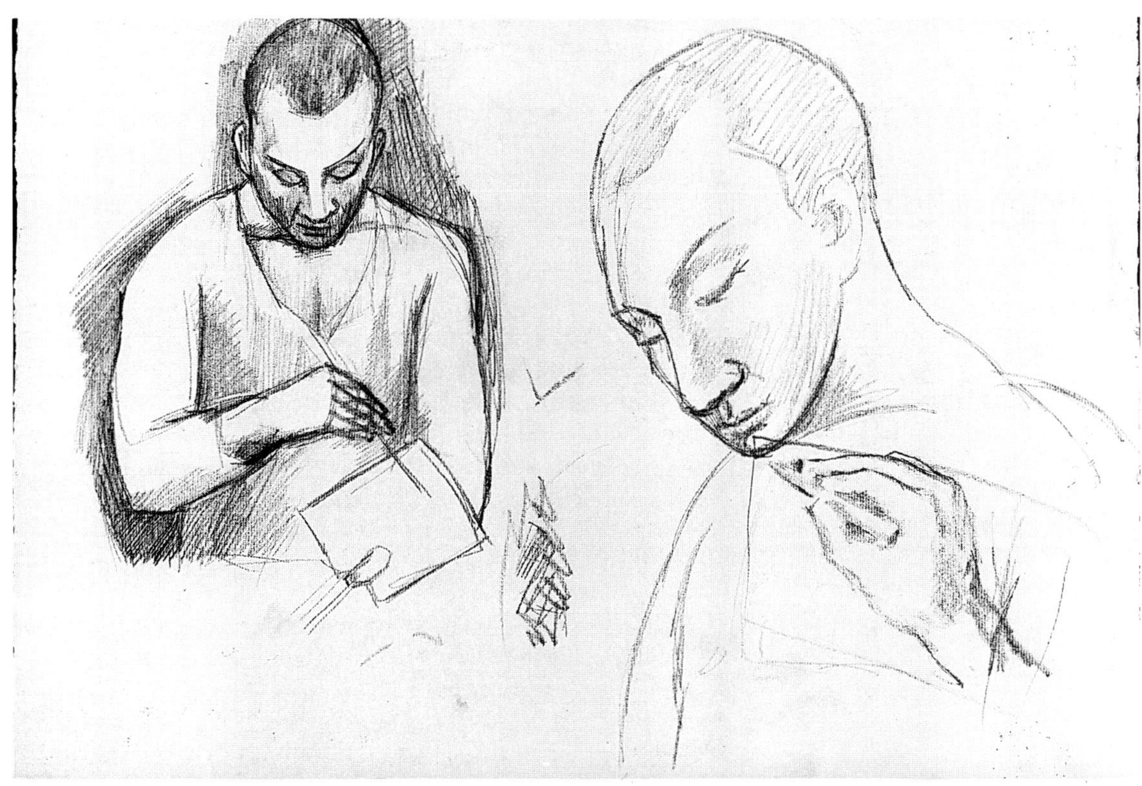

Picasso. *Man, Woman and Child.* Paris, 1906. Oil on canvas, 115×88cm. Kunstmuseum, Basel.

costs. Picasso had to make things ever more challenging for himself, and, by implication, for the public.

On his return from Gósol, Picasso put aside any doubts he may have had as to where he stood and where he was going. Judging by hints he dropped later in life, he realized that he had previously allowed himself to wander too far down the art-for-art's-sake path of symbolism; that the Blue period and, to a lesser extent, the Rose period had been detours. At Gósol he had put sentimentality, *poésie* and virtuoso effects behind him. After flirting with classicism, he had finally seen how primitivism—Gauguin's synthetic brand as well as the real thing—could enable him to fuse the conflicts inherent in his style and vision. He could now face up to the magnitude of the struggle that lay ahead. After the triumphant synthesis of the Stein portrait, the *Two Nudes* and the *Self-Portrait with a Palette*, Picasso realized that he had the confidence, imagination and power to execute a masterpiece that would 'free art from its shackles' and 'extend its frontiers' (Apollinaire); a painting that would provide artists of the new century with a licence to take every conceivable liberty, break every conceivable rule and 'demolish even the ruins' (Jarry).

There was, however, a small logistical problem: the prospect of doing another vast, enormously demanding composition was unthinkable in Picasso's Bateau Lavoir studio. Painting *The Saltimbanques* had been hard enough, but Fernande had not moved in with him until the last stages, so he had had the studio to himself. Now she had settled in and accumulated '*un tas de bric-à-brac*'. How was he to wrestle the whole tradition of European art to the ground with his mistress sitting by, fussing over her *toilette*, spraying herself with scent? What is more, Fernande was determined to adopt a child; so, in a halfhearted way, was Picasso. In the course of the winter he even painted a strangely tender Iberian group—Daix calls it '*la famille primitive*'—of a Picasso-like man intently contemplating a Picasso-like baby and a not-so-Fernande-like mother.[29] The wish embodied in the painting would come true, very briefly, a few months later. The prospect of a child made it all the more urgent to take another studio, where Picasso could work undisturbed by Fernande or the members of his entourage. The *rendez-vous des poètes* concept was all very stimulating; it was nonetheless distracting. When the Steins realized the problem, they came to the rescue. Early in 1907, they agreed to pay the rent for another studio on another floor of the Bateau Lavoir. Around the same time (February 1907) Vollard contracted to buy the remainder of Picasso's accumulation of early work for 2,500 francs—500 francs more than he had paid the previous year. With his future seemingly assured (Vollard did not come up with the money or collect the canvases until the following December), Picasso could now address himself to the task of painting the work that came to be known as *Les Demoiselles d'Avignon*, the great composition that he had had in mind ever since Gósol. He ordered a large, especially fine canvas, more or less the same size as the El Greco *Apocalyptic Vision* that he so much admired at Zuloaga's. Out of conviction that he was embarking on a masterpiece, he had it relined. Leo Stein had just had this done to one of his paintings, and Picasso had been much impressed.

* * *

It is at this point, the beginning of 1907, that I propose to bring this first volume to an end. The twenty-five-year-old Picasso is about to conjure up a quintet of Dionysiac *Demoiselles* on his huge new canvas. The execution of this painting would make a dramatic climax to these pages. However, it would imply that Picasso's great revolutionary work constitutes a conclusion to all that has gone before. It does not. For all that the *Demoiselles* is deeply rooted in Picasso's past, not to speak of such precursors as the Iron Age Iberians, El Greco, Gauguin and Cézanne, it is essentially a beginning: the most innovative painting since Giotto. As we will see in the next volume, it established a new pictorial syntax; it enabled people to perceive things with new eyes, new minds, new awareness. *Les Demoiselles d'Avignon* is the first unequivocally twentieth-century masterpiece, a principal detonator of the modern movement, the cornerstone of twentieth-century art. For Picasso it would also be a rite of passage: what he called an 'exorcism.' The *Demoiselles* cleared the way for cubism. It likewise banished the artist's demons. Later, these demons would return and require further exorcism. For the next decade, however, Picasso would feel as free and creative and 'as overworked' as God.

Picasso. *Les Demoiselles d'Avignon*. Paris, 1907. Oil on canvas, 243.9×233.7cm. The Museum of Modern Art, New York, Acquired through the Lillie P. Bliss Bequest.

FAMILY TREE

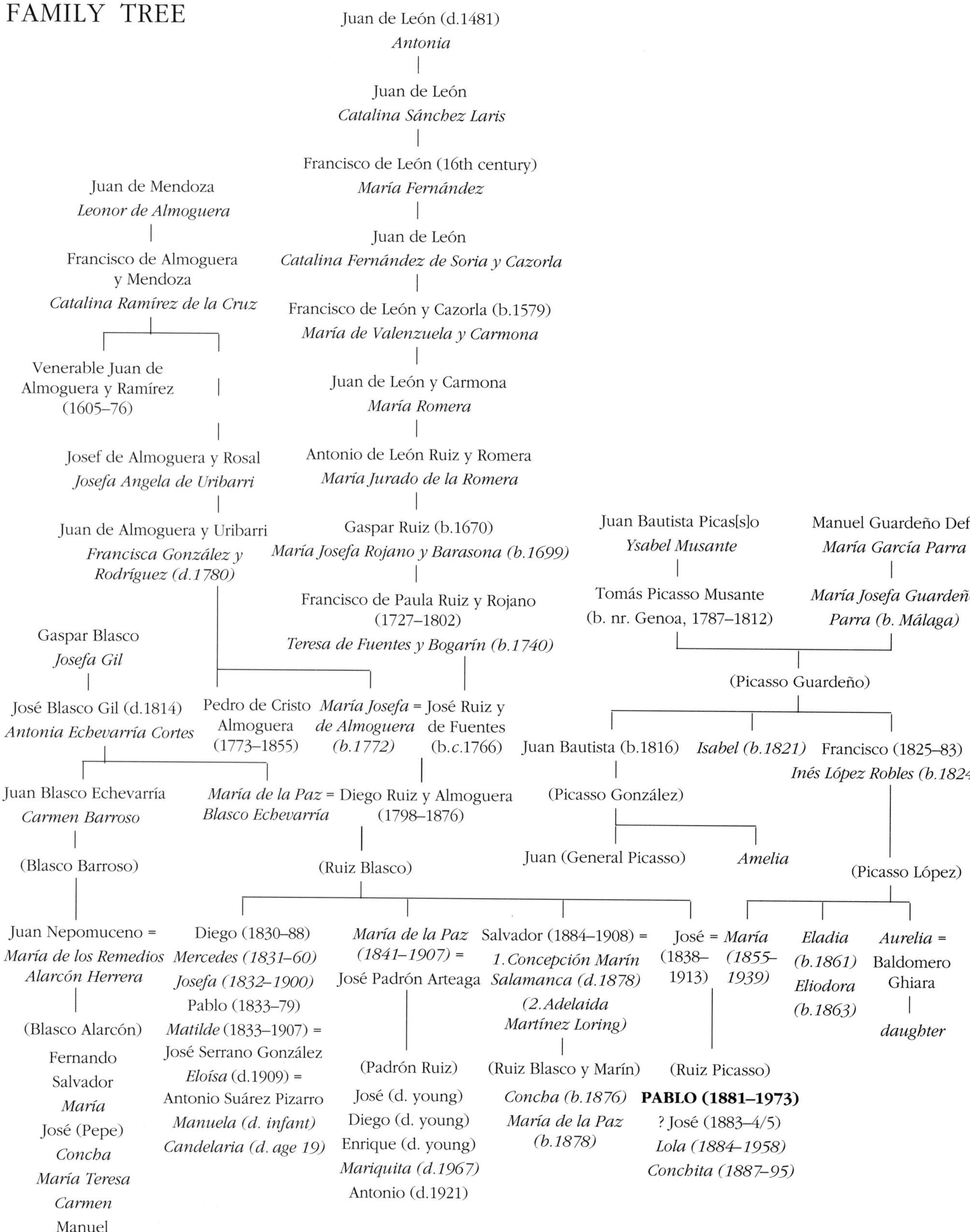

Juan de León (d.1481)
Antonia
Juan de León
Catalina Sánchez Laris
Francisco de León (16th century)
María Fernández
Juan de León
Catalina Fernández de Soria y Cazorla
Francisco de León y Cazorla (b.1579)
María de Valenzuela y Carmona
Juan de León y Carmona
María Romera
Antonio de León Ruiz y Romera
María Jurado de la Romera
Gaspar Ruiz (b.1670)
María Josefa Rojano y Barasona (b.1699)
Francisco de Paula Ruiz y Rojano (1727–1802)
Teresa de Fuentes y Bogarín (b.1740)
Juan de Mendoza
Leonor de Almoguera
Francisco de Almoguera y Mendoza
Catalina Ramírez de la Cruz
Venerable Juan de Almoguera y Ramírez (1605–76)
Josef de Almoguera y Rosal
Josefa Angela de Uribarri
Juan de Almoguera y Uribarri
Francisca González y Rodríguez (d.1780)
Gaspar Blasco
Josefa Gil
José Blasco Gil (d.1814)
Antonia Echevarría Cortes
Pedro de Cristo Almoguera (1773–1855)
María Josefa de Almoguera (b.1772) = José Ruiz y de Fuentes (b.c.1766)
Juan Blasco Echevarría
Carmen Barroso
(Blasco Barroso)
María de la Paz Blasco Echevarría = Diego Ruiz y Almoguera (1798–1876)
(Ruiz Blasco)
Juan Bautista Picas[s]o
Ysabel Musante
Tomás Picasso Musante (b. nr. Genoa, 1787–1812)
Manuel Guardeño Deff
María García Parra
María Josefa Guardeño Parra (b. Málaga)
(Picasso Guardeño)
Juan Bautista (b.1816)
Isabel (b.1821)
Francisco (1825–83)
Inés López Robles (b.1824)
(Picasso González)
Juan (General Picasso)
Amelia
(Picasso López)
Juan Nepomuceno = *María de los Remedios Alarcón Herrera*
(Blasco Alarcón)
Fernando
Salvador
María
José (Pepe)
Concha
María Teresa
Carmen
Manuel
Diego (1830–88)
Mercedes (1831–60)
Josefa (1832–1900)
Pablo (1833–79)
Matilde (1833–1907) = José Serrano González
Eloísa (d.1909) = Antonio Suárez Pizarro
Manuela (d. infant)
Candelaria (d. age 19)
María de la Paz (1841–1907) = José Padrón Arteaga
(Padrón Ruiz)
José (d. young)
Diego (d. young)
Enrique (d. young)
Mariquita (d.1967)
Antonio (d.1921)
Salvador (1884–1908) = *1. Concepción Marín Salamanca (d.1878)*
(2. Adelaida Martínez Loring)
(Ruiz Blasco y Marín)
Concha (b.1876)
María de la Paz (b.1878)
José (1838–1913) = *María (1855–1939)*
(Ruiz Picasso)
PABLO (1881–1973)
? José (1883–4/5)
Lola (1884–1958)
Conchita (1887–95)
Eladia (b.1861)
Eliodora (b.1863)
Aurelia = Baldomero Ghiara
daughter

Principal Sources

In the preparation of this volume I have drawn extensively on the memoirs of Picasso's friends of the period, particularly Jaime Sabartès (subsequently the artist's secretary), Fernande Olivier (his mistress from 1904 to 1911), and the writers Max Jacob, André Salmon and Gertrude Stein. Since their relationships to the artist and consequent bias are discussed in these pages, no introduction to them is needed here. However, there are a number of other writers —friends or associates of the artist at a much later date—whom we do not meet in this volume. As their names are often cited, a few explanatory notes are provided for readers who are not conversant with the Picasso literature.

The Catalan poet Josep Palau i Fabre, author of *Picasso: Life and Work of the Early Years 1881–1907*, was a late arrival in Picasso's life and never a very intimate friend. But his study, which covers more or less the same period as the present volume, is invaluable—the most detailed to have been devoted to any phase of the artist's life. Palau's vast corpus of plates and documentary material puts every student of Picasso in his debt.

Christian Zervos, whom Picasso had first met as a student newly arrived from Greece in the early years of the century, embarked on his great *catalogue raisonné* of Picasso's paintings and drawings in 1932. It extends to thirty-three volumes and covers the artist's entire career. Inevitably it is incomplete, and the dates are not always dependable. However, this catalogue is the foundation on which all writers on Picasso are obliged to build.

The first historian to classify and analyse the artist's work period by period was the American scholar and founder of the Museum of Modern Art, Alfred Barr. His methodology, with its preponderance of ideas inherited from Roger Fry, has been criticized by modern scholars for failing to take account of religion, mysticism or symbolism, let alone social history. Despite the justice of these reservations, the armature that Barr contrived holds up remarkably well.

Picasso's first full-length biographer, the English surrealist Roland Penrose, was a close friend of the artist from the summer of 1936, which he and his wife, the photographer Lee Miller, spent with Picasso and Dora Maar at Mougins. Penrose's *Picasso: His Life and Work* succeeds in charting the life as well as the art and seeing the one in terms of the other. The artist gave Penrose his fullest support, and the result is a book of incalculable value. My only reservation stems from Penrose's fear of causing Picasso offence. For better or worse his portrait of the artist is without shadows.

The task of subsequent biographers has been greatly facilitated by the pioneer studies of Barr and Penrose. Because Antonina Vallentin did not attempt to ask awkward questions or dig in forbidden areas, her *Picasso* met with the artist's complete approval. More informative are two posthumous biographies: Pierre Cabanne made a point of interviewing many of Picasso's closest friends and came up with much new French material. Patrick O'Brian has also written a biography aimed at the intelligent but unspecialized reader. O'Brian is an American living in Collioure: hence a certain bias in favour of Catalans and Catalonia, both French and Spanish.

Pierre Daix, who became a close friend of the artist after World War II, has written a succession of biographical studies (including *La Vie de peintre de Pablo Picasso* and *Picasso Créateur: La Vie intime et l'œuvre*), which set out to establish the facts of Picasso's life and work. He also compiled, with Georges Boudaille, the first *catalogue raisonné* of the Blue and Rose periods. Thanks to the full cooperation of the artist, Daix's accounts are by far the most accurate and up-to-date, and they avoid blind adherence to any particular methodology.

The Polish writer Hélène Parmelin and her husband, the painter Edouard Pignon, were close to Picasso from the early 1950s until the end of his life. Her books (including *Picasso Plain: An Intimate Portrait* and *Picasso Says*) brilliantly evoke the tenor of his personal life as well as the pace and rhythm of his work. Jacqueline Picasso maintained that Parmelin was the only writer to succeed in catching Picasso's idiosyncratic turn of phrase.

One of the most controversial contributions to Picasso literature is the book of memoirs, *Life with Picasso*, that the artist's erstwhile mistress Françoise Gilot brought out in 1964. As he had done in the early 1930s, when the first love of his life, Fernande Olivier, came out with an intimate memoir, *Picasso and His Friends*, the artist tried to have publication stopped. His failure to do so left him outraged and cast a shadow over the rest of his life. Picasso took issue with Gilot's overall story: young girl seduced, manipulated and betrayed by sadistic old Bluebeard, whom she leaves for a painter her own age. Not at all what happened, he said. He was the one who had been betrayed. With some justice Picasso also grumbled that too much jargon had been put into his mouth and that he sounded too pedagogical. Now that time has passed, it is possible to see that certain critics (myself included) were too censorious of the book. Gilot is invaluable when, instead of portraying the artist as a lecturer, she lets the quicksilver of his mind—the murderous quips, the baroque complaints, the insidious maxims—flow freely. For all that it focuses on a later period, Gilot's book is a valuable source of observations and anecdotes relating to the artist's earlier years.

During his liaison with Gilot (1943–53), Picasso carried on an affair with an even younger girl, Geneviève Laporte. She, too, has published a memoir: a far less ambitious one, entitled *Sunshine at Midnight* (recently revised and enlarged as *Un Amour secret de Picasso*), which shows Picasso as a lover—infinitely protective and beguiling—and includes many reminiscences of the artist's earlier years.

As for documentary sources, I am fortunate in having had permission to do extensive research in the vast archive at the Musée Picasso. Given the highly personal or confidential nature of much of this material, the artist's heirs, who retain ownership, have yet to declassify many of the documents: for instance, the hundreds of letters that the artist's parents (principally his mother) wrote to their son when he was away from Barcelona. Although most are said to be of minor interest, these cannot as yet be consulted. A pity—these letters would provide badly needed insights into the seemingly unclouded relationship between mother and son, as well as information about the basic dates and facts of Picasso's everyday life. Nor is it possible to consult the files of correspondence from Guillaume Apollinaire and Max Jacob.

These documents are being edited and published under the auspices of the museum. Despite these limitations, members of the museum staff have done everything in their power to further my project. They have provided me with an abundance of unpublished documents, photographs and other material. And when restrictions proved an obstacle, they found ways of answering my incessant questions, while respecting the letter of the law.

Two archives in Barcelona—especially important for the period covered by this volume—cannot as yet be consulted. The Vilatós, Picasso's sister's family, do not allow scholars to go through their family papers; however, my friend Javier Vilató has been generous with information. As for Sabartès's archive, we will have to wait until the year 2018 before we can peruse the documents that the artist's secretive secretary deposited in the Museu Picasso. According to Roberto Otero, Picasso was astonished by Sabartès's fifty-year embargo. 'Wasn't that a bit far-fetched?' Did his secretary want him 'to live another fifty years because of this secret bundle'?

These disadvantages were to some extent offset by the advantages of seeing Picasso regularly from the early 1950s until I moved from Provence to New York in the early 1960s. I had already envisaged writing a book about him, and so, whenever possible, I noted down his answers to my questions, as well as scraps of his conversation. Unless otherwise indicated, these jottings are the source of the artist's opinions quoted in the text. By luck rather than design, Douglas Cooper and I were present when the contents of Picasso's Paris studio were shipped to Cannes. His running comments as he went through portfolio after portfolio of his earlier work were the more revealing for being delivered in a spirit of total detachment. He seemed as awed as we were. After Picasso's death, I went on seeing his widow, Jacqueline, who continued to give me every assistance. Besides allowing me free run of the studios and storage area at Notre-Dame-de-Vie, she answered a barrage of questions and passed on many reminiscences that the artist had confided in her.

Most of the witnesses of the period covered by this first volume were dead by the time I started work on this project. And the few survivors of Els Quatre Gats whom I met—Sabartès, Pallarès and Vidal Ventosa—were not particularly forthcoming. However, I was fortunate in being able to obtain a great deal of firsthand information about the early years in Paris from D.-H. Kahnweiler, who was always ready to share his experiences with anyone who took a serious interest in 'his' artists. I was also fortunate in listening as Picasso discussed the past with Frank Burty Haviland and Alice B. Toklas, whom he had known since 1907. Last but not least, there was Douglas Cooper, to whom this volume is dedicated. After a feud that lasted twenty years or so, this difficult friend relented and put his phenomenal memory, library and archives once more at my disposal in the hope that I would produce the book that he had always aspired to write.

The ideal Picasso bibliography would run to many thousand items and require a publication to itself. Given lack of space, I have limited myself to listing the principal sources that have been consulted in the preparation of this volume.

Short Titles and Notes

Short titles of catalogues used to identify works by Picasso:

B.	Georges Bloch. *Pablo Picasso. Catalogue de l'œuvre gravé et lithographié.* 4 vols. Bern: Kornfeld & Klipstein, 1968–79.
Baer	Brigitte Baer. *Picasso Peintre-Graveur* (sequel to catalogues by Bernhard Geiser), 3 vols. (III–V). Bern: Kornfeld, 1986–89.
C.	Sébastien Goeppert, Herma Goeppert-Franck and Patrick Cramer. *Pablo Picasso, Catalogue raisonné des livres illustrés.* Geneva: Patrick Cramer, 1983.
D.	Pierre Daix and Georges Boudaille. *Picasso: The Blue and Rose Periods.* Greenwich, Conn.: New York Graphic Society, 1967.
G.	Bernhard G. Geiser. *Picasso: Peintre-Graveur*, 2 vols. Bern: Geiser, 1933; Kornfeld & Klipstein, 1968.
JSLC	Arnold Glimcher and Marc Glimcher, eds. *Je suis le cahier: The Sketchbooks of Picasso.* New York: The Pace Gallery, 1986.
MP	*Musée Picasso: Catalogue sommaire des collections.* 2 vols. Paris: Réunion des musées nationaux, 1985, 1987.
MPB	*Museu Picasso: Catàleg de pintura i dibuix.* Barcelona: Ajuntament de Barcelona, 1984.
PF	Josep Palau i Fabre. *Picasso: Life and Work of the Early Years 1881–1907.* Oxford: Phaidon, 1981.
S.	Werner Spies. *Picasso: Das plastische Werk.* Stuttgart: Gerd Hatje, 1983.
Z.	Christian Zervos. *Pablo Picasso.* 33 vols. Paris: Cahiers d'Art, 1932–78.

Short titles of principal sources cited in the notes:

Alberti 1983	Rafael Alberti. *Lo que canté y dije de Picasso.* Barcelona: Bruguera, 1983
Andreu	Pierre Andreu. *Vie et mort de Max Jacob.* Paris: La Table Ronde, 1982.
Ashton	Dore Ashton. *Picasso on Art: A Selection of Views.* New York: Viking, 1972.
Assouline	Pierre Assouline. *L'Homme de l'art: D.-H. Kahnweiler 1884–1979.* Paris: Balland, 1988.
Baer 1988	Brigitte Baer. 'Seven Years of Printmaking: The Theatre and Its Limits'. In *Late Picasso*, 95–135. London: Tate Gallery, 1988.
Barr 1939	Alfred H. Barr, Jr. *Picasso: Forty Years of His Art.* New York: The Museum of Modern Art, 1939.
Barr 1946	Alfred H. Barr, Jr. *Picasso: Fifty Years of His Art.* New York: The Museum of Modern Art, 1946.
Barr 1951	Alfred H. Barr, Jr. *Matisse: His Art and His Public.* New York: The Museum of Modern Art, 1951.

Beaumont	Keith Beaumont. *Alfred Jarry: A Critical and Biographical Study.* Leicester: Leicester University Press, 1984.
Benet	Rafael Benet. *El Escultor Manolo.* Barcelona: Argos, 1942.
Bernadac and Piot	Marie-Laure Bernadac and Christine Piot, eds. *Picasso: Ecrits.* Paris: Gallimard, 1989.
Blunt and Pool	Anthony Blunt and Phoebe Pool. *Picasso: The Formative Years.* London: Studio Books, 1962.
Brassaï	Brassaï. *Picasso and Company.* Trans. Francis Price. Garden City, N.Y.: Doubleday, 1966. Originally published as *Conversations avec Picasso.* Paris: Gallimard, 1964.
Brenan	Gerald Brenan. *The Face of Spain.* London: Penguin Books, 1987.
Breunig	LeRoy C. Breunig, ed. *Apollinaire on Art: Essays and Reviews 1902-1918.* Trans. Susan Suleiman. New York: Viking, 1972. Originally published as Guillaume Apollinaire. *Chroniques d'Art.* Paris: Gallimard, 1960.
Bugallal	José Luis Bugallal. *Cuatro retratos y cuatro retratistas de D. Ramon Pérez Costales.* La Coruña: Moret, 1956.
Burns	Edward Burns, ed. *Gertrude Stein on Picasso.* New York: Liveright, 1970.
Cabanne 1975	Pierre Cabanne. *Le Siècle de Picasso, 1: 1881–1937.* Paris: Denoël, 1975.
Cabanne 1977	Pierre Cabanne. *Pablo Picasso: His Life and Times.* Trans. (from Cabanne 1975) Harold J. Salemson. New York: Morrow, 1977.
Caizergues	Pierre Caizergues. *Apollinaire Journaliste—Textes retrouvés et textes inédits avec présentation et notes.* Thesis for University of Paris (May 1977), 3 vols. Lille, 1979.
Carnet Catalan	Douglas Cooper, ed. *Carnet Catalan.* Paris: Berggruen, 1958.
Cocteau	Jean Cocteau. *Le Passé défini.* 3 vols. Paris: Gallimard, 1985.
Crespelle 1967	Jean-Paul Crespelle. *Picasso and His Women.* Trans. Robert Baldick. London: Hodder and Stoughton, 1969. Originally published as *Picasso, les femmes, les amis, l'œuvre.* Paris: Presses de la Cité, 1967.
Crespelle 1978	Jean-Paul Crespelle. *La Vie quotidienne à Montmartre au temps de Picasso 1900–1910.* Paris: Hachette, 1978.
Daix 1977	Pierre Daix. *La Vie de peintre de Pablo Picasso.* Paris: Seuil, 1977.
Daix 1984	Pierre Daix. 'Picasso und Paris'. In *Der Junge Picasso*, 54–71. Bern: Kunstmuseum, 1984.
Daix 1987	Pierre Daix. *Picasso Créateur: La Vie intime et l'œuvre.* Paris: Seuil, 1987.
Daix and Boudaille	Pierre Daix and Georges Boudaille. *Picasso: The Blue and Rose Periods.* Trans. Phoebe Pool. Greenwich, Conn.: New York Graphic Society, 1967. Originally published as *Picasso 1900–1906.* Neuchâtel: Ides et Calendes, 1966.
Daix and Rosselet	Pierre Daix and Joan Rosselet. *Picasso: The Cubist Years 1907–1916.* Trans. Dorothy S. Blair. Boston: New York Graphic Society, 1979. Originally published as *Le Cubisme de Picasso. Catalogue raisonné de l'œuvre 1907–1916.* Neuchâtel: Ides et Calendes, 1979.
Dorgelès	Roland Dorgelès. *Bouquet de Bohème.* Paris: Albin Michel, 1947.
Flam	Jack D. Flam. *Matisse: The Man and His Art 1869–1918.* Ithaca: Cornell University Press, 1986.
Frèches-Thory	Claire Frèches-Thory, contributions to *The Art of Paul Gauguin.* Washington, D.C.: National Gallery of Art, 1988.
Frère	Henri Frère. *Conversations de Maillol.* Geneva: Pierre Cailler, 1956.
Gallup	Donald Gallup, ed. *Flowers of Friendship: Letters Written to Gertrude Stein.* New York: Knopf, 1953.
Gasman	Lydia Gasman. *Mystery, Magic and Lore in Picasso and the Surrealist Poets.* Ann Arbor: University Microfilms, 1981.
Gedo 1980	Mary Mathews Gedo. *Art as Autobiography.* Chicago: University of Chicago Press, 1980.

Gedo 1981 — Mary Mathews Gedo. 'The Archaeology of a Painting: A Visit to the City of the Dead Beneath Picasso's *La Vie*'. *Art News* (New York), Nov. 1981, 116–29.

Gilmore — David D. Gilmore. *Aggression and Community: Paradoxes of Andalusian Culture.* New Haven: Yale University Press, 1987.

Gilot — Françoise Gilot with Carlton Lake. *Life with Picasso.* New York: McGraw-Hill, 1964.

Giry — Marcel Giry. *Fauvism: Origins and Development.* Trans. Helga Harrison. New York: Alpine Fine Arts, 1982. Originally published as *Le Fauvisme: ses origines, son évolution.* Fribourg: Office du Livre, 1981.

Hobhouse — Janet Hobhouse. *Everybody Who Was Anybody.* New York: Putnam, 1975.

Huelin — Ricardo Huelin y Ruiz-Blasco. *Pablo Ruiz Picasso.* Madrid: Biblioteca de la Revista de Occidente, 1975.

Jacob — Max Jacob. 'Souvenirs sur Picasso contés par Max Jacob'. *Cahiers d'Art* (Paris) 6 (1927), 199–203.

Johnson 1984 — Ron Johnson. 'Picasso und die 98er Generation—"Arte Joven"'. In *Der Junge Picasso*, 156–65. Bern: Kunstmuseum, 1984.

Johnson 1988 — Ron Johnson. 'Picasso and the Poets'. Unpublished manuscript [1988].

Kahnweiler 1961 — Daniel-Henry Kahnweiler. *Mes Galeries et mes peintres: Entretiens avec Francis Crémieux.* Paris: Gallimard, 1961.

Langner — Johannes Langner. 'Der Sturz des Ikarus'. *Picasso: Todesthemen*, 121–36. Bielefeld: Kunsthalle, 1984.

Laporte 1989 — Geneviève Laporte. *Un Amour secret de Picasso.* Monaco: Editions du Rocher, 1989.

Leighten — Patricia Dee Leighten. *Re-Ordering the Universe: Picasso and Anarchism, 1897–1914.* Princeton: Princeton University Press, 1989.

Leiris — Michel Leiris. *L'Age de l'homme.* Trans. Richard Howard as *Manhood.* San Francisco: North Point Press, 1984. Originally published, Paris: Gallimard, 1946.

Leja — Michael Leja. '*Le Vieux Marcheur* and *Les Deux Risques*'. *Art History* (Norwich), 8:1 (Mar. 1985), 66–81.

Lorca — Federico García Lorca. *Poet in New York.* Trans. Ben Belitt. New York: Grove Press, 1977.

McCully 1978 — Marilyn McCully. *Els Quatre Gats: Art in Barcelona Around 1900.* Princeton: The Art Gallery, 1978.

McCully 1981 — Marilyn McCully, ed. *A Picasso Anthology.* London: Arts Council of Great Britain, 1981.

McCully 1984 — Marilyn McCully. 'Picasso und Casagemas. Eine Frage von Leben und Tod'. In *Der Junge Picasso*, 166–76. Bern: Kunstmuseum, 1984.

Malraux — André Malraux. *Picasso's Mask.* Trans. June and Jacques Guicharnaud. New York: Holt, Rinehart and Winston, 1976. Originally published as *La Tête d'obsidienne.* Paris: Gallimard, 1974.

Mayer — Susan Mayer. *Ancient Mediterranean Sources in the Works of Picasso, 1892–1937.* Ann Arbor: University Microfilms, 1980.

Mellow — James R. Mellow. *A Charmed Circle: Gertrude Stein and Company.* New York: Praeger, 1974.

O'Brian — Patrick O'Brian. *Pablo Ruiz Picasso.* New York: Putnam, 1976.

Olano 1982 — Antonio D. Olano. Interview with Picasso, quoted in Antonio L. Marino, 'Los cuatro años de Picasso en La Coruña'. In *Picasso e a Coruña*, 1–15. La Coruña: Gráficas Coruñesas, 1982.

Olivier 1933 — Fernande Olivier. *Picasso and His Friends.* Trans. Jane Miller. New York: Appleton-Century, 1965. Originally published as *Picasso et ses amis.* Paris: Stock, 1933.

Olivier 1988 — Fernande Olivier. *Souvenirs intimes.* Ed. Gilbert Krill. Paris: Calmann-Lévy, 1988.

Otero	Roberto Otero. *Forever Picasso.* Trans. Elaine Kerrigan. New York: Abrams, 1974.
Painter	George Painter. *Marcel Proust.* 2 vols. London: Chatto and Windus, 1961, 1965.
Palau	Josep Palau i Fabre. *Picasso: Life and Work of the Early Years 1881–1907.* Trans. Kenneth Lyons. Oxford: Phaidon, 1981. Originally published as *Picasso Vivent 1881–1907.* Barcelona: Polígrafa, 1980.
Parmelin 1959	Hélène Parmelin. *Picasso Plain: An Intimate Portrait.* Trans. Humphrey Hare. London: Secker and Warburg, 1963. Originally published as *Picasso sur la place.* Paris: Juillard, 1959.
Parmelin 1966	Hélène Parmelin. *Picasso Says.* Trans. Christine Trollope. London: Allen and Unwin, 1969. Originally published as *Picasso dit . . .* Paris: Gonthier, 1966.
Pazos Bernal 1981	María de los Angeles Pazos Bernal. 'En el umbral de Picasso: José Ruiz Blasco'. In *Picasso y Málaga*, 5–35. Madrid: Ministerio de Cultura, 1981.
Pazos Bernal 1987	María de los Angeles Pazos Bernal. *La Academia de Bellas Artes de Málaga en el siglo XIX.* Málaga: Bobastro, 1987.
Penrose 1958	Roland Penrose. *Picasso: His Life and Work.* London: Granada, 1981. Originally published London: Gollancz, 1958.
Pincus-Witten	Robert Pincus-Witten. *Occult Symbolism in France.* Ann Arbor: University Microfilms, 1968.
Pla	Josep Pla. *Vida de Manolo.* Barcelona: Llibrería Catalonia, 1930.
Podoksik 1984	Anatoli Podoksik. 'Die Entstehung der blauen Periode Picassos und das Pariser Gefängnis von St. Lazare'. In *Der Junge Picasso*, 177–93. Bern: Kunstmuseum, 1984.
Podoksik 1989	Anatoli Podoksik. *Picasso: La Quête perpétuelle.* Paris: Cercle d'Art, 1989. Originally published as *Picasso: Vechnyi Poisk.* Leningrad: Aurora, 1989.
Pool	Phoebe Pool. 'Picasso's Neo-Classicism: First Period, 1905–6'. *Apollo* (London) 81 (Feb. 1965), 122–7.
Purrmann	Barbara and Erhard Göpel, eds. *Leben und Meinungen des Malers Hans Purrmann.* Wiesbaden: Limes Verlag, 1961.
Reff 1971	Theodore Reff. 'Harlequins, Saltimbanques, Clowns and Fools'. *Artforum* (New York), Oct. 1971, 30–43.
Reff 1980	Theodore Reff. 'Themes of Love and Death in Picasso's Early Work'. In Roland Penrose and John Golding, eds. *Picasso in Retrospect*, 5–30. New York: Harper and Row, 1980.
Reventós	Jacint Reventós. *Picasso i els Reventós.* Barcelona: Gili, 1973.
Rubin 1972	William Rubin. *Picasso in the Collection of The Museum of Modern Art.* New York: The Museum of Modern Art, 1972.
Rubin 1984	William Rubin. 'Picasso'. In *'Primitivism' in Twentieth-Century Art*, 1:240–343. New York: The Museum of Modern Art, 1984.
Rubin 1988	William Rubin. 'La Genèse des Demoiselles d'Avignon'. In *Les Demoiselles d'Avignon*, 2:367–487. Paris: Musée Picasso, 1988.
Rusiñol	Santiago Rusiñol. *Obres completes.* Barcelona: Editorial Selecta, 1956.
Sabartès 1946	Jaime Sabartès. *Picasso: An Intimate Portrait.* London: W. H. Allen, 1949. Originally published as *Picasso: Portraits et souvenirs.* Paris: Louis Carré et Maximilien Vox, 1946.
Sabartès 1954	Jaime Sabartès. *Picasso: Documents Iconographiques.* Geneva: Pierre Cailler, 1954.
Salmon 1919	André Salmon. *Le Manuscrit trouvé dans un chapeau.* Paris: Fata Morgana, 1983. Originally published Paris: Société Littéraire de France, 1919.
Salmon 1955	André Salmon. *Souvenirs sans fin: Première époque (1903–1908).* Paris: Gallimard, 1955.
Salmon 1956	André Salmon. *Souvenirs sans fin: Deuxième époque (1908–1920).* Paris: Gallimard, 1956.

Schapiro	Meyer Schapiro. *Modern Art.* New York: Braziller, 1978.
Schiff	Gert Schiff. 'The Musketeer and His Theatrum Mundi'. In *Picasso: The Last Years, 1963–1973.* New York: Solomon R. Guggenheim Museum, 1983.
Schneider	Pierre Schneider. *Matisse.* Trans. Michael Taylor and Bridget Stevens Romer. London: Thames and Hudson, 1984. Originally published as *Matisse.* Paris: Flammarion, 1984.
Shattuck 1968	Roger Shattuck. *The Banquet Years.* New York: Vintage Books, 1968.
Silverman	Debora L. Silverman. *Art Nouveau in Fin-de-Siècle France.* Berkeley: University of California Press, 1989.
Spies	Werner Spies. *Picasso: Das plastische Werk.* Stuttgart: Gerd Hatje, 1983.
Stassinopoulos Huffington	Arianna Stassinopoulos Huffington. *Picasso: Creator and Destroyer.* New York: Simon and Schuster, 1988.
Steegmuller	Francis Steegmuller. *Apollinaire Among the Painters.* New York: Penguin Books, 1986. Originally published New York: Farrar, Straus and Giroux, 1963.
Stein 1933	Gertrude Stein. *The Autobiography of Alice B. Toklas.* New York: Vintage Books, 1961. Originally published New York: Harcourt, Brace, 1933.
Stein 1938	Gertrude Stein. *Picasso.* Boston: Beacon Press, 1959. Originally published in French, Paris: Floury, 1938.
Leo Stein	Leo Stein. *Appreciation: Painting, Poetry and Prose.* New York: Crown, 1947.
Steinberg	Leo Steinberg, 'Le Bordel philosophique'. In *Les Demoiselles d'Avignon,* 2:319–65. Paris: Musée Picasso, 1988. Revised version of 'The Philosophical Brothel', *Art News* (New York) 71:5 (Sept. 1972), 20–9, 71:6 (Oct. 1972), 38–47.
Sucre	José María de Sucre, *Memorias, I.* Barcelona: Editorial Barna, 1963.
Uhde	Wilhelm Uhde. *Picasso and the French Tradition.* Trans. F. M. Loving. New York: Weyhe, 1929. Originally published as *Picasso et la tradition française.* Paris: Editions des Quatre Chemins, 1928.
Valk	Gerrit Valk. 'Le Séjour de Picasso aux Pays-Bas en 1905'. Unpublished article [1990], 1–29.
Vallentin	Antonina Vallentin. *Picasso.* Garden City, N.Y.: Doubleday, 1963. Originally published as *Pablo Picasso.* Paris: Albin Michel, 1957.
Vollard	Ambroise Vollard. *Recollections of a Picture Dealer.* Trans. Violet M. Macdonald. Boston: Little, Brown, 1936.
Warnod	Jeanine Warnod. *Le Bateau Lavoir.* Paris: Mayer, 1986.
Weill	Berthe Weill. *Pan! Dans l'Œil: Ou trente ans dans les coulisses de la peinture contemporaine 1900-1930.* Paris: Librairie Lipschutz, 1933.

INTRODUCTION pp.3–11

1 Cocteau, 2:263.

2 Luis Miguel Dominguín, *Picasso: Toros y Toreros*. Trans. Edouard Roditi (New York, Alpine Fine Arts Collection, 1980), 12.

3 Alberti 1983.

4 Rafael Alberti. *A Year of Paintings: 1969*. Trans. Anthony Kerrigan (New York, Abrams, 1971), 72.

5 Alberti 1983, 105.

6 Gilmore, 161.

7 Ibid., 153.

8 Ibid., 156, 161.

9 Ibid., 161.

10 Góngora, quoted in Alberti 1983, 161.

11 Confirmed by Françoise Gilot to the author.

1 MÁLAGA pp.13–23

1 Recounted by Rosario Camacho Martínez, 'Pablo Picasso y Juan Temboury', in *Picasso y Málaga*, 129–37 (Madrid: Ministerio de Cultura, 1981); the postcard is reproduced as fig.3, p.135.

2 Archives, Ayuntamiento de Málaga.

3 O'Brian, 452. Although he later gave the bulk of his art collection to Barcelona, in 1953 Sabartès donated his personal collection of books and journals devoted to Picasso to the Museo de Bellas Artes de Málaga; see José Salinero Portero, *Libros sobre Picasso en el Museo de Málaga* (Madrid: Ministerio de Cultura, 1981).

4 The extent of permanent damage that phylloxera caused local winegrowers can be gauged from the fact that in 1878 vineyards in the province of Málaga covered 112,000 hectares; by 1900 only 25,000 were still under cultivation.

5 Sabartès 1954, 21–2.

6 Ibid., 294.

7 On May 24, 1849, don Diego sent a request to the director of the Instituto de Enseñanza asking that Pablo and José be admitted to the free drawing classes, as he could not afford a private teacher; see Pazos Bernal 1981, 12.

8 Sabartès 1954, 298.

9 According to Pazos Bernal, adults were given preference over children for entrance. The number of pupils increased dramatically from just over 300 at the end of 1851 to 1200 by the end of 1880; see A. Galbien, *Breve reseña del origen de la Escuela de Bellas Artes de Málaga* (Málaga, 1886), cited in Pazos Bernal 1987, 98, n.129.

10 The best source of information on the 'School of Málaga' is Teresa Sauret, *El siglo XIX en la pintura malagueña* (Málaga: Universidad de Málaga, 1987).

11 Brenan, 86.

12 Sabartès 1954, 24.

13 Reported by don José's grandson Javier Vilató to the author.

14 Manuel Blasco in conversation with Marilyn McCully.

15 Palau, 22.

16 After studying medicine in Granada, Salvador had stayed on as assistant lecturer at the faculty of medicine, in order to go on seeing his fiancée, Concepción Marín, the daughter of a local sculptor. However, teachers were so poorly paid that Salvador returned to Málaga in 1869, leaving Concepción behind. Seven years later, he went back to Granada and married her. In the meantime he had built up a large private practice; he was also principal medical officer of the port, local health inspector and co-founder of the Málaga vaccination centre.

17 Born a Heredia (the Heredias owned most of the Andalusian ironworks), doña Amalia had married into the Lorings, a Massachusetts family that had settled in Málaga around 1800 and done so well that the head of the clan, her husband, Jorge, had been created a *marqués* in 1865. Doña Amalia was all the more respected for being related to the powerful Francisco Silveta, subsequently prime minister of Spain.

18 In 1878 the Ayuntamiento de Málaga bought don José's *Palomar* for 1500 pesetas to celebrate the wedding of King Alfonso XII to his cousin Princess María de las Mercedes.

19 Pazos Bernal 1981, 34, n.33.

20 María de los Angeles Pazos Bernal and María Pilar Pérez-Muñoz Sanz, 'Hacia la línea Picasso: José Ruiz Blasco', *Boletín del Museo Diocesano de Arte Sacro* (Málaga), 1 (1980): 216.

21 The witnesses were Serafín Martínez del Rincón (the painter for whom José first worked at the Escuela) and Mariano Palomares y Castillo (listed as an unmarried businessman).

22 A Genoese portrait painter—also said (Sabartès 1954, 291–3) to have been a 'ship-builder'—named Matteo Picasso (1794–1879) may conceivably have been a relative of Picasso's great-grandfather Tomás Picasso Musante. Both men are recorded as born in a small village near Recco. Picasso believed in this connection to the extent of acquiring a small portrait of a man by his supposed kinsman. It is of little distinction; reproduced in Sabartès 1954, pl.2.

23 The Marranos were Jews forcibly converted under the Inquisition who practiced their faith in secret.

24 Palau, 18.

25 According to Javier Vilató.

2 PABLO RUIZ PICASSO, SON AND HEIR pp.25–35

1 Bernhard Geiser was tutor to Picasso's son Paulo, also the author of the first catalogue of the artist's engraved work.

2 Vallentin, 1.

3 Penrose 1958, 10.

4 This handsome square is named after General Riego, the liberal hero who briefly overturned the autocratic government of Ferdinand VII in 1820. He was executed in 1823. In the centre of the square stands an obelisk to the memory of General Torrijos, another liberal, who led an uprising against Ferdinand in 1831, only to be betrayed by the treacherous governor of Málaga and shot with forty-nine of his followers on the seashore. At the time of Picasso's birth, the square had two names: Plaza de Riego for civil affairs; Plaza de la Merced—after the church on one corner of the square—for ecclesiastical affairs.

5 Sabartès 1946, 26.

6 Picasso's father, don José, his aunts Josefa and Matilde and a servant called Antonia Martín Meléndez (who was succeeded sometime in 1881 by Màriana Montañés) were listed in the 1880 census as residents of a second-floor apartment at 36 Plaza de Riego, a corner building. The house was part of a larger block known as Casas Campos: a recent development built by a local nobleman, don Antonio Campos Garín, Marqués de Iznate, on the site of the former convent of Santa María de la Paz. The 1884 census indicates that in the course of the previous year the Ruiz Blascos had moved several doors down to an apartment on the third floor of 32 Plaza de la Merced (i.e., Plaza de Riego), facing directly onto the square.

The confusion about the birthplace originates with Palau (p.17), who took Sabartès's claim 'We know that Picasso was born in a room on a street close to the Calle Merced' (Sabartès 1954, 26) to mean that he had been born on a street other than the Plaza de la Merced. Unaware of the census records, Palau cites the commercial registry of 1882 that lists José residing on Calle Sucia (now Hinestrosa). This registry was years out of date: 15 Calle Sucia was where José had lived with his father, brother (Pablo) and sisters (Josefa, Matilde and Eloísa) up to his father's death in 1876. For the next four years José had lived in Canon Pablo's house at 8 Calle Granada.

Manuel Blasco, Picasso's cousin, has yet another theory. He told McCully that since his mother was Picasso's wet-nurse (doña María being too weak to suckle her own baby), it would have been more practical and in line with don José's social aspirations if the family had arranged for the birth to take place in the Blascos' large and comfortable house ('*una casa rica*') around the corner from the Plaza de la Merced on Calle Tejón y Rodríguez. Given that the entry in the 1880 census substantiates Picasso's assertion that he was born in the Casas Campos on the Plaza de la Merced, Blasco's theory can be dismissed.

7 Palau, 32.

8 Gilmore, 145.

9 See Rafael León, 'Papeles sobre Picasso', *Boletín de Información Municipal* (Málaga) 13 (1971), 8. Several details, including the ages of don José and doña María and the parish of Pablo's baptism (given as the church of La Merced instead of Santiago), are incorrect in the census, but a non-existent child is unlikely to have been entered.

At our request Javier Ordóñez Vergara has kindly undertaken further research in the Archivo Municipal de Málaga. The census records for 1884, 1885, 1886 and 1887 give conflicting information about ages of various family members, and the name of José (age 1) appears only in the record for 1885 (vol. 669, fol. 289v). No mention of the child's birth appears in the baptismal records for the church of Santiago. In view of the error about the church where Pablo was baptized, it is possible that José's baptism took place in the church of La Merced—but the relevant records were destroyed by fire in 1933. The name of José Ruiz Picasso is not listed in municipal records of deaths in 1885, 1886 and 1887, but Ordóñez suggests that the child could have died in another city or that his death may have been omitted by clerical error.

10 Penrose 1958, 13.

11 Brenan, 7–8.

12 Ibid.

13 Sabartès 1946, 6.

14 Ibid., 5.

15 In her 'psychobiography', Gedo 1980 (p.11) claims that the double trauma of the earthquake and the birth of a sibling left the artist's psyche permanently scarred. Alice Miller, *The Untouched Key* (New York: Doubleday, 1990), 3–18, goes even further; basing herself on Gedo's thesis, she maintains that this combination of events provides a more plausible explanation for Picasso's *Guernica* than the bombing attack by Spanish planes. Picasso, who remembered the earthquake as an exciting adventure and always had the easiest relationship with his sister, would have been much amused by this theory.

16 Huelin, 191.

17 Parmelin 1966, 73.

18 Laporte 1989 (p.31) recalls (late 1940s) that there were only two works hanging in Picasso's rue des Grands-Augustins bedroom: a Corot and a very small watercolour of a cock in a farmyard that he said he had done at the age of seven. I have been unable to trace it.

19 Otero, 43–4.

20 Parmelin 1966, 80.

21 Sabartès 1954, 305.

22 Ibid.

23 Gilot, quoted in Gedo 1980, 16.

24 Sabartès 1946, 31.

25 Palau, 31.

26 Sabartès 1946, 35.

27 Ibid., 36–7.

28 Isabel Rodríguez Alemán, 'El Examen de Ingreso de Picasso', *Jábega* (Málaga) 21 (Primer Trimestre, 1978), 9.

29 Sabartès 1946, 39.

30 Ramon A. Urbano and José Duarte, *Guía de Málaga* (Málaga, 1888).

31 Olano 1982, 3. Antonio Olano, a Galician journalist, interviewed Picasso in the 1950s.

32 Daix 1977, 16.

3 CORUNNA pp.37–55

1 Olano 1982, 5.

2 Pérez Costales was also the model for Dr Moragas in the Galician writer Emilia Pardo Bazán's novel *La piedra angular* (1891).

3 Olano 1982, 6.

4 Picasso doubted this story: 'Perhaps I may have done it once', he said. Palau, 56.

5 Modesto Castillo (or Castilla) was a journalist who wrote an account of his father's courageous and effective resistance to centralist authority in 1893: *Historia de La Junta de Defensa de Galicia* (La Coruña, 1894).

6 Over sixty years later the Pérez Costales family was still fresh in Picasso's memory, to judge by the following two lines from his 'play' *El Entierro del conde de Orgaz*: 'Hanging from two hooks in the ceiling a ham and sausages / Modesto Castilla natural son of D. Ramon Pérez Costales'. Facsimile in Bernadac and Piot, 355 (Aug. 14, 1957).

7 Sabartès 1946, 9.

8 Antonio Olano, 'Picasso en Riazor', article published in La Coruña in 1981, 2.

9 Olano 1982, 4.

10 Bernadac and Piot, 9 (Apr. 18, 1935).

11 Reported by Jacqueline Picasso to the author.

12 Otero, 160.

13 See Gasman, passim.

14 Olano 1982, 7.

15 Palau, 43.

16 MPB 112.057–112.090.

17 Palau, 43.

18 Brassaï, 86.

19 Vallentin, 5.

20 Olano 1982, 7.

21 Ibid., 8.

22 Palau, 48.

23 Olano 1982, 6–7.

24 Caizergues, 598. The interview probably dates from around 1910–11. The manuscript is preserved in the Bibliothèque Doucet (ms. 7540). Apollinaire may have had a hand in rephrasing the artist's words:

'The first thing I ever did was to draw, like most other kids, only I went on with it.

'The first paintings I ever sold were to a convent in Barcelona. I was fifteen years old when I did them, and it was a terrible blow to discover they had been burned during the troubles in Barcelona in 1909. The nuns commissioned me to copy two altarpieces by Murillo; the idea bored me, so I copied them up to a point, then rearranged things according to my own ideas. Considering my age, I must admit to feeling very satisfied.

'As for my purest emotional experience, this occurred at the age of sixteen, when I went off to the wilds of Spain [Horta] in order to paint.

'My greatest artistic revelation came about when I was suddenly struck by the sublime beauty of the sculpture done by the anonymous artists of Africa. In their passionate and rigorous logic, these works of sacred art are the most powerful and beautiful products of the human imagination.

'At the same time, I would hasten to add that I loathe exoticism. I have never liked Chinese, Japanese or Persian art.

'What touches me in the art of antiquity is the sheer beauty of its restraint, but I must confess to disappointment at the way the proportions of Greek sculpture are dislocated by rhythms that are all too mechanical.

'An artist worthy of the name should endow the objects he wants to reproduce with maximum plasticity. Take the representation of an apple: if one draws a circle one registers the basic form of the object. Should the artist want to endow his image with a greater degree of plasticity, the object in question may well end by taking the form of a square or a cube. These forms will not negate the object in the very least.

'These truths have been common knowledge to most great painters, and proof of my contentions can be found in any number of famous works.

'The point of art is not to represent an object according to perspectival conventions. There are an object's actual measurements to consider, the position it occupies, and much else besides.

'Above all else I love light.

'Colours are only symbols, and reality can exist only if there is light.

'I believe in nothing but work. You cannot have art without hard work: manual as well as cerebral dexterity.'

25 Olano 1982, 7.

26 Palau, 75.

27 Gilot told this story to Stassinopoulos Huffington (p. 30).

28 Pérez Costales recorded the tragedy in an article concerning the diphtheria serum in *La Voz de Galicia* (La Coruña), Mar. 12, 1895.

29 According to Gilot, reported by Gedo 1980 (p. 16).

30 Langner (p. 130) also discusses the parallel with Gauguin.

31 The death of Conchita was first reported in *La Voz de Galicia* (La Coruña) on Jan. 12, 1895 (with the date of death given incorrectly as Jan. 11); in the Civil Registry (Municipal No. 1, Death Records, vol. 51, fol. 37), details are given of Concepción Ruiz Picasso's death at 5:00 P.M., Jan. 10, at her family's home, 14 Calle Payo Gómez. This document is reproduced in Bugallal, App. 2.

32 Sabartès 1954, 38.

33 Penrose 1958, 20.

34 Sucre, 13.

35 Cabanne 1977, 33.

36 Ibid.

37 Daniel-Henry Kahnweiler, Introduction to *Picasso: Dessins 1903–1907* (Paris: Galerie Berggruen, May–June 1954), 1.

38 Caizergues, 598.

39 Kahnweiler, interview with Picasso Nov. 5, 1944; trans. in Ashton, 167.

40 Penrose 1958, 369.

41 Daniel-Henry Kahnweiler. 'Huit entretiens avec Picasso', *Le Point* (Souillac) 7:42 (Oct. 1952), 30.

42 Olano 1982, 6.

43 The Feb. 21, 1895, review was reprinted in *La Voz de Galicia* (La Coruña), Feb. 21, 1985.

44 Luís Caparrós, 'De cuando Picasso vivió en La Coruña', *La Voz de Galicia* (La Coruña), Dec. 4, 1949.

45 Palau, 68.

46 MPB 110.367R.

4 THE MOVE TO BARCELONA pp. 57–69

1 Bernadac and Piot, 89 (Jan. 12, 1936).

2 The undated oil sketch of a landscape (Z.XXI.50) that Palau (p. 520) credits Pablo with painting 'near Madrid' on the day of this rushed visit must surely have been done at another time and another place.

3 Penrose 1958, 24.

4 Sabartès 1954, 295.

5 Otero, 116.

6 Z.XVII.108. This story is recounted in John Richardson (ed.), 'Cordier-Warren Gallery: The Fifties', *Picasso: An American Tribute* (New York: Public Education Association, 1962), [136], pl. 23.

7 Palau, 76.

8 Ibid., 73.

9 Manuel Blasco Alarcón, *Picasso insólito* (Madrid: GEASA, 1981), 121.

10 Palau (p. 78) reports that Picasso's nephews always maintained that it was a dilapidated old boarding-house (3 Carrer Cristina) near the harbour; Sabartès 1946 (p. 9) says a gloomy apartment in the Porxos d'en Xifré, where don José had lodged when he came on his first visit earlier in the year.

11 In 1954 Sabartès told Bugallal (p. 20) that 'Picasso remembers having seen paintings of horses by don Román in the apartment on Carrer Llauder in Barcelona, the apartment given over to don José by don Román. The proprietor of the building owned works by the Corunna master.'

12 The development, known as the *Eixample*, was based on the master plan published by Ildefons Cerdà as early as 1859.

13 The minutes of this meeting are published in Palau, 82.

14 Penrose 1958, 32.

15 Ibid., 33.

16 Ibid.

17 The letter, dated Oct. 5, 1895, is reproduced in Palau, 88.

18 Cabanne 1977, 33.

19 Laporte 1989, 189.

20 Pallarès dictated his memoirs to Palau in 1966. Palau told McCully that when he showed the typescript to Picasso later that year, Picasso exclaimed: 'What a memory Pallarès has! Every detail, except one minor reference to some Germans living in Horta de Ebro, is correct.' Palau draws on these memoirs, but they have never been published in full, nor has the manuscript been made available to scholars.

21 Vallentin, 21.

22 Palau, 137.

5 SACRED SUBJECTS pp.71–87

1 Penrose 1958, 373.

2 Penrose (p.35) suggests that this might have been inspired by *Acolytes' Pranks* by Rafael Murillo Carreras, who had succeeded don José as director of the museum in Málaga. However, the subject of acolytes was widely popular among Spanish painters in the later nineteenth century; see Sauret, op.cit. (chap.1, n.10).

3 Picasso's second cousin Ricardo Huelin confirms that, according to family tradition, the painting was called *La Primera Comunión de Lola*. Huelin, 185.

4 Apropos the small painting of the *Holy Family's Rest on the Flight into Egypt* done shortly after the Ruiz Blascos' arrival in Barcelona, Gedo 1980 (p.9) has pointed out that the head of the Christ child blots out the face of his mother as he reaches across her to embrace his father, who crouches at his feet. Whether conscious or not, this solecism and the choice of subject fit too neatly into the Ruiz family story to be entirely coincidental.

5 In *Picasso i Barcelona* (Barcelona: Ajuntament de Barcelona, 1981), 68, Joan Ainaud de Lasarte mentions in passing that Picasso did preparatory drawings for a Sacred Heart composition—probably the one Kahnweiler reported as having burned during the Setmana Tràgica in 1909. That this was Picasso's first commission has not hitherto been noted.

6 Caizergues, 598.

7 MPB 111.211.

8 MPB 110.644.

9 John Elliott, 'Art and Decline in Seventeenth-Century Spain', *Bartolomé Esteban Murillo* (London: Royal Academy of Arts, 1982), 45.

10 Leiris, 138.

11 Lorca, 163.

12 Z.XVII.333–59 etc. (Mar.2–3, 1959).

13 The School of Olot had been founded by Joaquim Vayreda, an artist who had gone to France in the 1870s and studied the Barbizon painters. On returning to Spain, Vayreda had established himself and his followers at Olot in the mountains of Catalonia and preached a gospel of spiritual naturalism ('the painter's mission was to impart his own state of mind and soul to the natural spectacle he recorded').

14 Caizergues, 598.

15 Penrose 1958, 33.

16 MPB 111.453R, 111.475R etc.

17 Fortuny's *The Battle of Tetuan* would later become the object of a cult on the part of Salvador Dalí.

18 Palau, 120.

19 Luís Jiménez Aranda's *A Hospital Ward During the Doctor's Visit*, which won a prize at the Paris World's Fair in 1889; the Catalan religious painter Joan Llimona's *Last Rites* (1894); or Enrique Paternina's *The Mother's Visit* (1896), which (like *First Communion*) had been exhibited earlier the same year at the Exposición de Bellas Artes and illustrated in the catalogue. Similar subjects were also popular outside Spain; the English painters Herbert von Herkomer and Luke Fildes, for example, have been cited in this context. See Michael Harmer, Letter to the Editor, *Medical Defence Union* (London) 1:2 (Summer 1985), 23.

20 Don José resembled Degas to the extent that some of Picasso's biographers (e.g., Cabanne 1977, 556) have mistaken the frock-coated figure of don José in the late engravings for the French artist.

21 Brassaï, 56.

22 MPB 110.344, with the following annotations: '*Bendito sea tu cuerpo Lola / Lola Ruiz Picasso / . . . Lola Ruiz Picasso / familia Juan Vilató . . . Juanvi / Juanv / Lola / Juan Vil / Juanvilató*' (Blessed be your body Lola / Lola Ruiz Picasso / etc.).

23 Although he was in Spain at the time, Picasso did not attend his sister's wedding in 1909. The journey from Horta to Málaga would have been very arduous and taken several days.

24 Brassaï, 117.

25 André Verdet, prefatory text to *Picasso* (Geneva: Musée de l'Athénée, 1963); trans. in Ashton, 96.

26 According to Sabartès (Sabartès 1946, 49), the baptism took place at the Círculo del Liceo. Picasso remembered it happening at the Círculo Mercantil de Málaga. Otero, 191.

27 Ninety years later there would be another connection between the two families, when Dr Salvador's great-niece, Paloma Picasso, would win fame as a jewellery designer in New York, thanks to the sponsorship of John Loring, a director of Tiffany's, who descends from a collateral branch of the same family.

28 *Science and Charity* and the study for the altar boy in *First Communion* continued to hang in the house on the Alameda until 1918, when Dr Salvador's widow sent them to Picasso's sister, Lola Vilató, in Barcelona. Any other memorabilia were destroyed when the Málaga house burned down in 1936.

29 Huelin, 185.

30 Sabartès 1946, 40.

31 Huelin, 191.

32 Ibid., 189

6 MADRID 1897–98 pp.89–97

1 Palau, 133.

2 O'Brian, 54.

3 Penrose 1958, 39.

4 First published in Xavier de Salas, 'Some Notes on a Letter', *Burlington Magazine* (London), Nov. 1960, 482–4. After the words 'kisses to', the letter ends with a rebus: a hand holding a rose and a gold coin with a girl's profile on it—a reference to Rosita del Oro, the equestrienne he had left behind in Barcelona.

5 Munich would also be a lure for that other Spanish cubist, Juan Gris, younger than Picasso by a year, whose formative work in Madrid was heavily influenced by the *Jugendstil* illustrator Willy Geiger.

6 Palau, 137.

7 See Baer 1988, 110–12, for this interpretation.

8 Sabartès 1946, 41.

9 Ibid., 42.

10 Palau, 140.

11 Rafael Alberti, quoted in Otero, 116.

12 Sabartès 1946, 41.

13 Diego Pro, *Conversaciones con Bernareggi* (Tucumán, 1949), 21.

14 Ibid., 218.

15 Stassinopoulos Huffington's suggestion (p.41) that this might have been pleurisy or syphilis is without foundation.

16 Between them, Palau and Picasso have caused confusion as to dates (see Palau, 141). The drawing of Lola (dated May 1898) was surely done at the same time as the one of Picasso's room. This would fit with the artist's claim (Penrose 1958, 42) to have been in Madrid on June 12.

17 Lola's son Javier Vilató, in conversation with the author, said that there is no record of his mother going alone to Madrid, nor any likelihood of a girl of the bourgeoisie being allowed to make such a journey. But how else can we account for the date on this drawing, which was evidently done from life? Doña María may well have accompanied Lola.

18 Penrose 1958, 42.

7 HORTA DE EBRO pp.99–107

1 David Douglas Duncan, *The Private World of Pablo Picasso* (New York: Ridge Press, 1958), 122–3.

2 The village had always been known as Horta, but Pallarès added 'de Ebro' because of the proximity of the Ebro river; also to distinguish it from another village called Horta, near Barcelona. After 1910 the mayor officially changed the name of the village to Horta de Sant Joan, after its patron saint, but art historians still refer to the place as Horta de Ebro.

3 Sabartès 1946, 42–3.

4 Cabanne 1975, 50.

5 Confirmed by McCully, who had the greatest difficulty following in the footsteps of Picasso and Pallarès. The mule was presumably left behind at a certain point.

6 The mule boy who allowed the dog to devour dinner has been misrepresented by Stassinopoulos Huffington (pp.41–2). On no evidence whatsoever, she accuses Picasso of having 'a burning friendship' that burgeoned into a passionate love affair, 'physically as well as metaphorically true', with this child. Stassinopoulos Huffington claims he was a gypsy 'two years younger than Picasso and . . . also a painter'. Pallarès, who is a most reliable witness, says he was around ten years old—about what he looks in Picasso's drawings. He was certainly not a painter and is unlikely to have been a gypsy. Stassinopoulos Huffington's informant was apparently Françoise Gilot. She has confused the mule boy with Fabián de Castro (see p.296), who was staying in the Bateau Lavoir studio when Picasso moved there in 1904. A well-known performer of *cante jondo*, de Castro *was* a gypsy and developed such an admiration for Picasso's work that he later became a painter.

7 Laporte 1989, 26.

8 Palau, 150.

9 Ibid., 151.

10 O'Brian, 62.

11 It is customary for Spanish students to devise a '*rúbrica*', a stylized signature that functions almost as a stamp. The elaborate emblematic signatures on Spanish paintings in the Prado may also have appealed to Picasso.

12 Cabanne 1977, 38.

13 Brassaï, 68.

14 Otero, 84.

15 Ibid.

8 BARCELONA 1899 pp.109–127

1 MPB 110.290.

2 O'Brian, 68.

3 Picasso was indignant that his mistress Rosita del Oro, a well-known equestrienne, should have been mistakenly identified as his concierge (see Daix and Boudaille, 128). This confusion seems to have stemmed from the fact that (according to Picasso's friend Vidal Ventosa) the daughter of the owner of the Guayaba premises—and therefore conceivably a concierge—was also called Rosita. Josep Palau i Fabre, *Picasso: Les Noces de Pierrette, 1905* (Paris: Binoche et Godeau sale catalogue, Drouot Montaigne, Nov. 30, 1989), 14, points out that these two girls are not one and the same, but elsewhere he has perpetuated a worse error. He claims (Palau, 137) that Rosita was probably Picasso's 'favourite girl in one of the brothels he frequented'.

4 Sabartès 1946, 13.

5 'Discurs llegit a Sitges en ocasió de l'estrena de "L'Intrusa"', 1893. Rusiñol, 733.

6 'Discurs llegit a Sitges en la tercera "Festa Modernista"', 1893. Ibid., 735.

7 Casas's most powerful works are such socially conscious compositions as *The Garroting* (1894); his ominous pre-atrocity set piece, *The Procession of Corpus Christi Leaving Santa María del Mar* (1898); and *La Carga* (1899). These had little if any impact on Picasso.

8 Sabartès 1946, 19.

9 Angel, who was even younger than Picasso, was familiarly known as *Patas* ('footsteps'), because he walked everywhere, or *Patas arriba* (because he was so tall). Mateu was *Patas abajo* (because he was so short).

10 Olivier 1933, 23.

11 Penrose 1958, 71.

12 In 1913 Mateu de Soto returned to Spain: first to Madrid, then to Andalusia, finally (1915) back to Barcelona, where he made a modest name as a sculptor.

13 Olivier 1933, 168.

14 Sabartès 1946, 17.

15 Ibid., 18.

16 Ibid.

17 Ibid., 19.

18 Gilot, 166.

19 Ibid., 165.

20 Ibid., 167.

21 Sabartès's letters are said by those who have seen them to be more interesting and amusing than his published writings might suggest. His humour was similar to Picasso's: hence a farrago of gossip, fantasy and self-deprecating irony, contrived to divert the artist. Unfortunately these letters, like the rest of Sabartès's papers, cannot be perused or published until the year 2018.

22 Sabartès 1946, 103.

23 Ibid., 135.

24 Although Palau and others have claimed that Casagemas's father was the American consul, government records do not confirm this; presumably this was an honorary position.

25 Sucre, 147.

26 Benet, 52.

27 Sucre, 148.

28 Daix 1977, 49, n.12.

29 Gedo 1980, 267: 'An autopsy cannot evaluate genital function, but only genital anatomy. Even if the autopsy revealed an anomaly, the pathologist surely would not have assumed, in the absence of corroborative clinical evidence, that the defect caused Casagemas to be impotent.'

30 Pla, 104.

31 Ibid., 107.

32 Sucre, 148.

33 Palau, 185; Sabartès 1946, 14.

34 A young writer, Ramon Vives Pastor, had fallen for a young model and singer known as La Caterina (or Rina), who had sung in *Montserrat*, a musical dramatization of a poem by the Catalan laureate Maragall. This had been put on at Els Quatre Gats in 1897, and it was there, a year or so later, that Vives Pastor received the news that Rina was desperately ill at the Hospital de la Santa Creu. He arrived in time for her to die in his arms.

35 Marilyn McCully and Robert McVaugh, 'New Light on Picasso's *La Vie*', *Bulletin of the Cleveland Museum of Art* (Cleveland) 65:2 (Feb. 1978), 67–71.

36 Gedo 1981, 116–29.

37 This trip is confirmed by the draft of a letter, headed Málaga and dated July 14, 1899, from the artist to his cousin María Teresa Blasco (MPB 110.838R); also by a caricature inscribed 'Teresita Blasco' on the same sheet as caricatures of Casagemas (MPB 110.418). Paintings and drawings of Andalusian subjects provide further evidence of this trip.

38 Palau (p.162) has suggested—unconvincingly—that the portrait of Aunt Pepa might have been the work entitled *Portrait*.

39 The full text of the draft is transcribed in the catalogue of the Museu Picasso, Barcelona, p.486.

40 Palau, 210. As he is unaware of this trip, Palau has attributed certain events of summer 1899 to summer 1900.

41 Huelin, 195.

42 If the related studies of an Andalusian couple embracing, which culminate in a painted tambourine, have been excluded, it is because one of them is inscribed (albeit in writing that does not resemble Picasso's): 'Barcelona, April '99'. Either the inscription is erroneous, or this Malagueño subject had been thought up as a suitable present for one of the cousins.

9 ELS QUATRE GATS pp.129–141

1 Raimon Casellas, 'José Puig i Cadafalch', *Hispania* (Barcelona), 4:73 (Feb.28, 1902), 82.

2 The inn sign, which has survived, is surely not by Picasso, as its former owner, Manuel Rocamora, claimed.

3 McCully 1978, 18.

4 Benet, 53.

5 Fifteen issues of *Pèl & Ploma* were also published in Castilian, starting in June 1900.

6 'Desde el molino', *La Vanguardia* (Barcelona), Mar.31, 1892; Rusiñol, 1915.

7 It took Valadon seven years—what she described as her 'seven-years' war'—to persuade the father to recognize her child.

8 Rubén Darío, 'En Barcelona [Jan.1, 1899]', *España contemporánea* (Madrid, 1901), 16–17.

9 Palau, 175.

10 See p.490, n.11.

11 In addition to Mir, Nonell and Canals, the Colla del Safrà/ Colla de Sant Martí included Adrià Gual, a poster designer and important figure in the symbolist theatre, and Juli Vallmitjana, who gave up painting to become an expert on gypsies and their language. His writings encouraged Nonell to identify with the gypsy subculture.

12 In 1913 Trinxet commissioned Mir to do the decorative work—murals, stained glass, etc.—for an elaborate mansion that Puig i Cadafalch had built for him in Barcelona.

13 Their success included a well-received joint show (Jan. 1898) at Le Barc de Boutteville's gallery and another at Vollard's in 1899.

14 This etching is usually dated 1899, but since Canals, who supervised its execution, did not return to Barcelona until 1900, it should be assigned to the spring of that year. Further corroboration for this date is provided by Picasso's first sustained series of tauromachian scenes, also a woodcut of a torero (Z.VI.282)—all of 1900.

15 Palau, 164.

16 Olivier 1933, 31.

17 Jaume Socias, 'Ricard Canals', *Picasso, Barcelona, Catalunya* (Barcelona: L'Avenç, 1981), 64.

18 Reventós, 20. Picasso subsequently suggested to the Catalan publisher Jaume Canyameres that he republish these tales with a set of four illustrations by himself. In the end they were published by the Franco–Catalan firm Editorial Albor, in Barcelona in 1947, and with a different set of illustrations in Paris the following year (C.44, 45). In one of his sketchbooks of 1947 (JSLC 114), Picasso also included two portraits of Moni Reventós—one inscribed '*El Crepuscule d'un Faune*'.

19 Reventós, 28.

20 After Cinto died, in 1968, Picasso bequeathed the painting of the dead woman to the Reventós–Picasso Foundation, which had been set up in his memory. Picasso also contributed an engraving (a nude study of Geneviève Laporte, dated Aug.23, 1951) to a book of testimonials in Cinto's honour that was published in 1969 (see C.151), and an aquatint of a bearded cavalier dated May 17, 1971, to a book published in 1971 by Picasso's Catalan friend Gustau Gili (whose wife was born a Reventós) to raise funds for Cinto's Hospital de Sant Pau.

21 Josep Pichot designed gardens; Lluís was a violinist; Ricard, a cellist; Maria, a contralto, married the composer and pianist Joan Gay and frequently performed at Els Quatre Gats; Mercedes married the writer Eduard Marquina.

22 Besides introducing Picasso to the Pichots, Marquina was a friend of Casagemas, whose obituary he would write and Picasso illustrate for *Catalunya Artística* (Barcelona), Feb.28, 1901. He had also devoted one of his earliest articles to Rosita del Oro's equestrian performance at the Circ Tívoli in 1897. As the most gifted of the new generation of local writers, he almost certainly encouraged Picasso's early interest in modern literature; in return Picasso contributed a portrait of Marquina to the Castilian edition of *Pèl & Ploma*, Sept.1900.

23 The drawings for the chapter 'Els amics del sostre' ('friends of the ceiling'), in which the feverish Rusiñol visualizes fantastic fish, dragons with wings and apocalyptic monsters on the ceiling, foreshadow the paranoid vision that Salvador Dalí (a childhood friend of the Pichot family) would exploit thirty years later. The young Dalí, we should not forget, sprang from the same *modernista* roots as the young Picasso. All the more appropriate, then, that the only comfort of Dalí's last years should have been the nephew, also called Ramon Pichot, of one of Picasso's earliest protectors.

24 Stein 1933, 107.

25 Penrose 1958, 250.

10 YO EL REY pp.143–157

1 Raimon Casellas, in *La Veu de Catalunya* (Barcelona), Oct.31, 1899.

2 Palau, 184.

3 Sabartès 1946, 55.

4 Ibid., 54–5.

5 Palau, 186.

6 Trans. in McCully 1981, 25.

7 Sabartès 1946, 55.

8 According to Palau (p.187), Alexandre Riera purchased his portrait, but it is now lost. Palau believes that other works may have been acquired at this time by local collectors: Josep Sala and members of the Julià family.

9 O'Brian, 78.

10 Three years later, Casas would simply update and rename the painting *Barcelona, 1902*—the year of the city's notorious strike—whereupon it was immediately accepted by the Champs de Mars Salon in Paris and won the artist the title of *sociétaire.*

11 Stein 1938, 32–3.

12 Penrose 1958, 53–4.

13 Picasso probably moved into the Riera Sant Joan studio in late January. Earlier in the month Casagemas was still in Sitges, suffering from what he thought might be dengue fever.

14 Palau, 183.

15 Picasso drew Daix's attention to the fact that the arena in these scenes is only half full. It was usually that way, Picasso said, in the days before the sport had become vulgarized and commercialized—when it was still shockingly brutal. Daix and Boudaille, 120.

16 Pujulà i Vallès, who was an old friend of Casagemas's and one of the few witnesses to his suicide, gave his show a favourable review. He praised the sketches for being 'executed with the greatest ease and command of technique'. He mentioned 'a pastel copy of Velázquez's Count Duke of Olivares with the head of our writer Pompeu Gener substituted for that of the Count.' Frederic Pujulà i Vallès, *Las Noticias* (Barcelona), Aug.1, 1900.

17 Cabanne 1977, 52.

18 Penrose 1958, 53.

19 Sabartès 1946, 47.

20 Palau, 199.

21 Sabartès 1946, 46.

11 FIRST TRIP TO PARIS pp.159–175

1 Penrose 1958, 56. Picasso's visit to England in 1950 was made on the occasion of the third Peace Congress, held in Sheffield.

2 Victoria and Albert Museum, Dec. 1945.

3 Confusion as to this date has arisen because a letter from Joaquim Mir in Barcelona to the Mallorcan painter Antoni Gelabert contains a postscript in Picasso's hand: 'I've just turned 19!' This would imply that he did not leave Barcelona until after his birthday on Oct.25. On the other hand, the long letter from Paris to Ramon Reventós quoted in this chapter is dated Oct.25.

4 Oleguer Junyent's work failed to find any buyers in Paris, and he returned to Barcelona, where he had a modest success: sets for a Wagner opera in 1907 and illustrations to Catalan magazines.

5 Crespelle 1978, 142.

6 'Peio' refers to the writer Pompeu Gener.

7 The anarchist critic Alexandre Cortada is caricatured by Picasso in the letter with his own annotation: '*El seño[r] Cortada, jefe del comité separatista*' (Señor Cortada, chief of the separatist committee).

8 'Perico' refers to the Quatre Gats proprietor Pere Romeu.

9 Trans. in McCully 1981, 27–30.

10 Fornerod is the name of the Swiss painter whom Antoinette later married. In 1908 the Fornerods' daughter is recorded as giving André Salmon a white cat, Zamir (Salmon 1956, 66–7). This cat is the subject of the chapter 'Zamir ou le sofa d'occasion' in the second volume of Salmon's *Souvenirs.*

11 Stein 1933, 24.

12 Ibid., 25.

13 Trans. in McCully 1981, 31.

14 Ibid., 30.

15 Stein 1933, 25.

16 Palau, 204.

17 Weill (pp.65–6) says Manolo, but he was still in Barcelona. Picasso is more likely to have been in bed with Casagemas.

18 Ibid., 88.

19 Palau, 204.

20 Vollard, 219.

21 Weill, 67. The price was 60 francs.

22 Olivier 1933, 74.

23 Palau, 204.

24 Giry, 174.

25 Cabanne 1977, 56–7.

26 In her study *Paul Cézanne: The Bathers* (London: Thames and Hudson, 1990), 54, Mary Louise Krumrine sees Cézanne's early *Temptations of St Antony* as reflecting the artist's ambivalent relationship with the 'androgynous' Zola, also their very different (active/passive) rapports with women. As analysed by Krumrine, Cézanne's feelings for Zola have much in common with Picasso's for Casagemas.

27 Jehan Rictus was a former tramp whose recitations in shabby frock coat and top hat won fame for his vagabond verse.

28 The story of the falsification of the signature was reported by Joan Ainaud de Lasarte; see McCully 1978, 134. But, according to Sunyer's son (letter to McCully, May 16, 1991), the work in question with the signature 'Sunyer' was stolen from the collection of Fernando Benet during the Spanish Civil War; the artist never saw it again, and when it reappeared some years later in the U.S.A. the signature had been changed to 'Picasso'.

29 See Brossa's defense of '*L'avenir latin*' in response to Léon Bazalgette: Jacques Brossa [*sic*], 'Notre décadence', *La Plume* (Paris), Aug.15, 1903, 205–9.

30 Quoted in O'Brian, 71.

31 Brossa, quoted in O'Brian, 71; Picasso, in Zervos, 'Conversations avec Picasso', *Cahiers d'Art* (Paris), X (1935), 174; trans. in Ashton, 38.

32 To support her contention that Picasso was an anarchist and that anarchism 'had a profound impact on his development as an artist' (p.6), Leighten claims (p.44) that he became a close friend of a Catalan 'anarchist' in Paris, the literary and drama critic Alexandre Cortada. However, this was the man Casagemas singled out in his and Picasso's letter to Reventós (see pp.160–1) as a miserly bastard and an 'asshole'. She also claims that Brossa was 'a friend of Picasso's for many years'. But since Brossa had been an exile from Spain since 1896, he could not have been; their meetings were confined for the most part to Picasso's visits to Paris in 1900 and 1901.

33 Picasso's handwriting has been described as 'anarchic' by the graphologist Renata Propper, who has provided the author with a study of the artist's handwriting at different periods.

34 Kahnweiler 1961, 172. Furthermore, according to the staff of the Musée Picasso, no evidence of anarchist sympathy, let alone affiliation, has been discovered among the artist's papers.

35 Daix 1987, 78–9. Since Picasso's police dossier is still classified, there is no knowing what, if anything, aroused the authorities' suspicions.

36 *La Publicidad* (Barcelona), Dec.29, 1900.

37 Penrose 1958, 48.

38 This statement was made to John Golding.

39 Edna Carter Southard, *George Bottini: Painter of Montmartre* (Oxford, Ohio: Miami University Art Museum, 1984), 22.

40 Ibid., 24.

41 Sunyer is likely to have been the link between Picasso and Bottini. A further link would have been the critic and impresario Gustave Coquiot, who championed Bottini just as he would Picasso. After failing to persuade Picasso to finish a series of portraits of actresses and demimondaines for his 'book of beauty', Coquiot had Bottini illustrate his *Une Heure du Matin: Les Soupeuses* (1903)—one of the series *Les Minutes Parisiennes*, each of which was devoted to a different hour of the day.

42 Bottini was as unlucky in death as in life; in 1917 his body was disinterred because the bill for his burial plot had not been paid. Apart from Southard's study, his principal memorial is the considerable portion of his far-from-sizeable oeuvre in an anonymous Canadian collection.

43 Sabartès 1954, 51–2.

12 MADRID 1901 pp.177–191

1 Sabartès 1946, 44.

2 Trans. in McCully 1981, 32.

3 Palau is surely mistaken in his suggestion (p.226) that these scenes of a Toledano village are evocations or reconstructions of Horta de Ebro, or 'reminiscent of Galician landscape'.

4 Sabartès 1954, 53.

5 Ibid., 54.

6 Palau owned an unpublished account of this evening by Pujulà i Vallès, a hitherto unrecorded guest at Casagemas's farewell dinner. He has never published this document and claims that it is now lost.

7 L'Hippodrome had been a favourite haunt of Toulouse-Lautrec's in the nineties: it is now a café, called the Palace Clichy.

8 Manolo's account of Casagemas's suicide and the events leading up to it disagrees in certain respects with the one given here, which is based on the account given in Pallarès's memoirs (as reported by Palau). Picasso is said to have read Pallarès's manuscript and certified it to be 'the whole truth and nothing but the truth' (see p.490, chap.4, n.20). Manolo had little respect for facts and shamelessly played down Pallarès's role in the affair in order to play up his own.

Manolo's account, first published in Pla, 104–5, is translated in Reff 1980, 29–30.

9 The police record is reproduced in Daix and Boudaille, 338.

10 Pla, 106.

11 Ibid.

12 Palau, 213.

13 Daix 1977, 47.

14 'Picasso spoke to me more of Goya than of any other painter,' André Malraux claims in his book on the artist. Instead of telling us what Picasso said, he subjects us to his own ruminations (Malraux, 154). A pity, as Picasso was usually reticent about the master with whom he had so much in common. Malraux's principal quote from the artist casts more darkness than light on his reaction to Goya: 'He told me he had no need of style, because his rage would become a prime factor in the style of our time. . . . "Lautréamont ended up in deluxe editions, and the *Dances of Death* in a museum," [Picasso] added—and with such bitterness that I did not reply: "So did Goya." But that's where Picasso found him.'

15 For analysis of Goya's pictorial puns, see Eleanor Sayre's notes to the 1988–89 Goya exhibition, shown in Madrid, Boston and New York, in Alfonso E. Pérez Sánchez and Eleanor A. Sayre, *Goya and the Spirit of Enlightenment* (Boston: Little, Brown, 1989).

16 For additional discussion of parallels between Goya and Picasso in his late prints, see Baer 1988, 96.

17 The 'Generation of '98' also included Miguel de Unamuno, Angel Ganivet and 'Azorín' (José Martínez Ruiz).

18 Pío Baroja, *Red Dawn,* III, trans. Isaac Goldberg (New York: Knopf, 1924), 270.

19 Palau, 218.

20 Ron Johnson (Johnson 1984, 162) claims to have found omens for Picasso's future development in the '*Tres Sonetos—al Destino, Muerte y Niñez*' that Unamuno contributed to *Arte Joven*. 'An important source for Picasso,' he says, citing Unamuno's evocations of childhood: these struck 'major responsive chords in [his] painting [when] he returned to Paris' and took, briefly—and unaccountably —to painting children. This is possible, but studies of children, then as now, were a saleable item and more likely to have been Mañach's idea than Picasso's.

21 Stanley J. Kunitz and Howard Haycraft, *Twentieth Century Authors: A Biographical Dictionary of Modern Literature* (New York: H. W. Wilson, 1966), 76.

22 Ibid.

23 Pío Baroja, *Weeds*, trans. Isaac Goldberg (New York: Knopf, 1923), 9.

24 Pío Baroja, *Memorias* (Madrid: Ediciones Minotauro, 1955), 44.

25 Otero, 123.

26 Ibid., 125.

27 Ricardo Baroja, quoted in Enrique Lafuente Ferrari, 'Para una revisión de Picasso', *Revista de Occidente* (Madrid) 135–6 (June–July 1974), 300.

28 Pío Baroja, *Red Dawn*, III, 185.

29 *Arte Joven* was resurrected in Barcelona in Sept. 1909, with a different editorial staff. Picasso allowed his original masthead to be used, and four of his drawings (in addition to drawings by Torres García, Remigi Dargallo and a caricaturist called Cros) were included in no.1 (Sept. 1, 1909) and one drawing in no.4 (Oct. 30, 1909).

30 Sabartès 1946, 50.

31 Ibid.

32 Cabanne 1977, 60.

33 Efforts to locate the journal *Mercurio* in Spain have proved fruitless.

34 *Pèl & Ploma* (Barcelona), June 1901.

13 SUCCESS AT VOLLARD'S pp. 193–207

1 The Boulevard de Clichy is hallowed in the annals of French art. Seurat's studio had been at 128*bis*. At the time Picasso lived there, Degas had a studio at 6 and Signac at 130. The Atelier Cormon was at 140 and the Moulin Rouge at 90.

2 Daix 1977, 41, n.18.

3 Gustave Coquiot, *Cubistes, Futuristes et Passéistes* (Paris, 1914), 146.

4 Weill, 74–5.

5 Kahnweiler 1961, 33.

6 Vollard, 242–3.

7 In 1911 Iturrino showed at Vollard's and at the Salon d'Automne in a special room featuring 28 canvases devoted to Andalusian subjects. His work met with mixed critical reception, though Apollinaire (in *L'Intransigeant*) praised his paintings for their exceptional luminosity.

8 This large portrait, which can be seen in the background of a photograph taken in the Boulevard de Clichy apartment, does not resemble any other Picasso of the period. However, the artist has attested to its authenticity. That it was subsequently recycled is confirmed by its emergence in x-ray photographs of the *Young Acrobat on a Ball* (1905). Podoksik, who published these x-rays (Podoksik 1989, 157), has mistaken the Iturrino portrait for the one of don José done in Corunna.

9 Palau, 247–57; Daix 1987, 441–3. The only questionable suggestion is *The Greedy Child* (Z.I.51) as no.47. This was surely painted weeks, if not months, after the show.

10 Palau (p.259) claims that this title is an allusion to the recent Parisian success of the Catalan painter Anglada Camarasa, but he is not mentioned in the article.

11 Salmon 1955, 76.

12 Ibid., 75.

13 The work listed in the catalogue as belonging to Coll, *Au Bord de l'eau*, has been identified as Z.XXI.248 (Mellon Collection).

14 Daix and Boudaille, 154.

15 Daix 1977, 49, n.25.

16 Two of the Vollard exhibits, a painting of a child and a view of the pond in the Tuileries gardens, have been discovered by x-rays to be under Z.I.97 and Z.II.90. Podoksik 1989, 149, 163.

17 Zervos wrongly entitles this work *Le Moulin Rouge* instead of *Le Divan Japonais*, thereby confusing both Palau and Daix.

18 In Blot's memoir, *Histoire d'une collection de tableaux modernes* (Paris, 1934), about his activities as a *dénicheur*, he boasts that he was one of the first French collectors of Picasso, although the censorious tone of the book suggests that he turned against modern art.

19 Kollwitz's son told Daix (Daix and Boudaille, 158) that he did not recall his mother's owning a Picasso, so she may have disposed of it early on. However, it is significant that this work reappeared in the hands of Silbermann, a New York dealer who specialized in acquiring works from Germany and Eastern Europe.

20 Verlaine's poem '*A Bibi-Purée*' first appeared in his collection *Dédicaces* in 1894 (2nd ed.):

> *Bibi-Purée*
> *Type épatant*
> *Et drôle tant!*
>
> *Quel Dieu te crée*
> *Ce chic, pourtant,*
> *Qui nous agrée,*
>
> *Pourtant, aussi,*
> *Ta gentillesse*
> *Notre liesse,*
> *Et ton souci*
>
> *De l'obligeance,*
> *Notre gaîté,*
> *Ta pauvreté,*
> *Ton opulence?*

21 See note on PF 653 (Z.XXI.226) in Palau, 535.

22 Picasso, in conversation with the author.

23 Painter, 1:317.

24 Caizergues, 598.

25 Andreu, 38.

26 Ibid., 36, n.1.

27 Jacob, 199.

28 Leiris, 29.

29 Weill, 85.

30 Sabartès 1946, 72.

31 Olivier 1933, 34.

32 Liane de Pougy, *Mes Cahiers bleus* (Paris: Plon, 1977), 297.

33 Olivier 1933, 34.

34 Andreu, 61.

35 Cabanne 1975, 233.

14 PAINTER OF HUMAN MISERY pp.209–231

1 Cabanne 1977, 491.

2 Picasso annotated a photograph of this *alleluia* for the author.

3 Olivier 1933, 30.

4 Penrose 1958, 100.

5 Brassaï, 197.

6 Pla, 103.

7 Reported by Javier Vilató to the author.

8 Maurice Raynal, quoted by Brassaï, 199.

9 In 1937 Picasso paid Maillol a visit in an unsuccessful attempt to lure his assistant, Jean van Dongen (brother of Kees), away from him. On this occasion Maillol sang the Catalan song back to him, but Picasso did not even reply; see Frère, 153, n.3.

10 In another version of this story Manolo claimed to have been egged on by a foundryman, who went to America on the proceeds of this theft; see Pla, 134–5.

11 Daix and Boudaille, 175.

12 Lorca, 160.

13 See Alexandre Cirici-Pellicer, *Picasso avant Picasso* (Geneva: Pierre Cailler, 1950), 68. Cirici cites 'studies . . . which have been published', although nothing answering to this description has in fact appeared in print.

14 Daix 1987, 44.

15 Stein 1933, 25.

16 Gilot, 82.

17 Ibid.

18 Sabartès 1946, 58.

19 Ibid., 59.

20 Ibid., 61.

21 Picasso had recycled one of the canvases from the Vollard exhibition. Podoksik has published an x-ray photograph that shows a child with a large head and piercing eyes under the Sabartès portrait. Podoksik 1989, 149.

22 Sabartès 1946, 63.

23 Silverman, 233.

24 Sabartès 1946, 65.

25 Ibid., 67.

26 Ibid.

27 Ibid., 68.

28 Palau, 277.

29 Gedo 1980, 272, n.47.

30 Leja, 80, n.8

31 The most comprehensive history of Saint-Lazare is Dr Léon Bizard and Jeanne Chapin, *Histoire de Saint-Lazare* (Paris, 1925).

32 Jean Robiguet, *Saint-Lazare* (Lyon: Laboratoires CIBA, 1938), 26.

33 Adolphe Guillot, *Les Prisons de Paris et les prisonniers ('Paris qui souffre')* (Paris, 1890), chap. 10, 270–309. This book by Guillot, an examining magistrate, is a fundamental work, and chapter 10, on women, is devoted almost exclusively to the tale of Saint-Lazare. We owe the rediscovery of this book to a Soviet art historian, the late Anatoli Podoksik, who pioneered research into Picasso's Saint-Lazare paintings. See Podoksik 1984, 177–91.

34 Guillot, quoted by Podoksik 1984, 180.

35 Francis Carco, *L'Amour vénal* (Paris, 1938), quoted in Laure Adler, *La Vie quotidienne dans les maisons closes 1830–1930* (Paris: Hachette, 1990), 234.

36 Jules Hoche's article 'Une Visite à la Prison de Saint-Lazare' was published in *La Grande Revue* (Paris), Mar. 1901. The rediscovery of this article is due to Michael Leja, who has drawn on it extensively in his study of Picasso's attitude to the two 'dismal after-effects of sex that prostitution engendered': venereal disease and unwanted motherhood. See Leja, passim.

37 Penrose 1958, 83.

38 Leja (p.67) associates the Saint-Lazare paintings with 'an anarchist attitude' on Picasso's part and 'a view of prostitutes, particularly those of lower station, as victims of the economic and political status quo.' If Picasso subscribed to such views—and there is no evidence that he did—his work does them less than justice. Far from expressing the dismay he felt at their lot, Picasso depicts the inmates of Saint-Lazare in poetic and picturesque terms at odds with social criticism.

39 Salmon, in a poem inspired by the popular American song 'Poor Lily Dale': 'Lily, were you a poetic barmaid / In an old bar down east that was blue with smoke / and where drunkenness was sweet and romantic . . .'

40 Picasso, in conversation with the author in the mid-1950s: '*L'époque bleu n'était que du sentiment.*'

41 Sabartès 1954, [146], fig.70.

42 See, for instance, Steinberg, 344.

43 Leja (p.70) disdains the sacred and profane love theory, ('Careless assumptions have bred utter nonsense'), only to set up his theory of '*les deux risques*'—syphilis and unwanted motherhood—in its place: 'Such a reading corresponds closely to an attitude articulated at the time, especially by an anarchist contingent within the abolitionist movement.' Dogmatic assumptions can also breed 'utter nonsense'. The painting could as well be narrowed down to a feminist or lesbian reading, given the way these unjustly incarcerated females clutch at one another.

44 Sabartès 1946, 75.

45 Ibid., 77–8.

46 Ibid., 70.

47 Ibid., 71.

48 Ibid., 78–9.

49 McCully has discovered traces of newspaper buried in the underpaint of this portrait—possibly the consequence of recycling an old canvas.

50 Sabartès 1946, 79–80.

51 Daix 1984, 58.

52 Daix 1977, 69. Over thirty years later, Picasso would paint a portrait of his mistress Dora Maar with a green stripe (MP 166), specifically evoking Matisse's portrait of his wife.

53 See, for example, Gedo 1980, 42–3.

54 Olivier 1933, 29.

55 Sabartès 1946, 80–2.

56 Gedo 1980, 40.

57 Sabartès 1954, 310.

15 BARCELONA 1902 pp.233–249

1 Josep Rocarol Faura had studied painting at La Llotja and later stage design in Paris. His décors would subsequently have a certain local success. After accompanying Picasso to Paris in 1902 and briefly sharing a studio with him, Rocarol fades from his life.

2 Palau sees d'Ors's article exerting an important influence 'on the aesthetic ideas of the time, not only those of Nonell but possibly those of Picasso.' Palau, 287.

3 D'Ors, quoted in Palau, 287–8.

4 For example, Alexandre Cirici-Pellicer, *El arte modernista catalán* (Barcelona: Aymá, 1951), 360; Enric Jardí, *Nonell* (Barcelona: Polígrafa, 1969), 204.

5 Daix and Boudaille, 215.

6 A historical parallel can be drawn between Picasso's position and El Greco's. Almost exactly three hundred years earlier, Spain had been overrun by Greek refugees from Turkish oppression. The efforts of El Greco and his relative Manusso Theotocopuli to alleviate the suffering are reflected in the morbid attenuations of agony and grief which were the very traits Picasso was to borrow from El Greco's work.

7 Kahnweiler 1961, 172.

8 Quoted in O'Brian, 71.

9 Kahnweiler 1961, 140.

10 Reventós, 24.

11 So compact did the image of the crouching woman become that Picasso envisaged a sculpture or, more likely, a ceramic in this shape to be fired in Paco Durrio's kiln. See MPB 110.451.

12 Laporte 1989, 61.

13 Dr Fontbona was later acclaimed for editing the first gynaecological journal in Catalan, *La Ginecologia Catalana*.

14 See Sigmund Freud, *The Interpretation of Dreams*. Trans. James Strachey (London: George Allen and Unwin, 1961), 319.

15 In August 1903, Picasso's drawings after Rodin's bust of Jules Dalou, as well as works by Carrière and Puvis de Chavannes—three artists who left their mark on the Blue period—were published on the front page of his friend Junyer Vidal's newspaper, *El Liberal* (Barcelona), Aug. 10, 1903, to accompany Carles Junyer Vidal's article on art in the Exposition Universelle: 'La pintura y escultura allende los Pirineos'.

16 In the sketch for this painting that was bought from Sagot in 1913 by the Marquis de Ganay—the man who said he had never seen his wife's great Cézanne as 'it's in her bedroom, so I've never had occasion to' (see Painter, 2:253)—even the coiffures are dispensed with; and the two girls are portrayed as bald as de Chirico's mannequins.

17 Palau (p.304) cites the opening of the funicular as a reason for attributing this portrait to the spring of 1902.

18 Sabartès 1946, 85.

19 Ibid., 86.

20 Ibid.

21 MP Car. 102.

22 Sabartès 1946, 90.

23 Gilot, 229.

24 Gasman, 510.

25 Sabartès 1946, 87–8.

26 Ibid., 88.

27 This drawing must have been done before Sabartès returned to Barcelona. His hair is still depicted as Picasso remembered it in Paris: poetically flowing.

28 See McCully 1978, 33, fig. 11.

29 The regulars tended to be younger than those at Els Quatre Gats. The luminaries of El Guayaba included Vidal Ventosa's inseparable friend Joaquim (known as Quim) Borralleras; J. R. Ràfols, the future historian of Catalan art and *modernisme*; Eugeni d'Ors, who would soon give up the law to become a writer; and Diego Ruiz, an Andalusian turned Catalan activist and anarchist, who also practised as a doctor and wrote pioneering articles on psychological subjects. None of these local intellectuals played much more than a marginal role in Picasso's life, except possibly d'Ors, who later (1930) wrote an unilluminating monograph on his work, and then rounded on him in print, challenging him (1936) 'to produce a masterpiece' (trans. in McCully 1981, 202). 'Really a fool,' Picasso told Otero (Otero, 169).

30 Palau, 308.

31 This work may lurk under a layer of scumbled paint on the back of the large canvas that Picasso used for the *The Actor* of 1905. The brushwork and colour around the edges confirm that the covered-over painting is by Picasso, but x-rays do not enable us to identify the subject.

32 *La Revue Blanche* (Paris), Sept. 1902.

33 Ibid.

34 Trans. in McCully 1981, 38.

35 Palau, 310.

16 THIRD TRIP TO PARIS pp. 251–267

1 Palau, 311.

2 McCully 1984, 174, has suggested that the Louise in question might actually be Odette, Picasso's first Parisian girlfriend, whose real name was Louise Lenoir.

3 Palau, 312.

4 Picasso, in conversation with the author, c. 1962.

5 Maurice Joyant, quoted in Philippe Huisman and M. G. Dortu, *Lautrec by Lautrec* (London: Macmillan, 1964), 108.

6 Daix and Boudaille, 215. He later told Laporte (Laporte 1989, 48), quite untruthfully, that he was so disgusted that he threw the pastel down a drain near the Madeleine.

7 Stein 1933, 23.

8 Daix and Boudaille, 206.

9 To justify this bizarre label, the 'Dirty period', Palau dismisses the grave but anguished images in which the artist vents his despair as 'uncertain, much-rubbed doodles', 'this theatre of dirt'. Picasso's distress was so intense, Palau writes, 'that the entire drawing becomes a single great stain or a number of stains'. This 'dirtiness' is 'bound up with the physical dirt and squalor in which he was living'. Palau, 317–20.

10 For discussion of the influence of Puvis on Picasso, see: Richard J. Wattenmaker, *Puvis de Chavannes and the Modern Tradition* (Toronto: Art Gallery of Ontario, 1975), 168–77.

11 Ibid., 168.

12 Yet another transformation was in store for this figure. When the Junyer Vidal brothers decided to use Picasso's copy (captioned 'Puvis de Chavannes') to illustrate Carles's article in *El Liberal* (see p. 501, n. 15), it was redrawn in a form more suitable for engraving by another hand (possibly Sebastià's).

13 Trans. in McCully 1981, 41.

14 Sabartès 1946, 91.

15 Pla, 124.

16 Palau, 315.

17 Ibid.

18 Two months later Dalmau organized an *Exposició d'art cubista*. Significantly, it included works by Gris, Léger, Duchamp (*Nude Descending a Staircase*) and even Agero, but nothing by Picasso.

19 Palau, 316.

20 Jacob, quoted in Cabanne 1977, 81–2.

21 Especially Cabanne 1977, 82. Daix is a notable exception.

22 Andreu, 37.

23 On the back of this watercolour, Z.I.182, Jacob wrote a short biographical note about the poet, so he had presumably owned it. Barnaby Conrad III, *Absinthe: History in a Bottle* (San Francisco: Chronicle Books, 1988), 80, refers to this watercolour, 'sometimes titled *Absinthe*', and states that 'Cornutti [*sic*], an ether addict like [Jacob], had died in obscurity, probably from malnutrition.'

24 The story of the sausage appears in the memoirs of both Olivier and Gilot.

25 A note in Jacob's hand on the back of another drawing identifies her as Cécile Acker—wife of an employee at the Paris-France department store—with whom he was 'ferociously in love'. This does not tally with Jacob's other versions of this romance. See Andreu, 38.

26 Ibid.

27 Ibid.

28 Ibid.

29 Ibid., 39.

30 Jacob, 199–203.

31 Andreu, 40.

32 Quoted by Hélène Henry, 'Max Jacob and Picasso', *Europe* (Paris) 492–3 (April–May 1970), 204.

33 Friends and admirers were appalled to find a poem and photograph of Max Jacob opposite a photograph of Franco in the Christmas 1937 number of *Occidente*, the lavishly produced pro-Fascist magazine.

34 Trans. in Daix and Boudaille, 334.

35 Ibid., 334–5.

36 Claude Picasso, quoted by Johnson 1988.

37 Gauguin, *Cahier pour Aline*, quoted in Frèches-Thory, 281.

38 Daix 1977, 58, n. 18.

39 Penrose 1958, 85. When telling this story to Laporte, Picasso said that he had left the roll of paintings not with Pichot but with a couple of painters who lived at the Hôtel du Maroc. When he got back to Paris and went to recover his work, the friends had vanished. In every other respect the story is the same, but this version is probably apocryphal: Pichot is a more plausible person for Picasso to have used as guardian of his treasure. See Laporte 1989, 48.

40 O'Brian, 116.

41 Laporte 1989, 8.

42 Max Jacob and Claude Valence. *Miroir d'Astrologie* (Paris: Gallimard, 1949), 141. The book, published after Jacob's death, was written in 1928.

17 LA VIE pp. 269–279

1 Geneviève Laporte, *Sunshine at Midnight*, trans. Douglas Cooper (London: Weidenfeld and Nicolson, 1975), 19–20. Originally published as *Si tard le soir* (Paris: Plon, 1973).

2 Jacob, 199.

3 By the end of the nineteenth century the picturesque myth of the Tarot's 'ancient' origins in Indian mysticism, the Cabala, gypsy lore, etc. found credence in French avant-garde circles. Astrologers like Picasso's mentor Max Jacob made a point of forgetting or ignoring the Tarot's historic derivation from the Renaissance card game Tarocchi.

4 Langner, 132.

5 The juxtaposition of the sacred, the mystic and the sexual that we find in these allegories could have yet another source: the teachings of the sinister satanist Abbé Boullan (the origin of Dr Johannes in J. K. Huysmans's *Là-Bas*). Boullan preached the notions of redemption through religiously performed sexual unions and 'sexual promiscuity without original sin' (Pincus-Witten, 59–62)—notions for which he was excommunicated, also condemned by the Rosicrucians, who had once promoted him. Jacob is likely to have been familiar with Boullan's ideas and may well have passed them on to Picasso.

6 Per Palme, 'La Vie: ett dödsmotiv hos den unge Picasso', *Paletten* (Stockholm) 1 (1967), 21, has identified the bearded figure in these drawings as Pichot, which would imply that the woman is Germaine. An intriguing hypothesis. Unfortunately there is no physical resemblance to either of the Pichots and no evidence of Germaine's pregnancy.

7 Reff 1980, 14.

8 Rosalind Krauss, 'In the Name of Picasso', *October* (Cambridge, Mass.) 16 (Spring 1981), 11.

9 One drawing (MPB 110.470) bears a mysterious inscription in Picasso's hand: '*Aimez le bien pour sa beauté pour sa excellence sans crainte de rien, sans espoir de rien* [sic]' ('Love what is good for its beauty, for its excellence, without any fear and without any hope'). This dictum seems to have no special relevance to *La Vie*.

10 Blunt and Pool (p. 21 and fig. 115) claim that '*La Vie* probably alludes to the old theme of the Three Ages of Man, and particularly to the nineteenth-century version which took the form of Cycles of Life.' They do not, however, come up with an explanation for the gestures of the male figure. Palau (pp. 340–1) relates the left-hand gesture to the finger of Adam in Michelangelo's Sistine Chapel *Creation of Man*, while the upraised finger of the right hand in the drawing, he believes, evokes Casagemas and points upwards to suggest that Casagemas is in heaven. Reff 1980 (p. 14) also interprets 'the outstretched right hand evidently alluding to [Casagemas's] heavenly abode,' but he

perceptively adds that the contrast of the upraised arm and the downward gesture of the right arm reinforce 'the contrast between a higher and a lower condition'. Finally, Palme (op. cit., p.24) considers the meaning of the gestures in a narrative sense: the woman 'grips his shoulder with her right hand in sudden fright . . . he stretches his right hand towards heaven in a gesture of protest, the left is clenched aggressively and at the same time pointing, argumentative.'

11 Barr 1946, 26.

12 I am most grateful to my friend Peter Perrone for pointing out the significance of this gesture and other references to the Tarot.

13 Apollinaire's list of 'card-readers' is given in Salmon 1955, 305.

14 McCully 1984, 175, n.27.

15 Daix 1987, 396, n.37.

16 Vallentin, 46.

17 T. S. Eliot, 'The Waste Land', *Collected Poems 1909–1962* (London: Faber and Faber, 1970), 54.

18 Malraux, 11.

19 Schiff, passim.

20 Palau, 342.

21 Picasso annotated the illustration of *La Vie* accordingly for Jean Cassou in that author's own copy of his book, *Picasso* (Paris: Hyperion, 1940). MP Car.23.27.

22 Letter from Picasso to Max Jacob (Aug.6, 1903), Barnes Collection, Merion Station, Pa.

23 Trans. in McCully 1981, 54.

24 The August 6 letter reads: 'I've done a picture of a blind man sitting at a table. There's a piece of bread in his left hand and with his right he's groping for his jug of wine. There's a dog beside him who is looking at him. I'm quite pleased with it—it's still not finished.'

25 Said by Picasso on the occasion of his retrospective in Zurich in 1932; quoted by Cabanne 1977, 111.

26 Trans. in McCully 1981, 41.

27 Tom Ettinger, 'Picasso: The Pictorial Structure of Cubism and the Body-Image Construct', *Psychoanalysis and Contemporary Thought* (New York), 1989, 179.

28 X-rays also reveal a naked woman and a still life, so this canvas had evidently been used before. Podoksik 1989, 153.

29 Ibid.

30 Penrose 1958, 89.

31 Ibid.

32 Wollheim, who sees 'the malignity of the gaze' as one of the great themes of Picasso's work, suggests that for Picasso 'vision is the bad or aggressive side of sexuality and so needs to be punished'. Richard Wollheim, *Painting as an Art* (London: Thames and Hudson, 1987), 289.

33 Palau (p.362) thinks that '*El Loco*' had already served as the model for the noble-looking tramp, the *Man in Blue* of 1902. Any resemblance between them is hard to discern.

18 FAREWELL TO BARCELONA pp.281–293

1 Leighten (p.38) maintains that this bourgeois Catalanist, politically middle-of-the-road journal was 'a left-wing newspaper', and cites a drawing that Picasso did for a poster (never printed) to substantiate her claim. In fact the drawing portrays news vendors hawking the latest edition of *El Liberal*—rather than 'an angry demonstration of poor men and women, yelling angrily at us from underneath the inflammatory masthead'.

2 Trans. in McCully 1981, 42–5.

3 Thomas Hoving, in *King of the Confessors* (New York: Simon and Schuster, 1981), 83–4, has described a visit, circa 1969, to the 'secret' collection of the Junyer Vidal brothers with James Rorimer, then director of the Metropolitan Museum. Besides recounting how Carles 'would stop from time to time to urinate in his pants, his face taking on a look of sheer rapture', Hoving claims that José Gudiol, then director of the Instituto Amatller in Barcelona, told him that the Junyer Vidal collection included a number of dubious items by 'two gifted forgers,

Ozo and Ruiz, who by the way was Pablo Picasso's father'. Hoving goes on to claim that the three Romanesque items that Rorimer had purchased for the Cloisters from the Junyer Vidal collection were 'obviously painted by Ozo and Ruiz'. Fortunately, the eminently trustworthy Dr Gudiol nailed this preposterous aspersion on Picasso's father's reputation (see 'A Comment from Catalonia', *New York Review*, Jan. 21, 1982, 22). Hoving's entire story can thus be discounted.

4 Junyent arranged for the following works to appear in *Joventut*—in no. 204 (Jan. 7, 1904): *The Old Jew* (Z.I.175) and a drawing of a bearded man (Z.VI.430); in no. 256 (Jan. 5, 1905): a drawing of an old woman entitled *Capvespre* (Z.VI.600, formerly Junyent collection).

5 Palau, 349.

6 Penrose 1958, 87.

7 Ironically, the Nazis obliged the Wallraf-Richartz Museum to include this unusually conventional example of Picasso's work in their sale of 'degenerate art'; it was bought by the Musée des Beaux Arts, Liège.

8 For further discussion of this subject, see Adam Gopnik, 'High and Low: Caricature, Primitivism and the Portrait', *Art Journal* (New York), Winter 1983, 371–6.

9 Although Picasso inscribed the portrait to Sabartès, he never in the end gave it to him.

10 Sabartès 1946, 97–8.

11 Ibid., 98–9.

12 Gasman (p. 521) sees this maxim as reflecting Picasso's belief (reported by Gilot, 217–18) in 'the old notion of hair as a symbol of male vigour, as in the biblical story of Samson and Delilah'. She also relates it to a point made by Marcel Mauss in his *Esquisse d'une théorie générale de la magie* (1902–03), that a person's vital principle can be contained in a single hair.

13 Sabartès 1946, 93.

14 *Gamiani* is traditionally attributed to Alfred de Musset, but is probably by another author.

15 Sabartès 1946, 94.

16 See Rubin 1984, 252ff., for a discussion of the Eros and Thanatos theme in Picasso's work.

17 See Marilyn McCully, 'Picasso y "La Celestina"', *Batik* (Barcelona) 9:64 (Nov.–Dec. 1981), 22–8.

18 Ibid., 24.

19 In his student days Picasso had made a copy of one of these *Caprichos* (no. 17, entitled *Bien tirada está*), one of his very few overt references to Goya.

20 See John Richardson, 'Picasso's Apocalyptic Whorehouse', *New York Review*, Apr. 23, 1987, 40–7.

21 Palau (p. 360) accuses Sabartès of omitting this fact from his memoir because the secretary had always loathed and resented the gifted Gargallo ('the envious hostility of the failed sculptor towards the one who has been successful'); also because he was jealous of Picasso's regard for him.

22 A caricature of Nonell being fellated (MPB 50.493), drawn to amuse the Junyer Vidals, dates from this time.

23 Sabartès 1946, 92–3.

24 Ibid., 92.

25 Sabartès 1954, 62.

19 MONTMARTRE AND THE BATEAU LAVOIR pp. 295–307

1 After his parents' deaths this hoard ended up in the Passeig de Gràcia apartment of Picasso's sister, Lola Vilató. In the early 1930s unscrupulous acquaintances borrowed part of this collection ('to have it photographed') and put it on the market. To regain possession Picasso had to fight a long legal battle. Everything was ultimately returned to Lola in Barcelona. After her death, Picasso and the family presented the collection to the city of Barcelona, where it forms the basis of the Museu Picasso.

2 André Salmon, 'L'Europe Nouvelle', *Les Arts* (Paris), July 11, 1920. This review of Fabián de Castro's show at the Galerie Chéron was drawn to the author's attention by Jacqueline Gojard.

3 Ibid.

4 Stassinopoulos Huffington, 41–2.

5 Warnod, 37.

6 Olivier 1933, 26.

7 Salmon 1919, 85–7.

8 Dorgelès, 102.

9 Gilot, 81–2.

10 Malraux, 48–9.

11 Ibid.

12 Given that the Bateau Lavoir had always been a fire risk, hence uninsurable, it is a wonder this had not happened before.

13 Assouline, 72.

14 Olivier 1933, 28; *Acrobat and Young Harlequin* has yet to be x-rayed to determine the existence of this earlier image.

15 Ibid.

16 Ibid. 27–8

17 Daix 1987, 54, points out that zinc plates were cheaper than copper ones.

18 In 1913 Vollard steel-faced the plate and issued a second edition, including at least one example inked in blue, which is now in the Art Institute of Chicago.

19 Daix 1987, 78–9. See also chap.11, n.32.

20 Daix 1977, 61.

21 Picasso saw himself as being the sole owner of his mistresses' images. Daix cites the rage he triggered when he showed the artist a portrait of *Madeleine, the Friend of Picasso* (c.1907) by Daniel Vázquez Díaz, an Andalusian painter who lived between Madrid and Paris and who introduced Juan Gris to Picasso in 1906. Daix 1987, 401, n.2; the portrait is illustrated in Daix 1977, fig.11.

22 Ibid., 398, n.22.

23 Palau, 388–9.

24 Stein 1933, 23–4.

25 Olivier 1933, 40.

26 Given his reputation as the only mathematical mind in the *bande à Picasso*, Maurice Princet has often been credited with exerting an influence on cubist theory. However, Picasso and Braque emphatically denied taking any interest in Princet's ideas.

27 Daix 1977, 69.

28 Giry, 86.

29 Trans. in Breunig, 260.

20 LA BELLE FERNANDE pp.309–325

1 Stein 1933, 27.

2 Olivier 1933, 26–27.

3 Ibid., 46.

4 Cabanne 1977, translator's (Harold J. Salemson) note, 92.

5 Olivier 1988, 11.

6 Ibid., 9.

7 Warnod, 8.

8 Olivier 1933, 10.

9 Ibid., 115.

10 Olivier 1988, 194.

11 Olivier 1933, 29.

12 Olivier 1988, 178.

13 Ibid., 180.

14 Olivier 1933, 73.

15 Olivier 1988, 185.

16 Ibid., 186.

17 Ibid., 189.

18 Olivier 1933, 48.

19 Stein 1933, 20, 26.

20 Olivier 1988, 205.

21 For the most exhaustive interpretation of this theme, see Leo Steinberg, 'Picasso's Sleepwatchers', *Other Criteria: Confrontations with Twentieth-Century Art* (New York: Oxford University Press, 1972), 93–114.

22 Daix 1987, 55.

23 Olivier 1988, 100–1.

24 Gilot, 50.

25 Laporte 1989, 75.

26 Daix 1977, 65, n.5

27 Olivier 1933, 33.

28 Ibid.

29 Salmon 1955, 351.

30 Edouard Pignon and his wife, Hélène Parmelin, effected a reconciliation between Picasso and Salmon in the late 1950s.

31 Salmon 1955, 171.

32 For instance, the poem in which, as Reff observes (Reff 1971, 42), Salmon identifies himself as 'a tightrope walker who dances on the cord happy with his dizziness and tattered finery'—an image that is taken from Nietzsche.

33 Apollinaire, 'Poème lu au mariage d'André Salmon' (1909), included in *Alcools*.

34 Olivier 1933, 75.

35 Stein 1933, 58.

36 Jeanne Modigliani, 'Modigliani sans légende', in *Amedeo Modigliani* (Paris: Musée d'Art Moderne de la Ville de Paris, 1981), 74; see also André Warnod, *Fils de Montmartre* (Paris: Fayard, 1981), 128.

37 Salmon 1919, 78.

38 Olivier 1933, 50.

39 Ibid., 120.

40 The author is most grateful to Billy Klüver for bringing this photograph and the Pascin drawing to his attention.

41 Purrmann, 72–3. Apropos Wiegels's and Levy's sexual tastes, Purrmann quotes a letter from Pascin to Levy in which the former sets out to titillate the latter: 'This place is filled with beautiful boys,' he writes to him from a spa in the south of France in 1912, 'grooms, page boys, hairdressers, dish-washers. No wonder the waters have such a soothing effect on the gut.'

42 Salmon 1955, 24.

43 Ibid.

44 Purrmann, 75.

45 Ibid., 76.

46 Daix 1987, 95.

47 Olivier 1933, 73.

48 Dorgelès, 49.

49 Daix 1987, 95.

50 Cocteau, 2:76.

51 Olivier 1933, 133–4.

52 Ibid.

21 THE APOLLINAIRE PERIOD pp.327–349

1 Besides Picasso, the show, which opened on October 24, included several other young artists: Charbonnier, Clary-Baroux, Raoul Dufy, Girieud, Picabia and Thiesson (brother-in-law of Paul Poiret). The catalogue, which had an unmemorable preface by a certain Maurice Le Sieutre (Picasso 'is a good image-maker. A fine enameller, if one may say so'), lists eleven works and an unstated number of watercolours. Reprinted in Daix and Boudaille, 238.

2 Salmon 1955, 169.

3 Penrose 1958, 106.

4 Salmon 1955, 172.

5 Parmelin 1959, 124.

6 Shattuck 1968, 262.

7 Apollinaire would have had a certain standing at the Criterion, as his magazine *Le Festin d'Esope* had recently run an advertisement for the bar's 'Burton beer, invented by Lord Burton, sincere friend of His Majesty, Edward VII'.

8 Baron Jean Mollet, 'Les Origines du Cubisme: Apollinaire, Picasso et Cie.', *Les Lettres Françaises* (Paris), Jan. 3, 1947.

9 Trans. in Steegmuller, 125.

10 Ibid., 122.

11 Pierre-Marcel Adéma, *Guillaume Apollinaire* (Paris: La Table Ronde, 1968), 122.

12 Kahnweiler 1961, 64.

13 Salmon 1955, 53.

14 When this work was finally published in 1917—'dedicated to the poet André Salmon in memory of the rue Ravignan'—Picasso contributed an etching of a Pierrot as a souvenir of the days when *La Phanérogame* was being written at the Bateau Lavoir.

15 Adéma, op. cit.

16 Bernadac and Piot, 372–3.

17 See Apollinaire's introduction to *L'Œuvre du Marquis de Sade* (Paris, 1909).

18 Angela Carter, *The Sadeian Woman and the Ideology of Pornography* (New York: Pantheon, 1978), 91.

19 The series is usually said to number fourteen engravings, since the earlier *Frugal Repast* is traditionally included. One of them was used as a frontispiece to Salmon's *Poèmes*, published in 1906. Apollinaire put off publication of his poems until 1913, by which time the engravings had been sold *en bloc* to Vollard. Otherwise all or some would probably have appeared alongside the poems that inspired them, or were inspired by them.

20 *La Plume*, May 15, 1905; trans. in Daix and Boudaille, 335.

21 Palau, 398.

22 Peter H. von Blanckenhagen, 'Picasso and Rilke: *La Famille des Saltimbanques*', *Measure* (Bowling Green, Ohio) 1 (Spring 1950), 172.

23 *The Selected Poetry of Rainer Maria Rilke*. Ed. and trans. Stephen Mitchell (New York: Random House, 1982), 325–6.

24 Ibid., 175.

25 Barr 1946, 254.

26 Laporte 1989, 30.

27 Podoksik 1989, 151.

28 In May and June 1905 there was a festival of Italian *verismo* opera at the Théâtre Sarah Bernhardt, with works by Mascagni, Leoncavallo, Giordano and Orefice. The stars were Enrico Caruso, Lina Cavalieri and Tito Ruffo.

29 Andreu, 52, n.1.

30 Rusiñol's clown sings, 'We cry as much as we journey / we must cause laughter / we must sing in order to live.'

31 Theodore Reff has done an exemplary job tracing the historical origins of the genre. He has demonstrated that, towards the middle of the nineteenth century, harlequins invaded the work of one artist after another, from the most academic, e.g., Gérôme, to the most progressive, e.g., Cézanne and Seurat, though the latter had little, if any, influence on Picasso at this juncture. Reff has also shown that all over Europe, *fin-de-siècle* verse and drama teemed with harlequins, pierrots and *saltimbanques*. In Barcelona, there was not only Rusiñol but his friend Joan Pons i Massaveu (author of a *saltimbanque* novel called *En Mitja-galta*, illustrated by Picasso's detractor Opisso); in England, Ernest Dowson, who wrote *The Pierrot of the Minute* (with illustrations by Beardsley, whose androgynous shaven-headed Pierrot is similar to Picasso's); in Germany, Rudolph Lothar, author of a play called *König Harlekin*, which was given in Paris in 1902. Reff 1971, 31–43.

32 Ron Johnson, 'Picasso's Parisian Family and the Saltimbanques', *Arts* (New York), Jan. 1977, 91.

33 Trans. in Daix and Boudaille, 336.

34 See Pincus-Witten for a perceptive account of the waxing and waning of Péladan's star.

35 On Péladan's death of seafood poisoning (contracted at Prunier's in the early summer of 1918), Apollinaire wrote an obituary in the *Mercure de France* (July 16, 1918): 'This Magus of estheticism, this lover of dead arts, this herald of hypothetical decadence, will remain a singular figure, magical and religious, slightly ridiculous but of great charm and infinite delicacy, a lily in his hand!'; trans. in Pincus-Witten, 1.

36 Pincus-Witten, 44.

37 Trans. in McCully 1981, 57.

38 Parmelin 1966, 71.

39 Crespelle 1967, 68.

40 Laporte 1989, 201.

41 Olivier 1988, 206.

42 Daix says that it passed to Sarah Stein in 1910 (Daix and Boudaille, 268), but 1911, the year of the break-up, is more likely.

43 Olivier 1933, 51.

44 E. A. Carmean, Jr., *Picasso: The Saltimbanques* (Washington, D.C.: National Gallery of Art, 1980), 66–74.

45 Ibid., 31.

46 'Whenever I painted harlequin-musicians,' he told Hélène Parmelin, 'that's how I wanted to do them.' Parmelin 1966, 96.

47 Carmean, op. cit., 37.

48 The Goetz bronze is on exhibition in the nineteenth-century sculpture section of the National Gallery, Washington, D.C.; it was not included in *The Saltimbanques* exhibition (1980).

49 Podoksik (Podoksik 1989, 158) suggests that this diadem might have been inspired by the so-called Tiara of Saitapharnes, which the Louvre had acquired in 1896 under the delusion that it was a masterpiece of Scythian art. According to Catherine Metzger of the Louvre—see *Fake? The Art of Deception* (London: British Museum, 1990), 33—a 'Montmartre artist' (a certain M. Mayence, known as Elina) unmasked the fake in 1903 when he fraudulently claimed that he was the maker. It then transpired that the tiara was in fact the handiwork of a jeweller from Odessa called Israel Rouchomovsky.

50 Penrose 1958, 116.

22 DEALERS AND DÉNICHEURS pp.351–357

1 Crespelle 1978, 234.

2 Weill, 230.

3 Beaumont, 186

4 Crespelle 1978, 230.

5 Ibid., 231. There were at least two public sales of Libaude's collection at the Hôtel Drouot: March 9, 1918, and May 19, 1920. Among the works sold were Z.I.61 and 213, Z.VI.542, D.XI.15 and many more that are impossible to identify: four watercolours of dancers at the Moulin Rouge, a portrait of a young girl (on canvas, 73×50 cm) and watercolours entitled *At Table* and *Harlequin the Painter.*

6 Shattuck 1968, 66–7.

7 Brassaï, 21.

8 Vollard bought Picasso's series of *saltimbanque* engravings through Edmond Sagot in 1913.

9 Olivier 1933, 43.

10 Leo Stein, 168.

11 Ibid.

12 Olivier 1933, 43.

13 *L'Intransigeant*, Feb.13, 1913; trans. in Breunig, 272.

14 In a postscript Picasso informs Reventós that he has been reading Rabelais, La Bruyère and Pascal in French—'What a difference!' Letter trans. in McCully 1981, 51. Thanks to his entourage of poets, Picasso had developed a grasp of the language and a taste for the literature, but he was still ashamed of his heavy accent. This gives the lie to Fernande, who leads us to believe that Picasso never read a book.

15 Described by Vallotton as 'the Edgar Allan Poe of architecture', Trachsel was much admired by Coquiot (who classified him among his '*Nostalgiques*') for his architectural fantasies that look back at Boullée and Ledoux and forward to futurism and science fiction. His *Look into the Infinite* 'depicts a kind of anthropomorphic locomotive . . . [that] illuminates all manner of comets and asteroids' (Pincus-Witten, 135). Trachsel also exhibited a *Monument to Maternity*, a huge dome in the form of a female breast, at the Salon de la Rose+Croix in 1892. If, as seems likely, this was known to Picasso, it could have inspired his monumental projects for biomorphic sculpture in the late 1920s. Trachsel also wrote poems consisting of meaningless noises—e.g., 'Hou Hôôô'—that anticipate futurist experiments and Schwitters's *Sonate in Urlauten.*

16 Daix and Boudaille (pp.254–5) have identified most of the works listed in the catalogue. With regard to the vagueness of numbers 1–8 (*Saltimbanques*), they think 'that Picasso wanted his most recent works in the exhibition, but that he had not made the final choices at the time the catalogue was sent to the printers. No doubt he wished to feel free to finish some, to withdraw others, selecting only those he thought were best.' No.27, *Portrait de Mlle S.*, can be identified as the *Portrait of Suzanne Bloch* (Z.I.217). The sitter wrote to Picasso from Brussels, saying she was flattered that her portrait would be included in the exhibition.

17 Correspondence confirms that Picasso was dilatory in fixing the prices and coming up with titles, which was finally done with the collaboration of Morice.

18 Trans. in Daix and Boudaille, 335.

19 Ibid., 335–6.

23 THE ABSENCE OF JARRY pp.359–367

1 Laporte 1989, 14.

2 Olivier 1933, 44.

3 Ibid., 45.

4 Moréas had broken away from the symbolists in 1891 to found the Ecole Romane. His aim was to breathe new life into the French classical tradition—an aim that was in the end defeated by somewhat self-conscious archaism. Manolo's own brand of classicism owed much to the influence of Moréas, who apostrophized him in a poem that starts: '*De Don Caramuel Manolo suit la trace . . .*'

5 Cabanne 1977, 455.

6 Michael Holroyd, *Augustus John* (London: Heinemann, 1974), 365.

7 Penrose, for instance (Penrose 1958, 106): '[Jarry] became a friend whose talent, wit and eccentric behaviour made a profound impression on Picasso and his influence was remembered long after his death.' Shattuck, Johnson, Leighten and others have followed suit.

8 Beaumont, 5.

9 He followed up *Ubu Roi* with the even more scatalogical *Ubu Cocu* and later produced yet another offshoot, *Ubu Enchaîné*, which the *Revue Blanche* published in 1900.

10 Beaumont, 122.

11 Shattuck 1968, 213–14.

12 Parmelin 1959, 242.

13 Max Jacob, *Chronique des temps héroïques* (Paris: Louis Broder, 1956), 48–9.

14 Olivier 1933, 76.

15 Ron Johnson sees this as having thematic links with its coeval, the *Demoiselles*. Johnson 1988, 142.

16 Salmon 1955, 155–6.

17 Josep Palau i Fabre, *Picasso en Cataluña* (Barcelona: Polígrafa, 1966), 165.

18 Brassaï, 202. According to Salmon, Jarry had two owls, which were actually made of porcelain. Salmon 1955, 149.

19 Alfred Jarry, *Œuvres complètes* (Paris: Gallimard, 1972), 339.

20 Ibid., 591.

21 Roger Shattuck and Simon Watson Taylor, *Selected Works of Alfred Jarry* (New York: Grove Press, 1965), 193.

22 Beaumont, 81.

23 Parmelin 1966, 70.

24 Parmelin 1959, 79.

24 AU LAPIN AGILE pp.369–387

1 Olivier 1933, 128.

2 Laporte 1989, 45.

3 Brassaï, 20.

4 Olivier 1933, 127.

5 See the *Verve* series of 1953, for example, as well as many of the later prints.

6 Olivier 1933, 127.

7 Stein 1933, 27.

8 This self-portrait in harlequin costume seated next to the temptress, Germaine, provides an interesting thematic link between the *Temptation of St Antony* mural that Picasso had done for the Lapin Agile's predecessor, Le Zut, and the ambitious cubist composition *St Antony with Harlequin and Monk* (1909), which never progressed beyond the gouache stage.

9 John Richardson (ed.), 'M. Knoedler and Co. Inc: 1895–1909', *Picasso: An American Tribute* (New York: Public Education Association, 1962), [26], pl. 16.

10 Salmon 1955, 181. Walsey was a minor sculptor killed in World War I.

11 Francis Carco, *Montmartre à vingt ans* (Paris: Albin Michel, 1938), 106.

12 Sandricourt [Eugène Marsan]. *Au Pays des Firmans* (Paris: Société d'Editions Artistiques, 1906), 12–13. The passage (first cited by Daix and Boudaille, 336) is from the preface to the novel, in which Marsan—who signs this preface—introduces his 'author'.

13 Once rumoured to have been destroyed in a dispute between the heirs of a former owner, this lost work has now resurfaced and been sold at auction to a Japanese collector (at Drouot Montaigne, Paris, Nov.30, 1989; see p.492, chap.8, n.3). Daix dates *The Marriage of Pierrette* winter 1904–05. The blue tonality would seem to confirm this. However, the theatrical drawings for it relate to later Rose period works. Sketches for the Harlequin, Pierrette and the old man also appear in one of the Dutch sketchbooks (MP Car.002). It would therefore seem to be a throwback to the Blue period, more likely painted in the summer of 1905, slightly before *Au Lapin Agile*. For a full account of the vicissitudes of this painting, see Judd Tully, 'The Mystery of the Masterwork', *Washington Post*, Feb.25, 1990.

14 Laporte 1989, 30.

15 Francis Carco, *The Last Bohemia*, trans. Madeleine Boyd (New York: Henry Holt, 1928), 110.

16 Dorgelès, 26.

17 Ibid., 23–4.

18 Picasso was unenthusiastic about Dullin's performances. Although 'one of our group', he told Geneviève Laporte (Laporte 1989, 30–1), 'he always seemed to us the least gifted of all our actor friends. He was hunch-backed, ugly and talked through his nose. What was really funny about him were his brothers. Dullin came from Lyon, from a very poor family with fourteen or fifteen children—he himself did not know how many. At regular intervals he would get a letter asking him to . . . meet one of his brothers at the Gare de Lyon. The brother would arrive, they would embrace, and a few days later he would disappear. . . . And then another brother would arrive. Dullin did not know them.'

19 Quoted in Reff 1971, 43, n.97.

20 Trans. in Breunig, 73.

21 Dorgelès, 243.

22 Sabartès 1946, 131.

23 Kahnweiler 1961, 139.

24 Adriaan Venema, 'Nederlandsche schilders in Parijs, 1900–1914', *Engelbewaarder Winterboek* (Baarn), 1978, 181.

25 Guus van Dongen was a regular exhibitor at the Salon under her maiden name, Augusta Preitinger.

26 Jean van Dongen later became an assistant to Maillol; see p.499, n.9.

27 Schilperoort wrote about van Dongen's work first in *De Telegraaf* (Rotterdam), Nov.21, 1904, then in *Op de Hoogte* (Amsterdam) 2 (1905), 735–9.

28 According to Schilperoort, *Nieuwe Rotterdamsche Courant*, May 31, 1905, Mata Hari worked as an artist's model as well as a dancer. See Valk, 21, n.26.

29 According to Valk (p.10), Tom Schilperoort married for the first time in 1914. Nelly, who has hitherto been described as his wife, was a girlfriend.

30 Daix and Boudaille, 274.

31 Valk, 11.

32 Olivier 1933, 40.

33 Palau, 417.

34 Valk, 6.

35 Picasso was back in Paris by July 10, to judge by a card Schilperoort wrote from Schoorl, asking Picasso to look at a studio for him on rue Orchampt. On July 13 Schilperoort again wrote, to ask Picasso if he had posted some letters for him in Amsterdam; also to inform Picasso that a money order for him had arrived after his departure.

36 Olivier 1933, 40. According to Valk (pp.7–8), Schilperoort returned to Holland sometime around 1910, after which he was hospitalized for tuberculosis. He subsequently married one of his nurses, Odilia Frederika Akkerman. After his recovery he worked as a journalist in Holland and France and indulged his passion for motor racing until his death in 1930.

37 It may also have inspired the setting for *The Watering Place*, the major composition planned early in 1906 but never carried beyond the state of a sketch.

38 Valk, 14.

39 Cabanne 1977, 104. In one of the Dutch sketchbooks (MP Car.010/13) Picasso drew a woman with a baby.

40 Valk refers to an unpublished manuscript in the Alkmaar archives: A. H. J. Kok à Haaksbergen, 'Mata Hari by Picasso. The lost painting'. However, there is no evidence to support Kok's claim that the painting in question is by Picasso.

41 Palau, 417.

42 JSLC 33, 34.

43 If McCully is correct in thinking that the final setting derived from the sand dunes at Schoorl, all the states of *The Saltimbanques* except the last would predate the trip to Holland.

44 A version of the famous *La Halte du Cavalier* in the Victoria and Albert Museum was acquired from Paul Rosenberg in 1919; and *La Fête du Vin*, a decorative processional painting now given to the 'Maître du Cortège du Bélier', was acquired from Kahnweiler in 1923; it had formerly belonged to an aunt of André Malraux.

45 Reff 1971, 38ff.

46 Two drawings—one that includes a study of a low-crowned hat trimmed with roses (Z.XXII.194), and another sheet of studies of nudes, three of whom wear such a hat (Z.XXII.231)—suggest that this figure was formerly envisaged as a naked girl, standing not seated, and holding a staff.

47 Mayer, 192.

48 Daix 1987, 60, has rightly questioned this and other identifications. See also: Salmon, trans. in McCully 1981, 144, n.1; Reff 1971, 42–3; Penrose 1958, 112.

49 Gilot, 81. The child to whom Picasso refers is conceivably the girl with the hoop illustrated in a 1905 sketchbook (JSLC 35; illus. p.29). Picasso has transformed the hoop into the extravagantly large handle of the basket in *The Saltimbanques*—odd, since a hoop would have been less of an anomaly in this setting than a basket of flowers.

50 Reff 1971, 42, identifies these two acrobats as Max Jacob and André Salmon.

51 The three-verse '*Spectacle*' eventually became a five-verse poem called '*Crépuscule*'; and, after even more rewriting, the five-verse '*Saltimbanques*' became a totally different, three-verse poem, with its title unchanged and a new *dédicace* to Louis Dumur. Both are included in *Alcools*, Apollinaire's first volume of collected poems, which came out in 1913. For a discussion of the early versions and publication of the poems, see Marilyn McCully, 'Magic and Illusion in the Saltimbanques of Picasso and Apollinaire', *Art History* (Norwich) 3:4 (Dec. 1980), 425–34.

52 Daix 1977, 64–5.

25 COLLECTORS AND PATRONS pp.389–401

1 After Apollinaire's illustrated article in *La Plume*, nothing of importance concerning Picasso appeared in the French press for seven years.

2 Vollard held a show of these early works at his gallery in December 1910. Since no catalogue exists, this show has been omitted from previous lists of Picasso's exhibitions.

3 Picasso's exhibitions during the period 1908–14 are listed in Daix and Rosselet, 360–4, and Marilyn McCully, 'Chronology', *Picasso: The Artist before Nature* (Auckland: City Art Gallery, 1989), 43–5.

4 Olivier Sainsère seems to have been by far the most faithful of Picasso's early collectors. Other Parisians included the editor Adolphe Brisson; Dr Alexandre, Modigliani's patron; and Madame Besnard, the wife of Picasso's colour merchant. Libaude/Delormel accumulated a number of works, but he hardly qualifies as a collector. Nor does a speculator like Eugène Blot. There was also an in-between category of friends like Henri Bloch and Maurice Princet, who arranged occasional sales for the artist. As stated in chapter 13, some of Vollard's Gauguin collectors bought Picassos at the 1901 show. And it is surely no coincidence that three of the earliest and most discriminating buyers of the artist's work—Maurice Fabre, Gustave Fayet and Arthur Huc—hailed not from Paris but from southwestern France: Narbonne, Béziers and Toulouse respectively. Other early owners of Picassos tended to be friends, or writers (Coquiot, Fagus, Morice) who had to be rewarded for their articles.

The Spanish collectors of Picasso's work were mostly friends (Zuloaga, Sabartès, Vidal Ventosa, Sebastià Junyent and the Junyer Vidals), or friends of friends (Riera, Graells, Lluís Vilaró, Delmiro de Caralt). After the artist moved to Paris, Junyent did what he could to effect sales. Later Josep Sala, Josep Dalmau, Lluís Plandiura and Salvio Masoliver collected works principally of the Barcelona period.

5 Uhde, 19–20.

6 Ibid.

7 Stein 1933, 96.

8 Kahnweiler, quoted by Assouline, 70.

9 The Morozovs were Russia's most powerful industrial family (principally textiles), also prominent patrons of the arts. Mikhail was the most protean—historian, lecturer, *bon vivant*, gambler, art patron—and such a personality that he inspired a play called *The Gentleman* that ran for several years. He bought major works by Monet, Renoir, Degas, Gauguin, and van Gogh. He died in 1903, aged thirty-four. His brother, Ivan—an amateur painter —carried on where Mikhail had left off and built up a magnificent collection: thirteen Cézannes, five Monets, thirteen Bonnards, numerous Renoirs, Gauguins, van Goghs and Matisses. True, there were only three Picassos, but these included the *Young Acrobat on a Ball* (purchased from the Steins in 1913) and the cubist portrait of Vollard.

10 See Beverly Whitney Kean's study of the patrons of modern art in Russia before the Revolution, *All the Empty Palaces* (New York: Universe, 1983). I am also indebted to Hilary Spurling for her corrections to my original text.

11 Their mother came from one of Moscow's most cultivated families, the Botkins: rich tea merchants who were influential patrons of art and letters and counted Herzen, Tolstoy and Turgenev among their friends. Through the Botkins, the Shchukins were related to Pavel Tretyakov, whose collection forms the nucleus of Moscow's Tretyakov Gallery. The eldest of the Shchukin brothers, Pyotr, had followed suit and opened his vast accumulation of oriental art, historical documents, icons and Russian decorative arts to the public in the 1890s. Another brother, Dimitri, specialized in old masters (works by Rembrandt, Memling and eighteenth-century French masters), which he salted away at the time of the Revolution; neither he nor they ever reappeared. There was also an irresponsible younger brother, Ivan, who led a life of sybaritic indulgence in Paris and commissioned Picasso's friend Zuloaga to make him a collection of El Grecos.

12 Besides blossoming into the world's greatest collector of Picasso and Matisse, Sergei Shchukin bought thirteen Monets, eight Cézannes, five Degas, sixteen Gauguins, three Renoirs and four van Goghs. Unfortunately, Shchukin's archives have not survived, so it is not always possible to be precise about acquisition dates.

13 See Albert Kostenevich, 'The Russian Collectors and Henri Matisse', *Matisse in Morocco* (Washington, D.C.: National Gallery of Art, 1990), 248–9.

14 Olivier 1933, 118–19.

15 Quoted in Burns, 27.

16 P. P. Muratov, 'The Shchukin Gallery'. *Russkaya mysl'*, 8 (1908), 116.

17 Yakov Tugendhold, 'French Pictures in the Shchukin Collection', *Apollon* (Petersburg) 1 (1914); quoted in Podoksik 1989, 124.

18 Podoksik 1989, 127.

19 Kean, op. cit., 257.

20 Shchukin had hoped to marry Vera Scriabina, the former wife of Scriabin. When she refused, he laid siege to her friend Nadezhda Konius, the wife of a well-known pianist. She finally got a divorce and married Shchukin. The years 1911 to 1914, the time of his unstable private life, coincide with his last great period of collecting. See Kostenevich, op. cit., 249.

21 The only Picassos Gertrude Stein acquired after 1914 were a small watercolour of 1918 that the artist gave her and an unimportant gouache that may also have been a gift.

22 Calvin Tomkins, *Living Well Is the Best Revenge* (New York: Signet, 1972), 39.

23 Quoted in Hobhouse, 10.

24 Ibid., 11.

25 Stein did well enough to have some of her findings published in Harvard's *Psychological Review*: 'Cultivated Motor Automatism: A Study of Character in Its Relation to Attention' (May 1898).

26 Leo Stein, 146.

27 Mellow, 44.

28 Ibid., 44–5.

29 This turgid tale—Stein's *Well of Loneliness*—is of interest only in that it is at the root of her later writing. Because Alice Toklas would not give her imprimatur, *Q.E.D.* was not published until 1950, and then with a new title, *Things as They Are.*

30 Quoted in Hobhouse, 32.

31 Mellow, 17.

32 Leo Stein, 151–2.

33 Ibid., 154.

34 Mellow, 64–5.

35 In *Cézanne, the Steins and their Circle* (London: Thames and Hudson, 1986), 11, John Rewald writes that this 'was doubtless the portrait of the artist's wife shown at the Salon d'Automne of 1904'. Vollard claims to have sold the Steins this *Madame Cézanne with a Fan* out of the Salon d'Automne of 1905; see Vollard, 137.

36 The Steins' early acquisitions of Picasso include two of the finest Saint-Lazare paintings (1901), *Two Women at a Bar* (1902), *Woman with a Fan* (1905), *Young Acrobat on a Ball* (1905), *Acrobat's Family with Monkey* (1905), *Girl with a Basket of Flowers* (1905), *Portrait of Gertrude Stein* (1906), *Standing Nude* (1906), *Boy Leading a Horse* (1906) as well as countless drawings.

37 Hobhouse, 46.

38 Leo Stein, 166.

39 'Pablo so much dirtier than Raymond [Duncan] or Hutch [Hapgood],' Gertrude Stein wrote in her notebooks (Burns, 95). She meant subversive (like Bazarov in Turgenev's *Fathers and Sons*) rather than physically dirty. Later she turned violently against Hapgood.

40 Hutchins Hapgood, *A Victorian in the Modern World*, (New York: Harcourt, Brace, 1939), 247.

41 Mellow, 179.

42 Since we know that Leo Stein's purchase of the Matisse dates from October 1905, we can assume that the purchase of the Picasso dates from around November. What then is the 'exhibition' to which Stein refers? Surely not the Galeries Serrurier show; this had closed in March. Since Picasso had decided against exhibiting in galleries, we can only conclude that either Stein was mistaken, or that one of the smaller dealers had hung an assortment of Picassos on his or her walls.

43 Leo Stein, 169.

44 Gallup, 27.

45 Annette Rosenshine, quoted by Linda Simon, *The Biography of Alice B. Toklas* (Garden City, N.Y.: Doubleday, 1977), 43.

46 Stein 1933, 43.

47 Leo Stein, 173.

48 Through Raymond and Isadora Duncan—neighbours from Oakland who were now neighbours on the rue de Fleurus—Gertrude had met a young English sculptor, called Kathleen Bruce (later the wife of Scott, the Antarctic explorer, later still of Lord Kennet). And through Bruce, who had asked Gertrude's young nephew, Allan, to pose for her, she had met Roché. ('The sculpture ain't much,' Gertrude said, but the sculptor was 'very beautiful, very athletic'; see Stein 1933, 44.)

49 Stein 1933, 44.

50 Mellow, 86.

51 Leo Stein, 170.

52 Hapgood, op. cit., 131.

53 Stein 1933, 46.

54 Ibid., 59.

55 Mellow, 324.

56 Trans. in Breunig, 29.

26 TWO OR THREE GENIUSES pp. 403–419

1 It was Maillol who first observed Picasso's debt to the Ingres portrait of Bertin; see Frère, 152.

2 Andrew Green, 'a tall gaunt new englander', was so overwhelmed by Fernande's beauty that he told Gertrude Stein, 'If I could talk French, I would make love to her and take her away from that little Picasso. Do you make love with words, laughed Gertrude Stein. He went away . . . and he came back eighteen years later and he was very dull.' Stein 1933, 47–8.

3 Ibid., 46–7.

4 Ibid., 49.

5 Ibid., 52.

6 On November 2, 1905, Etta bought '1 picture and 1 etching' for 120 francs, and on March 3, 1906, the two sisters bought '11 drawings 7 etchings' for 175 francs, according to entries in their account books; see Brenda Richardson, *Dr. Claribel & Miss Etta* (Baltimore: The Cone Collection of the Baltimore Museum of Art, 1985), 167–8. However, a number of transactions with Picasso seem to have gone unrecorded.

7 Stein 1933, 52.

8 Ibid., 50.

9 Mellow, 73.

10 Ibid., 356.

11 Mabel Dodge Luhan, quoted in Hobhouse, 78.

12 Hobhouse, 78.

13 Ibid., 77.

14 The first portrait, written in 1909, was published in *Camera Work* in August 1912. The second, which will be discussed in a later volume, was written in 1923—originally in French, for the French edition, then translated into English by Alice Toklas for the English edition. The translation was subsequently revised by Stein and Toklas in two separate drafts. According to Edward Burns, 'No scholar who has had the opportunity to work on the Stein manuscripts at Yale University can ignore the role of Alice Toklas in Gertrude Stein's work.' Burns, 118.

15 Quoted in Edward Fry, *Cubism* (New York: McGraw-Hill, 1966), 55.

16 Stein 1938, 32–3.

17 Ibid., 16.

18 Leo Stein, 190.

19 Burns, 97.

20 Roché wrote perceptively to Gertrude in 1912: 'Quantity! Quantity! Is thy name woman? Of course it is very enjoyable to let oneself go . . . but why don't you finish, correct, rewrite ten times the same chaotic material till it has its very shape worthy of its fullness? A condensation of 60 to 90% would often do! Are not you after all very lazy?' (letter published in Gallup, 56). Roché had a point. Laziness was this prodigiously gifted woman's prevailing flaw, 'genius' the alibi for it. For all her minimalism, there is very little concision.

21 Virgil Thomson, in a letter to a correspondent dated June 20, 1983. Tim Page and Vanessa Weeks (eds.), *Selected Letters of Virgil Thomson* (New York: Summit Books, 1988), 393.

22 Picasso's huge, menacing *Dryad* of 1908 bears more than a passing likeness to Gertrude Stein.

23 Stein 1933, 49.

24 Hemingway, in a letter to Sherwood Anderson; quoted in Kenneth S. Lynn, *Hemingway* (New York: Simon and Schuster, 1987), 169.

25 Elizabeth Hardwick, 'Gertrude Stein', *Threepenny Review* (Berkeley) 31 (Fall 1987), 3.

26 Mabel Dodge Luhan, *Intimate Memories 2: European Experiences* (New York: Harcourt, Brace, 1935), 327.

27 Ibid.

28 BBC television documentary, *Bull in Winter*, 1988.

29 For a discussion of the controversies concerning the image of women prior to World War I, see Silverman, 63–74.

30 Stein 1933, 53.

31 Mellow, 92–3.

32 Unlike Gertrude, the Cone sisters were horrified by cubism: after the Rose period they bought nothing by Picasso until he adopted a neo-classical manner. And although they continued to visit Europe regularly, and kept in touch with Matisse, they bought nothing by him either. Between 1906 and 1922 they ceased collecting altogether. When they recommenced, the Cones concentrated mostly on Matisse. This time it was Claribel rather than Etta who made the acquisitions. In less than two weeks (July 11–24, 1922), she bought six paintings and (with Etta) four bronzes by Matisse.

33 Stein 1933, 54.

34 Barr 1951, 83.

35 Flam, 148.

36 Marcelle Nicole, *Journal de Rouen*; quoted in John Elderfield, *The 'Wild Beasts': Fauvism and Its Affinities* (New York: The Museum of Modern Art, 1976), 43.

37 Towards the end of World War II, Mauclair would accuse Picasso of being a Jewish fraud; see Charles Sorlier, *Mémoires d'un homme de couleurs* (Paris: Le Pré aux Clercs, 1985), 175.

38 *Gazette des Beaux Arts* (Paris), Dec. 1905.

39 See Maurice Denis's article concerning the salon in *L'Ermitage* (Paris), Nov. 15, 1905.

40 Daix 1977, 69.

41 Stein 1933, 53.

42 Like Picasso, Matisse had had a one-man exhibition at Vollard's gallery (June 1904). It had included forty-five paintings and a drawing and had a catalogue with a preface by Roger Marx. But the work did not sell well, and Vollard dropped Matisse, just as he had Picasso. Picasso would almost certainly have seen this show, which took place shortly after his move to Paris.

43 Brassaï, 252.

44 Daix 1987, 68.

45 James B. Cuno, 'Matisse and Agostino Carracci: A Source for the *Bonheur de Vivre*', *Burlington Magazine* (London), 122 (July 1980), 503–5.

46 Besides giving Matisse the theme of *Le Bonheur de Vivre*, Mallarmé's poem had (in 1894) inspired Debussy's 'Musical Eclogue', as it would (1912) Nijinsky's later ballet, *Prélude à l'après-midi d'un faune*.

47 For further discussion, see Flam, 164.

48 Olivier 1933, 139.

49 Leo Stein, 171.

50 Olivier 1933, 84.

51 Pierre Courthion reported the story to Flam; see Flam, 174.

52 Leo Stein, 170–3.

53 Penrose 1958, 101

54 Laporte 1989, 191.

55 Picasso, quoted in *Papeles de Son Armadans* (Palma de Mallorca) 17:49 (April 1960), trans. in Ashton, 89.

56 Ibid.

57 Schneider, 588.

58 Daix 1987, 74.

59 *The Blue Nude* was bought by Leo and Gertrude Stein, who sold it when they split up. After its *succès de scandale* at the Armory Show in 1913 this work was bought by John Quinn. In 1926 it was acquired by the Cone sisters and became the cornerstone of their collection. See Brenda Richardson, op. cit., 115.

60 Stein 1933, 64.

61 Although Picasso was categorical on this point in conversation with the author, it is only fair to add that Pierre Matisse was equally emphatic that neither his nor his brother's drawings had influenced their father's style. The very idea that the children could have exerted any artistic influence on their father's work struck Pierre Matisse as *lèse-majesté*.

62 Daix 1987, 74.

63 Olivier 1933, 88.

64 William Rubin, 'The Library of Hamilton Easter Field', *Picasso and Braque: Pioneering Cubism* (New York: The Museum of Modern Art, 1989), 63–9; these panels were never delivered.

65 In 1907 Sarah commissioned Matisse to do a full-length painting of her son Allan holding a butterfly net. It was an advance on the conventional gouache that Picasso had done of the same boy the year before.

27 PLUNDERING THE PAST pp. 421–431

1 Pool, 123.

2 Flam, 158.

3 Barr 1951, 91.

4 Douglas Cooper, *Picasso: Theatre* (London: Weidenfeld and Nicolson, 1967), 30, n.75; Schneider (p.502) attributes this same comment to Fermigier.

5 Z.VI.651.

6 Schapiro, 111–20.

7 Ibid., 114.

8 Plain Edition was the name of the press that Gertrude Stein founded and Alice Toklas briefly ran.

9 Mellow, 349.

10 Ardengo Soffici, 'Fatti personali', *Gazzeta del popolo* (Rome), Sept. 2, 1939, 3.

11 See Blunt and Pool, 26–7.

12 According to Rubin, 'Rosewater Hellenism' was a term applied to late nineteenth-century literary criticism, and Meyer Schapiro first applied the term to Puvis; see Rubin 1972, 193, n.5.

13 Pierre Aubery, 'Mécislas Golberg et l'art moderne', *Gazette des Beaux Arts* (Paris) 6:66 (Dec. 1965), 339–44.

14 See Mécislas Golberg, 'Puvis de Chavannes', *Cahiers mensuels de Mécislas Golberg* (Paris), March–April 1901, 33–4.

15 Silver points out the startling similarity between Picasso's 1918 composition *Bathers* (MP 61) and Puvis's *Young Girls by the Sea.* Kenneth E. Silver, *Esprit de corps* (Princeton: Princeton University Press, 1989), 242.

16 In his 1905 *La Plume* article Apollinaire commented on Picasso's fresco-like surfaces.

17 One of the studies for this figure has been taken directly not from Puvis but from an English counterpart, William Holman Hunt. See John Richardson, 'Your Show of Shows', *New York Review*, July 17, 1980, 17, where Holman Hunt's *Study for Rienzi* is illustrated.

18 'This hymn . . . to young male beauty should be interpreted as a stirring of male pride, a kind of refusal to give in to any woman or to back down from his own position.' Palau, 433.

19 For example, Rubin 1972, 34. Mayer, 203, has compared this figure to the boy with the horse on the western frieze of the Parthenon.

20 Rubin 1972, 34.

21 According to M. Le Bonheur of the Musée Guimet, the cast is likely to have been one of those made commercially at the time of the Paris 1900 Exposition. Another version was owned by van Dongen when he lived in the Villa Saïd—illustrated in *Kees van Dongen* (Paris: Musée d'Art Moderne de la Ville de Paris, 1990), 51.

22 Leighten, 78.

23 A page in one of the 1906 sketchbooks depicts a man in a top hat on a horse. There are no reins, and the drawing (MP Car. 1857/30) is inscribed '*Constantin Guis* [sic]'.

24 Spring 1906 is the date traditionally given for the installation (sometimes misleadingly described as an exhibition) of the newly acquired Iberian sculptures in the Louvre, in what is now Gallery XVIII on the ground floor of the north wing of the Cour Carrée. However, these objects may well have been on show as early as 1905. In a letter to Hélène Seckel of the Musée Picasso, Mlle Pic of the Louvre says that there is not a single document in the archives relating to the installation of the Iberian sculptures. All she can confirm is that the objects in question were excavated at Cerro de los Santos, Osuna and Córdoba in 1902, 1903 and 1904; that some were acquired from Pierre Paris; and that they were put on display as soon as they arrived from Spain.

25 Olivier 1933, 183–4.

26 For details of this trip, see Ghislaine Plessier, *Étude critique de la correspondance échangée entre Zuloaga et Rodin de 1903 à 1917* (Paris: Editions Hispaniques, 1983), 53, n.2.

27 Romuald Dor de la Souchère, *Picasso in Antibes* (London: Lund Humphries, 1960), 14.

28 Cocteau, 3:123.

29 Baer 1988, 110.

30 Otero, 80.

31 Olivier 1933, 29–30.

32 It is not known whether Degas, who by this time almost never went out, actually attended this party, nor whether he and Picasso met.

28 SUMMER AT GÓSOL pp.433–453

1 Reported by Jacqueline Picasso to the author.

2 Javier Vilató, 'Los Picassos de Barcelona y los Vilató', *La Vanguardia* (Barcelona), Apr.3, 1988, 23.

3 Reported by Jacqueline Picasso to the author.

4 William Rubin. *Picasso and Braque: Pioneering Cubism* (New York: The Museum of Modern Art, 1989), 341. To give an idea of Vollard's mark-up, it is worth noting that he charged Morozov 300 francs for the *Harlequin and Companion* of 1901 (Z.I.192). *The Saltimbanques* was not sold until 1909, when André Level bought it for 1,000 francs on behalf of Le Peau de l'Ours, a group of collectors

for whom he purchased modern art. The painting fetched 11,500 francs—a very large price—when it was sold in 1914 at the Hôtel Drouot. When Level's *Souvenirs d'un collectionneur* was published in 1959, Picasso contributed a lithograph, *Les Saltimbanques*: a tribute to the painting that Level had bought half a century before. The lithograph depicts the old hurdy-gurdy player with a monkey, familiar from so many Rose period compositions, confronted by a young pierrot.

5 Crespelle 1967, 68.

6 Trans. in Breunig, 122.

7 Daix and Boudaille, 292.

8 Palau, 440.

9 Correspondence from Picasso to the sculptor (1906) in the possession of Casanovas's son confirms these arrangements.

10 For a discussion of the Ecole Romane in the context of early twentieth-century sculpture, see Marilyn McCully, 'Mediterranean Classicism and Sculpture in the Early Twentieth Century', in *On Classic Ground* (London: Tate Gallery, 1990), 324–32.

11 Picasso wrote Casanovas on May 16: 'Monday (i.e., May 21), we arrive in Barcelona. I tell you this so that we can see each other. A good punch on the nose from your friend, Picasso.'

12 A couple of postcards (dated 1908 and 1909) from Picasso confirm that the obliging Casanovas was prepared to act as a courier between the painter in Paris and his family in Barcelona. In 1939, when the sculptor fled to France—he had been secretary of the Artists' Union during the Civil War—Picasso did what he could to help.

13 Olivier 1988, 212.

14 Stein 1933, 53.

15 Olivier 1988, 213.

16 Olivier 1933, 167.

17 The couple would not marry until 1909, whereupon they took an apartment in the building where Picasso's parents lived, on Carrer de la Mercè. Later they moved to Mahón in Minorca, where Dr Vilató directed a laboratory.

18 Olivier 1933, 93, 95.

19 Olivier 1988, 214.

20 Olivier 1933, 94.

21 The best of these portraits was presented to Fontdevila, and for many years it adorned the walls of Cal Tampanada. Eventually Picasso bought it back, but a reproduction of it still hangs in the inn.

22 When Shchukin purchased the colourful *Still Life with a Skull* (1907) from Kahnweiler in 1912, it bore the curious title *Tête de mort sénile* (Senile Skull). This title, which would have been authorized by the artist, seems to have been a black joke at the expense of Fontdevila.

23 Spies, 372 (S.10), mentions another hand-carved pipe with two bowls: one for good, one for cheap, tobacco.

24 JSLC 36.

25 The *Carnet Catalan* was published in facsimile in 1958, with an introduction and notes written by Douglas Cooper with the collaboration of Picasso and Sabartès.

26 One of the large paintings of two youths (Z.VI.715) was also worked on in Paris, according to Picasso's notes made in the margin of Jean Cassou's 1930 monograph (see p.504, n.21).

27 A drawing on newspaper of himself lowering his underpants in front of a mirror, dated December 30, 1906 (MP 527), would seem to confirm the identification with the figure in the prodigal son drawings.

28 This resemblance has been pointed out by Mayer, 209.

29 The '*bois de Gósol*' (*Buste de femme*, MP 233) became known only when it entered the Musée Picasso. In Cooper's notes to the *Carnet Catalan* (pp.5, 53), two drawings are related to 'a sculpture in wood as yet unpublished', i.e. this work.

30 The annotations read: 'if it were a painting / the dress [or robe] pink / white lace / a black mantilla / and the hair / black and glossy / the face very white / like an enamel / pink stockings / on a very small / foot / carin [carmine?] slippers / In full face she is like this / leaning against a door.'

31 Olivier 1988, 214.

32 Undated letter (late May) from Picasso to Casanovas.

33 Olivier 1988, 214.

34 These are the paintings on which Marie Laurencin—soon to become Apollinaire's mistress and, later, the *bête noire* of the Bateau Lavoir—would base much of her modish style.

35 Meyer Schapiro rightly sees the nude girl as an idealized beauty, but, failing to recognize the clothed figure as the painter's mistress, he concludes that the latter is beauty's servant—that is to say 'the painter himself'. Schapiro, 116.

36 This goat reappears in a group of sketches as a horned devil: in one case as a dandified Mephistopheles in evening dress tempting a little girl (the one who will appear in *The Blind Flower Seller*) with a mass of jewels.

37 Pool, 125.

38 Spies, 28; Rubin 1988, 396.

39 O'Brian, 147. This custom might explain the subject of this painting. Picasso left Gósol before the ceremony took place, but he would have known about it from hearsay.

40 *Carnet Catalan*, 40.

41 Olivier 1988, 214.

42 When Cooper was editing the *Carnet Catalan*, Picasso filled him in on the smuggling situation. Business, it seems, had boomed after the Civil War. Shortages made items like motorcycles well worth taking apart and transporting on muleback over the Pyrenees; and during World War II a lot of money was made out of smuggling refugees across the frontier. 'Now it's all over,' he said.

43 Olivier 1988, 215.

44 The influence of Iberian sculpture became an issue in 1939, when Alfred Barr claimed that the primitivism of the *Demoiselles* derived from the art of the Ivory Coast and the French Congo (Barr 1939, 55). Picasso insisted that the editor of his *catalogue raisonné*, Christian Zervos, publish a disclaimer: the *Demoiselles*, he said, owed nothing to African art, everything to the reliefs from Osuna that he had seen in the Louvre a year or so before. See Pierre Daix, 'Il n'y a pas d'art nègre dans les Demoiselles d'Avignon', *Gazette des Beaux Arts* (Paris), Oct. 1970, 247–70.

45 For instance by Leighten (p.81), who describes 'the hard linear rims, geometric arcs of eyebrow' of the *Self-portrait with a Palette* as 'exaggeratedly Iberian', whereas they are exaggeratedly Romanesque. As Palau has pointed out (p.171), the eyes are those of the Gósol Madonna.

46 Olivier 1988, 216.

47 In editing the sketchbook, Cooper wrongly assumed this itinerary to have been Picasso's route of arrival instead of departure. *Carnet Catalan*, 7.

48 Olivier 1988, 216.

29 THE MANTLE OF GAUGUIN pp.455–461

1 Stein 1933, 57.

2 Penrose 1958, 118.

3 Stein 1938, 8.

4 In the course of addressing mail to Fernande, Stein, who was at work on her autobiographical *The Making of Americans*, became sufficiently intrigued by the name of Picasso's Pyrenean retreat to change the name of her family's home town from Oakland to Gossols.

5 Cited in this context by James Johnson Sweeney, 'Picasso and Iberian Sculpture', *Art Bulletin* (New York) 23:3 (Sept. 1941), 191–8; John Golding, *Cubism* (New York: Harper and Row, 1968), 52; Rubin 1988, 398; et al.

6 *Carnet Catalan,* 5.

7 The whereabouts of all but one of the early stoneware pieces listed by Spies is still unknown; no examples were left in Picasso's possession at the time of his death.

8 Frèches-Thory, 58.

9 Gauguin also worked with other ceramists, including Delaherche, whom he came to loathe.

10 Frèches-Thory, 373.

11 On the grounds of his sarong, the sitter was formerly assumed to be a Polynesian. Peter Zegers has also tentatively identified a dramatic nude study—hitherto thought to depict 'a Maori'—as being of Durrio. In *The Art of Paul Gauguin* (Washington, D.C.: National Gallery of Art, 1988), 315, n.9.

12 Judith Molard was the daughter of Gauguin's friend William Molard, the Swedish composer.

13 Gerda Kjellberg, *Hänt och Sant* (Stockholm, P. A. Norstedt och Söner, 1951), 186–7; part of the story is also translated in Bengt Danielsson, *Gauguin in the South Seas* (Garden City, N.Y.: Doubleday, 1966), 69.

14 This mausoleum paved the way for the project that was to be Durrio's masterpiece: a colossal Temple de la Gloire that would commemorate heroes of World War I. It was never built, and the maquette was destroyed in World War II.

15 A pair of ceramics by Durrio is listed in the inventory of Picasso's estate, but their present location is not known.

16 Rubin 1984, 245–6, is an exception. He reproduces *Oviri* and relates the posture of the ceramic figure to Picasso's experiments in combining 'almost frontal shoulders with profile legs' in late 1906.

17 Shortage of money obliged Gauguin to put this piece on the market; and a bronze cast was not set up on his tomb in Atuona until 1973. *Oviri* is far more awesome than the *Woman with a Vase* of 1933 that presides over Picasso's grave.

18 For further discussion, see Frèches-Thory, 370–1.

19 Flora Tristan (1803–44) was a pioneer feminist and socialist. Gauguin's mother inherited her collection of Peruvian pottery; see Frèches-Thory, 58.

20 Roland Penrose, *The Sculpture of Picasso* (New York: The Museum of Modern Art, 1967), 12.

21 Confirmed by the artist in the notes he made in the margins of Jean Cassou's 1930 monograph (see p.504, n.21).

30 DIONYSOS pp.463–475

1 The first statement was made by Picasso on a number of occasions; see Gilot, 50; Malraux, 25; Louis Parrot, 'Picasso at Work', *Masses and Mainstream* (New York) 3 (Mar. 1948), 6–20; Gasman, 522. The second was overheard by Picasso's friend the Catalan sculptor Apelles Fenosa in the 1930s.

2 Olivier 1988, 204.

3 *Carnet Catalan*, 74.

4 Annette Rosenshine, 'Life's Not a Paragraph', unpublished manuscript in the Bancroft Library, University of California, Berkeley.

5 '*Le Cheval*' is not included in the poet's collected works.

6 Quoted by Jean Noëlle in his preface to the definitive edition of Max Jacob's *Le Roi de Béotie*, Paris, 1971.

7 Apollinaire's dedicatory poem:

Prince roumain, Mony convergea vers l'amour
Il périt en servant les princes de l'Amour
C'est un titre à la gloire énorme qu'il mérite
A toute heure il pouvait se servir de sa bitte
Son martyre lui vaut de flageller les dieux
Son nimbe est un gros cul qu'on nomme lune aux cieux
O Pablo sois capable un jour de faire mieux

G.A.

Reproduced in Guillaume Apollinaire, *Les Onze Mille Verges* (Paris: Pauvert, 1973), 23.

8 Laporte 1989, 43.

9 Guillaume Apollinaire, *Œuvres en prose* (Paris: Gallimard, 1977), 1155.

10 Ibid., 1332.

11 Ibid., 478.

12 Ibid., 423.

13 Salmon 1955, 199.

14 Degas's paintings and pastels never interested him, Picasso used to say. The monotypes of brothels, on the other hand, fascinated him. In the mid-1950s, the author gave an erotic monotype to the artist, who became an assiduous collector.

15 Olivier 1933, 50.

16 Picasso told the author that he owned a Rimbaud manuscript, possibly a childhood *cahier*.

17 See Steinberg, 344–7, for further discussion of this point.

18 This is a paraphrase of ideas that Picasso expressed to the author on more than one occasion in the late 1950s.

19 Years later (1956) Picasso would acquire a Cézanne *Bathers* that is remarkably like Matisse's. He would also own a magnificent *L'Estaque* and a *Château Noir*.

20 Emile Bernard, *Souvenirs sur Paul Cézanne* (Paris: Albin Michel), 37.

21 The author was able to study this drawing with the artist, when it was in Douglas Cooper's collection. With a number of other works, several by Picasso, it was stolen from Cooper's house in 1975 and has yet to be recovered.

22 The author wishes to thank Lydia Gasman for pointing out that Picasso's sketch of the Mercè procession, done for *El Liberal* in 1902 (see illustration, p.247), includes a float honouring the child Bacchus, with the same attributes that we see here.

23 Bloch II.1604.

24 Lorca, 154–66.

25 *Siguiriya* is a form of *cante jondo* that combines the Indian tradition at the root of gypsy music with Andalusian folk song.

26 Yu. A. Rusakov, 'Matisse in Russia in the Autumn of 1911', trans. John E. Bowlt, *Burlington Magazine* (London), May 1975, 285–91.

27 Matisse, 'Notes d'un peintre', first published in *La Grande Revue* (Paris) Dec. 25, 1908.

28 Leo Stein, 172.

29 Daix 1987, 73–4, raises the question as to why Picasso waited for Fernande's death before giving the painting to the Basel museum. She may have felt she had a claim to it. After they broke up, Picasso refused to allow Fernande to remove certain things she thought were hers from the Bateau Lavoir.

Index

Works by Picasso are listed by title (or subject) following the General Index. References to illustrations are in *italics*.

INDEX OF WORKS

Text Permissions

Every effort has been made to credit both the authors and the publishers of material reproduced in this book, and thanks are due to the Publishers Association, Book Trust and the staff of the British Library for their help in tracing copyright holders. The publishers apologise if inadvertently any sources remain unacknowledged.

We are grateful for permission to quote from the following:

Keith Beaumont, *Alfred Jarry: A Critical and Biographical Study,* Leicester University Press, 1984

Pierre Daix and Georges Boudaille, *Picasso: The Blue and Rose Periods,* translated by Phoebe Pool, New York Graphic Society, 1967

'The Waste Land', reprinted by permission of Faber and Faber Ltd from *Collected Poems 1909–1962* by T. S. Eliot

Françoise Gilot and Carlton Lake, *Life with Picasso,* Thomas Nelson & Sons Ltd, London, 1965

Fernande Olivier, *Picasso and His Friends,* translated by Jane Miller, London, 1964, reprinted by permission of William Heinemann Ltd

Fernande Olivier, *Souvenirs intimes,* edited by Gilbert Krill, © 1988 by Editions Calmann-Lévy, Paris

Roberto Otero, *Forever Picasso,* translated by Elaine Kerrigan, © 1974, reprinted by permission of Harry N. Abrams, Inc, New York

Josep Palau i Fabre, *Picasso: Life and Work of the Early Years 1881–1907,* © 1981, translation © Kenneth Lyons 1981, by Phaidon Press Ltd, Oxford

Roland Penrose, *Picasso: His Life and Work,* Victor Gollancz Ltd, London, 1958, reprinted by permission of A. P. Watt Ltd on behalf of The Executors of the Estate of Sir Roland Penrose

Jaime Sabartès, *Picasso: An Intimate Portrait,* W. H. Allen, London, 1949

André Salmon, *Souvenirs sans fin: Première époque (1903–1908)* © 1955 by Editions Gallimard, Paris

Gertrude Stein, *The Autobiography of Alice B. Toklas,* John Lane, London, 1933

Leo Stein, *Appreciation: Painting, Poetry and Prose,* Crown Publishers Inc, New York, 1947.

Picture Credits

The photograph on p.7 was presented to the Auckland City Art Gallery in memory of Brian Brake by a friend of the artist.

Works from the Baltimore Museum of Art bear the following museum numbers: (157a) 1950.267, (344b) 1950.272, (396b) 1950.276, (404a) 1950.275, (408) 1950.300, (410) 1950.12.481, (441b) 1950.12.487 (all from The Cone Collection, formed by Dr Claribel Cone and Miss Etta Cone of Baltimore, Maryland); (182b) 1960.183.19.

Photographs of works in The Barnes Foundation, Merion Station, Pa., are copyright © 1991 The Barnes Foundation.

Reproductions of works in The Art Institute of Chicago are copyright © 1991 The Art Institute of Chicago. All Rights Reserved. The following additional credit is due: (278d) Helen Birch Bartlett Memorial Collection, 1926.253. The museum number of illustration 303a is 1950.128.

Works in the Cleveland Museum of Art bear the following museum numbers: (197a) 58.44, (268 and 122a) 45.24, (324) 58.43, (446d) 58.45, (448) 54.865.

Reproductions of works in the Detroit Institute of Arts are copyright © 1991 Founders Society, The Detroit Institute of Arts. The following additional credit is due: (146e) Founders Society Purchase, D. M. Ferry, Jr Fund (38.34).

All rights in reproductions of works in the Metropolitan Museum of Art, New York, are reserved by the Museum. The following additional credits are due: (278c) Gift of Mr and Mrs Ira Haupt, 1950; (428a) Acquired from the Museum of Modern Art, Anonymous Gift.

Photographs of works in the following museums were supplied by the Réunion des musées nationaux: Musée Picasso, Paris; Musée du Louvre, Paris; Musée des Arts et Traditions Populaires, Paris; Musée d'Orsay, Paris; Collection Walter–Guillaume, Musée de l'Orangerie, Paris; Musée des Antiquités Nationales, Saint-Germain-en-Laye.

Grateful acknowledgement for supplying photographs is made to all those named in the captions and to the following:

A.C.L., Brussels: *422b, 456b*
Acquavella Galleries, New York: *172b*
Art Resource–Giraudon: *196b, 259b, 305a, 371a*
Galerie Berggruen, Paris: *193, 224, 245a, 263a, 265d, 289c, 300a, 305b, 442a*
Bibliothèque Nationale, Paris: *194b, 201b, 202a*
Maître Binoche, Paris: *373a*
Nane Cailler: (from Florent Fels, *L'Art Vivant*) *353a;* (from Jaime Sabartès, *Picasso: Documents Iconographiques*) *378b*
Marçal Casanovas: *423b, 434ab*
Christies: *ii, 111b, 196c, 212c, 217a, 232, 280e, 301b, 356b, 398, 456c, 465, 467a*
Douglas Cooper Archives: *470b*
Courtauld Institute of Art, London: *215b*
Jacques Faujour: *204*
Sala Gaspar, Barcelona: *298b*
James Neill Goodman: *280acb*
Hazlitt, Gooden and Fox, London: *173b*
Heritage of Music, London: *338b*
Wil Janssen: *378c, 379d, 381a*
Billy Klüver: *322a, 390, 414*
M. Knoedler and Co., Inc., New York: *197c, 240a, 280d, 368*
Galerie Kornfeld, Bern: *355*
Lefèvre Gallery, London: *92a, 94a, 111a, 146d, 152b, 179ab, 190a, 196e, 250, 251, 261b, 276b, 299, 306b, 342c, 346, 439b, 441a, 447a, 449a, 463*
Guy Loudmer, Paris: *310, 369*
Foto Luigi, Berga: *440b, 450a*
Arxiu Mas: *9ab, 39a, 59e, 65b, 67b, 69, 71, 76a, 77c, 86a, 92b, 93b, 97, 100b, 112d, 113a, 114b, 120, 131a, 134a, 135b, 136c, 138a, 139a, 140b, 143, 145, 147b, 149, 154b, 155b, 158, 159, 160b, 163a, 175, 180, 183a, 208ab, 234c, 238, 239c, 241b, 246a, 265b, 277a, 282a, 283a, 284c, 289a, 313b, 314, 435ab, 437a, 443b, 450b, 452*
Metropolitan Museum of Art, New York: *439a, 466b*
Musée Française de la Photographie, Bièvre: *297a, 309*
Musée Picasso, Paris: *4b, 62a, 75b*
Museu Picasso, Barcelona: *105b*
O'Hana Gallery: *283c*
Galerie Pierre: *289b*
Nimatallah–Artephot: *147e, 370e*
Phillips Fine Art Auctioneers: *90b*
Ricardo Rosello Saura, Málaga: *12, 24, 84b*
Archivo F. Serra, Barcelona: *5, 176, 185a*
Editions Aimery Somogy, Paris: *100a*
Sotheby's: *39c, 115a, 168a, 179c, 189, 192, 196a, 197d, 219a, 220c, 230, 252a, 264b, 352, 418a*
Archivo Temboury, Málaga: *58c, 60a*
Thames and Hudson Ltd, London: *411*
Roger-Viollet: (Collection Viollet) *297b, 370a, 455;* (Harlingue–Viollet) *361, 373b, 427*
Elke Walford (Hamburger Kunsthalle): *322b, 323b, 354b*

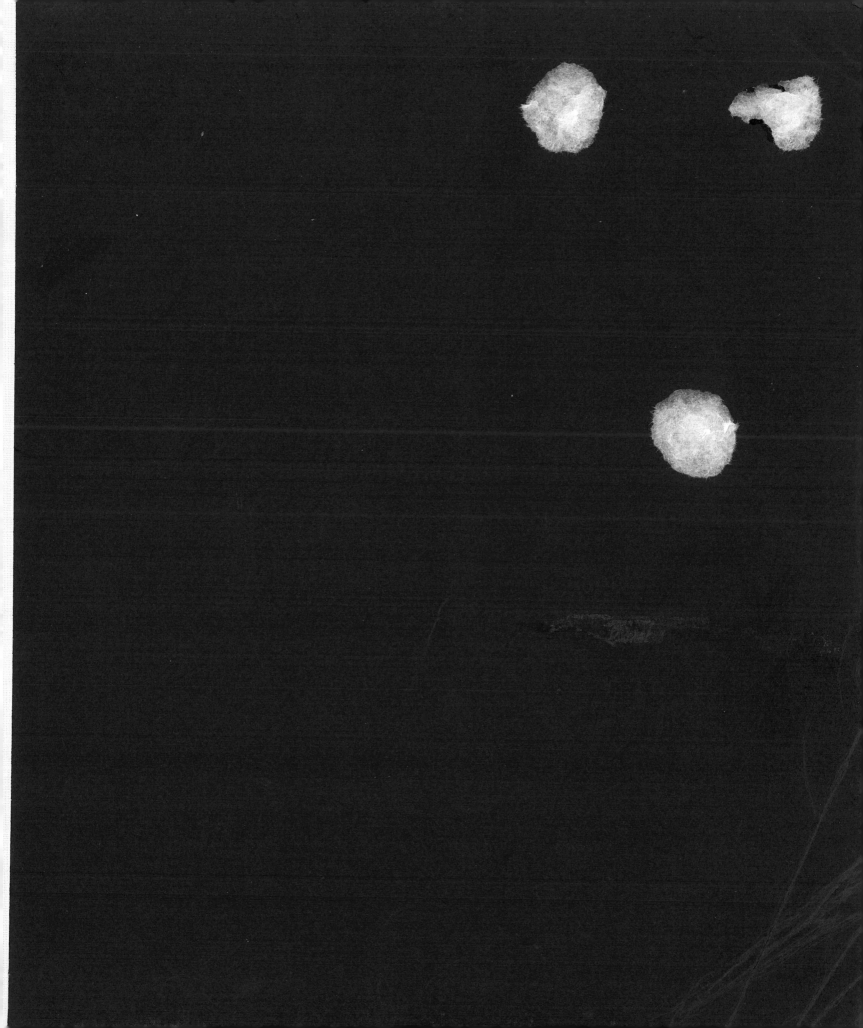